LEE

BOOKS BY
DOUGLAS SOUTHALL FREEMAN

R. E. LEE (4 volumes, illustrated)
WINNER OF THE PULITZER PRIZE FOR BIOGRAPHY

LEE (Illustrated)
AN ABRIDGMENT IN ONE VOLUME BY RICHARD HARWELL OF THE CLASSIC
FOUR-VOLUME *R. E. Lee*

LEE OF VIRGINIA (Illustrated)
THE LIFE OF THE GENERAL TOLD FCR YOUNG ADULTS

LEE'S LIEUTENANTS (3 volumes, illustrated)

GEORGE WASHINGTON (7 volumes, illustrated)
WINNER OF THE PULITZER PRIZE FOR BIOGRAPHY

ROBERT E. LEE: *April, 1865*

LEE

An abridgment in one volume

by RICHARD HARWELL

of

the four-volume

R. E. LEE

by DOUGLAS SOUTHALL FREEMAN

With a new foreword by
JAMES M. McPHERSON

COLLIER BOOKS
MACMILLAN PUBLISHING COMPANY
New York

MAXWELL MACMILLAN CANADA
Toronto

MAXWELL MACMILLAN INTERNATIONAL
New York   Oxford   Singapore   Sydney

Collier Books   Maxwell Macmillan Canada, Inc.
Macmillan Publishing Company   1200 Eglinton Avenue East
866 Third Avenue   Suite 200
New York, NY 10022   Don Mills, Ontario M3C 3N1

Macmillan Publishing Company is part of
the Maxwell Communication Group of Companies.

Library of Congress Cataloging-in-Publication Data
Freeman, Douglas Southall, 1886–1953.
    [R. E. Lee. Selections]
    Lee: an abridgement in one volume of the four-volume R. E. Lee by
Douglas Southall Freeman / by Richard Harwell; with a new foreword by
James M. McPherson.—1st Collier books trade ed.
        p.   cm.
    Originally published: New York: Scribner, 1961.
    Includes index.
    ISBN 0-02-019884-1
    1. Lee, Robert E. (Robert Edward), 1807–1870.   2. Generals—United
States—Biography.   3. Confederate States of America. Army—
Biography.   I. Harwell, Richard Barksdale.   II. Title.
[E467.1.L4F85   1993]   93-6528   CIP
973.7'3'092—dc20
[B]

Macmillan books are available at special discounts for bulk purchases for sales
promotions, premiums, fund-raising, or educational use. For details, contact:
Special Sales Director, Macmillan Publishing Company, 866 Third Avenue,
New York, NY 10022

First Collier Books Trade Edition 1993

10   9   8   7   6   5   4

PRINTED IN THE UNITED STATES OF AMERICA

CONTENTS

LIST OF ILLUSTRATIONS

Foreword

In 1986 a Virginia historian praised Douglas Southall Freeman's multi-volume biographies of Robert E. Lee and George Washington as "definitive portrayals of national heroes." Most Americans would read these words without a second thought. So pervasive has become the image of Lee as a "national hero" that we tend to forget that he fought four years to break up the United States, and came perilously close to accomplishing that goal.

The transformation of Lee from the foremost Rebel to a great American has been the product of many pens. But no author has done more than Douglas Southall Freeman to shape our image of Lee as a reluctant secessionist who was brilliant in victory, honorable in defeat, and admirable for his commitment to binding up the wounds of war in the re-United States. The sheer virtuosity of Freeman's prose, backed by twenty years of research, made Lee first in war, first in peace, and second only to Washington and Lincoln in the hearts of his countrymen.

Like all legends, the Lee legend that Freeman helped to create contains a great deal of truth. If Lee was not the greatest military strategist of the Civil War (a distinction now generally accorded to Grant), he was clearly its greatest tactician and most charismatic commander. If he was not as reluctant to support slavery and secession as myth would have it, until his own state seceded he did hope that disunion could be avoided and he used his powerful influence for reunion after Appomattox. If he was not the demigod enshrined in marble or bronze in countless Southern communities, he was nevertheless a "gentleman" in the classic sense of that word and a worthy representative of the Virginia gentry that did so much to shape the early history of the United States.

Freeman portrayed a Lee almost without blemishes or warts. In the index of the original four-volume biography is the entry "Personal Characteristics," which include: abstemiousness, alertness, amiability, boldness, calmness, charm of manner, cheerfulness, courage, courtesy, dignity, diligence, fairness, faith in God, friendliness, generosity, goodness, good judgment, good looks, grace, heroic character, humility, integrity, intelligence, justice, kindness, mercy, modesty, patience, poise, politeness, resourcefulness, sincerity, tact, thoughtfulness, wisdom. All of these characteristics stand out with even more clarity in this one-volume abridgment, which of necessity strips away much of the verbiage of the original but retains the essence.

Recent studies of Lee—particularly Thomas L. Connelly's *The Marble Man* (1977) and Alan T. Nolan's *Lee Considered* (1991)—have put in the warts and blemishes, perhaps too prominently. But the power of Douglas Southall Freeman's pen will probably keep the heroic image of Lee preeminent in the eyes of most beholders. "Lee," wrote Freeman in the concluding pages of the biography, "was one of the small company of great men in whom there is no inconsistency to be explained, no enigma to be solved. What he seemed, he was—a wholly human gentleman, the essential elements of whose positive character were two and only two, simplicity and spirituality." In a subsequent public lecture, Freeman described Lee as "one of the few, the very few of her sons, whom America offers at the altar of the ages as worthy by reason of his character to be exempted from the else-universal sentence of death." After reading this biography, we are almost prepared to believe it.

Freeman came honestly to his hero-worship of Lee. The son of a Confederate veteran who had survived to be one of the hardy few to surrender at Appomattox, Freeman learned the valorous legend of the Army of Northern Virginia at his father's knee. Moving with his family from Lynchburg to Richmond in 1891 at the age of five, Douglas attended a private school whose headmaster, also a Confederate veteran, gave his boys a weekly talk on moral conduct illustrated by anecdotes from the life of General Lee. At the age of seventeen, Douglas attended with his father a reunion of twenty-five hundred Confederate veterans at the famous battlefield of the Crater near Petersburg. Young Freeman there resolved, as he later recalled, "to preserve from immolating time some of the heroic figures of the Confederacy. . . . The memory of the tattered old ranks, the worn old heroes who charged up Crater Hill will ever be fresh in my memory."

That memory remained fresh through Freeman's years of graduate study at the Johns Hopkins University, from which he received a Ph.D. in history at the remarkable age of twenty-two. Unfortunately, the only copy of his dissertation, a study of Virginia's secession convention, went up in smoke when the downtown campus of Hopkins burned in 1908. The new Ph.D. chose a career in journalism rather than teaching. He went to work for the *Richmond Times-Dispatch* in 1909; in 1915, at the age of twenty-nine, he became editor of the *News Leader*, a post he held for thirty-four years. But Freeman never forgot those tattered heroes and their leader. In 1911 he came into possession of Lee's confidential wartime dispatches to Jefferson Davis, which had been missing and presumed lost since the Confederate evacuation of Richmond nearly half a century earlier. Freeman edited and published *Lee's Confidential Dispatches* in 1915, doing such a skillful job and writing such a brilliant introduction that he leaped into the forefront of historians of the Confederacy. "Lee the soldier was great," wrote Freeman in this introduction, but "Lee the man and Christian was greater by far. . . . Noble he was; nobler he became. The sufferings he endured were worth all they cost him in the example they gave the South of fortitude in disaster and courage in defeat."

Edward Livermore Burlingame, chief editor at Charles Scribner's Sons, was impressed by *Lee's Confidential Dispatches*. Burlingame signed up Freeman to write a 75,000-word biography of Lee. Freeman immediately set to work, confident that he could finish the job in two years. Those years passed, then two more. As America entered the roaring twenties, year after year went by with no manuscript from Richmond. Burlingame died, and the legendary Maxwell Perkins took over as editor of the still nonexistent biography.

The problem was not laziness. On the contrary, Freeman worked a schedule that would have destroyed a lesser man. He awakened each day at 2:30 A.M., put in a full day at the newspaper, gave two radio broadcasts every weekday and one on Sunday. He served on several boards, delivered dozens of public lectures a year—and worked fifteen to twenty hours a week on the biography. Nor was the problem inefficiency. Freeman became famous for the discipline and organization of his research methodology with its meticulous notebooks and color-coded notecards. The problem was thoroughness. Freeman worked his way through thousands of sources, many of them never before used. The project grew from one volume of 75,000 words to four volumes totaling one million words. Twenty years from the date he signed the contract, volumes 3 and 4 were finally published. The biography won rave reviews, a Pulitzer Prize, and honors beyond counting—including twenty-three honorary degrees for Freeman. Next only to *Gone with the Wind*, *R. E. Lee* was the publishing event of the decade. And it did more than *Gone with the Wind* to earn scholarly respectability for the Confederate viewpoint.

Two-thirds of the biography deals with four years of war in Lee's life of sixty-three years. This is a reasonable proportion, for the significance of those four years outweighs all the others. Freeman's technique in treating Lee as army commander became known as the "fog-of-war" approach. The author leads the reader through the complexities of a campaign or battle by viewing it through Lee's eyes, revealing only as much at any given point of the narrative as Lee himself knew at that moment. Thus if Union infantry are falling back or counterattacking, or Union cavalry are launching a raid in the Confederate rear, or A. P. Hill's division is nearing Sharpsburg after a forced march from Harper's Ferry, or Grant has slipped his forces out of the Cold Harbor trenches and headed for Petersburg, the reader does not know it until Lee learns of it from a courier or deduces it from intelligence reports or sees it with his own eyes. This technique, almost unique to Freeman, has both disadvantages and advantages in comparison with the usual "omniscient author" method of writing. For the reader who is a neophyte in military history, a clear depiction of the whole picture would have made a campaign or battle easier to understand. Yet the fog-of-war technique is truer to the confusing reality of military operations and enables the reader to understand the commander's thought processes and decisions as he picks his way through the fog of information, lack of information, and misinformation.

In any event, the fog-of-war method is less evident in this one-volume abridgment than in the original four-volume edition. To reduce one million words to 250,000, Richard Harwell had not only to eliminate footnotes and appendixes; he also had to cut out many of the quotations from dispatches and reports, many of the details of intelligence that Lee received and on which he based his decisions and orders. The narrative is thus paced faster, thought proceeds to action more quickly, and much of the fog is dispelled by events and results that follow hard upon information and decision.

As an example, consider Freeman's narrative of the Fredericksburg campaign. Lee's efforts to analyze and counter Union maneuvers, from November 7, 1862, when Ambrose E. Burnside replaced George B. McClellan as commander of the Army of the Potomac, until Union forces laid pontoon bridges across the Rappahannock on December 11, occupy fifteen pages of volume 2 in the original biography. These pages contain summaries of numerous conversations between Lee and his subordinates who were trying to figure out what Burnside was up to. Such close analysis is fascinating to the aficionado of Civil War military history, but may become tedious to the less dedicated reader. Without sacrificing any essential details, Harwell's abridgment boils these fifteen pages down to three (pp. 268–71 in this edition). Likewise, Freeman's narrative of the invasion of Pennsylvania in June 1863 that led to Gettysburg requires two chapters totaling thirty-five pages to get Lee from the Rappahannock to the Potomac, and includes long quotations from messages between Lee, Davis, Stuart, and others. Harwell's abridgment covers the same ground in eleven pages (pp. 307–18) that carry the story at a brisker, more readable pace that leaves out material of interest only to experts.

How well does Freeman's scholarship stand up two generations after publication of the original biography? Freeman's Lee was an unblemished Virginia gentleman who fought brilliantly for a good cause that he might have won had it not been for General James Longstreet's sullen lack of cooperation at Gettysburg. The Lee portrayed by some recent scholarship fought for the dubious causes of disunion and slavery; his aggressive strategy and tactics bled his army dry from the highest casualty rates of any commander on either side in the Civil War; by focusing Confederate resources on the Virginia theater, Lee's narrow strategic vision neglected the western theaters where the Confederacy ultimately lost the war; the Confederates suffered defeat at Gettysburg not because of Longstreet's failures but because of Lee's poor tactics and the Union army's stout fighting.

As with all Civil War controversies, neither side in this historiographical debate is wholly right or wrong. The dialogue will continue at Civil War round tables and symposia, in the pages of biographies, monographs, articles, and reviews, in the minds of readers. Lee will remain a titan of American history, a great military leader, an icon to many in the South. Douglas Southall Freeman did more to make him so than any other historian. This abridgment is the place to start for anyone who wants to understand the Confederacy's premier figure; it is still the best one-volume biography of Lee.

JAMES M. McPHERSON

Introduction

It has already been told: how Douglas Southall Freeman accepted a commission from Charles Scribner's Sons in 1915 to write a one-volume biography of Robert E. Lee; how his researches soon convinced him that previous biographers had not told the full story of the Confederate hero; how the single volume grew into four large ones. This much Dr. Freeman told in the foreword to his *R. E. Lee* in 1934. What he did not tell, for he did not then know and would have been too modest to write it had he known, was how his magnificent biography would win a Pulitzer prize, would crown years of painstaking work by bringing to him universal acknowledgment as the dean of Southern historians, would lead to new fame when he published *Lee's Lieutenants* a decade later, to another Pulitzer prize for his definitive biography of George Washington, and to a linking of his name with Lee's as irrevocably as Boswell's is linked to Dr. Johnson's.

The fame was in the future in 1934, but years of work were on paper. It was doubtless with feelings of mixed reluctance and relief that Dr. Freeman delivered his manuscript to Scribner's; for no author is ever completely satisfied that just one more look at his manuscript might not improve it. Mrs. Freeman tells a charmingly homely story of how "the Doctor," at complete variance with his usual habit of setting each moment of time to useful purpose, moved morosely about their home in the first days after releasing his manuscript. She commented on his restlessness. "My dear," he said, "when one has lived with someone as long as I have with General Lee it is a great loss to be parted from him." That was no momentary reaction, for when he wrote his foreword to *R. E. Lee* he echoed that remark in saying: "Prolonged as my investigation has been, and puzzling as some of its problems have appeared to be, I have been fully repaid by being privileged to live, as it were, for more than a decade in the company of a great gentleman. A biographer can ask no richer compensation."

Dr. Freeman was able to make Lee a real presence to the readers of history because Lee was a very real presence to Dr. Freeman. And he believed that something of the greatness of Lee could be transmitted to a later generation by a thorough knowledge of the man and his times. In an informal address to members of the Chicago and Richmond Civil War Round Tables Dr. Freeman said, just a few weeks before his death June 13, 1953: "There, gentlemen, is where we get the great reward of our study of this period. We are dealing four times in five, aye, nine times in ten, with men of character, and the great delight we have is that we can keep the company of truthful gentlemen. No honor that ever comes to a man in life is greater than the honor that may be yours by learning thoroughly the life of one of the great men of that era."

He spoke feelingly on that occasion, for he knew from experience whereof he spoke. In a day when history was emerging from its chastening period of muckraking that had been popular in the early 1900's into its "revisionist" approach of the 1920's and '30's and in a decade when the debunking biography, the subjective approach of Gamaliel Bradford or Lytton Strachey, was at the height of historiographical fashion, Dr. Freeman eschewed the tricks of the word-monger (though as a veteran newspaper editor he certainly knew them well) in favor of straightforward history. Concerning Lee, he wrote in 1934, that there was no occasion "to attempt an 'interpretation' of a man who was his own clear interpreter." He emphasized this respect for facts in his address to his fellow Civil War Round Tablers:

> I have often looked at Lytton Strachey's five-page account of what was happening in the mind of Essex after a famous interview with Queen Elizabeth. Five pages he devotes in his "psychography," so-called, to the thoughts of Essex at that particular time. Although I lived twenty years with General Lee and have lived for ten years with General Washington, I am prepared humbly to submit to you that I do not know what either of them ever was thinking at a given moment unless he happened to have written it down himself. We cannot be too sure. Of all the frauds that ever have been perpetrated on our generation, this "psychography" is, in my opinion, the worst. How dare a man say what another man is thinking when he may not know what he himself is thinking! That is the fate of a good many of us.

I knew Dr. Freeman only slightly, and only in his last years. But before I knew him as a person I had known him for twenty years as an impressive figure—from brief glimpses of him vacationing in the

Tidewater country of Gloucester, from hearing his daily radio summary of the morning's news (for years an essential of a Virginian breakfast) during long vacations I spent in Virginia, from his editorials in the *Richmond News-Leader,* from listening to his address at my brother's graduation from Emory University, and, eventually, from a timidly entered (on my part) correspondence concerning certain perplexing questions in Confederate history. Finally I had the privilege of meeting him and of enjoying the hospitality of his home. Then in the winter of 1953 I was a "visiting scholar" at the University of Virginia and was admitted to tireless conversations with this man who could truly claim scholarship, scholarship without quotation marks. Since his death a continuing friendship with Mrs. Freeman and other members of his family, a growing familiarity with his books, an affection for the surroundings that were his surroundings and for his books, and pictures, and bric-a-brac that were his home and that became to me a second home during the time I lived in Richmond have given me much of the regard for Dr. Freeman that the Doctor had for Lee and for Washington.

He was not the austere, removed figure that Richmonders who did not know him thought. He had little time for frivolities. ("Time alone is irreplaceable . . . Waste it not" was his rule.) But he had a wonderful sense of humor, genuine kindness, and unlimited affection both for people and, hardly second, for the English language properly used. As an editorial memorializing him in the *News-Leader* declared: ". . . There was really nothing remote, nothing cold, about him. Though he had slight patience with fools, he had boundless patience with any young Telemachus . . . who sought him out as Nestor. He was a superb host, and shared with his lovely wife a knack for hospitality that came from the heart as warmth comes from an open fireplace; he loved good stories and told them well himself; he read, of course, with a boundless appetite for learning, and the impact of his wide-ranging intellect was an unforgettable experience. To be sure, he had his human failings, his vanities and conceits; he was annoyed by whistling office boys and loud-voiced women and barking dogs . . . , but his satisfactions endlessly outnumbered his irritations, and he found in his books and his music and the serenity of his well-ordered life a world of peace and contentment."

I learned much from Dr. Freeman. I have continued to learn from him in the last three years by being associated with him and with General Lee in somewhat the way he was so long associated with Lee and with Washington. I too have been repaid by a long and close companionship in the company of great gentlemen.

This is a preface to another author's biography of a great man. If it has turned into a personal memoir of the biographer, I can plead only that these things I can say of Dr. Freeman because they represent what he was to me. The bare facts are easily read elsewhere: in the usual biographical sketches and, most luminously, in Dumas Malone's brilliant essay "The Pen of Douglas Southall Freeman" which is incorporated into volume six of *George Washington*.

Dr. Freeman's whole life was preparation for his achievements as biographer of Virginia's two greatest heroes and as chronicler of the army which defended the state throughout the Civil War. He was born and bred a Virginian. Though his authority as an editor and as a military historian eventually involved him in engagements which necessitated a travel schedule averaging twenty-thousand miles a year, he repeatedly declined any change of work that would separate him permanently from Virginia.

Douglas Southall Freeman was the son of Walker Burford Freeman (a veteran of the Army of Northern Virginia) and Bettie Allen Hamner Freeman. He was born in Lynchburg May 16, 1886. His association with Richmond, the city with which he was finally identified so completely, began when he moved there as a child, and his undergraduate training was at Richmond College. He continued his formal education at the Johns Hopkins University and received his doctorate there in 1908. From that time on he was wholly a Richmonder. An apprenticeship as a newspaperman was served as a member of the editorial staff of *The Richmond Times-Dispatch* in 1909–10. After an interruption to work as secretary of the Virginia Tax Commission he returned to the newspaper business as associate editor of the *News-Leader* in 1913 and became editor in 1915.

He completed in 1908, while still at the Hopkins, his *A Calendar of Confederate Papers* describing in detail the collections at Richmond's Confederate Museum and pleading for further collection and use of manuscripts relating to the Confederacy. His expressions in that book on the care with which materials concerning all aspects of history must be collected and studied as a prerequisite for the writing of adequate, truthful history are of significance in light of his later career. Worthy of particular note is the following paragraph:

Finally, material should be collected for military biography. It is useless to emphasize the importance of an intimate acquaint-

ance on the part of the investigator with the personal characteristics and methods of the great generals of the period; only
through their private as well as official papers, can these be disclosed.

Dr. Freeman's first large work with Lee was *Lee's Dispatches*, a com-
pilation published in 1915 of the until then unpublished military messages sent by the General to President Jefferson Davis. His editing of
the dispatches (then owned by Wymberley Jones DeRenne of Worms-
loe, Georgia; later presented to the Virginia State Library by Bernard
Baruch) led to his choice by Scribner's as the author of an authoritative
biography of Lee. That biography would, a score of years later, confirm all that is implied as a prophecy for it in Dr. Freeman's first
paragraph of his introduction to *Lee's Dispatches:*

> The passage of years and the death of his comrades-in-arms
> have increased rather than diminished the fame of General Robert
> E. Lee as a military commander. Detractors and panegyrists alike
> are dead. The careless overstatements of partisans have given
> place to the cool analysis of impartial investigators; rigid com-
> parisons of his strategy and tactics with those of other great
> captains have assured him a place higher than if somewhat dif-
> ferent from that assigned him by his contemporaries.

By 1915 Dr. Freeman's long and intense association with Lee had
begun. But it must be remembered that he was at the same time a
full-time editor of a major newspaper, from 1925 onward a radio
commentator broadcasting fourteen times a week, a lecturer in ever-
widening demand, and the head of a family of five. The rigorous
schedule needed to compress his multiple activities into a manageable
routine need not be detailed here. It is enough to say that the years
1915–1934 were the Lee years. No effort was spared to complete fully
and well the task the biographer had undertaken. It was this effort and
care and ability as an author that produced at last one of the great
biographies of our time, a biography that is the ultimate answer to the
question that Dr. Freeman posed (and briefly answered) in his pamphlet *The Lengthening Shadow of Lee* in 1936: "How is it," he asked,
"that his shadow lengthens daily? The answer is to the honor of man-
kind. A generation sometimes mistakes the theatrical for the dramatic,
the specious for the serious, the pretender for the defender. . . . The
'hero of the hour' may not have deserved his place even for that hour;
he who is a hero when his century is done has qualities that are
timeless."

* * * * *

There remains to say a word about what I have done in reducing Dr. Freeman's *R. E. Lee* from four volumes to one. In no sense is this single-volume edition a substitute for the student of history who wants all the facts. Obviously, many details had to be abandoned in reducing the text. All of the footnotes, all of the appendices were eliminated. But I hope the basic facts remain and that they remain undistorted by condensation. The broad story of Lee's life is here, if not each detail. In his own foreword to *R. E. Lee* Dr. Freeman noted: "On occasion I have tried to master some narrative of a campaign, written by an author who manifestly knew the facts, but I have found my guide hustling me from one opposing line to the other and back again so often that he hopelessly confused me . . ." In the four volumes Dr. Freeman's very wealth of detail may tend to confuse the reader inexperienced in reading of the Civil War or the reader not interested in knowing the war's every detail. Perhaps a reduction of detail can emphasize the most important aspects of Lee's life for many readers or heighten the dramatic progress of the war for others.

Few words in the condensation are my own; Dr. Freeman's language has been retained, and I have inserted only unimportant transitional words or sentences where absolutely necessary (and gratifyingly infrequently). As valuable as it is as an exposition of the facts about Lee, Dr. Freeman's full work is equally valuable for its interpretative passages, and I have strived to maintain Dr. Freeman's balance between fact and interpretation.

The latest printing of the *R. E. Lee* has been used in my work. Although Dr. Freeman himself freely said that he wished thoroughly to revise the biography when the plates for it became too badly worn for further printings he left no notes for such a revision. From time to time, however, as minor errors were discovered and pointed out to him, he had caused corrections to be made in the plates. The current printing of the four-volume edition, therefore, represents the best possible text of the biography.

* * * * *

Even such solitary work as the condensation of an existing text cannot be accomplished in a vacuum. In my work on this volume I am indebted to Mrs. Inez Goddin Freeman of Richmond for her constant faith and encouragement; to Mrs. Mary Wells Ashworth of Richmond, long Dr. Freeman's assistant and the co-author of the volume which completed his biography of Washington, for patient talk about the problems of condensation, for a careful reading of a portion of the present work, and for most helpful advice as to how to adjust some stylistic deviations to the rules Dr. Freeman developed for his later writing; to Peter David Barnes of London for a reading of my manuscript from the viewpoint of one not familiar with Civil War history; to my sister, Mrs. Marion B. Harwell of Greensboro, Georgia, for a careful typing of the completed condensation; to Miss Elaine Mitchell of Chicago for further typing; and, of course, to Mr. Wayne Andrews of Charles Scribner's Sons for prodding and encouragement and the conscientious performance of all the chores that befall a good editor.

Finally, readers of history and biography owe a continuing acknowledgment to Wallace Meyer, who was for many years the friend and editor of Dr. Freeman and who recently retired from his long association with Scribner's, for the editorial care lavished by him on the original edition of *R. E. Lee*.

RICHARD HARWELL

Chicago
18 February 1961

LEE

CHAPTER I

The Education of a Cadet

THEY had come so often, those sombre men from the sheriff. Always they were polite, but they asked so insistently of the General's whereabouts and they talked of court papers with strange Latin names. Sometimes they lingered about as if they believed Henry Lee were in hiding. That was why Ann Carter Lee's husband had placed those chains there on the doors in the great hall at Stratford. The horses had been taken, the furniture had been "attached," and tract after tract had been sold to cancel obligations. Faithful friends still visited, and whenever the General rode to Montross or to Fredericksburg the old soldiers saluted him and told their young children that he was "Light-Horse Harry" Lee, but she knew that people whispered that he had twice been in jail because he could not pay his debts. She could not help him, because her father had put her inheritance in trust. Robert Morris, poor man, had died without returning a penny of the $40,000 he owed Mr. Lee, and that fine plan for building a town at the Great Falls of the Potomac had never been carried out, because they could not settle the quitrents. If General Lee had been able to do that or to get the money on that claim he had bought in England, all would be well. As it was, they could not go on there at Stratford. Besides, Stratford was not theirs. Matilda Lee had left it to young Henry and he was now of age. So, the only thing to do was go to Alexandria, where they could live in a simple home and send Charles Carter to the free school and find a doctor for the baby that was to come in February.

That was why they had Smith and three-year-old Robert in the carriage and were driving away from the ancestral home of the Lees. Perhaps it was well that Robert was so young: he would have no memories of those hard, wretched years that had passed since the General had started speculating—would not know, perhaps, that the

3

long drive up the Northern Neck, that summer day in 1810, marked the dénouement in the life drama of his brilliant, lovable, and unfortunate father.

Fairer prospects than those of Henry Lee in 1781 no young American revolutionary had. Born in 1756, at Leesylvania, Prince William County, Va., he was the eldest son of Henry Lee and his wife, Lucy Grymes. But for the coming of the war he would have gone to England to study law. Instead, he entered the army as a captain in the cavalry regiment commanded by his kinsman, Theodoric Bland. His achievements thereafter were in keeping with his opportunities, for he seemed, as General Charles Lee put it, "to have come out of his mother's womb a soldier." A vigorous man, five feet nine inches in height, he had strength and endurance for the most arduous of Washington's campaigns. Washington praised him in unstinted terms and Congress voted him thanks and a medal; he was privileged to address his dispatches directly and privately to Washington, whose admiring confidence he possessed; he was given a mixed command of infantry and cavalry which was officially designated as Lee's partisan corps; when he wearied of inaction in the North he was transferred to the Southern department in October, 1780, with the rank of lieutenant colonel. In South Carolina and Georgia his was the most spectacular part in the most successful campaign the American army fought, and his reputation rose accordingly. Then something happened to him. In a strange change of mental outlook, the tragedy of his life began. As soon as the fighting was over he became sensitive, resentful, and imperious.

For a while all appeared to go well with him. He seemed to make his way "easy and comfortable," as he had planned, by a prompt marriage with his cousin, Matilda Lee, who had been left mistress of the great estate of Stratford, on the Potomac. Their marriage was a happy one, and within five years, four children were born. Two of them survived the ills of early life, the daughter, Lucy Grymes, and the third son, Henry Lee, fourth of that name.

Following the custom of his family, Henry Lee became a candidate in 1785 for the house of delegates of Virginia. He was duly chosen and was promptly named by his colleagues to the Continental Congress, which he entered under the favorable introduction of his powerful kinsman, Richard Henry Lee. To the ratification of the new Constitution he gave his warmest support as spokesman for Westmoreland in the Virginia convention of 1788, where he challenged the thunders of Patrick Henry, leader of the opposition. Quick to urge Washington to accept the presidency, he it was who composed the farewell address on behalf of his neighbors when Washington started to New York to be inaugurated. The next year Lee was again a member of the house of delegates, and in 1791 he was chosen Governor of Virginia, which honorific position he held for three terms of one year each.

His public service was all too plainly the by-product of a mind preoccupied. For the chief weakness of his character now showed itself in a wild mania for speculation. His every scheme was grandiose, and his profits ran to millions in his mind. He plunged deeply, and always unprofitably.

Though there never was anything vicious in his character or dishonest in his purposes, Henry Lee impaired his reputation as a man of business. His own father, who died in 1789, passed over him in choosing an executor, while leaving him large landed property. Matilda Lee put her estate in trust for her children in 1790, probably to protect their rights against her husband's creditors. Soon afterwards she died, followed quickly by her oldest son, Philip Ludwell Lee, a lad of about seven.

Desperate in his grief, and conscious at last that he had made the wrong decision when he had left the army, Lee now wanted to return to a military life. He was passed over for reasons that he did not understand. If he could not wear again the uniform of his own country there was an alternative, to which Lee turned in the wildest of all his dreams. He was head of an American state, but he would resign, go to France and get a commission in the army of the revolutionaries! But before setting out for Paris he decided to take counsel with Washington. Washington, of course, warned him to stay away from a conflict that was leading to chaos.

Despite his reverence for Washington, Henry Lee might have placed his sword at the disposal of the French terrorists had not his mind been turned to a softer subject: Like many another widower he found consolation for a lost love in a new. Visiting Shirley, the James River plantation of Charles Carter, then probably the richest man in Virginia except George Washington, he became attached to Ann Hill Carter, then twenty. Lee was seventeen years her senior but he must have appealed to her from the first.

Charles Carter did not look at Lee through his daughter's eyes. He would not permit Ann to marry a Virginian foolish enough to throw in his lot with the madmen of Paris. Parleys ended in Lee's decision to abandon his French adventure. Carter gave his consent to a union which he was considerate enough to say he had opposed on no other grounds. The two were joined in the marriage of which Robert E. Lee was born.

For a time Henry Lee seemed to be stabilized. Retiring on the expiration of his third term as governor, he was mentioned as a possible successor to Washington. Instead of that office, however, all that remained to him were a few years of service in the general assembly, a temporary commission as major-general at the time of the threatened war with France, and a single term in Congress, where he eulogized his dead chieftain, as "first in war, first in peace, and first in the hearts of his countrymen." Thereafter he held no political office of importance.

His old passion for wild speculation returned. He became involved in the purchase of a part of the vast Fairfax estates in the Northern Neck and endeavored to finance it through Robert Morris, but, in the end, advanced Morris $40,000, which the old Philadelphian could not repay. Next Lee was entrusted with the sale of Western lands in 1797. Certain of the owners assumed obligations they were unable to meet when settlement was delayed. Undeterred, he was lured by the mysterious Western adventure of Aaron Burr. It was at this stage of his speculative mania, when he was dreaming of a fortune that was to be won by conquest of a new frontier, that his son Robert was conceived.

Ann Lee's pregnancy was not happy. Too many shadows hung over it. Sickness had brought suffering and weeks of invalidism. Henry Lee had been more and more frequently absent for long periods; the pinch of poverty had taken from her the comforts she had known in girlhood; she had lost even her carriage; life had grown gray on the narrowed, untilled acres of Stratford. She had gone to Shirley after the death of her father and had found it a house of mourning. On her return home at the end of December, 1806, she had caught a cold from which she was suffering as the time for the delivery of her child approached.

On January 19, 1807, Ann Carter Lee's fourth child was born, an unblemished boy, who was named Robert Edward, after two of his mother's brothers, Robert and Edward Carter. His first cry was in the chamber in which, according to tradition, Richard Henry and Francis Lightfoot Lee, signers of the Declaration of Independence, had seen the light.

When Robert was sixteen months old, his half-brother Henry came into possession of Stratford. After that "Light-Horse Harry" and his family by his second marriage could only remain on the estate as guests of the young master. The old soldier could see no alternative to beating a retreat. He must leave the country, if he could, and find shelter where his creditors could not pursue him.

During the spring of 1809, when Robert was receiving his first impressions of Stratford as a place of beauty and of glory, his father came to the last humiliation: odds and ends of real estate that had been left to him after nearly thirty years of wild trading had to be deeded away. Of everything that could be sold, he was stripped bare. And even this did not save him. On April 11, 1809, he was arrested for a debt of some 5400 Spanish dollars, with accrued interest for nearly seven years, and was confined to jail. Not until the spring of 1810 was he at liberty, and then he had nothing left him except some lands he could not market.

At home again, he decided on the move to Alexandria. Henry could not be expected to supply food and shelter indefinitely. There was no money with which to employ a tutor for the three children. Everything left to Mrs. Lee and her young brood was the return from a trust that had been set up under the will of her father. When the estate was settled, the revenue from this fund, which Henry Lee could not dissipate, would provide shelter, food, and clothing but nothing besides.

The little caravan from Stratford ended its journey at a small house on Cameron Street in Alexandria. Life was easier there than in the sprawling Stratford mansion, but cares increased. During the winter, after the family settled in town, a new baby, a girl, was born to the burdened mother. There were now five children, ranging from the new-born infant to a boy of thirteen.

Then, when Robert was five and a half, the final blow came. Henry Lee's strong Federalism had led him to oppose a second war with Great Britain. When hostilities opened in June, 1812, Lee was unreconciled to the conflict and quick to sympathize with those who became the victims of war's passions. Among these was the young editor of The Baltimore Federal Republican, Alexander C. Hanson, whose plant, press, and building were wrecked by a mob which an antiwar editorial had inflamed. Hanson was no coward, and though he left Baltimore temporarily and came to Georgetown, he determined to return to the city and to resume the circulation of his journal. On July 27, 1812, he issued in Baltimore a paper which had been printed in Georgetown. Henry Lee had paid two visits to him after he had reached Baltimore, and when he observed the sensation created by the paper, Lee hastened to him again. He found the editor and a few friends assembled in a house that Hanson was using as a combined office and residence. Soon after Lee arrived, idlers in the street were swollen into a wrathful mob that threatened an assault. As an experienced soldier, Lee was asked to assist in protecting the premises. Firing soon broke out. One man was killed in the street and another was wounded. The mob would doubtless have attacked the building and would have slain the volunteer garrison then and there, had not the militia arrived and taken position in the street.

After a night of excitement, negotiations were opened between the troops and the friends of Hanson. Finally the occupants of the house submitted themselves to the officers of the law, who escorted them to jail as the safest place until passions cooled. After nightfall, a crowd of armed men gathered before the jail, intent on murder. An entrance was soon forced. Death seemed so certain that Lee proposed to his companions that they should take the few weapons they had and shoot one another rather than let themselves be torn to pieces by the mob. But better judgment prevailed, and when the door of the cell was beaten down, the defenders made a sally. Instantly there was a confused mêlée. When it was over, half of Hanson's friends had escaped, but one had been killed and eleven frightfully beaten. Eight were thought to be dead and were piled together in front of the building, where they were subjected to continued mutilation. Henry Lee was among this number. Drunken brutes thrust penknives into his flesh, and waited to see whether there was a flicker when hot candle grease was poured into his eyes. One fiend tried to cut off his nose. After a while, some of the town physicians succeeded in carrying him to a hospital. His death was reported in Washington, but his great physical strength sufficed to keep him alive and made it possible for him to return home later in the summer. But he was weak, crippled, and disfigured, doomed to invalidism for the remaining six years of his life, wholly dependent on the income of his wife, and of course incapable of accepting the military command that would almost certainly have been given him when the first tide of the war in Canada turned against the United States.

Hope was dead now in the heart of Henry Lee. His one ambition was to leave the country, both for his health and for his peace of mind. President James Monroe arranged for Lee to go to the Barbadoes. So, one day in the early summer of 1813, Robert must have shed tears with the rest, as he shared the final embraces of his father. Behind him, in his own household, "Light-Horse Harry" left only sorrow. For he had never lost the respect, much less the affection, of his family. Fully conscious of his failings, they still were awed by his dignity and fascinated by his conversation. But Henry Lee could not have been greatly comforted, as he went down the Potomac, by the knowledge that he was still king of his fireside. He was sailing away from the state he had governed, from the creditors he could never pay, from a family he might not see again, and he knew he was passing over the gray horizon of failure.

The city that Henry Lee left behind him, the Alexandria of Robert Lee's widening consciousness, was a pleasant place of 7500 people. Ties of blood or of common service joined the Lees to its society. Cousins uncounted lived in Alexandria. One of Henry Lee's brothers, Edmund Jennings Lee, was a luminary of the town. Their sister Mary had married Philip R. Fendall, a local lawyer of much social charm. Out at Ravensworth, in Fairfax County, lived William H. Fitzhugh, distant kinsman but close friend, the broad door of whose ample home was always open to Mrs. Lee and her children.

Nothing else meant so much to the town as did its associations with George Washington. By the time Robert was old enough to understand something of the spirit of the Father of his Country, Washington had been twenty years in his tomb at Mount Vernon. But he was alive in the hearts of old Alexandrians. Reminders of him were everywhere. Washington was a part of the life of Robert Lee from earliest childhood. Doubtless his mother remembered the letter in which Washington had written Henry Lee his congratulations upon the marriage. Pride in the friendship of the first citizen of the country had been the consolation of "Light-Horse Harry's" blackest days, and from his exile he was to write of "the great Washington" and repeat his old commander's words for the admonition of his son, Charles Carter. The family held fast to this reverence.

In Robert's young eyes the centre of Alexandria and of all its traditions was the home on Cameron Street. Over it presided his mother, charged for the rest of her days with the entire care of her five children, their finances, their religious training, and their education. Physically it overtaxed her, but spiritually she was equal to it. Ann Carter Lee was thirty-seven when they moved from Stratford, and forty when Henry Lee went to the West Indies. The contrast between the rich ease of her girlhood and the adversity of her married life was sharp. Yet it did not embitter her. She continued to love the author of her misfortune. And he, for all his distresses, kept his devotion to her and his high respect for her. But she had taken Henry's tragedy to heart, and the reasons for his fall, and she was determined that his grim cycle of promise, over-confidence, recklessness, disaster, and ruin should not be rounded in the lives of her children. Self-denial, self-control, and the strictest economy in all financial matters were part of the code of honor she taught them from infancy. These qualities were inculcated in Robert so deeply that they became fundamentals of his character.

Although Robert lived among the Lees, the atmosphere of his home was that of the Carters. His mother corresponded with them, talked of them, and at least once a year endeavored to take her younger children on a visit to Shirley. It was a gracious place. Built early in the eighteenth century, it had been adorned by each generation of Hills and of Carters, as though they owed it a debt they were eager to discharge with generous interest.

Young Robert had a friendly multitude of close Carter cousins, for hundreds, literally, were descended from the twelve children of "King" Carter. The size and endogamy of the Carter tribe made it socially self-contained. Every true Carter liked everybody, but most of all he liked his kinspeople. Often and joyfully they visited one another. Of journeying and letter-writing and the exchange of family news, the years brought no end. It was at Shirley, amid the infectious laughter and the kindly chatter of his cousins, that the youthful Robert developed early the fondness for the company of his kin that was so marked in his maturity.

When Robert was seven the war that his father had opposed before his departure for the West Indies had been in progress nearly two years and the time had come for Robert to begin his formal education. His first books doubtless were opened to him by his mother. Later he was sufficiently advanced in the rudiments to be sent away to the family school. For the Carters were so numerous and so intimate that they maintained two schools for their children, one for girls at Shirley and one for boys at Eastern View, Fauquier County.

The life of the family changed somewhat during the years Robert probably was at Eastern View. For a time the finances of Mrs. Lee had been less strained. By 1816, and perhaps a little earlier, the family had moved from Cameron Street to a house cn Washington Street at the corner of Princess. From this home, in 1816, the oldest of Ann Carter Lee's children, Charles Carter Lee, started for Harvard. Not long after Carter left, the elder Henry Lee's letters told of his plans to return home. He was determined to come back to his own state. But months passed, and no ship was available. Finally, Lee wrote that he would sail for Savannah, Ga., and would attempt to procure passage thence to Virginia. The next news was that Robert's father had been stricken mortally on the voyage and had been put ashore at Dungeness, Cumberland Island, Ga., the property of the daughter of his old commander, General Greene. He had died there, March 25, 1818. The details of his passing were not known to the family until the next autumn. The death of Henry Lee meant financial relief for them, but it was not mourned the less on that account.

Although Robert was only eleven when his father died, responsibility was soon to fall heavily on his shoulders. His sister Ann continued sickly; Mrs. Lee was slipping into chronic invalidism. Carter returned from Cambridge in 1819 but opened his law office in Washington and was not much at home to aid in the management of the household. The next year President Monroe gave a midshipman's commission to Smith, who went to sea. The duties of son and daughter fell on Robert.

Attendance upon his mother continued until Robert left Alexandria. More than anything else, perhaps, his filial attention to her was the prime obligation of his youth, precisely as care for an invalid wife was to be one of the chief duties of his mature years. He stayed at home uncomplainingly when his mother required him, but when he was free he delighted to swim in the Potomac, to share in the sports of the neighborhood boys with his cousin and playmate, Cassius Lee, or to follow the chase all day in the rolling country behind Alexandria. If he had a longer holiday he spent it at Chatham, or at Ravensworth with the Fitzhughs, or at Stratford with his half-brother Henry, who, about the time Robert was ten, married Anne McCarty of Westmoreland County. Robert developed rapidly in physique and in character, and by the time he was thirteen he had learned all that could conveniently be taught him at home and at Eastern View. Accordingly, by 1820, possibly before that year, Robert entered the Alexandria academy.

For approximately three years he studied the rudiments of a classical education. By the end of 1823 he had completed the course of study at the academy. What should he do next? It was a question not easily answered. He could not continue to follow cultural study and settle down as a country-gentleman, because he did not have money for the education, much less the land on which to live in leisure. He possessed no aptitude for public utterance and no taste for the law. He had never presented himself for confirmation and he probably never gave a thought to the ministry. There is no record that he ever debated the possibilities of a medical career, despite his contact with the sick and his growing skill in nursing. What, then, should he do?

His brother Smith had gone into the navy: why should not Robert go to the United States Military Academy at West Point and be a soldier? His love of mathematics would help; his education would cost him nothing. By this process of reasoning, it would appear, Robert E. Lee decided to become a soldier.

The age-limits for admission to West Point were fourteen to twenty years, for boys who were at least four feet, nine inches, free of physical defects, able to read and write well, familiar with arithmetic, and willing to sign articles to remain five years in the army, including the four years of cadetship. Robert could meet all these requirements, if he could have the good fortune to be named one of the 250 cadets for whom the government made provision. The appointments were at the pleasure of the President, on the nomination of the Secretary of War, who at that time followed no rule respecting their geographical distribution, but the number did not suffice even then, and the scramble was keen. Robert's age and his mother's circumstances were such that he could not afford to wait on a chance appointment. He must either begin soon as a soldier or turn immediately to something else. It consequently was decided in the family-circle that he should make personal application to John C. Calhoun, the Secretary of War. But who would introduce him to that august personage? The duty fell to the family's counsellor, William H. Fitzhugh of Ravensworth.

Robert presented Fitzhugh's letter in person. A strange interview it must have been between the man who was soon to be the "father of nullification" and the boy who, in maturity, was to carry the burden of the bloody struggle that was, in a sense, the unescapable consequence of the application of that doctrine. Calhoun could not have failed to be impressed by young Lee and probably told him that if he produced suitable recommendations, they would be considered.

Robert brought to bear all the influence his family could exert. Then he could only wait and hope. Finally there came notice from the War Department: As of March 11, Robert was appointed to West Point, but owing to the long list of applicants, he could not be admitted until July 1, 1825. That entailed a year's delay, but it meant opportunity then!

The very atmosphere of Alexandria seemed to lend itself to martial affairs after Robert learned that he would be admitted to the military academy. Lafayette was coming! "America's Friend," now an old man, was revisting the scenes of his greatest adventure. For no family in the town was Lafayette's visit more interesting than for the Lees. The marquis had not forgotten the brilliant cavalryman of Washington's army, who was only a year and a half his senior. Hearing that the widow of his comrade was residing in Alexandria, he made a call on the morning of October 14, 1824.

The very day before Lafayette called, a young Quaker named James Hallowell had brought his bride to Oronoko Street, where he proposed to open a boys' school in the house adjoining that of the Lees. This school Robert entered in February, 1825, and remained with Mr. Hallowell until he was ready to set out for West Point. The charges were $10 a quarter, no small item to a widow who had to count costs carefully, but the expense was justified. Hallowell was able to give the boy intimate and close instruction, and Robert responded to Hallowell's full satisfaction.

By steamer and stage, Robert Lee journeyed to West Point in June, 1825. There he had ample time in the relatively quiet summer to prepare for the work of the coming winter and to learn the "Thou-shalt-nots" that constituted a large part of life at West Point. No cadet could drink or play cards, or use tobacco. He might not have in his room any cooking utensils, any games, or any novel. With the consent of the superintendent, he might subscribe to one periodical, but to only one. Too much reading was accounted bad for a soldier: the library was open only two hours a week—on Saturday afternoons. Societies and meetings were forbidden without the consent of the superintendent. No visitors might call on Sunday, in study hours, or in the evenings. A cadet was forbidden to go beyond designated limits. And so for a still longer list of things that a gentleman and soldier should not do—if Colonel Sylvanus Thayer knew it. Such were the regulations; the practice fell far short of this stern assumption of the perfectibility of youth. There was drunkenness and fighting and abstention from parade and occasional visits after taps to North's, where supper and strong drink were to be had. Cadets were caught often and not infrequently were courtmartialled but were rarely dismissed.

It was a full routine on which Robert entered when recitations were begun September 1 after summer in camp. A long day was regulated overmuch and included too little time for recreation. In winter, cold, bad food, and lack of exercise—for drill had virtually to be suspended —made it too hard a schedule for boys who were not of the most robust. Robert was equal to it physically, and he found it academically easy. He had gone further in mathematics before he came to West Point than the curriculum carried him during the whole of the first year. Lee's only other academic study that winter was French, to which two hours of study and one hour of recitation were given daily.

Military instruction was limited in Robert's first year to what a private soldier would have received at an active army post under a good company-officer. Drill, however, ate up the little time that French and mathematics left. When the weather was good, there were few hours for outside study. Fortunately for the larger culture of the cadets, there came to the academy that year a man who taught the boys some things not set down in Colonel Thayer's tables of instruction and some they might not have sought out for themselves. This man was Reverend Charles P. McIlvaine, chaplain and professor of geography, history, and ethics. It was perhaps well for Lee, as for many another young man at West Point, that the zealous ministry of McIlvaine entered his life so soon after he left home.

The first six months at the school were probationary. The instructors made daily notes of individual proficiency and filed weekly reports. Not until examinations had been passed in January did a cadet receive his warrant and become a regular member of the corps.

On January 2, 1826, the semi-annual examinations began. The confident and the fearful alike were subjected to an hour's quizzing. Robert Lee came out well, though he discovered that some of his classmates had been working as hard as he had and were possessed of keen minds. Charles Mason, Catharinus L. Buckingham, and William H. Harford were tied with him in mathematics, and as his patronymic was alphabetically the third of the quartet he got that rating. In French, he was fifth. On conduct he was third, but had no offenses recorded against him. He received his warrant and settled down to a hard battle to improve his showing.

June came, and with it the board of visitors named by the Secretary of War to supervise examinations and to report on the needs and condition of the institution. Robert emerged the third man in his class. Charles Mason led and William Harford was second. Pressing close

SHIRLEY AND STRATFORD

LEE AS LIEUTENANT OF ENGINEERS

behind Lee were William Boylan and James Barnes. Neither Lee, Mason, nor Barnes had received a demerit during the year, but Harford had seven and Boylan thirty-five, which made the standing of Boylan all the more remarkable. In mathematics Lee was fourth, and received a credit of 197 of a possible 200. In French he was fifth, and was rated 98¼ of a possible 100. On the roll of general merit, he was put at the sum of these two ratings—295¼ of a gross 300.

This was a good showing and it brought immediate rewards. Robert was placed on the list of "distinguished cadets"—the first five in each class—whose names were certified to the Secretary of War for inclusion in the army register. His first appearance in that document was in the edition of 1826 when he was credited with special proficiency in mathematics and in French.

Another honor awaited him. Under the rules of the corps, the best soldiers of good standing acted as officers. From the boys who had just completed their first year's work were chosen the corporals. The second class previously had furnished the sergeants, and the first the lieutenants, the captains, and the most-sought-after post of all, that of adjutant. During the winter of 1825–26, the regulations had been so changed that the sergeancies did not all go to the second class. Robert had done so well in his drill, and had already developed such good military bearing that on June 23, when the appointments were read out, he was named staff sergeant, as high a position as any to which a man just finishing his first year at the academy could then aspire.

On July 1, 1826 Robert and his fellow-toilers ceased to be "plebes" and overnight became "upper-classmen," fit to hold fellowship with the lofty souls of the class of 1828, and permitted to look without apology on the faces of those who were now the first class. On the same day the annual encampment on the plain began. Lee, with his comrades, had the monotony of infantry drill broken by their introduction to artillery. For about nine weeks they had two hours daily with their muskets and four with artillery; work enough for warm days when the woods called and the river lured the boys who were sweating under canvas.

With the return to barracks on September 1, Lee and his class plunged into more advanced mathematics—calculus, analytical and descriptive geometry and difficult conic sections. French was continued. The one added academic study was free-hand drawing of the human figure. Infantry drill continued, in the school of the company, with instruction in the duties of corporals. Two hours every second afternoon during the academic term was devoted to artillery.

This was a busy routine, but Robert was now so well-grounded that he felt he could indulge himself in a little outside reading, and, in addition, he essayed some teaching. Lee and the three other members of his class who had stood first in that subject were made acting assistant professors of mathematics. The duties were largely tutorial, and they consumed hours that Lee must have wished he could have given to other subjects, but they were helpful. His mother was greatly pleased at the distinction and was delighted that he received compensation for it.

But Robert's outside activities proved too much for him. On the semiannual examination in January, 1827, his rating reflected the loss of the time he had devoted to reading and to teaching. In mathematics he was fourth, in French he was fifth, and in drawing fifth. He still had no demerits, and his drill-record was clean. William Boylan, who had stood next after Lee at the end of their first year, was no longer at the academy, but Catharinus P. Buckingham, No. 9 in June, 1826, was pushing ahead. Charles Mason and William Harford continued to do admirably. Warned by their progress, Robert forthwith abandoned most of his extra reading and buckled down to his classes.

But there was one historical work he probably could not resist. That was the new edition of his father's *Memoirs of the War in the Southern Department*. This had been prepared by his half-brother, Henry Lee. It contained some useful notes and addenda. Robert doubtless had read the first edition in boyhood, but now he could bring to bear on the book something of the understanding of a soldier, and could appreciate more fully the military qualities of his father. The effect the probable reading of this edition of his father's *Memoirs* does not show in any of his letters but it must have confirmed him in his determination to follow the career of a soldier.

Much closer to Robert in the winter of 1826–27 than any dream of emulating his father in military achievement, was the daily round of his study. He adjusted his hours to his teaching duties and began to form plans to win a furlough in July. No cadet could leave, except for serious illness, until he had been two years at the academy, and even then only those could go home who had received the written consent of their parents and stood well on Colonel Thayer's records. Robert procured Mrs. Lee's approval of his application; the money he was earning would suffice to pay his expenses; the rest depended chiefly on his own efforts. April arrived at last, and field exercises were resumed. May drew on, and the students settled to their special preparation for the June ordeal. Finally the examinations were over, and the results were announced. His total on the roll of general merit was 430½, and this put him second in the class. Charles Mason continued first. Robert remained staff sergeant, kept on the list of "distinguished cadets," and, of course, won his furlough.

This began in time to permit him to reach northern Virginia when sociable kinspeople of his name were starting their summer visits to one another. He found his mother residing in Georgetown, old at fifty-four by reason of disease and the burdens she had borne. He was able, however, to take her with him on at least one journey to the home of some of her Carter cousins. As her escort, dressed in his gray cadet uniform, with its white bullet buttons, his looks and his manners called forth admiring comment from the girls of his stock. He was becoming by this time an exceedingly handsome young man, with manners in keeping and at the academy was already styled the "Marble Model." A fellow-cadet testified years afterward, "His personal appearance surpassed in manly beauty that of any cadet in the corps. Though firm in his position and perfectly erect, he had none of the stiffness so often assumed by men who affect to be very strict in their ideas of what is military."

Shortly after his return to the academy on August 28 Lee resumed his work as acting assistant professor of mathematics. Simultaneously he entered on scientific studies that were entirely new to him. Mathematics was dropped. Drawing was continued and was given a higher credit. It called for two hours' work each week-day afternoon and included landscape and topography. Chemistry and "natural philosophy"—physics in modern academic terminology—became his major studies for the year. The subject interested Robert. It dealt with material, practical things that always appealed to him; it was an approach to engineering, which was the goal of nearly all ambitious cadets; and it meant much in determining a cadet's standing. In military study, Lee's class passed that year through the school of the battalion, learned the duties of sergeants, and was drilled in the exercise and manoeuvres of artillery pieces.

On January 7, 1828, the academic board met and the troubled cadets were commanded to give evidence of the knowledge that was in them. Robert Lee came out from the inquisition with an excellent showing. In natural philosophy he was rewarded by a standing of No. 2. He was third in chemistry, and in drawing fourth.

Encouraged by this showing and relieved after April 1 of his mathematical teaching, Robert had more time for independent reading during the late winter and early spring of 1828 than in any other period of his cadetship. Between January 27 and May 24, he drew fifty-two books from the library. They covered a wide field—navigation, travel, strategy, biography, and history. He indulged himself, moreover, in a reading of a French edition of Rousseau's *Confessions*.

Robert's reading did not interfere that spring with his studies or with his military duty. When the examinations were over in June, Robert had not headed Charles Mason but he was immediately below him on the roll of general merit. He was credited with 295 of a possible 300 in physics and was second in that subject. He stood No. 3 in chemistry, with 99 of the allowable 100. Drawing now yielded him 97 of a maximum 100 points. His general merit for the year was very high —491.

The academic mortality in the class had been heavy. Of the eighty-seven who had started in July, 1825, seventeen had fallen by the way at the end of the first session. Several had dropped out during 1826–27, and three more had failed by July, 1827. Now eight men went down, and others were despairing. Of the four Virginians who had entered together in 1825 only two were left, Lee and Joseph E. Johnston. These were drawn closer together when they realized they were the sole representatives of their state.

Robert's personal qualities and his high standing made him a contender in the mind of every cadet for that most coveted of West Point honors, the office of corps adjutant, which was awarded about July 1, when a class entered its final year. The appointment usually was awarded the first-classman of good standing who had the finest military bearing and the best record on the drill ground. Would it go now to Charles Mason, who had been No. 1 since the first examination? The answer came positively and promptly, as was the way with the decisions of Colonel Thayer and of Major William J. Worth: The adjutant of the corps for 1828–29 was to be Robert E. Lee of Virginia.

Now began the term for which all else was preparatory, the term into which was crowded all the technical military training, together with a second course in chemistry and a hurried, superficial survey of geography, history, ethics, and moral philosophy. Lee put aside all extra reading and concentrated his efforts. He spent a winter that was devoid of sensation and full of work. Tied with Buckingham at the head of the class in engineering after the critical semi-annual examinations, with even greater energy, he turned to the work of the final half term. On April 1 he procured relief as adjutant of the corps, got permission to board at Cozzen's Hotel, and thereafter, for two months, concentrated on his studies.

Quickly enough the finals approached, and the board of visitors arrived. At last it was done; all forty-six members of the class were examined; the credits were all computed. Lee's consistent good conduct and soldierly bearing now put him at the head of the class in artillery and tactics and gave him equal place in conduct with James Barnes, Sidney Burbank, Harford, St. John P. Kennedy, and Mason, who had received no demerits during the whole of their four years at the academy. In final class standing Mason was No. 1; Lee was No. 2; Harford, Joseph A. Smith, and Barnes followed in order.

Exercising the right accorded the class-leaders of selecting the arm of the service in which they desired to be commissioned, he asked to be assigned to the Engineer Corps. This was the usual choice of those who stood highest on the merit roll and it conformed to Lee's own inclination. No subject of study at the academy had enthralled him so much as that which he now made the basis of his professional work in the army.

Commencement at West Point in the 1820's was not the great event it is today. There was usually a valedictory address and sometimes a speech by the Secretary of War or some other dignitary, but that was all. Each graduate received a formal diploma, signed by the superintendent and academic board. Each was granted a two-months furlough and was given whatever balance of pay and allowances was due him. In Lee's case this amounted to $103.58, for while he had spent as much as the average cadet with the tailor, and something more than the average for postage, he had been most economical in other personal expenditures.

The tragedy of commencement was the separation of boys who had spent four years together in close and revealing companionship. Death was to claim seventeen of Robert's forty-five classmates and nine were to quit the service prior to the War between the States. Of the 323 who were with him at the academy and graduated in the classes of 1826–32, inclusive, 119 came to their end before 1861. Seventy resigned and, so far as is known, did not return to the service when North and South took up arms. Robert's intimates and his rivals for academic honors found varying fortune. Jack Mackay, who was perhaps his closest friend, served in the Artillery until 1846, when protracted illness forced him to procure sick leave. He died in 1848, aged forty-two. William Harford left the Army in 1833 and lived only three years thereafter. Charles Mason remained at the academy for two years, as principal assistant professor of engineering, then practised law in New

York and served as temporary editor of *The Evening Post* until 1836, when he went to Wisconsin. He later had a civil career of some eminence in Iowa, living to be seventy-seven.

The only men of '29 with whom Lee was closely associated in 1861–65 were Joseph E. Johnston and Theophilus H. Holmes, but eleven of the cadets who were at "the Point" during his four years were to become general officers in the Confederacy, and one was to be president. Lee's future chief of artillery, W. N. Pendleton, was in the class of 1830. L. B. Northrop, the commissary general, graduated in 1831, and Abraham C. Myers, quartermaster general of the South until 1863, was a "plebe" in Lee's last year.

Two of Lee's classmates, James Barnes, who was No. 5, and Sidney Burbank, No. 17, were later to face him in Virginia, though not as commanding generals. Silas Casey, of the class of 1826, was to stand stubbornly on the doubtful field of Seven Pines. Samuel P. Heintzelman, also of 1826, served with the Army of the Potomac, as division and corps commander, until October, 1863. W. H. Emory, a third classman in Lee's last year, came, in time, to command the Nineteenth Federal Corps in the Shenandoah Valley, in the campaign against Early. Erasmus D. Keyes, of the class of 1832, served with the Federals in the Peninsular campaign, as did Philip Saint George Cooke of '27. In the main, however, cadets who were with Robert Lee at West Point were not those with whom or against whom he was to fight. Such pre-war knowledge of his opponents as he was to use effectually in the 'sixties he acquired in the Mexican campaigns, or in his later service, and not during the years that came to a close that June day, 1829.

Robert Lee was then twenty-two and a half, full grown to his height of five feet, ten and a half inches, with brown eyes that sometimes seemed black. His hair was ebon and abundant, with a wave that a woman might have envied. There was dignity in his open bearing, and his manners were considerate and ingratiating. He had candor, tact, and good humor. The self-control he had learned from his mother was his in larger measure. His character was formed, and his personality was developed. It was easy for him to win and to hold the friendship of other people. His professional interest was fixed in engineering, and it never wavered until disappointment over slow promotion led him to accept a cavalry commission. He was not, of course, a finished, or even an accomplished soldier. But the training he had received was the best his country could give. The rest lay with him.

CHAPTER II

Lee Prepares for the War with Mexico

THE summer after his graduation should have been for Robert the happiest of all seasons, but it was, instead, one of the saddest periods of his life. The joy of home-coming was ruined by the illness of his mother. When Robert arrived, she was at Ravensworth in a worse condition than ever and was ready to die. Charles Carter was developing his practice; Smith was progressing in the navy; Ann in 1826 had married William Louis Marshall, a minister who later became an attorney of station; Mildred, in her nineteenth year, was in friendly hands. And now Robert was embarking on a career of high promise. Ann Carter Lee had seen it through, but the struggle had cost her all her vitality. She could fight for nothing further.

Robert resumed his old duties as a nurse. He mixed her medicines, administered them, and watched by her bed almost continuously. It was not a long siege this time. On July 10, Robert saw the light leave her eye and the last faint breath fail her. He turned from the bed in a grief that he never forgot. She was buried at Ravensworth, and there her ashes remained until they were moved to rest in a vault at Lexington, Va., near those of her son, whither also, in 1913, the bones of Henry Lee were brought from Cumberland Island.

For a time after her death, Robert apparently was in Georgetown, engaged in helping to settle his mother's estate. He doubtless was relieved when he was able to return to Virginia about August 1 and sojourn with relatives. But, with the buoyancy of youth, he quickly recovered from the immediate grief of his mother's death and, as one of his cousins remembered, was "as full of life, fun and particularly of teasing, as any of us." He visited much at Eastern View, but there was another mansion to which his interest and his horse were turning very frequently. This was Arlington, the home of George Washington Parke Custis, on the hills above Alexandria. Custis was the grandson of Mrs.

George Washington and was the adopted son of Washington. Having resided at Mount Vernon from 1782 until the end of his grandmother's life in 1802, he had observed Washington closely during the general's last years. His temperament was such that he delighted in the sentimental appelation, "The child of Mount Vernon," though he measured out his full seventy years and more. Arlington had been built by him after the death of his grandmother, when Mount Vernon had reverted to the Washington family. The house, named after an old Custis home on the Eastern Shore of Virginia, was distinguished more for its site and for the impressive columnated portico than for interior beauty or convenience. It gives the impression of being built to be looked at, rather than to be lived in.

To Arlington, in 1806, Custis brought as his bride Mary Lee Fitzhugh. Of their four children, only one survived infancy. She was Mary Anne Randolph Custis, born October 1, 1808, and reared in the amplest luxury. Twenty-one years of age when Robert came home from West Point, she had known him almost all her life, for the families were distantly related through the Lee ancestry of the Randolphs and they visited one another frequently. She was a frail, blonde girl. Her features were aristocratic but not beautiful. The nose was a trifle too long and the chin a bit too sharp, but she had freshness, bright eyes, a ready smile, and quick, sympathetic interest. If Robert did not actually love her from boyhood, he certainly put her in a place by herself. She it was who drew him to Arlington. When he went away, it was to come again, always with deepening delight in her company.

While Robert was visiting at Arlington and at Eastern View, his orders came. They read as follows:

Engineer Order No. 8.

Washington, D. C., Aug. 11, 1829

Brevet Second Lieut. Robert E. Lee . . . will, by the middle of November next, report to Major Samuel Babcock of the corps of Engineers for duty at Cockspur Island, in the Savannah River, Georgia.

C. GRATIOT,

Brig. Gen. Comndg.

Cockspur Island! A God-forsaken spot by all accounts, redeemed only by the fact that it was near Savannah, where lived the family of

Lee's chum, Jack Mackay. But orders were orders. Robert said farewell to his kinspeople and to the young mistress of Arlington.

Savannah, at which the young lieutenant arrived by packet, about November 1, 1829, was a place of some 7300 people, the largest city and the principal port in a state that had been settled less than one hundred years and then counted no more than 300,000 whites in a population of 516,000. Socially, the town was attractive and cultured. The Mackays, who welcomed Lee with open doors, were among the most distinguished of Savannah families, with daughters who were interesting even at first sight. In a few days Lee was introduced to all the civilians who were accounted worth knowing. As for the army, Savannah boasted a small garrison of United States artillery, among whom were several officers with whom Lee became friendly. Jack Mackay had been assigned to this garrison.

The post was by no means so pleasant as the town. It was, in fact, as drab and desolate as its reputation. Cockspur Island lies twelve miles down-stream from Savannah and is the easternmost islet of a number of flats in Tybee Roads. Very little of it was above normal tide level at the time of Lee's arrival, and most of it was marsh-land, flooded daily and completely covered in heavy storms. In summer, Cockspur had virtually to be abandoned because of mosquitoes, heat, and fever. It was, however, a training-school for Lee in the practical problems of military engineering and in the management of labor.

His engineering work was not always interesting but it usually was troublesome. The project at Cockspur Island was to locate and subsequently to construct a heavy fort on an island that afforded at best a doubtful foundation. Into the first stages of this hard work, Robert put all he had learned at West Point and all the strength of his staunch physique. He spent so many days in mud and water, up to his armpits, that a certain interested young woman, up in Virginia, wondered how he ever survived it, and to the end of her days she never ceased to marvel at it.

Finding friends in Savannah whenever he could go there, and occupying his leisure hours in letter-writing and in sketching, Lee passed the winter of 1829–30. Such social life as he could have in Savannah must have been less pleasant than it would normally have been to a young man of his temperament because the proud name of the Lee family had become involved in a humiliating public scandal in the very circles where it had stood highest. In 1817, Henry Lee, Robert's half-brother, had married a young woman of means in Westmoreland County. Living as a country gentleman, first at Stratford and then at Fredericksburg, Major Lee had dabbled in letters, much to the neglect of his estate, and had served as assistant postmaster general under President J. Q. Adams. In 1827, Henry Lee's affairs had become so much involved that a judgment of $9000 was procured against him by Henry Storke. As Lee could not meet this, Stratford had been sold for $11,000 and on June 30, 1828, had formally passed out of the Lee family. Impoverished and embittered, Lee had tried to make a living by writing. By inheritance he was a Federalist, but he had become a protagonist of Andrew Jackson. He had resided at "The Hermitage" after the sale of Stratford, had been engaged in arranging Jackson's military papers, and had written several polemics in behalf of "Old Hickory." Jackson felt much gratitude to Lee. When he became President, he named his defender United States consul to Morocco. It was a vacation appointment, which Lee was very glad to accept. He left the country for his post, only to find that he left a storm behind him. His wife had a younger sister, co-heiress to her father's estate. Henry Lee became enamoured of her and had been guilty of misconduct with her. The facts had been whispered about, but they had led to no public reprisals. Now, when Jackson submitted his name for confirmation by the Senate an open fight was made on him. Every senator who cast a ballot voted against him. The whole of the scandal became common knowledge in March, 1830. Henry Lee had to leave his post, and after a stay in Italy, removed to Paris, where he lived until his death, seven years later.

This affair must have been an intense humiliation to Lieutenant Lee. Much as he had cherished the memory of his father, he could not have been ignorant of "Light-Horse Harry's" financial reputation, and now to have his father's name disgraced by the son who bore it was to add the blush of shame to the ruddy complexion of the young engineer. So far as is known, he never referred in later life to Henry Lee. Such things in a man's life are not to be proved by citation or confirmed by footnotes, but there is every reason to believe that the stern morality of Robert Lee was stiffened by the warning of his half-brother's fall.

By the time summer and mosquitoes came in 1830, the embankment at Cockspur Island had been thrown over part of the island and the drainage canal had been dug. Because of the weather and the insect pests, the work was then suspended, and most of the force left the island. Lee went to visit among friends who lived close enough to Arlington for him often to see Mary Custis. He found Mrs. Custis not unsympathetic. Mr. Custis, however, was not pleased at the frequent appearance of the same horseman in the park at Arlington. Mr. Custis had nothing against Robert Lee personally, but he knew the financial tragedy of the Lee family and was aware that his daughter's admirer had very little beyond his pay as second lieutenant.

If Lee knew of Custis's opposition, he did not let it deter him. When Mary journeyed down to Chatham, her mother's former home on the Rappahannock, Robert appeared there also, and while sitting with her under a great tree on the lawn he talked to her of those gentle themes that make any suitor eloquent.

In company so delightful, the summer passed far too rapidly and the call to return to Cockspur Island came all too soon. Arriving at his station on the night of November 10, he found a situation from which a timid young man would have been glad to run away. A gale had broken the embankment erected during the winter and spring. The canal was choked. The wharf was in such condition that repair seemed impossible. It was Lee's duty to take hold at once and to resume the work with the help of the few men who had remained on the island during the summer. By the first of December, Lee had replaced enough of the embankment to keep the water off that part of the island on which the fort was to be erected, and he proceeded to strengthen this barrier so that the next storm would not beat it down or breach it.

As often as he could, Lee slipped up the river to Savannah and enjoyed the company of his friends. The family of Isaac Minis gave him welcome, made the more delightful by the presence of two daughters. Jack Mackay had been sent to a post in Alabama and was greatly missed, but the fine old house on Broughton Street was hardly less attractive on that account. Margaret Mackay, as charming as her name, had married Ralph E. Elliot, but there remained Catherine and Eliza. And Eliza was captivating, so captivating that the young lieutenant from Cockspur found some consolation in her presence for his long separation from the blonde girl at Arlington.

J. K. F. Mansfield, who succeeded Major Babcock, Lee's first commanding officer at Cockspur, had not long been on duty when he concluded that the original plan was not adapted to the site and that a new design would have to be prepared. It was apparent that the work would have virtually to be suspended for a season. This would involve the partial idleness of Lee, and that was no light matter to the bureau. The Corps of Engineers then had more contracts than the limited personnel could supervise. In these circumstances a lieutenant could not be kept unemployed at Cockspur Island. Lee had been expecting an assignment to Old Point Comfort, Va., and sometime before April 13, he received orders directing him to proceed thither.

When he reported at Hampton Roads on May 7, 1831, much of the labor on Fort Monroe itself had been completed, and the place was occupied by a garrison, but the outworks and the approaches had not been constructed. Lee's was the necessary but uninspiring task of computing costs, ordering supplies, and directing men in hauling earth, in grading, and in excavating the ditch that was to surround the fort. A little later he had to supervise the masons who erected a wall on the outer side, or counterscarp, of the ditch, which was exposed to the tide from the nearby waters of Mill Creek.

Out in Hampton Roads, less than a mile offshore from Old Point, was Fort Calhoun, later known as Fort Wool. This work had been started on rip-raps, or stones placed in deep waters to serve as a foundation. The walls were rising to the level of the second battery not long after Lee's arrival, but there was a dangerous subsidence, which showed the futility of immediate attempts to build higher. Thereafter, and for the whole of Lee's stay in Hampton Roads, when any work at all was done at Fort Calhoun, it was that of unloading and distributing stone, so as to bring to bear on the foundations as great a weight as they would have to carry when the walls were completed.

Life at Fort Monroe was mixed pleasure and controversy. The commander of the fort was Brevet-Colonel Abram Eustis. He and the engineers were not friendly. Lee's immediate superior was Captain Andrew Talcott. He was capable, careful, and considerate of his subordinate, and he speedily won the fullest respect of his new assistant. The year after Lee came to Fort Monroe, Talcott married Harriet Randolph Hackley, a lovely Virginia girl of high blood, with a fine coloring, brown eyes, a graceful figure, and a manner of much attractiveness. Lee, who was only three years her senior, admired Mrs. Talcott, "the beautiful Talcott," most extravagantly, both for herself and also because she was a cousin of the young mistress of Arlington.

Lieutenant Lee was a devotee of military promptness. If he must lay siege to a heart, he would do it with as little delay as he would countenance in investing a city. So, very soon after he returned from Georgia, he took a steamer up the Potomac to visit Miss Custis. Mrs. Custis watched with sympathy though the master of Arlington still frowned. One day soon after his arrival, the lieutenant was in the hall of Arlington, reading aloud to Mary and to Mrs. Custis from a new novel of Sir Walter Scott's. The interest of the narrative and of the

audience was such that Robert kept on until his weariness must have
been apparent to Mrs. Custis.

"Mary," she said, at a pause in the reading, "Robert must be tired
and hungry; go into the dining-room and get him some lunch."

Miss Custis obediently rose, and Robert, excusing himself, followed
her. At the sideboard, she stooped to get her guest a piece of fruit cake.
Robert leaned forward too, and then and there the question was put and
answered. If he ate his fruit cake, it was with a happy heart.

Mr. Custis reluctantly gave his consent to a marriage his daughter
was old enough to contract on her own account. The nuptials were set
for June 30, and the place, of course, was to be Arlington, with bridesmaids and groomsmen in a number becoming so important an event.
Robert was to get a furlough for as long a time as he could, and when
the festivities were over and the furlough had expired the two were to
live at Fort Monroe—live on his pay, as other young couples did, without any help from Mr. Custis. Mary was determined on that.

There followed many gay preparations, not least of which was Mary's
choice of six bridesmaids among her cousins. Robert called upon a
corresponding number of his friends, to support him in the hour when
the bravest man trembles. The desired furlough was procured through
the friendly help of Captain Talcott. Arlington, which usually wore a
somewhat neglected look, was put in order for the great day.

All was ready. The bridal party marched into the drawingroom.
Mary was nervous; Robert was pale but noted mentally that he was
not so excited as he thought he should have been. The minister, Lee
confided later to Talcott, "had few words to say, though he dwelt upon
them as if he had been reading my Death warrant, and there was a
tremulousness in the hand I held that made me anxious for him to end."

The wedding party remained at Arlington until the following Tuesday, July 5. Some of the bridesmaids lingered until the end of the week.
Then the young lovers were left alone for a day or two, with no company save that of Mr. and Mrs. Custis. But it was not for long. Robert
rode over to Washington on Monday, July 11, and got all the news of
the engineering office. The next day, or the day after, he and his bride,
accompanied by Mrs. Custis, went to Ravensworth, on the first leg of
a journey to visit Randolph and Lewis kin in Fauquier and Loudoun
Counties.

Robert was blissfully happy, and seemed already to bear unconsciously the air of a man destined to achievement. In love and merri-
ment the days ran rapidly on.

Lee's marriage to Mary Custis was one of the major influences that shaped his career. Although she was not often able to travel far or to share the hardships of an engineer's life on a frontier project, she bore him seven children in fourteen years. Ahead of her lay invalidism more nearly complete and more pitiful than that of Lee's mother. She was careless in her personal apparel to the point of untidiness. Her domestic management was complimented when it was termed no worse than negligent. In her engagements she was forgetful and habitually late, an aggravating contrast to the minute-promptness of her husband. Despite these shortcomings and later a nervous whimsicality that sometimes puzzled him, she held the love of Robert Lee through life. Ministering, rather than ministered unto, his first thought always was of her. She accepted this as her due from "Mr. Lee" as she called him, and even after the War between the States, when he was a demigod in the eyes of the South, she ordered him about. Yet rarely was a woman more fully a part of her husband's life. This, fundamentally, was because of his simplicity and her fineness of spirit. She was interested in people and in their happiness. A keen, if uncritical, interest in public affairs she retained all her days, nor did she hesitate to differ from Lee and to voice a fiery opinion in plain-spoken terms, when his sense of justice and his reserve alike disposed him to say little. Religion she had, of the same sort as that which her husband developed. A certain quick and understanding sympathy was shown in her kindling eye and ready smile. Her alertness made friends and brought admiring attention. She was wholly without personal ambition, beyond that of sharing in the experiences and confidences of her friends. Although she was never awed by his presence, she had for his character a respect that became in time a positive reverence. Next after binding him to her in deepest spiritual love, perhaps her greatest influence on him was that she strengthened his self-control, because, as her health became impaired, she required much care at his hands. They needed all the love and all the faith and all the self-mastery they could develop, for they were to endure more of tragedy than is measured out to most mortals.

When Lee married Mary Custis, he married Arlington as well, and that, too, was to have a profound influence upon him. The estate was to bring much harassment of spirit, but it was to deepen his reverence for the Washington tradition. Mr. Custis himself was, of course, the nearest link with the first President. Many of the Washington relics were at Arlington. To come into its atmosphere was to Robert Lee almost like living in the presence of his foremost hero, his father's old commander. "This marriage," wrote a kinsman-biographer, "in the eyes of the world, made Robert Lee the representative of the family of the founder of American liberty."

Early in August Lee and his wife reached Fort Monroe. Within a few weeks occurred the most exciting incident of their three years' residence there. On August 23, Colonel Eustis received word from the mayor of Norfolk that a menacing insurrection of slaves had broken out in Southampton County, forty miles from the city, and that the Negroes had procured arms and were mustering in large numbers. Help was needed. Eustis at once prepared three of his five companies of artillery for the field. The warships *Warren* and *Natchez* also supplied detachments. Setting out the next morning and using water transportation for a part of the distance, the force was able to cover sixty miles in twenty-four hours. It found, most fortunately, that the rising had been put down and that the Negroes had been scattered. Nearly sixty white people, however, had been slain. As a staff officer, Lee did not go to Southampton, but he was profoundly concerned over the outburst, and believed, on the basis of what he heard, that only the Negroes' misunderstanding of the date of the rising prevented "much mischief."

Apprehension spread throughout the South. In Richmond concern was so acute that Major Worth, Lee's old commandant at West Point, who was then in garrison at Fort Monroe, was sent on a special journey to Bellona Arsenal to see that the arms stored there were secure against seizure. At Old Point Colonel Eustis put into effect a series of regulations for the exclusion of Negroes from the post. This greatly embarrassed the engineers and increased the long-developing friction that was to lead to a "post war" between them and the colonel. The temper of some of the Negroes in tidewater Virginia was considered so menacing that five additional companies of artillery were brought to Fort Monroe and put on duty. This gave the fort a garrison of 680 men, no small part of the army of the United States.

The troops were not needed to suppress any further insurrection, but the presence of their officers added to the social life of the fort. To none was their advent more welcome than to Lee, for among the lieutenants who came with the artillery was his companion of West Point days, Joseph E. Johnston. The two took up where they had left off at the academy and were having a joyous time when their fellowship was interrupted by the Christmas holidays. The Lees went up the James River, probably to visit the Carters, and then journeyed to Arlington via Baltimore.

Mrs. Lee remained at Arlington after the Christmas holidays, and Lee went back to Old Point. He and Joe Johnston had a merry season. Johnston was impregnable in his self-discipline. Lee neither drank nor swore nor gambled. But if the pair walked not in the counsel of the ungodly, they had no compunctions about standing in the way of sinners, at least to see what the sinners were doing. There was no reproach in this, no shocked sensibilities. It was always so with Lee in his youth. He did not share in the excesses of his comrades but he did not wear a sombre face. Mrs. Lee returned with milder weather; the nightly vistation of quarters by the engineer and the artillerist became less frequent; the scare of a slave rebellion subsided; most of the officers slipped back into the leisurely routine of life at an army post.

Robert Lee's spirits were high during most of 1832, and his new domestic life was most happy. Mrs. Lee was sick part of the time, and was often away, but she bore him a fine baby on September 16. The youngster was named George Washington Custis Lee, after his grandfather, and he throve despite childish ills.

Now that he was *pater familias*, the company of the wives of the officers at Old Point interested Lee vastly. The news of expectancy and of birth found in him an amused and enthusiastic chronicler. "The population of the Point," he announced to Mackay, "has been increased by the little Huger boy, and I take it upon myself to predict the arrival of a small French." The coming of a new Talcott baby drew from him congratulations and avowals—the first of numerous such messages that he was to send: "I was sincerely delighted yesterday to learn by your note, of the *magnificent* present offered you by Mrs. T. and had some thought of taking the Barge this morning and presenting my congratulations to Mrs. T. in person. Do offer them in my stead in the kindest manner. We have been waiting for the event to decide upon the sex of our next and now determine it shall be a girl in order to retain the connection in the family." The joke was made the more pointed by the fact that the "next" was begotten soon thereafter, and, sure enough, was a girl.

For the company he kept, Lee's inclination and his disciplined neatness disposed him to wear handsome, well-cut clothing. It probably was about this time that he sat for the first of his portraits. It shows him in the full-dress uniform of his corps, with the side-whisker that was the *dernier cri* of fashion. Then, as in later life, he preferred the company of women to that of men, but even when Talcott was away from Old Point, Lee had a number of able men besides Johnston with whom

MARY CUSTIS LEE

ARLINGTON IN WARTIME

to consort. Benjamin Huger, West Pointer of 1825, James Barnes of his own class, Robert Parrott, who had been an assistant professor while Lee was at the academy, and Albert E. Church of the class of 1828, all of them brilliant, were at Old Point during Lee's service there.

In the better mastery of his profession, these years were a busy and a most important period with Lee. He came as an assistant of limited experience; he was to leave fully qualified to direct a large engineering project. Talcott was absent on other duty for part of the building season of 1832, and for virtually all the seasons of 1833 and 1834. The daily burden of the work rested on Lee.

He bore these responsibilities heavily, but he continued to learn. Lee did some designing of buildings, wharves, and fortifications; he supervised the preparation of accounts and of monthly and annual reports; he faced some of the problems of sanitation, with which the science of his day was quite unable to cope; he had a large experience in estimating construction costs; he acquired a further knowledge of the working of the commissary; he was inducted into the mysteries of banking and departmental finance. The art of dealing with labor he acquired so successfully that after an emergency in April, 1834, when all hands had been called out to build a barricade in a blinding blow of sand, hail, and rain, he had been able to say with pride, "I never saw men work better." He learned, also, how to combine initiative with deference, and in nearly all his personal letters to Talcott there was a tactful line asking, if that officer thought him in error, to forward further instructions. Most particularly did he shine in applying to public works the principles of economy he had been taught at home.

A burden to Lee were the constant jealousies and conflicts of authority between staff and line, between the engineers on one side and, on the other, the commandant at Fort Monroe. The line officers disliked the large liberty the engineers had to make contracts and to disburse public funds. Following the clash with Colonel Eustis in 1831 over the exclusion of Negroes from the fort there had been a continuing feud between Captain Talcott and the line. This quarrel was over the engineers' use of quarters within the fort and, more hotly, over the direction by the engineers of the remaining work at Fort Monroe. Talcott thought the engineers should complete the whole enterprise. The officers of the garrison wished it finished by the troops and laborers at the fort. Each side suspected the other of plotting against it. Early in 1834 the Artillery School of Practice at Fort Monroe was broken up and its officers and batteries were ordered to different stations. The engineers regarded this as a victory, though they had no part in compassing it. The number of idlers, in the eyes of the busy engineers, was graciously reduced. But for Lee this involved separation from Joe Johnston, and that was lamentable.

If the engineers rejoiced when the disappointed artillerists at last sailed away, their satisfaction was brief. Congress adjourned during the last week of June, and, among its final acts, confirmed all the *brevet* commissions in the army as regular grades. The exultation of the artillerists who remained at Fort Monoe aroused Lee's amusement and almost his disgust. Then, on July 18, though the regular inspection had already been made, Major General Alexander Macomb, the commanding officer of the army, came to Fort Monroe with the Secretary of War and examined the work being done at Old Point and at the Rip-Raps. He said little about his findings but went back to Washington and filed a report. Of its contents Talcott and Lee knew nothing at the time, though they attributed to Macomb the general hostility that line officers were supposed to feel toward the staff. Six days later the inspector general of the army, Colonel John E. Wool, arrived at the fort to examine the works. Talcott happened to be absent at the time, so Lee had to do the honors. When he waited on Wool for that purpose, the colonel asked if it were not a fact that General Macomb had recently made an inspection. As Lee confirmed this without comment, Wool said that he saw no reason for going over details of the work, but that, for his own information, he would like to see Fort Calhoun. Lee took him out to the Rip-Raps immediately. It was blistering hot, but Lee was determined, as he jestingly wrote Talcott, that the inspections "might complete our measure of Glory for this work." On the way, Wool "propounded several wise *querries,* and among them, whether there were not quarters for us outside, which," said Lee, "I take for a premonitory symptom."

That was all there was to inspection number three, but by no means all the story. On July 31 the adjutant general issued "Order No. 54 . . . received from the War Department." This stated that "on the report of the Major General Commanding the Army" the engineer department in Hampton Roads should be transferred to the Rip-Raps and that the commandant at Fort Monroe should be charged with the completion of the works at Old Point Comfort, "under directions and instructions from General Head Quarters."

When this order was received by Talcott he considered it a direct censure of his management of the work in Hampton Roads, and he be-

lieved every one else at Old Point so regarded it. He demanded a court
of inquiry. General Charles Gratiot, chief of the engineers, promptly
concurred in this demand, though he toned it down to a "request" in
his covering letter to the Secretary of War. Macomb, however, did
not approve of an investigation. "For my part," he wrote, "I cannot
see that any censure is either expressed or implied in any part of the
order from the War Department, and I am sure none was intended in
the report on which it is founded." Macomb was justified in this statement, because the report did not contain any criticism of Talcott. It
was, in a word, unexceptionable, whatever the feeling that prompted
it. The trouble was with the blunt, explicit language of the order from
the adjutant general's office.

Not realizing this, Lee went to Washington to see what lay behind
the report and the order. He learned that a modification of the offend-
ing order was in prospect, with high compliments to Talcott. The
engineer's workmen, however, were to go to the Rip-Raps, with Lee
in charge, and Talcott was to be sent to the Hudson River.

Despite his indignation at the political aspect of the matter, Lee did
not regard the change at Fort Monroe as a reflection on himself or
Talcott, or on their work, which he knew was creditable to them.
That the chief engineer did not consider the transfer of Talcott as a
discredit to Lee was soon evident. At the Rip-Raps, Lee's task was
simply that of supervising the piling up of stone on the foundations. It
was no work for a young and active man whose ability his chief in
Washington had already discovered. About October 25, 1834, Lee
received an invitation from General Gratiot to come to Washington. On
his arrival Gratiot told him that he was contemplating the transfer of
Lieutenant Bartlett, an assistant in the Office, and was considering Lee
for the place. Lee was as anxious for his family to be near Arlington as
he was to get away from Hampton Roads, but he frankly said he had
no desire for office work. Gratiot, however, was intent on having Lee,
and he painted the prospect alluringly. Lee agreed to try the work if
Gratiot desired him to do so. Shortly thereafter he was relieved at Fort
Calhoun by Captain W. A. Eliason and was ordered to report for
service as assistant to the chief of engineers.

When Lee took his wife and little son from Fort Monroe to Arlington in November he expected to rent a house in Washington, but as he
could not find suitable quarters he decided to leave them at Arlington
for the winter. And there they remained during the whole of Lee's
service in the capital. It was an arrangement physically taxing on Lee,

who rode to and from his office every day except in the very worst weather. For his family it was the most pleasant of lives. Mary Custis's marriage did not make the least difference in her status at home: she remained the "young mistress," the heiress to the estate. Her children were a delight to her parents. Mrs. Custis, whose warm heart, piety, and kindliness impressed Lee more and more as he lived at Arlington, watched ceaselessly over her daughter and her grandchild. And Mary's father soon abandoned his antagonism to her marriage.

The Washington tradition seeped more deeply into the spirit of Lee as he lived among the Arlington relics and heard Mr. Custis talk of the Father of his Country. Across the river he found a routine of labor that was pleasant only because his commanding officer made it so. In origin, Charles Gratiot, chief engineer of the army, was French-Louisianan, of the highest social station. With a brilliant career in the army Gratiot had received the thanks of Congress for his conduct during the War of 1812, and as chief engineer he had earned the reputation of being an indispensable officer—a model of military virtues. Every project aroused his interest. The welfare of each officer of engineers was his particular charge. Shortcomings on the part of his subordinates he was ready to overlook; their interests he was quick to defend against the rivalries of the line and the neglect of Congress. He had the warm good-will of the corps and when Lee went to Washington seemed fully entrenched in power, well able to care for himself.

Although Lee usually hurried home in fair weather, he was quick to find old friends and to enter again into their lives in the spirit of West Point or of Fort Monroe. Johnston was on duty in Washington and shared in Lee's social activities. On nights when the weather was too inclement for the journey home or the roads were too heavy, Lee often joined a "mess" at Mrs. Ulrich's, a boarding house where Johnston and James H. Prentiss and other army men resided, together with one or two Cabinet officers and a number of congressmen. It was a more expensive life than Lee's thrifty nature approved, and when a change in the army regulations reduced the allowance for rations, he vainly sought a transfer to another post.

Except for this expense and the dull duties assigned him, Lee enjoyed the life of Washington and of the Arlington neighborhood. All his social impulses were aroused by it. "Your humble servant . . . ," he confided to Talcott, "has returned to a state of rejuvenescency . . . and has attended some weddings and parties in a manner that is uncommon. My brother Smith was married on the 5th inst. and the Bride I think looked more beautiful than usual. We kept agoing till Sunday and last night I attended a Bridal party in Alexandria." Affairs of this nature were some compensation for a routine that made Lee exclaim—in the language of many a soldier of the same rank—"What a pity it is a man is a poor lieutenant."

The round of office work was pleasantly broken in the spring of 1835. The boundary between Ohio and the territory of Michigan was then in dispute. Talcott had previously been employed in making a survey of the line in controversy, and in May he was directed to make new observations to answer the rival contentions. "His old-time and able assistant, Lt. R. E. Lee of the Corps of Engineers"—in that gentleman's own bantering announcement to Mrs. Talcott—"will join him forthwith for same duty." The mission occupied the entire summer and involved a number of interesting calculations. The tour of duty added little, however, to his equipment for the duties that lay ahead.

Early in October, Lee got back to Washington and hastened on to Ravensworth, where the family was visiting. He found Mrs. Lee ill. Her second baby, Mary, had been born that year. The mother unfortunately got a pelvic infection of some sort, which the physicians attributed to overexertion on her part. Lee regarded her condition as serious and he removed her to Arlington the day after his return. She suffered acutely until two abscesses that had formed on her groin broke. Then she began to mend, though very slowly. It was the beginning of 1836 before she was able to walk about again. The children got the whooping-cough as their mother grew better—"whooping, coughing, teething, etc. and sometimes all three together," in the language of the despairing father. Whereupon, Mrs. Lee, not to be outdone by her youngsters, contracted mumps. As the summer of 1836 came on, her improvement was more rapid. Lee then took her to one of the mineral springs of Virginia, where she was able to resume her normal life except for a slight lameness. When he brought her back in the autumn he was himself much worn down by work and worry.

Lee's duties during these difficult months confined him closely to the office of the chief engineer, with no outside assignment except one inspection at Fort Washington. He would have tried to escape from it, by prevailing on General Gratiot to give him a post elsewhere, had Mrs. Lee's condition permitted him to leave her. Hearing all the department gossip and witnessing many of the controversies among his superior officers, he was drawn into the campaign to procure more consideration for the Engineers' Corps at the hands of Congress. His efforts at lobbying deepened his dislike of politicians. He was temporarily buoyed up by interest in Texas's struggle for independence and by the promotion he tardily received on September 21 when he was made first lieutenant. But the routine of the office continued to chafe him and made him restive. Talcott had quit the army for private engineering earlier in 1836, and Lee had almost been tempted to resign with him.

There was ebb and flow in his spirits for the next few years. In one letter he would joke merrily; in the next there would be ill-concealed depression. A sense of frustration was slowly stealing over him, and as Mrs. Lee came back to health he took refuge in his home life. He held patiently, if unhappily, to the routine of the engineer's office, but he kept working to get away from Washington and back to active duty on some interesting project of engineering.

His opportunity came at last. General Gratiot was a native of Missouri and vastly interested in the development of the Mississippi. He had kept there one of his best officers, Captain Henry Shreve, in charge of the force that had been clearing snags from the river. Shreve had done very well, but now a situation developed that called for further action: the ever-changing Mississippi was cutting a new channel on the Illinois side of the river and was throwing up a bar opposite Saint Louis. Another bar was forming in the stream from a point opposite the middle of the city as far down as its southern limits. The river commerce of Saint Louis was in danger of complete destruction. In 1836 Congress made an appropriation of $15,000, "with which to build a pier to give direction to the current of the river near St. Louis." Shreve thereupon drafted a plan for the pier but found that it was too late to begin work that year. He figured, also, that the appropriation would have to be increased by at least $50,000. Congress voted this amount. As a further improvement on the upper Mississippi the lawmakers provided money with which to cut a shipway through the rapids of the Mississippi near the Iowa-Missouri boundary. The work at Saint Louis had to be delayed because Shreve was occupied elsewhere and no other engineer was available. Lee was familiar with all this in 1837, knew the difficulties of the work, and sensed the loneliness of life so far from his home. But he was disgusted with official Washington and the spirit that prevailed there. So, as he subsequently confided, "I volunteered my services . . . to get rid of the office in W[ashington] and the Genl. at last agreed to my going."

The assignment of Lee for this enterprise was dated April 6, but he was not immediately dispatched, probably because Mrs. Lee was expectant. By the end of June, however, he had been presented with his third child, a boy whom he named after his own friend and wife's uncle, William Henry Fitzhugh of Ravensworth. Lee was free to go. He was in high spirits at the prospect of a change in his drab, uninteresting duties and immeasurably relieved at the improvement in Mrs. Lee's health. A new and stimulating period of his life was about to open, and he sensed it.

Lee set out for the Mississippi with Second Lieutenant Montgomery C. Meigs, a young engineer of twenty-one, who had graduated at West Point in the class of 1836. Meigs was a Georgian by birth and became quartermaster-general of the United States army during the War between the States. The two went to Pittsburgh, where they were lucky enough to find a new steamer bound for Saint Louis.

Saint Louis did not impress Lee at first. "It is," said he, "the dearest and dirtiest place I was ever in. Our daily expenses about equal our daily pay." He was lonesome and homesick. In his letters home there was constant thought of Mrs. Lee and of her heavy responsibility in rearing the children alone. He wrote her: "Oh, what pleasure I lose in being separated from my children. Nothing can compensate me for that; still I must remain here, ready to perform what little service I can, and hope for the best."

He was exasperated by the non-arrival of work boats from Louisville. When the boats at last reached Saint Louis, the river was still eight or ten feet above low water, but on the rapids it was reported to be at the lowest. So Lee packed off his force as soon as possible, intent on making a survey of the upper rapids, approximately 150 miles above Saint Louis.

That survey convinced Lee that a channel could be cut without great difficulty. By the end of September it was completed and he went back to Saint Louis, easy in his mind as to the upper rapids but puzzling over the engineering problem presented at the lower rapids. He was in Saint Louis by October 11, better pleased with the city and ready to make his examination of the sand bars that threatened the complete ruin of the harbor.

What could be done to save it? The first essential was an accurate map. Getting the finances of his enterprise in hand, and organizing his forces, Lee sent out parties on either side of the river to make surveys and to do the triangulations. The actual drafting of the map he put under the direction of Meigs. The surveying he handled in person, with the assistance of J. S. Morehead, his steamboat captain, and Henry Kayser of Saint Louis, employed for the purpose. As the survey revealed the depth of the water and showed what the current was doing, he developed his plan for utilizing the current to wash away Duncan's Island and the other sand bars.

Lee's solution was an adaptation of what both Gratiot and Shreve had earlier proposed. The plan was very simple: from the Illinois shore, a long dyke was to be run to the head of Bloody Island, with the object of diverting the waters of the river to the western, or Saint Louis side of the island. The face of the island beyond the dyke was to be revetted so that it would not be washed away by the current. At the foot of Bloody Island another dyke was to be made in order to throw the full force of the current against the head of Duncan's Island and against the shoals that were forming between that and Bloody Island. Lee confessed that the construction of these dykes would be "attended with great difficulty." The cost was estimated at $158,554.

By the time this report was finished in 1837 it was too late to attempt execution of the plan that winter. Lee procured permission to return to Washington, disbanded his party, laid up the steamboat on the Ohio, made contract for building another for the next year, ordered four new flatboats, and with Meigs started eastward.

Lee parted from Meigs when they reached Washington and was not again fortunate enough to have him as an assistant, but he was always affectionately remembered by the younger man, even when war divided them. Lee was then, Meigs wrote long after, "in the vigor of youthful strength, with a noble and commanding presence, and an admirable, graceful and athletic figure. He was one with whom nobody ever wished or ventured to take a liberty, though kind and generous to all his subordinates, admired by all women, and respected by all men. He was the model of a soldier and the beau ideal of a Christian man."

Lee got home about Christmas and spent the rest of the winter of 1837–38 partly on leave at Arlington and partly on duty in the engineers' office in Washington. Early in the spring he began to make arrangements and to assemble his supplies for his return to Saint Louis. Domestic preparations had to be made, also, because this time Mrs. Lee and the three children were to accompany him.

On May 1, Mrs. Lee and the children got their first view of Saint Louis, but as they found the rooms Lee had engaged for them had been otherwise disposed of, it was June 1 before they were finally placed in comfortable quarters, with meals at the home of Doctor William Beaumont, an army surgeon and the leading professional man of the town. Lee was happy to have his family so pleasantly situated, as he

expected his work up the Mississippi would require his absence from
Saint Louis often and for long periods.

On May 14 there arrived at Saint Louis Lieutenant Horace Bliss, who
was to be Lee's assistant for the year. Lee planned to put Bliss in immediate charge at the Des Moines rapids, and dispatched him up the
river on May 19 with boats and a force of men. Lee made several
journeys to the falls during the season, but most of his time he spent
on the Saint Louis project.

With the money available he could not construct both the dykes
during 1838, so he started the one intended to relieve the worst situation, directly in the harbor of the town. As the dyke was lengthened
he anxiously watched to see if it would have the effect he anticipated.
By the end of the construction season, 700 feet of the island had disappeared. The channel across the bar between Bloody Island and
Duncan's Island, below the foot of the dyke, had been deepened seven
feet. The old channel had been much improved, and on the Illinois side
the eighteen-foot channel had been filled in until it was only eight
feet deep. When boats once more could reach the lower part of the
city there was as much rejoicing among the merchants as there was in
the heart of the young engineer. The confidence of Saint Louis people
was restored, and a building boom began. In his annual report Lee
wrote with modest conservatism of what had been accomplished. In
his private correspondence he showed himself convinced that the harbor
could be saved if the height of the lower end of the dyke were increased and the projected dyke above Bloody Island constructed.

To that upper dyke, though he did not know when he would have
sufficient funds for constructing it, Lee gave much thought. During
the previous winter the shoal above the head of Bloody Island had
stopped the ice, which thereupon formed a barrier across the head of
the island. The channel on the Illinois side had accordingly been deepened, and more stream-flow had been diverted from the Missouri side.
The proposed dyke at the head of the island was more necessary than
ever. But how could the dyke withstand the pressure of the winter's
ice if the barrier were drawn on a straight line from the Illinois shore
to the head of Bloody Island? Lee had foreseen this difficulty the
previous year, but the alternative was the expensive one of starting the
dyke much higher upstream so as to present a slanting face to the ice.
The cost of this had made him hesitate in 1837. Now he saw the necessity in sharper terms. As he studied his problem he reasoned that the
longer slanting dyke would run through shallow water, whereas the

dyke he had originally planned perpendicular to the Illinois shore had to cross a twenty-two-foot channel. The expense of the longer dyke would not, therefore, be greater than the first estimates, if proper economy were shown in its construction. Lee accordingly proposed the change, frankly stating that the dyke designed the previous year might not be permanent.

The interest of Saint Louis in the project remained high. Citizens of the town advanced $15,000 to prevent a suspension of the enterprise. When Congress adjourned without allowing any money for Saint Louis, the mayor and the citizens authorized Lee to spend the balance of the fund they had raised. Acting on the authorization given by the city and approved by General Gratiot, Lee began construction of the upper end of the slanting dyke. Two rows of piles were industriously driven for a part of the way down this dyke, but cold weather came early in November and the river was so filled with running ice that it was not possible to fill all the space between the rows with stone.

During the months of this active work at Saint Louis, Lee's sense of frustration was diminished by the consciousness that he was achieving something. When he received notice that he had been commissioned captain of engineers, as of August 7, 1838, Lee was gratified but not quite sure the outcome would be for the best. "I do not know," said he, "whether I ought to rejoice or not . . . as in all my schemes of happiness I look forward to returning to some quiet corner among the hills of Virginia where I can indulge my natural propensities without interruption, and I suppose the more comfortably I am fixed in the Army, the less likely I shall be to leave it. As, however, one great cause of my not putting these schemes in execution arises from want of money, I shall in the meantime handle with pleasure the small addition arising from what the Genl. calls 'the tardy promotion.' " As promotion went in those days of a small army, his new rank was not "tardy," certainly as compared with his former advancement. He had been brevet second lieutenant from July 1, 1829, to July 19, 1832; he had been second lieutenant from that date until November 21, 1836; but he had been first lieutenant only one year and eight months. It was, however, to be more than eighteen years before he received further promotion, except by brevet.

Lee was well within the facts in saying he could "handle with pleasure" the additional pay of his new grade, for not long after he had completed most of his financial statements and had filed his reports on the season's work, he was given an intimation that he might expect a fourth baby in the early summer of 1839. The prospect was not inviting: his family was increasing more rapidly than his income.

Late in December, 1838, he received one of the worst shocks of his whole life. To Lee's bewilderment and distress there came news that Gratiot had been dismissed from the service of the United States for refusing to account for certain public funds. The General claimed that the money in dispute was due him as commissions and allowances; the Treasurer disputed this; the case went to the President, who decided against Gratiot. And when the engineer still refused to yield, the President ordered his name dropped from the roster of the army. The Secretary of War was not unfriendly to Gratiot, but that did not change the grim fact that the chief engineer was out of the service, disgraced. Lee was not a man to desert a friend. On his next visit to Washington he collected papers and data the General desired in his defense, but it was to no purpose: Gratiot retained Lee's affection and good opinion, but he ended his days as a clerk in the general land office in Washington. In Gratiot's place, Colonel Joseph G. Totten was named, an officer of whom Lee had seen little, and one who had no personal interest in the project Lee was directing.

While the Gratiot affair was still a fresh wound, Lee closed his accounts and formally ended his work for the year. He was free, then, to go home, but it was already January 5, 1839, and all navigation was closed on the river. His only means of getting back to Arlington would be to ride overland, and that, of course, was not practicable with three children and with his wife in a delicate condition. They were forced, therefore, to remain at Saint Louis. It was the first winter they had been away from Arlington since 1834.

Some hope had been cherished that Congress would appropriate money at the session of 1838–39 for rivers and harbors. In the acute financial distress of the government this hope was not realized. Not only so, but Lee was called upon to divide part of the money remaining from previous appropriations. Twenty thousand dollars of the balance left by his close economy were diverted to pay for the removal of snags from the Missouri River under the direction of Captain Shreve. Lee was enjoined to keep "operations in such a condition that they may be transferred to other hands on the briefest notice." This was discouraging to a man deeply interested in the completion of an improvement he believed of great value to the entire West.

Before he could begin work in 1839 Lee had to take his wife home. Sentiment and prudence alike dictated that the baby she was expecting be born at Arlington. The children, of course, had to go with her. The family set out on May 1. They proceeded as leisurely as possible, for Mrs. Lee's comfort, but they had very hard travel on May 11, the last day of their journey. No ill-effect followed, however, and the mother and her brood were safely placed in Mrs. Custis's care late that night.

Leaving Arlington about May 25, Lee started out alone for the West. Back in Saint Louis, Lee received word, about July 1, that he had a new daughter, who had arrived on June 18 and had been named Annie Carter Lee. The father was philosophical about the event: "Do you know," he remarked in a letter to Mackay, "how many little Lees there are now? It is astonishing with what facility the precious creatures are dressed up for the return of their Papa! I am sure to be introduced to a new one every Christmas. They are the dearest annuals of the season."

His domestic affairs settled in the fashion of his fecund generation, Lee dispatched Lieutenant Bliss to begin the removal of rock from the Des Moines Rapids as soon as the stage of the river permitted. For his own part he prepared to continue work on the dyke above Bloody Island, which had been somewhat damaged the previous winter by the accumulation of ice. To increase his funds for the enterprise he got permission from the bureau to sell the equipment he did not need for his reduced force. He had to abandon his revised plan for running the dyke and under orders from the chief engineer returned to the original project of a dyke perpendicular to the Illinois pier. There was added to the design an intersecting dam, which was intending to secure the head of the dyke on the Illinois side.

By August 12 the Mississippi was low enough for Lee to begin construction. It was undertaken with all his energy. "He went in person with the hands every morning about sunrise," the then mayor of Saint Louis wrote, "and worked day by day in the hot broiling sun,—the heat being greatly increased by the reflection of the river. He shared the hard task and common fare and rations furnished to the common laborers,—eating at the same table, in the cabin of the steamboat used in the prosecution of the work, but never on any occasion becoming too familiar with the men. He maintained and preserved under all circumstances his dignity and gentlemanly bearing, winning and commanding the esteem, regard, and respect of every one under him. He also slept in the cabin of the steamboat, moored to the bank near the works. In the same place, Lieut. Lee, with his assistant, Henry Kayser,

Esq., worked at his drawings, plans and estimates every night till
11 o'clock."

The driving of piles and the extension of the pier to the head of
Bloody Island had been going on just two weeks when a man named
Morris, a property holder on the Illinois shore, procured an injunction
against the further prosecution of the work. Work had to be suspended
after August 27, despite many grumblings and some protests that Lee
should go ahead in the face of the court order, but the improvement in
conditions on the river had been great. The dyke at the lower end of
Bloody Island was holding fast and had given so much added strength
to the current that a further section of Duncan's Island and a stretch of
1700 feet of the bar above the island had been swept away. Where the
bar had previously been dry, when the river was still six feet above low
water, a two-fathom channel gave access to the wharves. A new channel, a thousand feet wide, had been cut through what, as recently as
1838, had been a dry sand bar. Steamboats now had a straight course
down the river. The results satisfied Lee, but when he came to sum
them up he gave warning that the project had to be carried to completion if the improvement was to be permanent.

For work on the upper Mississippi in 1839 Lee had proposed that a
large party be organized, with ample machinery, and that the rocks in
the river be attacked simultaneously at several points, so that if interruption came at one place progress could still be made elsewhere.
Because of lack of funds, however, he was forced to confine his activities to the Des Moines Rapids.

Work began early and favorably, with Lieutenant Bliss in charge.
Lee himself was at the rapids about the middle of July. The upper
"English chain" at the Des Moines Rapids was the best point at which
to begin work. Under Lee's plan the narrow thirty-foot channel at
the lower end of the chain was widened to fifty to eighty feet, according to the position. The difficult windings above the right angle were
cut to a straight channel eighty feet wide and four feet deep. From
the "English chain" the whole force was moved down the river to
attack the "lower chain." Bliss removed nearly all the reef during the
period of operations and opened a passage fifty feet wide and nearly
four feet deep. When the boats were brought back to Saint Louis and
the men were discharged in the fall, some 2000 tons of stone had been
removed. Lee believed that "a tolerable season's work" had been done,
"considering the lack of cash."

He had few added opportunities to study costs and results that autumn, for after the injunction had halted operations in Saint Louis harbor Colonel Totten had no disposition to let Lee kick his heels idly off the side of the steamboat. Instead, he was sent to inspect improvement work on the Ohio, and then down the Mississippi, where he made a faithful count of snags. Lee was next ordered to the Missouri and again up the "Father of Waters" to "Lamallee's Chain," midway the Des Moines Rapids. Through this chain a very practicable channel was found that would admit of easy navigation simply by widening a narrow passage. In making these reports on the activities, particularly in that on the improvement of the Missouri River, he argued downrightly for internal improvements to help build up the West.

Having no duties to perform during the winter season, Lee procured leave and made the long journey overland to Arlington. He had been gone more than seven months and he was overjoyed to be home. His reward was the sight of his new baby, Annie. As he gathered his children about him he must have felt patriarchal for a man just thirty-three. His progeny now numbered four, a boy of eight and another approaching his fourth birthday, a girl in her sixth year and the newcomer in the cradle.

After four happy months of leave Lee was assigned to temporary duty in the office of the chief engineer, waiting for the decision of Congress on further appropriations for the Mississippi. Congress adjourned without allowing a dollar for the enterprise. Not only so, but the temper of the lawmakers was such that Lee doubted whether Congress would resume internal improvements for years to come. Nothing remained except to cover the long road once more and write "finis" to all the hopes of a completed Federal enterprise.

Receiving his orders on July 24, 1840, Lee started west shortly thereafter, and on his arrival in Saint Louis began a survey of the effects of the ice and freshets on the piers he had constructed in 1838–39. The dyke from the Illinois shore to the head of Bloody Island continued to operate in throwing the current west of the island, thereby deepening the channel on the Missouri side. The channel between Bloody Island and Duncan's Island was deep enough to pass the largest of the Mississippi steamboats to the Saint Louis wharves. The work, it appeared, would permanently serve its purpose, when finished. Up at the Des Moines Rapids, Lee found that the buoys he had placed the previous autumn had washed away. The new channels were being used exclusively and had facilitated navigation. The improvement, however, was incomplete and failed to give to passing ships the depth of direct channel growing commerce required.

It seemed a shame to have made so effective a beginning and not to finish it after so much labor. But orders were given to be obeyed! Maintenance of equipment was so expensive that it was uneconomical to retain some of the boats in the hope they might be useful when and if Congress authorized resumption. Lee accordingly sold at public auction all the boats, the machinery at Saint Louis and the greater part of that which had been employed at the rapids. It was with a heavy heart that he did this. "Lee expressed to me," the mayor of Saint Louis recorded, "his chagrin and mortification at being compelled to discontinue the work. It seemed as if it were a great personal misfortune to stop, when the work was about half finished."

On October 6, Lee completed his last work at Saint Louis, the writing of his reports. A few days later he started back home, where his presence was needed for the usual reason—the approach of still another baby. Lee naturally was not anxious to have a fifth child arrive while Annie was under two years of age, but, as usual, he accepted the inevitable.

Lee's return to Washington marked the end of his labor on the Mississippi. It was his initial independent detail as a responsible supervising engineer. It taught him little that he did not know already concerning the management of labor, the handling of accounts, and the award of contracts, but it did three things for him. First, it developed his ingenuity in the practice of his profession and it strengthened still further his quiet confidence in his ability to meet unexpected problems. The Saint Louis enterprise brought him, in the second place, into close relations with municipal officers and a critical public. He won the support of the officials, as he did of nearly all the men with whom he was closely associated. Finally, Lee's two years and a half on the Saint Louis project established his professional standing. He went to Missouri a promising young officer; he returned an engineer of recognized reputation in his corps. A difficult task had been brilliantly performed, and the fullest praise for it had been accorded him. From that time onward he had the highest esteem of his superiors. The opportunities that were to come to him in Mexico were created at Saint Louis.

His record at Saint Louis entitled Robert E. Lee to a good assignment, and he doubtless would have received it at once but for the fact that the very conditions that had forced him to leave the West, namely, the lack of government appropriations, prevailed equally in the East. Nothing better could be given Lee, therefore, after a month in Washington, than a tour of inspection of three of the forts in the Carolinas.

The first to be visited by Lee was Fort Macon, situated close to Beaufort, N. C. The site had been continuously subject to encroachment by the sea, and during flood tides, a part of it was overflowed. Examination in 1840 had indicated that strong jetties were necessary on the sea side, and that a dyke would be required to halt the overflow. Various repairs were needed, also, on leaky casemates, etc. Lee went to Beaufort about November 7, 1840, and made a close examination of the fort. This convinced him that it needed more protection from the battering Atlantic, and he set about devising a method for providing this.

From Beaufort it is likely that Lee went southwestward along the coast for about 100 miles to the mouth of the Cape Fear River. There he was to make a similar inspection of the breakwaters at Fort Caswell, which had been virtually completed in 1834, but had been injured by the sea the very next year. If Lee reached Fort Caswell he had scarcely begun his investigation there when the time came to go home for Christmas. After the holidays he drew up his reports on Fort Macon, covering both the repair of the fort and the extension of the jetties. It was March 20 before the last of the drawings was finished.

By that time an alternative assignment was open, and Lee had a choice of going to New York harbor or returning to North Carolina to supervise the improvements on the forts there. Either would involve much routine, but the Carolina forts were of relatively little importance, whereas the works in New York harbor were the most vital of the country's coast defenses. Lee quickly decided for New York.

Reaching New York on April 10, 1841, Lee soon discovered that his task was not as interesting as he had hoped it would be—that it was laborious but technically not difficult. His instructions were to institute somewhat elaborate repairs at Fort Lafayette and to make various changes in Fort Hamilton, particularly in the parapet, so as to adapt it to barbette guns. Both these forts were at "the Narrows," between the upper and the lower bays of New York harbor. Fort Hamilton was on the Brooklyn side, in a somewhat inaccessible location, with Fort Lafayette almost directly under its shadow, though separated from it by a channel. Lee received instructions to take over, in addition, Batteries Hudson and Morton, two fortifications formerly under state control on Staten Island that were to be modernized and rearmed. Four projects were thus under his superintendence, on either side of the Narrows and in it.

Because the work at New York gave promise of extending over a term of years, Lee brought his family to Fort Hamilton a month or so after he was ordered there. He established his wife and children in a house the government had acquired along with the site of Fort Hamilton. The young Lees who descended on the fort now numbered five, for the new baby was of course brought along with the rest. She had been named Eleanor Agnes, but the "Eleanor" was dropped early and she was always known as Agnes.

Into his new duties Lee threw himself with the same energy he had displayed at Saint Louis. He regularly visited the four forts under repair, and in a short time he was able to get results at each place. Much of the bookkeeping and virtually all the engineering he had to do in person. It was not until late in September that he felt justified in employing a draftsman to copy the drawings he made of Fort Lafayette. Diligent as Lee was, the routine soon became deadening. The old sense of frustration besieged him. He seemed to be weighted down by the very stones of the forts. During that first summer he left his station only twice—once to visit the Connecticut quarries from which he was getting stone and once to confer in Washington with Colonel Totten.

With the hardest of effort, Lee completed by September 30 the greater part of the work planned for Fort Hamilton. He closed the open embrasures in the parapet wall, raised the wall, and prepared the terreplein for twenty-three guns. He stopped the leaks in the casemates on the water front and renewed the floor and ceiling of the magazines. Meantime drawings of Fort Lafayette had been completed, the trusses of the second floor of that fort had been placed, materials for the construction of the other trusses and for paving one of the batteries had been assembled, and progress had been made in preparing the barbette battery for its armament. Battery Hudson and Battery Morton were completed except for the construction of a few magazines. Lee was much interested in Battery Hudson and believed that it would "prove more powerful in the defense of the passage than any other at the Narrows." Work continued on a diminished scale until January, 1842, and in March was resumed at all the forts. Shot furnaces were provided for Batteries Hudson and Morton, and the former was extended, as Lee had suggested, with provision for thirteen additional guns. By fall he had Fort Lafayette in good condition and was satisfied with the water front at Fort Hamilton. Much remained to be done on the land fronts.

No work being practicable at the Narrows during the winter of 1842–43, Lee and his family spent that time at Arlington, but by March, 1843, he was back in New York, pushing the repairs as fast as he could. Mrs. Lee and the children returned to New York with him, but journeyed homeward again in the early autumn, in order that the sixth baby might be born under its grandparents' roof. The young gentleman made his appearance on October 27, and was named Robert Edward.

Together with Major J. S. Smith and Captain Henry Brewerton, Lee was sent to West Point during the summer to report on the best location and suitable dimensions of proposed new cadet barracks. That pleasant break in the regular course of duty gave Lee his first close view of the changes that had been made at the academy since his own cadet days. The routine of the year was again interrupted, and not so pleasantly, on August 22, by a storm of unparalleled violence that caused several of the slopes at the forts to slide or to collapse.

Part of the winter of 1843–44 was spent in Washington and at Arlington on the unromantic task of verifying and tabulating the government's titles to the lands occupied by the public defenses. Lee came to the capital after January 10, 1844, and on April 15 was ordered back to Fort Hamilton. The construction during the season that followed was the simplest he had directed since he had been assigned to the Narrows.

For the first time in many summers Lee had a little leisure, which the vigilant chief engineer employed in the public service and to Lee's own gratification, by naming him one of the officers to attend the final examinations at West Point in June, 1844. This assignment lasted more than two weeks, during which time most of the visiting soldiers became well acquainted with one another. On the board were Lee's old cadet commandant, Major W. J. Worth, now a brevet brigadier general; a capable young captain of artillery, Erasmus D. Keyes, whom Lee learned to admire very highly; and above all—physically and in the vigor of his personality—Major General Winfield Scott, who had become the commanding general of the army two years before.

This period of association with old "Fuss and Feathers," as he later became known, was a major event in the life of the tired, frustrated engineer. Lee doubtless had met Scott many times in Washington, for the General essayed to be a lion in the society where Lee himself was not averse to bowing. The fortnight at West Point, however, was the first time the two ever sat down to a common task, where the intelligence and judgment of each was displayed at its real value, regardless of the differences in their military rank. Lee must have made a very deep impression on Scott, whose influence and good opinion were to become among the strongest forces in Lee's career.

With the approach of cold weather in the late months of 1844, Colonel Totten, the chief enginneer, ordered Lee to Washington to act once more as office assistant. It was pleasant to Lee to get back to Arlington with his family and to escape a winter of tempests in the harbor of New York. He went to Washington in time for the family to have Christmas at Arlington, but he soon found that the work assigned him under Colonel Totten's economical arrangement was much the same as that in which General Gratiot had first schooled him. It was so grim a battle with officialdom that Lee could not have been sorry when orders came on March 31, 1845, to return to Fort Hamilton. But his labors at the Narrows during the season of 1845 constituted, if possible, as dull a routine as that at engineering headquarters. The gray round of this uninteresting life was brightened somewhat in September by an appointment as a member of the board of engineers for the Atlantic coast defenses. This honor came to Lee in part because he had the leisure for the duties, and in part because of his general attainments as an engineer. Lee, as the junior officer, was made recording officer of the board, and, as it pursued its study, he filed frequent reports of its proceedings. While his part in the deliberations probably was not predominant, it added to his equipment as an engineer.

The winter of 1845–46 was the one period of Lee's service at Fort Hamilton, above all others, when he would most have wished, for personal reasons, to be at Arlington. Custis, who was now thirteen, was sent back to Virginia for his schooling. Mrs. Lee was pregnant again and wanted to be with her mother and to have the baby born at home. Lee naturally desired to attend her in the ordeal. But he had to remain near New York to discharge his duties on the board of engineers.

During the last week of November, Mrs. Lee made ready to leave. Her actual departure was delayed a short time because of an accident to the second boy, William Henry Fitzhugh, already nicknamed Rooney. This young man of eight succeeded in cutting off the tips of two of his fingers while experimenting with the chopping knife. For some days it was doubtful whether the ends of the digits would reknit where the doctor sewed them back. Rooney's fingers were saved and he grew up to manhood physically as magnificent as his father.

When the family went to Arlington, Lee was left for as lonesome a time as he had known since 1839 at Saint Louis. Early in 1846 word came from Arlington that the new baby had arrived—a girl, who was named Mildred Childe, after Lee's younger sister in Paris. The brood had almost doubled since he had left Saint Louis, and his responsibilities to it had increased even more, because his children were growing older.

Lee had been at the Narrows nearly five years. He had done much to improve the forts during that time, and had learned no little about the location of coast and harbor defenses. His logic had sharpened Colonel Totten's appeal for the better fortification of New York. But superintending dull repair work at the Narrows, sharing in the plans of the board of engineers, and contributing a few suggestions for the better defense of New York were, when all was said, a scant return for five of the most valuable years of his life. Lee was settling down to another year of the formalized routine of an army engineer when word reached Washington on April 7 that the Mexican Government had refused to receive the American minister, John Slidell. On May 9 dispatches were received from Brevet Brigadier-General Zachary Taylor, announcing that his forces and the Mexicans had clashed. On May 11 President Polk laid the facts before Congress, which declared war two days later. Meantime, unknown to the administration, Taylor had met a force of Mexicans at Palo Alto on May 8, and again at Resaca de la Palma on May 9, and had defeated it. Twenty thousand volunteers were soon called for from the Southern states. All the talk in Washington was of preparations, appointments, and expeditions. The line officers, of course, expected to be sent to Mexico as soon as a plan of operations was determined upon. But the engineers, especially those in charge of work at the forts—would they be given duty in the field? Lee could only wait and, like all soldiers, hope for a part in the campaign the administration was feverishly planning.

For three months he found work at the fort duller than ever, because Kearny was advancing on Santa Fe, Taylor was gathering troops at Camargo for a march on Monterey, and Santa Anna had slipped through the blockade at Vera Cruz. Then on August 19, 1846, Lee got the letter he was hoping to receive—orders to report to Brigadier General John E. Wool for service in Mexico. Opportunity had come to Captain Lee of the engineers.

CHAPTER III

Twenty Months in Mexico

LEE hurried to Washington, where he filed his accounts on August 28, 1846. Three days later he made his will. Under the spur of opportunity, he lost no time in adieux, even to the proud but anxious household at Arlington. On the first available steamer he travelled to New Orleans. From the busy Louisiana base he embarked for Port la Vaca, Tex. Arriving there, he took horse for San Antonio de Bexar, which he reached on September 21. Two squadrons of regular cavalry were there, one battery of regular artillery, three companies of the Sixth Infantry, two regiments of Illinois infantry, and a sufficient sprinkling of other volunteers to raise the total to 3400 men. The atmosphere was one of excited preparation, for the troops were to start an advance into Mexico as soon as supplies were accumulated and equipment was complete. The commander of this expedition, the officer to whom Lee reported, was Brigadier General John E. Wool. Wool had grizzled much since the hot day in July, 1834, when he had been rowed out to Fort Calhoun with Lieutenant Lee. He had received his promotion to the rank of brigadier in 1841, and in the years since Lee had been with him in Hampton Roads he had directed the transfer of the Cherokee Indians west of the Mississippi but otherwise had been engaged in routine duties.

The officer with whom Lee had the closest official relations, from the day he reached San Antonio, was Captain William D. Fraser of the corps of engineers, a New Yorker who had graduated from West Point at the head of the class of 1834. Fraser was seven years younger than Lee but had risen fast in the army and had been commissioned captain on the same day as Lee. Fraser had well in hand most of the engineering arrangements for the expedition. General Wool, therefore, did not supersede him on the arrival of Captain Lee, but associated Lee with Fraser, more or less as a supplementary officer.

Lee's first task was to assist in the collection of tools for use in road and bridge building. San Antonio had few artisans, prices were very high, and neither Lee nor Fraser had any government funds with which to make purchases. Progress accordingly was slow and results were discouraging.

Two days after Lee arrived the topographical engineers set out to find the best road for General Wool's advance. The expedition had not long to wait after the topographical engineers started. On September 28 a column of some 1954 men moved out of San Antonio, toward the Rio Grande.

General Wool's advance was in accordance with the tentative and incomplete plan of campaign that had been slowly formulated after war had been declared. Mexico had conceded to Texas a boundary line no farther south than the river Nueces, approximately 130 miles north of the Rio Grande. President Polk claimed the territory running south to the Rio Grande and in March, 1846, had sent General Zachary Taylor forward to occupy it. Taylor had reached the river on March 28 at a point opposite the Mexican town of Matamoras, where he had entrenched himself in the works later known as Fort Brown. The efforts of the Mexicans to force him to abandon the line of the Rio Grande had led to the battles of Palo Alto and Resca de la Palma. Following up his successes, Taylor had crossed the Rio Grande on May 18 and had occupied Matamoras. There he had remained until July 30, when he started up the river to Camargo to undertake his part of the larger operations upon which the administration had determined.

The plan was this: One small column was to be sent to seize New Mexico; another was to co-operate with the navy in upsetting the Mexican government of California. With these possessions taken from the enemy and held as war indemnity, General Taylor was to advance from the Rio Grande to Monterey, and General Wool, acting under Taylor's orders, was to go forward from the river to Chihuahua. The hope was that these operations and a strict blockade of the eastern coast would bring northern Mexico under American control.

An uneventful march of 164 miles in eleven days brought Wool's first column to the Rio Grande, just east of the presidio named after the river. The rapidity of this advance was attributed by one observer to "the indefatigable exertions of those distinguished officers, Captains Lee and Frazier [Fraser]," who built a road and bridged the streams. Being now on the boundary claimed by the United States, the army on its next advance would assume the offensive in Mexican territory. The ardor of every soldier was inflamed at the thought.

On October 12 the whole force passed over the Rio Grande. There a Mexican officer was awaiting General Wool. He brought news pleasant to the Americans: General Taylor had advanced to Monterey and after a battle there had forced the Mexican troops to withdraw. The articles of capitulation provided that the Mexicans should march out of the town with their arms, and should retire beyond a designated line. The "forces of the United States," the sixth article of capitulation read, "will not advance beyond the line . . . before the expiration of eight weeks, or until the orders or instructions of the respective governments can be received." This had been signed on September 24. The Mexican officer insisted that Wool's advance contravened the agreement. Wool was delighted at Taylor's success, but he did not consider that the first stages of the advance he had in contemplation were violative of the agreement. He accordingly sent back word that he would continue his march.

In the hearts of inexperienced soldiers, ambitious for battle, this incident raised hope of early action. Expectancy tightened. With high heart the army followed a route the topographical engineers selected, and on October 30 reached the environs of Monclova. Not an enemy was seen; not a gun was fired at a human mark; some of the enthuiasm of the army began to exhaust itself as the days passed in hard marches through dull country. General Wool considered that he had now reached a position where the Monterey armistice applied and that he could not go farther until it expired. This meant nearly three weeks around Monclova, a town of 8000, cleaner and more pleasant than most Mexican cities, but no place, surely, for a restive army to wait.

The Monterey armistice expired on November 19, according to Wool's interpretation of its terms; so, on the 18th, he pushed his advance guard forward. On November 24, leaving five companies of Illinois volunteers to guard Monclova, the column took up its southward march. A pioneer detachment that had been organized at Monclova from the Illinois troops was sent ahead under Fraser and Lee and prepared the roads for the main army.

Ten days after the start, the army halted near Parras, and on the following day took position about two miles north of the city. Nearly two weeks went by at Parras, with no alarms and no promise of excitement. Then, on December 17, came a hurried messenger from General Worth. The Mexicans were preparing to attack Saltillo, Worth wrote, and he wanted Wool, if possible, to reinforce him. Wool determined to move at once, because his only practicable road to Saltillo lay, in part, by the route the enemy would certainly take in moving on that city. If the Mexicans reached the hacienda of La Encantada, on the road from San Luis Potosí to Saltillo, a junction between Worth and Wool would be impossible and both American forces might be wiped out. Soon there was hustle and excitement everywhere, no man in the ranks knowing whether the enemy was a hundred miles away or just over the horizon. The head of the column moved within two hours after word had been given to break camp. For the next four days there was no rest for any one while Wool kept up a forced march.

On the evening of December 20, being close to the positions the foe might be expected to occupy, Wool sent forward a reconnoitring party. No enemy was to be found. The next day the little army encamped near Agua Nueva, seventeen miles south of Saltillo. The troops had come more than one hundred miles in four days but they were denied the battle they expected to fight upon arrival. The reported advance of the enemy was a false alarm and all Wool's haste had been to no purpose.

Lee now found himself with the largest body of troops he had ever seen, fully 6000 men! Once reconnaissances were made and the camp was laid out he had no special duties until Christmas eve, when Captain Fraser received orders to report at Monterey. This left Lee the senior engineer officer with Wool. For the time being, his new responsibilities were negligible.

Shortly after breakfast Christmas morning a hurried message was sent to headquarters: The enemy was coming! Great clouds of dust had been seen in the line of his advance. The alarm was sounded at once. Investigation proved that the clouds of dust had been raised by cavalry which had been out reconnoitring, but rumor and military logic still represented General Santa Anna as close at hand.

Wool was getting skeptical of alarms of Mexican activity near at hand, and when a new report came one evening of a great force marching down on the Americans, he determined to ascertain the enemy's position. Lee volunteered to make the required scout. The general told him to procure a guide, and gave orders that a company of cavalry should meet him at the outer picket line and go with him. Lee found a young Mexican, who knew the country, and prevailed upon him to act as his guide.

In some way Lee missed the cavalry escort at the picket line. Rather than search for it he determined to press on with no other companion than the native. A long ride brought him no sign of the enemy, but a little later he saw the light of numerous camp fires on a hill not far away. This was enough for the guide. He besought Lee to turn back. They must return or they would be caught! Lee rode on alone. Presently he was rewarded by the sight of what seemed to be a large number of tents on the hillside. Some impulse carried him still farther. He was now so close that he could see clearly—and could realize that the white objects he had taken for tents were a flock of sheep, part of a caravan that was moving to market and had stopped by the road for the night. Lee crossed the stream and, with the little Spanish he possessed, questioned the drovers. They told him the Mexican army was still on the other side of the mountains.

Lee had ridden forty miles, but with the information given him by the drovers he felt that he could speedily locate the Mexican forces. He rested three hours, changed mounts and started off again with a cavalry escort. This time he went much farther than during the night, and when he returned it was with fairly definite news of the position of the enemy.

Wool apparently believed that hard work was the best reward of men who had done it, and shortly after Lee's reconnaissance he named him acting inspector general without relieving him as engineer.

By the middle of January, 1847, it was whispered everywhere that another American army was mustering on the coast, and that a descent was to be made on Vera Cruz by General Scott. For once, camp-fire gossip was right. Campaigning without a cannon shot was about to end, for Captain Lee in particular.

He received orders about January 16, 1847, to proceed to Brazos and there to join General Scott. With hasty farewells and high hopes, he left Wool about January 17. Lee found General Scott immersed in preparations for the descent on Vera Cruz, fuming at every wasted hour. The newly arrived captain of engineers was recieved as a member of the general staff. He stepped overnight from the execution of small operations to the planning of great enterprises, and although he did not know it, he had started up the ladder of fame. He found himself, too, in the company of friends, among them "Joe" Johnston.

On February 15, 1847, Scott raised his pennant on the ship *Massachusetts* and led the way down the coast toward Tampico, where some 6000 American soldiers were awaiting transports. Three days later the convoy was off the mouth of the Panuco. The next morning Lee went ashore in the suite of General Scott, whose love of pomp and display was to be gratified to the fullest by the waiting regiments in Tampico. When Scott stepped on land, the band from Governor's Island struck up a tune, and all the high officers ashore came forward to pay their respects. They had a mount at hand for Scott, but the General declined to ride: His great bulk rising above that of all the large men of his staff and escort, he strode across the market place and up the streets to the quarters that had been selected for him. On February 20, Lee steamed southward again with Scott.

The *Massachusetts* arrived off Lobos on February 21, but did not discharge her passengers because of heavy weather. The end of riding the tides off Lobos came on March 3. By no means all of Scott's transport was then at the island, but he felt that what he had at hand was sufficient for the first stage of his operations. The red pennant was raised once more, and the fleet began to make its way down the coast, headed by the steam vessels.

The weather was favorable as the fleet continued southward before the wind. Shortly after noon on March 5 Lee saw Vera Cruz, with its castle, and a little later he sighted the American fleet that had been blockading the port for months. Commodore David Conner, senior officer of the navy in Mexican waters, had been in touch with Scott since December and had studied the coast carefully to determine where Scott's army could best effect a landing for the investment of Vera Cruz. The day after Scott's arrival, Conner invited the General, his principal officers, and his staff to make from the sea a reconnaissance of the landing places and of the town and fortress as well. Lee went with the rest aboard the steamer *Petrita*, and they ventured so close to the castle fort off Vera Cruz, San Juan d'Ulloa by name, that men on the other ships expected to see them blown out of the water. The castle opened on the *Petrita* when it was a mile and a half distant, but the fire went wild. It was the first hostile shot Captain Lee had ever heard as a soldier.

This reconnaissance brought General Scott to the opinion that the best available landing place was on a sandy beach about three miles southeast of the walls of Vera Cruz and he gave orders for a landing the following day. Dawn, however, brought rough weather and prompted postponement until the next morning.

March 9 was to Lee perhaps the most interesting day he had thus far spent as a soldier. Early in the morning the troops were placed in the surfboats and were rowed to the men-of-war, the decks of which were soon jammed with men, muskets, and equipment. The steamers started northward, passed over nine miles of calm seas, and dropped anchor at Sacrificios. Not a gun had been fired, though it was assumed that the Mexicans were in position behind the dunes and were merely biding their time. At last all was ready and the great moment was at hand.

The division of Lee's old drillmaster, General Worth, contained most of the regular infantry in Scott's expedition, and had been chosen as the van. When word came that the boats were all loaded, Worth stepped down into a swift gig and took his place. A gun boomed out from the flagship; the surfboats cast off from the *Princeton* and formed in line abreast. A few tense moments, and the men of the 6th Infantry sprang out on the beach. Not a shot greeted them. Quickly the contingents of the other leading boats joined them and made a rush for the crest of the nearby sandhills. In an instant this high ground was won, and the flag of the United States was planted in plain view of all the ships. Not until then did it dawn on every one that the landing was unopposed, through some unexplained miscalculation on the part of the Mexicans.

With the landing of the Vera Cruz expedition began Lee's first real opportunity in the field. He had every advantage. General Scott had already formed a high opinion of Lee's ability and had included him in what he termed his "little cabinet," consisting of Lee's own chief, Colonel Totten, Lieutenant Colonel Ethan A. Hitchcock, acting inspector general, Lee, and General Scott's son-in-law, Henry Lee Scott, who was the commander's assistant adjutant general and chief of staff. Lee was thus brought into close daily contact with Scott, who was a man quick to recognize merit and ready to take sound counsel, deferentially tendered, however pompous and dogmatic he seemed. Lee was, moreover, in the strongest branch of the general staff. Colonel Totten had seen to that. Directly under Totten was Major John L. Smith, next came Lee, and then a number of other officers of the highest promise, men who had stood at the very top of their respective classes at West Point. Among them was a youngster of twenty, Brevet Second Lieutenant George B. McClellan, who had been No. 2 in 1846 at the Military Academy. One step above him was First Lieutenant P. G. T. Beauregard, of the class of 1838. Another junior officer of fine abilities was Zebulon B. Tower of Massachusetts, a second lieutenant, and No. 1 in the class of 1841. In the affiliated corps of topographical engineers, besides Joe Johnston, was Lieutenant Gustavus W. Smith. George Gordon Meade was also in the topographical detachment.

Toward evening, on the 10th of March, General Scott and his staff came ashore. Establishing temporary headquarters in tents, Scott and his official family rode around the city. After his reconnaissance, Scott gathered the members of his "little cabinet" about him and raised the question of whether Vera Cruz should be stormed or taken by siege. He declared unequivocally for regular approaches. Somewhat to his surprise, Totten, Lee and the rest agreed with him. The investment of the city was accordingly ordered.

Owing to a succession of northers, March 12 arrived before the five miles of the line of investment had been taken up; and it was March 17 before all the entrenching tools had been brought ashore. The next day ground was broken for the batteries. It was one of the busiest times Lee had ever experienced. On the 19th, Lee very narrowly escaped death. From the position of one of the working parties, he started back to the lines, accompanied by Beauregard. At a turn in this path, they suddenly saw an American soldier. The soldier, thinking that the Mexicans were upon him, blazed away with his pistol, straight at Lee. The bullet passed between his left arm and his body, singeing his uniform.

General Scott was now ready to open the bombardment, but he had concluded that his army ordnance was not heavy enough, and he had asked the navy for the loan of six heavy pieces to be used against the walls. Lee was designated to locate these in battery. He picked a position within 700 yards of the Mexican defenses, and succeeded in masking it so completely that the enemy was unaware of what was being done.

The naval battery having been ordered to open on the morning of March 24, Lee pushed construction rapidly. By daylight on the 24th all the sandbags were filled, and soon thereafter the last gun was in place. The sailors were sponging it and were trying to get the sand out of it when well-directed shots showed that the battery had been observed by the Mexicans. Orders were given to unmask the pieces and to open on the enemy. It was then 10 o'clock, and Captain Lee, who was directing the fire, had his first experience in actual combat.

The fighting continued through two days. Not long after the guns opened on the morning of March 26, a flag of truce was sent out by the Mexicans through the flying sand of a severe norther. Ere long firing ceased. It was renewed no more at Vera Cruz, for though the Mexicans rejected Scott's first terms, they resumed conference during the forenoon of March 27 and that night signed the capitulation. The city and its armament were to pass into the possession of the United States.

In appreciation of the part the engineers had in this easy victory, General Scott entrusted his victory dispatch to Colonel Totten and commended him "to the very favorable consideration of the department." Before Colonel Totten left for Washington, he wrote Scott in warm commendation of the other engineers who had been engaged in the siege. He listed them by seniority and by name, Lee second on the list. Two days later Lee got his first mention in orders, when Scott included him among those who were, "isolated by rank or position as well as by noble services." The distinction Lee gained at Vera Cruz was much greater, in reality, than the orders indicated. Scott's good opinion of him was confirmed. On Totten's departure he became second ranking engineer officer of Scott's army; from the beginning of the subsequent operations he seems to have been consulted by the commanding general much more than was Major John L. Smith, the senior engineer, who was in ill-health.

Scott planned to find and to defeat the main army of the enemy, even if he had to march to Mexico City, and he tarried at the coast solely because of the slow arrival of transportation. No certain news was available concerning the strength, movements, or position of the enemy, though it was reported that General Santa Anna had hurried southward after his defeat at Buena Vista and had organized a new army with which to dispute the advance of the Americans. Units of the army marched inland from day to day until April 12, when General Scott himself left Vera Cruz, accompanied by Lee and the rest of his staff.

Travelling through rich plains the cavalcade came on April 14 to the Rio del Plan at a bridge leading to a village and a pleasant meadow styled Plan del Rio. All the troops that had preceded Scott were there, with Major General Robert Patterson in command. The men received their general in chief with loud cheers; but he had little time for their applause. His subordinates had grave news for him. The enemy had been located: in a mountain pass that rose above Rio del Plan, Santa Anna himself, with a force estimated at 12,000 or more, was awaiting the Americans.

Scott ordered a full reconnaissance. Lee was directed to ascertain whether the enemy's position could be turned. Going out on the morning of the 15th with his guide, John Fitzwalter, Lee found that Santa Anna had chosen his ground well. The army's only hope lay in finding a practicable way through the ravines on the Mexican left.

Slowly Lee worked his way up the ravines. The ground was very difficult, but to Lee it did not seem altogether impossible to construct a road over which troops might advance with proper caution. At last Lee stopped his stealthy movements to look about him. Near at hand was a spring, to which a path lead from the south. This path must have been well-trampled, for Lee at once concluded that he was in rear of the Mexican left flank. As he studied the ground he heard conversation in Spanish. Pausing a moment, he got a glimpse of a group of Mexican soldiers coming toward the spring. There was only an instant for reflection, then silently he dropped down behind a great log close to the water. Fortunately, the undergrowth was so thick by the side of the log that it formed a screen.

Louder the voices; louder, too, the sound of men making their way along the path. Soon the soldiers paused in the shade to talk of the Yankees that were gathering under the ridge. Quietly Lee lay under the log. More soldiers arrived. Was it to be all day? Was the spring the water supply for that wing of the army? Down on the log sat a Mexican; down sat another. Their backs were not three feet from Lee. At last they went their way. But others came and still others. Hours passed. Finally the last loiterer shuffled off. Silence then and tropical blackness. Slowly Lee lifted his stiff joints from his refuge and slipped out. He was safe!

And now to find the way down that treacherous ravine back to the American lines. Running now into a tree, slipping here down the side of the ravine, he at last reached headquarters. He reported his findings, but he was by no means satisfied with them. Major Smith had also been out that day and had reached the same conclusion as Lee, but he too was still in doubt whether the army could manoeuvre around the Mexican left. Scott directed them to continue the reconnaissance the next day and placed at Lee's disposal a working party with which to cut a trail. Lee accordingly went out on the 16th and before nightfall had pushed his reconnaissance much farther.

A decision had now to be reached: Either the army must remain in the valley, exposed to yellow-fever, which was expected to appear very soon, or else Scott had to attack at once; and if he attempted to drive the Mexicans from their perches he must deliver his main assault around the enemy's left flank, in the direction of Lee's and Smith's reconnaissance. There was no alternative. Scott decided to send Twiggs's division around Santa Anna's flank the next day, April 17, with Lee as guide.

As reveille was sounded for Twiggs's division on the morning of April 17, there opened for Lee two days of the heaviest responsibility he had ever known. With the greatest vigilance, Lee carried the men up the ravines that led around Santa Anna's left. About 11 o'clock the infantrymen found that a Mexican force from the direction of Atalaya was advancing against them in greatly superior numbers. A clash followed in a few minutes, and, as it was apparent that the movement was now discovered, General Twiggs ordered the men to advance on Atalaya.

The First Artillery and the Rifle Regiment sprang up the hillside, swept the Mexicans down the nearer hill, up Atalaya, over its crest, through a ravine—and had started up the sides of Cerro Gordo in hot pursuit before they heeded the recall. There was danger that the vanguard would be taken prisoner by a Mexican counterattack, but this was prevented by the fire of some light guns.

After nightfall the venturesome vanguard returned to Atalaya, and such of the men as were not designated for special duty threw themselves on the ground and went to sleep. There was no rest for Lee, however. As the attack on Cerro Gordo the next morning promised to be a more serious affair, Lee had two special duties to perform, first to locate a battery on Atalaya, and then to see that the heavy guns which were being painfully brought forward were ready to open at sunrise. Before daylight on the 18th all was ready.

At Scott's suggestion it was decided that a part of the division was to assault Cerro Gordo as soon as the artillery opened. Simultaneously, Lee was to conduct the men of another brigade around the northern flank of Cerro Gordo to cut off the enemy's retreat. Lee set out with Colonel Bennett Riley, commander of the Second Brigade. About the same time the direct assault on Cerro Gordo began. Lee saw little of this. The column he was conducting had not gone far before it came under raking gunfire from the northern and western sides of Cerro Gordo. Part of the command had to be turned to the left to protect that flank. With the remainder Lee kept on.

The attack on Cerro Gordo proceeded with success. The entire centre and left of the Mexican position was occupied, and the right of Santa Anna's army, near the river, was cut off from retreat. The

Mexicans on the right surrendered, and Patterson's division in the
centre undertook to pursue the enemy up the Jalapa road. Before nightfall the remnants of the enemy were driven ten miles and were broken
into small detachments. Approximately 3000 troops were captured,
together with thousands of small arms and most of the Mexican artillery. Santa Anna himself barely escaped.

Lee came out of the action at Cerro Gordo, his first open engagement, with a new realization of the hideousness of war. He wrote
Custis: "You have no idea what a horrible sight a field of battle is."
But if there could be glory for any individual in so much misery,
it came to Lee. He had been one of the two officers to find the route
on which the plan of battle had been based, and he had successfully
led the turning-column on both days. He had disclosed a special
aptitude for reconnaissance, and by the possession of this quality he
was commended anew to Scott, who leaned more and more heavily on
him.

When the reports came in, Lee was mentioned in the warmest
terms by each of the commanders under whom he had served. General
Scott named Lee twice in the body of his report and outdid his lieutenants in this studied tribute:

> "I am impelled to make special mention of the services of
> Captain R. E. Lee, engineers. This officer, greatly distinguished
> at the siege of Vera Cruz, was again indefatigable during these
> operations, in reconnaissance as daring as laborious, and of the
> utmost value. Nor was he less conspicuous in planting batteries,
> and in conducting columns to their stations under the heavy fire
> of the enemy."

No other officer of the army received such high praise; no other
gained so much in prestige by the action. On August 24, though he did
not get the news till much later, Lee was brevetted major, to date
from April 18, 1847, "for gallant and meritorious conduct in the battle
of Cerro Gordo." Opportunity had come in his first battle; he had
made the most of it.

With the vanguard of the troops that followed the defeated Mexicans, Lee entered the city of Jalapa on April 19. From Jalapa he hurried on to Perote, which General Worth took without opposition.
A few days later he rejoined Scott, who had established himself in
the governor's palace at Jalapa. Despite the recent victory the atmosphere of headquarters was not happy. Transportation was still below

JEFFERSON DAVIS

ABRAHAM LINCOLN, *1861*

the army's needs; there was no news of the arrival of reinforcements at Vera Cruz; the term of several thousand of the volunteers was about to expire, and they showed no disposition to re-enlist; Scott's suspicious nature led him to believe that the administration was withholding support at a time when he was sure that he could lead, with negligible losses, a properly equipped army straight to Mexico City.

Old "Fuss and Feathers" sent Worth forward to Puebla, which was entered on May 15, after a brush the previous afternoon with the enemy's cavalry. Puebla was at that time the second city of Mexico in population. Santa Anna's failure to defend so important a place could only mean he had not been able to collect an army capable of putting up a fight.

Here occurred another long period of delay and dark misgivings while Scott waited for reinforcements. He saw to it that his troops were occupied with hard drilling, and he held nightly levees to amuse and to instruct his officers. Touchy, pompous, and vainglorious though he might be, Scott none the less was the most scientific soldier at that time in America, and around his supper table he discussed for two or three hours with the heads of the various divisions of the general staff the particular problem that then confronted the army, whether of transport, supply, drill, gunfire, or march. These evening conferences were a very material part of the military education of Robert Lee. Equally instructive was his special duty. For Scott directed him and Major William Turnbull, chief topographical engineer, to make separate studies of the approaches to the city of Mexico and to prepare a map. Each collected what data he could from travellers and natives and pencilled these on his map. The result was a map of substantial accuracy, though faulty in many details.

On August 7, Franklin Pierce arrived at Puebla with reinforcements. The American force now numbered 10,738 officers and men. The size of this force led Scott to determine to abandon his line of communications and to undertake to live off the country while he pursued, found, and destroyed his adversary. The very morning after Pierce reported, Scott put Twiggs's division on the road to Mexico City.

Slowly the army crawled up the Rio Frio range, the great natural barrier to an attack on Mexico City from the east. No enemy was encountered until after the army had reached Ayotla, the last town on the road to Mexico. Here, on August 11, Scott established headquarters. To the west of Ayotla the road to Mexico, nineteen miles distant, ran on a narrow causeway through marshes, between Lake

Texcoco on the north and Lakes Xochimilco and Chalco on the south. The most casual examination of this ground showed that it was strongly occupied and fortified. Could the army assault the enemy's position or turn it successfully between the lakes? That was the question Lee was sent out on the 12th and 13th to answer. By evening on the second day he was able to report in some detail concerning strong fortifications protecting the hill El Peñón, and those guarding the village of Mexicalcingo.

Scott decided tentatively to mask El Peñón and to turn the enemy's positions via Mexicalcingo. Before this could be undertaken, word came from General Worth that some of his officers were convinced that the army could move around the lower end of Lake Chalco and advance on Mexico from the south, avoiding all the works between the lakes.

The reconnaissance to the south of Chalco had not been complete and some of the inferences drawn from it were erroneous. None the less, an advance in that direction offered so much the better chance of avoiding heavy losses that Scott promptly gave orders for the army to take the road around Chalco, leaving one division temporarily in front of Ayotla to delay the enemy. The distance from Ayotla to San Augustín, on the road from Acapulco to Mexico City, was estimated to be twenty-seven miles. While the army was slowly plodding around the eastern shore of Lake Chalco, Lee went ahead on the 17th and made a reconnaissance of the roads to the south and west of Chalco. Lee reported the facts and confirmed Scott in his purpose to advance on San Augustín. Scott did not deceive himself. Because he was sure the movements of his army had been observed and reported to Santa Anna, he expected to encounter the whole of the Mexican army in the vicinity of San Augustín. Advancing steadily on that village he met with no opposition, but when he arrived there on the morning of August 18 he received a message from General Twiggs that made him even more certain a battle was imminent. Twiggs reported that he had exchanged shots with a large force of Mexican cavalry, who must have discovered that the whole American army was moving to the south of Lake Chalco.

First reconnaissances showed singularly difficult terrain around San Augustín. The Acapulco road to Mexico City led northward to a hacienda known as San Antonio, distant about three miles. This highway was swept for a long distance by gunfire from San Antonio, which was found to be heavily fortified. East of it the ground was so soft that wheeled vehicles would be mired. Nor did it seem possible to turn San Antonio from the west, because the most conspicuous feature of the landscape was on that side—a great field of lava, broken into great blocks and fissures—a hopeless barrier to the advance of the guns or the trains. Such a tract of volcanic scoria was known locally as pedregal and bore an evil name. Even if a way for the infantry could be found through the pedregal, so that they could turn San Antonio without artillery support, their advance would be halted in another two miles at the town and river Churubusco, which were believed to be heavily fortified. An advance up the Acapulco road seemed an almost hopeless undertaking.

What was to be done; what alternative offered? Only one: About two miles west of San Augustín, the "San Angel" road led in a northeasterly direction to Churubusco, where it joined the Acapulco-Mexico City highway. If a passage could be made from San Augustín to the San Angel road, then San Antonio could be turned and perhaps no battle would have to be fought till Churubusco was reached.

Scott determined to ascertain whether the direct road northward toward Mexico City by San Antonio was as difficult as had been reported and whether a route could be opened across the pedregal to the San Angel road. To the important task of finding if there was a way over the pedregal he assigned Lee, accompanied by the 11th Infantry and two companies of dragoons.

Lee soon found a road that led over some mounds to the west of San Augustín and then followed the edge of the pedregal. It was no boulevard, to be sure, but it was passable for infantry and with some work it could be made practicable for artillery. For nearly three miles he made his way westward until he reached the side of an eminence in the pedregal known as Zacatepec. There his escort encountered a strong Mexican force, which exchanged shots and then fell back toward the western edge of the pedregal. Lee climbed to the top of Zacatepec and from that height was able to see that the enemy was in strength on the San Angel road and had thrown up a fortification on a hill near the village of Padierna. His long-range examination convinced him that this position could be occupied without great loss.

The immediate conclusion to be drawn from his reconnaissance was plain: the Mexicans he had encountered manifestly had come from the San Angel road; if they could cross the western part of the pedregal Scott's men could too. When they reached the other side of

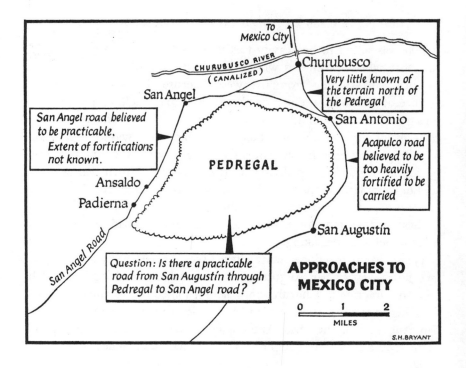

To Mexico City

CHURUBUSCO RIVER (CANALIZED) · Churubusco

San Angel

Very little known of the terrain north of the Pedregal

San Angel road believed to be practicable. Extent of fortifications not known.

San Antonio

PEDREGAL

Acapulco road believed to be too heavily fortified to be carried

Ansaldo

Padierna

San Augustín

San Angel Road

Question: Is there a practicable road from San Augustín through Pedregal to San Angel road?

APPROACHES TO MEXICO CITY

0   1   2
MILES

S.H.BRYANT

the lava field, they would be on the San Angel road and could avoid San Antonio altogether. Lee's judgment that this was the best strategy was confirmed in his mind by the news that the reconnaissance up the Acapulco road had been halted by fire from the hacienda of San Antonio.

That night Scott went over the reports one by one. Lee argued that the advance could be made by moving through the pedregal and up the San Angel road. Formal orders to this effect were issued before the night was over. The troops slowly advanced, covering the working party engaged in the difficult work of turning a mule path into a road fit for artillery and wagons. By 1 P.M., on August 19, the road had been constructed to within range of Padierna. The place was found to be armed with twenty-two guns, most of them heavy.

Lee saw that the road-making could go no farther till the Mexicans were driven off. He so reported to General Twiggs. A regiment was then advanced, and the enemy was driven back. Lee accompanied these troops, who halted on the edge of a ravine, 30 yards from the Mexicans.

The ravine that lay between the American troops and the Mexican position was deep and rough and was coursed by a rapid stream that flowed northward. Swept by the Mexican fire, the declivity was considered impassable. Some expedient other than a frontal assault had to be found, and speedily. Almost at the same hour, several of the commanding officers near the front realized that the best movement was to attempt to turn the enemy's left by advancing through the pedregal and westward across the San Angel road. Such a manoeuvre, if successful, would force the enemy from his high ground and would cut him off from a retreat to Mexico City. General Gideon Pillow ordered Riley's brigade to start the operation, and close behind Riley he sent General George Cadwalader. A little later General Persifor F. Smith filed away on his own initiative, and followed virtually the same route as Riley and Cadwalader.

All these troops, and a few others that General Scott sent on their heels, got safely across the pedregal and beyond the San Angel road. There they found themselves, some 3300 strong, in a situation full of advantage but, potentially, full of danger as well. The Americans were between two forces. If the Mexicans discovered the real situation and were good enough soldiers to make a simultaneous attack from north and south, the Americans might be wiped out.

Lee had come across the San Angel early in the evening, at the instance of General Scott, who was then at Zacatepec. Lee probably knew that the General believed it possible for the Americans west of the San Angel road to hold off the Mexican forces north of them while driving the other Mexican troops from the entrenched position at Padierna. Scott, indeed, had not been especially alarmed to find his advanced column between two Mexican forces. Lee may have known this to be Scott's estimate of the situation, but he brought no orders when he reported to General Smith.

After sundown Smith called Lee to confer with him and General Cadwalader. A decision was reached to deliver an attack on Padierna from the rear, before daybreak. To cover the attack on Padierna, a strong demonstration by the troops in front of that place was desirable. Smith stated that he would like to communicate his plan and position to Scott. Lee volunteered to carry the message to the commanding general, whom he believed to be still at Zacatepec. The understanding was, however, that Smith would deliver his attack, whether Lee returned from Scott or not.

It was near eight o'clock when Lee left San Gerónimo with a few men and started toward the pedregal. There was nothing to guide him but an occasional glimpse of the hill of Zacatepec when the lightning flashed. Groping his way along he reached the road and crossed it in safety. Next, at some point in that black maze—he did not know exactly where—he must find the American outposts and risk being shot before he could give the countersign. Ere long, above the roar of rain, he heard the slow, uncertain tramp of a large body of men. From the direction of their advance they must be Americans, but what if they were not? A crash of thunder, a ghostly glare for an instant, and he recognized them. They were General James Shields's men, moving to join Smith.

Leaving one of his companions to guide these troops, Lee plunged into the pedregal. Around great blocks of lava he felt his way, and across crevasses he was forced to jump in the dark. When the lightning showed an abysm over which he could not spring, he had to skirt it, with every risk of losing his direction. There were fully three tortuous miles of this. At last, drenched and sore, Lee stumbled to Zacatepec, only to find that Scott had returned to San Augustín.

Tired legs and bruised feet would have to carry him three miles more through the pedregal. Three miles must have seemed thirty, and Lee's strong body was close to exhaustion when finally he saw dim lights in the houses at San Augustín. Still wet from the rain, every muscle numb and aching, Lee stepped into Scott's headquarters at 11 o'clock. He found the General calmly writing his report of the day's operations, confident of the outcome but naturally anxious for news from the other side of the pedregal. Seven officers whom Scott had sent out in turn to carry messages to Smith had all returned without reaching him. The commander listened admiringly to Lee's report, cordially approved Smith's dispositions, and prepared immediately to order the desired demonstration.

The infantry were observed almost the moment they arrived, because the Mexicans were expecting a renewal of the attack from that quarter. Soon Lee found Colonel T. B. Ranson's men, whom he had guided into position, falling about him, as they answered the fire that was being poured into them. But the action did not last very long. Between 6 and 7 o'clock there was a nervous pause in the Mexican fire, visible confusion in the entrenched camp, and, in a few minutes, the roar of volleys from the crest of the hill above the Mexican guns. Then blue-coated men began to stream down the hillside through the growing light, and the Mexicans started to run. The attack that had been planned before Lee had left San Gerónimo was being delivered from in rear of Padierna, and the Mexicans were being routed.

General Smith realized that much depended now on the speed with which the enemy was followed up. He knew, as did the other commanders, that there was a crossroad north of the pedregal. At the village of Coyoacán, this crossroad divided. The upper, or nothern fork, ran to the village of Churubusco. As he rode steadily toward Coyoacán on the crossroad leading from the San Angel road, Scott was in his glory, enjoying every moment of his triumph and giving his orders rapidly and with a quick understanding of each new development. He soon ordered Lee forward to reconnoitre the lower fork which Pillow's division was to follow in the attack on the rear of San Antonio. Before this movement could be initiated, however, word came that the enemy had hurriedly evacuated San Antonio, and was retreating toward Mexico City.

Meantime, a hot fire was opened from the northeast through the standing corn beyond Coyoacán. The enemy was making a stand somewhere along the upper fork of the crossroad on the way to Churubusco. The Churubusco ran due east through cultivated fields, more a mill stream or a canal than a river. Where it crossed the Mexico-Acapulco road at the village of Churubusco a heavy bridgehead had been thrown up, with a deep wet ditch. About 450 yards to the southwest of the *tête-de-pont* was the convent of San Mateo. This enclosure covered the flank approach to the bridgehead, and had been converted into a temporary fort.

Worth advanced up the Acapulco road from San Antonio to Churubusco and deployed his troops against the bridgehead. Pillow joined him. The two divisions slowly but vigorously fought their way forward. Twiggs was ordered to take the convent. So confident was Scott of victory, despite the stubbornness of the Mexican resistance, that he decided to send Shields north of the river, with Pierce in support, to advance eastward to the Acapulco road and to cut off the enemy's retreat to Mexico City from the bridgehead. Lee was instructed to lead the troops across the Churubusco and to select a position for them.

Slowly the volunteers went forward in the face of a very heavy fire. When they saw the Mexicans waver they charged. As they reached the road they met Worth's troops advancing up it, for the bridgehead had been taken, the convent of San Mateo had been stormed, and the victory was won. Lee joined the infantry in pressing forward. Some of the cavalry pursued to the gates of Mexico.

Lee had been on his feet or in the saddle almost continuously for thirty-six hours and had been in all three of the actions, that of the

19th in the pedregal, that of Padierna, and that of Churubusco. He had his reward. Every general under whom he served at Padierna (Contreras) and Churubusco had praise for Lee, precisely as they had at Cerro Gordo. General Scott added a final tribute when he named the officers of his staff who deserve commendation, among them "Captain R. E. Lee (as distinguished for felicitous execution as for science and daring)"—the only officer for whom he had such words. Lee later received the brevet of lieutenant colonel, as of August 20, and gained much in professional prestige.

The day after the battle of Churubusco the Mexicans sought an armistice. This was signed on August 24, ostensibly that negotiators might agree on a treaty of peace. Scott observed both the spirit and the letter of the agreement, which forbade either side to construct or strengthen fortifications. Lee remained during this period of rest chiefly at the pleasant village of Tacubaya. Above the village, Scott had his headquarters in the bishop's palace. The height of Chapultepec, the main defense of Mexico City, was only a mile to the northward.

On the evening of September 6, when it was manifest that no peace would be concluded and that hostilities would be resumed shortly, Scott called Lee and several other officers to his quarters and discussed the best method of attacking the city. On the 7th the armistice was ended, and reconnaissance was at once undertaken. The burden of directing it fell on the Virginian.

The military problem was an unusual one. The only solid approach for an army was along one of the causeways that ran on straight lines toward the city gates. An approach from the south was difficult, but it avoided the fire of Chapultepec. On the other hand, if Chapultepec could be stormed, an advance into the city from that direction would be less arduous than by an attack from the south.

Scott learned that Mexican troops in considerable numbers had been observed around Molino del Rey, which lay at the western foot of the height of Chapultepec. He accordingly ordered General Worth, who was nearest the ground, to deliver a night attack on Molino del Rey. Later, on strong representation from Worth's staff, Scott consented that the attack be deferred until daylight.

Neither in the planning nor in the fighting of the battle of Molino del Rey on September 8 did Lee have any large part. While the action was on, he acted as an aide to Scott in reporting the movements of the opposing forces. By Worth's assault the enemy was driven from Molino del Rey and from the ground to the west, but Worth did not find the

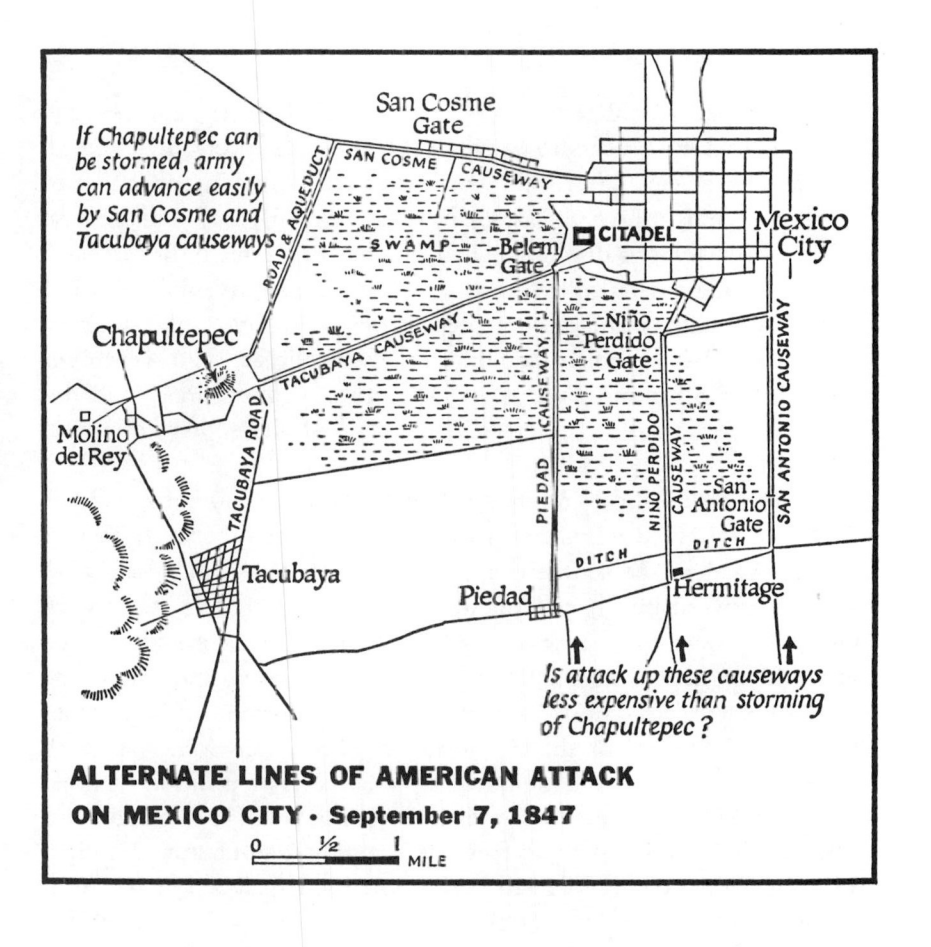

If Chapultepec can be stormed, army can advance easily by San Cosme and Tacubaya causeways

Is attack up these causeways less expensive than storming of Chapultepec?

ALTERNATE LINES OF AMERICAN ATTACK ON MEXICO CITY · September 7, 1847

0   ½   1
MILE

position sufficiently important to hold it after he had sustained 787 casualties in taking it.

No sooner was the battle over than Lee undertook his reconnaissances to the south of the city, assisted by Lieutenants Tower and Beauregard. The engineers discovered that the enemy was running an entrenchment in a northwesterly direction from the gate of San Antonio toward the gate on the Niño Perdido road. The Mexicans were expecting an attack in that quarter and were preparing for it. Lee's report of this situation was enough to induce General Scott the next morning, September 9, to make a personal examination in a wide sweep of the roads south of the city.

That night Scott called a council at Piedad. Scott announced that he wanted the judgment of his subordinates regarding the best method of attacking the city. It was of vital importance to strike a decisive blow with minimum casualties. Personally he favored an attack on Chapultepec and the western gates. He believed that one day's bombardment of Chapultepec would force its evacuation or make its capture easy, but he desired his officers to express their opinions freely. Lee and all the engineers except Beauregard announced themselves in opposition to Scott's plan and in favor of attacking the southern gates. The general officers, with Twiggs dissenting, also favored that course. Beauregard, however, made a detailed explanation of the comparative difficulties of the two operations and pronounced strongly in favor of assaulting Chapultepec. His argument convinced General Pierce, who went over to the side of Scott and Twiggs. With no further discussion, Scott decided that he would attack from the west, and thereupon adjourned the meeting.

The plan called for a continuing feint against the southern defenses while preparations were made for the real attack from the west. Troops were marched to the southern approaches in daylight and then were moved westward during the night. Lee was instructed to start work immediately on the construction of four batteries that were to be used against Chapultepec. As the batteries were put into position they one by one opened fire against Chapultepec on the morning of September 12. When the effect of the fire began to show, Lee went out with Lieutenant Tower to reconnoitre. Chapultepec was a position of great strength. A ridge of some 600 yards in length ran almost east and west, rising to a height of about 190 feet. On the crest a stout stone building had been constructed. This had been started as a palace but had subsequently been turned into a military college. The Americans always called it a fortress, but it scarcely deserved the name, for most of its armament had been extemporized for the expected assault.

The chief reliance of the Mexicans was on the difficulties of the approach. The whole ridge was enclosed on the north, east, and south by a high brick wall. On the western side were the buildings of Molino del Rey. Inside the enclosure the ground rose so precipitously on the northern and eastern faces that the position was impregnable there. On the south was the regular approach, by a ramp cut into the rock, with a single sharp turn about half-way up. This had been strengthened with sandbags and was a formidable barrier. From the west the approach was easier. East of Molino del Rey, within the enclosure, was an open field, and then a marshy cypress grove that ran to the edge of the rocky ascent. Precisely what fortifications had been constructed along this ascent the American engineers probably could not discover, but they doubtless could see the parapet rising from the rocky ground to the terrace of the palace, and they suspected, if indeed they did not actually observe, that there was a deep ditch below the parapet wall. A formidable position it was, weakened somewhat by the American guns, but by no means reduced!

Returning to the battery, Lee was soon visited by Beauregard, with a message that Scott wished to see him. Lee had not had any sleep for more than thirty hours, but rest had to wait on orders from the commanding general. Off he went to Tacubaya, accompanied by Tower and Beauregard. He found the general not in his best humor. Why had not Lee reported to him sooner? It was important that he know what the effect of the American fire on Chapultepec had been, so that he could decide whether to attack that evening or on the morning of the 13th. If he waited till the next day would the enemy be able during the night to repair the damage done by the bombardment? Lee answered that he feared the enemy would. "Then we must attack this evening," said Scott.

The three engineers hastily conferred and decided that there would hardly be time before nightfall to make preparations, to deliver the assault, and to follow it up. Lee thereupon approached Scott and told him that they believed it probably would be better to defer the attack until morning. Scott had cooled down somewhat, and, on second thought, he reasoned that if the Mexicans did reinforce Chapultepec that night the heavy batteries could drive them out the next morning. Moreover, he reflected, by attacking early in the day he would have a longer time in which to pursue whatever advantage he might gain. He acquiesced in the postponement and had Lee and the other engineers explain to him where the opposing batteries were located and what they had learned about the approaches to Chapultepec. Then he outlined fully his plan of operations, concluding with a request that Lee report to him that night.

Lee returned, as directed. Soon afterwards General Pillow rode up. At Scott's word, Lee sketched the plan of attack that Scott had described to him that afternoon. Lee spent the rest of the night visiting the batteries, to be sure that instructions were understood and that all damage done by the Mexicans during the day was being repaired. When dawn came on the 13th, he had been forty-eight hours without sleep and was close to collapse, but his orders took him very early in the morning to Pillow's division, which he was to guide in its advance.

Every one realized that the action about to open would be decisive of the war. A thrill passed through the ranks. Shortly after 8 o'clock in the morning Scott's messengers arrived at the headquarters of Pillow and of General John A. Quitman with word that he was about to give the signal for the opening of the battle. A moment's hush fell upon the army. Then the infantry were put in motion.

Lee set out immediately with Pillow from Molino del Rey and helped to guide the men of one storming party across the cultivated ground and into the cypress grove at the foot of the hill. They had not proceeded far when Pillow complained that he had been wounded. Lee saw the General safely placed out of the range of the fire, and probably had some part in carrying out Pillow's order that Worth be asked to support him immediately with his entire division.

Pillow's men pushed forward, while Colonel Newman S. Clarke's brigade came up from Worth, who held his other brigade for a turning movement north of Chapultepec. James Longstreet, Edward Johnson, George E. Pickett, and other young officers within the enclosure, urged their men on—past a temporary entrenchment the Mexicans had drawn up, over a mine field which the enemy had no time to explode, and on to a deep ditch directly under the ramparts of Chapultepec itself. Here there was a short pause while the scaling ladders were brought up. A little more, and the most daring were mounting the wall. They were thrown back, but others quickly gained a foothold, and the whole storming column was streaming up the terraces. Regimental flags were soon flung out from the elevation. Cheers drowned the clash of arms.

Quitman had been making his way toward the enclosure from the south, and part of his troops soon mingled with the rejoicing regiments of Pillow. Worth was thrown forward by Scott, on the northern side of the Chapultepec enclosure, to deal with a large force observed in that direction. A part of Pillow's command that had been unable to share in the assault was already there, and Lieutenant T. J. Jackson was serving a gun, almost single-handed, in an unequal duel with Mexican artillery.

There is no record of Lee's movements from the time he saw Pillow carried to a place of safety until he reappears on the terrace of Chapultepec shortly after the palace had been stormed. Lee may have gone on with Pillow's men, but it is more probable that he returned to Scott with a report of what had happened. Now he hurried forward, under Scott's orders, to reconnoitre the approaches to the San Cosme gate, and to bring up the siege and engineering trains. Scott sensed the demoralization of Santa Anna's troops and was determined to push Worth and Quitman on the heels of the enemy into Mexico City itself.

By this time strain and sleeplessness almost paralyzed Lee. It was with the greatest difficulty that he kept his saddle, but he started on his mission. While he was discharging it he received a slight wound, which he did not even stop to have dressed. He examined the ground over which Worth had to advance. The wagons he got under way. Somehow he managed to return to Scott at Chapultepec, and he rode with the commanding general on the line of Worth's advance. Then he fainted—for the first and only time in his life.

Before sunrise the next morning Lee was himself again and was soon dispatched by Scott with orders for Quitman. After Lee had left the field the previous evening Worth had fought his way to the San Cosme gate and Quitman to the Belem gate. Darkness had found them both practically within the city. About 4 A.M. a delegation from the city council had arrived at Scott's headquarters and had announced that Santa Anna had evacuated the city. All the Americans had to do was march in!

Lee carried the orders for Quitman to move cautiously to the centre of the city. He discovered that Quitman had placed his entire command under arms soon after daylight and had occupied the citadel. On report that a mob was looting the public buildings, Quitman sent a column to the grand plaza. Lee went with it and doubtless was in the square when Captain Roberts of the rifle regiment raised the United States flag over the palace amid the huzzas of the soldiers. About 8 o'clock Scott rode into the plaza from the Alameda, at the head of Worth's division. He and his staff were in full dress, and Scott did not lose a single thrill of the dramatic climax in which he was the central figure.

There followed twenty-four hours of scattered fighting in the streets with ruffians and with convicts that Santa Anna had released from prison before abandoning the city. Scott did not hesitate to employ a strong hand in dealing with these miscreants. In these bloody street encounters of the 14th and 15th, Lee did not share. Scott praised him for his conduct at Chapultepec, and the Department of War later gave him the brevet of Colonel, but his fighting in Mexico was at an end.

Labor did not end with active hostilities. While the tired little army awaited reinforcements, Lee set himself and his brother engineers to making surveys and to preparing maps of Mexico City and the nearby defenses and battlefields. Not until April 21, 1848, were certain of the maps finished and forwarded to the engineers' bureau. A little later Lee joined Beauregard and McClellan in reconnoitring Toluca, but apparently he made no further surveys. During almost the whole of this work he had, in addition, the troublesome supervision of the engineering company.

Hostilities ended on March 6, but the Mexican Congress was slow to ratify the peace. When word came at last on May 21 that the treaty had been ratified by the chamber of deputies, the favorable action of the senate being taken for granted, Lee rushed off the news to his brother Smith: "We all feel quite exhilarated at the prospect of getting home. . . ."

Lee lost little time in realizing his hopes. On May 27 he received orders to march the engineering company to Vera Cruz, and, as soon as he heard that ratifications of the treaty had been exchanged, to embark them for the United States. He reached Vera Cruz on June 6, sent off some of the officers and all of the men the next day, and sailed after them as soon as he could purchase a few gifts for his family and find a place aboard the steamer.

Twenty months of service in Mexico had been ended when Lee saw the castle and the towers of Vera Cruz fade from view. They were probably the twenty most useful months of his training as a soldier. Their effect on him can be seen during nearly the whole of the War between the States. The lessons he learned on the road to Mexico City he applied in much of his strategy. Warnings he read in that campaign he never forgot.

He carried home with him the highest admiration of his former commander and the good opinion of his brother officers. As a result of their labors together, Scott had an "almost idolatrous fancy for Lee, whose military genius he estimated far above that of any other officer of the army," according to E. D. Keyes. When there was talk of war between America and England, Scott is said to have declared that it would be cheap if the United States could absolutely insure the life of Robert E. Lee even at a cost of $5,000,000 a year. In 1858 Scott referred to Lee in an official letter as "the very best soldier that I ever saw in the field." Among other officers in Mexico, Lee gained a high professional reputation. Yet he did not return from Mexico a national figure, in any sense. His skill in reconnaissance and his contribution to Scott's victories were known only to the army and to his intimates. At the same time, if Lee was not a national figure when he returned to the United States in 1848, his reputation increased thereafter, as the admiration expressed by Scott and by other friends during the decade after 1848 caused an appreciation of his soldierly qualities to spread gradually from the army to the general public.

Lee's Mexican experiences gave him close observation of an army in nearly all the conditions, except those of retreat, that were apt to arise in the field. He had acquired his experience under an excellent, practical master, and in an army that, though small, was efficient and well-trained. All this helped him and made it easy for him in 1855 to transfer from the staff to the line. Even more valuable was Lee's training in strategy while in Mexico. As a member of Scott's "little cabinet" he sat in council when the most difficult of Scott's strategical problems were being considered by the General. His views, which were usually based on a better knowledge of the ground than his superiors possessed, were expressed fully and were received by Scott with respect. More than once he had a part in planning operations that were executed where he could see the correctness or the errors of his reasoning—a very different matter from the blackboard studies of West Point.

Seven great lessons Lee learned from Cerro Gordo to Mexico City in strategy and in the handling of an army, seven lessons that were the basis of virtually all he attempted to do in Virginia fifteen years later:

1. Lee was inspired to audacity. This was, perhaps, his greatest strategical lesson in Mexico, for all the circumstances favored a daring course on the part of his teacher. The nucleus of Scott's army was professional; the forces that opposed them were ill-trained and poorly led. Scott could attempt and could achieve in Mexico what even he, bold as he was, would not have undertaken against an army as well disciplined as his own. When it is remembered that the son of "Light-Horse Harry" received his practical instruction under as daring a soldier as Scott, and followed that by a study of Napoleon, it will not be surprising that audacity, even to the verge of seeming overconfidence, was the guiding principle of the strategy he employed as the leader of a desperate cause.

2. Lee concluded, from Scott's example, that the function of the commanding general is to plan the general operation, to acquaint his corps commanders with that plan, and to see that their troops are brought to the scene of action at the proper time; but that it is not the function of the commanding general to fight the battle in detail. Whether he was right in this conclusion is one of the moot questions of his career.

3. Working with a trained staff, Lee saw its value in the development of a strategical plan. Scott was very careful on this score. He relied

on the young men who had been trained at the Military Academy, and they did not fail him. Lee kept this ideal of a trained staff and had become so accustomed to efficient staff work in the regular army that when he first took command in Virginia he did not realize how vast was the difference between trained and untrained staff officers.

4. The relation of careful reconnaissance to sound strategy was impressed on Lee by every one of the battles he saw in Mexico. He left Mexico convinced for all time that when battle is imminent a thorough study of the ground is the first duty of the commanding officer.

5. Lee saw in Mexico the strategic possibilities of flank movements. Cerro Gordo had been passed and San Antonio had been turned by flanking the enemy. At little cost of life, positions of much strength had been rendered untenable.

6. Lee acquired a confident view of the relation of communications to strategy. It is possible that this was one reason why Lee was emboldened to expose his communications in the Maryland campaign of 1862 and in the Pennsylvania campaign of 1863.

7. Lee acquired in Mexico an appreciation of the value of fortification. The proper location of the batteries at Vera Cruz and at Chapultepec had contributed to the American victory. At Cerro Gordo and at Padierna he had examined fortifications that had been poorly defended but had been well laid out by Mexican engineers. Lee may well have told himself that a competent defending force could have added much to Scott's difficulties by intelligent use of earthworks.

Between his return from Mexico and his participation in the War between the States Lee had no first-hand opportunity of observing large-scale field operations. His practical training in war prior to 1861 thus covered twenty months. His only additional lessons were theoretical, acquired from limited study at West Point in 1852–55. However, he was of a nature to apply readily what he had learned, and as there was comparatively little advance in military science between 1848 and 1861, except in the development of ordnance, his Mexican training was not seriously deficient.

CHAPTER IV

From West Point to Texas
and Secession

LANDING at New Orleans on his way home, Lee came up the Mississippi
with his mare, Grace Darling, and his orderly, Jim Connally. When his
steamer reached Wheeling he left Jim to bring on the horse, and himself
"took the cars" for Washington, which he reached June 29, 1848. No
time was lost in returning to the duties of peace. On July 3 he was
assigned to "special duty" in Totten's office. On the 21st he was again
named a member of the board of engineers for the Atlantic coast defenses. During this time, he had the pleasure of receiving his brevet
commissions. He could not have hoped for more—brevet major for
Cerro Gordo, brevet lieutenant colonel for Contreras-Churubusco, and
brevet colonel for Chapultepec. After the publication of general orders
on August 24 he was "Colonel Lee," as army usage gave the title of
highest brevet.

Now came a new assignment to duty. The port of Baltimore, Md.,
had been neglected by Congress in its appropriations for coast and
harbor defenses. Between the city and bombardment, in case of attack,
stood only old Fort McHenry, famous as inspiring "The Star Spangled
Banner," but too close to afford adequate defense. Army engineers had
long recommended a new fort on Sollers' Point Flats, and the United
States had at last acquired jurisdiction of the flats from the Maryland
legislature. Major Cornelius A. Ogden of the corps of engineers had
laid off the site in 1847 and during 1848 had begun preliminary work.

To the construction of the fort Lee was assigned on September 13,
and on November 15 he reported for duty in Baltimore, but he could
do little more than officially take over the undertaking as he had to
leave almost immediately for Boston on duty with the board of engineers. He was in the latter city by November 18 and remained there

until December 1. On his return to Baltimore the state of the work, the weather, and the scarcity of funds, led him to conclude that building operations should be suspended until the spring of 1849.

General Totten—for he had been brevetted brigadier for his service at Vera Cruz—was careful, now as always, to keep his engineers occupied, so he set Lee to finishing maps begun in Mexico. Soon after these maps were done, Lee was sent off again with the board of engineers to make a study of the lands that should be held as public domain for the construction of fortifications in Florida. The engineers left Washington early in January, 1849, and by the middle of the month were in Mobile. Thence they made a circuit of the Florida coast from Pensacola all the way to Cumberland Island.

About April 1, Lee returned to resume work at Sollers' Flats. The family moved and took up residence on Madison Avenue in Baltimore. Their house was quite pleasant, but the rooms were small in comparison with those of Arlington. To reach his station Lee had to take a bus daily to the wharf, where two oarsmen met him with a boat. He was rowed to Sollers' Point, and thence, after construction got under way, out to the flats.

Late in July Lee developed a fever that probably was malaria, and sought refuge at Ravensworth. Returning to Arlington when he began to improve, he remained there until the end of the first week in August. On August 12 he placed his assistant, Captain J. G. Foster, in charge at Sollers' Point and took train for Newport, R. I., where he joined the other members of the board of engineers in a study of the best location for new barracks, quarters, and a hospital at Fort Adams. Lee's sickness still dogged him. It was not until the end of August that he returned to Baltimore after the first and only illness prior to 1863 of which there is any record. Work then settled into its usual channels at Sollers' Point. By the end of September, when the report-year closed, he was able to record the completion of nearly all the preliminary work and the erection of one hundred feet of the outer wharf.

Two brief visits to Washington and Christmas at Arlington seem to have been Lee's only absence from Baltimore during the period from October 1, 1849, to the end of the report-year, twelve months thereafter. With longer residence in Baltimore, the social life of the Lees became far more active. Colonel Lee's sister Ann (Mrs. William Louis Marshall) was still in the city and her husband had successfully made the change from the pulpit to the bar. Through Mr. and Mrs. Marshall and through other connections of Lees and Custises, the family made many new friends. Colonel and Mrs. Lee attended Mount Calvary Church and were active in the city's social life. The two older girls lived in an ever-widening circle of young misses of their own age. Similarly, the boys were soon at ease in their new environment. The chief difference in the household was the absence of Custis. He was eighteen in 1850 and decided to follow the profession of his father. Lee succeeded in procuring for him an appointment to the Military Academy. In midsummer, 1850, Custis went to West Point. He had abundant ability, but at first he was somewhat indolent. Lee had to deal tactfully with him in order to arouse in him a determination to excel.

Life in Baltimore was not all enjoyment. Construction did not progress quite so satisfactorily at Fort Carroll in 1850–51 as during the previous report-year. The work of the board of engineers necessitated two journeys—one to Boston in December and one to New York in March. Worse still, the Thirty-first Congress adjourned without making any appropriation for Fort Carroll, and construction had to be reduced.

The driving of piles and the laying of stone continued, as the weather permitted, into the spring of 1852, with Lee more than ever confined to the fort because of a change of assistants late in March. Work was progressing regularly, when on May 28, Lee received the following letter from Totten, dated at Washington on the 27th:

"You will prepare yourself to transfer the operations now under your charge temporarily to Lieut. [W. H. C.] Whiting, in order that you may proceed to West Point towards the close of the month of August and on the 1st of September next relieve Capt. [Henry] Brewerton of the Superintendency of the Military Academy, and of the command of the post of West Point, Capt. Brewerton to succeed to duty at Fort Carroll."

This was a surprise, and not a pleasant one, to Lee. The superintendency of West Point was an honor, one of the few "plums" of the hard-worked engineer service. The superintendent was the titular head of a considerable command and the centre of a very pleasant society, but Lee felt that he lacked experience for the position. Accordingly he wrote:

"I learn with much regret the determination of the Secretary of War to assign me to that duty, and I fear I cannot realize his expectations in the management of an Institution requiring more skill and more experience than I command.

"Although fully appreciating the honor of the station, and extremely reluctant to oppose my wishes to the orders of the Department, yet if I be allowed any option in the matter, I would respectfully ask that some other successor than myself be appointed to the present able Superintendent."

The bureau must have given consideration to Lee's request for it was June 8 before an answer was sent him. It was official and positive: the chief engineer had to decline to change the assignment. Lee began to prepare for the change. He completed his annual financial statement, and on August 21 announced to the department that he had turned over all balances to Lieutenant Whiting. On August 23, 1852, he set out for West Point.

When Lee, on September 1, became ninth superintendent of the United States Military Academy, he found a plant very different from the one he had known in the days of his cadetship. Scarcely any of the old buildings remained. Of the old faculty only two remained, W. H. C. Bartlett and Albert E. Church. Both of them were now full professors, but they were paying for rising fame with multiplying gray hairs.

The work of the institution was on a high general level, but Brewerton had some problems that Lee inherited. Many boys were being sent to the academy without proper preparation, and sometimes when they were dismissed for failure or for misconduct, discipline was impaired because the Secretary of War yielded to political considerations and ordered them restored to duty. The curriculum was crowded, and some important subjects were being omitted; but neither Congress nor the War Department had acted on the recommendation of successive boards that the course of study be lengthened to five years.

While Lee was adjusting himself to his routine, his family was settling itself in the superintendent's house. Agnes and Annie remained in Virginia for at least part of the winter, but the other children came with their mother to West Point. The family horses were brought from Arlington, as was some of the furniture, so that the household was quite comfortable. Living expenses were high, because the superintendent had to do much official entertaining, but fortunately, soon after he entered on his duties, Lee was assigned according to his brevet rank, with higher pay and allowances. Every social pleasure was sharpened by the knowledge that Custis was nearby. The boy usually came home on Saturday afternoon for a call, accompanied by one or more of the other cadets.

Lee engaged in a study of the printed regulations of the school, preparatory to the publication of a new edition. In this way he familiarized himself with the modifications adopted during the twenty-three years he had been away from West Point. Without any overnight revolution or even a shakeup in personnel, he began to tighten discipline and academic standards. His first step was to make the midyear examinations mean more to the cadets. Prior to 1849 the regulations had provided that only members of the fourth (freshman) class could be dismissed for failure to pass the January examinations. In 1849 the academic board had been given authority to dismiss at midterm any cadet who failed, regardless of the class to which he belonged. Until Lee's time, however, this new rule had never been applied to members of the first (senior) class. In the earliest examinations held after Lee became superintendent three cadets of the graduating class failed engineering, and their case was brought before the academic board. Had their deficiency been in any other subject the board might have given them until June to regain their standing. But engineering had a certain sacrosanctity. First-classmen failing in it had been dismissed, as Lee subsequently explained, "on the very eve of graduation." The board voted to dismiss the three men who had fallen behind. One of them carried his case to Washington and precipitated a correspondence in which Lee vigorously defended the action of the board. Politics proved more potent than high scholarship. The young man was returned and, in the class of 1853, was duly graduated.

A case of this sort was most destructive of discipline, but Lee made no protest. He found the Secretary of War, C. M. Conrad, very much disposed to sacrifice morale to save a friend, however, and it must have been with inward satisfaction that, on March 4, 1853, Lee saw Conrad retire, and a new secretary take the oath. The change marked the transfer of the government from Lee's own party to the Democrats, but it brought a personal friend to the head of the department, under a President who knew something of war at first hand. The new President was Franklin Pierce, whom Lee had often seen in Mexico. The incoming secretary was Jefferson Davis. From the very hour that Davis assumed office, reversals of the superintendent of the academy virtually ceased. Himself a West Pointer, the secretary understood that discipline at the academy could be no stronger than the faith of the War

Department in the discretion of the superintendent. Lee's troubles were accordingly reduced. New confidence and respect between himself and Davis were built up.

Suddenly, in April, came word that Mrs. Custis was very ill. Mrs. Lee started for Arlington at once, only to find on her arrival that the gracious mistress of the estate was already dead. Mrs. Lee sustained the shock courageously. Mrs. Custis's death grieved the son-in-law almost as deeply as it did the daughter. To Markie Williams, daughter of his friend and fellow officer, Capt. Seth Williams, he said: "The blow was so sudden and crushing, that I yet shudder at the shock and feel as if I had been arrested in the course of life and had no power to resume my onward march."

The first commencement of Lee's superintendency came not long after the death of Mrs. Custis. No man could have been otherwise than proud of the four companies he presented the board of visitors when those functionaries arrived on June 1. The board forwarded a report in which the academy and its administration were warmly praised.

After commencement, summer leave—in the sequence that seemed more logical to third-classmen than any syllogism in the book! During this vacation occurred an important event in the life of Lee. In early boyhood he had been drilled in his catechism by Reverend William Meade. From his youth he had lived in the spiritual atmosphere Meade had created in northern Virginia, but he had not joined any church. As he grew older all his religious impulses were deepened, and he felt an increasing dependence on the mercy of a personal God. It is probable that the Mexican War, the death of Mrs. Custis, and his sense of responsibility for so many young men brought the great questions of faith closer to him. More particularly, as both Mary and Annie were now of an age to be confirmed, Lee decided that he ought also to submit himself formally to the Christian faith. On July 17, 1853, he and the two daughters were confirmed at the chancel of Christ Church, Alexandria, by Right Reverend John Johns, Bishop of Virginia.

His vacation over on August 27, Lee had comparative quiet at the academy until almost the end of the year. All was proceeding peacefully when the commandant came to Lee and reported that on the night of December 16 a trio of third-class cadets had been absent from barracks from twelve o'clock until five, and that two fourth-class men had been away for an hour. The fourth-class men had liquor in their possession when they returned, and one of them, as well as one of the third-class men, was in citizen's clothes. The men had been caught red-handed. The infraction was rendered worse by the fact that among the offenders was Fitz Lee, the superintendent's nephew and son of his beloved brother Smith Lee. Fitz had entered the academy in 1852 and had not distinguished himself, but this was the first time he had been in serious trouble. Colonel Lee resolved embarrassment by the simple expident of declining to be embarrassed. He recommended the dismissal of all the culprits from the academy, or their trial before a court-martial.

But in his youth, as always, Fitz Lee had the ability to make friends who would stand by him in trouble. All the members of the third class offered, if the superintendent would relieve the trio of the charges against them, to pledge themselves for the remainder of the session not to commit the offense of which their comrades were accused. Lee forwarded the tender of this pledge to General Totten. Jefferson Davis passed on the paper and declined to accept the pledge. The case went to court-martial, which put stiff punishment on Fitz Lee and two of his comrades. The two fourth-class men were allowed to resign.

Light-hearted Fitz Lee did not regard his narrow escape very seriously. Because he then had 197 demerits he was required to remain at West Point during July and August. Wearying of this dull life he slipped out of camp with another cadet one night and did not return until 2:30. He was caught and placed under arrest, with every prospect of ending speedily and ingloriously his career as a cadet. Colonel Lee could only forward the papers and recommend a court-martial. Again all Fitz's classmates then at the academy offered to make a pledge not to commit his offense during the academic year. When the rest of the class returned the pledge was made unanimous, and in the third class all but two members proffered a like pledge for Fitz's companion in misadventure. This time the secretary authorized acceptance of the pledges, and Fitz Lee was saved for the cavalry corps of the Army of Northern Virginia and for a long life of varied public service.

As Lee dealt with his night-walking nephew, so he dealt with all the cadets. He carried them on his heart, and spent many an anxious hour debating how best he could train them to be servants of their country by making them masters of themselves. "When . . . I visited the academy," Jefferson Davis wrote years afterward, "and was surprised to see so many gray hairs on his head, he confessed that the cadets did exceedingly worry him, and then it was perceptible that his sympathy with the young people was rather an impediment than a qualification for the superintendency." Earnestly, however, Lee studied the boys. By the summer of 1854 he had come to know most of their frailties, their adolescent dodges, and all their good points, and he had made a consistent "administrative policy" out of the school's precedents and his own observations.

He believed that the best age for a boy to enter the academy was between seventeen and eighteen, and he thought adequate preliminary training could be had at home. From the hour they were admitted his attitude toward them he put into a single sentence: "These young gentlemen are not considered exactly in the light of enlisted men, and as much deference as possible is paid to their convenience and wishes in relation to personal matters." Individual rights were not overriden and freedom of religious worship was always regarded. In official dealings his fundamental was equal treatment for all.

If a cadet stood well in his classes and had little demerit, Lee was not apt to see much of him, but if the boy got into trouble of any sort, Lee was quick to know of it. If a cadet did not write home, Lee found out why. In cases of serious illness he promptly notified the family, visited the boy, and gave him the best treatment possible in the academy hospital. In the rare instances of death in the corps, his sympathy was personal and instant.

Lee kept a close eye on class reports, and when he perceived that a boy was in danger of failing he watched his standing week by week, consulted his instructors, and on occasion would call him in to discuss his case during his cadet office hour, which was between 7 and 8 A.M. Sometimes he wrote parents urging them to prod an indolent son or to encourage a disheartened student. In those instances where a boy was in danger of dismissal for demerit, without having been guilty of any serious offense, Lee always took pains to explain that the cadet's character was not involved.

In case a cadet fell hopelessly behind in his work, or showed himself incompetent and certain to fail in his examination, Lee often urged parents to permit the boy to resign and thereby to save him the humiliation of dismissal. Whenever he received the list of cadets deficient in conduct Lee went over it and reduced the demerit of those in whose behalf any valid excuse could be urged. If the number remaining was more than one hundred for six months, Lee held strictly to the rule that denied the privilege of resignation to cadets who exceeded that figure.

Serious offenses at West Point often provoked Lee to urge that the cadet be brought before a court-martial, or be dismissed by the Secretary of War. When dismissal occurred, Lee was opposed in every

instance to re-examination or readmission. It was painful to mete out
punishment, especially to the young, he once wrote Totten, but "when
it is necessary, true kindness requires it should be applied with a firm
hand, and not converted into a reward."

Some of the young men who had tasted Lee's discipline were included
among the forty-six who graduated in June, 1854. At the head of the
class, to Lee's gratification, stood his son Custis, who had maintained
his improvement in his senior year and had qualified for the engineer
corps. The graduate whom Lee had come to know best after his own
son was a stout gray-eyed lad of middle height and broad shoulders,
with abundant hair and a dashing manner, a boy born to be a cavalryman and known already from his three initials as "Jeb" Stuart. He had
visited the superintendent's home often and had wholly won his heart.

At this commencement the board of visitors had nothing but compliments for the cadets themselves, for the academy, and for the superintendent. "The board cannot conclude this report," it said after
summarizing conditions, "without bearing testimony to the eminent
qualifications of the superintendent for the honorable and distinguished
post assigned him by the government. Services conspicuous in the field,
and when our country was engaged in a war with a foreign nation, have
lost none of their luster in the exalted position he so worthily fills."

The board had two definite suggestions, that Spanish be taught the
cadets, and that the course be made five years instead of four. Instruction in Spanish had been previously proposed by the visitors of 1850
and the extension of the course had been favored by every board after
1850. This time the board argued that a fifth year was necessary in order
that the instruction might be given in important omitted subjects and
also in order to make good the poor preparation of many boys appointed to the academy. Secretary Davis saw the logic of this argument.
He ordered instruction in Spanish begun with the next school year, and
on July 8 he opened a lengthy correspondence with Lee on the scope
of the projected five-year course and on the fairest way of separating
the fourth class into two sections, to graduate a year apart. The cadets
who entered in June, 1854, were rearranged in two classes in September,
not without some complaints, but only a few new courses were undertaken for the session of 1854–55. Lee had no part in initiating this five-
year system. It was not his proposal, though he has generally been
given credit for it. After a few years' trial it was abandoned.

While Lee was effecting these changes at the academy, changes that
were directly to affect him were being made in the army. Davis had

pointed out the weakness of the regular armed forces of the United States and had asked that they be strengthened. Congress had not acted. On August 19, 1854, Lieutenant John L. Grattan, who had graduated under Lee the previous June at West Point, had been sent out with thirty men from Fort Laramie, Wyo., to make an arrest. The detachment had been attacked by Indians and every man in it save one had been killed. The survivor was badly wounded and subsequently died. This massacre created a sensation and sharpened Davis's argument when he appealed in December for new regiments. This time Congress heeded the warning and authorized the establishment of two new regiments of infantry and two of cavalry.

Who would command the new troops? Almost as soon as the bill increasing the army had been signed by the President, Davis announced the appointments: As of March 3, 1855, Albert Sidney Johnston, hero of Davis's West Point days, was named colonel of the new 2d Cavalry and Lee lieutenant colonel. Lee was surprised and not altogether pleased. The change from staff to line would bring no new compensation, for Lee was already drawing pay as colonel by brevet. Transfer meant farewell to the corps he loved and would involve separation from his family. On the other hand, there was little prospect that he could rise to be chief engineer, for Totten was still vigorous and not disposed to retire. Even if he should, two lieutenant colonels of engineers, four majors, and three captains were ahead of Lee. In the army the outlook was different. All the general officers and most of the colonels were old and there was talk of increasing the number of generals. Still again, service in the line meant a healthful, out-of-door life in pleasant contrast to the confinement and office work of the superintendency. But none of these things weighed heavily with Lee. He did not hesitate. "Promotion, if offered an officer, ought in my opinion to be accepted, but it need not be sought unless deserved," he afterwards said. On March 15 he accepted and on March 31 turned over the command at West Point to Brevet Major Jonathan G. Barnard and went to Arlington.

He left the academy in good condition. The school was the better for Lee's administration of its affairs, though he worked no revolution, in teaching or in discipline, and was no more, in the annals of the school, than an efficient, diligent superintendent. As for the effect of the academy on Lee, it was immensely valuable in giving him added experience in dealing with one type of the young men he was to have under his command six years after he left West Point. He learned how to elicit their best endeavors and how to cope with their weaknesses. Without dreaming that he was doing so, he likewise equipped himself to be a college president: when he went to Washington College he had to apply a different discipline, but it was with a confident understanding of how the head of a school should deal with trustees, faculty, and students. It is hardly probable that he would have accepted the post at Lexington in 1865 if he had not been superintendent of the military academy.

On April 12 Lee received orders to repair to Louisville, Ky., and to take command of the new 2d Cavalry, as its colonel was not ready to report for duty. It was the first time since the Mexican War that he had left home without the assurance that the family would speedily join him. The 2d Cavalry had been established for frontier duty. Whether to Texas, to the plains, or to California, Lee had to go with it. Without ado or long farewell, he left beloved Arlington. Following the oft-travelled route he reached Louisville, and on April 20 assumed direct command of troops for the first time in his military career.

As the establishment of the two cavalry regiments had been at the instance of the military authorities in the face of stiff opposition, Secretary Davis had been put on his mettle to provide competent commanders and good recruits. Major E. V. Sumner, who well merited the honor, had been transferred from the 2d Dragoons and had been made colonel of the 1st Cavalry. Joseph E. Johnston had been named lieutenant colonel. In the 2d Cavalry, with Albert Sidney Johnston as colonel and Lee as second in command, W. J. Hardee and William H. Emory were commissioned major. Emory served only a short time, whereupon Davis offered the post to Braxton Bragg, and when he declined, the secretary named George H. Thomas, one of Lee's associates for a part of his superintendency at West Point. Among the captains were Earl van Dorn, E. Kirby Smith, and George Stoneman. Charles W. Field and John B. Hood were lieutenants. It was a roster of picked officers.

Almost before Lee was able to form an estimate of his brother officers and his men, the 2d was ordered to Jefferson Barracks, Saint Louis. Thither Lee went, and soon found himself temporarily in command as ranking officer at the station. He speedily got his first unpleasant dose of what was to become the irksome physic of his changed military life. This was court-martial service, which during the next five years was to compel him to ride hundreds of miles, and sit for tedious hours while witnesses testified and advocates argued. Both he and Albert Sidney Johnston were ordered across Missouri to Fort Leavenworth, on the edge of Kansas, there to hear charges brought against several officers.

The court convened on September 24, and when it was adjourned, Lee was sent to Fort Riley, farther westward in Kansas, to sit in judgment on a surgeon who was alleged to have abandoned his post of duty in the midst of an epidemic. When he at last was free at Fort Riley, he got still another assignment to court-martial duty, but this time he was lucky: the court was held at Carlisle Barracks, Pennsylvania, early in January, so he had opportunity of coming east and seeing his family again. His stay was brief, and from Carlisle Barracks he was ordered to West Point for his fourth court-martial in as many months. Hardly was he back home from West Point when orders arrived for him to join his regiment in Texas. Leaving on February 12, 1856, a long journey brought him on March 6 to San Antonio. In that city he had to wait two weeks before he could set out for regimental headquarters, located temporarily at Fort Mason, one hundred miles from San Antonio. Five days' fast riding northward brought him to the fort, where Albert Sidney Johnston welcomed him.

On March 27 Johnston assigned Lee to command the two squadrons of the regiment then at Camp Cooper, 170 miles north of Fort Mason. At this outpost, which he was to call his "Texas home" for nineteen months, Lee arrived on April 9, relieving Major Hardee. The camp was part of the Comanche reserve, on the clear fork of the Brazos River, 35 miles from the point of its junction with the main stream. Snakes were everywhere. Wolves prowled and howled at night. West of the camp wild country stretched away to the "Staked Plains." North of the camp the Comanches roamed and hunted, always ready to send an arrow after the white man. Downstream were the lodges of a part of the tribe, under Chief Catumseh, whom the government was trying to "humanize," as Lee put it, with free clothing and food. These Indians professed friendship, but they were not trusted. Lee's impressions of them were anything but favorable.

Indians or no Indians, it was Lee's nature to make the best of his surroundings, but his cheerfulness did not keep him from seeing the hardships and the futility of the life he was leading. Only one professional interest was offered him at Camp Cooper: the War Department considered it desirable to locate a fort in that area, and it designated Lee to suggest a site. For a time he made long rides almost daily to study the terrain and to find the most desirable location. Often he was attended by one of his lieutenants, John B. Hood, who had graduated from West Point during the first year of Lee's superintendency. Lee was fond of Hood and he talked with him of many things besides fortification and drills. Perhaps he had an idea that Hood might be tempted to marry some girl of the frontier, simply as an escape from loneliness and he told him very earnestly, "Never marry unless you can do so into a family that will enable your children to feel proud of both sides of the house." The search for a good site for a fort did not require many days. Monotony of the darkest and dullest descended again, but, like most woes, it was relieved at length.

Indians had been carrying on depredations on the edge of the Staked Plains and in the vicinity of Fort Chadbourne. The department had determined to pursue them and, if possible, track them down. Lee was placed in charge of one expedition against them and was given four squadrons of cavalry. From a fruitless and tiring expedition he returned to Camp Cooper on July 23, after an absence of forty days. The distance covered by all the units had been 1600 miles, and the results had been negligible. He came back convinced that the Indians did not inhabit the country on the upper waters of the Colorado and Brazos and simply passed through on their raids. No opportunity was given him for justifying or demonstrating this conclusion. His first long scout proved to be his last.

Lee tried to keep cheerful, but was depressed by the heat and by the arrival of news that his sister Mildred, Mrs. Edward Vernon Childe, who was only forty-five, had died in Paris.

Soon after the tidings of Mrs. Childe's death, there came orders for the detail that Lee must by this time have learned to expect along with changing weather and hard fare: once again he was summoned to court-martial duty—not at Fort Mason or Fort Chadbourne, but 700 miles away, on the Rio Grande, at Ringgold Barracks. The assignment meant weary days of riding across Texas. He was twenty-seven days on the road, but he enjoyed the company of his friend Major George H. Thomas, who met him at Fort Mason.

At Ringgold Barracks, where he arrived on September 28, work was tedious, and the principal case before the court was protracted by two Texas lawyers. On October 30, 1856, the court adjourned to Fort Brown, on the site of the present Brownsville. Lee was now in closer touch with the outside world, and he had already made friends among the families of the other officers, who, like himself, had to travel about to form the courts-martial. His duties were not heavy. Soon he recovered his old poise and wrote home in better spirits.

During the week before Christmas he scoured the poor shops of Fort Brown for presents, and on Christmas morning he had something for every officer's child in the garrison, though he had known them only a few weeks and expected to leave them soon.

His own best Christmas gift was a full file of his Alexandria newspaper, the most recent issue only three weeks old. In writing to his wife of this happy arrival, Lee set down for the first time, as far as is known, his reflections on the slavery question that was then inflaming sectional hate. He had participated in the discussions among the officers at West Point during his superintendency; while he was on court-martial duty at Fort Leavenworth he may have seen at first hand some of the passions aroused in "bleeding Kansas"; he had been in contact with slavery all his life, though he had never owned more than some half-dozen slaves, and they had probably been inherited or given him by Mr. Custis. He believed in gradual emancipation, and had sent to Liberia such of his servants as wished to go. But of all he thought and said on a subject that puzzled open-minded Southerners, nothing of any consequence remains prior to this letter, written about seven weeks after the first national election in which the Republican party had presented a candidate:

"In this enlightened age, there are few I believe, but what will acknowledge, that slavery as an institution, is a moral & political evil in any Country. It is useless to expatiate on its disadvantages. I think it however a greater evil to the white than to the black race, & while my feelings are strongly enlisted in behalf of the latter, my sympathies are more strong for the former. The blacks are immeasurably better off here than in Africa, morally, socially & physically. The painful discipline they are undergoing, is necessary for their instruction as a race, & I hope will prepare & lead them to better things. How long their subjugation may be necessary is known & ordered by a wise Merciful Providence. Their emancipation will sooner result from the mild & melting influence of Christianity, than the storms & tempests of fiery Controversy. This influence though slow, is sure. The doctrines & miracles of our Saviour have required nearly two thousand years, to Convert but a small part of the human race, & even among Christian nations, what gross errors still exist! While we see the Course of the final abolition of human Slavery is onward, & we give it the aid of our prayers & all justifiable means in our power, we must leave the progress as well as the result in his hands who sees the end; who Chooses to work by slow influences; & with whom two thousand years are but as a Single day. Although the Abolitionist must know this, & must See that he has neither the right or power of operating except by moral means & suasion, & if he means well to the slave, he must not Create angry feelings in the Master; that although he may not approve the mode by which it pleases Providence to accomplish its purposes, the result will nevertheless be the same; that the reasons he gives for interference in what he has no Concern, holds good for every kind of interference with our neighbours when we disapprove their Conduct; Still I fear he will persevere in his evil Course. Is it not strange that the descendants of those pilgrim fathers who Crossed the Atlantic to preserve their own freedom of opinion, have always proved themselves intolerant of the Spiritual liberty of others?"

This was the prevailing view among most religious people of Lee's class in the border states. Lee shared these convictions of his neighbors without having come in contact with the worst evils of African bondage. He had never been among the blacks on a cotton or rice plantation. Lee was only acquainted with slavery at its best and he judged it accordingly. At the same time, he was under no illusion regarding the aims of the Abolitionists or the effect of their agitation.

When writing in this wise on the slavery question, Lee had been in Texas nearly ten months. Although oppressed often by the separation from his family and by the news that Mrs. Lee was ill again, he was becoming inured to the life of camps and courts-martial. After that Christmas at Fort Brown he had little to say in his letters home about the hardships of a soldier's life. Those hardships continued, however. He passed his fiftieth birthday at Fort Brown, and from there he went to San Antonio on February 6, 1857, only to be ordered to a new court at Indianola. Before the time arrived for that tribunal to sit he was ordered back to Fort Brown once more. Thence he went to Indianola, arriving by March 20.

The court at Indianola adjourned within ten days, and Lee started back to Camp Cooper by way of San Antonio and Fort Mason. By April 18 he was back at Camp Cooper. Return there did not bring immunity from the perennial nuisance of court-martial duty. If Lee was not to go to a court, a court would be brought to him. A week after he pulled up the flap of his old tent he was entertaining a court-martial, was its president, in fact, and was embarrassed, besides, to provide decent food for Mrs. George H. Thomas, who accompanied her husband on his journey thither. The court adjourned, leaving no com-

ment on the diet Camp Cooper provided. Summer came, with heat and
sickness. A soldier's child died, and Lee for the first time had to officiate
in reading the Episcopal burial service.

It was quite indicative of Lee's relations with his men that one of
them should have asked him to read the burial service. There was
already between him and them the fullest understanding. They knew
him to be a capable soldier; he saw to it that their rights were fully
respected and that justice was done them. In fact, that very reputation
for fair dealing sometimes made the men a bit concerned when they
were called before him.

Although he had no idea that such fortune awaited him when he next
rode away, Lee was never to see Camp Cooper again. Arriving at Fort
Mason in time for the assembly of a court on July 15, he had been
there only eight days when an express arrived with orders to proceed
at once to San Antonio and to take command of the regiment, as
Colonel Johnston had been called to Washington by the War Department. Lee reached San Antonio on the 28th and assumed command the
next day. Life was now much more pleasant. San Antonio was immeasurably a more acceptable post than poor Camp Cooper. Instead of
a tent there were quarters, a whole house, indeed, which Lee occupied
on August 1. He found friends there, too, among them the family of
Major R. H. Chilton, paymaster, who was to serve later as his chief
of staff.

Life flowed quietly on at San Antonio, with daily duties none too
exacting and with pleasures moderate enough. Although Lee had now
been in Texas a year and seven months, there seemed to be no prospect
of an early summons home. The months stretched out ahead, with no
promotion and little opportunity. Then, on October 21, with no
warning, there came news that on October 10 Lee's father-in-law had
died at Arlington. This meant grief to Mrs. Lee and heavy responsibility besides. There was nothing for Lee to do except to procure
leave and start for Virginia.

He had gained some new experience, of course, during the nineteen
months he had been on duty in Texas. He had adjusted himself to camp
life, to hard riding, and to rough fare. Physically, he had unconsciously
been training for desperate years ahead. His leading of troops taught
him little, but his acquaintance with the private soldier's state of mind
was invaluable. Tedious as was his endless court-martial duty, it was
instructive. As he listened to case after case, he understood better than
ever before how weak, jealous, indolent, and sensitive men reacted to

GENERAL GEORGE BRINTON McCLELLAN AND WIFE

GENERAL JOSEPH E. JOHNSTON

army life. He saw why they lapsed in their duty, and what were the temptations before which they most often fell. At West Point, during his superintendency, he had seen the raw material of command; in Texas he had dealt with the worn as well as with the recently finished product.

On November 11 Lee reached Arlington on the saddest of all his ante-bellum home-comings. The shadow of Mr. Custis's death still hung over the plantation. The absence of his father-in-law was less of a shock to Lee than the plight of his wife. When he had left home in 1856 she had been in her usual health, which had been fair after she had recovered from the pelvic infection which had caused her so much suffering in 1836. Lee had heard in January that she was ill, but he does not seem to have realized the seriousness of her condition. Arthritis had assailed her right hand and arm. Lee now found her scarcely able to move about the house, and, though she was only forty-nine, aging very rapidly. Overnight, and without warning, he had to face the fact that his wife had become an invalid.

Lee soon found that Mr. Custis's will had put a heavy burden on him. He had to discharge all the duties of settling a troublesome estate under a complicated testament. Mr. Custis had drawn up the paper in 1855, apparently without consulting counsel. He left Mrs. Lee a life interest in Arlington and its contents and in adjacent properties. On her demise all this property except the minor plate was to pass in fee to Custis Lee, "he my eldest grandson taking my name and arms." His "White House" plantation of 4000 acres in New Kent County, Mr. Custis left to Rooney Lee, and the "Romancock" property of like acreage he bequeathed to his youngest grandson, Robert E. Lee, Jr. To Colonel Lee he left a lot in Washington City. Each granddaughter was to receive $10,000. One paragraph of the will provided that Smith's Island, off Northampton County, and sundry lands in Stafford, Richmond, and Westmoreland Counties, should be sold to provide these legacies. Another section said that these properties and "my estates of the White-House in the County of New Kent and Romancock in the County of King William" were to be "charged with the payment of the legacies to my granddaughters." The will then read: "Smith's Island and the aforesaid lands in Stafford, Richmond and Westmoreland only are to be sold, the lands of the White House and Romancock to be worked to raise the aforesaid legacies to my four granddaughters." All the Custis slaves were to be emancipated, "the said emancipation to be accomplished in not exceeding five years from the time of my decease."

The courts manifestly would be required to construe this document and to determine the nature and extent of the liens on White House and Romancock. The beneficiaries under the will were of the same family. If, therefore, all went well and the miscellaneous landed properties yielded enough to pay the greater part of the legacies without draining the White House and Romancock for too long a time, a settlement would be a matter of no great difficulty. The immediate trouble was that Mr. Custis left more than $10,000 of debts and virtually no money with which to operate the estate. He had always been a negligent farmer and an easygoing master, and he had become more careless as he had grown older. His Arlington tract of 1100 acres was sadly "run down." Instead of inheriting easy luxury, the Lees found themselves "land-poor."

Lee saw that if his daughters' legacies were to be paid, Arlington must be made self-supporting. If the house was to be saved from ruin, it had to be repaired. To do all this called for the expenditure of at least a part of his salary and also for his presence. He had no choice except to ask for a lengthy leave. He applied for two months' leave soon after he reached home, and before that expired he got an extension to December 1, 1858.

So Lee settled down in the winter of 1857–58 to become temporarily a farmer—with scant equipment, little money, many debts, and indifferent help. He had often longed to lead the life of a planter, but now that he had to do so he entered upon one of the darkest, most unhappy periods of his life. He soon became restless and unsettled regarding his future. Should he stay in the army, or was it his duty to resign and devote himself to Arlington?

Desire and ambition alike were subordinated to the need of the family. He was not alone in this. If he was willing to abandon his profession in order to improve Arlington for his son, Custis was equally anxious to increase his father's happiness and at his own expense. On March 17 Lee received a letter from Custis, written February 18, in which the boy sent his father a deed to Arlington. Lee sat down at once and thanked his son but declined the gift. Lee must have felt that his boy's generous letter was full compensation for all the labor he put on Arlington. His own affairs were not so embarrassed as Custis may have thought. The Custis property was in distress, but Lee himself had always lived within his income and had been able to save a part of his salary.

On April 26, Lee had to leave for Newport Barracks, Kentucky, to serve on a court-martial, convened to try Brigadier General Twiggs, but he was back in Washington on May 5. He was at work again in time to put in a good crop of corn, his first large venture as a planter.

The condition of Mrs. Lee was somewhat better, but she had to be taken to the Hot Springs during August, while the younger children were left with the ever-generous Mrs. Fitzhugh at Ravensworth. Later in the year, two of his daughters were ailing. He had to play the nurse, while attending to the farm, but he contrived to do both and still kept in contact with the army. Unknown to him, James M. Porter of Pennsylvania, founder of Lafayette College, and former nominee for Secretary of War, had been urging Lee's promotion as brigadier general to succeed Persifor F. Smith, who had recently died. The recommendation came to naught, but it shows that Lee's professional reputation was spreading. When Scott was ill about this time there was talk in the army of Lee as his successor.

There was beginning to creep into his correspondence some of the misgiving of a man long separated from his profession. His leave was to expire on December 1, but as that date approached, Lee realized that he could not quit Arlington with his work as executor half-done. He requested and was allowed an extension of his leave to May 1, 1859. Not all this additional leave, however, was spent at home. On December 15, Lee was at West Point, sitting on an irksome court of inquiry. This held him until after Christmas, and forced him to hurry back home for the necessary but unpleasant task of hiring out some of the idle Arlington Negroes.

The winter of 1858–59 and the spring of 1859, were in many ways the gloomiest Lee had experienced. The circuit court adjourned in November without construing the Custis will, and the pressure on Lee's finances, for the improvement of the property, was so manifest that the always thoughtful Mrs. Fitzhugh was constrained to send him $1000 to be used as he saw fit. Lee had determined to keep the expenditures at Arlington within his means and he could not accept the check, which he acknowledged with warmest gratitude. Remaining continuously at home, except for about seven weeks' service on a board convened in Washington he worked hard, but, as he thought, to very little purpose.

His other worries continued. Mrs. Lee's health at the end of the spring of 1859 was as bad as it had been when Lee returned from Texas. By July, Lee had begun to despair of her recovery. His ailing daughters, except Mildred, got no better. He did not spare himself to make

those young Lees happy. Whatever the load he carried, he had a cheerful mien in their presence.

Lee's only relief from nursing his family and managing the farm in
1859 was in a number of brief visits. In March he travelled to Richmond
and thence to Shirley, the beloved old home of his mother, where, on
the 23d, Rooney was married to his distant cousin, Charlotte Wickham.
Lee was one of the trustees under the marriage settlement, and on
April 1 he was in Richmond, probably in connection with the recording of the deed of trust. The next month he made a brief trip to Good-
wood, his first vacation since his return to Virginia. He went, also, to
the White House at the end of May, to prepare it for Rooney and
Charlotte, who were soon to move there, and journeyed to Baltimore
in July to see Mrs. Marshall, whose eyesight was endangered. But even
changes of scene, which he regarded as the best physic, did not raise
his depressed spirits. Absence from his command troubled him deeply.
He had hoped to return to his regiment on May 1, but he had to ask
once again that his leave be prolonged, and on June 14 had it extended
four months more.

The handling of slaves, always a difficult matter to a conscientious
man, added to Lee's distress. The Negroes at Arlington numbered
sixty-three, and the majority of them belonged to a few large families.
They were more than Lee could work advantageously with his available capital and land, consequently he had to hire out a few of them by
the year in order to supplement the income from the property. He was
compelled to send some of the Arlington Negroes to work in eastern
Virginia. This may have caused something of a rebellion among them,
for two of them, a man and a young woman, ran away in the hope of
reaching Pennsylvania. They were captured and returned to Arlington. Thereupon Lee sent them to labor in lower Virginia, where there
would be less danger of their absconding. That probably was the extent
of the punishment imposed on them.

The summer dragged itself out. A visit to Capon Springs, for the
health of Mrs. Lee and of Agnes, was interrupted by a hurried call from
Lee's niece, Mary Childe, who begged Lee to join her at Saratoga
Springs, N. Y., were her father was very ill. Lee dutifully started from
the Capon spa, but fortunately got a letter, as he was passing through
Alexandria, stating that Childe was better and that Lee need not come.

On October 6, he was at Fort Columbus, New York harbor, for a
brief court-martial. Then, or about that time, General Scott offered
him the position of military secretary, with the same rank as Lee then

held, that of lieutenant colonel. But Lee had made the change from the staff to the line, and though he was devoted to the old General and would have done anything in his power to serve him, he did not wish to return to staff duty. Scott expected he would decline and was not piqued when he did so.

Lee returned home from the court-martial in New York and put all his energy behind the work at Arlington in the belief that he could soon complete the necessary repairs and rejoin his regiment. He was busy at this on the morning of October 17 when Lieutenant "Jeb" Stuart arrived with a sealed note from the War Department. The message was a brief order for Lee to report to the Secretary immediately.

Setting out at once, in civilian clothes, Lee soon learned that the government had received from John W. Garrett, president of the Baltimore and Ohio Railroad, news of a mysterious insurrection at Harpers Ferry, Va. Trains had been stopped; firing had been heard; rumor had it that strangers had entered the town in large numbers and were inciting the slaves to a rising. It might be a serious affair, calling for instant action. Troops had been ordered from Fort Monroe during the morning; the service of Maryland militiamen had been accepted; a detachment of marines from the Washington navy yard had been ordered to the scene; Lee was to take command of all the forces, acting with his brevet rank of colonel. Orders were quickly issued, and Lee went with the secretary to the White House, accompanied by Lieutenant Stuart, who had been at the War Department negotiating for use of his patent on a sword-attachment when he had been requested to carry the message to Arlington. Sensing trouble, Stuart had immediately asked the privilege of going with Lee.

Lee hurried with Stuart by train to the Relay House, eight miles from Baltimore, whither the marines had gone from Washington at 3:30 P.M. to take the train for Harpers Ferry. The two arrived after the cars had left, but Lee was told that a locomotive would be brought up to carry him to his destination. He telegraphed orders to the marines to stop at Sandy Hook, slightly more than a mile from Harpers Ferry, and to await his arrival. By this time alarm was general.

Lee reached Sandy Hook at 10 o'clock and found the marines waiting for him along with four companies of Maryland militia under a brigadier general of that state. Lee learned quickly that the bridge to Harpers Ferry was open, that the number of the insurgents had been greatly exaggerated, and that those who had survived a day of desultory fighting with the militia had taken refuge in the fire-engine house, within the armory enclosure. They had carried with them a number of hostages. Firing, slow and half-hearted, was still in progress. The leader of the band, Lee heard, was a man styling himself Smith, who had been seen at Harpers Ferry and in Maryland before the attack. Lee ascertained, too, that Harpers Ferry was already swarming with Virginia militia and armed citizens and that the engine house could be surrounded with little difficulty. There were troops enough, and to spare, for the only work ahead—that of storming the place. At 11 o'clock P.M. that night he crossed the river and placed the militia in the armory enclosure with the marines. His inclination was to attack at once, but he feared that if he entered the engine house in the darkness the hostages might be slain in the mêlée. He determined to survey the ground, to make ready for an assault on the engine house at daylight, and, meantime, to draw up a summons to the insurgents, in case they might be induced to yield and to give up their prisoners. This was the letter he addressed to the men in the armory, of whose identity he was not yet certain, though it was reported that the leader was one John Brown, a notorious antislavery partisan from Kansas:

Headquarters Harper's Ferry,
October 18, 1859.

Colonel Lee, United States Army, commanding the troops sent by the President of the United States to suppress the insurrection at this place, demands the surrender of the persons in the armory buildings.

If they will peaceably surrender themselves and restore the pillaged property, they shall be kept in safety to await the orders of the President. Colonel Lee represents to them, in all frankness, that it is impossible for them to escape; that the armory is surrounded on all sides by troops; and that if he is compelled to take them by force he cannot answer for their safety.

R. E. LEE
Colonel Commanding United States Troops.

Lee gave this message to Stuart about 2 A.M. and told him to deliver it, under a white flag, at the door of the engine house when directed to do so. Lee intended to have the militia paraded and drawn up around the armory so that the insurgents would see he was not bluffing when he said the place was surrounded. He had to figure on the possibility that after they had refused his terms they might actually slay their captives, unless allowed safe conduct from the place. How would Lee guard against this? He told Stuart not to entertain any counter-proposal, but to give a signal the very moment the insurgents rejected his demand. On that signal, a storming party was to batter in the door and attack the insurgents with the bayonet. No shots were to be fired, lest some of the hostages be hit.

Lee felt that as the insurrection was apparently directed against state authority, the militia, if they desired to do so, should have the honor of capturing the invaders. Colonel Shriver, head of the Maryland volunteers in Harpers Ferry, declined. Colonel Robert W. Baylor, senior officer of the Virginia militia companies, also declined. Lee thereupon turned to Lieutenant Israel Green of the marines to know if he wished the honor of "taking those men out." Green doffed his hat and warmly thanked Lee, who thereupon told him to pick twelve men from his detachment as a storming party. Green immediately did so and selected a dozen others as a reserve.

It was 7 o'clock on the morning of October 18 when arrangements were complete. Lee took his stand on a slight elevation, about forty feet from the doors of the engine house. Stuart was ready with his flag of truce. Green and his selected twenty-four men were close by but out of the line of fire, which had virtually ceased during the night. The militia were in position, surrounding the building at a little distance. The whole population of the town and most of the countryside had gathered to witness the assault. Fully 2000 people were looking on when Stuart advanced with his flag to the entrance of the engine house. In answer to his summons, a gaunt, begrimed old man opened one of the doors about four inches and thrust out a carbine. Stuart, who had been on duty in Kansas, immediately confirmed the identification of this man. He was none other than "Ossawatomie" John Brown. Stuart read Lee's terms, which Brown at once began to argue. Almost before Stuart could announce that Lee would entertain no counter-proposal, Brown was advancing another compromise. Stuart continued trying to explain that Lee would not consider any other terms. Brown babbled on. Finally Stuart broke away, stepped from in front of the house, and waved his hat. Three minutes after Stuart had given his signal, the affair was over. There were four dead men on the floor, two of whom had been killed prior to the assault that morning. One man was dying from an earlier bullet. Brown was bleeding from wounds inflicted by Lieutenant Green's sword and was thought to be mortally wounded. Two others were uninjured. The hostages, thirteen in number, were dirty and half-famished, but all of them had escaped bullets and bayonets.

The dead and the wounded were carried from the building and laid on the grass. Brown was soon removed to the paymaster's adjacent office. The day before there had been talk of violence on the part of half-drunken rowdies, but Lee's authority was fully respected. He had not regarded the affair at any time after his arrival as of great consequence. He now considered the "invasion" at an end. In a brief report for the Secretary of War he no longer dignified John Brown's men as insurrectionists, but dismissed them as "rioters."

As for the troops, Lee thought the militia might readily be dismissed but he deemed it necessary to keep the marines on the ground temporarily. His one concern was over the disposition of Brown and the other prisoners, and on this point he asked the instructions of the Secretary of War. The Department instructed Lee to place Brown and the other survivors in the joint custody of the United States marshal and of the sheriff of the county (Jefferson) where the insurrection had been attempted. Lee made a final check of the conspirators on the morning of October 19 with Andrew Hunter, whom Governor Henry A. Wise had designated as prosecutor; then Lee had the prisoners removed by train to Charlestown, the county seat.

As this seemed to him the last scene in his part of the drama, he began to draft his final report and to prepare the marines for their return to Washington. That night a wild tale came to Harpers Ferry that an attack had been made by insurrectionists on the village of Pleasant Valley, Md., some five miles away. Lee thought the story improbable but proceeded there in person with Stuart, Green, and twenty-five marines, only to find the report entirely false. He returned to Harpers Ferry, brought his report down to that hour, took his command back to Washington on the train leaving at 1:15 A.M., and the next morning, October 20, completed the report and presented himself at the War Department. The Virginia state authorities had not complained at the withdrawal of the marines but shortly after Lee's departure Governor Wise entered a protest at the withdrawal of the Federal force and pointed out the unprotected condition of Harpers Ferry.

After a few days at home, and about a fortnight's service on a board of officers considering the form of ceremonials and parades, Lee was ordered back to Harpers Ferry. The radical abolitionist element in the North had been aroused to a frenzy by the assumed "martyrdom" of Brown. Governor Wise had become deeply alarmed lest these threats be carried out, and had asked President Buchanan to send Lee to Harpers Ferry again with sufficient troops to repel any attempt to seize the arsenal. The President had regarded the reports Wise forwarded him as "almost incredible," but on November 29, he had the Secretary of War issue the necessary orders to Lee. Lee first went to Baltimore to make arrangements for transferring the four companies of troops that were being sent him by steamship from Fort Monroe. Then he proceeded with them to Harpers Ferry, where he arrived on November 30 and posted guard. The next day he met Mrs. John Brown. She had come to ask permission to say farewell to her husband, who was to be hanged at Charlestown on December 2. Lee had no control over the prisoner or the execution and could only refer the sad woman to General William B. Taliaferro, commander of the Virginia troops.

The day of Brown's execution passed without the appearance of any of the desperadoes who were supposed to be massing. Although Lee improved the idle time of the troops by drilling them in target practice, he and the men alike were glad when orders came on December 9 for a return on December 12 to their station. The country continued to debate bitterly the rights and the wrongs of Brown's attempt, but the affair seems to have affected Lee very little. "The result," he said in his report of October 19, "proves that the plan was the attempt of a fanatic or madman. . . ." He did not believe that the Negroes would respond to such appeals as Brown had made, and he troubled himself no more about it.

Lee had expected that the work at Arlington would have progressed far enough by the end of October to make it possible for him to leave for Texas, and he had procured an assignment of duty in Washington for Custis so that the prospective master of Arlington might supervise the estate. Orders had been issued prior to December 14 for him to join his regiment, but these were suspended in order that he might be a witness in the Harpers Ferry investigation. This duty discharged, Lee was assigned on February 6, 1860, to temporary command of the Department of Texas, according to his brevet rank, with headquarters in San Antonio. It was a distinction to have departmental command, but as it was an accidental appointment, due to the fact that no colonel of the army was in Texas Lee attached no importance to it.

He waved good-bye to his family and set out for Texas on February 10. Those months of homely hard work at Arlington had rendered his destiny more certain. Some Southern-born officers, sent for long tours of duty on distant stations, had lost contact with their states and with the implications of the doctrine of states' rights. It had never been so with Lee. Often his post of duty had been close to Virginia. Always he had come back to Arlington as frequently as he could. The spirit of Virginia had been alive in his heart every hour of his life. It had become more potent than ever during 1857–59, when he had sensed her feeling, had seen her reaction to the hostility of abolitionists, and had mingled much with his countless cousins, whose faith in Virginia's political rightness was as unquestioning as their belief in God. During the next fourteen months, he was to read of the coming crisis in a full understanding of how Virginia interpreted it. Having ploughed her fields, he had a new sense of oneness with her. He was a United States officer who loved the army and had pride in the Union, but something very deep in his heart kept him mindful that he had been a Virginian before he had been a soldier.

Lee reached New Orleans on the afternoon of February 13. From New Orleans he sailed by steamer for Indianola, and thence he went to San Antonio, arriving on February 19. The next day he assumed command. He found part of the forces disorganized by a series of plundering raids, made by Indians in northern Texas. The War Department authorized a large expedition against the Indians as soon as the grass on the prairies would suffice for the horses. Until this could be undertaken, Lee worked as best he might to restore order.

From the time of his arrival at San Antonio until late in the autumn he had only routine duties to occupy him. He had a few things to cheer him, such as the arrival of his first grandchild, whom Rooney and Charlotte insisted on naming after him. He interested himself in the building of an Episcopal church at San Antonio. Despite his separation from his family, he tried to be philosophical. ". . . We want but little," he wrote Rooney. "Our happiness depends upon our independence, the success of our operations, prosperity of our plans, health, contentment, and the esteem of our friends." But under the surface of cheerfulness, this was a time of deep depression with Lee.

Slow promotion, as well as homesickness, had something to do with this mild but melancholy expression of frustration. He was now fifty-three, and had been twenty-two years in advancing from the grade of captain to that of lieutenant colonel. Between him and the rank of general officer stood nineteen colonels and three lieutenant colonels, while four other lieutenant colonels had been commissioned the same day that he had been. Twenty-two men at least were between him and titular brigade command. After holding a commission for thirty-one years his pay was only $1205 per annum, and his gross return from the government—pay, rations, quarters, travel, and everything—only $4060. This was discouraging to the father of four unmarried daughters and husband of an invalid wife.

In this depression, as the autumn of 1860 opened, Lee found himself involved in the darkest of American tragedies. It was his nature to leave politics to the politicians, but it could no longer be so. Politics had become the affair of every man and the concern of every soldier, for the old amity among the states was gone. Men all around Lee were talking of secession.

Lincoln was elected. In four days the South Carolina legislature issued a call for a convention to withdraw the state from the Union; sentiment for secession grew stronger over night; and everywhere in Texas the people were flying the "Lone Star" flag. Governor Sam Houston was opposed to secession, and his opponents began to agitate for a "popular convention" chosen without a formal legislative call.

From Lee's own state newspapers told of much dissatisfaction and of many appeals for secession. Lee was profoundly concerned but not despairing. "The Southern states," he wrote Custis, "seem to be in a convulsion . . . My little personal troubles sink into insignificance when I contemplate the condition of the country, and I feel as if I could easily lay down my life for its safety. But I also feel that would bring but little good."

His distress over the threat to the Union and his lack of sympathy with extreme policies caused Lee to withdraw into himself. From this period date references to the reserve he showed so strongly in later years that it has been mistakenly assumed to be a part of his personality from youth. "I knew him well," wrote a Kentuckian, who was thrown with him often in the fall of 1860, "perhaps I might say, intimately, though his grave, cold dignity of bearing and the prudential reserve of his manners rather chilled over-early, or over-much intimacy." There is no earlier comment on Lee's "coldness." On the other hand, his exuberance of spirit was often noted, especially in his youth.

As the exciting days passed it looked for a time as if secession might be accomplished peaceably and by consent. General Scott believed the Southern states should not be forced to remain in the Union or punished for leaving it, though he had no sympathy with secession. Horace Greeley said in the *Tribune:* "We hope never to live in a republic whereof one section is pinned to the residue by bayonets." Lee momentarily, too, reasoned that the Union might simply be dissolved, though he did not admit the unity of Southern interests. Save as he felt that the citizens of every state had equal rights in the territories, he had no regard at the time for the South as a section, much less as a confederation. His mind was for the Union; his instinct was for his state. He felt powerless to help in preserving the Union, but with the religious faith that had been growing steadily since the Mexican War, he could not believe a beneficent Providence would permit its destruction. As for his state, he looked on Virginia much as he did on his family. He did not then or thereafter stop to reason out the nature of this instinctive feeling.

Lee declared himself fully after Charles Anderson lent him a copy of a confidential pamphlet General Scott had sent. Anderson was with Doctor Willis G. Edwards when Lee returned the pamphlet. The conversation shifted, inevitably, to crisis. Doctor Edwards raised the question whether a man's first allegiance was due his state or the nation. Lee instantly spoke out, and unequivocally. He had been taught to believe, he said, and he did believe, that his first obligations were due Virginia.

His own position plain to all his intimates, Lee left San Antonio on December 19 for the comparative isolation of Fort Mason, the headquarters of the 2d Cavalry. Neither Lee nor his men were in a mood to improve their renewed acquaintance by hard drilling or field manoeuvres. They discharged their duties, of course, but in bewilderment of mind they saw their world being dissolved about them. Every mail brought reports of new tragedy. South Carolina's convention had voted unanimously for secession, and hotheads had rejoiced as though the division of the Union were as great an act as its creation. In Congress the Crittenden compromise was voted down. On December 26, Colonel Robert Anderson moved his troops from an exposed position at Fort Moultrie to the security of Fort Sumter.

The new year came, the blackest in American history. On January 9, the steamer *Star of the West* was fired on by South Carolinians. On the same day Mississippi seceded. Florida followed on the 10th, Alabama on the 11th, and Georgia on the 18th. Every hour the prospect seemed darker.

At Fort Mason, Lee watched events.

On January 22 he wrote Markie Williams:

"I wish to live under no other government, and there is no sacrifice I am not ready to make for the preservation of the Union save that of honour. If a disruption takes place, I shall go back in sorrow to my people and share the misery of my native state, and save in her defence there will be one soldier less in the world than now. I wish for no other flag than the 'Star spangled banner' and no other air than 'Hail Columbia' I still hope that the wisdom and patriotism of the nation will yet save it."

The plain inference from these sentences is that if secession destroyed the Union, Lee intended to resign from the army and to fight neither for the South nor for the North unless he had to act one way or the other in defense of Virginia. In this, he showed that he was no constitutional lawyer. Apparently he did not stop to reason that Virginia could not be neutral in a war between the states, but must either fight with the North or with the South. Mrs. Lee correctly stated his position when she later said, "From the first commencement of our troubles he had decided that in the event of Virginia's secession, duty . . . would compel him to follow." In light of his words and hers, it is hard to understand why it has been so widely believed that he waited until the secession of Virginia to determine what he would do. There is not the slightest doubt that before he left Texas he had decided, without any mental struggle or thought of personal gain or loss, to stand with Virginia, though he hoped with all his heart that the Union would be preserved.

After Louisiana seceded, on January 26, and the Texas convention met in belligerent temper on the 28th, he wrote in deepest distress: "The country seems to be in a lamentable condition and may have been plunged into civil war. May God rescue us from the folly of our own acts, save us from selfishness and teach us to love our neighbors as ourselves." On February 1 the Texas convention passed an ordinance of secession by a vote of 166 to 7. Secession was now a reality in seven states, and plans for the establishment of a separate Southern government were under way. Offsetting, to some extent, these grim omens was the news that a peace conference, called at the instance of Virginia, had met on February 4 in Washington. On the same day the people of Lee's state elected a convention but chose to it a two-to-one majority of delegates opposed to secession. Virginia voters overwhelmingly decided, further, that no ordinance of secession should be valid unless and until it was approved by the voters at the polls.

For these reasons, hope was not dead when Lee received a wholly unexpected message from Twiggs's headquarters in San Antonio: by direct order of the War Department Lieutenant Colonel Lee was relieved of duty with his regiment and was directed to report in person to the general in chief in Washington by April 1. Hurrying away from

San Antonio, Lee reached New Orleans February 25 and made his way homeward through a troubled country. A separate government, the Confederate States of America, had been set up at Montgomery, Ala., and Jefferson Davis had been chosen its President. The mails, however, were still passing freely between the North and the South, commercial intercourse was as yet unhindered, the free navigation of the Mississippi had been pledged by the Confederate Congress, and, what was infinitely more important, not a blow had been struck. Tense as was the situation, there was nothing to compromise Lee's status as an officer of the United States army when on March 1 he joined his loved ones at Arlington.

"Our country," he had written one of his sons before leaving Texas, "requires now everyone to put forth all his ability, regardless of self." That maxim he applied in the bewildering situation he faced when he reached home. On the Virginia side of the Potomac opinion was divided concerning the occasion for secession, but there was almost complete agreement touching the right. North of the river, just half-an-hour's ride from Arlington, cross-currents of sentiment were sweeping. In Congress and at the White House efforts were still being made to avert war; in the departments preparations were under way to face any emergency. [President Buchanan was fighting to save the Union.]

Lee called at General Scott's office soon after he reached home. For three hours the old General and his favorite lieutenant talked together. What they said to each other in the confidence of long and trustful association neither ever revealed, but Scott's known opinion of secession, his admiration for Lee, and his desire to assure good leadership for the army make it possible to reconstruct the substance of at least a part of what was said. Scott told Lee that he was soon to be made a colonel and then, probably, hinted that if he found himself too feeble to take the field he would recommend Lee as his second in command. There can be little doubt that Scott sought to appeal to Lee's ambitions, but that, knowing Lee as he did, Scott did not try to buy his allegiance with promises, which, indeed, Scott was not authorized to make. If Lee replied to Scott's overtures it was to repeat that if Virginia seceded he would follow her because he considered that his first obligation was to her. Scott, of course, was of a temper to argue this and probably ended a lengthy oration with the request that Lee go home, think the subject over, and await further developments.

Lee went home and in agony of spirit watched events. All the while Scott probably was quietly at work, seeing if he might not hold Lee to the Union. Erasmus D. Keyes, then Scott's military secretary, thought that Scott did not expect Lee to fight against the South, but that the General believed it possible to put Lee at the head of an army so powerful that war could be prevented. General Twiggs was dismissed from the army on March 1 for his surrender of Texas. Colonel E. V. Sumner of the 1st Cavalry was named brigadier general to succeed him on March 16. Lee was made colonel and given Sumner's regiment. This commission, signed by Abraham Lincoln, Lee did not hesitate to accept when, on March 28, it was forwarded to him.

Between the date he was promoted and the time he received his commission, Lee probably got a letter written him on March 15 by L. P. Walker, Confederate Secretary of War. This was a direct offer of a commission as brigadier general, the highest rank then authorized in the army the South was raising. After the long years of slow promotion honors were coming fast—a colonelcy in one army and an offer of a generalship in the rival service. There is no record of any reply by Lee to this tender from the new Confederacy. It is probable that he ignored the offer. He owed allegiance to only two governments, that of Virginia and that of the Union.

This was Lee's state when all the passions that had been rising since 1830 in South Carolina suddenly overflowed, and at daylight on April 12 the bombardment of Fort Sumter began. On the 14th Sumter surrendered. The next day, to a nation gone mad, Lincoln issued his proclamation calling for 75,000 soldiers "to suppress combinations" and "to cause the laws to be duly executed." The North and the South were arrayed, and blows had passed, though no blood had yet been shed—what would the border states do? What would be the action of Virginia? For the answer, Lee turned his eyes from Sumter to Richmond.

Late on April 16, or on the 17th, he heard that the Virginia convention had gone into secret session. That was the only news from Richmond; but from Washington, on the 17th, there arrived a letter and a message. The letter bore Scott's signature and requested Lee to call at his office on the 18th. The message was conveyed in a note from a Washington cousin, John Lee. It was that Francis P. Blair, Sr. formerly editor of *The Congressional Globe*, desired Lee to meet him the next morning at his house in Washington.

What was afoot? The answer, in its entirety, Lee did not learn during his lifetime. He never realized how anxious some men high in office and influence had been to save his services to the United States army. In addition to what General Scott had done, Blair had been at work. He had been to President Lincoln, who had authorized him to "ascertain Lee's intentions and feelings." Blair had also discussed the subject with Secretary Simon Cameron and had been directed to make a proposition to Lee. It was to explain this that Blair had sent the message to Arlington.

On the morning of April 18 Lee rode up to the Blair son's house on Pennsylvania Avenue. Francis Blair promptly explained his reason for asking Lee to call. A large army, he said, was soon to be called into the field to enforce the Federal law; the President had authorized him to ask Lee if he would accept the command.

Command of an army of 75,000, perhaps 100,000 men; opportunity to apply all he had learned in Mexico; the supreme ambition of a soldier realized; the full support of the government; many of his ablest comrades working with him; rank as a major general—all this may have surged through Lee's mind, but if so, only for an instant. Then his Virginia background and the mental discipline of years asserted themselves. He had said: "If the Union is dissolved and the government disrupted, I shall return to my native state and share the miseries of my people and save in defence will draw my sword on none." There he stood, and in that spirit, after listening to all Blair had to say, he made the fateful reply that is best given in his own simple account of the interview: "I declined the offer he made me to take command of the army that was to be brought into the field, stating as candidly and as courteously as I could, that though opposed to secession and deprecating war, I could take no part in an invasion of the Southern States."

Bidding farewell to Blair, Lee went to Scott's office. He sensed Scott's deep interest in his action, and as soon as he arrived he told him what Blair had offered and what he had answered. "Lee," said Scott, deeply moved, "you have made the greatest mistake of your life; but I feared it would be so."

Deep as was the difference between the two men on a public question that made personal enemies of many lifelong friends, Scott did not stop with this sad observation but expressed the belief that if Lee were going to resign he ought not to delay. "There are times," Scott is reported to have said, "when every officer in the United States service should fully determine what course he will pursue and frankly declare it. No one should continue in government employ without being actively employed."

This added a complication that Lee pondered as he left his old commander for the last time. Though willing to resign rather than to fight against the South, he had clung to the hope that he would not have to act unless Virginia seceded. But Scott had now said that he should not remain in the army if he was unwilling to perform active duty. As his brother Smith was on duty in Washington, Lee stopped to discuss this new question with him. They could come to no conclusion on it and parted in the expectation of meeting again before either of them took action. But Lee did not leave his problem behind him as he turned his back on his country's capital. He felt that Scott was right, but his own mind was so opposed to secession, and his devotion to the Union and to the army proved so strong now it was put to the test, that he delayed the actual writing of his resignation, hoping against hope.

The next morning, April 19, Lee went into Alexandria and there read the news he had hoped he would never see: Virginia had seceded! To his mind that meant the wreck of the nation, "the beginning of sorrows," the opening of a war that was certain to be long and full of horrors. But of all that he thought and felt, his only recorded observation is one he made when he went into a shop to pay a bill. "I must say," he remarked sadly, "that I am one of those dull creatures that cannot see the good of secession."

When other hopes had failed him Lee had told himself that secession could not become an accomplished fact until the voters of Virginia had passed on the ordinance of secession, as they had specifically reserved the right to do, but now Lee's judgment told him that war would not wait on a referendum. Virginia would certainly consider that her safety required the seizure of Federal depots within her borders. The time had come. All the Lees had been Americans, but they had been Virginians first. Virginia had seceded; her action controlled his; he could not wait for the uncertain vote of the people when war was upon him. So after midnight on the 19th he sat down and wrote this letter:

> *Arlington, Virginia (Washington City P.O.)*
> *20 April 1861*

Hon. Simon Cameron
Secty of War
Sir:

I have the honor to tender the resignation of my commission as Colonel of the 1st Regt. of Cavalry.
> Very resp'y Your Obedient Servant.

> R. E. LEE
> *Col 1st Cav'y.*

His resignation was not prompted by passion, nor did it carry with it resentment against the Union. On the contrary, if there was any resentment, it was against the authors, Northern and Southern, of the consummate wickedness of bringing about division within the Union. There was a pang and a heartache at the separation from brother officers. He was willing to defend Virginia, whatever her allegiance, but he did not desire to fight against the flag under which he had served. It was in this spirit that he wrote farewell to General Scott, that loyal old friend, who had admired him, taught him, and advanced him.

He came downstairs when he had finished the letters. Mrs. Lee was waiting for him. "Well, Mary," he said calmly, "the question is settled. Here is my letter of resignation and a letter I have written General Scott."

She understood. Months later she wrote a friend, "My husband has wept tears of blood over this terrible war, but as a man of honor and a Virginian, he must follow the destiny of his state." The other members of the family understood, also. Arlington became as if a death had occurred. Rooney, who hastened to consult his father as soon as the state seceded, was in deep depression as he saw how jubilant the people were. They had no conception of what a terrible mistake they were making. Custis was no believer in secession. Had he been able to dictate policy, he said, he would have called the movement revolution and would forthwith have seized and fortified Arlington Heights.

Lee dispatched his resignation to General Scott that morning, probably by special messenger, and before night it had been forwarded to the Secretary of War.

After he had sent off the paper, he sat down to explain his act to his sister, Mrs. Marshall, and to his brother Smith. Mrs. Marshall's husband was Unionist in his sympathies. Her son Louis was now a captain in the United States army. She herself sided with her husband and son, though she could not quite forget her Virginia uprearing.

He had left Smith Lee on the 18th with the understanding that they would confer again regarding their course of action. He therefore wrote to explain why he had resigned before consulting with him further. Lee gave no advice to Smith regarding his own course, nor did he counsel Custis, who was as loath as he to quit the service of the United States.

The rest of that fateful 20th of April nothing of consequence occurred except the receipt, late in the evening, of a letter from Judge

John Robertson, of Richmond. The judge asked for an interview the next day. Lee set 1 o'clock as the hour and offered to meet him in Alexandria. Sunday morning, April 21, dressed in civilian clothes, Lee went into Alexandria with one of his daughters to attend service at Christ Church. At length the service was over. When Lee reached the open air he became engaged in conversation with three men whose identity has never been established. It seems probable that they were companions of Judge Robertson, who explained that the judge had gone to Washington and had been detained there but would soon arrive to keep his appointment. Lee waited and chatted several hours and then, concluding that Robertson would not return, rode back to Arlington.

That evening a messenger arrived with a letter from Robertson. He apologized for his delay and—this was the important item—invited Lee, in the name of the governor, to repair to Richmond for conference with the chief executive. Lee realized, of course, that this meant participation in the defense of Virginia, but he did not hesitate. The very reason that had impelled him to resign from the United States army, his allegiance to Virginia, prompted him to sit down at once and answer Robertson. Virginia's action in withdrawing from the Union carried him with her, and if she called him now it was his duty to obey. He notified the governor's representative that he would join him in Alexandria the next day in time to take the train for Richmond. The road from Arlington, though lit with glory, led straight to Appomattox. But Lee never regretted his action. With the war behind him, with the South desolate and disfranchised, and with her sons dead on a hundred battlefields, he was to look back with soul unshaken and say: "I did only what my duty demanded. I could have taken no other course without dishonor. And if it all were to be done over again, I should act in precisely the same manner."

Lee departed from Arlington on the morning of April 22, never to enter its friendly portals again. Driving to Alexandria, he joined Judge Robertson and, with sombre face, climbed aboard the train, bound for Gordonsville, whence he was to travel via the Virginia Central to Richmond. At Orange and at Louisa he had to go to the rear of the car and bow to the crowds that insistently called for him. For the rest of the long journey he observed and pondered.

He was then fifty-four years of age and stood five feet eleven inches in height, weighing slightly less than 170 pounds. In physique he was sound, without a blemish on his body. In the whole of his previous life he had suffered only one recorded illness and that had not been severe. Without having the bulging muscles of bovine strength, he was possessed of great powers of endurance. When he was past forty he had competed with his sons in high jumps at Arlington. He had skated and danced and had been an excellent swimmer. His vision and teeth were fine, his hearing was unimpaired, and his voice was rich and resonant. Few men were inheritors of a stronger nervous system.

In appearance one fellow-traveller, who saw him that April day, considered Lee "the noblest-looking man I had ever seen." His fine large head was broadly rounded, with prominent brows and wide temples, and was set on a short, strong neck. His hair was black, with a sprinkle of gray; his short mustache was wholly black. Brown eyes that seemed black in dim light and a slightly florid complexion gave warmth and color to his grave face. His mouth was wide and well-arched. His lips were thin. A massive torso rose above narrow hips, and his large hands were in contrast to very small feet. Sitting behind a desk, or on a horse, his shoulders, neck, and hands made him appear larger than he was. His finest appearance was when mounted, for he was an admirable rider, with the flat legs of the ideal cavalryman.

His manners accorded with his person. In 1861, as always, he was the same in his bearing to men of every station, courteous, simple, and without pretense. Of objective mind, free of any suggestion of self-consciousness, he was considerate in his dealings with others, and of never-failing tact. He made friends readily and held them steadfastly. Close relations never lowered him in the esteem of his associates. He was clean-minded and frank with his friends, and confided in them more freely than has been supposed. Always he was unselfish, talked little of himself, and was in no sense egotistical. Although he was slow to take offense and was not quick to wrath, his temper was strong. Except when he was sick, he rarely broke the bounds of self-mastery for more than a moment. Then he was best left alone.

The company of women, especially of pretty women, he preferred to that of men. In the presence of the other sex, he displayed a gracious, and sometimes a breezy gallantry; but no suggestion of a scandal, no hint of over-intimacy, was ever linked with his name. His conversation with his younger female friends was lively, with many touches of teasing and with an occasional mild pun, but it was not witty. He had a good sense of humor, which his dignity rarely permitted him to exhibit in laughter. In dealing with children his manners were at their finest. For them he always had a smile, no matter where he met them, and won their confidence almost invariably.

His manners reflected his spiritual life. His was a simple soul, humble, transparent, and believing. Increasingly religion had become a part of his very being. Creeds meant little to him. Reading daily his Bible and his prayer book, spending much time on his knees, he believed in a God who, in His wisdom, sent blessings beyond man's deserts, and visited him, on occasion, with hardships and disaster for the chastening of the rebellious heart of the ungrateful and the forgetful. In every disaster, he was to stand firm in the faith that it was sent by God for reasons that man could not see.

Self-denial and self-control were the supreme rule of life. It was the basis of his code of conduct. He loved good food—but he was ready to eat thankfully the hardest fare of the field. In the confused councils he was doomed to share, he bore the contention of braggarts and swaggerers with self-control because it was his duty as a soldier to be patient and his obligation as a Christian to be humble. He had built up a dislike for tobacco, which he never used, and a hatred for whiskey. Wine he drank rarely and in small quantities.

In intellect he was of an even higher order than had been demonstrated in thirty-two years of army service without a single failure to his discredit. His mind was mathematical and his imagination that of an engineer. The best of his results always were attained when originality and initiative could be employed. Routine office duties bored him. His culture was wider than that of most soldiers. Well-grounded in Greek and in Latin, he kept some of the spirit of the classics when he had forgotten the texts. French he had mastered when he was in his first full vigor of mind. For Spanish he had an enthusiasm born of a belief in its utility. Of some phases of American history he had a measure of precise knowledge. Fiction he avoided, but poetry he enjoyed. He delighted to look at a sunset or at a garden. Birds were a particular care to him. His own contribution to physical beauty was through the promotion of orderliness and in the planting of trees. Outside his profession his chief interests were agricultural and social. The ideal life, had he been able to fashion it, would have been to entertain or to visit pleasant people while riding daily over a small plantation. As for society, he learned more from men than from books. All manner of acquaintances were his—generals, professors, planters, politicians, engineers, laborers.

In those two unchanging fundamentals of military service, discipline and co-operation, Robert E. Lee had received the precise training of a professional soldier. Obedience to orders was part of his religion. Adverse decisions he had schooled himself to accept in the same spirit as approval. He could elicit the support of his superiors without flattery, and in the few instances where he had ever had subordinates, he had won their allegiance without threats. He was a diplomat among engineers. Fully qualified to deal with the politician in executive office, he was suspicious of him in the field or in the forum, though he was meticulous in subordinating himself to civil authority. His dealings with his brother officers had never been darkened by scheming or marred by jealousy.

Familiarity with the history of war was his in limited measure. The American Revolutionary campaigns he had surveyed carefully. Napoleon was the great captain whose battles he had carefully followed. To the Crimean War he had devoted at least casual study. With Hannibal and with Julius Caesar he was not wholly unacquainted. From these masters of war, and most of all from General Winfield Scott, he had learned the theory of strategy and had learned it well. He had participated, too, in nearly all the strategical preparation of the most successful series of battles ever fought prior to 1861 by an American army. The strategical function of high command he had learned from those battles in Mexico. That function, as he saw it, was to develop the lines of communication, to direct the reconnaissance, to ascertain the precise position of the enemy, and then to bring all the combatant units into position at the proper time and to the best advantage. Thanks to Scott he had far more than the staff officer's approach to the duties that awaited him. In reconnaissance his experience had been sufficient to develop great aptitude. He was an excellent topographer and not without training as an intelligence officer. He had seen something of what sea power meant. Fortification he knew thoroughly.

Such was the positive equipment of Robert E. Lee. It was the best equipment with which any soldier entered the struggle.

Admirable as was the training of Lee it was not complete. Only the regular soldier did he know well. From the narrowness of his subordinate command, there was danger that his view would be microscopic. All his battle experience had been on the offensive, though the situation and comparative weakness of the South were to compel it to hold a defensive in the larger sense of the word. Furthermore, having labored so long on detached projects, he was disposed to do work that could have been passed on to others. Most of all was he lacking in any detailed knowledge of the service of supply.

There remained the basic, if less tangible, factor of temperament. He was a gentleman in every impulse: was he too much a gentleman for the dirty business of war? Was there enough of steel in his soul? That respect for civil authority—would it tie his hands in a revolution? Feeling that his duty was performed when he had obeyed his orders and had done his utmost, would he fight for his opinions? Would he escape the "subordinate complex" which is all too familiar in war? If the Southern cause ever depended on him and on him alone, was there in him the stuff of which military dictators are made?

If he thought at all of these things, as his train rolled down to the valley of the Chickahominy, it must have been in the humble conviction that he was not equal to the task that lay ahead. The crowds that filled the stations along his route may have been talking of easy victories and early independence, but he had measured the strength and determination of the North, and he foresaw a bloody test, a long war, a doubtful issue.

CHAPTER V

The First Campaign

ON THE afternoon of April 22, 1861, Colonel Lee rode through Richmond streets to the Spotswood Hotel where he took a room. Conversation was all of defense against invasion, of preparation, and of speedy alliance with the Southern Confederacy. The day before, while the ministers had been dismissing their anxious, prayerful congregations, the tocsin had been sounded from the guard house in the Capitol Square, and word had quickly spread that the *Pawnee*, a Federal warship, was steaming up James River to bombard the unprotected city. She had not appeared, but the excitement of this first of Richmond's many war scares had not died away when Lee arrived.

The town was buzzing, also, over the arrival of Alexander H. Stephens, Vice-President, as special commissioner from the Confederate States of America to Virginia. All secessionists welcomed Mr. Stephens and advocated a speedy union of Virginia with the other Southern States. Most Whigs, now that war was upon them, favored the same course. Virginia, as they saw it, could not remain neutral. Would the convention display the same spirit and vote Virginia into the Confederacy, pending final action by the people on the ordinance of secession?

Virginia alone could not resist. If there must be war there must be alliance with the South. Lee did not mingle with the noisy debaters, however. Instead, he hastened to the capitol, where he met Virginia's governor, John Letcher. Lee was to see much of Letcher during the next few months and he was to profit by Letcher's integrity, his determination, his common sense, and his familiarity with the mind of the Virginia people.

The governor had an explanation to make and a question to ask. The state convention, he said, had provided by an ordinance of April 19 for the appointment of a "commander of the military and naval forces of Virginia," with the rank of major general and with authority to direct the organization and operations of the troops under the governor's constitutional control. The advisory council had recommended Lee for this post. Letcher had formally tendered it to him on April 21 and had sent a messenger, whom Lee had probably passed on the road. Would Lee accept the office created by the convention?

Lee's answer had been shaped by the reasons that had led him to resign from the army. There was no hesitation now; in a few brief words he accepted the task of defending his native state. That was all. Before the convention adjourned its night session Lee's name was sent in by Governor Letcher for confirmation, with a simple note that Lee had determined to resign from the United States army before the convention had created the office to which Lee was nominated. The convention at once and unanimously approved the choice; word that Lee would take command was telegraphed to Norfolk, and the weary new general retired to his bed in the Spotswood Hotel with greater burden than he had ever borne.

The next morning, Lee opened a temporary office. Without an adjutant, or even a clerk, he drafted his General Order No. 1, announcing that he had assumed command. Before Lee was able to do much more a committee from the convention waited on him to escort him to the capitol, where he was to receive formal notice of his appointment.

President John Janney addressed Lee in full and rounded periods:

> "Sir, we have, by this unanimous vote, expressed our conviction that you are at this day, among the living citizens of Virginia, 'first in war.' We pray God most feverently that you may so conduct the operations committed to your change, that it will soon be said of you, that you are 'first in peace,' and when that time comes you will have earned the still prouder distinction of being 'first in the hearts of your countrymen.' . . .
>
> "Yesterday, your mother, Virginia, placed her sword in your hand upon the implied condition that we know you will keep to the letter and in spirit, that you will draw it only in her defense, and that you will fall with it in your hand rather than that the object for which it was placed there shall fail."

Some of the very qualities that Lee's admirers saw in him were put to the test within a few hours. Vice-President Stephens wished to see him that evening. The Confederacy, Stephens explained, of course desired an immediate military alliance with Virginia. This would involve the control of military operations in Virgina by the Confederate authorities—a manifest necessity of war. The Confederacy had no military rank at the time higher than that of brigadier general; Lee, a Virginia major general, might find himself under orders of a titular subordinate. What did Lee propose to do? To use Stephens's own language: "With a clear understanding of its bearing upon himself personally, he expressed himself as perfectly satisfied, and as being very desirous to have the alliance formed. He stated, in words which produced thorough conviction in my mind of their perfect sincerity, that he did not wish anything connected with himself individually, or his official rank or *personal* position, to interfere in the slightest degree with the immediate consummation of that measure which he regarded as one of the utmost importance in every possible view of public considerations." With this assurance, Lee bade good-evening to Stephens, who prepared to press for an early alliance. Lee was fully committed to the Confederate cause.

The seven weeks that followed the appointment of Lee to the command of the Virginia forces are the least known of his military career, but certainly among the most interesting. They are little known because the confused events of the period were eclipsed by his conduct of field operations the next year. They are interesting because they disclosed Lee's powers as an organizer and also because they represent the solution adopted by a trained military mind for problems that recur in every democratic society that is forced to raise an army from untrained citizens on the outbreak of a war for which there has been no adequate preparation.

Lee found himself the military and naval commander, under the governor and convention, of a state of 1,596,652 people, of whom only 1,047,579 were whites. Virginia was the most populous state of the South and the fifth in the union. Her territory extended from the Atlantic Ocean to the Big Sandy River. On the longest axis in the general direction of east and west, Virginia was then 425 miles in width.

That this large state would have to be prepared immediately for defense was apparent to all. She had already committed acts of war, though for self-preservation, and she must accept the consequences. The Federal authority had been overthrown everywhere in Virginia except at Lee's old post, Fort Monroe, which had been too powerful for the state's volunteers to assault. Harpers Ferry had been mistakenly believed by the Virginians to have in its Federal arsenal not less than 16,000 modern small arms, badly needed for the defense of the state, together with immensely valuable machinery for the manufacture of muskets and rifles. On the night of April 18 Virginia volunteers had descended on the place, only to find that the commander had set fire to the buildings. The machinery had escaped the flames, but most of the small arms had been destroyed.

At Norfolk, the United States had maintained a large navy yard. Volunteers had sunk some hulks at the mouth of the Elizabeth River in an effort to prevent the escape of naval vessels, but the sloop *Pawnee* steamed through the obstructions on the night of April 20, landed at the navy yard a contingent of about 500 men who proceeded to set fire to the buildings and vessels and, about midnight, left aboard their ship, with the Cumberland in tow. The next day the Virginians had occupied the yard.

These overt acts would certainly be answered, and speedily, by the Federal Government. It could not permit its power to be flouted. President Lincoln, in his proclamation of April 15, had given the Southern forces twenty days in which "to disperse and return peaceably to their respective abodes." This was generally interpreted to mean that the President would wait until May 5 and then would begin the invasion of the South. Twelve days, then, Lee had—from April 23 to May 5—in which to prepare Virginia for the first shock of the invasion.

How did Lee view this prospect? He was convinced that war would come; that it would be prolonged, he feared for reasons all too valid. "The war may last ten years," he wrote Mrs. Lee, when he had been in Richmond only eight days. His plan had to be shaped virtually as it was being executed, in an atmosphere of excited haste and with scant trained assistance. Yet as Lee's successive steps are retraced from his dispatches, their logic appears, and it is possible to see why he acted when he did.

He postulated everything on the maintenance of a strict defensive as long as possible. He enunciated this policy as soon as he entered upon his duities. There were seven questions he had to ask himself:

1. How could he offset the sea power of the North, with its constant threat to Virginia?

2. Should he attempt to hold Harpers Ferry, and could he retain Norfolk?

3. How were competent officers to be procured in sufficient numbers?

4. On what basis and with what personnel was the general staff to be organized?

5. Prompt mobilization and early training were necessary: how were they to be effected?

6. In what way were the necessary arms and equipment to be provided?

7. When mobilized, armed, and trained, where could the Virginia forces be disposed to meet effectively the advance of a superior enemy, that not only controlled Chesapeake Bay, but was able to move into Virginia simultaneously from the north, the east, and the west?

His answer to the first of these questions was a vindication of all that Mahan was later to argue regarding sea power. Virginia must be saved from the possibility of a fleet movement up the Rappahannock, the York, or the James, all navigable to points within striking distance of Richmond. Governor Letcher had been quick to sense this danger. Embarrassed as he had been by the lack of military experience and of trained advisers, he had proceeded to organize for the defense of the rivers. Lee pushed this work with the most insistent vigor. The state engineer proved to be none other than Lee's chief of happier days, Colonel Andrew Talcott.

Lee left the location of works entirely to the discretion of the energetic old colonel, in whose judgment he had full confidence. But when the batteries had been designed and staked off, who was to construct and to arm them? He turned over this part of the task to the navel personnel of Virginia, which had been quickly and efficiently organized from resigning United States officers. An admirable job the navy made of it. The fortification of the rivers progressed satisfactorily from the beginning and occupied so little of Lee's time that he was able at an early date to turn to the defense of Norfolk and of Harpers Ferry.

The property seized by Virginia at the Norfolk shipyard was found to include 1198 guns, and was worth some $7,307,000, but the value to the new government of such a plant and dry dock, with much of the machinery intact, could not be computed in terms of money. If Norfolk could be held, at least one and perhaps three of the scuttled warships could be raised and refitted, and the South would have the means of building other naval vessels until perhaps a formidable fleet might be gathered to dispute control of Hampton Roads. Norfolk, moreover, was strategically located in relation to North Carolina. To possess Norfolk was to hold the key to eastern Carolina.

The machinery at Harpers Ferry was scarcely less important to the Confederate army than the Norfolk dry dock and shops were to the sea forces. Mainfestly, if Virginia could retain Harpers Ferry, the manufacture of small arms would go on more rapidly than if the shops were moved. But there was one great difficulty about retaining the shops at Harpers Ferry. The town was badly placed to stand a siege, because it was in a flat dominated on three sides by very high ground.

Lee decided to continue the removal of surplus machinery from Harpers Ferry and to haul all the machines to Richmond as speedily as possible, but, meantime. to operate the shops as long as any part of the equipment remained. While he was planning this there came into his office a tall, sober-faced young professor, in the uniform of the Virginia Military Institute, to consult with him regarding the use of the cadets of that school. Lee had not seen him, so far as is known, since they left Mexico in 1848, but he recognized him as Major Thomas J. Jackson. Governor Letcher had known Jackson in Lexington, where the institute was located, and he nominated him to the convention for a commission as colonel of infantry. Simultaneously, he directed Lee to put Jackson in command at Harpers Ferry as soon as he was confirmed. The convention accepted the appointment. Promptly and cheerfully enough Lee ordered Jackson to his post, doubtless without imagining that circumstance and Governor Letcher had combined to bring under his command the one Southern soldier, above all others, who was to show himself the ideal lieutenant.

When Jackson arrived at Harpers Ferry he found something more than 2000 volunteers and militia there. Increasing hourly, they had little equipment and less powder and shot. Jackson acted with the greatest energy. The machinery immediately required in Richmond was moved rapidly; more volunteers were brought up, organized and drilled; arms taken from the arsenal at the time of the fire were traced; outposts were established; and a spirit of confidence was gradually created.

Lee was much gratified at Jackson's accomplishments. He prepared to send new troops to him and decided to increase the force already sent to Manassas Junction. He had to gamble whether he would be able to hold Harpers Ferry, but he felt that the machinery in the shops and the strategic value of the position justified the risks.

As soon as these first defensive measures had been taken he turned to the third aspect of his problem, the selection of officers and the creation of a staff. For the first operations, Governor Letcher, of necessity, had chosen the most available men, chiefly of the militia. As respected field officers, this arrangement was unsatisfactory and had to be changed as speedily as possible. The convention had provided that the field officers should be appointed by the governor. The convention also invited all "efficient and worthy Virginians . . . in the Army and Navy of the United States to retire therefrom and to enter the service of Virginia." The governor had been directed to assign these officers "such rank as will not reverse the relative rank held by them in the United States service and will at least be equivalent thereto." The invitation assured ultimately a limited supply of trained soldiers, for nearly all the Virginians of distinction in the Federal army had resigned, except General Scott and Major George H. Thomas. Caution was shown from the outset in giving high commissions to politicians—even to so influential a person as ex-Governor Wise. By May 1 Lee was sending out commissions in the army of Virginia to a number of men who later attained distinction. Besides Jackson, Virginia called on Joseph E. Johnston, John Bankhead Magruder, Richard S. Ewell, Harry Heth, Samuel Jones, J. C. Pemberton, and others. Lee had reasonable prospect of procuring competent brigade officers and a fair number of good colonels and lieutenant colonels by the time he was ready to bring the full force of volunteers into the field. His task was complicated, however, because neither he nor any one else knew how desirable a commission in the army of the commonwealth might be. On April 25 the state convention had ratified a pact for temporary union with the Confederacy. This might well mean that every Virginia commission would be vacated.

The organization of the general staff proceeded simultaneously, if less satisfactorily. The adjutant general's, quartermaster's, subsistence, medical, and pay departments and an engineers corps were set up. By a series of brief general orders Lee sought to establish system as rapidly as practicable within the departments, and as a short cut he adopted the old regulations of the United States army wherever applicable.

Virtually no attempt was made to set up an intelligence service as a part of the general staff. Reports of the plans and movements of the Federal forces were gleaned from Northern newspapers, or were gathered from travellers and private letters. Some of the most important movements were wrongly reported or were not discovered at all. The Virginia press, in its zeal to inform its readers, informed the enemy as well, and helped to create in Lee a dislike for newspaper methods.

The personal staff of the commanding general, like the general staff, had to be built up in an atmosphere of impermanence. Although he had started without a single assistant, Lee was determined to employ only trained men, so far as they were procurable. "It is necessary," he wrote in an early veto on nepotism, "that persons on my staff should have a knowledge of their duties and an experience of the wants of the service to enable me to attend to other matters." It was an ideal he never fully realized.

Fortunately, R. S. Garnett, who had been Lee's adjutant at West Point, joined Virginia early and accepted the new post of adjutant general. With Garnett in charge of the office, Lee soon collected a few clerks and the staff of two aides and a military secretary allowed him. Lieutenant Walter H. Taylor quickly made himself indispensable at Lee's headquarters. Other officers assisted him during the summer, notably Lieutenant Colonel George Deas and Lieutenant Colonel John A. Washington.

All work had to be done at a furious rate. Every one wanted to fight; few were willing to recognize that war calls, first of all, for ordered preparation. The public seemed to think that all that was needed was the word to go forward and overwhelm the enemy. Lee had to do a prodigious volume of work, but he kept his head. This initial stage of his labors brought him close to May 5, the expiration of the period that Lincoln had allowed for the dispersion of the secessionists.

Immediately following secession the governor and the advisory council had seen the folly of calling out more troops than Virginia needed at exposed points. Lee had postponed a general mobilization in the knowledge that arms were limited, that field officers were lacking, and that the general staff had not been organized to transport, to quarter, and to feed the thousands who were anxious to defend their state. Now that invasion was imminent he had to bring the volunteers into the field. Delay after May 5 might be as dangerous as haste before that time would have been confusing.

Mobilization meant training, and that was the fifth aspect of Lee's labor of preparation. In addition to the simple drilling provided at the mobilization centres, a camp of instruction named after Lee was established at Richmond. The cadets of the Virginia Military Institute were speedily put to work as drillmasters and some of them were subsequently sent to Harpers Ferry for similar service. An artillery school of instruction was established at Richmond College, with V. M. I. cadets again in charge.

Beyond a certain stage, mobilization was futile and training was impossible without arms and equipment. Providing these was the sixth aspect of Lee's problem. In order that the best use might be made of the arms that were available the convention authorized Lee to distribute them. It was a burdensome assignment. He had to dole out arms very cautiously in advance of actual enlistment, and he used his scant supply of percussion and "altered" muskets where he expected the troops to be called speedily to the field. A thousand muskets were procured from North Carolina and were sent to Jackson. New efforts were made to recover arms seized by individuals at Harpers Ferry, and the shops there were operated as long as he believed it could be done without subjecting the machinery to the risk of capture. The store of percussion muskets was exhausted by the end of May, but through economy, the supply of flintlocks held out. Every requisition from Virginia troops was met, and probably more than 10,000 muskets were issued to troops from other states. When the Virginia forces were taken over by the Confederate States, Lee's report showed some 46,000 guns in the hands of the mustered volunteers. It is enough to note, for comparison, that during 1861 the North was able to issue to its soldiers 1,276,686 firearms.

As it was with infantry small arms, so it was with arms and equipment for cavalry. The same story seemed in a fair way of being repeated with percussion caps and small-arms ammunition. As for powder, the state had only 50,000 pounds and some 226,000 ball cartridges on December 15, 1860. The increase of this scant stock was very much in mind when the capture of the Norfolk navy yard was undertaken. The seizure of 300,000 pounds in that city met immediate needs.

Of field artillery the twelve volunteer companies in Virginia had thirty pieces in December, 1860, including about a dozen new Parrott guns. The state had some 300 old light cannon in addition, but most of these were unmounted and lacked harness and equipment. The principal task of the ordnance bureau, therefore, was to provide gun

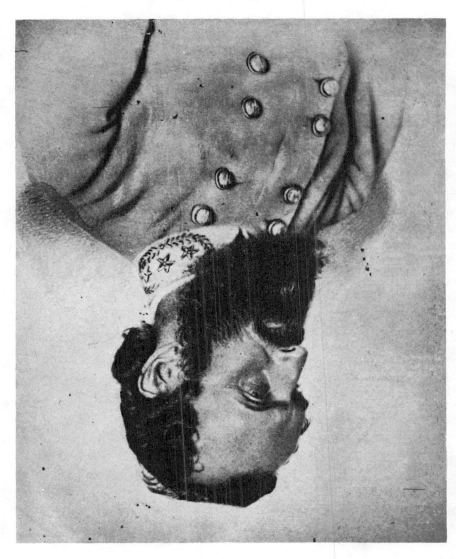

GENERAL T. J, "STONEWALL" JACKSON

Top: SEVEN DAYS: MILITARY BRIDGE ACROSS THE CHICKAHOMINY
Bottom: WHITE OAK SWAMP, *June, 1862*

carriages and caissons and then to distribute the ordnance to best advantage. Thanks to the great store at the Norfolk navy yard, the supply of heavy ordnance was ample.

In all supplementary equipment Virginia was dismally lacking. No tentage, no knapsacks, no cartridge boxes, no flags were ready for issue. In the first brush with Federal gunboats, the battery at Sewell's Point, near Norfolk, had to fly the state colors of a Georgia company in the small garrison as it possessed no others. To avoid the hopeless task of attempting to uniform 51,000 men, Virginia required that the volunteers supply their own clothing.

The need of a large supply of field transport was in Lee's mind from the first, for despite the mobility that the railroads made possible, he knew the armies must often operate at a distance from tracks. Failure to provide adequate transportation was, perhaps, the worst shortcoming of Virginia's preparation, and it was to cost the South dearly.

While Lee was working in these and other ways to prepare the state forces for the field, the Confederacy was beginning to send Southern volunteer regiments into Virginia to dispute the expected Federal advance. There was immediate confusion, which it took much time to straighten out. Conflict was in the air, and the personal representative of the Secretary of War began to crowd the wire with suspicions of Lee and of Letcher, intimating that Lee was "troubled about rank." In a personal exchange of telegrams with the President, Lee explained that he was satisfied with his place in the Virginia service. Friction was definitely relieved on May 10 by an order from the War Department authorizing Lee to "assume control of the forces of the Confederate States in Virginia, and assign them to such duties as you may indicate, until further orders." Four days later Lee was made brigadier general in the regular army of the Confederacy, the highest rank then existing. He continued to discharge all the duties of his Virginia commission, however, for some weeks, and certain of the duties much longer.

Western Virginia, concerning which Lee was beginning to be very apprehensive, was strategically important and open to the Federals. Its rivers flowed into the Ohio or into the major tributaries of that stream. Harpers Ferry was easily turned from western Virginia. United States troops operating from Grafton could advance southeastward and by a shorter march than that to Harpers Ferry could reach Staunton and the upper valley of the Shenandoah. In the larger strategy, railway communications in Kentucky and Tennessee might be interrupted by an armed force based on the westernmost counties of Virginia.

Sentiment was divided in this wide area, which was potentially a source of considerable man-power either for or against Virginia. Finding that nothing had been done to secure western Virginia, except to warn the president of the Baltimore and Ohio not to permit the Federals to use the railroad for military purposes, Lee proceeded to rally the doubtful counties even before he issued the general call for volunteers. On April 29–30 he designated officers to undertake the organization of troops at Wheeling, in the lower Kanawha Valley, and at Grafton.

By May 6 the bulk of the news from western Virginia became distinctly unfavorable. Jackson reported much disaffection in that section and urged that troops be sent there. Other information was to the same effect, especially from Grafton, where the people were said to be verging on a state of "actual rebellion" against the authority of Virginia and were confidently expecting Federal support from Pennsylvania and Ohio. Lee was very much concerned at this, but aside from ordering arms hurried forward, he felt that he could do little.

Lee took up the final aspect of Virginia's defensive preparations, that of disposing the state's enlarged forces to meet the Federal offensive. With Norfolk and Harpers Ferry reasonably well strengthened, he decided he must concentrate more troops at Manassas Junction. A small force under General P. Saint George Cocke had been placed there by Letcher. On May 6 Lee warned Cocke to prepare for an attack directed from Alexandria, because seizure of the Manassas Gap Railroad, leading from Manassas Junction to Strasburg, not only would deprive the Confederate forces at Harpers Ferry of direct railway connection with Richmond, but would similarly cut off the scant force that was trying to rally the states' rights men in northwestern Virginia. As quickly as he could, Lee began to dispatch additional officers and men to Manassas Junction.

Every effort that he made to strengthen Virginia's hold on her exposed northern frontier was seconded with the greatest energy by Jackson at Harpers Ferry. Thanks to his diligence and military judgment, it became apparent that Harpers Ferry not only was measurably safe, but that the troops there might be utilized to meet an offensive directed against it by way of Manassas Junction.

Lee left Richmond on May 16, and made a thorough inspection of Norfolk. He found the situation confused and unsatisfactory. Progress

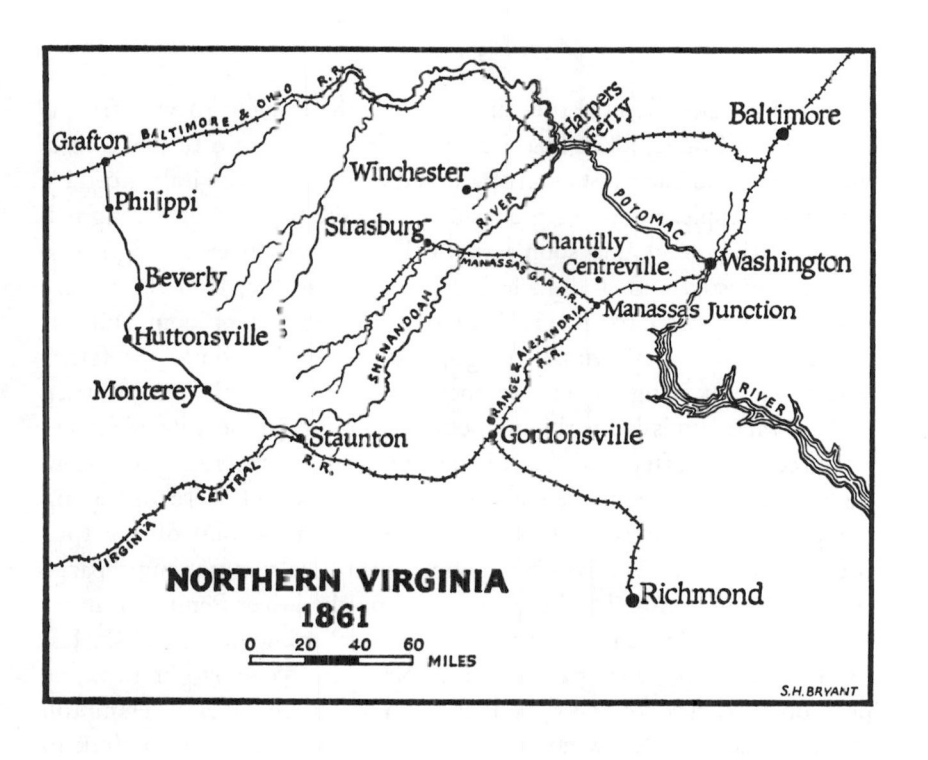

NORTHERN VIRGINIA
1861

0   20   40   60
MILES

S.H.BRYANT

on the fortifications was slow. Hastening back to Richmond as soon
as he was convinced that he had found the trouble, he relieved General
Walter Gwynn, who had not seen regular military service since 1832.
In his place Lee put Brigadier General Benjamin Huger. Under Huger's
direction the construction and arming of the batteries went on with
less delay.

On May 24, the day after the people of Virginia ratified the
ordinance of secession, came long-expected news: the Federals that
morning had occupied Alexandria and the Virginia side of the Potomac.
Lee promptly forwarded to Manassas reinforcements and gave orders
for dispositions in case the Federals continued their advance.

The occupation of the Virginia side of the Potomac had a personal
aspect that Lee could not wholly overlook. It meant that Arlington was
in the hands of enemies. His concern was for his invalid wife, not for
himself. Mrs. Lee had been very loath to leave Arlington. Not until
about May 14 did she betake herself temporarily to nearby Ravensworth. Even then she left many of the family's possessions and some
of the Washington relics within easy reach of marauders. Lee knew
that Mrs. Lee could not remain at Ravensworth without causing embarrassment to Mrs. Fitzhugh for housing the wife of a "rebel general,"
but he was unwilling to have her come to Richmond, inasmuch as he

expected to take the field speedily. The daughters went to visit friends in Fauquier County, Virginia. Lee had left his sons free to make their own choice and had most carefully urged Custis not to be influenced by his own example. But all of them sided with the South. Custis resigned, came to Richmond, and soon was working as an officer of engineers; Rooney enlisted and was made a captain of cavalry; Robert was ere long to be chosen to like rank in one of the student companies at the University of Virginia, though, because of his youth, his father was as yet unwilling for him to enter the service. Smith Lee returned his Federal commission early and became a captain in the Virginia navy.

Three days after the occupation of Alexandria and Arlington, Federal transports appeared in Hampton Roads and were unloading troops in large numbers at Newport News. The second of the four probable Federal offensives was taking form. Lee was not unprepared for it. He had consolidated the command on the lower Peninsula under Magruder on May 21, and had been strengthening him steadily, but the Federal troops being collected at Newport News might turn the position at Yorktown and thus open the York River or cross Hampton Roads, ascend the Nansemond River, cut the railroad from Norfolk to Petersburg, and mask Norfolk. Lee hastened to send more troops to the Norfolk district and to dispatch artillery to defend the approaches to Suffolk.

Before the object of the landing at Newport News had become apparent, Lee felt it necessary to visit Manassas Junction on May 28. He made a hurried inspection of the junction and the next morning went on to Fairfax Courthouse. The troops were increasing rapidly in number but were in every conceivable state of efficiency or lack of it. The officers ranged from wholly inexperienced civilian volunteers to men with West Point training and a solid background of service in the regular army. Lee made new dispositions to cover the flanks and to place a detachment for observation at Fairfax Courthouse.

The selection of the best available commander for the force at Manassas Junction had been giving Lee much concern. Cocke had worked zealously, but the Virginia convention had concluded that the state had too many general officers and reduced their number. Letcher had renominated Cocke, along with others, for rank in the volunteer forces one grade lower than previously held. There was no alternative to the selection of an officer of commanding rank to take charge of the Manassas line. Brigadier General M. L. Bonham of South Carolina had reported in Richmond with a brigade of South

Carolina volunteers, and as these troops were most needed at Manassas, Bonham was sent there. Being the senior officer he was given command on May 21, with detailed instructions to hold to the defensive. Lee now concluded that a more experienced soldier than Bonham was needed for Manassas.

When Lee returned to Richmond he found that President Jefferson Davis had arrived from Montgomery, Ala., to make Richmond the capital of the Confederacy in accordance with the invitation of the Virginia convention. This invitation had been extended on April 27 and had been accepted on May 21. Strategically it was a serious mistake, for it placed almost on the frontier of the Confederacy the capital that was so surely to become the emblem of the South that its retention took on a moral significance out of all proportion to the industrial importance of the city.

The preliminaries of this removal of the capital to Richmond had not been wholly cordial, and the separate efforts of the state and of the Confederacy in Virginia had not been without friction. Governor Letcher had been in no hurry to effect the transfer of the Virginia forces. But the Montgomery government had gradually asserted its authority and on occasion had ignored both Letcher and Lee. General Joseph E. Johnston had been ordered on May 15 by the War Department to take charge at Harpers Ferry, without reference to Lee, and had been directed to forward from Lynchburg to Harpers Ferry certain Confederate troops that Lee had previously earmarked for Richmond. Lee had recommended that Johnston be given rank equal his own in the army of Virginia. Johnston had preferred a commission as brigadier general in the Confederate army. It was in this capacity that he had been assigned to Harpers Ferry. He was doubtful of his ability to hold Harpers Ferry, and, though he recognized Lee's authority and even went so far in one letter as to style him "commander in chief," he was out of sympathy with Lee's plan to retain Harpers Ferry as long as practicable.

Johnston's attitude, the conflict of authority, the arrival of Davis, and the near approach of the day when the Virginia forces would be taken over by the Confederacy added to the difficulties of Lee's position. However, with a President and a governor, a Confederacy and a state alike to be served, Lee had one asset in his steadfast refusal to be incensed by slights or provoked by the clash of authority. Another asset was the esteem of the President.

Jefferson Davis was then close to his fifty-third birthday. His instincts, his, bearing, and his manners were those of an aristocrat. His well-chiselled features and his fine head bespoke high intelligence; his thin, erect form was commanding and gracious. He had dignity without austerity. His experience had been long and varied, as planter, as volunteer in the Mexican War, as senator, and as Secretary of War. His understanding of military matters was sound and his viewpoint in war essentially that of the professional soldier. In administration, he was of average capacity or better, occasionally disposed to delay decisions but usually reaching them promptly and reasonably. He had in him, in fact, some of the qualities essential to the success of a revolution, but these were coupled with serious weaknesses. His nature was exceedingly sensitive. His health was uncertain. He was too much of a constitutionalist to be a daring revolutionary. In his dealings with men he applied to the fullest the political maxim of loyalty to friends and of hostility to foes. His stubborn loyalty to friends of mediocre mind was to cost the Confederacy dearly, but in the case of Lee his loyalty was to be, perhaps, his largest service to the South. Lee had his "unqualified confidence, both as a man and a patriot, and had the special knowledge of conditions in Virginia that was most useful." From the time of his arrival in Richmond, Davis kept Lee near him and consulted often with him. Together, on Lee's return from Manassas Junction, they conferred on the choice of a commander for that exposed line. The President decided to entrust the post to Lee's friend of earlier days, the "Hero of Charleston," General P. G. T. Beauregard, who was then in Richmond.

The dispatch of Beauregard to Manassas put three of the four exposed posts in Virginia under the charge of professional soldiers of experience: Huger and Magruder were on opposite sides of Hampton Roads, Johnston was at Harpers Ferry, Beauregard faced the enemy below Washington. Conditions in each of these areas were improving hourly. Very different was the situation in the fourth zone of probable Federal advance, western Virginia. For two weeks news from that quarter had been bad.

On June 1 a messenger arrived from Johnston with dispatches. One contained a rumor that Colonel George A. Porterfield had evacuated Grafton, and that the Federals had occupied it. A few days later Porterfield had been surprised at Philippi, fifteen miles south of Grafton, and had lost most of his equipment. A third Federal offensive of unknown strength was developing ominously. State and the Confederate authorities moved to redeem the situation. Porterfield was relieved. The militia in seven counties were ordered out. Colonel R. S. Garnett was commissioned brigadier general and hurriedly sent to the Allegheny Mountains.

As soon as these measures had been initiated, Lee paid a visit on June 6–8 to the York and James Rivers, for the Confederate authorities were about to take over the Virginia forces, and he wished to satisfy himself that the batteries had been properly placed and armed. He found the work almost finished, and the ceremony of transferring the Virginia forces to the Confederacy was completed on June 8. In one sense Lee's immediate task was accomplished. The rivers were defended by the batteries he had just inspected. The navy yard was operating. As far as practicable, Norfolk had been secured from direct attack and from a turning movement by way of Suffolk. Approximately 40,000 troops from Virginia had been enlisted and armed and had been supplied with field officers, staff, and partial equipment. One hundred and fifteen field guns had been issued, including twenty batteries of four guns each. The whole mobilization had cost Virginia $3,779,000, and it had been effected in slightly less than eight weeks, during seven of which Lee had been responsible.

The record speaks for itself. As an achievement in mobilization it would seem to be without serious error. As a feat in the preparation of a force for service under the conditions of combat prevailing in 1861, it was deficient only in the failure to provide adequate field transportation and in the inability of the state properly to equip the cavalry. In the larger view of strategy, the disposition of the forces, as mobilized, was sound otherwise than as respected western Virginia. Lee doubtless was deceived by the first reassuring reports from that area of disaffection. Limited as his forces were, he had to take chances somewhere. The import of the loss of that section was not foreseen, or else Lee yielded more readily than was his habit to obstacles which were bad enough yet scarcely more serious than others his energy and strategic sense overcame.

Heavy as were the calls on Lee's energy and patience, during these weeks, his strength of body and of character was equal to them. Anxious as he was to take the field, he met patiently the vexations of office work. No homesickness was discernible in his letters, and there must have been distinct relief for him to know that Mrs. Lee, having left Ravensworth, was at Chantilly, cheerful and reconciled to indefinite absence from Arlington. He had committed his loved ones, along with his own destiny, his strategy, and his prepartions for

Virginia's defense, into the hands of a God who was never more personal or more real to him than in those days of a divided nation's insanity.

An empty title was left Lee when the Virginia forces were transferred to the Confederate States. For the moment he seems almost to have forgotten that he was a brigadier general in the regular army of the Confederacy. Considering that inquiry about his status would smack of place-hunting, Lee had no intention of asking, and the President had not thought to discuss it with him when, on June 10, there came news of something approaching a battle at Big Bethel, eight miles northwest of Newport News. Major General Benjamin F. Bulter had planned a surprise attack on a troublesome Confederate outpost of Magruder's command, but one of his regiments, becoming confused, fired into another and had given the alarm. A force of some 1400 Confederates met the poorly organized attack of seven Federal regiments and drove them back. This little action was evidence that the Federals were prepared to take the offensive on the lower Peninsula. Magruder's position had to be strengthened. To this task Lee was assigned immediately.

Operations on the Peninsula were closely bound up with those around Norfolk and on the Rappahannock. In the course of a few days, still without formal orders which would clarify his status, Lee was directing the defense of eastern Virginia, including Richmond, while the War Department and the President took over the preparation of the forces at Harpers Ferry and Manassas Junction. Western Virginia remained in some sense a charge both on Davis and on Lee, but the latter was authorized to carry on correspondence with Garnett and to receive that officer's reports.

Much of the now-familiar routine was resumed. Lee expedited the construction of the system of earthworks for Richmond, and he undertook some defenses for the Rappahannock River. The probability of an attack on Norfolk he kept constantly in mind as he steadily built up its garrison and the forces on the Nansemond. In a short time the Norfolk line was completed and fully armed.

Daily Lee's duties were enlarged, though they were not defined. Jealous as was President Davis of his prerogatives, and instant as was his resentment of all interference, he made the most of Lee's abilities. Soon Lee was in one sense an acting assistant Secretary of War and in another deputy chief of the general staff, to borrow a later military term, for Davis at this period was his own chief of the general staff.

Fortunately for Lee, though his own military family had changed, it was still adequate to serve him in the discharge of his miscellaneous duties.

There were ample reasons why Lee could not be certain whither he would be sent. Apart from Hampton Roads and Tidewater Virginia, a sudden blow might be struck in northern or in western Virginia. The next move came at Harpers Ferry, where Johnston continued pessimistic of his prospects. On June 13 the Federals made a raid on Romney, fifty-five miles west of Harpers Ferry. Johnston evacuated Harpers Ferry and took position at Bunker Hill. On July 2 General Robert Patterson crossed the Potomac and on the 3d drove into Johnston's outposts and occupied Martinsburg. There he halted. Daily expecting an attack, Johnston called out two brigades of militia and asked for the loan of 6000 or 7000 men from Beauregard's army.

Meantime the situation in northwestern Virginia grew ominous after Porterfield had been driven out and Garnett sent to relieve him. On his arrival at Huttonsville, on June 14, Garnett had found only twenty-three companies of infantry, and these, he had reported, were "in a miserable condition." Still, he regimented these troops, pushed forward with them, and, with a single battery, occupied the passes on Rich Mountain and Laurel Hill. By July 1 his force had not mounted above 4500 effectives, and Garnett had felt compelled to ask for further reinforcements. Before the receipt of this appeal Lee had sent one more regiment to Garnett, and on hearing more fully of the situation he directed two others to be forwarded under the command of able professional soldiers.

After fortifying the mountain passes Garnett underwent a change of opinion as to the outlook. On July 5 he reported that he did not believe the enemy would attack him, primarily because he supposed the Federals had occupied as much of northwest Virginia as they could want. Lee did not take this optimistic view. "I do not think it probable," he wrote on receipt of Garnett's dispatch, "that the enemy will confine himself to that portion of the northwest country which he now holds, but, if he can drive you back, will endeavor to penetrate as far as Staunton. Your object will be to prevent him, if possible, and to restrict his limits within the narrowest range, which, although outnumbered, it is hoped by skill and boldness you will accomplish."

This warning never reached Garnett. Two days before it was

written General George B. McClellan arrived in front of Rich Mountain. His communications were well covered and his dispositions were admirably made. The absence of anything even approaching an intelligence service on the Confederate side enabled McClellan to advance with all the elements of surprise. Deliberately employing the strategy that Lee had helped to develop in Mexico, McClellan planned and executed another Cerro Gordo. General W. S. Rosecrans found an unguarded path to the crest of Rich Mountain, stormed the battery there on July 11 and opened the road for McClellan, who advanced rapidly to Beverly on the 12th. Garnett, finding his flank turned, attempted to withdraw from Laurel Hill, but was pursued. In a rearguard action on the 13th he was killed at Corrick's Ford. The remainder of his force precipitately withdrew to Monterey.

First news of the disaster reached Richmond on July 14. Lee hurried troops forward and placed General W. W. Loring in temporary command, with instructions to organize a counter offensive as soon as he thought proper. Lee had overtaxed his endurance, but he would have gone at once to attempt to redeem the evil day had not President Davis desired him to remain in Richmond, in view of the imminence of a hard battle in front of Manassas.

On that sector Beauregard had been receiving reinforcements, and had organized his forces into brigades placed somewhat in advance of the position that Lee had selected for defense. On July 14, James Chesnut, Jr., member of the Confederate Congress, came down from Manassas with a grandiose strategic plan that Beauregard had directed him to submit for approval. Davis and Lee opposed this plan. In discussing the situation, however, Davis and Lee again considered a plan previously formulated for co-ordinated action by Beauregard and Johnston.

What followed was under the personal direction of the President, rather than of Lee. On the 17th, Beauregard reported his outposts attacked. Davis promptly ordered Johnston to go to Beauregard's help, if practicable. Meantime, from Richmond and from Lynchburg every company that the railroads could transport was hurried forward. Lee wished to go to Manassas, but Davis considered it more important that he remain in Richmond. On Sunday morning, July 21, President Davis found himself unable to endure the inaction he felt compelled to enjoin upon Lee. Taking a special train for the scene of the battle he left Lee to agonize.

Rumor did its worst with wild tales of a Confederate *débâcle* and a victorious Federal march on Richmond. After dark fell the official dispatches began to trickle in. Presently this one arrived:

Manassas, July 21, 1861.

We have won a glorious though dear-bought victory. Night closed on the enemy in full flight and closely pursued.

JEFFERSON DAVIS.

It was the first time in Lee's life that he had experienced the anguish of a battle from afar. His relief was greater, perhaps, and his emotions came more completely to the surface than in any other crisis of the war. His part in the victory was hardly less than if he had been present. More than a fourth of the army had been raised and put in the field under his direction. He was responsible for the selection of the line taken up by Beauregard, and it had been his military judgment which dictated the concentration at Manassas Junction. In large part he fashioned the strategy of a junction between Johnston and Beauregard.

The public, however, did not reflect on the preparation that had made victory possible. It saw only the victory itself. Beauregard became as popular in Virginia as he had been in South Carolina or Louisiana. Johnston took the place that Lee had occupied in the affection of Virginia people. Circumstances had denied Lee a share in the battle of Manassas. The next unlucky turn of the wheel was to bring him an unpopularity that might have ended his military career before his great opportunity came.

On the morning of July 28, Lee started from Richmond to perform his first field duty for the Confederacy. It was not an impressive departure. His only military companions were John A. Washington and Walter Taylor. He had no more than two private attendants, Meredith, his cook, and Perry, another Negro, who was now acting as Lee's body servant. His baggage was of the smallest proportions. Many a brigadier, starting for the front, had a far larger *entourage* and a more ostentatious leave-taking. It was not precisely to the command of an army that Lee was going. As the President's confidential military adviser he was being sent to western Virginia. His mission was to co-ordinate—not to direct operations.

From the hour he arrived at Staunton, however, Lee encountered a state of affairs unlike anything he had ever seen in war. Into the quiet valley town had rolled the backwash of Garnett's little command—men whose zeal for war had been quickly dampened by contact with its

dirty, bloody realities. It was not soldiery that Lee saw at Staunton; it
was panic exhausted in paralysis.

On the morning of July 29, he left Staunton and started on horseback for Monterey. At Monterey he came to the headjuarters of Brigadier General Henry R. Jackson of Georgia, commander on that part
of the front. A strange fortune it was that brought such a man into so
precipitous a wilderness. Judge Jackson was a Yale graduate, an art
lover, a poet, an ex-judge, and a former United States minister to
Austria. But, in a new capacity and in an unfamiliar country, he kept
his head, used his strong, native intelligence, and made in the crises what
were probably the best dispositions possible with the small force at
hand. Although he had acted with decision, Jackson had displayed unusual modesty. He had urged that Lee come in person to western
Virginia and he had suggested that a man of greater military experience than himself be placed in direct command. Those of the troops
that had not shared in Garnett's campaign were in good condition. So
were the reinforcements that were now coming up from Staunton. But
many of the survivors of Garnett's command were in a pitiable plight.
Their recovery of morale was slow. Added to other miseries was an
epidemic of measles. Hospital facilities were too crude for classification.
The soldiers who kept their health were wet and dejected, for rain had
been falling steadily since July 22.

The feebleness of the army seemed all the worse when measured
against the assumed strength of the enemy. And the strength of the
enemy was increased by the geographical position he then occupied.
The two forces had come together on the watershed of the Allegheny
Mountains, an imposing range that runs northeast and southwest
through the whole of Virginia. The contest was for the mountain passes
and the roads that wound through them.

The strongest of the passes was that on Cheat Mountain, where there
was a long crossing at an elevation in excess of 3500 feet, easily swept by
artillery on the summit. The Federals had occupied the eminence while
the Confederates were demoralized by the early successes of Mc-
Clellan. All the advantages of position was on the Northern side.

Where the strength of the Federals was unknown, the first step had
to be defensive. Lee must make certain that the troops were numerous
enough, vigilant enough, and well enough fortified in the mountains to
keep the Union forces from reaching the Virginia Central Railroad. It
was not until some time after his arrival at the front that he was entirely satisfied the enemy could not break through the defenses and

strike the railway. Offensively, the key position in the campaign was the high ground north of Huntersville, dominating the road in rear of Cheat Mountain. To ascertain the exact state of affairs Lee set out for Huntersville in the rain that had been falling steadily and miring the roads. As soon as he reached the village Lee went to call on Loring, who, on July 30, had established his headquarters there. He met with a distinctly cold reception. Not two weeks had passed since Lee had given Loring discretionary orders in Richmond and had sent him forward. Loring did not feel that he needed supervision. It was apparent from the moment of Lee's meeting with Loring that another difficulty had been added to the inexperience, the demoralization, and the sickness of the Confederates: jealousy had come into the campaign.

If Loring would advance with all his forces, the enemy might be driven back. Everything depended on speed. And Loring showed not the slightest disposition to move fast! Before he went forward he was determined to establish a base and stock it adequately. When he would be ready to move, Loring did not say. Of course, a long offensive could not be sustained without building up supplies as Loring proposed. To that extent Loring was right. But a brief advance was all that was necessary to seize the key positions, and that was worth risks, even if the men had to carry their own rations

Lee's alternatives were plain: he must wait on Loring and coax him into action, when and if he could; or else he must overrule his authority, and order the troops forward. Lee could not bring himself to impose his will on Loring. Instead of hurrying Loring to Valley Mountain, he set out to conciliate him and to shape a new plan of campaign in place of the one the Federals had carelessly presented and Loring was negligently letting slip by. Lee chose the rôle of diplomatist instead of that of army commander.

All his life Lee had lived with gentle people. In that atmosphere he was expansive, cheerful, buoyant even, no matter what happened. Now that he encountered surliness and jealousy, it repelled him, embarrassed him, and well-nigh bewildered him. He showed himself willing to go to almost any length to avoid a clash. In others this might have been a virtue; in him it was a positive weakness. Doubtless he was unconscious of this weakness; but from those days at Huntersville until Longstreet was wounded in the Wilderness on May 6, 1864, there always was a question whether Lee would permit his battles to be lost by it. It became necessary to ask whether his judgment as a soldier or his consideration as a gentleman dominated his acts.

Four days he waited on Loring. Growing desperate then, Lee set out on August 6 for Valley Mountain, where he arrived the same day. A single reconnaissance showed that the opportunity for a surprise attack on the western side of Cheat Mountain was fading fast. By now the solitary alternative to a march straight into the mouth of the Federal guns, was the discovery of some obscure, unguarded trail to the rear of Cheat Mountain. The only way of finding such a route was to reconnoitre with the greatest care. As Lee had about him scarcely any officers experienced in this difficult work he felt that he should do a part of it.

Hourly the rain continued to pour down. By August 10, when twenty successive days of rain had passed, the roads were bottomless in mud. Measles had spread through the commands, bringing men down by hundreds and provoking fever and intestinal ills. Half the army was sick.

While Lee continued his reconnoitring, Loring slowly brought the rest of his troops forward, but until Lee could find a new line of advance they could do nothing against an adversary now fully alive to the danger on his flank. McClellan had been recalled to Washington. General W. S. Rosecrans, named as his successor, had placed J. J. Reynolds in direct command on the Cheat Mountain sector. Lee drew such comfort as he could from the fact that the Confederates had at least closed to the Federals the roads leading to Saunton and to Millborough.

The wretchedness of the green troops grew deeper daily. The weather gave no promise of change. Ice formed on the night of August 14-15. Supplies were brought forward with increasing difficulty. Lee had to guard at long range against a Federal advance up the valley of the Kanawha. He never knew what news of fatal contention the next courier from the south might bring. Nor did he know what the enemy was doing or what Reynolds's numbers were, though every move of the Confederates was quickly reported to the enemy. Still he held tenaciously to the hope of an offensive against the Federals.

On August 31 Lee was confirmed as a full general in the regular army of the Confederate States. On the same day Samuel Cooper, the adjutant general, Albert Sidney Johnston, and P. G. T. Beauregard received like rank. Commissions were so dated that Cooper and Albert Sidney Johnston were his seniors. Joseph E. Johnston and Beauregard were rated his juniors—an arrangement that aroused in Johnston a resentment that colored his views throughout the war.

Loring began to show himself more amenable. He interposed no objection as Lee gradually took over the strategy of operations. Step by

step a route had been found by which a column could make its way
from Valley Mountain along the western ridges of Cheat Mountain to
a point two miles west of its crest and on the road by which the force
was being supplied. Before Lee could fit this discovery into a plan of
attack, General Loring sent to him a civilian engineer along with
Colonel Albert Rust of the Third Arkansas Regiment. They had ridden
over the mountains from General H. R. Jackson's command and had
information that set every ear tingling. The engineer had set out from
Greenbrier River and, after days of scrambling through thickets, had
reached a point from which he believed the Federal position on the
mountain top could be taken. The engineer had taken Colonel Rust
with him on a second journey to the position he had discovered. Rust
explained all this to Lee, and was emphatic in his assertion that a column
could reach the point. The enemy's flank was exposed, he insisted. A
surprise attack from the height would give Lee Cheat Mountain and
would open the way to a general advance against the enemy. All he
asked, Rust confidently went on, was that if General Lee decided to
attack, he would give him the privilege of leading the assault on the
crest. It was to prove a most expensive "Yes."

Lee decided to fight the battle and went about preparations with an
eye to every precaution. By September 8 he had worked out the plan
to the point where the order could be issued—tactfully in the name of
Loring. Rust was secretly to take a column of about 2000 men to the
position he had selected. General S. R. Anderson was to move down
the western ridge of Cheat Mountain until he reached the road that
led to the summit from Tygart's Valley. He was then to occupy the
western crest and was to block the road. Jackson, on the eastern side
of the mountain, was to take position for a march up the Staunton-
Parkersburg turnpike. General Daniel S. Donelson and Colonel Jesse S.
Burks were to be ready to advance down either side of Tygart River
toward Elkwater. The date set for the advance was September 12. Dawn
found Lee where he had every reason to hope for success. Anderson
was where he could reach the Staunton-Parkersburg pike in a rush;
Donelson occupied a position whence he could reinforce either Loring
or Anderson. The troops that had marched down the valley under
Loring were close to the enemy. If Rust and Jackson were doing their
part on the eastern side of Cheat Mountain, that barrier might easily be
seized and the enemy driven down Tygart's Valley.

The attack was to open when a volley from the crest of Cheat Mountain announced that Rust was storming the block house. What was

delaying the confident colonel? It was long past light, 8 o'clock in fact, and not a sound had come from the summit. Had Rust lost his way? Now a courier reported that Anderson's men were across the Cheat Mountain road. The Federal pickets had been driven in. The movement would soon be known: was Rust never going to give the signal?

Presently the silence was shattered by the sound of guns. But it was not a volley. And it came from the wrong direction—from up Becky Run. What was afoot there? Lee spurred down the ridge to find out, and made for the main road. As he was about to emerge a strong Federal cavalry outpost dashed by in the direction of the firing. Lee was within the enemy's position. There were shouts, bugle-calls, more firing, and the Federals came back. They had run into Donelson's pickets and were carrying back the news of his advance. When the Federals had vanished, Lee went into Donelson's lines and learned, to his chagrin, that the firing had been done by impatient soldiers who hoped in this way to clean their guns more quickly.

It did not matter greatly, for 10 o'clock had come and passed. Something had gone wrong with Rust. What could be done to reshape the plan? Nothing, except to give battle with the troops west of the mountain, regardless of Rust and Jackson. Quickly Lee undertook to do this. He went from regiment to regiment, urging the colonels to get their men in hand. Lee encountered a curious and invincible passive resistance among the officers. The men were wet and too hungry, he was told, to undertake a battle. Morale was gone. By noon it was apparent that nothing could be accomplished. All the high expectations had evaporated. Lee's first battle had ended in utter fiasco. Not one word did Lee receive to explain why the attack on the crest of Cheat Mountain had not been delivered.

The morning of September 13, the men now rested somewhat, Lee determined to see if he could find a new way of reaching the rear of the Federals. West of the river, in the direction of Rich Mountain, a turning movement might be possible. Reconnoitring parties were sent out. As a part of the reconnaissance, Colonel Washington and Rooney Lee decided to explore the right branch of Elkwater Fork. Late in the afternoon Rooney returned with the news that they had encountered a Federal picket and had been fired upon. Washington had fallen at the first fusillade, and his body had not been recovered. This was the only incident of consequence during the day. On the 14th Lee sent a flag of truce to the Federals, requesting the body of Colonel Washington, if dead, or news of him, if captured. On the way the bearers were met by a party of Federals bringing the remains of the unfortunate officer. In deep personal grief Lee wrote the first of the many letters he was doomed to address to those who lost friends known intimately to him in the army.

Before this letter was penned, Lee learned what had happened east of Cheat Mountain, in the form of a curious and confused report from Rust. His column had safely reached the designated position. Rust in person had captured the first of several pickets who were silently disarmed. These prisoners were costly, however, and served their cause with their tongues. They told him that there were 4000 to 5000 men on Cheat Mountain; that they were strongly fortified; that they knew of his approach; and that they had already telegraphed for reinforcements. Rust concluded that their capture was a providential warning against making the assault, and he looked out on the enemy's position with very different eyes from those he had hopefully turned on it when he had made his reconnaissance. Rust simply waited, without firing a gun, and then withdrew as he had come. He did not know the troops on the crest numbered only 300.

"We must try again," Lee said, but what was left to try? The enemy could not advance. But if the enemy could not advance, neither could Lee. It was useless to continue to keep on that front more troops than were required to hold the passes. Especially was it wasteful to camp a large force there when Rosecrans was advancing up the valley of the Kanawha against Generals Wise and John B. Floyd, with troops withdrawn from the northern sector. So, Lee struck his tent, ordered Loring to follow, and started for the headwaters of the Kanawha.

His first campaign had ended ingloriously. Everything had been against him—weather, sickness, and circumstance. The larger opportunities had been lost before he came. But Lee's own performance must be adjudged disappointing. First was his failure to push Loring forward from Huntersville when he reached that village. Second, he consented to let Rust lead the attack against a position that no trained soldier had reconnoitred. Rust had superb troops and was himself no coward, but it was a mistake to entrust to him the most difficult part of the operation. The task called for a trained soldier, not for an unskilled volunteer who, until that day, had never been in action. The third question that must be asked regarding Lee's conduct of his first campaign is whether he should have overridden the objections of the officers who told him their men were in no condition to deliver an attack. This may or may not be a valid ground of criticism. In 1863 or in 1864 Lee's officers would not have dared such an objection, and he would not have heeded them if they had. In 1861 it may have been different. The evidence is so scanty that no final judgment can be based on it.

Contemporary criticism was that Lee was too much of a theorist and overcautious. The press that had praised him now turned upon him. But he had learned much. On the positive side, this campaign and the one that was to follow in the valley of the Kanawha disclosed in Lee's dealings with the man in the ranks the aptitude and the understanding that later made it possible for him to build the superb morale of the Army of Northern Virginia.

When the disaffection of western Virginia became apparent, Wise had been summoned to Richmond by President Davis, given a commission as a brigadier general, and hurried off to the valley of the Kanawha. He had been the champion of that section, and it was believed that his presence would rally the wavering. He went into the disputed territory early in June. By eloquence and personal appeals, he contrived to raise some 2850 men whom he organized as a "Legion" and mustered into the Confederate service. 1800 state volunteers were enlisted or brought from nearby counties to co-operate with him. Most of these men were wretchedly equipped and many of the state volunteers considered that they had entered the ranks solely to protect their own homes against invaders. Undependable as was this force, and inexperienced as were the commander and his officers, Wise advanced boldly down the valley of the Kanawha to Charleston. On July 17 he had a successful brush with a Federal force at Scarey Creek, near Charleston, but a week later he began to fall back to refit at White Sulphur Springs.

While Wise was in the Kanawha Valley, Brigadier General Floyd was completing the enlistment of the "brigade of riflemen" that President Davis had authorized him to raise, to the great impairment of regular recruiting in southwest Virginia. Floyd was as ambitious as Wise. He had been like Wise, Governor of Virginia. Serving as Secretary of War during most of Buchanan's administration, he had been accused of favoring the South by scattering the regular army and by piling up arms in arsenals located in the disaffected states. Floyd was not altogether devoid of native military talent, but he was rash and was to disclose a temperament readily confused in action. His troops, on the whole, were much better equipped than those of General Wise, but they lacked good muskets, artillery, and cavalry.

On August 6, at White Sulphur Springs, the two ex-governors met for their first council of war. Each came in a determination to yield nothing to the other. Floyd was intent on asserting his authority over his rival. Wise was resolved to retain the independence of his command. The two parted without a final decision. Foreseeing what was certain to follow, Wise appealed to General Lee to separate his command from Floyd's, but Lee was apprehensive of a Federal advance against the Virginia and Tennessee Railroad, and rejected Wise's appeal and directed Floyd to assume command of all the troops unless he had orders to the contrary from Richmond. Floyd promptly availed himself of this new authority.

About that time, word came that the Federals were advancing. Floyd determined to push forward and directed Wise to send one of his regiments to move with his column. Wise protested. Lee sided with Wise as to the policy of a general advance, but he could not sustain him in his defiant insubordination. The quarrel was past mending. Floyd proceeded to take the state troops entirely from under Wise's control. He showed no disposition to compromise or conciliate. There was an appeal by Wise to Lee for a transfer; again Lee had to sustain Floyd and had to explain to Wise that the army of the Kanawha was too small to be divided.

In contention and excitement, Floyd moved after the middle of August to the vicinity of Carnifix Ferry. Wise unwillingly followed. On August 25, when the cavalry covering his advance broke and fled, Wise was forced to halt temporarily. The next day Floyd surprised the 7th Ohio at Cross Lanes and, without assistance from Wise, routed it. This victory increased Floyd's self-confidence and indirectly led to new friction between him and Wise. There followed a brief season of alarms and rumors. Disgusted by what he termed Floyd's "vacillating and harassing orders," Wise made a successful demonstration on his own account though his command was still at half its strength because of sickness. This brush salved Wise's pride and served momentarily to offset Floyd's victory at Cross Lanes.

The condition in the upper valley of the Kanawha added no little to Lee's troubles in his mountain camp, but until the second week in September the situation on the scene of the Wise-Floyd war was not alarming. On September 8, however, a new danger developed. Floyd's principal adversary had been Brigadier General Jacob D. Cox, who had been based on the Kanawha River. Now Lee learned that Rosecrans was preparing to reinforce Cox with troops from the Huntersville-Elkwater sector. Floyd at that time was on the northern bank of Gauley

River, at Carnifix Ferry, with Wise at Hawk's Nest, twelve miles southwest of the ferry. Floyd might be caught between two attacks or overwhelmed from the north.

On the night of September 8–9, Floyd received positive news of an advance from the north and called on Wise for one regiment of the state Volunteers and one from Wise's Legion. Wise sent the state troops but protested against the dispatch of any part of his own small command. Before Floyd could answer with a new order, he was attacked, on the afternoon of September 10, by Rosecrans at Carnifix Ferry. He beat off several assaults, but fell back during the night to the south bank of the river, whence he again ordered Wise to reinforce him. This time Wise obeyed, but ere his men reached Floyd they were told to return, as Floyd was retreating farther to the east. Floyd had been slightly wounded at Carnifix Ferry and was almost bewildered. On the 11th, when Wise met him, he was so little master of himself that he admitted in the presence of his rival he did not know what orders to give. The next day he had somewhat recovered his composure and decided to retreat to Big Sewell Mountain. There, on the 16th, he held a council of war, to which he invited Wise and such of his officers as Wise saw fit to bring.

Up to this point on the retreat he and Wise had staged three distinct controversies. At the council, however, everything began amicably. As Floyd seemed to have no definite plan, Wise proceeded to tell his superior what should be done. The council ended with Wise apparently in control of the situation. But as Wise left Floyd's camp one of his officers called his attention to activity among the troops. Soon there came a dispatch from Floyd, announcing that he had decided to fall back beyond Sewell Mountain to the vicinity of Meadow Bluff, twelve miles away. Wise was instructed to hold himself in readiness to cover the rear.

This was too much for Wise. Outraged, he remained where he was and contended that he could better co-operate with Floyd and more readily repulse the enemy there than at Meadow Bluff. Very soon the enemy appeared in strength and took the position Floyd had evacuated. Wise had not more than 2200 men and faced at least twice that number. The road between him and Floyd was steep and difficult, crossing many streams and liable to be rendered impassable by rains. Friction, rival ambitions, and military insubordination had reached their climax. Wise seemed in danger of being cut to pieces before Floyd could reinforce him.

Thus matters stood on September 21 when General Lee, accompanied only by Taylor and a small cavalry escort, drew rein in Floyd's camp at Meadow Bluff.

The course that Lee had urged in the Kanawha Valley was simple: Floyd was to advance if he could but was to secure his rear and was not to take chances whereby the enemy would reach the railroads. Lee had directed Floyd to concentrate and fortify in the strongest position west of Lewisburg. His first determination had been to bring all the troops together. Loring had been ordered to follow Lee to the Kanawha Valley. When he arrived with his troops the Confederates would be strong enough to combat the Federals. Until that time division might mean disaster.

Lee's argument did not shake Wise's conviction that he had chosen the better of the positions. It was his contention that for all practical purposes he was united with Floyd. Meantime, Lee or no Lee, he held on to the heights in the face of the approach of Rosecrans's army.

The situation called for action. The following day, the 22d, Lee rode forward to Sewell Mountain and made a reconnaissance. The position was as strong as Wise had affirmed. It was stronger than that of Floyd. If the main attack was to be directed along the line of the James River and the Kanawha turnpike, across Sewell Mountain, then it was the course of wisdom to bring up Floyd and to fight where Wise stood. There was but one military argument on the other side: north and south of Wise ran a few inferior roads by which a vigorous enemy might flank his position. In this uncertainty, Lee left Wise without making a decision or explicitly ordering him to retreat.

On Lee's return to Floyd he found that officer more satisfied than ever that the Federals were outflanking Wise and moving against him. Floyd, however, had no tangible evidence of this. Consequently, Lee determined to await the development of the enemy's plans. The next morning word came from Wise that the Federals were preparing to attack him and that he could not withdraw. As Floyd still insisted that the enemy was moving around Wise's position, Lee again urged Wise to unite with Floyd if possible and prepare for a quick retreat on the first evidence of a move against Floyd. Wise replied that the enemy in his front was not as strong as he had thought. His statements as to the position of the enemy were contradictory and made the situation more involved than ever.

The absence of any large force in front of Wise might mean that the Unionists were turning his flank; but, on the other hand, the lack

of positive information of any Federal movement on either side of
Wise's position might indicate that the whole Northern army was
facing Wise on the mountain though only a part of it was visible. Lee
had to warn Wise of the risks he was taking by remaining in his exposed position, but, at the same time, he had to assume that Wise correctly stated the case when he said he could not draw away from the
enemy without disaster. The reinforcement of Wise with a part of
Floyd's men might make him strong enough to beat off the enemy even
if the whole force were in his front. It was dangerous to keep the
forces divided, but if they must be divided, they could be equalized.
On September 24, therefore, Lee started for Wise's position, and had
four of Floyd's regiments brought up at once to his support.

When Lee arrived at Sewell Mountain, in no good humor, he found
the enemy in sight, a mile and a half from Wise, on the crest that Floyd
had first occupied on his withdrawal from Carnifix Ferry. The whole
of his experience in Western Virginia had been a satire on everything
he had learned about war, but here, in the very face of the enemy,
conditions were worse than any he had yet encountered. Wise's sick
troops were wretched and without shelter. Many of the officers were
discontented, ignorant of their duties, and bitter toward Floyd and his
command. Disorganization and demoralization were widespread. And
amid this military chaos, like a stubborn old seneschal in the last hour
of a hopeless siege, General Wise strode defiantly. It was a terrible
experience for a man like Lee, who had dealt only with soldiers taught
to make discipline their religion.

That night Lee bivouacked on the mountainside covered by his overcoat, for his wagon had not come up, and the next morning he gathered
what information he could concerning the operations of the enemy on
the roads north and south of Sewell Mountain. All the reports he could
collect were that the enemy was not moving in either direction. It was
probable, then, that the main force was in front of Wise and might
remain there. If that should be the case, then, the thing to do was to
bring up Floyd and fight on the ground Wise had chosen. But to this
course there was one objection, political rather than military, but
serious none the less. To order Floyd to come to Wise, after Wise had
refused to go to Floyd, would be regarded by Floyd as a distinct
rebuff. As tactfully as he could, he wrote Floyd of his conclusion
that the enemy was not moving against him. Then he added:

"I suppose if we fall back the enemy will follow. This is a strong
point if they will fight us here. The advantage is, they can get no

position for their artillery, and their men I think will not advance without it. If they do not turn it, how would it do to make a stand here? In that event we shall require provisions and forage. Of the latter there is none, and the horses are suffering. This command is now in movable condition, and can retire or remain at pleasure."

This was not an order, but it hinted very broadly. The answer came most unexpectedly in a dispatch from Floyd later in the day of the 25th, while the enemy was demonstrating and Wise was at the front. This dispatch contained a copy of an order for Wise from acting Secretary of War Judah P. Benjamin:

> Sir: You are instructed to turn over all the troops heretofore immediately under your command to General Floyd, and report yourself in person to the Adjutant-General in this city with the least delay. In making the transfer to General Floyd you will include everything under your command.

Lee forwarded this paper to Wise without comment. Explicit as were the terms of the order, Wise debated whether to obey. In his hesitation he wrote Lee. Lee urged Wise's immediate compliance. Wise thereupon drafted a "farewell" to his men, announcing his recall and stoutly affirming that when the President instructed that he be relieved, Davis could not have foreseen that the order would be received when the troops were in the face of the enemy in hourly expectation of attack. A few hours afterwards he left for Richmond.

The conditions that forced President Davis to recall Wise had been a military scandal for days before the chief executive acted. Wise had made no bones of his distrust of Floyd's judgment, and even in his official correspondence he had indulged in language that no superior could overlook. He had actually written Lee of Floyd: "I feel, if we remain together, we will unite in more wars than one." Mr. Davis's growing willingness to take the political risks and to recall Wise as a military necessity was probably quickened into final action by a letter written him on September 15 by Floyd. This was restrained in language, but dwelt on the "peculiar contrariness" of Wise's "character and disposition" and left the matter in Davis's hands with the assertion that Wise's presence was "almost as injurious as if he were in the camp of the enemy with his whole command." Davis had to relieve Wise or else supplant Floyd.

Three days of uncertainty followed Wise's departure. As the enemy

gave every indication of attacking at any hour, Lee proceeded to
fortify the position. A downpour on the 27th swept away bridges,
turned roads into morasses, and cut off the troops at Sewell Mountain
from Floyd's support and from all supplies.

The situation was relieved in part, but only in part, on the 29th by
the arrival of the vanguard of Loring's little army of 9000. Thereafter
Lee had "great strength," as he wrote Floyd—sufficient men to meet
any attack the enemy was apt to make. He found it exceedingly difficult, however, to procure food for the men and provender for the
horses, to say nothing of building up a supply for an offensive. Troops
and horses lived only from day to day, the soldiers were still dogged
by sickness and the animals so thin they manifestly would break down
under heavy duty. Lee looked to Floyd for supplies; Floyd did what
he could to forward them, still convinced that Meadow Bluff was the
proper position for the army.

What should Lee do with his enlarged army? Obviously, in a country
that presented such formidable natural barriers, it was far better to
meet an attack than to deliver one. In case the enemy did not assume
the offensive, the Confederates could do so by several routes to the
rear of Rosecrans, provided the necessary supplies were available. From
day to day Lee waited and waited, with greater resignation, because
no reserve of supplies to sustain an offensive was being accumulated
at Sewell Mountain.

On the night of October 5–6, it seemed as if Lee's decision to await
the enemy's attack was to be rewarded. The pickets heard the creaking
of wheels on the mountain and concluded that the Federals were moving up their guns. A Federal advance against Lee's strong works meant
certain victory for the Southerners. The artillery would mow down
the Union troops; the infantry would finish off those that escaped the
cannon.

Lee must have awaited dawn in expectancy almost as high as that he
had cherished September 12 in the hope of hearing Rust's opening
volley. When day came there was silence. For a time it seemed
omnious; then it became suspicious. When full light came over the
ridges not a Federal soldier was visible. While Lee had waited for
Rosecrans to attack, Rosecrans had reasoned in precisely the same
fashion, that it was better to receive assaults than to deliver them.
Despairing of having that advantage, he decided not to throw away his
men. During the night he had slipped away.

The escape of the Federals was accounted another failure for Lee.

"One favorable opportunity to expel the enemy has been lost," said
The Examiner. "Shall we lose another? General Lee is able and accomplished. In this campaign accidents have baffled his best plans. He
has been delayed by incessant rain and unfathomable mud. After two
disasters to our arms in that section, he may well have been cautious lest
a third should finally ruin our interests there. But excess of caution or
malignant chance has wrought, by mere delay, much of the mischief
that was dreaded from defeat. The general, we doubt not, now feels
the necessity of a more adventurous policy, and he is quite able, we
hope, of adapting his plans to the exigency . . ."

Without waiting for the approval of arm-chair strategists, Lee
drafted a new plan of advance on the very day of Rosecrans's retreat
and delivered the preliminary orders for its execution. His hope now
was to move Floyd quietly to the south of the Kanawha and to have
him advance to a point where he could cut the communications of the
Federals on the Gauley. Lee was then to press forward to the Gauley,
attack the enemy, and, with Floyd's help, drive them out of the
Kanawha Valley. Success would achieve one main purpose of the
campaign in that it would free the more fertile part of western Virginia
of the enemy.

Floyd set out with all the troops under his immediate command except Wise's Legion. But no sooner were the soldiers on the march than
obstacles to the execution of the strategic plan were encountered. Sickness still thinned the ranks. The departure of Floyd's wagon train so
curtailed the transport that the horses had no forage and the troops on
Sewell Mountain lived literally from barrel head to frying pan. The
weather was so cold that Lee had to propose one night that he and
Taylor pool their blankets and sleep together under them. As for the
roads, the like of them had never been seen. Besides all this, General
H. R. Jackson, on the Greenbrier, had been attacked by a considerable
force on October 3, and though he had very handsomely beaten off the
enemy, the movement of the Federals in that quarter might be the first
step in a new offensive directed against Staunton and the Virginia
Central Railroad. If this were so, Loring would have to return to support Jackson. And, finally, there was soon no prospect of surprise. For
the newspapers had learned of Lee's plan and were printing the precise
details of what was intended to be a secret move.

On October 20, Lee gave up the idea of an offensive and ordered
Loring back to Jackson. Floyd took this in bad part, protesting that Lee
remained idle when an advance would have made it almost certain that

they could have captured the whole of the Federal Army. Lee, however, was fully satisfied that the Confederates could not and that the Federals would not advance during the few days of open weather that remained, so he completed the evacuation of Sewell Mountain and sent Wise's Legion back to Meadow Mountain, after all.

The campaign in the Kanawha Valley was over—in barrenness and disappointment. Lee is to be credited with some measure of success in that, with negligible losses, he kept the enemy from reaching the railroad. On the other hand he did little to achieve a positive result. Lee cannot fairly be criticised for waiting for Rosecrans to attack. But his operations after October 6, when the launching of an offensive depended on the quick accumulation of supplies, raise a doubt. If there was a chance of a successful drive, Lee displayed a willingness to wait on the wagon trains that can be given no less a name than inertia. As a strategist, he showed himself facile, but in all that pertained to the commissariat, he seems to have been well-nigh supine at this time.

All this was behind Lee after October 20, and nothing was to be gained by remaining in the mountains. On October 30 he turned his horse's head eastward and left western Virginia—left it to the enemy. Failure to drive Rosecrans out had strengthened the Unionist and cowed the secessionists. On October 24 a majority voted to establish a separate state and West Virginia was lost to the Confederacy and to the Old Dominion.

On the afternoon of October 31, accompanied by Taylor, Lee reached the Confederate capital. He had been gone a little more than three months. He had suffered greatly in prestige, not only in the opinion of the fire-eaters perpetually preaching an offensive policy, but also in the eyes of the public. Cynics began to call him "Granny Lee" and affirmed that his reputation was based on an impressive presence and an historic name rather than on ability as a field commander. His first campaign might have been his last, but for the faith President Davis had in him. When Lee called on the President, after his return to Richmond there was nothing to indicate that his confidence in Lee had in the least been impaired. The political experience of the President gave him quick and ready understanding of Lee's difficulties with Wise and Floyd. His knowledge of war made him put full valuation, or more than full valuation, on the other obstacles Lee had encountered. The interview ended with the President as convinced as ever both of the high character and of the high ability of the man at whom the people were sneering.

CHAPTER VI

Lee Wins the Command

THE FIRST personal concern of General Lee on his return to Richmond was to visit his wife, whom he had not seen since he had left her at Arlington on April 22. Mrs. Lee had been brave in her separation from the home in which she had spent almost all her life, and after she had moved twice she had declared, greatly to her husband's amusement, that the enemy would have to take her, as she would shift her abode no more. She had changed her mind, however, and about September 15 had travelled to the Hot Springs. Lee had been anxious for her to reside for the winter with her daughters at some safe and quiet place in North Carolina or Georgia, but having a will of her own she had gone instead to Shirley, where she was when her husband reached Richmond. It was a delight to Lee to think that his long separation was to be ended in the pleasant atmosphere of his mother's first home, and on November 2 he prepared to join Mrs. Lee. Unfortunately, before he could get away darkness was almost upon him and he was forced to defer his journey. On Monday, November 4, he conferred at length with the new Secretary of War, the brilliant Judah P. Benjamin, who had succeeded the overworked and disillusioned L. Pope Walker. The next morning he had an appointment with the President, and before the 5th of November was over, news arrived that postponed to the uncertain future all hope of seeing his wife.

A large fleet of Federal warships and transports had been gathering in Hampton Roads in October, and on the 20th had sailed for an unknown destination. On November 1, Secretary Benjamin had received an intimation that the flotillas were bound for Port Royal Sound, South Carolina. Nervous reports from the Palmetto State now told of the arrival of the ships at that destination. Any offensive in Port Royal Sound was potentially most serious. The Confederate forces in that quarter were weak on land and almost helpless at sea. Manifestly, the situation would be a difficult one. President Davis for some time had felt that the Southern coast needed additional defenses, and he at once directed that it be organized as a single military department. By the same order, and to his complete surprise, Lee was named as commander there.

Lee doubtless would have preferred some other assignment, but he was delighted at the prospect of field duty. His experience in western Virginia had shown him the dangers of divided command and he overcame his reticence for once and asked the President what his position and authority would be at his new post. He was told *instanter* that he would go to South Carolina as a full general in the regular army of the Confederacy, the senior officer in the department, and with the entire support of the administration.

The announcement that Lee had been chosen to command on the threatened southeastern coast of the Confederacy was not received with general favor. "Granny" Lee was not the man, in the opinion of many, to conduct a vigorous campaign for the defense of Charleston and Savannah. The opposition to him was so strong that Davis deemed it necessary to advise Governor Francis W. Pickens of South Carolina, and the chief malcontent of the southeastern states, Governor Joseph E. Brown of Georgia, that Lee, in his opinion, was the best soldier available for the duty assigned him.

On the morning of November 6 Lee left for Charleston, where he arrived the next day. He hastened by special train to Coosawhatchie, the station nearest Port Royal Sound. When he arrived he learned that a heavy engagement at the entrance to the sound was in progress between the Federal fleet and the Southern forts, Walker and Beauregard. Excitement was fevered. Brigadier General R. S. Ripley had ridden down the river to ascertain the situation. Lee took horse as quickly as possible and hurried in the same direction.

During the evening he met Ripley. His news was bad: the Confederates at Fort Walker and Fort Beauregard had been overwhelmed during the day by the fire from the enemy's ships and would have to evacuate their island positions at once. It seemed, at the moment, another disaster.

Lee at once gave orders for the withdrawal of the garrisons and of their supports from the two islands on which the forts had been located. Then he went back to Coosawhatchie, established his headquarters, organized his staff, and proceeded to make his first hurried survey of a problem that the nature of the country and the scantiness of his resources rendered exceedingly complex.

From Georgetown as far south as the Saint John's River, a distance of fully 300 miles, the inland waterways cut off from the mainland a multitude of islands, some of them mere mudbanks, some of them the fertile plantations of wealthy planters. Near the northern end of the most vulnerable part of this coastline was Charleston, symbol of secession. Toward the southern end was rich Savannah. Between these two cities ran the Charleston and Savannah Railroad, 100 miles in length, crossing a number of rivers that could be ascended by light vessels to within a few miles of the railroad bridges. The Federals had complete control of the waterways, with heavy ships for the deeper channels and gunboats for the upper stretches of the rivers; the Confederates had only four converted steamers, armed with two guns each. Of land forces, Lee found not more than 6800 between the Savannah River and the defenses of Charleston. Around Savannah were about 5500, few of whom could be moved, lest Savannah be exposed. These troops were widely scattered. Some of them were equipped only in part and had scarcely any efficient field artillery.

What could Lee do? He determined on three courses of action. The first was to prepare the defenses of Fort Pulaski, of Savannah, and of Charleston for far more serious bombardment than they had been built to sustain. The second was to obstruct the waterways up which the Federals might send their ships. The third was to assemble the scattered Confederate forces at the most probable points of Federal advance toward the railroad. Orders were issued accordingly.

These three measures of immediate defense called for intense activity. Fortunately, the Federals showed no signs of capitalizing quickly their victory at Port Royal. There were, at the same time, some evidences of encouraging activity and co-operation on the Southern side. Brigadier General A. R. Lawton, commanding at Savannah, assured Lee of his gratification at his arrival and pledged support; a hurried visit to Savannah and to Fort Pulaski on November 10–11 showed Lee that Lawton meant what he said. A number of trained naval officers had been sent to the department and were promptly dispatched to Charleston, to Georgia, and to Florida, where they quickly performed admirable service in obstructing waterways. In addition, the *Fingal* came into Savannah on November 13 with a cargo of arms and munitions, from which Lee was authorized to take 4500 Enfield rifles for the use of such new troops as he could collect in Georgia and South Carolina.

As soon as the first defensive measures were under way, Lee determined to inspect the coast defenses. He went first to Charleston. In the harbor forts Lee found the best-trained artillerists in the department. They were capable of giving the Federal naval gunners shell for shell, but unfortunately, were so few in number and entrusted with so vital a defense that it was doubtful whether any of them could be transferred to other endangered points. Officers at Charleston were not in every instance so well-qualified as the enlisted personnel. The work of obstructing the nearby streams was not progressing rapidly enough. Showing none of the hesitancy that had marked his dealings with sensitive leaders in western Virginia, Lee shifted a few men of doubtful capacity or questionable habits, placed Captain D. N. Ingraham of the navy in general charge of the armament of the batteries, and determined as soon as practicable to name General Ripley to command the Charleston district.

General Lee held a long conference on the night of November 15 with Governor Pickens. Lee wanted five additional regiments of South Carolina troops mustered into Confederate service. The question to be decided was how the troops were to be armed and for what term they were to be enlisted. Pickens could arm only a part, and the War Department refused to issue rifles to any that did not enlist, as units, for the duration of the war. Lee and Pickens agreed on a compromise: South Carolina was to arm two regiments, or the equivalent, of men willing to serve until peace was declared, and Lee was to issue 2500 of the Enfields recently received through the blockade on the *Fingal* to South Carolina commands who pledged a similar period of enlistment. On November 16 Lee returned to Coosawhatchie. He waited there only long enough to send Ripley to Charleston and to issue a few necessary instructions. Then he hurried to Savannah and proceeded thence on a two-day inspection of the Brunswick district and the northern part of the east coast of Florida.

The examination of these scattered defenses led to the most important decision of Lee's entire stay in the department. He determined on three related steps: first, to withdraw all the guns and garrisons from the minor, outlying positions; second, to strengthen still further and, if possible, to hold the entrance to Cumberland Sound, the approaches to Brunswick, Fort Pulaski, Savannah, and Charleston; and third, to construct in front of Savannah and the lower end of the Charleston and Savannah Railroad a deep interior line, so drawn that he could concentrate and hold it with the troops at his disposal, while compelling the enemy to fight where the heaviest guns of the warships could not be used.

The decision to organize the defense by these successive steps was made about November 19 and was the basis of all that Lee did during the remainder of his service on the southeastern coast. Every day there were new vexations, new developments, new complications, but every day there was effort to speed up the work on the principal forts and obstructions, to further the preparation of the inner line, and to procure and train more troops. It was a gruelling pace. One day he covered 115 miles, 35 of them on Greenbrier, a young gray horse he had seen in Western Virginia and had purchased when his owner's command had joined Lee in Carolina. The strength and endurance of this fine animal won him the reputation of being a "fine traveller" and ere long his old name was dropped and he became thenceforward simply Traveller.

Following a futile demonstration by the Federals in the vicinity of Garden's Corner, Lee went to Charleston again on December 11. For nearly a week he studied the city's defenses. He placed new obstructions in the rivers and changed batteries without removing guns from the principal forts, which he insisted on keeping at full armament in view of the possibility that the enemy contemplated an attack. Before he had completed this work there came a letter from the adjutant general of the state placing all the troops of the state at his disposal. This was a triumph of diplomacy and honest effort. Lee had already received 1400 reinforcements from other states, and soon after he returned to Coosawhatchie on December 17 he had notice from Richmond that six regiments of infantry, the Phillips Legion, and two batteries of field artillery were moving to his support.

This greatly improved his prospects, though he was still embarrassed by the shortage of artillery and by the rival purchasing of state and Confederate troops in the same territory. Numerical superiority in land forces was shifting, for once, to the Confederate side; but on the rivers and deep estuaries, heavy guns were needed to combat the Federal fleet.

Lee was engaged in correspondence on this subject and was pushing hard for the completion of the inner line when he received announcement on December 20 of an event that was materially to modify his strategic plan. Federal warships had convoyed to Charleston more than a dozen old ships loaded with stone and had sunk these in the main ship-channel. Fortunately for the port of Charleston, the sinking of the "stone fleet," as it was called, closed only one of the three ship-channels. It served an almost useful purpose in that it indicated to the Confederates that the enemy apparently wished to "bottle up" Charleston and had no immediate intention of attacking there. Lee, however, did not consider that the action of the enemy lessened the necessity of making Charleston as strong as possible. At the same time, he felt that Ripley would now have opportunity of employing some of his force to protect nearby islands and to break up raids. In a larger strategic view, he made ready to meet an attack farther south. Increasingly he concentrated his forces and centred his defensive measures on the Savannah sector.

In the midst of these preparations, Lee came to the first Christmas of the war. After distributing a few gifts to the children of his officers and to his servants, he devoted the greater part of the day to writing letters to the members of his family. Almost before these Christmas letters had reached their Virginia destination, the decisive year of Lee's life had opened. Before 1862 ended, the general who had never fought a battle was to have four bloody campaigns to his credit, and the people were acclaiming him the savior of the South. There was little at Lee's Carolina headquarters to suggest such an early reversal of fortune, but there was much to indicate that a bitter test awaited the Confederacy.

Lee pressed vigorously for the completion of the inner line, the obstruction of the rivers, and the strengthening of the principal forts. At the beginning of the second week in January, he went to Savannah and thence on a tour of the east coast of Florida, stopping at Cumberland Island, where he visited the grave of his father for the first time. He found much discontent in Florida. "Our defences are growing stronger, but progress slowly," he wrote Custis several days after his return to Coosawhatchie on January 16.

A week later Lee was called to Charleston by news that another Federal fleet had appeared off the harbor. On the 25th and 26th he witnessed the sinking of a second "stone fleet" consisting of twelve old merchantmen. This time it was the Maffitt channel the enemy sought to obstruct. Simultaneously the Federals began to clear the obstructions from Wall's Cut on the waterway linking Port Royal Sound to the Savannah River. These moves fully convinced Lee that the enemy was preparing for operations in the vicinity of Savannah. He went to Savannah on the evening of January 28, and by February 3 he had transferred his headquarters there. He found an admiring welcome at the homes of the Mackays and in a circle of cultivated, sympathizing friends; but he also found that work which should have been finished by this time had "lagged terribly." Fort Pulaski had been victualled for a siege the day Lee had left Coosawhatchie; he followed this with changes in the bearing of some of its guns and with calls on the War Department for additional heavy ordnance; he had to arrange to withdraw all cannon from below the fort; facing attempted profiteering in iron, he was quick to take what the government required at the old price; plans had to be made to induce re-enlistment for the war by Georgia troops; pourparlers had to be opened with Governor Joseph E. Brown for the destruction of Brunswick, a then deserted resort which Lee did not want the enemy to occupy; an effort had to be made to get trained artillerists from Charleston in case Ripley thought they could be transferred.

While Lee was struggling with inertia, incompetence, and a multitude of troublesome duties, the Confederate cause elsewhere had suffered two disasters. On February 6, Fort Henry, on the lower Tennessee River, was captured by a Federal army under a general who then came prominently into the news for the first time, Ulysses S. Grant. A week later, the Union forces, supported by a flotilla of gunboats, invested Fort Donelson, Tenn., and on the 15th, after two days' hard fighting, forced 15,000 Confederates to surrender. The disaster shook the hold of General Albert Sidney Johnston on Tennessee. On February 8, General Wise, with 3000 men, was attacked at Roanoke Island, N. C., and was driven from the island with the loss or capture of two-thirds of his little command.

The immediate result on Lee's command of the disasters in Tennessee and in North Carolina was a double call from the War Department— to withdraw all units from the islands to the mainland for a more concentrated defense and to abandon Florida, except for the line of the Apalachicola River, and to send the troops from that state to Albert Sidney Johnston. The loss of force amounted to nearly 4000 men, and the change in the situation meant that Lee could expect no further reinforcements.

Much remained to be done on the Savannah sector, where it was now apparent the enemy was making preparations to deliver his long-delayed offensive. Progress had been substantial but the inner line took form slowly. Anxiety was great. On March 2 Lee confided to one of his daughters: "I have been doing all I can with our small means and slow workmen to defend the cities and coast here. Against ordinary numbers we are pretty strong, but against the hosts our enemies seem able to bring everywhere, there is no calculating. But if our men will stand to their work, we shall give them trouble and damage them yet."

On the evening after he wrote this letter, there was handed to Lee a telegram that read as follows:

If circumstances will, in your judgment, warrant your leaving, I wish to see you here with the least delay.

JEFFERSON DAVIS.

Lee knew no reason for this unexpected summons, but he must have felt it meant his final separation from the coastal command, for he promptly replied that he would leave on the morning of March 4, and began immediately to make disposition of his staff officers. His chief concern was for the Savannah defenses, and he gave minute instructions to Lawton concerning the places that remained to be fortified and the measures that should be taken to halt the further progress of the enemy up the Savannah River. Lee disposed of these details so quickly that he was able to start on the evening of the 3d instead of on the 4th.

His mission on the southeastern coast was ended. He had done his work thoroughly. He was fortunate, to be sure, in having as his adversary General Thomas W. Sherman, a man cautious and indecisive. Lee nevertheless had prevented the development of an offensive that had threatened serious damage. Without the loss of a single soldier from the fire of the enemy, he had held the railroad, and had put so many difficulties in the way that the Federals had nowhere moved beyond the cover of their warships.

Lee departed with the curious distinction of having been ten months in a command without having fought a single battle. It was a period of preparation for action, rather than of action itself, but it was preparation of the most valuable sort. His touch had been more nearly sure. He had not conquered his excessive amiability, as time was to prove, but he had not let it ruin him as a commander. Much was learned, also, while on the coast, about handling larger bodies of men. He was lucky, moreover, in having an opportunity of studying how a railroad could be utilized for the movement of troops and how it could be defended. He had learned something of new transportation methods during April–July, 1861; but the responsibility was entirely his in South Carolina and Georgia. It was a useful lesson, well learned, and it convinced him that the proper defense of a railway lay in guarding strategic bridges and crossings and in concentrating force where it could be moved rapidly to endangered points. Finally, this command confirmed Lee's faith in the indispensability of earthworks. Such works had been little used in America before that time and were despised by the Confederate volunteers as representing labor no white man should do and cover behind which no Southerner should take refuge. Lee had believed in digging dirt and though his men complained all along the coast, he persisted in giving them the protection of field fortification. He could hardly have had better training for the task that awaited him at the Confederate capital to which he now returned.

During the terrible months Lee had been in western Virginia, South Carolina and in Georgia, he had heard little of the confidential news that came to the President and to the War Department. Back at the storm-centre of the Southern struggle, he soon learned the dark inwardness of a situation that had changed for the worse since he had left in November.

Disaster was in the air. The defeats at Fort Henry and Fort Donelson had led the Confederates under Albert Sidney Johnston to evacuate most of Kentucky and part of western Tennessee. The newspapers contained the gloomy intelligence that Fort Columbus, the advanced Confederate position on the Mississippi, had been abandoned by Leonidas Polk. Nowhere, since a small Federal column had been destroyed at Ball's Bluff on the Potomac, October 22, had there been a substantial Confederate success on land to relieve the gathering gloom. Southern commissioners in Europe had not been received at a single court. "Foreign intervention" seemed much more remote than immediately after the victory at Manassas.

The worst was not known, even to Congress. The Confederacy's supply of powder was nearly exhausted. Arsenals were almost bare. Expected arms from across the Atlantic were being delayed by a blockade that was demonstrating the decisive influence of sea-power. The army might soon be without the means to fight. Hope of relieving the blockade was raised for a day when the frigate *Merrimac*, cut down to the water's edge and covered with railroad iron, awkwardly steamed forth from Norfolk on March 8 as the Confederate ram *Virginia* and destroyed the *Congress* and the *Cumberland*, but she was challenged the next day by an ironclad as curious as herself, the *Monitor*.

The faith of the public had fallen with misfortunes. Gone was the old boastfulness. Silent were the platform-patriots who had predicted defeat of the United States within ninety days. The prophets had been confounded, the weak were despairing, the courageous were anxious. In the passion of 1861, hotheads had relied on "Southern valor" and

had refused to concede that 23,000,000 people had any advantage over
an opposing 9,000,000; but now that Northern ports were receiving
hundreds of tons of equipment from Europe, and Northern factories
were being made ready to supply every want of any force that might
be called into the field, Confederates no longer scoffed when indiscreet
Northern newspapers and occasional Southern sympathizers who made
their way through the lines told disquieting stories of the might and
magnitude of the host that McClellan had brought together since he
had taken command in Washington.

Not only were the Confederates depressed and outnumbered but
they were preparing to abandon the lines that Joseph E. Johnston had
held, close to Washington, since the victory of Manassas eight months
before. That news was the most alarming of all the secrets that Lee
heard in the electric atmosphere of the President's office.

Johnston's withdrawal had been agreed upon at a conference between
himself and Davis February 20. The President had accepted the view
that the army could not successfully resist a heavy offensive by superior
forces that could use their sea-power to land troops in rear of Johnston's
right flank on the Potomac, just north of Fredericksburg, which Johnston believed they were preparing to do. Yet no sooner had the withdrawal been sanctioned than the nervous Davis and the irascible
Johnston disagreed as to the time it should begin and the necessity of
leaving stores behind. Davis admonished, but Johnston kept his own
counsel, determined to withdraw when and whither his judgment
dictated.

A week and more Lee spent in study of the general situation, without definite assignment of duty. On March 13 there were important
developments. Davis received official information that Johnston had
evacuated the Manassas line on March 8-9, had retreated twenty-five
miles southward and had halted his army on either side of the north
fork of the Rappahannock River. The same day a Union council of
war at McClellan's headquarters decided on the line of advance for the
vast Army of the Potomac that was now equipped to the last tent-peg.
And Lee received an impossible assignment to duty.

Behind it lay conflict between the President and Congress. The dissatisfaction of that body had been directed first to a campaign against
the Secretary of War, who had been assailed for failure to send munitions to General Wise at Roanoke Island, N. C. Benjamin had the most
valid of excuses—that there were no munitions to send—but both he
and the President deemed it better to accept unmerited censure than to

expose weakness. The attack on Benjamin was not the only grievance of
Congress. Mr. Davis's disposition to direct military operations had provoked much criticism. Reasoning that the first need was a new Secretary of War, and that the President had confidence in Lee, Congress
passed an act providing that, if a general of the army were appointed
Secretary of War, he would not lose his rank. When the President
signed the measure it was assumed that Lee would be named, but the
President concluded that a soldier would not make a good secretary
and made no appointment. Instead, he asked in effect that Congress
provide him with two secretaries, one civil and one military, and that
legislation creating the post of commanding general be enacted, so
that the appointee could act, in a sense, as military or technical head
of the War Department. Congress acquiesced, but in drafting a new
bill the President's enemies seem to have had equal hand with his
friends. The measure provided for a commanding general, directed the
President to nominate such an officer to the Senate, and authorized the
officer so named to take personal command of any army in the field at
any time. Again it was expected that Davis would name Lee, but
the President saw in the move an invasion of his constitutional rights
as commander-in-chief of the army and navy. On March 10 the bill
came to him. Within three days his political experience suggested a
means of maintaining his rights as commander-in-chief and of accomplishing the desired object. He vetoed the measure and assigned Lee
"to duty at the seat of government," charged "under the direction of
the President with the conduct of military operations in the armies of
the Confederacy." Congress sustained his veto and re-enacted that part
of the original bill providing a staff for the general so designated to
duty. Davis won a tactical victory and followed it by reorganizing his
Cabinet, naming Benjamin as Secretary of State and placing the war
office under George W. Randolph. Lee's new position was difficult and
anomalous. Lee himself said: "It will give me great pleasure to do anything I can to relieve [the President] and serve the country, but I cannot see either advantage or pleasure in my duties. But I will not complain, but do the best I can."

Once appointed, Lee was not given an hour to organize his staff or
to add to such understanding of the situation as he had been able to get
from the tangled records between his arrival in Richmond and his
assumption of command March 14. The duties were vexing and varied
and were never to be finished. He could not know when the President
would call him to a long, futile conference, or what new problem from

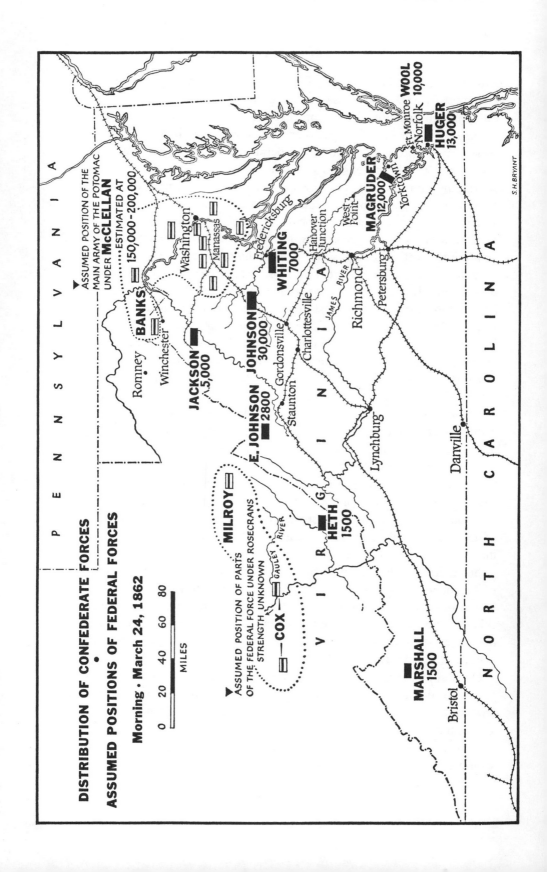

DISTRIBUTION OF CONFEDERATE FORCES
•
ASSUMED POSITIONS OF FEDERAL FORCES

Morning • March 24, 1862

0   20   40   60   80
MILES

PENNSYLVANIA

VIRGINIA

NORTH CAROLINA

▼ ASSUMED POSITION OF THE
MAIN ARMY OF THE POTOMAC
UNDER McCLELLAN
ESTIMATED AT
150,000–200,000

▼ ASSUMED POSITION OF PARTS
OF THE FEDERAL FORCE UNDER ROSECRANS
STRENGTH UNKNOWN

COX

MILROY

BANKS

Romney
Winchester

JACKSON
5,000

E. JOHNSON
2800

Staunton

HETH
1500

MARSHALL
1500

Bristol

Washington
Manassas

JOHNSON
30,000

Gordonsville

Charlottesville

Lynchburg

Danville

Fredericksburg

WHITING
7000

Hanover
Junction

Richmond

Petersburg

JAMES RIVER

West
Point

MAGRUDER
12,000

Yorktown

Ft. Monroe
Norfolk

WOOL
10,000

HUGER
13,000

GAULEY RIVER

S.H.BRYANT

an unfamiliar field would plead for instant answer. Some dispositions were to be left completely to him by the President. Other matters Mr. Davis was to handle in person or was to take from him, half-completed. Within less than three months he was to be called upon to pass on operations in every Southern state. Broadly speaking, Davis entrusted to him the minor, vexatious matters of detail and counselling of commanders in charge of the smaller armies. On the larger issues the President usually consulted him and was often guided by his advice, but in no instance was Lee given a free hand to initiate and direct to full completion any plan of magnitude. He had to work by suggestion rather than by command. In his whole career there was not a period of more thankless service, but there were few, if any, during which he contributed more to sustain the Confederate cause.

It had been his singular ill-fortune to assume each of his previous Confederate commands in an atmosphere of disaster. Now almost the first dispatch that reached his desk announced that a strong Federal expedition had descended from Roanoke Island on the important North Carolina town of New Berne, had swept past the feeble Confederate lines that protected it, and had routed the defending forces of 4000 men. The possibilities were so serious and the available Confederate forces so small that the President authorized Lee to detach a few regiments from Huger's force at Norfolk and two brigades of infantry, with two companies of artillery, from Joe Johnston's army, and to dispatch them to North Carolina.

This detachment weakened by more than 10 per cent the strength of the principal Confederate army in Virginia and carried still further a deplorable if unescapable policy of scattering the troops. "Our enemies are pressing us everywhere," Lee recorded at the time, "and our army is in the fermentation of organization. I pray that the great God may aid us, and am endeavoring by every means in my power to bring out the troops and hasten them to their destination."

All agreed that the enemy would assume the offensive speedily, for his numbers were vastly superior and his equipment was complete. At Johnston's headquarters the belief was that Richmond would be the immediate objective by one of four routes, but there was no agreement as to which of the four would be adopted. Johnston withdrew a few miles southward on the 18th and put the Rapidan as well as the Rappahannock in front of him, but he was entirely in the dark as to the enemy's movements. Lee was no better informed. He suspected that an attempt might be made on the Peninsula but he did not believe a real offensive could be launched until the roads were firmer.

On March 24 there came a sensational telegram from General Huger at Norfolk: more than twenty steamers had begun to disembark troops at Old Point. A little later, General Magruder notified the Secretary of War that he believed the force confronting him had risen to 35,000. Magruder did not suggest that the troops had come from McClellan's army, nor could Lee be sure, but by the next morning the information in hand rendered it probable that the new arrivals belonged to the Army of the Potomac. If this were true, Lee had to consider three possibilities:

1. McClellan might have detached the troops to co-operate with Burnside in North Carolina.

2. The new troops might be designed to join with the 10,000 already at Fort Monroe in an attack on Norfolk or up the Peninsula, while McClellan advanced on Richmond from the north.

3. The reinforcements at Old Point might be the advanced guard of McClellan's whole army which was preparing to march up the Peninsula.

In dealing with these possible movements it was not enough to draw a line and defend it. Norfolk could readily be cut off, as Lee had pointed out during the mobilization of Virginia. The Peninsula afforded at least three good defensive fronts, drawn from river to river, that could be held by an alert force against odds, provided the James and the York were not opened by the enemy. But if the attacking Federals used their sea-power wisely and passed the batteries on either of these streams, they could land in rear of the Confederates. This condition had led Lee in April, 1861, to put the obstruction and defense of the rivers first in his programme and it was an important factor in his strategy now. Time was of even greater importance. The army must not be thrown into a campaign, if this could be prevented, until the reorganization had been completed.

Lee developed a plan that is a most interesting example of provisional reconcentration to meet an undeveloped offensive. Perhaps the most remarkable thing about this plan is that it was devised and put in process of execution within thirty-six hours after Lee received news of the landing at Old Point. The course he chose was this:

1. Holmes's force in North Carolina was to be strengthened, so as to occupy Burnside, if possible, and to prevent his advance into North Carolina or his co-operation in any operations against Norfolk.

2. Both Huger and Magruder were notified to prepare their forces so that Huger could help Magruder if the attack were on the Peninsula, and Magruder could assist Huger if Norfolk proved to be the Federal objective.

3. The ironclad *Virginia* could cover the mouth of the James River and prevent Federal interference with troop-movements by Magruder or Huger of Confederate forces across that stream, but she was then in drydock at Norfolk. Pending her return to service, Lee undertook the improvement of the water-batteries on the James, accumulated transportation on the river, and selected a point above the probable reach of Federal gunboats, where the infantry could cross.

4. The scanty available reserves—a couple of regiments of infantry and some squadrons of cavalry then around Richmond—were at once ordered to Magruder.

5. Magruder was urged to stand on the first defensive line on the lower Peninsula and was instructed not to evacuate it voluntarily unless the Federals were able to turn it by carrying their gunboats up the York or the James.

6. In case the lines on the lower Peninsula should be turned, Magruder was directed to prepare for a withdrawal to the third defensive line, that of the Chickahominy. In doing this, Magruder was to destroy the river landings. He was, moreover, to use his artillery to prevent the passage of the enemy high up the James or up the Pamunkey.

7. The enemy must be kept as far down the Peninsula as possible. It might not be possible to do this with the force Magruder had. Lee accordingly decided on this major movement: he would withdraw the greater part of Johnston's army from the Rapidan, would move it quickly to the lower Peninsula, would attack the Federals there, and then, if need be, would return Johnston's troops to their old position. Lee believed the situation in northern Virginia would make this possible, without excessive risk of losing Richmond, because he reasoned that so large a part of McClellan's army had already been transferred that McClellan would not quickly advance on Richmond from the north with the forces left him.

This bold plan displayed the facility that Lee always exhibited in strategy, and it embodied all that he had learned in South Carolina and in making dispositions for First Manassas. Execution, however, was not so easy as conception. Obstacles were encountered in such numbers that the plan had to be revised almost as soon as it was formulated. Magruder held a council of war which decided that unless 10,000 reinforcements could be at once dispatched to that front, Yorktown should be evacuated. Lee reassured him and urged him to stand where he was as long as possible. Magruder acquiesced, and that tangle was straightened out. It was otherwise with Johnston. He was a sworn devotee of concentration and he argued that all or none of his army should be transferred to the Peninsula. Soon he reported that Jackson was threatened by superior forces and that the enemy showed activity on his own front. Several days' exchange of correspondence with Johnston convinced Lee that his old friend would not willingly fall in with his plan. Then Lee displayed a quality of mind that was to become one of his greatest assets as a commander. It was this: he would make the best, for the time, of what he could not correct, but he would hold to what he believed sound strategy and would look to time and circumstance for an opportunity of executing his plan. If Johnston would not consent to the dispatch of enough troops at one time to strengthen Magruder, Lee would take what Johnston would give him immediately and then would get more as soon as he could. Such patient persistence was to become the measure of the man in many a difficult hour.

In place of a general movement he effected a series of small transfers to the Peninsula. Johnston was willing, at the outset, to detach only two brigades. One of these was sent to the Peninsula; the other to North Carolina. As Magruder needed much more, Lee ordered one of Huger's brigades to be ready to cross the James and sent two Alabama regiments to Yorktown. He even dispatched 1000 unarmed men to Magruder, in the hope that Magruder could give them, if necessary, the guns of soldiers then in hospitals. Not even old flint-lock muskets could be supplied from Richmond, and preparations were being made to manufacture and issue pikes. To this desperate plight had the battling Confederacy been brought!

During the march of these troops to Magruder's support, the Federals made no demonstration against his lines. This aroused Lee's suspicions and led him to apprehend that the real objective might be Norfolk. He accordingly began to strengthen Huger's little army and called for two of Johnston's brigades, to be employed on the Peninsula, at Norfolk, or in North Carolina as the situation might demand.

It seemed as likely on April 4 that the main offensive would be in northern Virginia as on the Peninsula. That day, however, Lee received news through Stuart that a flotilla of transports was under way down the Potomac. Simultaneously, word came from Magruder that heavy columns of Federals were moving in his direction as if to give battle. Lee concluded immediately that the two reports were related and that McClellan was moving more of his men to the Peninsula; but as Lee still was uncertain how large a part of the Army of the Potomac remained in Johnston's front, he decided for the time being not to attempt to send the remainder of Johnston's forces to Magruder's support. He continued, however, to order detachments until, by April 4, he had called a total of three divisions from the line of the Rapidan-Rappahannock. It was done so quietly and so gradually that few protests were made.

Reinforcements to Magruder gave that officer the prospect of a force of 31,500 by April 11. This piecemeal reconcentration was a matter of great delicacy. Success depended on maintaining the morale both of Johnston and of Magruder, while interpreting accurately available information of the enemy's movements. If Lee underestimated the strength or the initiative of the Federals either in northern Virginia or on the Peninsula, Johnston or Magruder might be overwhelmed. A simultaneous attack on both, in such numbers as the Federals were known to have in the state, would inevitably be disastrous.

For while Lee was in conference with Davis, hour after hour, calculating the risks in Virginia, the rival armies of Grant and of Albert Sidney Johnston were grappling on April 6–7 at Shiloh, near the Tennessee-Mississippi boundary. The Confederate press claimed a victory but the losses were heavy and Johnston was killed. Island No. 10, a Confederate stronghold on the Mississippi, was captured on April 8, with 7000 men. The bold bid of the South for the control of the upper Mississippi had been rejected by the fates. There was imminent danger that the Confederacy would be split in twain and that the Federals would proceed to break up the riven halves.

The troops sent southward from the Rapidan moved steadily to the Peninsula, where the enemy was placing batteries and bringing up heavy artillery but showed as yet no disposition to assault. No general advance in northern Virginia was reported. The threat against Jackson had not materialized. By April 9 Magruder was satisfied that the greater part of the Army of the Potomac was in his front.

On April 9, doubtless with Lee's full approval, the President made the final move in the reconcentration, ordered Johnston to report in Richmond, and directed that his two strongest divisions, Longstreet's and G. W. Smith's, be set in motion for the capital. Ewell's division of some 7000 or 8000 men was left on the Rappahannock to observe the enemy and to co-operate with Jackson, whose division of 5000 was slowly increasing in numbers. One brigade of Smith's command was left temporarily at Fredericksburg. By this time it was understood from Northern newspapers that the Federals remaining in northern Virginia were under Major General Irvin McDowell.

When Joe Johnston arrived in Richmond, his command was enlarged to include Norfolk and the Peninsula, and he was directed to visit that part of the front to see his problem at first hand. On April 13 he left. The next morning Lee received a summons to come to the President's office. When he entered, he learned that Johnston had returned unexpectedly and had made a disheartening report. The President was so much concerned that he had called a council of war, to which he had summoned Lee, Johnston, Secretary Randolph, and Major General Longstreet and Gustavus Smith, the two last-named at Johnston's instance. Johnston pronounced the situation at Yorktown an impossible one. The line, he said, was entirely too long for the force defending it. Magruder's men were beginning to show the effects of strain. Inundations that had been prepared along the Warwick River might hold off McClellan on the land side but they would render an offensive by the Confederates impossible. The superior Union artillery would soon batter down the Southern batteries covering York River, and when that happened McClellan's gunboats and transports could pass up the stream and turn the Confederate position. The most that could be done on the lower Peninsula would be to delay McClellan temporarily. It would be better, Johnston went on, to discard the plans under which they were operating, to abandon Norfolk and the Peninsula, to concentrate in front of Richmond all the troops in Virginia, the Carolinas, and Georgia, and to strike McClellan at a distance from his base. As a less desirable alternative, he proposed that Magruder stand siege in Richmond while the other Confederate forces carried the war into the enemy's country.

The Secretary of War promptly opposed this change of plan because it would necessarily involve the evacuation of Norfolk, where the

Virginia was based and where other ships were under construction. To lose Norfolk was to give up all hope of creating a navy to cope with the Federal sea-power.

Lee was then asked to express his opinion. An early withdrawal, to his mind, would bring the armies dangerously close to the nerve-centre of the Confederacy and would complicate the reorganization then in progress. It would likewise make heavy fighting inevitable before the full armed strength of the South was in the field. No large reinforcement could be expected immediately. Stripping the South Atlantic coast of men might involve the fall of Savannah and of Charleston. Lee had faith in the line on the lower Peninsula. He believed that invaluable time could be gained by delaying McClellan there as long as possible.

Lee and Randolph argued against Johnston and Smith, with Longstreet saying little and Davis reserving judgment. The debate kept up till 1 o'clock the next morning. Then Davis declared himself in favor of defending the lower Peninsula. It was a sound decision. Had Johnston's plan been adopted, the Confederacy could hardly have survived long.

Davis's decision in overruling Johnston had a direct effect on the operations of the next six weeks. Johnston made no protest at the time and seemingly acquiesced in the orders of the commander-in-chief, but he prepared to go to the Yorktown front in the conviction that he would soon fall back on Richmond and would leave the President no alternative to that of bringing all possible forces for a battle near the capital.

On April 17, Johnston assumed his new command. Operations on the Peninsula and the conduct of affairs at Norfolk were thereafter, until May 31, entirely under Johnston's direction. Lee's part in the reconcentration was done. The military achievement of Lee in effecting it speaks for itself. His had been the guiding hand in shaping a policy that had held the Yorktown line with trifling losses until Magruder's 11,000 were in a fair way of being raised to 53,000 without any advance by the enemy south of the Rapidan River. He had benefited by the extreme caution of his opponent. How much of that caution was due to the temperament of McClellan, and how much was dictated by sound dispositions that might have been mismanaged by a Confederate commander less capable than Lee, is a question that cannot be answered.

Ever since the early winter, Lee had been looking forward with the deepest concern to March and April, when the men who had clamored to join the colors in the first fervor of secession would come to the end of their twelve months' enlistment. Many, of course, would continue in service, but a sufficient number would leave the army to reduce its strength most dangerously. He had seen no way of meeting this condition except by conscripting the man-power of the South, and as early as December 26, 1861 he had written Governor Letcher advocating a general draft in Virginia of all soldiers who did not re-enlist. President Davis had advocated a like policy for the entire Confederacy, but he had encountered the opposition of extreme states-rights politicians and had faced the inertia born of the belief that European countries would intervene to stop the war before another campaign opened. Not until December 11, 1861, had legislative action been taken, and then the law had been fashioned to please rather than to strengthen the army. A worse law could hardly have been imposed on the South by the enemy. Its interpretation was confusing, its effect was demoralizing, and it involved nothing less than a reconstruction of the entire land forces of the Confederacy in the face of the enemy.

This mischievous measure had been enacted before Lee had returned to Virginia from the South Atlantic coast and its evil consequence·· were only too apparent when he assumed nominal control of military operations. Seeing no way of preventing disorganization of the army except by conscription, Lee made an opportunity, even during the crisis that followed the landing at Old Point to review the subject fully with the new lawyer-member of his staff, Major Charles Marshall of Baltimore. Marshall was directed to draw up a bill providing for the conscription of all white males between eighteen and forty-five years of age. The finished paper Lee took to the President, who approved its principles and had it put into shape by Mr. Benjamin. Introduced in Congress, the bill was amended and mangled. Provision was made for the election of officers in re-enlisted commands, and other useless paraphernalia of the bounty and furlough act were loaded on it. The upper age-limit was reduced from forty-five to thirty-five years, and a bill allowing liberal exemption was soon adopted. The press had applause for the object of the bill and sharp words on its weaknesses. In the army, those who had intended not to re-enlist charged bad faith on the part of the government, but those who were determined to carry on the war to ruin or independence rejoiced that those who had stayed at home were at last to smell gunpowder. In the well-disciplined commands, men who went home at the expiration of their twelve months and returned as conscripts soon settled down to army routine. The election of new officers resulted in the defeat of many good soldiers and in the choice of "good fellows" in their places, but on the whole, the elections wrought less evil than could reasonably have been expected. For his part Lee realized the danger involved in reorganizing the army to the accompaniment of Federal bullets, but he read in the law a promise that recruits would ere long fill the regiments, and for that promise he must have been grateful. It probably never occurred to him that chief credit for the conscript act was his own.

The enactment of the conscript law and the assumption by Johnston of command on the Peninsula turned Lee's labors into other channels. Affairs on all the fronts were tangled and on some were desperate. Lee was called upon by the President to advise regarding the movements of the army in northern Mississippi. In East Tennessee, a small force under General Kirby Smith was in need of equipment and reinforcement, and the task of helping it was assigned to him. The regiments in western and southwestern Virginia were threatened by superior Federal forces; unable to send more men, he could only urge a slow withdrawal and preparation for defense. To him was given also the difficult rôle of diplomatist in dealing with Governor Brown of Georgia; on his shoulders fell part of the burden of apportioning such arms as reached the Confederacy from abroad; on occasion he helped in the work of the commissary and quartermaster-general. From West Florida and Alabama, from the trans-Mississippi, then and thereafter, came calls for reinforcements and appeals for instruction. In dealing with these distant operations, Lee laid down the principle that where he did not know the "particular necessities" of a local situation he could only make general suggestions and would not send "definite instructions."

His chief attention, after April 17, he gave to operations in northern Virginia and in the Shenandoah Valley. When Johnston had left the Rapidan, he had directed Jackson and Ewell to communicate with him through the adjutant general's office. The President evidently reasoned that Johnston would be engrossed in operations on the Peninsula and that the campaign north and northwest of Richmond could be managed more satisfactorily from the capital than from Johnston's headquarters. No formal orders were issued and the nominal command of Johnston over Ewell and Jackson was not reduced, but dispatches from them were referred to Lee, evidently with instructions to supervise the movements of these two officers. It was a most embarrassing arrangement. Johnston was excessively sensitive on all that touched his authority. Lee had to defer to the chief executive, as always, while avoiding offense to Johnston. His work, in short, had to be one of tactful substitution, now for Davis, now for Johnston.

It was pressing work, too. The strength of the Federals in northern Virginia was still unknown but was assumed to be great. On April 21 this army, or a large part of it, was believed to be debarking at Aquia Creek, north of Fredericksburg. Its advanced guard, estimated at 5000, had reached the Rappahannock opposite that city. In its front was only Field's brigade, about 2500 men.

Forty-seven miles west, at Gordonsville, lay the greater part of Ewell's division, now 8500 strong. This force was the mobile reserve designed to be moved as required. Twenty-five miles northeast of Staunton, Jackson had 6000 men, in the face of General N. P. Banks, whose strength was thought to be much in excess of Jackson's.

On April 21 the Federals had the greatest opportunity the war in Virginia was to offer them until the late winter of 1864–65. Correspondingly, the Confederate position was one of acutest danger. The odds against the troops north, west, and northwest of Richmond were even greater than the Confederates supposed—65,000 to 24,000. If Banks and Frémont occupied Jackson and Ewell, then a sudden thrust across the Rappahannock would overwhelm Field's little command. Richmond would be only sixty miles to the southward, less than five easy marches, and McDowell would be on Johnston's line of communications before that officer could return to Richmond. A quick attack by McClellan might mean the destruction of Johnston ere he could reach the defenses of the capital. Even if the Federal armies were not capable of launching four offensives simultaneously, it seemed almost certain that McClellan and McDowell could unite in front of Richmond. They could invest the city from the north, the east, and the south and either reduce it with their superior artillery or force the immediate retreat of Johnston to North Carolina. The least result of vigorous, joint action by the Federals would be that they would soon occupy the whole of Virginia. The downfall of the Confederacy by midsummer was a distinct possibility.

Johnston and Lee were both alive to this danger, but they took fundamentally different views of the best method to meet it. Johnston continued to urge that concentration be met with concentration—that McClellan and McDowell be allowed to advance to a great distance from their bases and then be attacked by all the Confederate forces from the Rapidan to the Savannah. Lee's strategy was to occupy the Federals on the Peninsula and to undertake an offensive-defensive in northern Virginia. Lee's was the bolder policy, but in a long view it was the more prudent course. Lee never willingly accepted investment in a fixed position. When a siege was threatened, his impulse was to avoid it by a counter-stroke. If a siege was inevitable or the enemy was concentrated in a single army, then, of course, Lee was as insistent as Johnston could have been on the fullest possible concentration.

Lee's fundamental problem was to prevent the reinforcement of McClellan from any quarter. Immediately the point of danger was Fredericksburg, where McDowell might establish a base for an advance to McClellan's flank. The city was so feebly defended that Field's little brigade could not retard, much less halt, a Federal offensive. The Fredericksburg line had to be strengthened. Lee adopted the expedient of calling for small forces from several quarters, on the theory that he would not take enough men from any army to destroy its powers of resistance. Like a hard-pressed debtor, he had to borrow where he could to meet his most pressing obligations, trusting that, if his new creditors became troublesome, the future would bring the means with which to repay them. In this way the force at Fredericksburg would be raised to 13,000 men by April 28, or about that time.

Thirteen thousand troops on the Rappahannock manifestly could put up a more formidable resistance than 2500 could, but they could not prevent an advance by such an army as McDowell was rightly assumed to command. Something more must be done. On April 21 Lee wrote one of the most historic of all his military dispatches. It was addressed to Jackson. In it, Lee outlined the situation and suggested three possibilities. First, if Jackson felt that he could drive Banks down the valley by calling up Ewell's division, he was advised to do so. If Banks was too strong to be attacked and Jackson thought that Ewell should be in supporting distance, it would be well to place Ewell between Richmond and Fredericksburg, whence he could be moved with equal speed by rail to support Jackson, Field, or even Johnston. If Jackson believed that he could hold Banks without assistance, then Lee recommended that Ewell be made ready to reinforce Field. In a word, Lee proposed to take the initiative, and so to occupy McDowell that he could not advance. "I have hoped," he wrote Jackson, "in the present divided condition of the enemy's forces that a successful blow may be dealt them by a rapid combination of our troops before they can be strengthened themselves either in position or by re-enforcements."

Lee favored an attack by Jackson and Ewell on Banks. He was altogether for an immediate offensive-defensive. "The blow, wherever struck, must, to be successful, be sudden and heavy"—such was his admonition.

Jackson did not feel strong enough to attack Banks, even with

Ewell's support, unless Lee could send him 5000 men. Lee could not do this. As an alternative, Jackson proposed that he unite with Edward Johnson, who was being pressed back on Staunton. Doubtful whether it was practicable at that moment to attack Banks, Lee, on May 1, approved Jackson's plan for joint operations with Johnson west of Staunton.

Lee's dispatch of May 1 marked the end of the preliminaries to Jackson's renowned valley campaign. Jackson silently marched away on his mission and entrusted neither to mails nor telegraph any intimation of his purpose or progress. Lee had to wait, and wait not less to see his judgment of Jackson vindicated than to see their joint strategy work. For Lee was gambling on Jackson. Jackson did not then have great reputation. Stern in his discipline, uncommunicative with his officers, darkly Calvinistic in his manner, this strange soldier was regarded by some of his comrades as eccentric to the point of madness. Yet Lee from the outset saw in Jackson qualities that some overlooked or discredited. To Jackson's discretion he now entrusted operations that affected the whole strategic plan for saving Richmond.

On the very day Lee sanctioned Jackson's move against General R. H. Milroy, word came from Johnston that he intended to evacuate Yorktown on the night of May 2-3. Davis at once urged Johnston to delay long enough to permit the removal of naval supplies from Norfolk. Believing that the enemy could be delayed on the lower Peninsula, Lee undertook to see if Johnston would not try to hold on a few days longer. Johnston had changed his mind about general strategy and had reverted to an alternative he had presented at the council of war on April 14—a plan for a general offensive across the Potomac. Lee assured him the President was considering the feasibility of such a move and the next day, May 2, he wrote Johnston again, explaining that time was needed to complete the evacuation of Norfolk and, if possible, to bring the unfinished gunboats up James River.

It was in vain that he held out the possibility that the administration might approve Johnston's plan for a new offensive in the territory from which his army had withdrawn. On the 4th came news that Johnston was retreating up the Peninsula. Simultaneously Lee received the ominous tidings that Federal gunboats had passed up the York and had reached West Point. He at once telegraphed to Johnston, inquiring if light artillery might be sent to prevent the Federal ascent of that river from West Point. No reply came from Johnston. The authorities in Richmond were as much in the dark as the enemy concerning the plans of the general whose 55,000 troops were the chief reliance of the Confederacy.

Monday brought rumors of a bloody action at Williamsburg; Tuesday added dark details of a stubborn rearguard battle, so closely contested that Johnston had been forced to leave his wounded in the rain. And still nothing official from Johnston! All that Lee could do was to prepare for a battle close to Richmond. He endeavored to speed work on the James River defenses and channel obstructions, seven miles below the city. From Norfolk, he sought to remove to Richmond the heavy guns. His chief hope of saving Richmond he still pinned to the projected operations in northern Virginia. Looking beyond Jackson's attack on Milroy to his cherished offensive against Banks, he was scouring the seaboard for troops to reinforce Ewell.

At last, on May 7, came a dispatch from Johnston. It told of the presence of a fleet of ironclads and transports at West Point and of Johnston's apprehension for the safety of Richmond. There was no reference to a plan of operations and no hint of any early stand. The only reassurance was that Johnston held a position from which he could meet any offensive directed against his flank by way of York River.

The next day brought even more disquieting evidence of the field-commander's state of mind. His known and deplored jealousy as to his prerogatives broke out, most inopportunely, in a long, sharply phrased letter of many complaints. The feeling disclosed in this letter had been shown before by Johnston in smaller things, when the possible consequences of discord had not been so serious. Johnston possessed very great ability as a strategist and was in many of his impulses generous and warm-hearted, but his temper was apt to get out of control when he felt his authority was ignored. Knowing and admiring the man, Lee had no intention of permitting Johnston's testiness to endanger a cause to which he knew Johnston was sincerely devoted. With patient tact, he smoothed down Johnston's ruffled sensibilities. The incident, however, added to the difficulty of a situation that now hurried to a tragic climax.

For Johnston's army had continued its retreat and now was less than thirty miles from Richmond and only fifteen from the Chickahominy, the last natural barrier in McClellan's way. Stragglers were streaming into Richmond; on May 10 the Federals entered Norfolk—an irreparable loss; the valiant *Virginia* was blown up on the 11th; Huger was in retreat up the south side of the James; Federal gun-

boats were in the river; the defenses below the capital were so weak
that field artillery had to be hurried down to support the guns in
fixed positions; panic had again seized Richmond; the archives were
packed for removal and a conference was held on the disposition of
reserve rations; committees waited on the President to know if he
intended to hold the city, and went away scarcely reassured by his
calm announcement that he would. News reached Richmond that
Jackson had won a victory over Milroy on May 8, but this did not
ease the mind of a public which did not understand that the battle
was the auspicious preliminary to the fulfillment of larger plans.

Every energy was bent on the preparation of the defenses at
Drewry's Bluff. The Federal ironclads were coming up the James; the
lower defenses of the river had all been abandoned; nothing stood between the Union fleet and Richmond except the incomplete batteries
perched on the cliff at Drewry's. All the resources of the breathless
capital were requisitioned to finish the obstructions and batteries before
the enemy's ships hove in sight. The seasoned, confident gunners of
the *Virginia* were sent to reinforce the garrison. Ships that had been
brought up from Norfolk were sunk below the bluff. Troops were
posted on both sides the river to punish the incautious when the
ships appeared. General William Mahone, as the most experienced construction engineer, was placed in charge of the defensive preparations.

Early May 15, Lee rode down the valley of the James for examination of the river defenses. He had not gone far when there came the
roar of the heaviest guns that had ever echoed over that quiet country.
The Federals were attacking Drewry's Bluff! Quickly the ordnance
on the cliff took up the challenge. Farther down the river, on either
bank, there was the bark of small arms as sharpshooters sought to
hold the Federal sailors below decks. For three hours and twenty
minutes thunder followed thunder. Then the fire died away and the
calm of the countryside settled once again.

The redoubtable *Monitor*, the ironclad *Galena*, and three other ships
had steamed up the river almost to the obstructions and had engaged
the garrison of the unfinished fortification. The Southern gunners had
met this attack with a deliberate, accurate fire. The Confederate
Patrick Henry had added the weight of its metal. The *Galena*, badly
mauled, had finally quit the fight, and, with the other vessels, had
dropped down the stream, out of sight. The repulse was as decisive as
it was surprising.

Following the defeat of the Federal gunboats Johnston decided to
bring the greater part of his army across the Chickahominy both to
give it safety and to cover the land defenses being constructed on
the north side of the James opposite Drewry's. Johnston put part of
one division north of the Chickahominy. The right flank of his main
force he gradually drew in until on May 22 it was across the Charles
City Road, about five miles from Richmond. Thence his line ran
generally northward to the vicinity of the Chickahominy. His left was
close to the Fairfield race-course, almost within the northeastern
suburbs of the city, but his outposts were north of the Chickahominy
as far as Mechanicsville. It was a line so dangerously close to Richmond that the sound of a heavy action would almost certainly be
heard in President Davis's office. Should the Confederate line break in
a rout, two hours' pursuit would bring the Federals into the streets
of Richmond.

Close as Johnston was to Richmond, he had shown no intention
of giving battle, and had not informed the President when he intended
doing so. Soon after he crossed the Chickahominy, Davis and Lee rode
out to his headquarters in order that the President might be apprized
of the situation. It was not a satisfactory conference. Johnston was
reticent and seemed to have no definite plan. Subsequently, Lee asked
Johnston to come to Richmond to review the situation with the President, but Johnston did not answer. At length, probably on May 24,
Johnston came into Richmond and doubtless had an interview with
Davis, but apparently he did not explain his plan. The same day the
enemy occupied Mechanicsville. Everything indicated the loss of northern Virginia and the early junction of the two Federal forces, immediately in front of Richmond, with a strength not much below
150,000. To oppose them, Johnston would not have more than 72,000.
Only one of three things could save Richmond—a miracle, a successful attack by Johnston, or the failure of McDowell to advance.

Impatient at Johnston's failure to make any movement or to con-
fide his plan, despite their recent interview, Davis expressed to Lee
his deep dissatisfaction. The President's concern was so manifest that
Lee once more volunteered to act as a peacemaker. "General Johnston,"
he said to Davis, "should of course advise you of what he expects or
proposes to do. Let me go and see him, and defer this discussion until
I return." Riding out to Johnston's headquarters, Lee must have had
a more satisfactory interview with Johnston than on his previous visit

in the company of the President, for he brought back news that Johnston intended on the 29th to attack that part of the Federal army north of the Chickahominy.

At last the prospect of an offensive against McClellan! And with it the news of an event that might add vastly to its success. Rumor had been bringing reports of battles in the valley, but there had been nothing definite. Now, on the 26th, came dispatches from Jackson. The very first word was an assurance of a victory, for the paper was dated at Winchester, which had been eighteen miles behind Banks's lines at last reports:

"*General S. Cooper:*

"During the last three days God has blessed our arms with brilliant success. On Friday [23d] the Federals at Front Royal were routed, and one section of artillery, in addition to many prisoners, captured. On Saturday Banks's main column, while retreating from Strasburg to Winchester, was pierced, the rear part retreating towards Strasburg. On Sunday the other part was routed at this place. At last accounts Brig. Gen. George H. Steuart was pursuing with cavalry and artillery and capturing the fugitives. A large amount of medical, ordnance, and other stores have fallen into our hands.

T. J. JACKSON,
Major-General, Commanding."

Faith in the eccentric Jackson had been vindicated. What would be the effect? On the answer might hang the outcome of the battle in front of Richmond. "Whatever movement you make against Banks," Lee had written Jackson on May 16th, "do it speedily, and if successful drive him back toward the Potomac, and create the impression, as far as practicable, that you design threatening that line." Jackson had executed the first part of this plan and could be counted on to spread the fear of a farther advance. If the threat on the Potomac halted or delayed McDowell's advance, until Johnson could drive against McClellan, then a victory at Richmond might break up the combination against the capital. So much depended on Johnston's proposed offensive that every nerve of the Confederacy was strained to reinforce him.

Everywhere, on the morning of May 27, the question was the same —What news of McDowell? Had he started across the Rappahannock? Before noon, the worst possible news reached Johnston's head-

quarters: Anderson's videttes reported that McDowell had started to
march on Richmond! The main Federal column was already six miles
south of Fredericksburg and the advanced guard was less than forty
miles from Richmond. Had Jackson's demonstration been in vain?

Later in the day a strong Federal force struck Branch's brigade
at Hanover Courthouse and forced it back. Southern strategists reasoned
that McClellan was extending his right flank to meet McDowell.
With Hanover Courthouse in Federal hands, the gap between Mc-
Dowell's advanced guard and McClellan's right was reduced to less
than twenty-five miles. The outlook seemed almost hopeless.

Thick clouds obscured the sky on the morning of the 28th. Lee
spent the morning in final efforts to bring up the troops hurrying
northward from the Carolinas. Johnston was satisfied that McDowell
was approaching. There seemed nothing to do except to prepare for a
stubborn defense against overpowering odds. Night brought no news
to Richmond. On the morning of the 29th nervous thousands strained
their ears but heard no sound of battle. Did contrary wind drown the
roar of the guns, or had there been some unexplained change of plans,
when a day's delay in attacking McClellan might mean ruin?

Davis hurried through his office-work and took the road to Mechanicsville. Lee could not remain behind. To wait and know nothing
when he yearned to be a participant was a more terrific ordeal than
he could endure. He ordered his horse and went out, probably to
Johnston's headquarters. He found no battle in progress but he heard
news that meant as much as victory. Jeb Stuart had put a cavalry outpost close to McDowell on the previous day and late in the night had
reported that McDowell had halted his columns in the road and then
turned them around and marched back to Fredericksburg!

There might be speculation as to the reasons for this deliverance,
but what was more reasonable than to suppose that the victory at
Winchester, the rout of Banks, and Jackson's discharge of his orders
to threaten the line of the Potomac had led the Washington government to order McDowell closer to Washington? Relief had come when
it might be the salvation of the Confederacy. It was not Lee's nature
to exult or to count personal performance, but he could have reflected
that Johnston might fight the battle, but that he had made the victory
possible with the stout aid of Jackson.

The great news that McDowell was marching away from Richmond,
instead of toward it, had led to a decision to call off the battle and
to regroup the forces for an attack south of the river. That was why

Lee found no action under way. Lee rode back to the city that afternoon but he had been in the tense atmosphere of approaching conflict and he could no longer restrain himself. On the morning of May 30 he sent Colonel A. L. Long, his military secretary, out to Johnston's headquarters with a personal message. He had no desire, he bade Long tell the general, of interfering but he would be glad to serve in the field in any capacity during the coming action.

In the anxious twilight Long came in, bringing a polite, indefinite answer to his message: Johnston would be happy to have him ride out to the field, and, meantime, would Lee send him all the reinforcements he could collect? Johnston did not tell Long when the battle for Richmond would open. Still uncertainty; still suspense!

May 31 found Lee still restless. No commanding duties held him at his office. An irresistible desire to see what was happening on the front of the opposing armies led him to ride with some of his lieutenants to Johnston's headquarters. Learning that Johnston had gone forward, Lee went on. He found Johnston at a new headquarters. There was a tenseness in the air. Officers were coming and going. Johnston was preoccupied. A general movement evidently was afoot. That obvious fact Johnston must have announced to Lee, but he did not explain his plan in detail or tell Lee when the battle was to open.

Noon passed. Presently, from the southeast, came the intermittent mutter of heavy guns and, very faintly, after 3 o'clock, a sound that Lee's ear took to be the sound of musketry. But, no, Johnston explained; it could only be an artillery duel. Ere long, orders reached the troops waiting at the forks of the road, the word of command was passed, and Whiting's men hurried down the road that led toward the enemy.

Now a familiar mounted figure turned into the lane from the road. It was the President. A moment later—either by chance or with intent to avoid an embarrassing meeting—Johnston rode away across the field, in the direction of Whiting's march. Lee went out to meet Mr. Davis. The President's first question was what the musketry-fire meant. Lee explained that he had thought it was musketry, but had been assured by Johnston that only artillery was in action. Together the two walked to the rear of the house and listened. There was now no mistaking the sound, faint though it was. Either a heavy skirmish or a battle was in progress.

Davis, always a soldier at heart, could never resist the impulse to ride to the sound of firing. He returned to his horse and started for-

ward. Lee rode with him. It was now late afternoon. If a battle was
being fought, night would soon end it, one way or another. They
went down the road for nearly a mile, with a thick wood on their
right and open ground on their left. Then, beyond a lane leading off
toward the Chickahominy, they found a heavy tangle of timber on
their left also. Whiting's and Pettigrew's brigades had left the road
near this point and had deployed on the left, driving back Federal
pickets to an unseen line.

Before they knew it, Lee and Davis were under hot fire. To their
left, hidden Federal batteries were pouring a regular and well-placed
fire into charging ranks that floundered over fallen logs and through
the bushes, vainly seeking the Federal infantry. On the right another
column was engaged. Smoke was everywhere. Wounded were limping
to the rear; the line on the left was making little or no progress.
Johnston was somewhere down the road in the thickest of the fire.
Nobody seemed to know anything except that the enemy was strong
and resisting hotly, and that, away on the right, an even more desperate action was in progress. It was apparent that unless the Federal
flank was turned and the batteries in that locality silenced, Whiting's
troops would sustain a bloody repulse. Lee was merely an observer and
could not act, but Davis made a hurried reconnaissance and sent off
one messenger and then another to find General Magruder and to
direct him to throw a Confederate brigade beyond the Federal right.
Magruder, like the others was in the battle. Search for him was vain.
Davis was starting in person to look for him when a courier reported
he had located General Richard Griffith, one of Magruder's brigadiers,
and had delivered the message to him.

It was beginning to get dark. From the right Hood's Texas brigade
was coming forward. Griffith's men were being assembled on the left.
But it was too late. Before the flanking column could start, Whiting's
troops began to stream back from the thickets. They had not been
able to reach the Federal line. Dusk made it almost impossible to
distinguish blue from gray. Further effort would be a waste of life.
Davis suspended Griffith's movement.

The Federal fire continued. The troops waited to see if it would
be followed by a counter-attack. Presently up rode Postmaster-General
Reagan. He had been farther south and had found Johnston in great
danger. Davis, he instantly observed, was taking chances needlessly.
He protested against the President's remaining where a bullet might
strike him down. Davis refused to leave. And now a courier passed by

from the left, with the news that General Wade Hampton had been shot. On his heels rode another messenger who told them that Johnston had been wounded, some thought fatally. Darkness, a joined battle, crowded confusion, a multitude of wounded and the army left without the one man who knew all the dispositions.

Before Lee and Davis had time to think of the possible effects of this loss, up the road came litter-bearers bringing General Johnston, conscious, but in so much pain from two serious wounds that he had not been able to stand the jostling of the ambulance in which he had first been placed. It was a desperate hour and it promised a desperate tomorrow. Fortunately, the enemy had suffered heavily and was quite content to leave the issue as it was. No counter-charge was pressed. The broken regiments reformed beyond and across the road and prepared to sleep on their arms.

And now Smith had come up. From him Davis and Lee learned as much as he knew of the battle they had witnessed but had not understood. Johnston, they were told, had expected by a sudden attack to overwhelm that part of McClellan's army on the south side of the Chickahominy at a time when he believed the rise in the waters of that river would prevent the dispatch of Federal reinforcements from the ample divisions north of the stream. D. H. Hill, with four brigades, was to have advanced down the Williamsburg road and was to have opened the battle, with Huger on the Charles City road to turn the left of the enemy. Smith had understood that Longstreet was to have moved down the Nine Mile road to form on Hill's left, but, he explained, in some manner unknown to him, Longstreet had gone over to the Williamsburg road and had attacked there. Smith's own command, Johnston had told him, was to occupy the extreme Confederate left, to serve as a support for Longstreet, if needed, and to watch against a possible movement by the Unionists from across the Chickahominy. For reasons that Smith did not know, the opening of the action had been long delayed. Then heavy fighting had broken out on the right and Longstreet had called for help; Federal troops had unexpectedly arrived from the north of the Chickahominy, and the greater part of Smith's troops, under Whiting, had been brought up and thrown into action. Whiting, Smith concluded, had been heavily engaged. Did Davis know anything of the battle on the right? Had he received any word from Longstreet later than a message sent to Johnston at 4 o'clock?

Davis had no information, and, as Smith was the senior major-general on the field, the President asked him what his plans were. Smith was manifestly under heavy nervous strain. He could make no decision, he said, until he could ascertain how the battle had gone on the front of D. H. Hill and Longstreet. It might be necessary to withdraw closer to Richmond. He might be able to hold his ground. Davis suggested that the Federals might fall back and thereby give the Confederates the moral effect of a victory. Smith could only reply that he would not retire unless compelled to do so.

After a few minutes, Davis turned his horse's head toward Richmond. Lee went with him. Along the deeply trampled highway and on by the endless line of ambulances the two rode in darkness. At length, Davis uttered the words that were to change the course of the war in Virginia. "General Lee," he said, in effect, "I shall assign you to the command of this army. Make your preparations as soon as you reach your quarters. I shall send you the order when we get to Richmond."

CHAPTER VII

The Seven Days

THE BATTLE probably would be renewed with the dawn. Lee could not attempt to direct the fighting immediately, for that would be as dangerous to the army as it would be unfair to General Smith. What, then, could he do to help Smith?

Over that question Lee wrestled after he returned to Richmond. Before 5 o'clock on the morning of the 1st, a courier was knocking with a dispatch from Smith. Lee answered at once: "Your letter of this morning just received. Ripley will be ordered and such forces from General Holmes as can be got up will be sent. Your movements are judicious and determination to strike the enemy right. Try and ascertain his position and how he can best be hit. I will send such engineers as I can raise. But with Stevens, Whiting, Alexander, etc., what can I give you like them. You are right in calling upon me for what you want. I wish I could do more. It will be a glorious thing if you can gain a complete victory. Our success on the whole yesterday was good, but not complete."

He addressed his reply to "Genl. G. W. Smith, Comdg. Army of N. Va." Then he set himself to redeeming the promise of his letter. At this he was laboring when he received a communication from the President. Davis explained that the wounding of Johnston "renders it necessary to interfere temporarily with the duties to which you were assigned in connection with the general service, but only so far as to make you available for command in the field of a particular army." Other dispatches came; every hour brought new calls; preparations had to be made. It was about 1 P.M., June 1, when Lee was able to start with his staff for the battlefield.

In what spirit did he approach the army he was to lead? His feelings probably were those he put on paper the next day in a letter to his daughter-in-law. "I wish," he said, "that [Johnston's] mantle had

186

fallen upon an abler man, or that I were able to drive our enemies back to their homes. I have no ambition and no desire but the attainment of this object, and therefore only wish for its accomplishment by him that can do it most speedily and thoroughly." It was the profession of a simple soul, and such a soul was Lee's.

Riding out the Nine Mile road, Lee found Davis and Smith at the Hughes house, about a mile closer to Richmond than the headquarters occupied the previous day. The battle around Seven Pines had been renewed during the morning, but Smith had not been successful in winning a victory. The action seemed to be dying indecisively away. Davis had notified Smith that Lee was to supersede him, so explanations were unnecessary, and an immediate conference could be held. At its conclusion Lee and Smith went to the headquarters of Longstreet on the Williamsburg road. Longstreet's troops had broken off the battle, but their commander was anxious to renew it. The forces on the flanks, however, were not in hand for immediate co-operation, so Lee ordered the whole army back to the lines it had occupied before the battle of the previous day.

Lee returned to the Nine Mile road, where he opened headquarters. One of his first acts was to issue an address he had prepared before leaving Richmond. It was the first of a series that was to range every chord of resolution, triumph, and exhortation before the solemn finale was sounded at Appomattox. This order gave the army the name it was to make famous. Lee had already styled it "The Army of Northern Virginia" but never before had it been so addressed in its own orders. The troops politely cheered when this order was read to them, but no enthusiasm attended the announcement of the selection of Lee as commander of the army. Aside from Davis, the only man of station who seemed to realize what Lee might accomplish was Johnston himself. In some quarters, "disparagement, sarcasm and ridicule" were the lot of Lee.

The new commander bent himself to the task of saving Richmond. McClellan had been shaken by the impetuous attacks at Seven Pines, and his cautious nature prompted him to delay until reinforcements made good his casualties. Lee had no information of this, of course, but he could judge the effects of the weather. And that weather was of the worst. The Chickahominy bottom was covered with three or four feet of water; the whole face of the country was a bog. Behind the temporary barrier of these mud-courses, Lee reasoned fast. After a conference with Longstreet, he decided to hold the ground on which the troops then rested, as he believed this would keep McClellan's army astride the Chickahominy.

This settled, Lee's next task was to prevent the capture of Richmond. It was manifest that Richmond could not be held indefinitely against McClellan's larger army. The way to save the capital was to drive McClellan off, before his army was overwhelming or his guns close enough to shell the city. To attack McClellan, Richmond must be so protected by earthworks that it could be defended by a small force while the rest of the army attacked. Lee's first move was to provide for the construction of the earthworks. With good speed and good fortune, Richmond would be safe enough, in two or three weeks, for him to make a thrust at his adversary.

How was he to keep the industrious McClellan from pounding his way within striking distance of Richmond? The roads, Lee reasoned, were so heavy that McClellan could not haul siege guns over them. If, therefore, some method could be devised to keep the Federals from employing the railroad for this purpose, a bombardment might be avoided until Lee was ready for an offensive. Lee solved this problem by proposing to mount and armor a heavy gun upon a railroad truck, which could be run down the Richmond and York River line, out-ranging the Federal ordnance on the swampy ground. This was the birth of railway ordnance. Simultaneously, he directed an immediate reorganization of the Confederate artillery to render it more mobile and more efficient.

Cover was being prepared for an offensive. An untried weapon for halting the movement of the Federal heavy artillery was to be fashioned. How, next, was he to guard against the possibility that McDowell would reinforce McClellan and envelop Richmond with a force against which an offensive would be merely a waste of life?

Jackson's victory at Winchester had been an immense relief, but the demonstration on the Potomac had been short-lived. Frémont and Shields had threatened the rear of the Army of the Valley and forced Jackson to withdraw. Once out of the Federal pincers, Jackson had immediately projected a new thrust at the enemy. He sent to Lee a Confederate congressman, A. R. Boteler, with a statement of his situation. Jackson believed he could strike successfully at Shields, but if Lee could raise his army to 40,000 men, he could invade the North. In talking with Boteler, about June 3 or 4, Lee did not see how he could do more than replace Jackson's losses, and he perhaps told Boteler that before he could give Jackson reinforcements, Jackson would have to unite with him and drive McClellan from in front of Richmond—a possibility which he had discussed with Davis.

Lee saw the immense possibilities of an offensive in the North. "After much reflection," he wrote the President on June 5, "I think if it was possible to reinforce Jackson strongly, it would change the character of the war. This can only be done by the troops in Georgia, S. C. and N. C. Jackson could in that event cross Maryland into Penn. It would call all the enemy from our Southern Coast and liberate those states. If these states will give up their troops I think it can be done." Heretofore, Lee had held strictly to the defensive, in order that the South might gather strength. Looking beyond the relief of Richmond, Lee could consider a new phase of the war, an offensive-defensive at a distance from Richmond. The immediate success of such a change of policy depended not merely on good strategy but also on the attitude of the Georgia and Carolina people. The influences that were to thwart the efforts of the administration in later attempts to effect large-scale concentration already had to be taken into account. The Southern states were allies, not a united nation. Were the much-cherished states' rights, which were so potent a factor in leading the South to declare its independence, to prove an obstacle to the attainment of that independence?

While Davis undertook to negotiate for the transfer of troops from the South Atlantic states, in order that Jackson might invade Pennsylvania, Lee gave himself for a few days to expediting the construction of the defenses. Scorning the shelter of fortifications as unworthy of gentlemen in arms, the troops were not disposed to construct them. Much they grumbled at the orders of their engineer-general the "King of Spades" as they dubbed him. Lee did not stand back because of antagonism of doubting minds. Almost daily he went out to the lines, encouraging the soldiers and complimenting them on their progress. The work began to rise satisfactorily, not a strong line but ample for the immediate purpose.

To stiffen the discipline and improve the organization of the army was a task even more difficult. The obstacles were manifold. In some of its aspects, discipline had been lax under Johnston; drunkenness had been frequent; many things were at loose ends. Lee worked as fast as he could to improve the condition of the men. The commissary and the quartermaster's service were improved. Favoritism in granting details for service in the rear was ended.

The labors took many hours of the busy days of June. Lee was

ceaselessly astir. Not only did he have to supervise a hundred under-
takings on the line, but he had to direct, in some measure, those distant operations that had been under his care when he was assigned to
field duty. In dealing with the officers, he proceeded as though there
was no opposition to him. The day after he took command he summoned all the generals to a council of war. The division commanders
were somewhat scandalized at what they considered incaution on Lee's
part in discussing a plan of operations in the presence of the brigadiers.
They might as well have spared their feelings. Lee simply asked for
opinions on the state of affairs and listened as the brigade commanders
reported. He at length bade his lieutenants good-day without the
slightest intimation of what he intended to do.

The generals rode away none the wiser for their conference, some
of them assured of Lee's ability, others convinced that he had simply
called them together to see what manner of men they were. He could
hardly have been disappointed in them as a group. The policy of the
administration had put at the disposal of Lee an unusual number of
professional soldiers of high intelligence. Counting those who were yet
to join him, Lee was to go into the Seven Days' Battle with forty-nine
general officers, whose average age was slightly over forty years.
Thirty-one of these were West Point graduates, and only a handful
could be accounted as "political generals" in the accepted Northern use
of that unhappy term.

With surprising rapidity, considering their devotion to Johnston
and their secret disdain of the staff, nearly all of these officers were
won over to Lee's support by his manner, his energy, and his modest
but unmistakable willingness to assume responsibilities. He neither
flattered them nor dealt with them austerely, but they could not fail
to see that he knew his duty and was determined to discharge it. He
was careful in his appointments to fill vacancies, studiously just in his
judgment of qualifications, and unwilling to recommend officers of
whose ability he was doubtful. One thing helped him greatly—the
confidence imposed in him by those who knew him well. Such confidence begat confidence.

Before Lee had progressed far in preparing for the offensive against
McClellan, it became apparent that no such reinforcements as Jackson would require for an invasion of Pennsylvania could be expected
from the South Atlantic seaboard. Brigadier-General A. R. Lawton
had a large Georgia brigade that he was anxious to bring to Virginia
and he started northward. But large detachments from that quarter

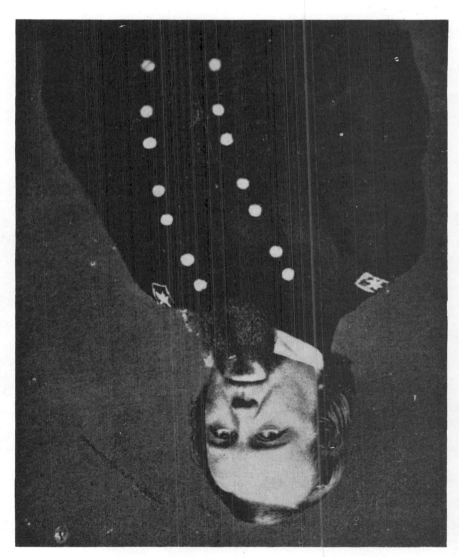

GENERAL JOHN POPE

MILITARY TRAIN DESTROYED BY CONFEDERATES

might break morale. The War Department continued its efforts to get troops, but Lee had to abandon his project for an invasion of Pennsylvania almost as soon as he formulated it. He determined, however, to send Lawton to reinforce Jackson. "We must aid a gallant man if we perish," said he. Beyond this, he had not decided what should be undertaken in the valley when, on June 8, he received an important letter from Jackson. His forces, the valley commander reported, were so disposed that if Shields attempted to advance and join Frémont, the Federal column would have to cross his front. If, Jackson went on, his command was required at Richmond, he could have part of his troops at the railroad after one day's march. Lee wrote Jackson to rest his men and to be prepared to move to Richmond, but meantime "should an opportunity occur for striking the enemy a successful blow, do not let it escape you."

The next morning, June 9, there came news that once again changed Lee's plans for Jackson: Jackson had struck Frémont at Cross Keys and had halted him, bewildered. The other wing of Jackson's army had grappled furiously with Shields's advanced guard at Port Republic and had hurled it back on the main force. As these battles of great tactical brilliance gave Jackson the advantage again, Lee decided to make the most of it. He ordered Lawton's brigade and a few North Carolina regiments united at once with Jackson's force. Lee still had no way of sending Jackson enough men to undertake the offensive in Pennsylvania, but he had learned something from the quick recall of McDowell after Jackson had defeated Banks. He had made a discovery, in fact, that was to influence his strategy many times in the next two years and on occasion was to shape it: any Confederate movement that threatened the Federal capital would be apt to prompt Mr. Lincoln to call troops from Virginia to its defense. Might not Jackson undertake a sharp offensive that would crush the enemy in front and so alarm the Northern President that McDowell's army would be summoned to Washington? With the valley cleared, Jackson might join in the attack on McClellan. His troops might give Lee sufficient strength to hope for a victory in the field.

On June 11, Lee detached W. H. C. Whiting, with eight regiments, ordered the men through Richmond, and sent a staff officer thither to create the impression that much importance was attached to the speedy departure of the reinforcements in order that an offensive might be launched in the valley. Jackson's orders were explicit: "The object," Lee wrote, "is to enable you to crush the forces opposed to you." This done, Jackson was to leave in the valley his weaker infantry units, his cavalry, and his artillery, in order to screen the movement and to guard the passes. With the rest of his troops he was to move eastward and assail McClellan's right flank while Lee attacked in front.

Lee at once turned to preparations for the offensive to be undertaken when Jackson arrived. The first step was to procure exact information concerning McClellan's position and line of communications. To ascertain the facts, he determined to order a cavalry raid to the rear of McClellan's right and called to headquarters Brigadier General J. E. B. Stuart, now at the head of the cavalry. Lee was in no position to risk the loss of his cavalry and, after talking with Stuart, gave lengthy instructions explaining the information he desired and cautioning against too great exposure. ". . . be content," said he, "to accomplish all the good you can without feeling it necessary to obtain all that might be desired." Happily Stuart picked some 1200 men and disappeared with them on the 12th, pretending that he was bound for the valley to reinforce Jackson.

Other concerns now crowded Lee's mind, along with that for Stuart. There were evidences that McClellan was being reinforced. The fickle weather had turned Unionist again. There had been no rain since the 10th and the roads were drying. McClellan would soon be able to advance his heavy guns, despite the railway battery, which was not yet ready for service. Every man would soon be needed on the Richmond front.

June 14 was a day of anxiety. Before it ended, there arrived an exhausted courier, Corporal Turner Doswell, with a message from Stuart—the first to be received from that daredevil since he had started on the reconnaissance. And what a message it was! Stuart had ridden to McClellan's rear, had destroyed a wagon-train, had captured some 165 men and more than that number of horses, with only one casualty, and had circled entirely around the rear of the Federal army. On reaching the Chickahominy, more than thirty miles below Richmond, he found the ford so deep and swift that Fitz Lee had nearly lost his life crossing it. There was no bridge and no other ford close by. Stuart was on the far side of the stream when Doswell left, and all his men were with him. He had been quite confident he would get back to the Confederate lines and had directed Doswell to request Lee to make a diversion so that the Federals would not be able to send a force to cut him off.

With the dawn of the 15th, Stuart rode up to headquarters. His iron frame was weary, but he was triumphant and full of information. He had found the skeleton of a burned bridge a mile below the ford, had repaired this and had crossed the entire command.

There was much more than adventure about the raid. To Stuart's report of the ground and of the Federal dispositions Lee gave instant and serious ear. The roads behind the Federal lines, Stuart said, were worse than those on the Confederate front. The Federals were supplying their lines by wagon-trains from the vicinity of the White House, as well as by the railroad. There were no signs of any intention on McClellan's part to change his base to James River. All this indicated, of course, that if the Confederates could turn the Federal right, they might get on McClellan's line of communications, perhaps cut him off from his base. Beyond the headwaters of Beaver Dam Creek, Stuart had found no Federals on the long ridge that Lee had especially enjoined him to examine. There was nothing to keep Jackson from turning Beaver Dam Creek and sweeping on toward the White House. That news justified all the risks that Stuart had taken.

Stuart's information about McClellan's position resolved the ground-factor in Lee's equation of an offensive. While Stuart was on the raid, the time-factor was brought closer to an answer. Colonel Boteler arrived again at Lee's headquarters on the evening of June 14 with a confidential message and a formal dispatch from Jackson. The message was a renewal of the suggestion that Lee bring up Jackson's strength to 40,000 men so that he could invade the North.

Lee then made inquiries as to conditions in the valley and examined the dispatch. It was a confusing document. Jackson acknowledged Lee's hint that he might call him to Richmond, but he said nothing about the letter wherein Lee had told him he was sending him reinforcements so that he could crush the enemy in his front before joining the Army of Northern Virginia. Yet Jackson said, "You can halt the reinforcements coming here if you so desire, without interfering with my plans provided the movement to Richmond takes place." Boteler did not know what letters Jackson had received; so, telling the colonel that he would have an answer for him, Lee bade him good-night and began to study anew the condition that "Stonewall" faced. It was clear from Jackson's dispatch that when he wrote he was close to Port Republic, where he had fought his most recent battle. He could not hope to reach the Federals, attack them, and return to the railroad in time to reach Richmond before McClellan was ready to open with his heavy guns. The course to follow was to bring Jackson to Richmond at once.

Thus was the climax approaching. The next step was to work out precise details of the offensive. Lee lost no time in doing this. A few hours after he had written Jackson, he left his headquarters with Colonel Long and rode out to the north of the Chickahominy. As far as the outposts of the enemy, he made a careful examination of the countryside. There was no question as to the general wisdom of attacking McClellan's exposed right flank. It seemed providentially extended for a turning-movement. The question now to be decided was whether Lee should launch his drive on both sides of the stream or should maintain a strict defensive on the south side of the Chickahominy and transfer the greater part of the Confederate army north of the river to co-operate with Jackson.

When Lee had returned to headquarters, Longstreet called and, by odd coincidence, proposed that Jackson be brought down from the valley and hurled against the Federal right. Lee had no hesitation in confiding to Longstreet that this had already been ordered and sketched a plan for an attack north and south of the river. From his experience at Seven Pines, Longstreet knew the difficulties of bringing the whole Army of Northern Virginia simultaneously into action, and he raised the practical question of what would happen if, for any reason, the frontal attack south of the Chickahominy were delayed when Jackson advanced. Might not the enemy concentrate and drive him back against the Pamunkey, the fords and bridges of which it was reasonable to assume a vigilant enemy had destroyed? Lee weighed this objection and decided to move the greater part of his troops north of the river.

When Lee next met Davis, he laid this plan before him. The President was quick to ask if Lee thought McClellan would permit him to take the initiative north of the Chickahominy and not deliver a counter-attack south of the river. The line south of the river was much too weak to sustain long assaults. If McClellan was the man he had taken him to be when he had been Secretary of War he would march into Richmond. If, on the other hand, said Davis, the Federal commander acted like an engineer officer and considered it his first duty to protect his communications, he would not attack. Lee's plan was based in part on knowledge of McClellan. It was founded on the belief that if he could once drive McClellan eastward on the north side of the Chickahominy, till he passed New Bridge, he had nothing to fear

on the south side. Once in control of that bridge, Lee felt he could
reinforce that part of his command south of the river or get in the
rear of McClellan's forces if they attempted an advance on Richmond.
The outcome fully justified Lee.

After receiving Lee's letter by Boteler, Jackson elaborately masked
his movements and on June 17 left his old battleground. On Sunday,
the 22d, he arrived at Fredericks Hall ahead of his men and spent the
day attending religious meetings. That evening Jackson waited till
the Sabbath was ended. Then, at 1 A.M., he left and, on relays of
commandeered horses, covered the fifty-two miles to Lee's headquarters in fourteen hours. Lee was at work when he arrived. Jackson
refused to interrupt him and waited in the yard of the house. Presently
D. H. Hill rode up, for Lee had received advance notice of Jackson's
coming and it had been to summon Hill and two other division commanders to a council of war that he had sent off couriers earlier in the
day. They talked for a few minutes, and then went in to Lee's private
office. Lee was awaiting them and offered the tired Jackson some
refreshment, but the traveller would take only a glass of milk. In a
short time, Longstreet and A. P. Hill arrived.

Lee had already made the decisions regarding the offensive, but
much remained to be discussed in an historic council that brought together for the first time the men who were to direct the opening battle.
Lee promptly and briefly explained the conclusions to which he had
come. These were:

1. Richmond could not be successfully defended in a formal siege.

2. It was necessary to assume the offensive.

3. The offensive could not take the form of a direct assault because
the troops were inexperienced, the positions strong, and the Union
artillery too powerful.

4. If there could be no direct assault, there must be a turning movement.

5. This was invited by the fact that McClellan was astride the
Chickahominy, with his forces divided by that stream.

6. McClellan's right wing, north of the Chickahominy, could be
more readily attacked than his left wing south of that stream.

7. A successful attack north of the river would threaten McClellan's
communications. The Federal commander would then be forced to

call his whole army north of the Chickahominy to defend his base
or would have to seek a new base on James River.

8. To overwhelm the Union right, north of the Chickahominy, it
would be necessary to concentrate very heavily there.

There was risk that the Federals might attack south of the river
while the greater part of the Confederate army was north. If the
Federal right rested on Beaver Dam Creek, that would be a difficult
position to attack directly. The Unionists were on good ground and
could dispute the crossing of the Meadow Bridges and the Mechanicsville Bridges, over which Lee would have to pass three of his divisions.

How could these difficulties be overcome? Jackson was to move
his army to Ashland, sixteen miles north of Richmond. Then, on the
day before the battle opened, he was to march southeast. This would
put him above the Chickahominy. Early on the day of the action he
was to start a march that would carry him past the head of Beaver
Dam Creek as he moved toward Cold Harbor en route to attack
McClellan's line of communications. In this way he would turn the
troublesome stream. The army should not have to fight for the high
ground along the creek.

A. P. Hill was to send a brigade under General L. O'B. Branch
up the Chickahominy to a place known as Half Sink. When Jackson
started his march on the day of battle, Branch was to move to the
enemy's side of the Chickahominy and advance toward Mechanicsville. In this way he would establish contact with Jackson and would
brush aside any outposts that might molest Jackson's right flank. And,
finally, as he moved down the river, Branch would uncover the
Meadow Bridges. When this was done, A. P. Hill would cross at the
Meadow Bridges and would advance on Mechanicsville. He would
thereby open the Mechanicsville Bridges to D. H. Hill and Longstreet.
D. H. Hill would then march past A. P. Hill's rear and form in support
of Jackson. Thereupon Longstreet would cross and take position in
support of A. P. Hill. By this time, Jackson would have turned
Beaver Dam Creek, and from left to right the advancing force would
be *en échelon*.

The attack would progress down the Chickahominy and would
have as its intermediate objective the Federal position in front of
New Bridge. When this was stormed, the last of the known difficulties
would be removed. Contact with the Confederates on the south side
would be re-established and the danger of a successful Federal attack

on that bank of the river would be passed. The advancing columns could press on toward the final objective, the York River Railroad. The two divisions of Huger and Magruder that were to be left in front of Richmond were to demonstrate on the day of battle. If they needed help, they were to call on the commands of General Holmes and General Wise who were on either side the James, and if the enemy withdrew from their front, Huger and Magruder were to pursue vigorously.

Having explained all this, Lee did something he had never done before and was never to do again: He excused himself for a time and left his subordinates to discuss among themselves the proposed movement. When he returned he was told that the four had agreed to launch the offensive on June 26. It is not certain he was informed that Jackson had first stated that he would be in position to attack on the 25th but had been urged by Longstreet to set the following day for the turning movement. The conference adjourned about nightfall and Jackson set out at once to spend another sleepless night in the saddle, returning to his command.

On the 24th Lee drafted his general order and had it distributed. He was determined not to repeat the misunderstandings of Seven Pines. Unfortunately, he did not make it altogether unambiguous.

The only pressing duty that remained was to see that the six excellent North Carolina regiments of Robert Ransom's brigade, then in Petersburg, were brought to Richmond. The arrival of these troops gave Lee a strength of about 67,000 men. Jackson would bring 18,500, so that Lee hoped to open the battle with about 85,500 soldiers of all arms. Of this number, he intended to employ some 56,000 against the Federal right flank north of the Chickahominy.

Of the strength of his opponent, Lee had no definite information, though he had estimated the Federal strength at 150,000 or more. He was convinced that the Unionists heavily outnumbered him. He expected, however, to concentrate on the north side of the Chickahominy a force superior to that which the Union commander-in-chief had left there.

The 25th dawned with the rain falling intermittently. Scarcely had routine camp duties been discharged than there came a development not on the schedule. The Federal artillery opened on a wide front, north and south of the Chickahominy. The Federals were attacking· the pickets along the Williamsburg road and were driving them in. Had McClellan learned of the approach of Jackson? Was he launching an

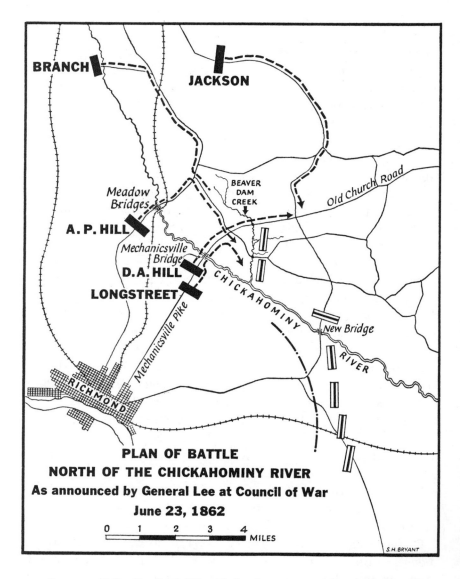

PLAN OF BATTLE
NORTH OF THE CHICKAHOMINY RIVER
As announced by General Lee at Council of War
June 23, 1862

0   1   2   3   4   MILES

S. H. BRYANT

attack to spoil Lee's plan? The Federals were seeking nothing more than to advance their picket line. But this action raised a question: Should Lee execute his plan for a battle the next day or await development of the enemy's movement? He concluded that McClellan was not attacking because he was aware of Jackson's advance, but that the Federal commander would assume the offensive shortly. He let his plan for the offensive stand.

Toward evening, the charges and counter-charges on the Williamsburg road ended with the Confederate main line untouched. Artillery-fire at length fell away. The rain ceased, too.

On June 26 Lee was early astir. Bad news came with breakfast. Down the river, opposite New Bridge, artillery fire broke out hotly and lasted half an hour. From Jackson arrived a dispatch explaining that his command had been delayed and had not reached Ashland until the evening of the 25th, whereas the plan had stipulated that the divisions were to camp that night about six miles nearer the chosen field of battle. That was a poor beginning, and it could not be wholly redeemed by the assurance Jackson gave that he would start at 2:30 on the morning of the 26th. At best, Jackson could not cross the railway until 6 o'clock—three hours late. Jackson reported, also, that his cavalry pickets had been driven in and that the telegraph wire had been cut near Ashland.

Lee's apprehension increased but his purpose was not shaken. He rode over to the Mechanicsville turnpike, out of which the regiments of D. H. Hill and Longstreet were streaming. By 8 A.M. all the units of the two divisions were in position. If Jackson were delayed in crossing the railroad, it followed that Branch would be later in marching on Mechanicsville than had been contemplated. It would be afternoon before the village could be taken. Still, the sun did not set until 7:17, and Lee would have at least six hours in which to drive the Federals. Everything depended on Jackson and on Branch.

An anxious hour crept by, and another. The President, the Secretary of War, and a number of public men had ridden out. There was enough of conversation and of high company. But to Lee, the suspense must have been torture. The sun was beginning to slant. Three o'clock was drawing on, and it began to look as if the whole plan might have to be cancelled, for the Federals who had driven in Jackson's pickets had certainly reported his advance by this time. Night would give McClellan opportunity of covering his threatened flank. The fates that thus far had kept Lee from fighting a single battle seemed to be leagued once more against him.

At 3 o'clock Major W. H. Richardson reported that he was satisfied the enemy was evacuating the gun-positions immediately opposite him. With Longstreet and D. H. Hill, Lee went out on the redoubt to see for himself. Although there was some movement around Mechanicsville, there was nothing definite, nothing to indicate any sudden alarm.

The hour had not long passed when there rolled down the valley a rattle of musketry. It grew into volleys, loud and furious. Bluecoated figures began to emerge from the fringe of woods on the far side of the river, below the Meadow Bridges. The attack was being delivered at last! Quickly on the heels of the Federals a Confederate skirmish line appeared. Behind the skirmishers the woods seemed suddenly alive with men, spreading rapidly northward. They halted, formed line of battle, and began to sweep eastward toward Mechanicsville. The effect was electric. Bugles echoed. Horsemen sprang to saddle. Orders rang out. The gunners stood to their pieces, anxiously awaiting the word of command.

The Confederate line on the other side of the river was now moving steadily eastward, almost unopposed by the fleeing Federals. Soon it was evident that some of Hill's artillery had reached the road that led from the Meadow Bridges toward Mechanicsville, for, while the road could not be seen, the boom of guns could be heard from beyond the advancing infantry and the smoke of their fire was visible.

There was other smoke, too, across the Chickahominy. Rising faintly over the village and far beyond the Federal line, it was in a most significant position—directly on the line of Jackson's expected advance. "Stonewall" and his famous valley soldiers must be close at hand. Late as it was, the plan seemed now to be working out! Hill was coming down the heights to clear the Mechanicsville bridges, and Jackson would soon be turning Beaver Dam Creek. Victory might still be won.

A. P. Hill's advancing line was nearing Mechanicsville now. No Federal batteries remained on the plain to oppose it. The Federal infantry was withdrawing rapidly. But as the Confederates approached Mechanicsville a heavy artillery fire was opened upon their columns. The Federals behind Beaver Dam Creek were ready for them. The whole stream seemed to be covered with the smoke of the Union batteries. Hill must not advance too far before Jackson turned the creek. On Hill went, the fire upon him heavier every minute. The situation was becoming confused. The Federal stand on Beaver Dam Creek did not indicate that Jackson was close enough to turn that stream. What was wrong?

Four o'clock found Hill in the village. The turnpike was cleared. D. H. Hill could cross at last to go to support Jackson—if Jackson were there. Longstreet would follow and form on A. P. Hill's right. Down the hill from the south side went D. H. Hill's leading brigade. R. S. Ripley was leading it.

Lee had waited to see the column well under way. It was nearly 5 o'clock before he left Richardson's battery-position to cross the river. When he arrived at Mechanicsville, he found chaos. Hill, he discovered, had not waited till Jackson and Branch were opposite the Meadow Bridges. Instead, Hill had despaired of their arrival and moved on his own responsibility. He did not know where Jackson was. The village was his. But what good did this do? The men had no cover.

Evening was drawing on—what could be done? It was Lee's to decide. The decision was made quickly. Ripley was ordered to move to the right and to turn the enemy's flank. Ripley did not know the ground, and he took the exposed route. Casualties were sustained that might have been avoided. By 9 o'clock the infantry action was over. The artillery-duel continued for another hour, and, on some parts of the line until even later.

Lee's first battle was finished. Fought where he had not expected to be engaged, it had carried the Confederates no farther than the prepared position of the Federals, and there it had been a ghastly failure. With 56,000 men north of the Chickahominy, or crossing it, Lee had been able to get only 14,000 into action and had lost nearly 10 per cent of them with no other gain than to drive the enemy from the plain around Mechanicsville. The Federal loss could only be surmised, but it had to be regarded as trivial. And this was the result of days of hard planning and careful preparation! Where Lee had expected to turn Beaver Dam Creek and to sweep down the Chickahominy, with all the advantage of surprise, something had gone wrong with Jackson, and A. P. Hill had been halted and bloodily repulsed.

The whole element of surprise was lost. The Federal commander could reinforce his right or attack Richmond on his left. Lee could only hope that Jackson would turn the creek during the night, so that the original battle plan could be carried out. Until 11 o'clock he worked to prepare the troops and to make the dispositions for an attack at dawn and then, wearily, he went back across the river to rest.

On the morning of June 27 Lee had two tasks: he must drive the Federals from Beaver Dam Creek and he must pursue them down the north bank of the Chickahominy and force them to fight away from their entrenchments and heavy guns or else retreat. He snatched up a hasty breakfast and started for Mechanicsville. He dispatched Major Walter Taylor to find Jackson and show him his route and then prepared to turn on Beaver Dam Creek. Before the turning movement could be organized, the Federals ceased fire and evacuated the position.

Now for the pursuit and the new attack! Maxcy Gregg soon had his brigade across the stream. By 9 o'clock, A. P. Hill and Longstreet were well under way. Waiting near Mechanicsville until the last brigade of Longstreet's division was moving, Lee followed the line of march. He had not gone far before he found that contact with the enemy had been established. A. P. Hill's advance had brushed the rearguard of the enemy, and, what was equally exciting, had been fired upon by Jackson's artillery. Jackson was at last on the ground.

Lee rode to near Walnut Grove Church to confer with the redoubtable commander of the valley army. Jackson considered that he had discharged the first part of his mission, and he made no apologies for his delay. Lee appears to have raised no question: he simply told Jackson to hasten his march on Cold Harbor. Jackson would have under his command considerably more than half the army on the north side of the river. His advance would turn Powhite Creek. If this movement did not force a Federal retreat, it would put Jackson on the line of the Federal communications and in position to fall on the Unionists when A. P. Hill and Longstreet drove them.

The interview over, Jackson rejoined his command, and Lee rod᠂ on to the head of Hill's column, which he instructed to attack the enemy as soon as located. It was now about noon, and so far as the situation was known to Lee, it was altogether favorable. Just east was the military road that led down to New Bridge, Lee's intermediate objective. The most serious danger in his plan seemed to be safely overcome. A. P. Hill and Longstreet were advancing rapidly, and if Jackson and D. H. Hill did equally well it could not be long before the battle was joined, with every promise of success.

News began to come in that indicated the proximity of the Federals. General W. N. Pendleton, chief of the reserve artillery, sent word that he could see the enemy in great force east of Powhite, Doctor Gaines's house, which occupied a knoll, three-quarters of a mile down the Chickahominy from Selwyn. The topography of the country made it probable that the Federals would give battle there. It seemed altogether probable that the Federals held a continuous front along Powhite Creek and were awaiting attack. Lee proceeded to make his first plan of the day in the expectation that the battle would be fought on Powhite Creek.

Meantime, about 11 o'clock, D. H. Hill had found the enemy in strength across a road that linked Old Cold Harbor with Grapevine Bridge over the Chickahominy, and about noon, he had attacked hotly. The first intimation Lee had that the infantry had come together was the sound of rapid volleys about 1 P.M. from the Cold Harbor road. Riding thither, he found that Gregg's South Carolinians had reached the point where the Cold Harbor road crossed Powhite Creek at Gaines's Mill. Gregg crossed with slight difficulty about 1:30 P.M., and was soon in pursuit of the enemy. This was a suspiciously easy beginning if the Federals had really intended to make a stand on Powhite Creek. Why did not the enemy contest the crossing? Passing uphill from the creek, Lee came to an open plateau. At that moment, from a stretch of woods to the southeast, in the vicinity of what was known as New Cold Harbor, some of Gregg's troops began to roll back. The panic was local and short-lived. Gregg led his men quickly and steadily back into the woods. Soon the fighting was as hot as before.

The enemy was at bay. Reconnaissance showed the terrain falling away on the south and southeast into a wooded, boggy bottom, through which ran a stream known as Boatswain's Swamp. This water-course was not on Lee's map and its presence explained why McClellan had not stood on Powhite Creek. The position selected by the Federals was stronger and more compact. It was a terrible position to have to assault.

The volume of fire and the calmness of the Federals in taking position and awaiting attack convinced Lee that the greater part of Mc-Clellan's army was in his front. A. P. Hill engaged the enemy, and Longstreet waited with his fresh troops till they began to move. There was every reason to hope that McClellan would be trapped by Jackson.

Then the Federal artillery opened a devastating fire. Men began to fall fast, but the lines swept on. Right and left the fire swelled along the swamp and echoed against the ridges. On the left, Gregg was advancing. In the centre and on the right, as well as they could be distinguished, the Confederate volleys for a while seemed farther away; then they remained stationary for a time; then they were closer. And soon, with a sinking of heart, observers on the fringe of the wood saw men struggling back over the shell-swept crest.

They had a dreadful tale to tell. Archer had been compelled to fall back. J. R. Anderson had made three charges, but when his centre had wavered, he had retreated, and in doing so had confused Field's brigade, which was supporting him. Two of W. D. Pender's regiments had entered the Federal lines but had been beaten back. Branch's command had been confused. Only Gregg had succeeded in crossing the swamp on the left, and there he remained.

Some of the units were rallying, even as the others withdrew, and

were now pressing a forlorn, second assault, but it was nearly 4 o'clock
and there was no denying that A. P. Hill had sustained a costly repulse.
From the sound of the firing in the swamp, it was believed that the
Federals had themselves taken the offensive.

Lee had to scrap his previous plan of action, and to arrange for a
general assault as soon as the troops could be put in position. Thus far,
only A. P. Hill had attacked. Help must be had at once. Lee kept sending messengers to Jackson, urging him to hurry forward. He dispatched
orders to Longstreet to make a diversion in Hill's favor. He ordered
Ewell to support A. P. Hill and directed him to send back staff officers
to quicken the march of Whiting and Lawton. As Ewell prepared to
throw in two brigades on the ground where A. P. Hill's left had been
fighting, Longstreet started a demonstration with four of his brigades,
and the second phase of the battle began on a wider front. Jackson
ordered D. H. Hill to advance against the enemy.

Hill's progress to the southern end of the woods along the upper
waters of Boatswain's Swamp had been easy, but beyond that point his
every attack was met with a quick counterthrust. When Samuel
Garland's and G. B. Anderson's brigades found their progress halted
by the fire of a battery near the McGhee house, Hill ordered the artillery stormed by a separate column. Guns were taken and retaken, but
the two brigades meantime reached the road on the crest in front of the
house and found shelter there. D. H. Hill was not so close to victory
at this point as he subsequently thought, but he was in position to co-
operate effectively if a general assault was ordered. Jackson, meantime,
was busily employed in bringing up his own division and in arranging
artillery support for D. H. Hill. As the battle roared toward its climax,
Jackson's spirits rose. Sending officers to all his division commanders,
he said, "Tell them that this affair must hang in suspense no longer;
sweep the field with the bayonet!"

By this time Isaac Trimble's and Richard Taylor's brigades of Ewell's
divisions were feeling the strength of the Federal centre. Richard
Taylor's brigade was driven off the field. Gregg's men were being
forced slowly back. Trimble fared better. His regiments extended their
flanks and contrived to keep up a vigorous fire. A. P. Hill's survivors
were holding on to the crest in front of the Parsons house. Longstreet's
demonstration was taking form. No sooner did the demonstration
disclose the strength of the position in his front than Longstreet saw
that a diversion would simply be a waste of life. He could only help

A. P. Hill by converting the demonstration into an assault and he paused to bring up troops for that purpose.

Such was the situation after 5 P.M. With the issue still in doubt, down the road from Old Cold Harbor rode Jackson.

After a brief conference with Lee on the proper disposition of the troops not yet in line, Jackson rode away. Meantime Lawton, with his 3500 Georgians, the largest brigade in the army, had joined Ewell and was making his fire felt. Soon Lee saw Whiting, his brilliant assistant of Sollers' Point, who had been feeling his way to the right from Old Cold Harbor. Lee at once ordered Whiting to support A. P. Hill's right, just as Ewell had been thrown in to relieve A. P. Hill's left.

Soon the head of Whiting's division was in the road. Lee rode toward it and inquired for General John B. Hood, leading the Texas brigade of that command. Hood came up on his horse and saluted. Briefly Lee told him what had happened—how the troops on the front were fighting gallantly but had not been able to dislodge the enemy. "This must be done," he said quietly. "Can you break his line?"

"I will try," answered Hood, stoutly enough.

It would take time for Hood and Law, who commanded Whiting's other brigade, to deploy for action. Meantime, more weary soldiers were seeking the rear. Whiting would help, but Longstreet must not delay. Unless he acted speedily, the day might be lost. Lee hurried a staff officer to Longstreet to tell him so. Louder and louder the battle roared through a half hour of uncertainty. Then came a strange, shrill, sustained cry, as if thousands of men were calling on the dogs in a fox hunt. It was the "rebel yell." Whiting's men were going into action. They had established contact with Longstreet, and his brigades also were pressing forward.

It was a drama that gave Hood's Texans a place in Lee's heart no other command ever won. E. M. Law's brigade was on the right, next Pickett, who held Longstreet's left. Hood was on the left of Law. As they went forward, Hood saw an open field and he quickly moved the 4th Texas across Law's rear and into this gap. The movement was flawless; the whole division swept onward, the 4th Texas ahead of the others. The fire grew faster. So did the pace of the men. They were passing through Hill's ranks; they were plunging down the grade to the swamp. A thousand had fallen now, but scarcely a musket had been fired from the attacking division. The men were within twenty yards of the Federal front line—within ten—and then, suddenly, as if the same fear had seized every heart, the Federals were leaving their works, were running, were throwing their arms away. The Texans crashed in pursuit; and then, as the bluecoats spread in a confused mass, the Confederates loosed their volley where every bullet reached its mark. A break had been made. If it could be widened, the enemy would be routed.

Lee had in line every man he could hope to place there. It was time for the final thrust. He gave orders to A. P. Hill to start a general advance. It was scarcely necessary. Longstreet's columns were moving; Lawton had not halted since his brigade had gone into action; Ewell was full of fight; every one knew that Jackson had arrived; D. H. Hill had seen his opportunity, and his regiments had rushed for the McGhee house about the time the Texans had broken through the swamp. In fifteen minutes, as if some animated jig-saw puzzle had suddenly fallen into place, the full design of the assault showed itself. The Federals yielded, slowly and stubbornly in front of the Confederate left, rapidly in the centre and on the right. Two Union regiments were taken on Whiting's front and large detachments everywhere. Elsewhere the Union troops made for the Chickahominy flats south of the hill, where it was futile to pursue.

Lee had won his first victory, but it was a heavy price he had paid. The slaughter of officers had been tremendous. The total Confederate dead and wounded, though never separately tabulated, could not have fallen below 8000, and in some brigades the slain were so numerous that twenty-four hours scarcely sufficed to bury them.

On the morning of June 28 couriers began to gallop back to Lee, all of them with the same message: the enemy was gone from the north side of the Chickahominy. Jackson's men had met a cavalry detachment, but it had fled at the first fire. Many prisoners had been taken. Longstreet found only the dead, the wounded, and the straggling in his front. The bridges over the Chickahominy had all been burned. The enemy appeared to be concentrating south of the river, and apparently had evacuated none of his positions there. All the approaches to the destroyed crossings were under fire of massed artillery. It seemed scarcely conceivable that McClellan, after only one general engagement, had abandoned the railroad. He must be preparing to renew the battle, somewhere.

Lee directed Stuart to move down the Chickahominy, destroy the railroad, and get on McClellan's supply line. Ewell's division was likewise ordered to march in support, on a similar mission, preceded by one regiment of cavalry. Longstreet was told to bring up such long-range guns as he could and open on the enemy across the river. This was all that could be done at the time.

As often as they surveyed the bloody battleground, Lee's eyes turned anxiously to the opposite side of the river. What was the enemy doing behind those trees that covered the hills above the Chickahominy? Before noon, Trimble, of Ewell's division, reported that one of his officers had climbed a tree and had seen the enemy moving southward. Soon the bright panorama beyond the river-valley began to be obscured. An ever-lengthening cloud began to rise. It was not the smoke of a silent battle; it was dust, and it could only have been raised by laboring horses and marching men. Now there came distant flashes, echoing heavy explosions. Magazines were being fired! McClellan was on the move—but why and whither? A message from Trimble confirmed his earlier report. There was no misreading the great news: McClellan was so hard hit or so frightened that he was abandoning his base at the White House. Either he was retreating down the Peninsula, by the way he had come, or else he was changing base to the James River, where the Federal sea-power would suffice to refit and revictual him. But which? Lee was disposed to believe that McClellan would do the latter rather than endure the humiliation of a retreat down the Peninsula.

If McClellan was establishing a base on the James, the whole of the Army of Northern Virginia should be concentrated south of the Chickahominy and hurled against the enemy while he was in the confusion of change. But if the Federal commander were preparing to retreat down the Peninsula, there was compelling reason for keeping a large part of the army north of the Chickahominy. Risk and probability seemed balanced. As far down the horizon as the dust clouds could be observed, they rose from roads that McClellan would follow whether he was moving down the Peninsula or toward the James. It was such a situation as often paralyzes the initiative in pursuit. All that Lee could safely do was watch and guard the downstream bridges of the Chickahominy, to which McClellan would soon be coming if he were moving eastward. Through the long, hot afternoon, Lee waited for further news. Silence strengthened his belief that the enemy's objective was the James. He began to plan for pursuit on the morning of the 29th.

Soon after sunrise on June 29, he received a message of great import from the two engineers who had been sent from Longstreet to attempt a reconnaissance across the Chickahominy. Their report sent a thrill through the army: the great, frowning Federal works around Golding's Farm were empty! This was the key position south of the Chickahominy. McClellan had abandoned his attempt to take Richmond. Lee's spirits rose. The aim of the campaign had been to force McClellan to retire or to come out from behind his entrenchments so that he could be attacked to advantage. McClellan had done both.

The plan of operations now took form rapidly. Ewell and Stuart would be held guarding the lower bridges of the Chickahominy. The remainder of the army should be put in pursuit of the enemy. Lacking information as to the line of McClellan's probable withdrawal, Lee had to dispose his forces in the most practicable manner to meet his adversary on any route that he might follow. This was a difficult task in detail, but if it were rightly performed Lee believed that he could keep McClellan from reaching the James.

The distance to the James was too great for the whole army to get in front of McClellan's moving army before nightfall of the 29th. The main battle would have to be fought on the 30th. In his retreat, however, McClellan would have to cross White Oak Swamp. If his rear was pressed with vigor part of his army might be cut off north of that stream.

A. P. Hill's and Longstreet's men were able to start as soon as orders were received. Lee hurried ahead to explain to Magruder and to Huger in person what was expected of them.

Smoke climbed high from piles of abandoned stores. Dust rose in a mighty column. Here and there houses, barns, and haystacks were smouldering. The fields were littered with accoutrements and arms. By the roadside stood abandoned wagons and broken ambulances. At Lee's temporary headquarters there was the same "fog of war" that somehow had prevailed from the beginning of the campaign. Either the majority of the division commanders did not appreciate the necessity of keeping headquarters informed, or else each of them was acting as if he were exercising independent command. Stuart, who had gone to the White House, reported that base abandoned, vast stores burned, and Rooney Lee's historic home destroyed.

As the day closed, the news had become less favorable. Confusion and delay had marked the pursuit. Magruder and Huger had misunderstood orders and had made little progress. Magruder had engaged in a severe action and had driven a portion of the Federals back to Savage Station. The sitution was by no means what Lee had hoped it would be. The Union rearguard had not been caught on the north side of White Oak Swamp; the columns pursuing the Federal rear were not yet close to the swamp. The day's operations had been a failure, not to say a fiasco.

Still, the enemy would be within striking distance the next day. Mc-
Clellan doubtless was crossing White Oak Swamp and might have
the rear of his army across before morning, but he would be strung
out along the roads. And he would be bound for the James River. Of
that, Lee was now satisfied.

Was it possible to dispose the Army of Northern Virginia so as to
cut McClellan off before he reached the James? Lee saw a possibility
of attacking the enemy on the move. Then, if he demoralized and defeated the Federals, he would have a chance of enveloping them. A great
opportunity was presented for a convergence of force in a simultaneous
attack on a moving enemy, encumbered with a great wagon train. Lee
determined to make the effort, hopeful of large results.

The decisive day, June 30, broke "cloudless and calm" upon thousands of confident soldiers who expected McClellan's army to be destroyed ere night fell again. Lee's first concern was for Magruder. Riding down to Savage Station, he found that Jackson had joined "Prince
John" at 3:30 A.M. The two greeted each other warmly but wasted no
time upon the greeting. Jackson began talking in a jerky, impetuous
way, drawing a diagram on the ground with the toe of his right boot.
He traced two sides of a triangle with promptness and decision; then
began to draw a third. This he traced with hesitation, alternately looking at Lee's face and at the diagram, meanwhile talking earnestly. When
at last the third line crossed the first and the triangle was complete,
he raised his foot and stamped it down with emphasis saying "We've
got him." There is no further record of what passed between the two,
but it is certain that Jackson understood the plan of operations and his
part in it. Jackson hurried on; Lee sought out Magruder. In person he
gave him orders to move over to the Darbytown road and supplied
him with a guide who knew the terrain.

Then Lee went across the country and joined Longstreet's marching
men. As far as could be ascertained, the enemy was in motion southward down the Willis Church road, some two miles to the east of the
Confederate van. Soon the advancing infantry came upon a small force
of Confederate cavalry engaged with Federal skirmishers. McClellan
evidently was on the alert and had troops west of the road on which
he was hurrying southward. Close to 2:30 P.M., there came from the
direction of Huger's advance the sound of light artillery fire.

It was now almost 3 o'clock and the fire from Huger's position did
not swell any louder or seem any nearer. Soon R. H. Anderson's
brigade of Longstreet's division became lightly engaged with the

enemy's infantry, and by 3 o'clock the artillery on both sides was barking viciously.

At field headquarters a courier handed Lee a note from Colonel Thomas L. Rosser. Lee must have read it with a sudden consciousness that the outlook was not so favorable as it seemed. Rosser reported that the enemy's column, with much haste and confusion, was then moving southward over Malvern Hill, which was within little more than gun shot from the James River. Lee perhaps remembered Malvern Hill as one of the large estates of his grandfather, Charles Carter, but he knew little or nothing of the sinister strength of its heights. What shook him now was the realization that if the enemy was retreating over Malvern Hill, McClellan might already be escaping before the battle was joined. Lee might have in prospect little more than a bootless rearguard action.

Returning from his reconnaissance, conscious that opportunity was slipping through his fingers, Lee met Holmes riding forward and directed him to do what damage he could to the retreating column. The General then galloped back to the main field of action, whence there rolled an increasing volume of artillery fire. As he rode on, there came from the opposite direction a still louder roar of heavier ordnance: Federal gunboats in the river were opening fire across the flats over which Holmes's green troops had to advance. If McClellan's army were already getting under the cover of those guns, the game was up!

When Lee reached the troops on the Long Bridge road he found the artillery blazing away but the infantry not yet fully engaged. Magruder had been ordered by Longstreet to march to the support of Holmes. Nothing further had been heard from Huger and nothing from Jackson. Neither of them could be attacking successfuly, if at all, because such reconnaissance as could be made by Lee showed that the Federal right and centre, which would have been exposed to assaults by Jackson and Huger, were standing staunchly, apparently inviting the Confederates to attack. Dangerous as it was to order an advance with only two divisions against a force of unknown strength, Lee had either to use the troops he had or else let slip all opportunity of striking McClellan. Without hesitation Lee ordered an attack.

As far as the enemy's position had been developed, when this order was given, McClellan, unprotected by earthworks, seemed to be across the Charles City road and west of the Willis Church road. The country was flat, except on the Confederate right, where it was uneven and, at some points, almost precipitous. The nearby settlement was known as

Glendale, and the largest property in the neighborhood was Frayser's Farm. The battle was to bear both names.

The advance began, about 5 o'clock.

J. L. Kemper's Virginians included many of the earliest volunteers of 1861, who had chafed at the fate that had denied them an active share in the earlier battles of the campaign, and now that they had an opportunity they swept wildly forward. Through the wood they rushed, across a little field, through another boggy wood crowded with underbrush, and into a second field some 600 or 700 yards square. In this they discovered a barricaded log house, surrounded by a crude breastwork of rails. Undeterred by the fire from the breastwork, the house, and the artillery, Kemper's men stormed onward, overran the house, captured six of the eight guns, and pushed on to the woods east of the clearing. They had far outrun the brigades on either side of them. Determined to hold their ground, they made the best of their bad position and maintained a vigorous fire.

Wilcox was detained by conflicting orders, but at 5:40 he advanced. His fine Alabama infantrymen pressed on, through woods, down to a little stream with a dense growth of trees along it, then through another wood, thin on the left of the road and heavy on the right. Here the brigade emerged into open ground and came under rifle fire. In the field could be seen infantry and two batteries, one on either side of the road. The 8th Alabama became engaged with the force in the woods but the 11th Alabama got within 100 yards of the battery before the Federal defense forced it back. The regiment renewed the attack and this time came within fifty yards of the Federal guns. Once more the 11th gave ground. Then a bitter clash, and the Union troops were forced to flee. This time the Alabamians were on their heels. The Federal gunners rallied with infantry support and soon delivered a counterattack. Bayonet crossed bayonet in a fierce mêlée. Heads were mashed with rifle butts. Primal rage possessed the struggling men. Decimated at last, the Alabamians were driven back.

Kemper on the right and Wilcox on the centre were spearheads held fast in the heavy blue line, but neither brigade could be extricated or pushed farther to reach the vitals of the enemy. Both on the left and on the right the Federal lines overlapped those of the Confederates and threatened to envelop them. There was nothing to do but to throw in the remaining brigades in an effort to consolidate and hold the ground already won.

Forgetful of the slaughter of Mechanicsville and unmindful of their frightful losses at Gaines's Mill, regiments moved forward at the order of command. The left of the line was threatened anew, but it was held against a vigorous fire. Finding the Federals in strength, the right regiments charged bayonets and soon were at grips with the enemy. One private was confronted by four Federals at the same instant. Although several times stabbed with bayonets, he killed three of his four antagonists. The other was dispatched by his brother. Soon the 56th and 60th Virginia outdistanced the troopers on the left of the road and found themselves far in front. Field now withdrew his right regiments from their exposed position. The enemy, however, by this time was closing in from the right, and was actually in rear of Field, but Pender's fine brigade was in support of Field, and when the enemy was within seventy-five yards Pender opened and quickly scattered it. Ere long, Archer was in touch with Pender on his right.

Still the enemy fought hard. Close as the Confederate front had advanced, its ability to hold on was doubtful. Fortunately, A. P. Hill had followed the changing situation with a clear eye and had already ordered forward his last reserve, J. R. Anderson's brigade, with instructions to raise the rebel yell in full voice. Through gathering darkness Anderson moved up on a wide front and delivered a volley at close range. The loud outcry of his troops deceived the Federals into thinking that heavy, fresh reserves were at hand. They broke and ran. In a short time, with night lying black on the field, the infantry action was over. Confederates had won the field.

But the field was not the battle, and on the battle the campaign had hung. The enemy might resume the fighting at dawn, and even if he did not, it was certain that his wagon train by that time would be safe on the James River. The ambitious plan for the convergence of Jackson, Huger, Longstreet, A. P. Hill, Magruder, and Holmes had failed tragically. Every man of Longstreet's and Hill's 20,000 had been thrown into action, leaving not a soldier in reserve—and more than 50,000 other Southern troops had stood virtually idle within sound of the guns.

Magruder had not been able to bolster Holmes in an offensive below Malvern Hill. The advance of Holmes's infantry had raised so much dust that it had disclosed his presence to the enemy. An overwhelming artillery fire had paralyzed Holmes until nightfall, and some of his raw artillery and cavalry had behaved very badly. Why had Huger failed to attack on Longstreet's left? What had happened to him? The answer was not given until the next morning and was then as brief as it was unsatisfactory. Huger had started down the Charles City road from Brightwell's at daybreak. Before he had gone a mile he found trees felled across the road. Instead of leaving his artillery and pushing on through the woods, he started to make a new road around the obstructions. As his men chopped away with poor tools, the Federals continued to cut trees along the highway. In this unequal contest between road-making and road-blocking, the greater part of the day was passed.

And what of Jackson on the Federal rear? Why had he, too, failed to do his expected part? Jackson had not moved across the Chickahominy at Grapevine Bridge until after midnight on the night of June 29–30. The advance on the morning of June 30 was so delayed that Jackson himself did not cover the seven miles to White Oak Swamp until about noon, and some of the troops did not come up till late afternoon. Had Jackson been a few hours earlier he would have caught the enemy in the act of crossing the bridge on the main road. As it was, the last of the organized rearguard was beyond reach when Jackson arrived, and the enemy's wagons were moving slowly up the road toward Glendale, out of range. The bridge had been broken up and burned by the Federals, and the miry ford had thus been rendered almost impassable. A Federal battery was in waiting across the stream, with infantry in support.

Jackson had been in a "peculiar mood" early in the day but had been smiling and hopeful when he had reached the swamp. During the afternoon, however, a strange inertia overwhelmed him. General Wade Hampton found a good sandy bottom and shallow water. He rode across the swamp and discovered that he was beyond the right flank of the Federals. They were lying down at ease, not suspecting that an enemy was at hand. Hampton reported his findings to Jackson. Could he build a bridge over the swamp at the point he had described? Jackson asked. Easily for infantry, Hampton answered, but not for artillery. Jackson told him to set about it. In a few minutes the bridge was made, and Hampton went across again. He found the Federals still unaware of their danger. When he returned, he again reported to Jackson, who was sitting alone on a log by the roadside, his cap down over his eyes. Hampton announced that the bridge was ready. Jackson sat silent for a time and then got up and stalked off without saying a word. No orders were issued and nothing was done, though the sound of the opening of the battle at Frayser's Farm soon was audible. Instead of reconnoitring in person, Jackson sat down and penned a letter to his wife describing his loss of rest and advising her what money she should contribute to the church. It is said that Jackson fell asleep and either was not or could not be aroused by his staff officers. Night came. The roar of the battle at Frayser's Farm continued to crash over White Oak Swamp. Jackson's artillery ceased firing. The men prepared to bivouac. The General started to eat supper with his staff but was so weary that he fell asleep with his food between his teeth.

Myths have grown up regarding Jackson's strange lapse that day. Most students probably will conclude that the most likely explanations are these: either the position, in Jackson's judgment was so strong that he did not think he could take it without unwarranted casualties; or else, the none-too-robust frame of Jackson had been exhausted by loss of sleep, on which his physique was especially dependent. Perhaps the two reasons are one: well-rested, Jackson might have stormed the Federal positions.

However this may be, Frayser's Farm was one of the great lost opportunities in Confederate military history. It was the bitterest disappointment Lee had ever sustained, and one that he could not conceal. Victories in the field were to be registered, but two years of open campaign were not to produce another situation where envelopment seemed possible. He had only that one day for a Cannae, and the army was not ready for it.

On the morning of July 1 the depleted army was not united again for the last stage of a pursuit that every one felt was well-nigh hopeless. Lee's disappointment at the outcome of the previous day's failure to concentrate was apparent to all; his temper was not of the best and he was feeling unwell, but he bore himself calmly and talked quietly with Longstreet, A. P. Hill, and Magruder of the battle of the previous day.

The orders for the march were issued. Jackson was directed to take up the pursuit at once down the Willis Church road. Magruder offered to lead the van, but Jackson insisted on doing so as his troops were fresher. Word was sent to Magruder to form on Jackson's right. Huger's division was divided. Two of his brigades, those of Armistead and Wright, were to advance, by a track through the woods. Mahone and Ransom, leading Huger's other brigades, were to follow Jackson. The divisions of Longstreet and A. P. Hill were to remain in reserve. Holmes was to hold his position and co-operate.

It was tactically bad, of course, to send Jackson, Huger and Magruder one behind another down a narrow road, but there was no alternative. Lee may, however, have read an omen of disaster in the crowding of so many on one wooded route, for his grip on his temper began to fail him. When General Jubal A. Early expressed concern lest McClellan escape, Lee answered grimly and with some impatience, "Yes, he will get away because I cannot have my orders carried out!" His mind could not cease dwelling on the lost opportunity.

A ride of two miles and a half with Jackson's division brought Lee to the northern foot of the Malvern Hills. Anxious eyes could not fail to see that it was just such a position as the Federals had chosen at Ellerson's Mill and behind Boatswain's Swamp. It was an exceedingly formidable position. Had the Union engineers searched the whole countryside below Richmond, they could not have found ground more ideally set for the slaughter of an attacking army.

One sweep of the field with his glasses was enough to show Lee the difficulty of attacking such a natural fortress. Nothing could be accomplished unless the enemy was badly demoralized, and even then an attack could not wisely be undertaken without a careful reconnaissance. Lee sent Longstreet to the right to study the ground and started toward the left himself. At the time, however, he did not undertake a detailed examination of the land in that quarter.

Longstreet reported Magruder far to the right on a road that he insisted was the Quaker road Lee had directed him to follow, when, in reality, Lee had intended him to march down the Willis Church road and take position to the right of it. The error, due to poor guides and poorer maps, meant that Magruder would be forced to make another troublesome countermarch.

On the right of the Confederate position, Longstreet had found an admirable artillery position. It was an elevation equalling that on which the Federal batteries were standing. On the Confederate left a large open field afforded a direct line of fire to the Union gun positions. Longstreet expressed the opinion that if the Confederate batteries were employed in full force on the knoll to the right and in the field to the left, they would bring to bear on the enemy a converging fire that would demoralize the Northern artillerists and open the way for the Confederate infantry. It seemed feasible to concentrate ordnance as Longstreet suggested and to deliver one more blow at an enemy who apparently was inviting further punishment. Lee approved the plan. Longstreet was sent to locate the batteries on the right flank; word was given Jackson to concentrate his artillery on the left. When the Confederate guns had demoralized the enemy, all the infantry were to make a simultaneous assault and wrest Malvern Hill from the enemy.

If the action was to be a heavy bombardment, followed by an assault all along the line, how was the order to be given? Lee directed that if Armistead found the Confederate fire breaking the Union line, he was to charge with a yell. This was to be the signal for all the divisions to assault together. This order was issued about 1:30 P.M. Now to bring up the artillery and to begin the bombardment! At last, from the knoll behind Armistead, the sound of firing was heard. It was taken up on the left. Before men could do more than ask one another why the fire was so feeble, the Union guns answered with a defiant roar. In roaring crescendo the Federal batteries found their target. Confederate guns were fast silenced in an unequal exchange. The preparatory bombardment, in short, was little more than a bloody farce. If the infantry advance depended on artillery preparation, there could be no general assault!

By 2:30 P.M., the first phase of the battle was over. The Federal artillery had not been shaken, and the Union infantry, except for some of the skirmishers, had not been engaged. Confusion and uncertainty prevailed everywhere. Longstreet, and perhaps others, got the impression that no assault was to be made because of the strength of the Federal position. But Lee was waiting and pondering and planning. He had pursued McClellan too long and at too heavy a cost to permit escape without one last challenge: If he had failed with his artillery, he would attempt a turning movement.

Summoning Longstreet, he rode hurriedly to the east to see if there was any point beyond the Federal flank from which he could advance and force McClellan to evacuate Malvern Hill. Arriving on the left, a hurried examination of the terrain convinced him that if high ground in that quarter could be seized he could accomplish his object. How could Lee make this shift to the left? The two divisions of Longstreet and of A. P. Hill could be utilized. Lee ordered Longstreet to move these troops to the left.

Whiting with his division had long been waiting under shell fire, but about this time, close to 4 o'clock, the Federal batteries suddenly ceased firing on Whiting's front. Soon a horseman galloped up from that officer to Lee. Whiting, said the messenger, could see Federal baggage trains and troops in motion, apparently in retreat from the field. This news put the whole situation in a new light. The course to follow was to scrap the plan for a turning movement on the left and to attack on the whole front at once.

The centre of gravity in the battle shifted to the right. Magruder had arrived on the right about 4 o'clock, very hot but vigorous and in high spirits. He found that Armistead had not received the additional artillery for which he had called out had repulsed the enemy's skirmishers about 3 o'clock and had then thrown forward three of his regiments. Although these Virginians had rashly advanced too far ahead of the main positions, they had found some cover and had stubbornly held their ground. Sending immediately for his artillery, Magruder, in great excitement, began a characteristically reckless examination of the ground. Almost before he could complete it, he received for the first time the order Lee had sent him about 1:30 P.M. telling him to advance at the sound of Armistead's cheering if the artillery preparation broke the enemy's line. As this paper did not carry the time of its dispatch, it was accepted by Magruder as a current order.

Magruder was fully conscious of the inadequacy of his artillery, but he did not consider that Lee's orders permitted delay. He determined to assault the front of the Crew house hill and, simultaneously, to move troops down the flank of the hill into the edge of the wheat field so that he could attack from the west, also under the brow of the hill.

Almost as soon as the line started forward the Federal gunners redoubled their fire. Ere long the supporting Federal infantry could make its musketry count. Every foot of advance brought heavier casualties. Still the men kept on until they were within 300 yards of the Federal gunners and in danger of being cut off by a force of Union soldiers that was deploying as if to flank them. The fighting was close, and the cross-fire enough to shake the morale of veterans. To the men of the attacking brigades it seemed as if they had been sent out alone, to make a futile charge and then to be killed off, one by one, huddled under the edge of the hill. They began to waver as they feverishly loaded and fired. It would be only a matter of minutes before they would break for the rear—to be wiped out as they ran.

Just then there came the roll of nervous musketry on the left, and soon D. H. Hill's division was advancing from the Confederate centre. Hill had heard cheering as Wright and Mahone had advanced, and he had taken this to be the signal for the charge. He had pushed all his brigades forward. Now they were advancing up an incline of 700 or 800 yards that Nature seemed to have set at that very point to lure on the incautious. The enemy had an almost perfect field of fire.

Inspired by the appearance of Hill's men, Armistead made another attempt. Wright and Mahone dashed across the shoulder of a ridge and reached a hollow not more than seventy-five yards from the enemy.

Garland's brigade covered 400 of the 800 yards to the Federal batteries and then had to lie down and await reinforcements. Colonel John B. Gordon of Georgia led Rodes's brigade forward and brought it within 200 yards of the nearest battery—only to be compelled to halt. Ripley advanced with the other brigades and like them had to stop. Colquitt was brought to a standstill; G. B. Anderson could not reach the batteries that were decimating his North Carolinians.

The confusion was maddening. The Willis Church road, the only direct avenue of approach, was crowded with artillery and fugitives and was almost impassable. As General Early tried to carry his brigade toward Hill's right he encountered so many skulkers and disorganized troops that he lost touch with his own men.

The clear, hot day was about to end. The last moment was at hand when a Confederate victory could possibly be wrested from the chaos of a costly contest. Would the climax of Gaines's Mill be repeated in a sudden, resistless charge at twilight, with every brigade somehow finding its place in the line of battle?

The confident roar of the unwearied Federal batteries gave a mocking answer. The move on the left that Whiting had taken as a sign of retreat had not weakened the enemy's resistance. Toombs's brigade came up to support D. H. Hill. It reached the crest of the hill, broke in blood and flowed back to the woods. Even Gordon retreated. Winder and Trimble were pressing forward. All the troops were moving as rapidly as the ground permitted, but none of them could hope to reach the line in time to support the assault before night fell. The gory remnants of Wright's and Mahone's brigades were facing over the brow of the Crew house an enemy that seemed strong enough to smother them. Armistead delivered three more assaults. There was a moment when the furious onslaught of these men made the issue doubtful. An hour more of daylight and a little more vigor on the part of Magruder's weary troops might have spelled triumph. But it was too late. Darkness had now settled. The assault had been "grandly heroic," but "it was not war—it was murder."

Lee had to admit to himself that the day had ended in failure. With a heavy heart, he made such dispositions as he could for the safety of the lines and the comfort of the fallen. Though McClellan had been forced to abandon his lines under the very shadows of Richmond's spires, and had been struck hard and often, he had escaped the destruction Lee had planned for him.

A heavy mist hung over the battlefield when July 2 dawned. From the Confederate side it was impossible to tell whether the enemy still held Malvern Hill or had retired. Lee's brigades were still hopelessly confused. On the crest of the hill a mixed Federal force of cavalry and infantry was waiting. It made a show of advance, but drew back at the first fire of scattered Confederates. From the woods the ambulance details began to trickle slowly out; officers rode forward; soon an informal truce prevailed and thousands of hungry, restless men emerged from the woods to search for missing comrades or to look for food in the haversacks of the fallen. Shattered bodies were everywhere and dead men in every contortion of their last agony. Weapons and the keepsakes of soldiers, caps and knapsacks, playing-cards and pocket testaments, bloody heads with bulging eyes, booted legs, severed arms with hands gripped tight, torsos with the limbs blown away, gray coats dyed black with boys' blood—it was a nightmare of hell, set on a firm, green field of reality, under a workaday, leaden, summer sky, a scene to sicken the simple, home-loving soldiers who had to fight the war while the politicians responsible for bringing a nation to madness stood in the streets of safe cities and mouthed wrathful platitudes about constitutional rights.

Toward 10 o'clock the last of the Federals disappeared. Lee once again had to ask the question, where had McClellan betaken himself? An immediate Federal offensive against Richmond could be left out of consideration, inasmuch as the Federals were in retreat. Eliminating that, there were three possibilities: The enemy might be nearby, preparing to refit and again offer battle; he might be retiring farther down the river to take ship and renew the struggle on some other front; or, lastly, he might be about to pass over the James, as he had crossed the Chickahominy, unite with Burnside's army from North Carolina, capture Drewry's Bluff and open the way for his men-of-war to reach Richmond. Canvassing these possibilities, Lee determined: (1) to send the cavalry immediately in pursuit; (2) to move a part of the army down the James to be at hand if the enemy proved aggressive, and (3) to return Holmes to Drewry's Bluff at once.

As Jackson was nearest the line of the Federal retreat and had suffered least in the campaign, he was ordered to leave D. H. Hill's battered division at Malvern Hill and to move against the enemy with the rest of his force. Longstreet and A. P. Hill were to follow. The remaining units of the army were to remain for the time in their positions, burying the dead, caring for the wounded, and collecting arms and accoutrements from the field. Rain was falling heavily by the time these orders were issued. The enemy also must be suffering. Persons in the neighborhood whom Jackson had interviewed earlier in the morning told him the the Federals were retreating down the River road in the greatest demoralization. The opportunity seemed great if the endurance of the men sufficed and the deluge did not prevent pursuit.

Jackson remained with Lee by the fire in the dining room of a plantation house until his men could take the road. Presently Longstreet came in. He was not cheerful. The weather and the condition of the troops depressed him. After awhile he sloshed out in his wet garments. Soon another visitor came—the President, attended by his brother, Colonel Joseph Davis. Sitting down with the President at the table, Lee reviewed the military outlook.

As the two talked, the rain continued mercilessly. The more the situation was considered, the more confused it appeared. At last Lee and Davis agreed that the weather and the uncertainty of the army made effective pursuit impracticable that day. Jackson sat silent as the reasons for this decision were canvassed, and when he was asked for his opinion, he remarked quietly, "They have not all got away if we go immediately after them." He believed that the enemy could and should be pursued, for his experience with a retreating enemy persuaded him that McClellan was beaten and not merely retiring for new manoeuvres.

Undoubtedly Jackson was right regarding the condition of the enemy, but insistence on a swift pursuit, in such weather, was the counsel of perfection. The Army of Northern Virginia at the close of the action at Malvern Hill was in the condition in which both it and the Army of the Potomac were to find themselves after nearly every major engagement of the next two years. The margin of superiority was so narrow, on either side, that a victory could rarely be developed into a triumph.

The rain ceased on the morning of July 3, and pursuit began. It had hardly started before Lee learned from Stuart that the Federals had reached Harrison's Landing. Rumors were current that McClellan was preparing a great shift across the James, but Stuart's dispatches, arriving every few hours, indicated no such movement.

On the morning of July 4 Lee rode forward to examine McClellan's position. The Federals' ground had been chosen with the same care that had been displayed in the selection of all McClellan's defensive positions during the campaign. Harrison's Landing was on a long, low promontory extending into the James River. Federal gunboats lay in the river, with the batteries trained across the meadows.

Longstreet was chafing to attack; Jackson's judgment was against it; Lee did not attempt a decision until he had thoroughly surveyed every approach. Finding the Federal position protected on all sides, except for a narrow stretch on the northwest, he concluded that an offensive was not justified. This decision in reality marked the end of the campaign.

The tangible results of the campaign were for every man's reckoning. The whole plan of Federal operations in Virginia had been disrupted after its success had seemed inevitable. On June 26 McClellan's army of 105,000 effectives had been like a sharpened sickle, ready to sweep over Richmond. Now it was crowded into an entrenched camp eighteen miles away. Fifty-two fine Federal guns were in Confederate hands. Ten thousand prisoners had been captured, and upwards of 31,000 needed small arms were gleaned from the fields. "The siege of Richmond was raised," Lee reported, "and the object of the campaign, which had been prosecuted after months of preparation at an enormous expenditure of men and money, completely frustrated."

Yet too many Confederate dead were buried between Mechanicsville and Malvern Hill, and too many men lay wretched in the hospitals for Lee to feel any elation. Of the 85,500 men with whom he had opened the campaign, 3286 were dead, 15,909 were wounded, and 946 were missing, a total of 20,141. Half the wounded roughly, were doomed to die or to be permanently incapacitated for field duty. In other words, 11,000 men, the "first line" of the South, had been lost to the Confederacy for all time. Federal losses were assumed to be higher, but actually they were less by nearly 4300.

Lee had achieved less than he had hoped, less than he believed he should have accomplished. "Under ordinary circumstances," he stated in his report, "the Federal army should have been destroyed." The causes were plain.

The Federal army was not destroyed for four reasons: (1) The Confederate commander lacked adequate information for operating in a difficult country because his maps were worthless, his staff work inexperienced, and his cavalry absent at the crisis of the campaign; (2) the Confederate artillery was poorly employed; (3) Lee trusted too much to his subordinates, some of whom failed him almost completely; and (4) he displayed no tactical genius in combating a fine, well-led Federal army. When these four factors are given their just valuation, the wonder is not that an honest commander had to admit that he had failed to realize his full expectation. Rather is the wonder that so much of success was attained. In the face of obstacles and failures, how was

Lee able to break the grip of McClellan on Richmond and to pen up that splendid Federal army at Harrison's Landing?

There would seem to be three major explanations. The first, of course, was the fundamental soundness of Lee's strategy. The campaign may well be cited as an example of the manner in which the highest type of strategy, if consistently followed, will sometimes overcome difficulties and atone for tactical blunders. Second, Lee accomplished the major object of his campaign because the valor of his infantry was neither shaken by losses nor impaired by long campaigning. Through the worst hardships of the campaign, the men remained wholly confident of victory and convinced that they would soon end the war. Finally, there was the singular temperament of Lee's chief opponent. Though General McClellan was certainly the ablest organizer and probably the best military administrator developed in the North during the war, possessing his men's affection as did no other Federal general in chief, he was not far from panic during the Seven Days. It is impossible to state the precise cause or combination of causes for his condition. Whatever it may have been, it aided Lee to a degree past all reckoning. Lee could not have asked for a more favorable state of mind on the part of his adversary.

Hostile critics of President Davis and of General Lee, balancing successes against failures, professed disappointment with Lee's generalship and with the results obtained. But the public saw the successes, not the shortcomings. Especially in Richmond, press and people did not judge the Seven Days as a series of close battles but in their proper light, as a campaign of strategy that began with the first move to transfer Jackson from the Valley and ended when McClellan was caged and impotent at Harrison's Landing with his plan of operations hopelessly shattered. They remembered the panic of May; they did not forget how they had seen the glow of bombardment and had heard above the anxious beating of their own hearts the defiant challenge of the enemy's guns. And in the contrast between June 1 and July 4, they read mighty achievement.

More important, far, than popular acclaim was the confidence and admiration aroused among the soldiers in the ranks. Within a month the "King of Spades" became the father of his men, trusted and idolized. Stories of his simplicity, devotion, and humility began to go the rounds. The troops felt that he was superior to the best general the enemy had and that their lives and their cause were safe in his hands. After this first campaign their faith in him was unbounded.

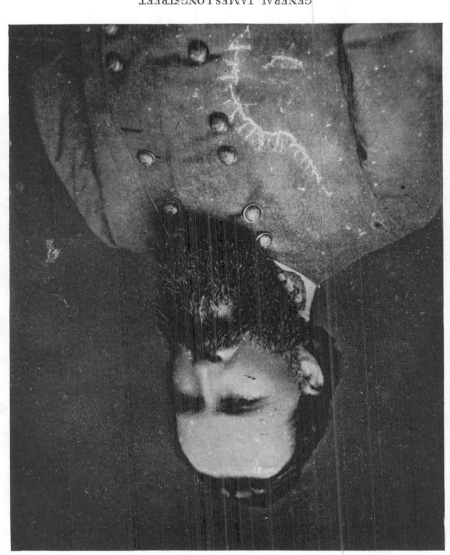

GENERAL JAMES LONGSTREET

GENERAL AMBROSE EVERETT BURNSIDE AND AIDES

Lee gave little time and less thought to reading the newspapers that were discounting his performance or sounding his praises. His immediate task was to reorganize the army. The most pressing part of that task was to provide better divisional leadership. Longstreet had emerged as the most dependable man, at the moment, among his lieutenants. More fully than any other division commander he had shown himself worthy of trust with a larger command. D. H. Hill had been admirable. A. P. Hill had marched well and had fought hard. Magruder was too excitable for such fighting as lay ahead Fortunately, the question of disposing of him had been solved in advance: he had already been offered command in the Trans-Mississippi department. Huger's failure had been unrelieved and was irredeemable. He was now named inspector of artillery and ordnance. His division was assigned to R. H. Anderson of South Carolina, who was promoted major general. Holmes had not exhibited brilliance and was slow and deaf, besides. Like Magruder, he was given command in the Trans-Mississippi department. D. H. Hill was assigned in his place.

There remained Jackson—what should be done about him? By every test, Jackson had failed throughout the Seven Days. Had Jackson fought as hard and done as well as Longstreet and A. P. Hill, there would have been a different tale to tell. Lee may have felt this. He never had the slightest doubt concerning Jackson's ability, his discretion, or his daring independent command, but he may have feared that Jackson was ambitious and ill-disposed to fight under another. Yet Jackson had to his credit the amazing campaign in the Valley that had shown of what he was capable. Lee could not overlook past performance. He retained his faith in Jackson, but he made a significant change in the organization of the army. He left Lawton's brigade to fill out Jackson's old division and retained Ewell under the control of Jackson. Thus, if required for separate use, the Army of the Valley was intact. Whiting's division was joined with Holmes's former force under D. H. Hill. The rest of the infantry divisions were entrusted to Longstreet. In short, Jackson fought the Seven Days with fourteen brigades; in the reorganization, he was allotted seven. Longstreet had carried six brigades across the Chickahominy; he soon had twenty-eight. What did Jackson think of all this? He never told any one that he felt he had failed to do his part in the campaign. His report contained no apologies. If he did not blame himself, however, it is certain he did not blame Lee or criticize the distribution of force.

No reorganization of the artillery was undertaken. The general staff was not modified, and Lee's personal staff was not changed. Lee came gradually to act as his own chief staff officer. It seems strange, at first glance, that a man so mindful of the value of military details should have done so little to prepare maps, to make his artillery more efficient, and to build up the staff. Lee, however, realized that Confederate success depended on utilizing the means at hand, without waiting to perfect them in competition with an enemy whose resources were greater. Whatever the Southern States could hope to do must be done quickly. Lee had to leave much to chance and more to the accumulating experience of the army, as he prepared for a dramatic new stage of the war in Virginia.

CHAPTER VIII

Second Manassas and Sharpsburg

DURING the six weeks following his hard battles around Richmond, Lee sought to rest, refit, reinforce, and reorganize the Army of Northern Virginia. Most of the troops had only routine duties to perform, and even these were suspended on Sunday. Leisure and decent rations quickly restored the health of men. Reinforcement was more difficult. Lee had to rely on the flow of conscripts, on the return of wounded men, on the prevention of absence without leave, and on the stoppage of wasteful details. Reorganization was retarded by slow action on recommendations for promotion and, except for the cavalry, was dangerously far from completion when the army again entered on active operations. The mounted arm was taken vigorously in hand. Stuart was given command of all the horse; two brigades were created, Hampton at the head of one, and Fitz Lee, the other. Reorganization of Jackson's cavalry was deferred.

The Federals were not idle. Three hundred thousand volunteers had been called for on July 1. Defeat stiffened the determination of the North. By July 10, besides the main force under McClellan, Lee had to watch three Federal armies. The shattered divisions of McDowell, Banks, and Frémont had been organized into a new "Army of Virginia" under Major General John Pope. Lee did not know whether these forces had been consolidated, but he assumed them to be in the general vicinity of Manassas. A second additional column was known to be around Fredericksburg. The third force had come from Burnside in North Carolina and was on transports off Fortress Monroe.

Lee had to plan as information accumulated. The starting point was the fact that the battles for Richmond had given the retention of that city a moral value out of all proportion to its importance. Richmond must be fortified further. Improvement of the fortifications, while of high importance in protecting the city against McClellan, would make it less difficult for Lee to detach troops in case the forces in northern Virginia seriously threatened an advance. Jackson, now rested and full of ardor, was for an immediate offensive that would sweep past Pope's army and carry the war into the enemy's country. With Mc-Clellan still dangerously close to Richmond and at the head of an army larger than his own, Lee was averse to weakening himself, at least until he knew what Pope would attempt to do.

The first shift in the army was brought about by the receipt of news on July 12 that the Federals had occupied Culpeper Courthouse that morning. A serious threat in that quarter was an immediate menace to an indispensable line and had to be met at any cost. Desirable as it was to await the development of the enemy's plan, Lee did not feel that he could delay. On the 13th, therefore, he ordered Jackson with his own and Ewell's division, to proceed by train to Louisa and, if Pope had not anticipated him, to proceed to Gordonsville. Part of Jackson's cavalry was sent to Hanover Junction.

This was the first time Lee had been called upon to apply in Virginia a principle he doubtless had learned in South Carolina. He did not scatter infantry along the railroad, which was perpendicular to the line of Pope's advance and consequently exposed for a long distance. Instead, he kept Jackson's troops together to strike the invader as he approached the railway.

Thus far Lee had developed only two of the fundamentals of a new campaign, namely, to strengthen the Richmond fortifications, so as to make a detachment of force possible, and to guard his communications with the Valley. He began to study the third step in the development of a new plan: He began to ask himself whether he could send enough men to Jackson to defeat Pope and then return them to Richmond in time to meet McClellan.

From July 23 to July 27, Lee wrestled over the logistics of this plan. Lee was uncertain whether McClellan was demonstrating to deceive him, testing the strength of the Confederates, or preparing for a serious advance. In any case, unless some decision was soon reached and put in execution, both Lee and Jackson might be assaulted. So reasoning, Lee reached this solution: the two brigades that were coming from South Carolina would arrive on July 28. Lee would incorporate them in his army and send 18,000 veterans forthwith to Jackson for a blow against Pope. This would leave 56,000 men on the James. Lee would take his chances of holding Richmond with that number. He would organize a diversion on the south side of the James against McClellan's base and would endeavor to interrupt the transport of supplies to McClellan. Jackson might be strong enough to dispose of Pope, and McClellan might be held back until this was done, or, if McClellan advanced, a sufficient force would be at hand to maintain a good defensive. On July 27 A. P. Hill was ordered to Gordonsville. Hill's men moved quietly away on the day their orders were received.

McClellan was believed to have received an accession of numbers and was known to have a force much larger than Lee's. If Burnside should reinforce McClellan, an advance on Richmond would be a serious matter. If Burnside should join Pope, he would give the Army of Virginia a number of men in excess of the 30,000 to 36,000 that Lee calculated Jackson would have on Hill's arrival. Burnside's movements consequently became of the utmost moment.

About this time there arrived the young captain who had been made prisoner on July 20 at Beaver Dam Station by the Federal cavalry. This officer was John S. Mosby, subsequently head of the famous "Rangers" that bore his name. Mosby had been sent to Fort Monroe and, while awaiting exchange, had kept his eyes open and had shrewdly questioned his guards. He had concluded that Burnside's expedition was about to sail to Fredericksburg to join Pope and hastened to communicate to Lee that conclusion.

But on August 5 the evidence seemed to indicate that the long-awaited offensive by McClellan was under way: the Confederate cavalry reported a heavy force advancing toward Richmond. Lee set himself for a shock. He put three divisions in motion the next day and found McClellan drawn up at Malvern Hill. This time the Confederate lines were deliberately drawn. The Confederate right skirmished briskly with the Federals; there were many signs of approaching battle. Then, on the morning of August 7, when a clash seemed certain, an amazing situation was disclosed: the Federals had gone as they had come and soon were back at Harrison's Landing! Lee concluded that his opponent must have made the demonstration to cover an advance on the part of Burnside in northern Virginia.

The argument in Lee's mind pursued a circle, caution bringing him back to the waiting policy from which his desire to suppress Pope and his concern for the Virginia Central Railroad constantly were drawing him. He did the only thing he could do at a distance from a situation he could not fathom—he gave discretion to Jackson. Jackson did not wait for the discretionary orders. On August 9 he found the Federals on Cedar Run in the vicinity of Slaughter Mountain. He attacked viciously and after suffering a temporary reverse on part of his line, swept forward and drove the Federals from the field. Jackson was himself again.

Jackson soon realized, however, that he had met only the vanguard of Pope's army and that the remainder was coming up. On the night of August 11, he decided to withdraw closer to Gordonsville, there to await reinforcements. This move decided Lee on his course of action. Whatever the risks, Jackson must be strengthened to strike a blow at his adversary. On August 13, therefore, Lee ordered Longstreet with ten brigades to move to Jackson's aid.

On the very day when Lee decided that he must face the risk involved in these further detachments from the James it developed that the risk might not be so great as he had previously believed. There had been rumors that McClellan was reducing his force at Harrison's Landing, but nothing definite was reported until August 13, when a deserter came into the Confederate lines and stated that part of McClellan's army had embarked for a move. Lee immediately instructed D. H. Hill to send scouts down the right bank of the river to ascertain the facts. The next day Hill reported there was no doubt that Fitz John Porter had left McClellan. Three deserters from Burnside's army averred that he had reached Fredericksburg with 12,000 men and there had been reinforced by twenty-one regiments.

This was news of the greatest moment. Pope would soon present a most formidable front on the line of the Virginia Central Railroad. Unless Jackson were still further reinforced he would be overwhelmed. But, along with a great danger, a large opportunity was presented. If Lee could concentrate against Pope before troops from the Army of the Potomac could reach him, a great victory might be won. Lee acted with dispatch. He immediately decided to go to Gordonsville himself.

Thanks to Jackson's forethought, when Lee sat down in council with him and Longstreet on the 15th he had a good map and adequate intelligence reports. The Rapidan River on the south and the Rappahannock on the north form a great "V" laid on its side with its apex to the east, where the two rivers unite, about nine miles west of Fredericksburg. Across the open end of this "V," at an average distance of twenty miles from the confluence of the streams, ran the Orange and Alexandria Railroad, which constituted Pope's line of supply. Into the angle between the two rivers Pope had brought a force estimated at 45,000 to 50,000. Pope's front was to the Rapidan. Behind him lay the Rappahannock. Reinforcements, the Confederates computed, made Pope's full strength 65,000 to 70,000 men.

Pope's ignorance of Lee's movements had caused him incautiously to present his adversary as fair an opportunity as ever a soldier was offered. If the infantry of the Army of Northern Virginia concentrated close to the Rapidan, the cavalry could be dispatched quickly to burn the bridge at Rappahannock Station and the veteran brigades from the Peninsula could be hurled across the Rapidan. Pope would thus be caught within the "V" between the two rivers and might be destroyed.

But this must be done quickly, for the whole instead of merely a part of McClellan's army was probably moving to reinforce Pope. Lee must strike before Pope became alarmed and put the Rappahannock between him and the Army of Northern Virginia. What was the earliest date at which the army could cross the Rapidan? The decision was to approach the fords of the Rapidan on the 17th and to give battle to Pope on the 18th.

Stuart reached Orange Courthouse by train on the afternoon of the 17th and came out to Lee's headquarters. He reported that he had moved Fitz Lee's brigade from Hanover Courthouse on the 16th to the vicinity of Beaver Dam, and had left him there with orders to march on the 17th toward Raccoon Ford on the Rapidan, where Stuart expected to cross the river. Preparations went on all day of the 17th. The army was in excellent spirits, confident of its ability to defeat Pope. There was no sign that the Federals were aware of the thunderbolt Lee was forging for them. Everything pointed to an early and an overwhelming victory. But when the morning of the 18th came, the army was not prepared. R. H. Anderson's division, arriving from Richmond, was not in position. There was no news from Stuart as to his whereabouts and none as to the arrival of Fitz Lee. The cavalry on the Confederate left was not disposed to suit Lee. The commissary did not have enough hard bread on hand. Lee had to defer the crossing of the river until the 19th.

Even had all else been ready, Fitz Lee's cavalry would not have been at hand for its important work. Stuart had been the victim of a curious misadventure that morning. Late in the afternoon of the 17th he had ridden eastward from Orange to Verdiersville, where he expected Fitz Lee to halt for the night. The quiet people of the slumbering countryside had answered with blank looks Stuart's questions regarding the location of the Confederate cavalry camp. Much puzzled, Stuart had sent his assistant adjutant general, Major Norman Fitzhugh, down the road to find Fitz Lee and to hurry him on. Then Stuart and his aides had lain down on the porch of a private house to await the troopers. As day was breaking on the 18th Stuart saw a body of horsemen some 400 yards away and heard the clatter of advancing hoofs. There was a moment's wait, loud voices, a shout of "Yankee cavalry," a few nervous shots—and in an instant Stuart was up, mounted, and dashing for the nearby woods, while his aides were galloping off with a Federal patrol in avid pursuit. All escaped except Major Fitzhugh, but the Federals rode off triumphantly with Stuart's hat and coat.

It probably was late in the morning of the 18th when the general in chief heard from Stuart of this mishap, and still later when he received a telegram from Fitz Lee reporting where he was. Either because his orders had been carelessly drawn, or else because he had misinterpreted them, Fitz Lee had not understood that he was to press on to Raccoon Ford by the evening of the 17th. Regretfully, the commanding general was forced to postpone the crossing of the Rapidan one day more, until the morning of the 20th.

To Lee's disappointment over his inability to strike Pope in his exposed position at the time he had appointed there was added on the 18th a fear that the enemy had discovered his presence. Before nightfall the worst apprehensions seemed realized in reports from the lookouts that the Federals were breaking up their camps and retiring toward Culpeper Courthouse, but the magnitude and meaning of this move were not wholly apparent then. Lee went ahead with his preparations.

The air was tense. The men knew that an advance was immediately in prospect. Before noon the signal station announced another move-ment by the enemy. Without waiting for particulars, Lee sent for Longstreet and rode with him to the crest of the mountain. "From its summit," wrote Longstreet, ". . . the white tops of army wagons were seen moving. Half an hour's close watch revealed that the move was for the Rappahannock River. . . . Little clouds of dust arose which marked the tramp of soldiers, and these presently began to swell into dense columns along the rearward lines. Watching without comment till the clouds grew thinner and thinner as they approached the river and melted into the bright haze of the afternoon sun, General Lee finally put away his glasses, and with a deeply-drawn breath, expressive at once of disappointment and resignation, said, 'General, we little thought that the enemy would turn his back upon us thus early in the campaign.' "

Unknown to Lee, a copy of one of his orders to Stuart, showing something of the whereabouts of the army, had been found on Major

Fitzhugh when he had been captured, and this document had been sent to Pope. A spy, moreover, on the morning of August 18, had reported the Confederate preparations to General McDowell. General Reno had also discovered the Confederate dispositions. At 1:30 P.M. on the 18th Pope had started to withdraw.

But whither was Pope withdrawing? As far as Lee could make out he was moving by the road to Fredericksburg, but that road led into the narrow part of the "V" formed by the Rappahannock and Rapidan, where his condition would be worse than before. It was obvious that the Federals must intend to cross the Rappahannock and go northward. As the course of the Orange and Alexandria Railroad was from southwest to northeast beyond Culpeper, Pope could cross well down the Rappahannock and still not be at a dangerous distance from his communications.

It was too late to begin pursuit on the 19th, and if the men started that night they would not be fresh for battle the next day. Lee consequently decided to cross the Rapidan at 4 A.M. Orders were amended. On the morning of August 20 the Army of Northern Virginia crossed the undefended fords of the Rapidan. Its seven divisions and two unattached brigades of infantry numbered about 50,000 men. The cavalry division and the artillery brought the total effectives to some 54,500. Pope's army was above the Rappahannock, with the fords heavily guarded. To effect a crossing without excessive losses, Lee had to move up the Rappahannock, by his left flank.

After Taliaferro's division of Jackson's command reached Beverley Ford it began a hot artillery action with Federal batteries on the opposite bank. The passage of the infantry was apt to be costly. Lee examined the ground, weighed the chances of success, decided not to attempt a crossing, and recalled Stuart to the south bank. The presence of the enemy near Beverley Ford did not mean that the turning movement up the Rappahannock was to be abandoned. On the contrary, Lee was more intent upon it than ever. From his imperfect information of the enemy's movements, he concluded that part of Pope's army was moving toward Fredericksburg and part toward Warrenton, and he considered it desirable on every count to attack and dispose of the force nearest him.

The news that came to headquarters on the morning of the 22d was not particularly encouraging. The enemy seemed fully apprized of Lee's purpose to turn his right by outflanking him up the Rappahannock. When Stuart reached the next good crossing, Freeman's Ford, there were the Federals strongly placed on the opposite bank as if defying the Confederates to force a passage.

The operation was becoming tedious. Wherever Lee moved, there was Pope, apparently confident and fully the master of the situation. Lee decided that something must be done to shake and demoralize the enemy. No means at Lee's disposal so readily promised this as a quick dash that Stuart asked that he be permitted to make, with torch and carbine, against the Federal rear at Catlett's Station. Orders for the raid were accordingly issued.

The rainy night of the 22d settled on a situation still unpromising. Stuart had started off on the raid against Catlett's Station with all except two regiments of the cavalry. Jackson, at Warrenton Springs Ford, had eight small regiments and two batteries, under Early, cut off by the raging Rappahannock. Longstreet and Anderson, downstream, were facing superior artillery. All that was known of Pope was that he was conforming to the Confederate left-flank movement. Nothing definite could be planned for the next day beyond a strong artillery demonstration at Rappahannock Bridge for the double purpose of driving back the Federals at that point and of creating the impression, if possible, that the Confederates intended crossing there.

At dawn on the 23d Longstreet's artillery was brought up to demonstrate at Rappahannock Station. A small force of Federals was promptly forced to seek the north bank, and the opposing Federal guns were silenced. While Longstreet was making this demonstration, Jackson was trying to rebuild the burned bridge at Warrenton Springs Ford and was instructing Early regarding the defense he was to make in his threatened position. More important was the news from Stuart. After receiving his orders on the 22d, that officer had ridden to Catlett's Station. A friendly Negro had guided him to Pope's headquarters. The commander had been absent but his uniform coat had been in his tent, and several of his staff had been there. A miscellaneous mass of Pope's military papers, including a dispatch book, had been carelessly placed where the Confederates could seize them. They had been gathered up and brought off, together with General Pope's quartermaster, who had subsequently done some indiscreet talking. This loquacious officer affirmed that Cox's army in western Virginia had been ordered to move to Wheeling and then to join Pope.

When Lee received the more important of Pope's papers he discovered that Pope had 45,000 men on August 20, exclusive of the rein-

forcements from Burnside and that he had not detached any of these
eastward toward Fredericksburg. Pope's expectation was to hold the
line of the Rappahannock until McClellan could join him from the
vicinity of Fredericksburg. The reading of the dispatches showed that
the race between Lee and McClellan to reach Pope was getting dangerously close. That knowledge was the turning-point of the campaign.
Lee now knew that Pope was numerically superior to him, besides
having a great advantage in artillery. As soon as McClellan's divisions
joined Pope, the odds would be hopeless. If luckily, a part of Pope's
army could be caught, it would of course be attacked, but an offensive
leading to a battle between the whole of the two armies would entail
losses to the Confederates that could not be replaced, even if a victory
were gained. The proper course was to avoid a general engagement and
to force Pope away from McClellan and out of the fat agricultural
districts of northern Virginia. What form of manoeuvre would accomplish the largest result in the shortest time? Lee fixed his eye on the
Orange and Alexandria Railroad. He hoped to cut that supply line. In
doing so, he might be able to put part of his army between Pope and
Washington.

Lee wrote Davis of his discoveries from Pope's correspondence and
tactfully ordered the remaining units of the Army of Northern Virginia
to rejoin him. Lee sent for Jackson to come to his headquarters. The
conference that followed between the two was one of the most important Lee ever held. He told Jackson to take his command up the
Rappahannock, to get in rear of Pope's army, and to cut his communications with Washington.

Jackson would carry with him in his three divisions approximately
23,000 men. That would leave Lee only some 32,000. Such a division
of force in the face of an enemy of known superior strength was a
violation of the strategic canon of concentration in the face of the
enemy. Lee deliberately violated that canon. He did not do so because
of contempt for Pope, as has been alleged. The reason was that an
attack on Pope's line of communications seemed to be the only means
of manoeuvring into a retreat an opponent whom he did not feel strong
enough to fight. Had he any intention to give battle, it is unlikely that
Lee would have adopted such a dangerous course. Years afterwards,
when told that his move had been criticized as over-rash, he said: "Such
criticism is obvious, but the disparity . . . between the contending
forces rendered the risks unavoidable."

The last of Jackson's "foot-cavalry" filed off about daybreak on

August 25. All the morning and most of the afternoon of the 24th the artillery had exchanged its challenge across the river, but the demonstrations ended in smoke and sound. In the evening General Stuart rode over to headquarters to report and to get his orders. Lee gave him detailed instructions for his march in support of Jackson, and, in the knowledge that Jackson's operation required an abundance of cavalry, Lee authorized Stuart to take all his troopers with him, an over-generous act for which he was soon to pay.

There was something suspicious about the movements of the enemy the next morning. The bridgehead was still occupied and the fire was strong, but the bustle was not that of a foe expecting to receive or intending to deliver an attack. Lee interpreted what was happening as an indication that the enemy was beginning to move away. If Pope was moving away from the Rappahannock, he would soon be within striking distance of Jackson, even if he had not already had wind of the march of "Stonewall." The Army of Northern Virginia must be re-united. Calling to him the stocky, hardheaded Longstreet, Lee told him he intended to join Jackson as soon as possible. Orders were issued accordingly. R. H. Anderson was told to cover Warrenton Springs Ford, and the "right wing" that was soon to be the famous "First Corps" stole quietly away during the afternoon under cover of the hills and headed north.

On August 27 two and a half miles from Salem the march was broken by the arrival of a courier. He brought from Jackson a dispatch that made every heart beat faster. By an astounding two days' march Jackson had covered fifty-four miles and the previous evening had reached Bristoe Station. There he had captured two trains, though two had escaped. Then, while some of their men had been tearing up the track, Trimble with two regiments and Stuart with part of the cavalry had gone seven miles farther up the Orange and Alexandria Railroad to Manassas Junction, where Jackson had heard that the Federals had accumulated vast stores. The junction had been taken with slight op-position. Jackson was precisely where Lee wanted him to be—in rear of the Federal army and between it and Washington. Not only so, but, with good fortune, the two wings of the army could unite again before Pope's retreat, which was now inevitable, brought him in superior force to Manassas.

Lee saw possibilities of high manoeuvres from Jackson's position, if more men were forthcoming, and in customary manner he wrote of the next move as he read of the last. In a dispatch to the President he urged once again that reinforcements be sent forward with all speed. The messenger that carried this dispatch to the telegraph station at Rapidan probably passed a courier bound from that place with a message from Davis. In this, the President told Lee of the advance of the troops already sent to his assistance. With a mind to the criticism that would overwhelm him if Richmond were taken because it was stripped of its defenders, Mr. Davis concluded: "Confidence in you overcomes the view which would otherwise be taken of the exposed condition of Richmond, and the troops retained for the defense of the capital are surrendered to you on a new request." Reinforcements coming, Jackson between Pope and Washington, the railroad cut, the enemy's advanced base destroyed—it was enough to strengthen men to endure even the torture of that endless day's groping through dust that burned eyes and parched throats.

Lee was now on the watershed of the Potomac, the dividing line between the Union and the Confederacy. If Jackson was still at Manassas, the remainder of the Army of Northern Virginia on the morning of August 28 was just twenty-two miles from him, a long but not an impossible day's march. All the news was reassuring. Couriers arrived at intervals during the morning from Jackson. They brought the cheering tidings that Jackson had left the exposed position at Manassas and was resting his men, undisturbed and apparently unobserved, at a place called Groveton, seven miles northwest of Manassas.

The soldiers rose on the morning of August 28 from their short night's slumber and moved toward Thoroughfare Gap. The highest ground was reached before the gap was visible and the down grade began; but the progress of the wagon train was slow and the day was hot. The morning had dragged to noon and noon to 3 P.M. before the head of the column approached the gap. Lee was disposed to call a halt and give the men twelve hours' sleep, so that they would be fresh the next morning to descend the Bull Run Mountains and join with Jackson in a manoeuvre that would throw Pope back on Washington. As a precaution, however, he determined to send forward Longstreet's leading division, that of D. R. Jones, to occupy the pass against possible seizure by the Federals.

Jones went briskly forward. Soon there rolled the sound of an angry fire. Presently the message was glumly brought back: The enemy in undetermined strength held the pass and commanded it from a ridge at the opposite side. The Federals stood squarely between the two wings of the Army of Northern Virginia. If the Union force was large enough

and stubborn enough, Longstreet could be held off while the rest of
Pope's army demolished Jackson. Then the united forces of Pope and
McClellan could fall upon Longstreet.

Lee rode forward to the summit of the hill west of the pass and there
dismounted and studied the gap closely. Lee's quick eye for topography
convinced him that Thoroughfare Gap was not so formidable as it was
reputed to be—that there must be trails or minor passes by which
resolute men could turn the position of the enemy. He gave his orders
briskly. D. R. Jones was to press the enemy on either side of the gap.
Hood's division was to search for a nearby route over the mountain,
and Wilcox, temporarily commanding three brigades, was to move
them quickly to the northward and to try Hopewell Gap, three miles
to the left.

In the late afternoon the troops who were climbing and crawling
over barren rocks and through tangled mountain laurel heard in the
intervals between the slow Federal artillery fire a low and ominous
mutter from the eastward—gunfire, artillery, a battle undoubtedly in
progress in the distance. It must be Jackson, found and assailed by the
enemy. At the gap, the Federals pushed forward artillery and swept
the defile. Finally the 1st Georgia regulars got within effective range. It
made its fire count. An attempt by the enemy to hurl back the
Georgians was quickly repulsed.

Twilight began to fall in the pass, but the fire continued, as if the
Federals, in confident possession of a dominating position, seemed determined to hold off the Confederates until Jackson was finished. The
situation gave every promise of a long, ugly fight. But the threat of the
advancing Confederates had its effect. The enemy was preparing to retreat. Jones waited a while and then boldly marched his division unopposed through the pass. When the anxious day ended, the danger was
past, as if by some miracle. Lee sent a courier to Jackson, announcing
the outcome of the fight. Two stout divisions of the Army of Northern
Virginia slept on their arms with their faces toward "Stonewall's"
battleground. There was hope in their hearts. Only the open road lay
before them now, and they were determined that all the might that
Pope could muster should not halt them on the morrow.

The road to the eastward led to Jackson's position on the morning of
August 29, but south of that road, nine miles away, lay Warrenton,
where Pope, by the latest report, had a large force. During the early
morning a detached cavalry company rode into the lines at Thoroughfare Gap. Lee took this company, collected all available mounted men,

placed them under Stuart's quartermaster, Major Samuel H. Hairston, who happened to be with the infantry, and sent them off, 150 strong, to ascertain if any Federals were still in the vicinity of Warrenton.

Before Hairston could set out, the infantry were on the road. Hood's division was in advance, and picked Texas riflemen acted as skirmishers. Contact was soon established with the rearguard of the Federals who had held the gap the night before, but they fled fast and soon disappeared altogether. The steady tramp of Longstreet's regiments was uninterrupted. The dust was thick and the air already hot by the time Haymarket was reached and passed. Soon, on the left, in the edge of a wood, horsemen were seen. As their leader galloped ahead, his flowing beard and familiar garb identified him as Stuart.

The arrival of the cavalry was most reassuring, because it could guard the exposed right of Longstreet's column from sudden attack. The infantry were halted in the road so that the cavalry might cross to the south for this purpose. Refreshed by the rest this pause afforded them, the regiments took up the march and soon were close to Gainesville. The sound of desultory artillery fire had beaten an uncertain accompaniment to the tramp of the troops for several miles, and now it swelled in faster time. Lee's mind was busy as he rode with Longstreet's troops. Was there a prospect of victory, beyond the ridge where the smoke was rising?

As Lee pondered, the head of the column reached Gainesville. Lee came up shortly thereafter and established his headquarters. Presently there galloped up from the left a solitary courier to ascertain whether the troops who were taking position with so much composure were Federals or the long-awaited divisions of Longstreet. The courier paused only long enough to make sure and then returned as fast as spurs could force his jaded horse toward the waiting and weary captors of Manassas. "It's Longstreet," he cried joyously, so that every listening ear caught the words. A mighty cheer went up, and Jackson's men knew for the first time that the worst danger was past, that the Army of Northern Virginia was united again. Jackson's "foot-cavalry" had reason both to rejoice and to be proud, for their performance from the time Lee had heard of their arrival at Bristoe Station and at Manassas had been almost as splendid as their march to Pope's rear.

The whole operation had been conducted on Jackson's part without a serious mistake of any sort. His troops were weary and were sadly deficient in senior officers, but their spirit was high, and when they saw their old comrades of the Seven Days file into position, they turned

again defiantly to the enemy, who was massing on the front as Longstreet came up.

Longstreet's line was formed promptly. Hood's division was placed
perpendicular to the turnpike, with its left close to the right of Jackson's line. Evans was in immediate support. Three brigades under Wilcox were put in rear of Hood's left, and three others under Kemper
were behind Hood's right. D. R. Jones's division was sent to the right
of Hood, where his flank rested on the Manassas Gap Railroad. It was
an admirable position in which to meet an attack, though not quite so
good for hurling quickly the full weight of the army in assault.

Lee had at hand all the troops he could hope to put into action,
whereas troops arriving from McClellan might so strengthen Pope that
he could seize the initiative. The thing to do was to attack at once. He
so informed Longstreet. But "Old Pete" was not satisfied. He was
granted time in which to examine the ground more fully and to ascertain what force was gathering on his right. When Longstreet returned
he was full of misgiving. Lee was disappointed. As the two debated, a
message arrived from General Stuart, who was on reconnaissance down
the road leading to Manassas. Stuart said that a column was approaching
from that direction. Longstreet hurried off to see the situation and to
dispose Wilcox's men as they came up on the right. Again Lee had to
wait. Longstreet came back somewhat reassured. The force opposite his
right was hardly large enough as yet to threaten his flank, he said, but
there was more dust down the road toward Manassas. Further troops
might be moving in that direction.

"Hadn't we better move our line forward?" Lee asked.

"I think not," Longstreet answered cautiously; "we had better wait
until we hear more from Stuart about the force he has reported moving
against us from Manassas."

Lee hesitated to order an attack where the man who was to deliver
it was opposed to it, so he consented to await developments a while
longer. Soon Stuart arrived, to confirm what Longstreet had said of a
movement up the road from Manassas. Pope's command was being reinforced still further by the Army of the Potomac—dark news! The
last lap of the race to Pope was being run on the field of battle. Lee
determined now to ascertain the facts for himself. He made a personal
reconnaissance. After an hour, he rode back to the hill. For the third
time Lee declared himself for an attack. Longstreet was obdurate. Lee
hesitated. Judgment and consideration for the opinion of his subordinate
were at odds. At length, though unconvinced, he assented. His decision

was reached after far too little deliberation and probably was expressed
in a very few words, but the moment was an important one in the
military career of Lee. In all the operations since Lee had taken command of the Army of Northern Virginia he had not shown any of the
excessive consideration for the feelings of others that he had exhibited
in West Virginia in his dealings with General Loring; now it appeared
again.

The roar from the left now told of such a battle as even the Army of
Northern Virginia had seldom fought. A. P. Hill, on Jackson's left, had
his six brigades in a double line. Against this line, now swinging to the
right and now to the left, Pope threw his troops in successive charges
from 3 o'clock until 6. On some parts of the front the ammunition was
exhausted after the second Federal assault, and the men had to meet the
enemy with the bayonet. The enemy was across the railroad cut, and
the survivors of the regiments that had fought in the swamp at Gaines's
Mill were preparing to meet them with steel when there was a shout
behind them. Thinking that they were surrounded, they turned in
dread—and saw the familiar gray of Early's brigades and a part of
Lawton's, comparatively fresh. There was a brief, wild encounter; then
the Federals were repulsed once more and were forced to retreat beyond the line of the unfinished railroad.

Of all this Lee could see nothing, but as he received no call for assistance from Jackson, he knew that all was well. About sunset, Hood
was sent forward along the turnpike to make the reconnaissance that
Longstreet had favored. He encountered a Federal force advancing to
attack him. A quick, fierce clash occurred in gathering darkness. It was
late when Hood came back to Lee and Longstreet and reported that he
had advanced so far that he could not distinguish bluecoat from gray.
He advocated a withdrawal to his original line. He had made, at Longstreet's instance, as careful a study as possible of the enemy's position.
His conclusion was disconcerting, almost disheartening. The ground
held by the enemy was very strong, he said. An attack the next morning would be dangerous. General Wilcox, who made a separate report,
was of the same opinion. The information supplied by Hood and
Wilcox threw Lee back on his original plan to avoid a general engagement and to rely on manoeuvre in forcing Pope from northern Virginia.

Day broke clear and bright on the 30th, in a stillness that did not
suggest a renewal of the enemy's attacks. Such slight movements as
could be observed from headquarters indicated a withdrawal. When
Lee sat down to write an early-morning dispatch to the President, his

mind was not on an offensive battle but on the possibility of further manoeuvres to clear the enemy from fruitful northern Virginia.

About 8 o'clock the enemy's batteries opened a slow fire, but this caused no apprehension. With guns so advantageously placed to support the batteries attached to the infantry commands, Lee felt that he had little to fear in an artillery engagement, even from the superior ordnance of the Federals. The fire kept up for about an hour; then it died away in a silence more profound than before.

Straining ears heard the distant rumbling of artillery wheels about noon, and anxious eyes ere long saw rising clouds of dust on the left. Couriers were dispatched to put the troops on the alert. Jackson joined Lee and Longstreet at headquarters. Stuart was summoned and came up quickly. Preparations were complete, the generals reported. Unless more of McClellan's troops had come to swell Pope's numbers to invincible odds, Lee had only to fear that the army would run out of ammunition or that Jackson's thinned regiments would be overborne.

As Lee, at headquarters, waited and watched, there arrived an unexpected visitor in the person of General Pendleton. Along with dispatches from President Davis he brought the good news that the rest of the reserve artillery was on the march to Lee and that D. H. Hill's division was at Rapidan Station. On the next move, whatever it might be, Lee would have reinforcements. He sent General Pendleton off to rest and turned to ascertain the meaning of the fire that was now rolling heavily from Jackson's front.

The Federals had begun a new attack. At first it was heaviest on Jackson's right. Opposite the second brigade of Jackson's old division the enemy got so close to the cut that the opposing flags were only ten yards apart. For half an hour the battle raged; then it appeared to be directed chiefly against the left flank, as on the previous afternoon.

Lee turned to his signal officer and had him flag to Jackson, two miles off, "What is the result of the movements on your left?" Presently the answer came back: "So far, the enemy appear to be trying to get possession of a piece of woods to withdraw out of our sight."

But "Old Jack" was wrong. Quickly the Federals returned in force that made their first assault seem no more than a skirmish. Hill's men, fighting hard, began to waver, and Jackson quickly sent word to Longstreet and to Lee, asking for reinforcements. Lee forwarded an order to Longstreet to hurry a division to Jackson. Longstreet received this message while standing on high ground near the centre, whence he could see the left flank of the Federals who were then renewing their assault on Jackson's right at the same time they were pounding his left. As the Federal left was within easy artillery range of his guns, Longstreet reasoned that a well-directed fire would break up the attack before he could possibly march a division to Jackson's relief. He had noticed, as he had ridden up, that the battery commanders had been anticipating an order to advance and had their horses harnessed and the men standing to the guns. It now took him only a minute to send an aide dashing back to bring up these batteries.

A moment later Lee heard the crash of Longstreet's guns. Perceiving soon the effect of Longstreet's fire, Lee signalled Jackson: "Do you still want reinforcements?" and, as the Federal flank began to melt away, he saw that a great opportunity had come. Instantly he seized it: Let R. H. Anderson move from reserve to support Longstreet; order Longstreet to attack at once with his full force; pass the word to right and to left for a general assault; throw every man in his army against Pope. Quick action would engulf the whole of the Federal left and left-centre. As the lines prepared to move forward, the answer to Lee's signal came back from Jackson, half an hour after it had been sent. "No," Jackson said, he did not need reinforcements, "the enemy are giving way."

The battle smoke drifted back to headquarters; the roar of the guns shook the hills. There was victory in the air. The assault began with far greater precision than at Gaines's Mill or at Malvern Hill. Instead of wasteful attacks in detail, nearly the whole of the right went forward simultaneously. Very soon the resistance was stiff and the field confused. Jackson's division did not come up promptly. The advance of Longstreet's left was exposed to an enfilading fire from batteries that had been placed in front of Jackson's right. Time was lost in silencing these guns, though Lee hurried orders to Jackson to hasten his advance. Despite these checks and complications, the line swept on. The enemy was in general retreat except where stubbornly resisting at strong points opposite the Confederate right.

But the end of the pursuit had to come before the objective was reached. Scattered by their advance of more than a mile and a half, weakened by losses and confused by strange ground, Longstreet's men were overtaken by darkness as they approached the ridge of the Henry house. Visibility was low. A storm threatened. There was danger that a farther advance would throw Federal and Confederate so close together that the Southerners would fire into their own ranks. Through a rain that soon began to fall the Federals surged back across Young's

Branch and the Stone Bridge at Bull Run, protected in their flight by a few regiments that held the hill of the Henry house with magnificent resolution.

Lee had not been able to remain at headquarters in the unparticipating rear while his troops were making the most triumphant advance their banners had ever shone upon. Headquarters for the night were established in an open field, and a fire of boards was lighted for the reading of dispatches. These were unanimous in asserting a victory on every part of the field. Lee's spirits rose and his gratitude to God increased as the good news continued to come in, especially when the commanders were able to report that though many a good man had fallen, the losses of the day had not been excessive.

In this atmosphere, Lee sat down to compose his victory dispatch that would be carried all the way back to Rapidan, telegraphed to Richmond, and announced to the anxious Southern people.

> *Groveton, 30 Aug. 10 o'clock P.M.*
>
> Presdt Davis: This Army today achieved on the plains of Manassas a signal victory over combined forces of Genls. Mc-Clellan and Pope. On the 28th and 29th each wing under Genls. Longstreet and Jackson repulsed with valour attacks made on them separately. We mourn the loss of our gallant dead in every conflict yet our gratitude to Almighty God for his mercies rises higher and higher each day, to Him and to the valour of our troops a nation's gratitude is due.
>
> R. E. Lee

When a short night's rest ended with daylight the rain was still falling. Clad in rubber overalls and with a rubber poncho over his shoulders, Lee rode out early on a short reconnaissance across Bull Run accompanied by Jackson. Soon he came under fire of the enemy's pickets. Pope evidently was still close at hand. Lee was satisfied that his only possible course was to continue to manoeuvre and, if possible, once more to interpose his army between Pope and Washington or so to threaten Pope's flank as to force him into a further retreat. Lee explained this to Longstreet and to Jackson and gave his orders for the day: Jackson, being nearest the exposed flank of the enemy, was to take his entire command and cross Bull Run at Sudley Springs. He was to move north until he struck the Little River turnpike. Then he was to turn southeast again. If all went well this would put Jackson on the enemy's line of retreat and would force the evacuation of Centreville. To aid Jackson, Stuart and his cavalry, supported by a brigade of infantry, were to pass over Bull Run and create a diversion. Longstreet was to remain on the battlefield, looking after the wounded and burying the dead, until Jackson had a good start. Then Longstreet was to follow, and D. H. Hill, when he arrived from the South, was to complete the gruesome work Longstreet left unfinished. The plan was as simple as it was bold.

Later in the day Lee was standing by Traveller, with the reins on the animal's neck. Suddenly a cry was raised, "Yankee cavalry!" Traveller started at the sudden commotion, and Lee stepped forward to catch the bridle. He tripped and fell. He caught himself on both hands and was up in an instant, but it was soon apparent that he was hurt. The scare of Union cavalry proving unfounded, the nearest surgeon was sent for. He found a small bone broken in one hand and the other hand badly sprained. Both had to be put in splints. As this of course kept Lee from riding, he had much against his will, to enter an ambulance.

The road the army had to follow to Sudley Springs on Bull Run was narrow and muddy. Night found Longstreet not yet across Bull Run. Jackson was on the Little River turnpike with his front toward Fairfax Courthouse, but his weary men had not been able to move fast enough to get in rear of Pope. Stuart had been hovering on the enemy's flank, but he had accomplished no substantial result. The exhaustion of the hungry men and the condition of the roads cost Lee virtually the whole advantage he had hoped to gain on the critical first day after the victory.

The rain had ceased falling on the morning of September 1, but the army was still hungry. Jackson's column, though covered by Stuart's cavalry, moved very slowly. Not until late afternoon did it reach the vicinity of the friendly mansion of Chantilly. It was then apparent that the enemy was aware of the threat to his flank and was prepared. At Jackson's order, A. P. Hill forwarded Branch's and Brockenbrough's brigades to feel out the enemy. The Federals met the attack with vigor. Massing on the flank and front of Branch, they drove him back on his supports, along with Brockenbrough; and when three more brigades of Hill's division were thrown into the battle, they, too, were roughly handled. The battle soon engulfed a part of Ewell's division in the midst of almost continuous thunder that drowned the roar of the guns. Night was falling before there was any wavering in the

Federal line and even then it was darkness rather than defeat that led the enemy to withdraw slightly.

When the skirmish line went forward the next morning it was found that the enemy had evacuated his position both at Centreville and in front of Jackson. Stuart's cavalry went in pursuit only to discover that the long Federal columns were moving steadily toward the Washington entrenchments whither it would be futile to pursue them.

About the hour Lee realized from these reports that this phase of his campaign of manoeuvre was at an end, President Davis was sending to the Confederate Congress the recent dispatches from Lee, including the message written on the field of Second Manassas after the battle of the 30th. There was pride and jubilation in Davis's closing sentence. "Too much praise," said he, "cannot be bestowed upon the skill and daring of the commanding general who conceived, or the valor and hardihood of the troops who executed, the brilliant movement whose result is now communicated."

The words did not exaggerate the fact, nor did they even touch upon the contrast between the situation Mr. Davis described and that which had existed three months previously. On June 2, Lee's first full day in command of the Army of Northern Virginia, McClellan had been in front of Richmond, Jackson was being pursued up the Shenandoah Valley by three strong forces, western Virginia was completely in the hands of the Federals, and the North Carolina coast was overrun. Now, western Virginia was almost evacuated, Confederate cavalry were soon to cross into Ohio at Ravenswood, Winchester was about to be abandoned, the North Carolina coast was safe, and the wrecked Army of Virginia, together with most of the Army of the Potomac, was in full retreat on Washington. Despairing officials in the Federal capital had given orders to ship all movable government property to New York. The government clerks were called out to share in the anticipated defense of the city. Except for the troops at Norfolk and at Fort Monroe, the only Federals closer than 100 miles to Richmond were prisoners of war and men busily preparing to retreat from the base at Aquia Creek.

Lee's operations had improved in excellence as they had developed. By every standard, Second Manassas was better than the Seven Days. Staff work was incomparably superior. The artillery had been more effectively employed. So had the cavalry. The intelligence service was much improved. The superiority of the tactics was attested by the relative losses. From the crossing of the Rapidan to the final pursuit of the Federals into the Washington defenses, Confederate casualties had been 9112, and an exceptionally large percentage of these were men but slightly wounded. Pope's casualties August 16 to September 2 were 14,462, including 4163 prisoners. Like his tactics, Lee's strategy was better at Second Manassas than around Richmond. It was better because it was somewhat simpler, and, still more, because it placed responsibility in the hands of fewer men. This concentration of authority was one reason for success. Another reason was the excellent logistics. Lee's troop movements had been prompt and rapid. Lee's strategic plan succeeded, thirdly, because at nearly every stage of the campaign his reasoning from his evidence was sounder than his adversary's. He had drawn the right conclusion concerning the movement and destination of McClellan's army, and he had been correct to the very day in his calculation of when Pope received his first substantial reinforcements from the Army of the Potomac.

Only three reasonable criticisms can be made of Lee's handling of operations from the time he reached Gordonsville until the Federals disappeared from his front on the morning of September 2. The first, that he should have crossed the Rapidan earlier than the 20th, is based on the valid assumption that if he had been able to catch Pope between the Rapidan and the Rappahannock, he could have destroyed him. But this criticism leaves out of account the shortage of provisions, a subject about which, unfortunately, there is little specific information. The second criticism is that Lee should have forced Longstreet to attack on the afternoon of August 29 instead of permitting him to delay until the 30th. Had Longstreet attacked successfully on the 29th, Lee would have been able to pursue on the 30th in clear weather. The gain would have been substantial and might conceivably have resulted in very heavy losses to Pope. This criticism must be given due weight. Lee knew he was not omniscient and he did not believe he could be omnipresent. He held to his theory of the high command. Having put the army under the best officers at his disposal, he felt that on the field of battle he should trust their discretion. This is a sound general rule. In the study of war it is futile to canvass what cannot be decided, and for that reason it cannot positively be asserted that Lee should have given Longstreet a peremptory order to attack or would have been sure of a greater victory if he had. The third criticism is that Lee should have organized a prompt pursuit of Pope. Circumstances and the hunger of his own men deterred him. To have moved a hungry army through the mud against heavy defenses, readily manned, would have been to flirt with ruin. Manoeuvre, his prime aim, was still possible if the army kept the field, but manoeuvre would be impossible and starvation might threaten if the army were committed to a siege at a long distance from its base. Lee's thought was of the next manoeuvre, not of a bootless investment of Washington, as he saw the rearguard of Pope's army fade into the horizon on the morning of September 2.

Lee's manoeuvring after the second battle of Manassas had to be extensive and not a mere matter of shifting a few miles in this direction or in that, because Fairfax County, in which the army had halted, had already been stripped of food and of forage. The scant and overworked wagon train could not be relied upon to bring from Richmond an adequate supply of provisions. Likewise, manoeuvre had to be prompt. Quick action might deter the Federals from aggressive moves until the coming of winter, but delay would place in front of the Army of Northern Virginia a larger force than it had yet encountered. The weaker side could not wait.

Destiny beckoned northward, across the Potomac. Maryland and Pennsylvania invited the next stage of manoeuvre. They offered positive advantages. The enemy could be drawn away from the Washington defenses. With Maryland occupied, Virginia would be free. No Federal army based on Washington would dare advance on Richmond so long as Lee was north of the Potomac.

Political not less than military advantage seemed to be offered in Maryland. The South believed that strong sentiment for the Confederacy existed in Maryland and would have exhibited itself in extensive volunteering and possible secession had it not been repressed with the overwhelming power of a Federal Government that was charged with brushing aside constitutional rights. The presence of a large Confederate force above the Potomac would give the people of Maryland what they had never had—a chance to express their will.

There were risks in undertaking promptly an extensive maneouvre. The army was not equipped for it. Uniforms were in rags. Thousands of men were shoeless. The horses of many of the cavalrymen were exhausted. The Federals were still in the lower Valley, lingering at Winchester and garrisoning Harpers Ferry and Martinsburg, though it was reasonable to assume that when the army crossed into Maryland these posts would be evacuated. Weighing necessity, advantage, and risk in the scales of his judgment, Lee virtually decided on September 3 to enter Maryland. The next day he was fully persuaded of the benefits to be gained, and wrote the President that he would proceed unless Mr. Davis disapproved.

Where should he enter Maryland, east of the Blue Ridge or west of it? His conclusion was to advance east of the mountains, because this would be regarded by the Federals as a direct threat to Washington and to Baltimore. The administration, he reasoned, would at once call north of the Potomac the forces operating south of that river. This would remove all danger to his supply line.

On September 5-6, the head of the columns prepared to cross the Potomac. The first dusty troops halted, stripped, or pulled frayed trouser legs high over aching knees, and plunged into the shallow water of the boundary river. As they clambered up the northern bank they cheered in the proud knowledge that they had carried the war into the enemy's country. The few and battered bands played "Maryland, My Maryland," and the soldiers cheered the more. They were confident of their ability to win new victories, confident of their cause, and confident of their commander.

Once in Maryland, Lee rode with the infantry straight for Frederick, within two miles of which he established his headquarters on September 7. The first impressions made by the army on the people of Maryland were not wholly unfavorable. Firm discipline was enjoined on the army. Sentinels were posted at the stores in Frederick. The soldiers who had to march through the town had a varied reception. Some women brought out food; others held their noses and waved the Union flag.

Dispositions were made promptly. The cavalry was stationed at Urbana. The infantry and artillery were encamped around Frederick, with the exception of Early's division, which was moved a few miles southward. It was soon known that McClellan had replaced Pope in general command, and that was not pleasant news, for Lee regarded McClellan as the ablest of the Federal commanders. Lee's plan was to wait at Frederick until the people showed their sentiments or until McClellan appeared in his front. On September 8 he addressed the people of Maryland in a proclamation:

> "No constraint upon your free will is intended; no intimidation will be allowed within the limits of this army, at least. Marylanders shall once more enjoy their ancient freedom of thought and speech. We know no enemies among you, and will protect all, of every opinion. It is for you to decide your destiny freely and without constraint. This army will respect your choice, what-

ever it may be; and while the Southern people will rejoice to
welcome you to your natural position among them, they will
only welcome you when you come of your own free will."

Lee looked to something more than recruits. It seemed to him
that the Confederacy should make a peace proposal, based on the
recognition of its independence. On the day that he issued his statement to the people of Maryland he suggested to the President a move
to this end. "Such a proposition," he wrote, "coming from us at
this time, could in no way be regarded as suing for peace; but, being
made when it is in our power to inflict injury upon our adversary,
would show conclusively to the world that our sole object is the establishment of our independence and the attainment of an honorable
peace."

There were only two circumstances that seemed in any wise to
cast doubt on the continued ability of Lee to manoeuvre in Maryland
and in Pennsylvania as he had in northern Virginia. One of these was
the unexpected development of a dangerous degree of straggling in
the army. The other was the approaching exhaustion of supplies in
the country around Frederick. When he carried out his original plan
and moved to Hagerstown, Lee would still have no guarantee of
sufficient food for his army and would have to draw from Virginia,
whence, also, his ammunition must come. His proposed new line
would run down the Shenandoah Valley directly by Martinsburg and
within sixteen miles of Harpers Ferry. And there was the rub. Winchester had been occupied by the Confederates on September 3, but
the Federals were still at Harpers Ferry and at Martinsburg in strength.

The desirability of reducing these posts had suggested itself strongly
to Lee during the early stages of the advance into Maryland, but
Longstreet had argued so warmly against a division of force that
Lee had determined to wait and see if the Federals would abandon
the towns. Now there seemed no alternative to sending a force to take
them. Nor did the risk seem greater, in dealing with a deliberate
opponent like McClellan, than the risk that the weaker army always
must take to win advantage. Once the army was reunited and its line
of communications clear, dazzling possibilities of manoeuvre would
open. The Baltimore and Ohio Railroad could be held or destroyed,
and the army could move from Hagerstown to Harrisburg, a distance
of only seventy-one miles. West of Harrisburg, the Susquehanna bridge
of the Pennsylvania Railroad could be broken. Then the East would

be cut off from the West, except for the slow and circuitous route by the Great Lakes. Lee would be left free to deal with McClellan, assured that no reinforcements could reach his adversary from the West. A march on Philadelphia, Baltimore, or Washington would be practicable, and the war might be won. Such an opportunity justified the danger incident to dividing the army.

If Harpers Ferry and Martinsburg were to be cleared of Federals before these great manoeuvres were undertaken, Jackson was the man to do the work. He was perfectly familiar with the country by reason of his long service there. Lee called him to headquarters, on or about September 9, and discussed the best way to accomplish his object. While they were talking, Longstreet's voice was heard outside. Lee invited him to share the council. Longstreet was not sympathetic, but as he saw it had been determined upon he made no other suggestion than that, if Jackson should be detached, the remainder of the army should be kept together.

Harpers Ferry was one of the most vulnerable of positions. Artillery could rake the town and make it untenable. But if the garrison was to be captured along with the place the task was not easy. Lee reasoned that the garrison should be taken along with the post, and to effect this he had to close all the exits by organizing three columns to converge simultaneously—one on Loudoun Heights, one on Maryland Heights, and one from the rear of Harpers Ferry on Bolivar Heights. The last of these three columns could readily force the Federal troops at Martinsburg to retreat to the ferry. For the occupation of Loudoun Heights, Lee chose the small but fresh division of Brigadier General John G. Walker. To seize Maryland Heights he selected McLaws's and R. H. Anderson's divisions of Longstreet's command. And for the most serious part of the work, cutting off the retreat of the garrison from in rear of Harpers Ferry, so that it would surrender to McLaws, Lee designated the whole of Jackson's "left wing of the army." That Walker might know precisely what was expected of him, Lee summoned him to headquarters, went over the plan in detail, and then told him of his intention to march from Hagerstown to Harrisburg.

Walker could not conceal his astonishment. Lee observed it. "You doubtless regard it hazardous to leave McClellan practically on my line of communication, and to march into the heart of the enemy's country?"

Walker had to admit that it seemed so to him.

"Are you acquainted with General McClellan?" Lee inquired. "He is an able general, but a very cautious one. His enemies among his own people think him too much so. His army is in a very demoralized and chaotic condition, and will not be prepared for offensive operations— or he will not think it so—for three or four weeks. Before that time I hope to be on the Susquehanna."

No time was to be lost in launching the enterprise. The main army was to be moving toward Hagerstown while the detached columns were on their mission. Harpers Ferry itself was to be captured Friday, September 12. Then the army would be ready to reconcentrate at Hagerstown or at Boonsboro and to advance into Pennsylvania.

All these details were covered by Special Orders No. 191, issued on September 9, and destined to have a memorable place in American military history. Copies were made for all those division commanders who were to participate in the movement, and as D. H. Hill was not formally attached either to Jackson's or to Longstreet's "wing," the text was delivered directly to him. Jackson, however, had never been notified that Hill had been taken from under his control, so he also sent the paper to that officer. This copy from Jackson Hill carefully preserved. The other, being superfluous, was used by some staff officer of Hill's—the world will never know by whom—to wrap up three cigars against the time when the owner should want them. It was to prove the costliest covering ever used for such a purpose.

At the designated time, the march began. Lee remained with Longstreet and then rode westward with him. Before the 10th of September ended, a rumor reached Lee that a Federal force was moving southward on Hagerstown from the direction of Chambersburg, Penna. Hagerstown must be secured. Longstreet was therefore directed to proceed thither the next day, instead of remaining at Boonsboro.

Lee was loath to abandon altogether the strategic position at Boonsboro for there was no other point from which he could move so quickly toward Harpers Ferry in case of emergency. He determined to leave Hill at Boonsboro while Longstreet went on to Hagerstown. This meant splitting the army into five detachments. Still, so long as McClellan lingered under the shelter of Washington a dispersion that violated all the canons of war might serve the needs of the situation and involve no undue risks.

Lee rode on with Longstreet to Hagerstown on the 11th. He found no signs of any Federal advance from Pennsylvania and nothing to create alarm. The 12th did not bring the news of the capture of Harpers Ferry that Lee had hoped to receive. Instead, Stuart reported through Hill that the enemy was advancing on Frederick. This intelligence was most disquieting. McClellan was not running true to form! The next morning there was still no information of the capture of Harpers Ferry. As it was reasonable to suppose that the advancing Federals had occupied Frederick, Lee warned McLaws to watch the road from Frederick to Harpers Ferry. The outlook was vaguely darkening.

During the evening of the 13th Stuart reported that the Federals had driven him from the gap in the Catoctin Mountains, a minor range that lay about seven miles east of South Mountain. McClellan, still contrary to all expectation, was pushing on—and shrewdly. Lee was puzzled that a Union army that had suffered a demoralizing defeat at Second Manassas and that was now under a commander who was deliberation incarnate should suddenly begin to march on him. A new McClellan seemed to emerge, a McClellan who divined the movements of his opponent and whom Lee did not understand. Not until the publication, much later, of McClellan's report of the operations did he learn that at Frederick on the 13th McClellan had received from a soldier who had picked it up in the street a packet of cigars wrapped in a headquarters copy of Special Order 191, covering the movement to Harpers Ferry and the march of all the units of the army. This information had dissipated the "fog of war," had galvanized McClellan, and had made it possible for him to advance in full knowledge of where Lee was and what Lee intended to do. Once the enemy covered the distance from the Catoctin Gap to Turner's Gap, in South Mountain, the whole situation would be changed. It was a prospect so serious that there was but one thing to do—to hurry D. H. Hill back to South Mountain, which Lee had not intended to defend, and to hold off McClellan at that point until Harpers Ferry fell or McLaws, at the least, was out of danger.

Lee at once dispatched a messenger to Hill with orders to defend Turner's Gap. Longstreet was called to headquarters. Lee told "Old Pete" of the state of affairs and instructed him to leave Toombs at Hagerstown with one brigade and with the rest of his command to march at daylight the next morning to support Hill. In the darkest uncertainty as to the situation, Lee on the morning of the 14th joined Longstreet in his advance.

As the column approached the mountain, Hill could be heard, furiously engaged. Ere long there came a dispatch from him asking that the reinforcements come forward with all speed. Reinforcements had not come an hour too soon for Hill's necessity. He had been fighting against a much stronger force in a position of extreme difficulty. Placing Rodes on the left, with Colquitt astride the main road, he had stationed G. B. Anderson and Ripley on the right to support Garland's brigade, which had been thrown in early and had been demoralized after its commander had been killed in a most brilliant defense. The right had held thereafter, but at the time Longstreet came up it was evident that the Federals were massing heavily to turn the Confederate left, maintained with much stubbornness and skill by Rodes's brigade.

Longstreet threw in his troops before he familiarized himself with the terrain and in a short time sent back word to Lee to prepare to retire that night as it would not be possible to hold South Mountain. The troops, however, were determined not to yield their ground. When nightfall ended this battle of South Mountain, as it was subsequently called, some 1800 Confederates and a like number of Federals lay dead or wounded on the ridges, and the greater part of Garland's brigade had been captured. The Federal lines extended beyond both flanks of the Confederates. Unless the Army of Northern Virginia was reinforced, the pass would be stormed the next morning. And there was no prospect of reinforcement.

The hours that followed were among the most anxious Lee had known. Never before in his campaigning had the situation changed so often or so perplexingly as between dark on the 14th and dawn on the 15th. Lee looked squarely at the facts: the day had been bad; the morrow might be worse. The enemy's advance through the mountains would put him directly in rear of McLaws. McLaws must get across the Potomac as soon as possible, by some ford that the Federals did not command. There was no alternative. All the high hopes of manoeuvre had to be abandoned. The Army must seek the friendly soil on the south side of the river, and await a new opportunity. So reasoned Lee. He dictated orders to McLaws:

"General: The day has gone against us and this army will go by Sharpsburg and cross the river. It is necessary for you to abandon your position tonight. Your troops you must have well in hand to unite with this command, which will retire by Sharpsburg."

Further bad news confirmed Lee's decision to withdraw: The Confederate cavalry sent to defend Crampton's Gap had lost it; the

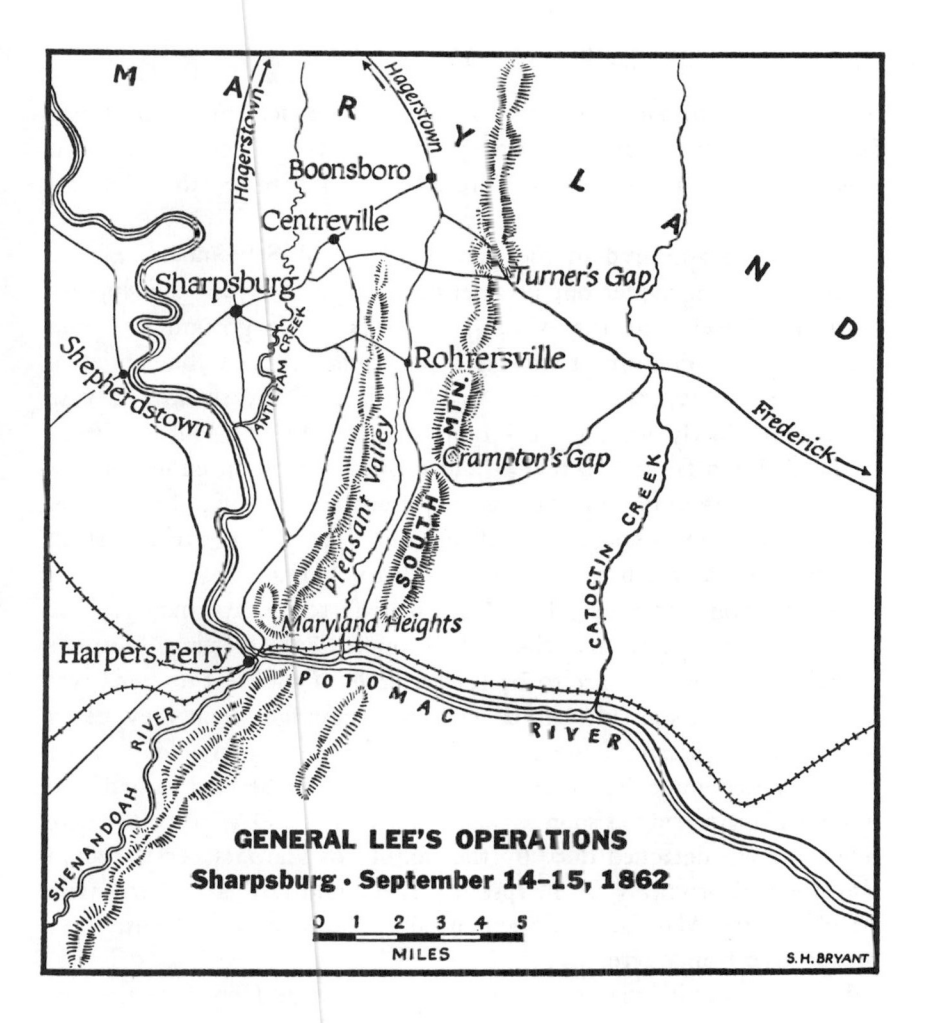

GENERAL LEE'S OPERATIONS
Sharpsburg · September 14–15, 1862

0 1 2 3 4 5
MILES

S.H.BRYANT

Federals were pouring through directly in McLaws's rear. The army manifestly must lose no time in reaching Centreville, both to protect McLaws and to guard its own line of retreat. On the heels of the messenger bringing this grim news a report from Jackson reached headquarters. It was not specific in promise, but it led Lee to believe that Harpers Ferry would fall the next morning. That suggested a possibility of retrieving the situation. If Jackson took Harpers Ferry, his orders were to rejoin the army and he could be counted on to do so promptly, perhaps at Sharpsburg, which was only twelve miles from Harpers Ferry by the most direct road. If McLaws could also get to Sharpsburg, the army might be able to resume its campaign of manoeuvre.

The army was set in motion. The dead and the seriously wounded had to be left behind. On the road, Lee sent another urgent note to McLaws. He told McLaws to move to Harpers Ferry if it had fallen by the time McLaws received his dispatch. Then Lee decided it would be better to march direct to Sharpsburg than to halt at Centreville.

Sharpsburg appeared in the morning light of September 15, as a quiet town lying under one of a series of ridges between the sluggish Antietam Creek and the winding Potomac. The ground Lee had chosen for his concentration was a peninsula between the Antietam and the Potomac, reasonably strong but dangerously shallow in case of disaster. Slowly and doggedly Longstreet's and D. H. Hill's divisions tramped down from Centreville, and took positions on either side of the road. All the morning the dusty veterans moved toward the town. They were only 18,000, all told and they seemed a pitifully small command with which to face the army in pursuit.

About noon a courier galloped up to Lee's temporary quarters. He brought a message from Jackson: "Through God's blessing, Harper's Ferry and its garrison are to be surrendered." Quickly the word was passed; the men seemed charged with new courage when they heard it. The worst danger from the division of the army would soon be over: for Lee immediately ordered Jackson's stout-hearted brigades to rejoin the main army as soon as possible. McLaws and Walker, likewise relieved from detached duty by the capture of Harpers Ferry, would also proceed promptly to Sharpsburg. Lee could now afford to invite attack on the Maryland side and need not forego the advantage of prospective manoeuvre.

Lee was over his map at 2 P.M. when a message from Fitz Lee advised him that the enemy was approaching the Antietam. Soon the Union troops began to appear. Steadily through the afternoon moving clouds of dust, far-off flags and glimpses of blue on distant hills showed that the Federals were coming up in great strength. They made no attack, however. Lee watched guns and moving columns with apparent unconcern. Jackson would surely be up the next day with all his force, and McClellan was not a man to attack hurriedly.

On the next morning Lee exhibited no fear of the fast-swelling mass of Federals in front of him. He had as yet only the 18,000 infantry who had marched from South Mountain. He had to allow time for the removal of the booty taken at Harpers Ferry; he was dealing with a cautious adversary who had never yet fought an offensive battle; he would soon have together all the units of an unbeaten army that had established its superiority over Pope's greater host only a little more than a fortnight before. A quick withdrawal in the face of his proclamation to the people of Maryland would mean the definite and probably the permanent loss of that state to the Confederacy. If McClellan should attack and could be defeated, all the promising manoeuvres Lee had projected at Frederick might still be executed.

So, Lee waited. A little after 12 o'clock, Jackson and Walker rode up to headquarters and reported that their troops were behind them, en route to Sharpsburg. Jackson's troops were directed to the left. Walker's men received instructions to move before light the next morning and to occupy the extreme right.

The artillery had been active most of the forenoon. About sundown, the Union artillery quickened its fire. Soon there came the rattle of musketry and the shouts of engaging troops. The enemy was attacking, but as his advance was against Hood's veteran division, Lee probably felt no concern. The attack ended with darkness and left the opposing wings about where they had stood when it commenced.

At headquarters, during the evening, Lee waited in vain for the arrival of three divisions that Jackson had left on the south side of the river. It would be a difficult matter to hold off the whole of the Army of the Potomac if three divisions were missing. A message was dispatched to A. P. Hill to hurry forward. It was a brief last night of earth for hundreds of the soldiers, such a night as the army had not known since the field of Seven Pines. Always before, the graycoats had expected to attack; now they must stand on the defensive. Odds they had always faced, and with confidence; this time, the odds were appalling, both because of straggling and because of the arrival of the enemy before the whole army had been reconcentrated. The Confederates numbered less than 25,000, artillery and cavalry included. Twenty-four brigades faced forty-four. Even if all the troops engaged in the Harpers Ferry operations could be brought up, Lee would have less than 40,000 with which to face twice that number. Lee had no breastworks on any part of his line. About 50 batteries, slightly more than 200 guns and 3000 men, were on the field, though some of them were in exposed positions where they could not cope with the heavier metal of the enemy. Except for Hood's division no reserves were at hand, and none could be expected until McLaws and Anderson arrived in advance of A. P. Hill. They were expected hourly —but when would they come up?

It was still black night on September 17 when sporadic fire broke into the steady rattle of an approaching general engagement. With three divisions not yet reported from Harpers Ferry, the dangers of a prolonged battle begun at daylight were apparent. Lee, to keep open a line of retreat, took the precaution of warning General Pendleton, who had moved his batteries across the Potomac, to guard well the fords. General J. B. Kershaw rode up about daylight and reported that McLaws and R. H. Anderson, after a hard march from Harpers Ferry, were approaching Sharpsburg.

The heavy fire of the skirmishers was taken up by the artillery as soon as it was light. By 6 o'clock news began to filter back to head-quarters. Soon thereafter, a powerful Federal force, later identified as Hooker's corps, struck furiously. Lawton's brigade was wrecked. Trimble and Hays were hurled back. Jackson's old division was swept aside. A great gap was torn in the Confederate flank.

This was a threat of immediate disaster. Still, if the line could be held until McLaws and Anderson were thrown into action, the day might be retrieved. But was it possible to maintain the left against such heavy assaults as were being delivered by the Federals? The infantry of Hood were moving into the gap or standing stubbornly on either side of it, but with the odds so heavy and the stake so great they must have help, and speedily. Whence could it come? Only from the right. So Lee sent orders to Colonel G. T. Anderson to march at once to support Hood. About an hour later he directed General J. G. Walker to take the two brigades of his division to Jackson. This meant that he was to employ thirteen of his twenty-four brigades and most of his cavalry on about one mile of his four and a half miles of front. On the right flank he left only seven brigades to defend one and a half miles, with one of these brigades, that of General Toombs, to defend the important crossing at the lower bridge over the Antietam. The centre of the line, held by D. H. Hill's 3000, was already engaged and "in the air" on its left. All the reserves that had come up were promptly moved into action, with no assurance that they would stem the tide.

To see the situation for himself, Lee rode toward the firing. Colonel Stephen D. Lee reported from Hood that the Texans and Law's brigade had plunged into the gap created by Hooker's attack. By the fiercest of fighting they had driven back the Federals almost where the battle had opened. Hill had given gallant support from the right, and Early held the line on the left of the gap. At the moment of their farthest advance, a second Federal onslaught had been made with an overwhelming force of fresh troops. Hood's ammunition had been exhausted, and his weary men had been forced to give ground. The left of Hill's division had been heavily engaged. The gap had been opened a second time; Walker had then gone in; G. T. Anderson had reinforced Hill; the line had been restored in part and the Federals had been driven back once more from the ground they had taken. Already, however, the Federals were preparing for a third assault. The left of Hill's line was being slowly pushed back, and he was urgently calling for reinforcements.

In the lull that came while men deployed for the third counterattack of the morning, Lee turned back from the left, and rode toward the centre in anticipation of an attack there. He found R. H. Anderson's division, less than 4000 men, arriving to support Hill. Soon Hill joined Lee. Together they rode down the line. Lee told the regimental officers he met that they must prepare themselves for an attack at any moment and he encouraged them as best he could.

Before another Federal advance McLaws's troops attacked with splendid *élan*. Cobb's brigade moved at too wide an angle to the right, lost contact with the rest of the division, and joined the left of Rodes's brigade. Semmes, on the left of McLaws, was obliqued to the left by Jackson's order to support Stuart's cavalry, whose artillery under Pelham was plastering the Federal right. The brigades of Kershaw and Barksdale drove back from the woods a strong force that proved to be a part of Sumner's corps—the third corps hurled against the Confederate left that day. The pursuit carried McLaws to a fence where Walker had been halted by the enemy's fire. There McLaws's men, too, had to stop. In a few minutes they had to fall back to the edge of the West Wood. But this time they were not followed. Anything might happen where three assaults had been delivered with so much pertinacity, but for the moment it looked as if the worst were over on the left.

But on the centre intense bombardment and the massing of distant blue lines could mean only that the enemy was about to open the second battle of the day and was to assail the thin line of D. H. Hill. His left, which had held the right of the gap at the angle in the line, had already been roughly handled. The brunt of the attack would have to be borne by Rodes's and George B. Anderson's brigades, which stood in a sunken road, aptly styled thereafter "The Bloody Lane." Soon the troops of Franklin's corps began to stream forward in heavy masses. They were met and hurled back. Again they attacked and again met a repulse. A third assault had the same fate, thanks alike to the valor of the infantry and to the enfilading fire of some guns that D. H. Hill brought up.

The attacks on the centre seemed about to die away when a lieutenant colonel of Rodes's brigade reported that a force of the enemy had worked around to a point whence it could enfilade a part of the sunken road. Rodes at once ordered one flank drawn in, but the officer understood that this was to involve the withdrawal of the whole brigade. Before Rodes looked up from caring for one of his aides who had been wounded at that instant the whole of his line retired. General G. B. Anderson held his brigade together for a short time, but he too was enfiladed and fell mortally wounded. His men broke and came across the road. Soon the enemy was in hot pursuit and was within a few hundred yards of the high ground on which stood the Dunker Church. R. H. Anderson's division by this time was fighting hard and incapable of giving D. H. Hill any support. A gap yawned in the centre, and there were no troops to fill it. Disaster seemed at hand, but Hill refused to admit that the day was lost. He found Boyce's battery near by and set it firing furiously. Personally, Hill gathered a few men together and led them against the enemy. About 200 other soldiers, collected by a few diligent officers, were launched against the right of the Federals who were pouring into the gap. There was wild confusion for a time and then, most mysteriously, the enemy halted, though his artillery continued to pour its fire against a line that had almost disappeared.

Despite this pause, a renewal of the attack on the centre seemed so nearly certain of success that Lee had to undertake some movement to lessen the pressure on D. H. Hill. He had no reserves on the field, though A. P. Hill was supposed to be on a forced march from Harpers Ferry. The roar of guns from the right told of an impending attack that forbade the withdrawal of troops from that flank. He must create a diversion and the one point at which he could attack with any promise of success was on his left, where the assaults of the enemy had not been renewed. Orders were at once sent to Jackson to attempt to turn the enemy's right near the Potomac, while Walker brought his worn regiments together and renewed the offensive on the Hagerstown road at the point where the line bent to the left.

Before Jackson could deploy, the action on the Confederate right became so heavy that Lee had to ride in that direction to see what

had befallen D. R. Jones's division. That command had been holding
the whole of the line south of the Boonsboro-Sharpsburg road. The
right of Jones's position had been defended by three regiments of the
brigade of Robert Toombs, with the help of a few scattered companies.
Toombs had placed his men close to the creek and had engaged early
the Federal skirmishers and sharpshooters. After 10 o'clock four attacks had been delivered on him. Each had been repulsed bloodily
by the 2d and 20th Georgia regiments. Now the Federals massed
opposite the fords below the bridge in such numbers that it was
manifest Toombs's weary men could no longer prevent a crossing.
The best that could be hoped was that they could retreat and hold
the high ground until A. P. Hill came up. If he arrived in time, the
enemy might be pressed back to the creek. If he were delayed, nothing
could prevent the Federals from pushing forward.

As Lee waited in the streets of Sharpsburg, where every wall echoed
the roar of the guns, Captain Thomas M. Garnett, of the 5th North
Carolina, Garland's brigade, approached and asked for orders. Lee
ordered Garnett to support Evans, the nearest command, in the outskirts of the town, facing the Antietam. Then he rode to an eminence
west of the town, where he watched Toombs's men form with the
rest of Jones's division for a last stand on the ridge to which they had
skillfully withdrawn.

It was now nearly 2 o'clock. No new attack had been delivered
against the Confederate left since McLaws had fallen back. Such a
day of suspense and instant danger Lee had never known, and now
crisis piled on crisis. Jackson reported that the enemy's guns so completely commanded the Confederate left that he could not turn the
Federal right. Immediate hope of a counterstroke vanished. Lee had
only one recourse—the concentration of all available artillery. As
he found batteries, he had them put in action on the right, firing over
the heads of the Confederates and into the ranks of the enemy, who,
by this time, had brought across the creek some guns that were
supporting the Union left with vigor. Still the concentration against
the Confederate right grew; still the Federals hammered at the centre.
An army that had never known defeat was perilously close to it.

Then, at 2:30, when the very seconds seemed to be ticking doom,
from the south a group of officers rode up at the gallop on frothing
horses. A. P. Hill had come at last! Starting from Harpers Ferry at
7:30, only an hour after he had received Lee's order to move to

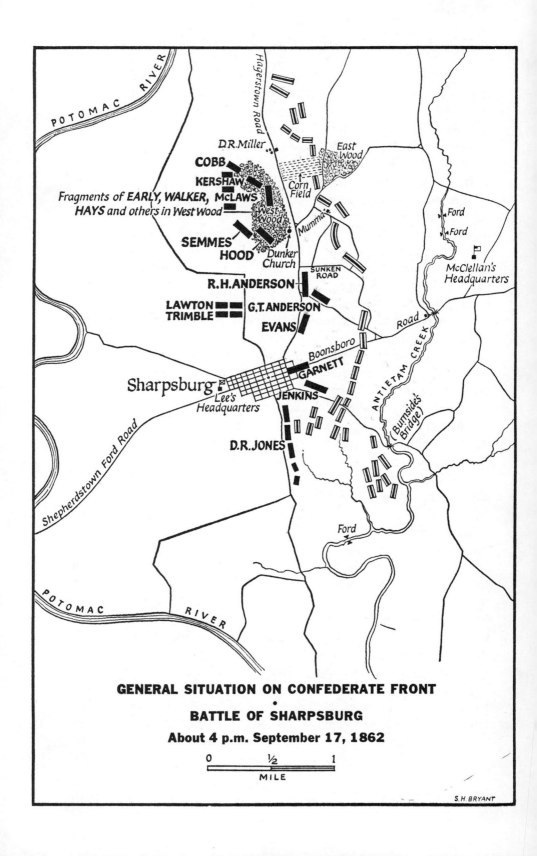

GENERAL SITUATION ON CONFEDERATE FRONT

•

BATTLE OF SHARPSBURG

About 4 p.m. September 17, 1862

0 ½ 1

MILE

S.H.BRYANT

Sharpsburg with the utmost speed. Hill had covered seventeen miles in seven hours. He had only 3000 men and they were an hour and more behind him, panting on the road. Would they be too late?

The situation grew tense. Then, at 3 o'clock, the threatened attack on the right broke in fury. Up the hill came the Federals, disdainful of losses. The southern lines bent and shifted and almost broke as the weary men slowly gave ground. Everything now depended on the speed with which the four brigades of Hill could reach the field and go into action. Steadily the Northerners advanced; stubbornly for an hour the Confederates resisted.

The concentration against the Confederate right was overwhelming. As Lee watched the columns that were plunging toward Jones's little division under a pall of smoke, a section of the Rowan Artillery passed by. Noticing that its commander, Lieutenant John A. Ramsay, had a telescope, Lee pointed to a distant column and asked, "What troops are those?" The lieutenant focused the telescope: "They are flying the United States flag." Lee pointed to the right, where another line was now visible. He repeated his question. "They are flying the Virginia and Confederate flags," Ramsay reported. Lee did not move a muscle, though the words spelled salvation. "It is A. P. Hill from Harpers Ferry," he said quietly, and, with no other word of explanation, he hastened to tell Ramsay to open on the enemy he had first sighted.

Hill's advance came late, but it came with explosive power. Archer's brigade was on Hill's left as the division formed line of battle. Quickly his men were hurled against a Federal column that had overrun McIntosh's battery, sent to the field ahead of Hill's infantry. Raising a defiant rebel yell, Archer's troops swept forward without a halt, recovered McIntosh's guns, and continued to press the enemy. Gregg and Branch, on the right of Archer, awaited the Federal advance, repulsed it, and then followed steadily the swift retirement of the enemy. Pender was brought up from A. P. Hill's extreme right, but before he could engage, the bluecoats were surging back from the edge of the town and over the ridges to the shelter of the stream bank. Toombs and Jones joined in the pursuit, and Toombs was for pressing the advance beyond the creek.

The Federal artillery continued to challenge the hills; the heavy blue columns could still be glimpsed in overmastering strength across the creek and far around to the Federal right, where D. H. Hill and R. H. Anderson and McLaws and Walker and Jackson himself were counting the army of the dead. But the enemy had enough. The fine divisions of Burnside's corps—for he it was who made the attack on the Confederate right from across the bridge that has since borne his name—were content to find such cover as they could away from the avenging rifles of A. P. Hill's infantry. Shining as red as if it reflected the blood on the Maryland hills the September sun set at last, and the battle was abruptly over, within an hour and a half after A. P. Hill's division had gone into action. Three thousand men, only 2000 of whom had been engaged in the final counterstroke, had saved Lee's army from almost certain destruction.

The battle had taken heavy toll. The dead were everywhere. Of the 36,000 infantry or thereabouts that Lee had in action from sunrise to nightfall more than 10,000 were casualties. Some units had been almost wiped out. Grievous as the losses had been, and desperately as the outcome had hinged, time after time, on the arrival of Lee's scant reinforcements, what could the morrow hold except disaster more nearly complete?

So, at least, thought nearly all the officers who made their way during the evening to headquarters. When the last of the reports had been received, Lee concluded that an offensive was out of the question the next day, but he was confident that the army could and would defend its position if McClellan again attacked. Artillery was to be placed to cover the bridge across which Burnside had attacked; rations were to be cooked and delivered to the men who slept on their arms almost where the battle had opened; guards were to be sent back to collect stragglers between the lines and the Potomac. After all this had been arranged without a touch of the theatrical, the division commanders were allowed to return to their troops, some of them frankly amazed at Lee's daring. What manner of man was he who would elect after that doubtful battle against vast odds to stand for another day with his back to the river?

The seemly silence of a vast cemetery lay over the green ridges on the morning of September 18. The Confederate line had been drawn in about 200 yards on the centre; elsewhere it remained where it stood at the close of the battle. Numerous stragglers had come up during the night. For the first time in days, meat and bread were eaten in reasonable abundance by all.

Nowhere on the long front did the enemy stir. Reconnaissance showed that he had massed his artillery on the east bank of the Antietam, as if expecting an attack. Encouraged by this Lee ordered another examination of the left, to see if it would be possible to break through the enveloping lines on that flank and resume manoeuvre. He rode there himself to prepare for the move, but the enemy's guns were too strongly posted.

Lee was confident that he could resist successfully a Federal attack and he waited expectantly. The spirit of the men was reviving. Still, the strength of the army was too low to consider an offensive. Every sign indicated the early arrival of substantial Federal reinforcements. If Lee could not attack where he stood, and if the enemy would not do so, it was the policy of prudence for the army to retire across the Potomac and to choose some new line of advance for a continuance of the campaign of manoeuvre. So, at 2 o'clock, Lee notified Longstreet of his intention to withdraw that night.

The day ended as quietly as it had opened and witnessed no challenge of the Confederate position. After midnight of the 18th–19th, Longstreet led the way over the Potomac and formed line of battle on the right bank.

Safely on Virginia soil again, Lee had only to fear a strong and vigorous pursuit by the Federals. To guard against this, he directed General Pendleton to cover with his reserve artillery the ford by which the army had passed. The tired army moved from the river and spread itself out on the hills to rest from its battles. Darkness on the 19th found Lee and his staff bivouacked under an apple tree, supperless but fed with the promise of long-desired silence.

Lee withdrew his command on September 20 to the vicinity of Martinsburg, in order to manoeuvre to the westward, to pass over the Potomac again at Williamsport, to move on Hagerstown, and to defeat McClellan. If that could not be done, his plan was to occupy the enemy on the frontier, and, should the occasion require, to enter the Shenandoah Valley. But it could not be. Even with the stragglers who had come up, he had only 36,418 infantry present for duty on September 22. Absentees were scattered through a wide country. Thousands had no shoes, no blankets, and scarcely any garments. Lee called vigorously for clothing and footgear and urged stern measures against straggling, but for the time his initiative was paralyzed. He had to forego all his plans for further manoeuvre in Maryland. The "Maryland phase" of the campaign—it should not be regarded as a campaign in itself—was at an end.

The greatest development of the Maryland operations was in Lee himself. He did not abandon his view that the chief duty of the commanding general was performed when he brought the troops into position on the field of battle. He continued to leave the tactical details of action to the brigade and division commanders. But in the emergency of the day at Sharpsburg, when every general had been occupied on his own front, the larger tactical direction of the action had fallen to Lee and he had discharged it flawlessly. Walker had been moved from the right to the left at precisely the right moment; Mc-Laws had been directed to that part of the line where he was most needed; R. H. Anderson had been at hand to support D. H. Hill when that officer's own division had been shattered; A. P. Hill had been sent to precisely the place where his timely arrival, and only his arrival, could save the day. In a word, Sharpsburg was the first major battle that Lee had completely directed, and if he had ever believed, deep in his own heart, that his ability as a tactician was less than his skill as a strategist, Sharpsburg must have given him new confidence. For that action remains a model in the full employment of a small force for a defensive battle on the inner line.

CHAPTER IX

Fredericksburg and Chancellorsville

PRECISELY two months after the exhausted survivors of the Maryland operations dragged themselves back across the Potomac they were marching swiftly in long, confident columns to meet the enemy on the Rappahannock. Never, except during the dreadful last retreat to Appomattox, was the army more disorganized than when it returned to Virginia on September 19, 1862; never, unless after Chancellorsville, was its spirit so high or assured as when it was moving on November 19, from the hills around Culpeper to the heights at Fredericksburg.

Rest, food, refitting, and discipline—that was Lee's prescription. Rest was largely the gift of General McClellan, who was slow to start across the Potomac for a renewal of the campaign. Most of the divisions got five full weeks for recuperation. Food he procured in an enlarged ration by using nearby mills and by collecting cattle. It was not an easy task. Increasingly Lee had to devote his time to commissary duty. Refitting was a large undertaking because the army was in tatters, but he continued the appeals made immediately after his return from Maryland. Ere long clothing and blankets in considerable quantities were forwarded to the army. Lee's disciplinary measures were incident to his effort to increase the army's strength and were of three sorts—the collection of stragglers, recruitment, and reorganization under competent officers.

The most important step in reorganization was the division of the armies into two corps, the first under Longstreet and the second under Jackson. Congress had passed an act providing for the appointment of lieutenant generals, and Davis had written for recommendations. Lee unhesitatingly endorsed Longstreet. In advocating like rank for Jackson, Lee employed language which records the final dissipation of all his doubts as to "Stonewall's" willingness to co-operate. Lee said: "My opinion of the merits of General Jackson has been greatly enhanced

265

during his expedition. He is true, honest and brave; has a single eye to the good of the service, and spares no exertion to accomplish his object."

While Lee labored to raise the efficiency of his forces, two other influences, very different in their nature, operated on individual soldiers. By proclamation of September 23, President Lincoln announced that he would emancipate on January 1, 1863, all slaves in districts where the people were "in rebellion against the United States." This confirmed the belief of Southerners that the election of Lincoln was a conspiracy against the Constitution. A new sense of justification showed itself in the resistance of the South. A little later there began in the army a "revival of religion" that spread from division to division for more than a year. This improved discipline and helped to give the army the quality that Cromwell desired when he said he wanted only such men as "made some conscience" of what they did.

The first stages of the reorganization were passed while Lee was still handicapped by the injury he had received on August 31. It was not until approximately October 12 that he was able to dress and undress himself with his left hand, and, with his right, to sign his name.

The last days of his convalescence were brightened by a visit from Custis, but within a few weeks he was dealt a personal blow far worse than physical injury. His second daughter, Annie, had gone to the Warren White Sulphur Spring, North Carolina, and had been stricken ill there. On October 20, she died. "I cannot express the anguish I feel at the death of my sweet Annie," he wrote Mrs. Lee. "To know that I shall never see her again on earth, that her place in our circle, which I always hoped one day to enjoy, is forever vacant, is agonizing in the extreme. But God in this, as in all things, has mingled mercy with the blow, in selecting that one best prepared to leave us. May you be able to join me in saying, 'His will be done' . . ."

Meantime, tragedy was shaping itself again to a bloody climax. Lee knew too well the weakness of Harpers Ferry to attempt to hold it. He retired with the greater part of the army a few miles higher up the valley pike. His headquarters were established at Falling Waters.

Federal activity in North Carolina and signs of an advance from Norfolk up the south side of the James about this time created some alarm in Richmond and led to an agitation for the return of the Army of Northern Virginia. Lee was not unmindful of the safety of the capital, but he believed that McClellan's first advance would be toward the Virginia Central Railroad, which he thought he could protect by manoeuvring on the flank of the enemy.

Although he considered that Richmond was in no immediate danger, he believed that if McClellan found it impossible to advance southward to the Virginia Central Railroad, he would later move against Richmond from the south side of the James. Meantime, the longer the Army of Northern Virginia could delay the enemy on the frontier, the shorter the period McClellan would have for field operations. This last consideration became the major factor in Lee's plan of campaign. Whatever was done and whatever had to be risked, Lee reasoned that he must fight for time. A junction with his ally, winter, was his main objective.

On October 16 word reached headquarters that a Federal force had crossed the Potomac and was making its way southwestward toward the Confederate front. Convinced that the blow would fall soon, Lee made his preparations with care. Then, on October 26, the outposts reported that the Federal army was crossing the Potomac, apparently in full strength. More than a month had been gained; the gray regiments were rested and ready; and Lee, though conscious of the odds, faced his old antagonist with steadfast heart.

From the time of his return to Virginia after the Maryland expedition, Lee had hoped that McClellan would enter the Shenandoah Valley, but he considered it more likely his foe would move southward on the eastern side of the Blue Ridge, and he had to provide for either contingency. Semi-independent command was given "Stonewall," with instructions to act at discretion when he could not readily communicate with army headquarters. Longstreet was to march for Culpeper, accompanying Lee. If the enemy advanced up the Valley in force, Jackson was to delay him, retire before him, and then make for the gaps through which, if necessary, he might form junction with Longstreet. In case the enemy marched southward east of the mountains and gave him an opening, Jackson was to move on the rear of the Unionists and cut their communications. Longstreet was to defend the direct line of advance east of the Blue Ridge.

By November 6 the enemy was advancing with some vigor between the Blue Ridge and the Orange and Alexandria Railroad and was holding all the passes on his right flank and in rear of his right. Lee learned on the 7th that the advance of the enemy had reached Warrenton and that his cavalry was on the Rappahannock. During the next few days he was apprized of the arrival of further units around Warrenton. But nothing happened. To the surprise of many, the general advance stopped. On the 10th, within twenty-four hours after the reason for this halt became known to the Army of the Potomac, it was reported to Lee: McClellan had been superseded on the 7th by Major General Ambrose E. Burnside and on the 9th had transferred command.

The news was received by the Confederates with regrets and rejoicings curiously mingled. Lee was sorry that his old associate of the Mexican War was no longer to oppose him. "We always understood each other so well," he said to Longstreet. "I fear they may continue to make these changes till they find some one whom I don't understand." Longstreet was glad of the change, because he thought McClellan was developing as a general and, if left in command, would have given the Army of Northern Virginia no further breathing spell. Others reasoned that the change was to the advantage of the South, since Burnside was regarded as less able than "Little Mac."

On November 12 Lee began to suspect that the change of commanders would involve a change of plan. Although the only definite evidence he had of this was the failure of the Federals to move southward, he thought it likely that the enemy might turn down the Rappahannock to Fredericksburg. On the 17th scouts reported that three brigades of the Union infantry were moving against the city and that several Federal transports and gunboats had entered Aquia Creek.

Lee gave orders for one division of Longstreet's corps to take the road toward Fredericksburg, and he determined to send the rest of the corps after it the next morning if the news of the Federal march was confirmed. Lee had no desire to make a stand on the south bank of the Rappahannock at Fredericksburg. The position had no depth and was dominated by heights on the north bank which the enemy was certain to occupy. Strategically, it was far preferable to withdraw to the line of the North Anna. But during the day of the 18th one of his spies reported that the force advancing toward Fredericksburg consisted of Sumner's corps only. Lee decided that if no other force were moving to Fredericksburg he should endeavor to hold Sumner on the line of the Rappahannock until Burnside's purpose was disclosed. It might even be possible to surprise Sumner in an attempt to cross the river. Most particularly, Lee decided to oppose Burnside on the Rappahannock because he could not afford to lose the supplies in the lower valley of that river or to open to the enemy territory south of Fredericksburg which the Federals had not previously pillaged.

The rest of Longstreet's corps was ordered to move for Fredericksburg on the 19th. The same day Lee broke up his headquarters at Culpeper and started to the new scene of action, confident that the enemy was preparing to advance via Fredericksburg on Richmond.

As Lee rode toward Fredericksburg Burnside was hurrying his troops forward by the roads on the opposite side of the Rappahannock. Lee had anticipated the movements of his new opponent with a precision that was almost prescience. With all the advantage that the initiative normally offers, the Federals had a start of only one day.

The gracious little city of Fredericksburg, to which Lee came through a rising storm on November 20, is among the fairest and most ancient of Virginia. As Lee saw it through a rain that had whipped the last of the leaves from the oaks and maples, his eye swept swiftly over its beauties to the Stafford Heights. There they were—the encampments and the fires of the enemy, the batteries and the hurrying dispatch bearers.

Scarcely had Lee made his preliminary dispositions on the 21st than a flag of truce with a message for the mayor of the town was reported on the river front. The flag came from Brigadier General M. R. Patrick, commanding General Burnside's provost guard, and was delivered to Lee. In a letter, General E. V. Sumner, commanding the Right Grand Division of the Army of the Potomac, demanded the surrender of Fredericksburg on the grounds that his troops had been fired upon from the streets, while the manufactories had been used to assist the Confederate cause. Capitulation was demanded by 5 P.M. that day, under penalty of a bombardment at 9 A.M. on the 22d. To save the town from destruction, if possible, Lee informed Mayor Slaughter that he would not occupy Fredericksburg or use its factories, though he could not consent to an occupation by the enemy. Later in the evening, Lee was told that Sumner had notified the mayor that he would accept the assurances given him and would not begin to shell the town the next morning. Welcome as was this reprieve to the defenseless townspeople, Lee felt that he had to advise them to evacuate the town as promptly as possible.

Although the storm was still at its height, the brave women and the old men accepted his advice without a murmur. That night and the next morning a long, dolorous procession moved out from

Fredericksburg. Many of the civilians had neither food, transport, nor protection against the rain. As Lee met these brave townsfolk his admiration rose. "History," said he, "presents no instance of a people exhibiting a purer and more unselfish patriotism or a higher spirit of fortitude and courage than was evinced by the citizens of Fredericksburg. They cheerfully incurred great hardships and privations, and surrendered their homes and property to destruction rather than yield them into the hands of the enemies of their country."

When no advance followed the threatened bombardment of Fredericksburg Lee was puzzled. The rebuilding of the wharfs at Aquia Creek seemed to indicate that Burnside intended to use that admirable landing as a base for an advance on Richmond, but there remained a possibility that he might be screening a movement southward to the James.

By November 23 Lee felt that the Army of the Potomac was so definitely committed to the line of the Rappahannock that a further change of base would be regarded in the North as equivalent to a defeat. "I think, therefore," he said, "he will persevere in his present course, and the longer we can delay him, and throw him into the winter, the more difficult will be his undertaking."

The probability of a general offensive on the Rappahannock increased as five days passed, and with it grew the desirability of uniting the army. Still Lee had faith in the advantage of holding Jackson on Burnside's flank, where he had been ordered on November 23. It was not until he found that the next storm would probably make the roads almost impassable that he, on November 27, urged Jackson to move to Fredericksburg and take position close to Longstreet.

On the evening of November 29, while snow was falling heavily outside his headquarters tent at Hamilton's Crossing, Lee heard some commotion and, on going out, saw the familiar figure of Jackson, who had ridden ahead with one aide to report the advance of his corps. Lee greeted his incomparable lieutenant warmly and then confirmed the directions he had already issued that Jackson place his corps to the right and rear of Longstreet. He ordered Jackson to establish himself around Guiney's Station, whence he could easily move to support Longstreet, to extend the right, or to face an advance from farther down the Rappahannock.

Jackson's troops began to take their position on December 1. Many of them had marched 175 miles in twelve days, and though some were barefooted, the physical condition of the whole corps was good and its spirit was high. Their commander did not like his new position, and protested against it to Lee. Active preparations for the inevitable battle went on apace, in weather that made war impartially against the armies. On the hills back of Fredericksburg, artillery positions were chosen and the ranges set. Absentees were brought into the ranks until, on December 10, Lee had 78,511 men with the colors.

Ten dark December days passed. Headquarters labored to meet the attack when it should come. The night of December 10 arrived and a rumor spread through some of the camps that the Federals had received a large issue of rations with orders to cook them at once. The ranks had learned to read the signs and knew that the cooking of extra rations almost invariably meant an army movement on the morrow. Would the attack come with the dawn? Was Burnside about to challenge the confident Army of Northern Virginia? At every camp fire the questions were argued. They doubtless were still vaguely ranging in the sleeping minds of the soldiers when, about 4:45 o'clock on the morning of December 11, there came from Marye's Heights, behind the town, the roar of a cannon, then of another, and then silence. Two guns . . . signal guns . . . the agreed warning that the enemy was attempting to force a crossing of the Rappahannock.

By a half-obscured moon at 2 o'clock on the morning of December 11, through a rising haze the Confederate pickets in Fredericksburg had observed the first preparations of the Federal engineers to throw pontoons across the Rappahannock. Word reached General McLaws about 4:30 that General William Barksdale, who commanded in the town, would open fire as soon as the *pontoniers* were within easy range. A few minutes later McLaws sent a courier to Lee and ordered Captain J. W. Read's battery of reserve artillery to fire the signal guns.

As Lee rode forward in answer to McLaws's summons the haze reduced visibility to less than 100 yards, but he took pains to examine all the artillery positions he passed. To the sharp accompaniment of musketry from the river bank, he climbed an eminence about a mile and a half southwest of the lower end of the town, an eminence known from that day as Lee's Hill. There he learned that the Federals were attempting to throw pontoon bridges across the Rappahannock at three points—the first at the foot of Hawk Street in the town, the second just below the railroad bridge, and the third near the mouth of Deep Run.

The first and second bridges were within effective range of the artillery on the long ridge west of the town, but they could not be bombarded without danger to the houses and population of Fredericksburg. The third bridge was within range of the better guns on that part of the line, but the ground in front of it on the right bank of the river was open and so dominated by the Federal artillery that the Confederate infantry would be too exposed to offer effective resistance. As Jackson's corps had not been brought up, the crossing had to be delayed as long as practicable at all three points.

Opposite the first and second bridges General McLaws had posted Barksdale's Mississippi brigade. The third bridge, near Deep Run, was in front of General Hood's lines. From the outset it was apparent that Hood could not prevent the laying of the bridge. The action and the outcome were largely in the hands of Barksdale's men, who were already engaged hotly when Lee rode to the front. The determined Federals would rush to their farthest boat and would attempt to throw another into position—only to meet a sharp and accurate fire from the Mississippians. Down would drop the tools, back would run the Federals, and the same drama would be repeated in all its parts. By 9 o'clock the line of boats was almost complete to the southern side of the river, opposite Deep Run, but the work on the upstream bridges had progressed scarcely at all since dawn.

A little later the fog began to lift, and the impatient Federals on the Stafford Heights could make out the houses from which the Mississippi volunteers were sharpshooting. A hundred guns were soon in action, pouring their fire indiscriminately into the buildings occupied by the soldiers and into those where only trembling children and anxious mothers were. The roar was continuous, and, like the bed of some vast volcano, the haze seemed to bubble with the smoke of explosion. Ere long, darker clouds of smoke began to rise from houses set afire by the shell. In the still air these clouds mounted up and up, as if from rival altars kindled to the god of war. Riding untroubled over all were two great balloons, the eyes of the Federal army.

Fifty rounds per gun, 5000 shell, the Union batteries fired, while frightened women prayed in cellars and the riflemen of Barksdale's brigade found such shelter as they could behind shaking walls in smoke-stifled streets. Then the fire slackened. Soon the artillery ceased altogether, for the Confederates had not wasted their all-too-scant ammunition in practice beyond their range. But the silence lasted only a few minutes. Out from their cover rushed the bridge builders once more, and from the houses along the waterfront echoed again the

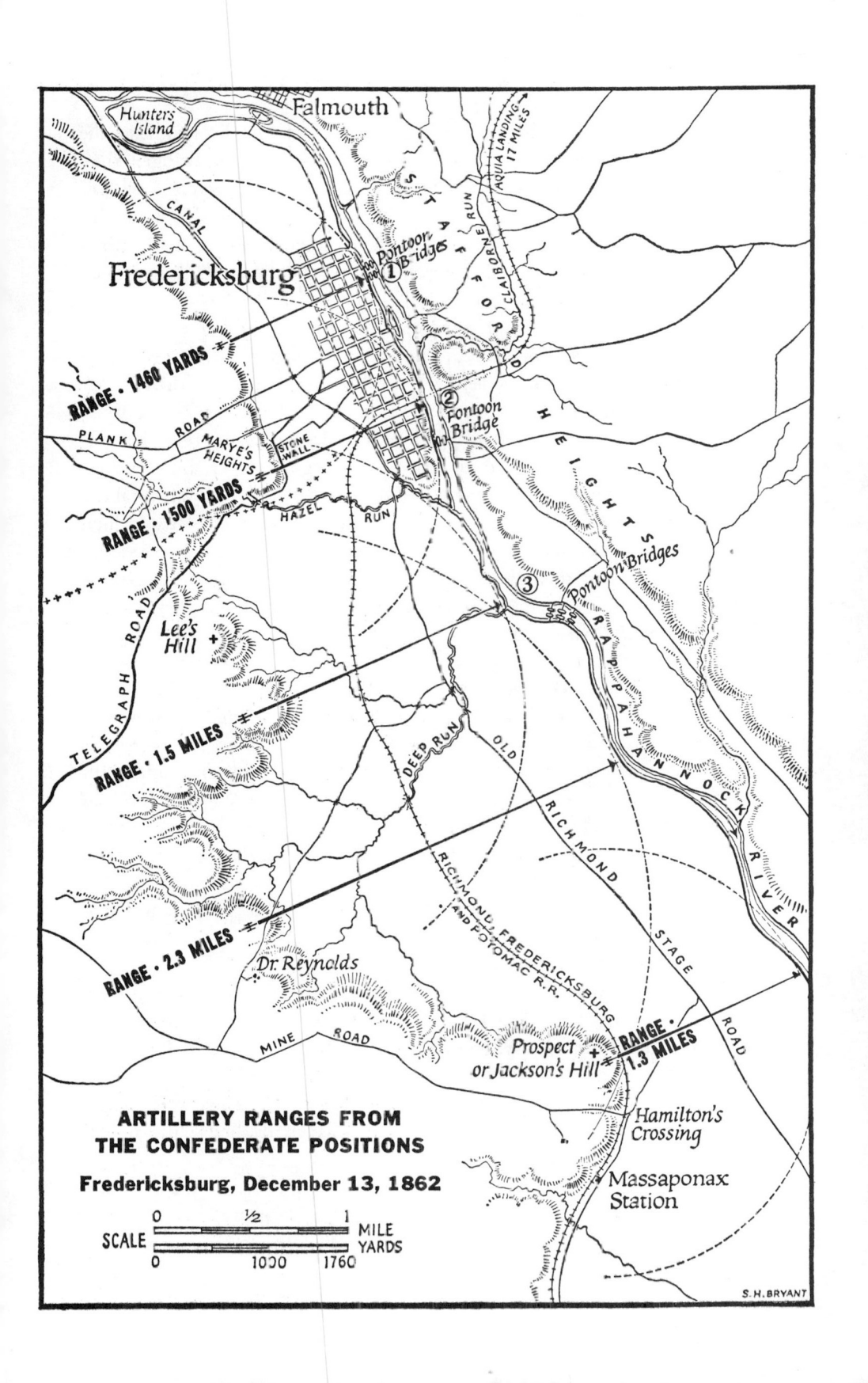

ARTILLERY RANGES FROM
THE CONFEDERATE POSITIONS

Fredericksburg, December 13, 1862

defiant fire of the Mississippians. They had suffered little during the
bombardment, and now, at the first and second pontoon bridges, they
were ready as ever to dispute the passage of the river. Lee had
listened to it all and had watched as much as was visible from his
station. Reports from the town continued at short intervals. And each
time that Barksdale proudly announced that a new attempt had been
beaten off, Lee's countenance lighted up.

A double pontoon bridge near Deep Run was completed by 11
o'clock, though the infantry did not attempt to pass over. Still Barksdale's men hung on. Six, seven, eight, even nine times they drove back
the detachment of engineer troops. Before noon, Barksdale was notified
by Longstreet that the disposition of the defending force was complete and that he could retire when he thought proper, but he continued to dispute the crossing. About 1 o'clock Federal infantry
streamed down the heights and leaped into waiting bateaux, which
immediately put out, with strong arms at the sweeps. The Federals
were determined to cross the river and establish a bridgehead. As the
purpose of the enemy became plain, the riflemen quickened their
fire. In every bateau bluecoats began to drop, but the stream was
narrow, the oarsmen numerous, and soon the first contingent sprang
ashore and deployed. Others followed quickly.

The game was up. Nothing material was to be gained by prolonging the action in the town, but the fighting blood of the men was
aroused and they contested the enemy's advance stubbornly and skillfully. It was 7 o'clock that evening before the last of them crossed
the open ground between the town and the ridge and left Fredericksburg to its captors. By that time both the upper bridges had been
completed.

Meanwhile, of course, Jackson had been notified to prepare to bring
up his troops, if it should develop that the enemy was not attempting
to cross the river farther downstream.

There was much, in fact, to suggest the situation at Sharpsburg
when Lee had faced McClellan with Jackson's entire command; yet
Lee did not hurry Early from Buckner's Neck or D. H. Hill from
Port Royal. The reason was simple. He could hardly believe he was to
have the good fortune of receiving Burnside's attack at Fredericksburg.
Concentration could be neglected for a day in dealing with an adversary who seemed about to defy all the rules.

Haze again covered the river valley on the morning of the 12th and
screened the enemy from the expectant army. About noon Lee rode to

the right, where he was joined by Jackson and, a little later, by Major von Borcke of Stuart's staff. Von Borcke bore a message from Stuart, reporting the rapid concentration of the Federals in front of the Confederate right, and he said he had been within a few hundred yards of advanced units. At Lee's instance, he led him and Jackson to the vantage point. Within 400 yards of the enemy, so close that when they used their glasses, they could distinguish the features of the men opposite them, they carefully examined the enemy's line.

Lee saw enough to convince him that this was a major advance, and not a feint. Everything indicated a general advance. Moreover, the activity of the enemy indicated that an attack would probably come the next day. D. H. Hill and Early, therefore, must be recalled at once and the army must be made ready for the morrow. As Lee rode back to the centre of the line he was more than satisfied at the outlook, even though all signs indicated that the Federals were massing to attack at his weakest point, his right flank. It was better to have them there than farther down the Rappahannock. "I shall try to do them all the damage in our power when they move forward," he said simply.

The fog at daybreak on the 13th was so thick that nothing was visible beyond fifty or sixty yards, but by the time Lee reached his observation post the camps were astir. General officers began to ride up with reports and reassurance. Early had arrived on the right. D. H. Hill's long march from Port Royal had put him in position. The entire army was concentrated to the last regiment. Every rifle that the Army of Northern Virginia could muster was at Lee's instant command. Three hundred and six guns were in position. Seventy-eight thousand men were ready for the worst that Burnside's 125,000 could do.

Jackson was for business. There must be no defensive, said he, but instant attack under cover of the fog, which would keep the Federals from employing their artillery across the river. Stuart seconded him. But Lee said no. He would meet the Federals where he stood, wear them down, let them break their fine divisions in hopeless assaults on his position, while he held back and conserved his strength. Then, when their losses had reduced their numbers, *then* he would strike, but not sooner.

Longstreet had reported early that the orders of command which he had heard through the fog confirmed the general belief that the attack would be on the right. Jackson was of the same mind. Lee rode in that direction. Attended by Jackson and Stuart he covered the whole of the long flank. Leaving Jackson, Lee crossed with Stuart to a field on the flank of the Federals and tried to ascertain if the enemy was moving. Soon sharpshooters' bullets began to hum about and a few shadowy forms could be glimpsed. Lee took his time, regardless of the Federal riflemen, and did not retire until it was apparent that further reconnaissance in the fog would yield no result.

Imperceptibly the baffling fog began to dissipate. By 10 o'clock impatient captains of a few enterprising Union batteries opened a desultory fire on the right. Then the white steeples of Fredericksburg's churches were visible above the gray mist. The blurred outlines of the Stafford Heights could be vaguely seen.

"Test the ranges on the left," Lee ordered at 10:30, and soon a quick blaze of fire swept from Marye's Heights northward. The enemy seemed to take it for a challenge. Scarcely had the Federals started forward than white smoke-puffs could be seen on the enemy's left. They were from two of Pelham's horse artillery, only two, set boldly out in the field. Soon their fire was enfilading the approaching column. The lines halted. Busy batteries could be seen hurrying to silence Pelham. Four opened quickly on him. It seemed certain that he would be destroyed. One gun was disabled, but he shifted his other rifle and put the enemy off his range. Again and again he moved, one piece against sixteen, but he was not silenced. The Federal attacking column remained where it was. The whole army waited, as if to watch the single combat of the paladin gunner. Lee's judgment told him that Stuart had opened too soon, but his admiration for Pelham's fine fighting rose with each round. "It is glorious to see such courage in one so young," he exclaimed. Stuart had thrice to recall Pelham before the young artillerist abandoned the unequal fight.

When at last Pelham withdrew, the Federal artillery began to plaster the front of A. P. Hill's division spitefully. Not a gun answered them. "Old Jack" was unwilling to show his hand for the small stakes his hidden batteries might claim. Soon Lee saw the Federals marching undisturbed down the Richmond stage road to extend their left flank. Presently they halted and faced about. No sooner were they in position than they surged forward in a long line for their first attack. Still the ridge in their front sent no challenge. They were only 800 yards away when, in a single crash, Hill's artillery swept their lines. The startled troops halted, wavered at the second salvo and then in confusion fell back. A first repulse: the enemy must try again!

Longstreet on the left had opened his batteries at 11 o'clock to create a diversion, in the belief that the attack on the Confederate right was a

major assault. His fire swept across Fredericksburg and played on the
bridges. The 30-pounder Parrott and the smaller guns on Lee's Hill
added their metal. The artillery had a commanding field of fire. So
wide and so open was the zone of fire in front of Lee's Hill that no
troops could hope to endure shelling long enough to reach the sides of
the hill from the plain below. Marye's Heights were closer to the
enemy and seemed to be easier. The town gave cover for massing the
assaulting columns. In front of the heights, diagonally from left to
right, ran a deep ditch that offered good shelter. Between this ditch and
the heights the ground rose gradually, with one "dip" about midway
that was not under direct fire. But from this "dip" the incline was
steady and open, though not very steep, to the Telegraph road. This
road was sunken, scarcely visible from the town side. The outer
retaining wall was four feet high and constituted a perfect parapet for
infantry. Above the sunken road were the Confederate guns. Behind
the stone wall in the sunken road stood a North Carolina regiment of
Cooke's brigade and a Georgia brigade, commanded by General
T. R. R. Cobb.

The heights and the sunken road constituted a death trap; were the
Federals foolish enough to venture into it? The Confederates speculated
and doubted until, at 11:30 o'clock the incredible answer came. Out
from the streets poured the Federal infantry, headed straight for Marye's
Heights, precisely as Lee had hoped, yet scarcely had dared hope.
General Burnside most obligingly was preparing to waste in costly
assault the great odds his country had given him. The Unionists did not
even choose the weakest part of Marye's Heights for their assault. They
made their advance against the steepest part of the heights and directly
against the sunken road. They planted three standards defiantly, but in
the very act received the full blast of the artillery almost in their faces.
So intense was the fire and so perfectly laid that the ranks thinned at
the very first round and soon were melting back to the ditch in blue
and blood. The Confederate infantry had scarcely anything to do in
repulsing this first advance. Shellfire sufficed.

First blood for Longstreet as for Jackson—but every indication was
that heavier assaults against both positions were to be delivered speedily!
On the right, as 1 o'clock approached, Lee could see the stout columns
slowly massing. Almost on the hour the Federal left wing swept forward
against Jackson. It was a major assault this time. Quickly the Confederate batteries opened in reply. Gaps were cut in the charging
columns. Windrows of dead were left behind.

The advance seemed resistless. Gradually it concentrated on a neck of woodland that extended from the Confederate front across the railroad. Presently whenever the sound of the enemy's cheers could be heard in the din, they were pitched to a note of triumph. Something had gone amiss. Ere long, keen eyes could distinguish figures making their way to the rear in garb of a different color from the blue dots on the plain. Prisoners! Some disaster had overtaken A. P. Hill.

The enemy was farther into the woods now—was Jackson being whipped? Advanced batteries had been withdrawn. There was fury and confusion, and, on Lee's Hill, wonder and misgiving. More prisoners, wounded streaming back; but no withdrawal. If the Union troops were not advancing they were at least holding their ground. In front of Marye's Heights they soon formed again, were advancing, and were being hurled back over their own dead and wounded—but there on the right, what was happening?

Suspense was now at the highest. Reports from the right told only that the enemy had made his way between the brigades of Lane and Archer and was fighting savagely. Another column had crept up the ravine of Deep Run and had engaged the left of Pender's brigade. At last, above the deep roar of the artillery, there came the echo of the high, quavering rebel yell, an "unearthly, fiendish yell, such as no other troops or civilized beings ever uttered," as a Federal chaplain reported. It must be a Confederate countercharge. A few minutes later, as anxious eyes and ears were strained, the Federals began to run out of the wood they had entered. Louder swelled the yell, faster rolled the fire, until, with a gasp of excited joy, the observers on Lee's Hill saw the familiar ragged men in butternut burst from the wood and down Deep Run in all the passion of pursuit.

Lee's eyes flashed as he saw them. Turning to Longstreet he revealed the whole man in a single brief sentence: "It is well that war is so terrible—we should grow too fond of it!"

Whatever had happened on the right—and Lee did not know—it had been rectified, the front had been restored and the enemy had been driven back. It was not yet 3 o'clock, and the enemy might renew his assaults in that quarter, but there was scarcely time for speculation on this, because the enemy was again madly hurling his brigades against Marye's Heights in a third attack. This was repulsed, but it was pushed so far and with so much vigor that Lee began to wonder if his troops were numerous enough to hold the ground. Again, and with fresh troops, the Federals came forward, and again they were hurled back before a single man could reach the stone wall. Attack followed attack until the soldiers in the sunken road lost count of the number.

About 3:30 there came a lull in front of Marye's Heights, while new brigades were prepared for the slaughter. Though the artillery continued to roar, there were no infantry charges. The enemy had enough of Jackson's fire. His battle was over, with his lines completely restored. Taking advantage of the pause in the assaults, Colonel Walton on Marye's Heights asked that his Washington Artillery, the caissons almost empty, be relieved by other batteries. Word was sent to E. P. Alexander to bring up fresh guns. His shortest road to the Heights was across the front and up a ravine. Without hesitating he hurried his pieces forward in the very face of the enemy, down the Telegraph road. One gun was overturned and the column was delayed, but the piece was quickly righted and the wild rush began again. Officers shouted and urged the men on; the batteries turned up the grade, exposed to the full fury of the fire, reached the crest, swung to the right, and unlimbered. Then, and not till then, did Walton's exhausted men drag their scorching, smoke-covered guns to the rear. The Federals saw the withdrawal and assumed that a retreat was beginning. With a shout, they sprang forward again. But Alexander's guns opened instantly, the infantry in the sunken road were well warmed to their bloody work, and the combined fire repulsed the enemy once more.

The day was nearly done, but the bewildered Burnside stubbornly pushed in fresh troops in a mad determination to achieve the impossible by the weight of his numbers and the immensity of his sacrifices. On the enemy came, with strong supports. The whole field seemed alive with a blue that by this time was beginning to blend into the twilight on the chill ground. Each time the folly of the blind assault seemed more criminal. Still the gallant columns pressed on toward the stone wall. It was nearly 7 o'clock when the final assault withered in the face of artillery that now was firing by the flashes of the Federal small arms.

When the artillery at last died away in black night, the very skies seemed to reflect the blood that had been spilled to no purpose in front of the sunken road. The mysterious shafts of such an aurora borealis as the soldiers from the far South had never seen were, in their eyes, a warning of what the morrow would bring, for nearly every one expected Burnside to renew the attack. At headquarters, whither Lee rode under the glow of the aurora, his generals were all but unanimous in expressing this view. Only Hood insisted that Burnside would not resume the battle. Lee himself was of opinion that Burnside would make his major attack the next morning. In the highest spirits he predicted that further Federal assaults would be repelled and that the Army of Northern Virginia would then assume the offensive. He voiced the expectation of a renewal of the battle in the first telegraphic report of the day's action, sent the Secretary of War at 9 P.M. Before midnight his judgment seemed to be confirmed by the capture of a messenger bearing a memorandum of Burnside's plan for the next day's fight.

A brief and troubled night broke in heavy fog on the morning of December 14. Sun quickly scattered the fog and gave to the expected new battle the setting of a perfect winter's day. When the field became visible, the enemy was seen holding the ditch in front of Marye's Heights, but the men were flat on the ground and showed no disposition to stir. The ends of the streets facing the Confederate positions were barricaded, and the walls of many of the houses were loop-holed for infantry. Manifestly, Burnside did not intend to resume the attack on Marye's Heights, and as no reports came of any activity farther to the left, Lee concluded that the offensive would not be renewed on that wing. Sending fresh long-range artillery to Jackson, Lee rode to the right and, with "Stonewall" and Hood, went to Prospect Hill, the eminence from which Lindsay Walker's artillery had broken up the first demonstration on the morning of the 13th. "We had a magnificent view of the Federal lines on their left, some seven in number, and each, seemingly, a mile in length," Hood wrote. ". . . Strange to say, amid that immense assemblage of Federal troops, not a standard was to be seen; the colors were all lowered . . ."

What did all this mean? Could it be possible that the enemy had abandoned the offensive? With the question puzzling him, and almost unwilling to believe the evidence before his eyes, Lee returned to his own post of observation and examined the ground again. The Union troops were burying the dead within their lines and were carrying off such of the wounded as they could reach. Now and again skirmishers engaged in angry exchanges, and the Federal batteries fired a few half-hearted rounds. That was all. Noon and afternoon brought no change. Evening came, and not a man had been engaged at close range. Still, it did not seem credible that so great an army was ready to abandon so elaborate a manoeuvre after only one day's partial engagement of his forces.

On the morning of the 15th, with his own line still further strengthened, Lee observed that the enemy had dug rifle pits and had thrown
up fortifications on the outskirts of the town, as if to repel attacks. He
saw a ghastly sight besides: The Federal dead that still remained between the lines had changed color. They no longer were blue, but
naked and discolored. During the night, they had been stripped by
shivering Confederates.

Jackson came during the morning for a conference, but so far as is
known there was no discussion of a counterstroke. How could there
be one, when the Federal lines were now well fortified, and the superior
artillery was still in position on the plain and across the river to blast
the Confederate lines? Lee's spirits sank. If the Federals did not intend
to renew the attack, the victory would be barren, save for the losses inflicted. It was a heavy price to pay for having to defend the line of the
Rappahannock in order to procure supplies from the lower valley of
the river. The strategy of the commissary might be inescapable but it
was disheartening.

During the afternoon of the 15th, Burnside sent out a flag of truce
for the burial of the dead and for the relief of such of the wounded as
had survived forty-eight hours on the ground. Lee readily consented
to a truce on that part of the front where the Federals had fallen. Soon
their surgeons, ambulance detachments, and burial details mingled with
the Confederates in the field. The horror of the scene was far greater
at close range than it had appeared from the lines. In the space of an
acre or so were 1100 dead Federals, some of them piled 7 or 8 deep.
There could be no reasonable computation of the gross casualties. Not
until months afterward was it known that the Federals had lost 12,653,
compared to 5309 on the Confederate side, many of the latter having
trifling wounds. In front of Marye's Heights, where 9000 Federals had
fallen, McLaws had lost only 858—in Cobb's brigade but 235—and
Ransom's casualties had been 534. The toll on the entire Confederate
left, from McLaws's division to the end of the line, including Kemper's
and Jenkins's brigades, had not exceeded 1676.

Rain was falling and the morning was dark when Lee started to the
front again on the 16th. With "Stonewall," he went out to the eminence
near the railroad whence he had observed the silent army resting on the
morning of the 14th. D. H. Hill met them with the announcement that
the enemy had disappeared. Under the cover of the darkness, with the
south wind shutting off all sound from the Southern lines, Burnside had

retreated and had removed his bridges. It had been an easy task and Lee felt that it could not have been prevented. He was deeply depressed that he had not been able to strike a decisive blow.

That was all. There was no pride in the quick discovery of Burnside's plan to move from Warrenton to Fredericksburg, no boasting that an army of 78,000 had blocked the advance of 125,000 Federals on the Confederate capital, and had captured 11,000 stands of arms, no rejoicing that the great preparations of the enemy had been set at naught with casualties nearly two and a half times those the Army of Northern Virginia had sustained. There was only regret that more had not been done.

The army passed a bleak Christmas. Lee spent the forenoon in writing letters. For dinner he went to Jackson's headquarters, where the doughty "Stonewall" entertained him, Pendleton, and their staffs.

On the last day of the year Lee published his congratulatory order on the battle of Fredericksburg. "The war is not yet ended," said he. "The enemy is still numerous and strong, and the country demands of the army a renewal of its heroic efforts in her behalf. Nobly has it responded to her call in the past, and she will never appeal in vain to its courage and patriotism. The signal manifestations of Divine mercy that have distinguished the eventful and glorious campaign of the year just closing give assurance of hope that, under the guidance of the same Almighty hand, the coming year will be no less fruitful of events that will insure the safety, peace and happiness of our beloved country, and add new lustre to the already imperishable name of the Army of Northern Virginia." This final flourish showed the hand of Major Charles Marshall rather than that of Lee.

The year had, indeed, been one of victory in Virginia, at least during the seven months Lee had commanded the army. Port Republic, Cross Keys, Mechanicsville, Gaines's Mill, Savage Station, Frayser's Farm, Malvern Hill, Cedar Mountain, Second Manassas, Boonsboro, Harpers Ferry, Sharpsburg, and Fredericksburg—thirteen battles great and small —had been fought during that time, and the Confederates had remained masters of the field in every instance except at Boonsboro and at Sharpsburg. Leaving out of account the actions at Cross Keys, Port Republic, and Cedar Mountain, which were tactically Jackson's though Lee had a part in the general strategy, the troops under Lee's command had this account of gains and losses: They had sustained 48,171 casualties and had inflicted 70,725. They had taken from the enemy approximately 75,000 small arms and had yielded scarcely more than 6000. With the loss of 8 cannon, they had secured 155. The infantry practically had been rearmed with improved, captured rifles, and half the batteries boasted superior ordnance that had belonged to the Army of the Potomac.

The morale of the Army of Northern Virginia was vastly higher than it had been when Lee took command, yet there was a consciousness in the ranks, though not in the Richmond executive offices, of the persistent, determined spirit of an enemy who could replace every fallen soldier, make good every captured arm, and supply every necessity of the Army of the Potomac from ample manufactories and open ports. Richmond was fearful of military defeat but refused to admit the inevitable consequences of economic attrition. The Army of Northern Virginia was confident of victory in the field but fearful of economic disaster behind the lines. Before the winter was to end, the danger of starvation and of immobility, resulting from a collapse of transportation, was to be plain to every private in the ranks.

The improvement in organization wrought after July was amazing. Gone were the excitable Magruder, the slow Huger, the gloomy Whiting, and the deaf Holmes. Gone was the cumbersome arrangement of divisions operating as if they had been independent armies. In its place were two well-administered corps, commanded by officers of proved capacity. The divisions and brigades were becoming conscious of their relation to the military machine, and were led, in most instances, by men who relied on sound tactics and good discipline rather than on the costly valor of untrained soldiers. Fifteen of the brigadier generals who had entered the Seven Days' Battle with Lee were no longer present. Some of the best of the fifteen had been killed, notably Garland, Gregg, and Winder, but the incompetents had in part been supplanted and the political generals had been sent elsewhere—and all so quietly, so tactfully, that few realized how the army had been transformed by the time the men tumbled out of their blankets and wished one another a Happy New Year on the morning of January 1, 1863.

On January 14, Lee ordered D. H. Hill to Richmond, and on the 16th he went there in person, at Mr. Davis's request, to confer on the situation. He found the administration concerned over the immediate outlook but confident that the war should soon be won, an optimistic delusion he did not share.

Lee was hurriedly recalled to Fredericksburg by the news that Burnside's army was on the move and seemed to be threatening to cross the

Rappahannock. When he reached headquarters on the 18th, Lee found Jackson and Longstreet at odds concerning the disposition of the army for the expected attack. Quickly settling this, he spent two busy days riding to the left and to the right of the line, and concluded, in the end, that the enemy's effort would be on the upper Rappahannock, above Fredericksburg.

Signs multiplied by January 20 that the enemy again was preparing to adventure across the Rappahannock. In a heavy rain, the shivering Confederate troops remained on the alert. At length all Federal activity ended, and Lee concluded that Burnside's attempt had been frustrated. He was correct. The Federal commander had contemplated a general offensive but had found the roads so nearly bottomless that his advance had degenerated into what his disgusted army styled a "Mud March."

During the five weeks that separated the beginning of the "Mud March" from Burnside's defeat at Fredericksburg, Lee had been fortifying the entire front of the Rappahannock. After the "Mud March" he had this work continued on the whole line of twenty-five miles from Banks's Ford to Port Royal. These fortifications marked a definite stage in the evolution of the field defenses that were to be one of Lee's most historic contributions to the science of war. From this type of work there was only one step to field fortification.

While the lines were daily growing stronger, Lee was warning an overconfident administration that the next few months might be decisive. "The enemy," he said, "will make every effort to crush us between now and June, and it will require all our strength to resist him." He renewed his perennial appeal for the completion of the Richmond defenses; he exhausted his arguments and almost exhausted his patience in trying to end wasteful details and to bring men into the ranks. Congress's failure to act to this end aroused to indignation even a nature that had been disciplined from boyhood to respect civil authority. "Our salvation will depend on the next four months," he said prophetically, "and yet I cannot get even regular promotions made to fill vacancies in regiments, while Congress seems to be laboring to pass laws to get easy places for some favorites or constituents, or get others out of active service. I shall feel very much obliged if they will pass a law relieving me from all duty and legislating some one in my place, better able to do it."

Lee's apprehension of a new crisis kept him from resting, inactive, behind his cavalry outposts, which were extended by this time from Beverley's Ford on the upper Rappahannock far down the river to the watershed between the Rappahannock and the Pamunkey. With the energy that always surged under his calm exterior, he now turned his attention to Federal General R. H. Milroy. That officer, or some one misusing his name, was putting into effect in parts of western Virginia a system of organized blackmail. Southern sympathizers were notified that loss had been inflicted on Union supporters and that an assessment had been levied against them to make this good. From Confederates there came complaints that Brigadier General W. E. Jones had not been active in dealing with Milroy's raiders. Lee had defended Jones, whose difficulties he understood, and he now resolved to detach Fitz Lee's brigade of cavalry to reinforce Jones for an attack on Milroy.

Just at the time this expedition was moving through the mud toward the Valley on February 14, a fleet of Federal transports, loaded with men, steamed down the Potomac. As reports immediately indicated a concentration at Newport News, Lee ordered Hood and Pickett to Richmond, and, on the 17th, directed Longstreet to proceed southward and take command of the two detached divisions. The departure of Longstreet left Lee with a total force not exceeding 62,600 officers and men, of whom only 58,800 were on the line of the Rappahannock. Yet Lee's chief regret was that he could not take the offensive against the diminished Federal command opposing him.

General Joseph Hooker had now replaced General Burnside in command of the Army of the Potomac—a change that Lee accepted with complacency. In his personal letters he jested mildly over the apparent inability of Hooker to determine on a course of action. By February 26, Lee concluded that Hooker had decided to do nothing on a large scale until the weather improved. Rest in winter quarters became more of a reality.

During March the army passed through a series of alarms and preparations, while Hooker kept his balloons in the air as if he were expecting an attack. Attention to details was interrupted by a call to Richmond for consultation with the President on the military situation. This visit, like that in January, was ended by a report that the enemy was massing cavalry, this time at Kelly's Ford. Assuming that this was the beginning of a general offensive, Lee ordered Longstreet's detached divisions to rejoin the army, but when he reached headquarters on the 18th, he found that the enemy had not attempted to move any infantry across the river and had withdrawn his cavalry after a spectacular battle between 3000 Federal horse and Fitz Lee's mounted brigade.

The wise employment of Longstreet's force, who was operating near Suffolk south of the James, was becoming a matter of serious moment to Lee. Longstreet had 44,000 effectives. The force opposing him was estimated to be about equal. If Longstreet had opportunity of striking at the Federals, he might reasonably hope to defeat them. But was it wise to force a fight on that front? The Army of Northern Virginia badly needed supplies, and if it was able to assume the offensive, it must have food. Longstreet was within reach of eastern North Carolina, where a large volume of provisions, especially of bacon, was known to be available, but could only be collected with army wagons. Which meant more to the cause—a commissary campaign by Longstreet or a military campaign at a time when Lee might have desperate need of the best units of Longstreet's command? It was a difficult choice.

His impulse was to have Longstreet take the offensive against diminished forces in his front while he drove the Federal cavalry from the Valley and thereby played once more on Mr. Lincoln's fears for the safety of Washington. But the roads made immediate operations in the Valley impossible. Lee did not feel able to do more than once again to trust to Longstreet's discretion. "You are . . . ," he wrote Longstreet, "to make any movement that you may consider advisable; but, as stated in former letters, so long as the enemy choose to remain on the defensive and covered by their intrenchments and floating batteries I fear you can accomplish but little, except to draw provisions from the invaded districts. If you can accomplish this it will be of positive benefit. I leave the whole matter to your good judgment."

At this juncture, when a right decision on Lee's part might affect the outcome of the war, the fates that had so often conspired against the Confederacy at critical hours again intervened on the side of the Union. For the first time since 1849, Lee fell ill. He contracted a serious throat infection which settled into what seems to have been a pericarditis. His arm, his chest, and his back were attacked with sharp paroxysms of pain that suggest even the possibility of an angina.

On April 6, after Lee's sickness had begun to abate somewhat, the Secretary of War sounded him out on something that meant even more than the detention of Hood and Pickett in southern Virginia: would it be possible, the secretary asked, to dispatch part of Longstreet's command to Tennessee to reinforce Bragg? Lee put forward a bolder plan. On April 9 he wrote the Secretary of War: "Should Hooker's army assume the defensive, the readiest method of relieving the pressure upon

FREDERICKSBURG, *December, 1862*

GENERAL JOSEPH HOOKER

General Johnston and General Beauregard would be for the army to cross into Maryland. This cannot be done, however, in the present condition of the roads, nor unless I can obtain a certain amount of provisions and transportation. But this is what I would recommend, if practicable."

Expecting the campaign to open in northern Virginia, Lee made preparations to carry out the plan he had outlined to Seddon. If Hooker did not seize the initiative before May 1, Lee intended first to sweep Milroy from the Valley. Then he intended to carry the war again into Maryland in the hope of relieving pressure on the other Confederate armies. But even to move the army on the first leg of its advance toward the Potomac, Lee must have the supplies from North Carolina, and to collect those supplies Longstreet must be kept there as long as practicable.

Risk increased hourly. Evidence began to multiply that Hooker had no intention of waiting until Lee could take the situation in his own hands after Longstreet had collected his bacon and rejoined the army. A raid was made on Port Royal on April 23. Lee took it to be a warning that the campaign was soon to open, and he notified the troops to be on the alert. Spies informed Lee that all the troops in rear of Hooker's lines had been brought up. Lee watched every development intently. He was satisfied that if Hooker delayed until the army could be reunited, he could defeat him. But with the army divided, the horses feeble, and provisions low, he doubted his ability "even to act on the defensive as vigorously as circumstances may require."

Sunday morning, April 26, Lee went with Jackson to a religious service. That evening, on both sides of the Rappahannock, regimental adjutants were beginning to put together the returns of personnel due on the 30th. Hooker's officers had a magnificent total to compile—138,378 present for duty. Lee's strength cannot be stated with absolute certainty, as events were to prevent the completion of the returns, but the total was not much, if any, in excess of 62,500. Except on the day before the battle of Sharpsburg, he had never faced such crushing odds, yet he had been planning to take the offensive if Hooker did not!

Before daybreak on April 29, Lee was aroused by a distant roll that he took to be gunfire, but he was overtaken again by drowsiness and was soon asleep once more. Presently he was awakened by some one calling his name. Opening his eyes, he saw the grave face of Jackson's aide, Captain James Power Smith. Smith announced that Jackson had sent him to inform the General that Hooker was crossing the Rappahannock in force.

"Well," said Lee, "I thought I heard firing and was beginning to think it was time some of you young fellows were coming to tell me what it was all about. You want me to send a message to your good general, Captain? Tell him that I am sure he knows what to do. I will meet him at the front very soon."

It was dawn, but it was close to the high noon of the Confederacy.

When Lee rode through the early morning fog to the front he found that the Federals had quietly pushed their boats over the Rappahannock just below the mouth of Deep Run. The Conferedate pickets had seen nothing and heard nothing until the boats were grounding. Retreating before superior forces, the outposts had no information except that the enemy was on the Confederate side. Downstream another Union column had attempted to cross but had been delayed. The troops that reached the Confederate side did not attempt to advance immediately but sheltered themselves under the bank of the river, covered by the artillery that lined the Stafford Heights. A very large supporting force was in sight on the other shore, as if waiting its turn to move forward. Everything indicated that the Federals were launching a general offensive.

The reasons that had prompted Lee in December not to attempt to resist the enemy in the plain along the river applied with equal weight now. Orders were given to prepare on the ridges to meet the attack. For the moment, Lee could do no more. He conferred with Jackson on proper dispositions. President Davis was notified and was asked to send forward any available reinforcements from south of the James, though Lee had no expectation that Longstreet could return to him in time for the coming battle or that any other help on a large scale could reach him speedily.

Before noon on the 29th Stuart reported that about 14,000 infantry with six guns and some cavalry had crossed below Kelly's Ford on the upper Rappahannock and apparently was moving toward Gordonsville. During the afternoon a telegram arrived from Stuart announcing that he had engaged the enemy at Maddens, nine miles east of Culpeper, and had captured prisoners from the V, XI, and XII Corps of the Army of the Potomac. Stuart stated that these columns of the enemy were headed for Germanna and for Ely's Ford on the Rapidan. This was news of the greatest moment. It indicated that some or all of these men were moving to turn the left flank of the Confederate army.

There was danger that if the Federals crossed at Ely's and Germanna Ford they might throw themselves between Lee and Stuart and deprive the army of its cavalry at a time when every road should be watched. Lee deliberately took the chance that the enemy's horse might prey upon the railroads in his rear and ordered Stuart to rejoin the main army as soon as possible, delaying the Federals on their march.

Shortly after 6:30 that afternoon a courier arrived with a report that the Federals had crossed at Germanna Ford. Another brought intelligence that the enemy was over the Rapidan at Ely's Ford. This removed all doubt as to the direction of the advance: the roads from Ely's and from Germanna met at Chancellorsville. The Federals evidently were seeking to turn the flank and, presumably, to get in the rear of the Army of Northern Virginia.

R. H. Anderson had three of his brigades above Fredericksburg, guarding two of the fords. Another brigade was near at hand. The fourth had been ordered up. Lee decided to pivot the right of this division on the Rappahannock, above Fredericksburg, and to swing it back roughly at right angles to the river. This would cover his left and would enable him to hold Chancellorsville.

This movement began at 9 P.M. Anderson, to whom it was entrusted, was an able officer of high courage but indolent and difficult to arouse. Lee accordingly took the precaution specifically to order Anderson to direct the troop-movement in person. Lee ordered McLaws to put his troops in condition to move the next day with cooked rations if needed to support Anderson. Lee did not place these two under McLaws, the senior. Instead, he took their movement in his own hands, leaving to Jackson the management of the Second Corps.

Morning of the 30th saw little change on the front below Fredericksburg. The enemy showed no disposition to attack. Lee turned to measures for aiding Anderson. Engineers were hurried to him to draw entrenchments and Alexander's battalion of artillery, which had come up from the rear, was sent him. Nothing was heard from Anderson during the morning, but between noon and 1 P.M. a courier arrived announcing that Federal infantry were advancing. The columns were moving on Chancellorsville. A little later, Anderson reported that he had been as far as Chancellorsville and had been joined by the brigades from the United States Ford. He had withdrawn to a good position east of

Chancellorsville and had encountered only cavalry, moving from the direction of Chancellorsville, but he needed reinforcements.

Lee promptly sent Anderson careful and detailed orders: he was to dig in at once and, if he could do so, prepare a line adequate for the additional troops that Lee hoped to be able to send. Anderson was to advise whether he desired additional artillery. He was to have his men keep two days' cooked rations on their persons and was to be prepared to remove his trains at any time. These orders to Anderson were of historical importance. It was the first time in open operations that Lee had ordered the construction of field fortifications.

Lee had now to decide on his general plan. He believed the Federals had advanced almost as far as he could permit them without getting between him and Richmond. A retreat was the easier and safer course, so far as the immediate situation was concerned. The alternative policy —to divide the army and to give battle on the left—was to take great risks of destruction. He probably reasoned that a retreat was what Hooker might reasonably anticipate. An immediate offensive against the columns advancing down the south bank of the Rappahannock might disconcert his adversary and give the Confederates the advantage of surprise in a broken, wooded country. Lee's decision, therefore, was to prepare the army for a retreat, if that became necessary, but to retain a limited force at Fredericksburg and to strike swiftly on his left.

Instead of riding forthwith to the left, Lee prudently went back on the morning of May 1 to the old lines on the heights behind Fredericksburg. Finding that the Federals were not preparing an immediate advance, he directed that more artillery be brought up. From Lee's Hill, he approved the disposition already made of the artillery and sent a battery down the Rappahannock to deal with two gunboats reported to be shelling Port Royal. To General Early, who was left in charge, he gave precise instructions: Early was to conceal the weakness of his numbers and was to endeavor to hold his position against attack.

With a final look at the lines, Lee started during the early afternoon of May 1 to the threatened sector. He was playing a desperate game, and he knew it. He was about to lead 51,000 against a foe who, if he were making his major offensive, might have nearly twice that number in and around the gloomy Wilderness of Spotsylvania. There was no news of any Confederate reinforcements. The weakened Army of Northern Virginia would have to rely upon itself, and itself only, to escape the jaws of the gigantic pincers that seemed to be closing upon it.

In a short time the Federals began to give way before McLaws and Anderson, who were advancing along the Orange Turnpike and the Plank roads. There was something suspicious about the situation. The advance of Anderson and McLaws was much too easy. What had happened? Was Hooker screening a movement farther around the flank? Stuart should know; Lee sent him a message to ask what had become of the other Federal columns.

After sunset Jackson sent word that the enemy had stopped his withdrawal and had checked the Confederate advance. To ascertain more, Lee went forward and joined Jackson. Jackson explained how promptly the enemy had abandoned his advance and how easily he had been driven back to Chancellorsville. The movement was a feint or a failure, he said. The enemy would soon recross the Rappahannock. "By tomorrow morning," he insisted, "there will not be any of them this side of the river."

Lee could not believe that this would happen. He hoped that Jackson's prediction might be realized, he said, but he thought that the main army of Hooker was in their front, and he could not persuade himself that the Federal commander would abandon his attempt so readily.

Lee decided against a frontal attack. "How," he asked, half to himself, "can we get at these people?" Jackson answered, in substance, that it was for Lee to say. He would endeavor to do whatever Lee directed. Lee took his map, which showed most of the roads and, after a few minutes' study, pointed out the general direction of a movement around the Federals' right flank and to their rear. An attack must be made from the west, to turn the strong Union positions around Chancellorsville, so that the two wings of the army could make a united assault. Jackson at once acquiesced.

"General Stuart," Lee went on, "will cover your movement with his cavalry." Jackson rose, smiling, and touched his cap: "My troops will move at 4 o'clock," he said.

Jackson was thus entrusted with the execution of the plan that Lee had determined. Caution and speed were urged upon him. The council then ended. Jackson retired promptly to get a few hours' rest, as he would have to be up early to procure detailed information about the roads, before he set his column in motion.

Lee had left the execution of the movement to Jackson, and had not prescribed a definite route or designated how many troops were to follow it. As they made last-minute plans Lee turned to "Stonewall," who was still studying the map. "General Jackson," said he, "what do you propose to make this movement with?"

"With my whole corps," Jackson answered.

That was Jackson's own conception, his major contribution to the plan. He would not attempt a simple turning movement that would merely confuse the enemy and give an opening for a general assault. He would march with all his 28,000 men and would attack in such force as to crumple the enemy. It was a proposal Lee had not expected. "What will you leave me?" he said, in some surprise.

"The divisions of Anderson and McLaws," Jackson answered.

Two divisions to face an enemy who might easily have 50,000 men in a strong position! In case the enemy should learn that Jackson had been detached and should then resume the offensive at Chancellorsville and at Fredericksburg. However, the movement around the left flank to the rear of the Federals was the only means of retaining the initiative. The boldness of the proposal stirred Lee's fighting blood. If Jackson could turn the flank, he would hold the line. "Well," said he, calmly, "go on." And as Jackson sketched his march, Lee jotted down notes for his own dispositions.

He was there, about 7 A.M., when the head of Jackson's column began swinging to the southwest. A short distance behind the leading regiments rode "Stonewall" and his staff. Jackson drew rein for a minute or two and said a few words to Lee that nobody overheard. "Stonewall" pointed significantly ahead. Lee nodded. Jackson rode on. As Lee looked, it must have been with confidence, affection, and admiration. "Such an executive officer," he said not many days thereafter, "the sun never shone on. I have but to show him my design, and I know that if it can be done, it will be done. No need for me to send or watch him. Straight as the needle to the pole he advanced to the execution of my purpose."

The mission of Jackson was daring. Equally daring was the task to which Lee turned when Jackson's figure faded into the forest. For Lee, defying the lesson of Sharpsburg, had divided his army into three parts —into four, if Rooney Lee's two regiments of cavalry, facing Stoneman, were counted as a separate unit. Jackson was carrying 28,000 men with him toward the right flank and rear of Hooker. Early's 10,000 were watching Sedgwick on the Fredericksburg sector, and Lee, with a scant 14,000, was left to hold off the main army of the Federals on a front of three and a quarter miles.

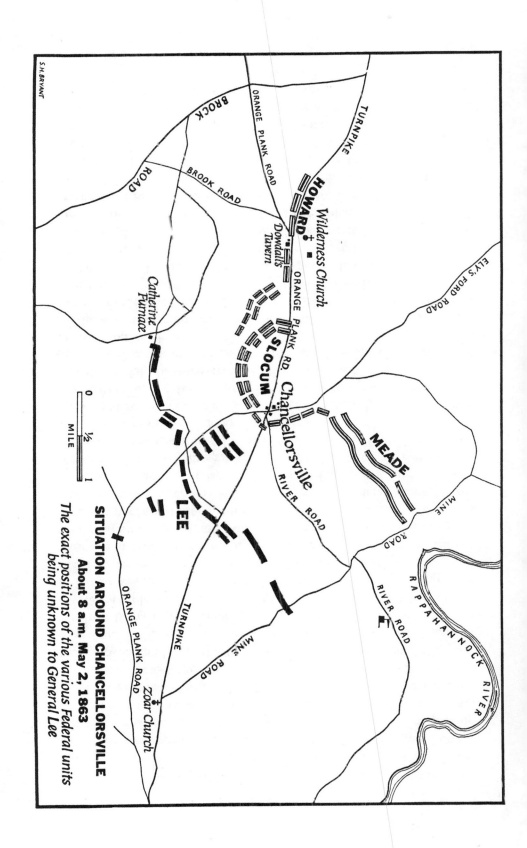

SITUATION AROUND CHANCELLORSVILLE
About 8 a.m. May 2, 1863
The exact positions of the various Federal units
being unknown to General Lee

S.H.BRYANT

HOWARD

Wilderness Church

Dowdall's Tavern

BROCK ROAD

ORANGE PLANK ROAD

BROOK ROAD

ROAD

Catherine Furnace

TURNPIKE

SLOCUM

ORANGE PLANK RD.

Chancellorsville

MEADE

ELY'S FORD ROAD

RIVER ROAD

MINE ROAD

LEE

ORANGE PLANK ROAD

TURNPIKE

MINE ROAD

Zoar Church

RIVER ROAD

RAPPAHANNOCK RIVER

0   ½   1
MILE

Lee planned his dispositions quickly. Orders were to hold the line, with skirmishers well out, but not to provoke attack. The guns were placed as advantageously as possible to cover the approaches, but the prospect remained one of dire danger. The men were six feet apart on some sections of the line. They could not possibly hold their ground against a determined attack by the powerful enemy that faced them.

About 10 o'clock there was a sound of artillery fire by a few guns to the westward, and at 11 this grew heavier. As noon shortened the shadows, a sudden outburst of infantry fire was audible from the vicinity of the iron furnace past which Jackson's column was moving. Soon a courier brought ominous tidings—the enemy was attacking the wagontrain that was following the rear of the turning column! Ere long came the reassuring news that the enemy had been beaten off.

As the afternoon wore on, it became apparent that Jackson had not been held up a second time. Nor had the enemy shifted troops to meet him. On McLaws's front there was some lively firing by Wofford's brigade around 3:15, but nothing to indicate a general attack by th᷾ Federals. Just as the fusillade on Wofford's lines began to die away, a message in Jackson's autograph was delivered to Lee: "The enemy has made a stand at Chancellor's which is about 2 miles from Chancellorsville. I hope as soon as practicable to attack."

Suspense was rising. Unless Jackson's guns were soon heard, his action would have to be deferred until morning, and, being postponed, would almost certainly be discovered. Orders were issued to press the enemy as soon as Jackson opened, so as to prevent the dispatch of reinforcements to oppose him.

The next news did not come from the west but from the east. Early had left Fredericksburg! Without firing a shot, he was marching to join Lee; the strong positions on the heights had virtually been abandoned to the enemy. The rear was open to Sedgwick! It was all due to a mistake in the transmission of ever-dangerous verbal orders. Colonel Chilton had confused the instructions he had been directed to deliver. He had told Early that he was to leave one brigade and was to march at once to Lee with the rest of his command. Early had protested in vain and then obediently had drawn out his guns and had put them on the road. It was a desperate moment in a desperate campaign. If Fredericksburg were occupied in force, or if Jackson had been balked, then . . . but what was that rumble from the west? Every ear was strained; every heart stopped for a moment. Then, as the fury of a cannonade swept over the Wilderness, every eye brightened. It was

Jackson at last, hurling his veterans desperately against the Federals!

Quickly the word was passed to the right: Advance and hold the attention of the enemy. Not one man must Hooker be permitted to withdraw from his left to reinforce the right that Jackson was now crumpling up. As diligently as if engaged in a real offensive, the thin line sprang up and straightened and stiffened and began steadily to move forward.

The demonstration served its purpose, for in the darkness that now settled over the Wilderness the Federals could not move troops to their right in time to strengthen it. Lee with the rest of the army listened in fascination to the swelling roar of Jackson's attack. It was evident that Jackson was advancing rapidly, but the volume of sound indicated a growing resistance. Now the din diminished, now it rose again; salvoes and volleys, the nervous uneven fire of scattered, frantic batteries, the rattle of long lines of muskets. The night battle continued. At 11 o'clock it was still in its fury; not until midnight did it die away into silence.

Weariness overcame the questionings of an anxious mind, and Lee went to sleep on the ground. About 2:30 he was awakened by Captain R. E. Wilbourn, Jackson's signal officer. He had to tell a tale the like of which had never been recounted in all the grim annals of America's wars. Jackson had discovered the right flank of the XI Corps, "in the air" just north of the turnpike, a mile beyond the Wilderness Church. The Federals had been unsuspectingly cooking their supper. Jackson quietly extended his men in three lines on a wide front. The bugles sounded through the woods, and the corps went forward with a demoniac yell. The startled enemy offered brief resistance and then fled, Jackson in full pursuit. Such a victory the army had never won, but . . . in the confusion, Jackson had ridden forward with a few of his officers, had been fired on by overanxious soldiers among his own men . . . and had been wounded three times in the arms. He had been carried to the rear and was under a surgeon's care.

Lee heard Wilbourn without a comment or even an exclamation. At the announcement of Jackson's injuries, though Wilbourn said they were only flesh wounds, he could not contain himself. With deep feeling he said, "Ah, captain, any victory is dearly bought which deprives us of the services of General Jackson, even for a short time!"

Wilbourn volunteered that from what he had heard Jackson say, he thought the General had planned to seize the road to the United States Ford and to cut the enemy off from it that night or the next morning. This reference to the resumption of the battle galvanized Lee. He rose on the instant. "These people must be pressed today," he said. He wrote immediately to Stuart: "It is necessary that the glorious victory thus far achieved be prosecuted with the utmost vigor, and the enemy given no time to rally. As soon, therefore, as it is possible, they must be pressed, so that we may unite the two wings of the army."

When Lee rode off to do battle for a junction with Jackson's corps the situation was much confused. The brigade commanders knew nothing of the difficult ground through which they had to lead their troops. Their force was much too small to cover their assigned front adequately. They went to their task, however, with fine initiative, their left supported by three guns that Lee personally ordered into position. Perry cleared the ground on his part of the front. Posey engaged hotly. Wright found himself called upon with 1600 to sweep the tangle of woodland on a front of one mile. Lee himself started to the left to direct the junction of Stuart's column and his own.

As he approached Catherine Furnace the fury of a battle to the northwest was borne upon him. Stuart had attacked before sunrise and was pushing forward. Thanks alike to the good judgment of Colonel E. P. Alexander and to a bad blunder on the part of the Federals, Stuart had been able to seize an excellent artillery position known as Hazel Grove, about 2000 yards southwest of Chancellorsville, and had massed thirty guns there. This strong battery gave him an immediate advantage. But on the left of Stuart's command the enemy was attacking violently. Stout brigades were shaken. The centre of the Second Corps was hard beset also. Its dispositions had not been tactically good. Still Stuart's men pressed on; still their leader rode recklessly up and down the line as if he were a cavalry colonel in the first exuberant days of the war.

As the battle raged beyond the furnace, men were carried beyond themselves and fought as if the fumes of gunpowder were a mysterious hashish that gave them the strength of madness. Rarely in the whole war did frenzy mount to wilder heights; never before had the exaltation of a common cause so completely possessed the Army of Northern Virginia. Mistakes were disregarded, enfilading fire was ignored, and attacks from flanks and rear were met without a tremor and repulsed without a stampede. Above the din could be heard the fiendish rebel yell rolling clear and defiant.

The Confederate flags were planted on the works at Fairview and then went down under a wave of blue; again the flags went forward; again there was a Federal rally and the lines gave way. From the southeast, Union troops threatened the rear of the attacking force in front of

Fairview. But the Confederates were following them fast. With one more thrust the enemy might be pushed back, the two wings of the army united, and victory driven home. Lee rode over in person to Hazel Grove and ordered the men forward. For 400 or 500 yards they advanced and then halted. Again they went on, dividing on either side of the open ground in front of Fairview and disappearing in the woods. In this manoeuvre, the right flank of Archer established contact with the left of Perry. A continuous line was now moving forward. Quickly Lee sent word to Stuart that junction had been formed. Lee was ready for the final blow: Stuart was ordered to advance with his whole command up the Orange plank road; McLaws and Anderson would co-operate.

The line now swept on without a break. The newly formed artillery battalions hurried their batteries to Fairview. By 10 o'clock these guns were beating a fast accompaniment for the approaching climax. The resistance to the advance of Stuart's left wing was immediately reduced. The Chancellor house was breaking into flames from chance shots. Anderson's men worked their way almost unopposed to the plank road.

The Federal artillery fire fell off. The batteries limbered up and disappeared. The blue infantry were making for the thickets that lay between Chancellorsville and the river. Everything indicated a precipitate retreat to the fords and pontoon bridges on the Rappahannock. If all went well, the enveloping lines would tighten, the retreat would become a rout.

And now word came back that Chancellorsville had been taken. From Hazel Grove, Lee rode eastward to the clearing. Everywhere was the debris of the battle, wrecked caissons, dying horses, abandoned rifles, knapsacks thrown away in the flight, blankets, oil cloths, cartridge boxes. Past woods on the left of the road, Lee rode beyond Fairview, where jubilant artillerists were firing at retreating fragments of broken regiments. The woods on the left gave place to the Chancellorsville clearing, in itself a paltry stake on which to gamble the lives of 125,000 men. But what a sight it was in the wild jubilation of victory. As Lee rode toward the Chancellor house the soldiers recognized him. Sensing that he had fashioned their victory, they broke into the wildest demonstration they had ever made in his presence.

It was the supreme moment of his life as a soldier. The sun of his destiny was at its Zenith. All that he had earned by a life of self-control, all that he had received in inheritance from pioneer forbears, all that he had merited by study, by diligence, and by daring was crowded into that moment. The life of stern duty that had carried him from a West

Point classroom through the mud flats of Cockspur Island, across the pedregal to Padierna, over the passes in West Virginia, and to the brink of the Potomac at Sharpsburg had brought him to that peak of military glory.

But it was not given to this man ever to know as a Confederate soldier a single hour when the fates that had favored him did not threaten him with ruin. As he turned modestly from the acclaim of his troops, a courier placed a dispatch in his hand. It was from Jackson. Nothing in it indicated that Jackson had dictated the paper after an operation for the amputation of the wounded left arm. Jackson expressed his congratulations on the victory, and announced that he had been compelled. by wounds to turn over the command of his corps to Major General A. P. Hill. Not for a moment had Lee forgotten his great lieutenant, but this note and the accompanying news that it had been necessary to remove the injured arm shook Lee more violently than if one of the shells that were still roaring overhead had exploded under the flank of Traveller. What was another victory if it meant that Jackson's flesh wounds were serious and that he might . . . ? With shaking voice, choked by emotion, he bade Major Marshall reply to Jackson that the victory was his, that the congratulations were due him, and that he wished he had been wounded in his stead.

At the moment, success seemed to promise the immediate retreat of the enemy across the Rappahannock. Speed was necessary if the victory was to be capitalized, but Lee felt compelled to call a temporary halt to rest the men and to organize the next stage of the offensive, which had to be conducted in one of the densest parts of the Wilderness.

Then fate again rode into the Wilderness. Just as Lee was about to give the orders for the resumption of the attack Lieutenant Andrew L. Pitzer, of General Early's staff, reached him with news of a disaster. Before dawn the enemy had thrown a bridge across at Fredericksburg. A demonstration below the town on Early's right had been easily repulsed. Then an attack above Beck's Island had been beaten off. Thereupon the enemy had assailed Marye's Heights. Twice the Federals had recoiled and then, in a heavy assault, had overwhelmed the position. The enemy, by this time, was almost certainly in Lee's rear, marching down the plank road. Fredericksburg lost, the main army now between Sedgwick and Hooker—this in the hour when one more blow had seemed to promise overwhelming triumph!

Lee did not blanch at the news of the disaster at Fredericksburg. Nor did he hesitate. When a Mississippi soldier rode up a little later with another excited report, Lee simply said: "We will attend to Mr. Sedgwick later." His position dictated his action. He would demonstrate against Hooker's crippled host, hold it in the Wilderness, and detach troops immediately to deal with Sedgwick's column. McLaws must go, for his front was not in danger and his troops had not been heavily engaged.

Establishing headquarters in a tent by the side of the Orange plank road, Lee, left with only 36,000 to 37,000 men, now undertook to make a demonstration that would discourage Hooker from taking the offensive on the strength of the news from Fredericksburg. Lee assumed, of course, that the knowledge of the success on that sector would lead Hooker to halt the move back to the north side of the Rappahannock, but he believed he could hold him within his lines. It was a grave state of affairs, but the confidence neither of the commander nor of the army was shaken. About 5 P.M., there came the sound of a cannonade from the direction of Salem Church, followed by reports of an infantry engagement. Now, if ever, Hooker would assume the offensive; yet the Federals did not attempt an advance.

For two hours and more the firing from the east continued. Taking it to mean that McLaws was attacking, Lee determined to develop whatever advantage McLaws might gain. The combined strength of Early and of McLaws should suffice to demolish Sedgwick. So, to the music of the cannonade, he wrote to Early and to McLaws outlining a plan whereby Early should come up on the enemy's left while McLaws attacked in front. Just as he had seized the initiative in dealing with Hooker by advancing toward Chancellorsville, so now Lee purposed to put Sedgwick on the defensive.

The first news from McLaws's column indicated that the way had been prepared for the execution of this plan. Wilcox, who never appeared to better advantage than on that day, had made a stand at Salem Church, on the plank road, where he had been joined by McLaws. The Federals had come forward about 5:20, after artillery preparation. They had gained an initial advantage and had broken the front of one regiment but had been savagely repulsed. A second attack had been beaten off easily. Then Wilcox and Semmes, who was on the left, had rushed forward and driven the enemy nearly half a mile.

In the security this news afforded Lee prepared to bivouac for the night. He read near midnight a message from McLaws enclosing one from Early, in which that officer proposed that he return to Marye's Heights, cut Sedgwick's communications with Fredericksburg, and then move against the enemy in co-operation with McLaws. Lee had one of his staff write approving the scheme. Then, in an atmosphere of alarms and distress, with the wounded crying out from nearby copses for water, he sought a little rest.

When Lee took up his duties on the early morning of Monday, May 4, reports were that Jackson was doing well. He was resting comfortably in a tent. Lee felt, however, that there still was danger of a raid by the enemy's cavalry from the direction of Ely's Ford, so he instructed Doctor Hunter McGuire to remove Jackson to a place of safety at Guiney's, as soon as this could be done.

Reconnaissance showed that Hooker had strengthened his position. On well-chosen ground he had a heavy line. Lee quickly decided that it would be a waste of life to attack with less than his entire force. He must first dispose of Sedgwick and remove the threat against his rear. He must take no chances with this. McLaws and Early might suffice to hold Sedgwick or even to defeat him, but it was wise to send Anderson to reinforce them.

Scarcely had Anderson started when Lee received a dispatch from McLaws in which that officer explained the details of Early's plan. Mc-Laws expressed doubt as to his ability to co-operate adequately and asked for reinforcements. Lee replied that Anderson was marching to McLaws's support, and he decided to ride to the right in person.

When Lee reached the vicinity of Salem Church he found the situation less favorable than the dispatches had indicated. At length, with Anderson on his way, he rode around to Early's sector.

Early's plan was to advance up the high ground in rear of the heights and to turn the Federal position on the plank road while Anderson attacked on his left and McLaws closed in from the west. It was a plan that involved no little manoeuvring over difficult terrain, but as it seemed feasible, Lee approved it and rode back toward the centre. The troops there were still having much trouble in getting into position. Six o'clock came before the troops were all satisfactorily disposed. At last the signal guns were fired, and Early and Anderson advanced. Despite difficulties, the enemy was pushed back. Reports from the brigade commanders during the next hour led Lee to believe that if the enemy were immediately assailed, he would be forced across the

Rappahannock that night. Lee determined to push the advance in the darkness—the first time he had ever undertaken a night attack.

Stuart reported during the evening that he could hear the enemy moving vehicles on the Confederate left, beyond Chancellorsville, but whether this presaged a retreat or the beginning of an attempt to turn that flank he could not say. Through the night the artillery boomed away at the unseen target. At daylight, when the skirmishers advanced, the bird had flown. Sedgwick was across the river. Lee could accordingly prepare to march again to Chancellorsville and confront Hooker. But as Sedgwick could readily return to the right bank of the river, Lee took precautions that his final blow at Hooker should not again be halted at the very moment it was poised. Early was sent back to Fredericksburg with his own division and Barksdale's brigade.

Lee was free to strike again. If the army had been able to turn the Federal right on the evening of the 2d and to break the line on the morning of the 3d, what was there to keep it from driving the enemy into the Rappahannock on the morning of the 6th?

At dawn the camps were astir, scant rations hastily eaten, skirmishers sent forward. The line of battle was being formed. Lee was on the point of giving the order for the general advance when General Pender galloped up. His skirmishers had already moved forward, he said—but Hooker was gone! The frowning lines in the woods were empty.

"Why, General Pender!" Lee exclaimed in amazement that nothing of this had been reported during the night. "That is the way you young men always do. You allow those people to get away. I tell you what to do, but you don't do it!"

Pender could say nothing. "Go after them," Lee cried, with an impatient gesture, "and damage them all you can!"

There was no damage the advancing divisions could inflict. Federal troops, guns, horses, and wagons were safely over the Rappahannock. Leaving a few regiments to care for the wounded, to bury the dead, and to collect the prizes of war, Lee started back to Fredericksburg with the main army. The weary army had now to be refreshed, the gaps had to be filled, and officers had to be designated to replace those who had been killed or disabled.

But there was a more immediate concern than for the increase of the cavalry or the reinforcement of the infantry. Jackson was worse. Doctor McGuire had found unmistakable symptoms of pneumonia. There was fear, for the first time, that his illness might be fatal. Lee would not admit the possibility. He said to Chaplain Lacy: "Give [Jackson] my affectionate regards, and tell him to make haste and get well, and come back to me as soon as he can. He has lost his left arm, but I have lost my right."

That evening Jackson was reported better. But the next morning, Friday, May 8, gloom settled again. Jackson was weaker. The pneumonia was advancing: he was in mild delirium at intervals. Lee was unable to go to Jackson, both because he could not trust his emotions and because there was no one in whose hands he would feel safe in leaving the army. There was one thing, only one, that he could do. That was to pray for him. While the army slept, Lee on his knees implored Heaven to grant to his country the mercy of the deliverance of Jackson from death.

When the troops began to gather for worship during the forenoon of a beautiful Sabbath, Lee was still unconvinced that Jackson would be taken. Eagerly he met the chaplain who came from Guiney's at Jackson's request to preach at headquarters. The face of the clergyman told his story: The doctors had given Jackson up and did not believe he could survive except by a miracle. Even in the face of this, Lee refused to believe it could happen. The minister preached to a multitude who had escaped the fangs of death in the Wilderness, but it is doubtful if Lee heard much. His mind was with Jackson and so were his prayers.

Going to his headquarters tent, Lee found that his staff officers had just completed decoding an important dispatch from the War Department. It was an argument for sending Pickett's division to Vicksburg. In Lee's eyes the proposal represented a choice between holding Virginia and holding the line of the Mississippi, and he so answered the message from Seddon.

Then . . . there was a stir outside the tent, a moment of hesitation, and some one brought in a bit of folded paper. It contained the brief and dreadful news. In the little cottage at Guiney's, Jackson had roused and had struggled to speak. His mind had been wandering but with an effort, in his even, low voice, he had said: "Let us pass over the river, and rest under the shade of the trees." And then he had led the way.

Lee never dreamed of claiming what military critics have since been disposed to assert—that Chancellorsville was perhaps more nearly a flawless battle, from the Confederate point of view, than any that was ever planned and executed by an American commander. Facing an army two and a half times as large as his own, better equipped in every way

and supplied with more numerous artillery, Lee had been on the defensive at the opening of the operation and had been threatened in
front and on the left flank by a well-planned and admirably executed
advance. In the face of his opponent's superiority, Lee divided his army,
wrested the initiative from Hooker, again divided his force and overwhelmed the XI Corps. On the 3d he drove the enemy back to the
lines, and on the 4th, the least successful day of the operations, he
forced Sedgwick to retreat. He took a great risk in leaving so small a
force at Fredericksburg, and he seemingly took still longer chances on
May 2 when he detached Jackson and faced Hooker with only two
divisions; but except for the capture of the Fredericksburg Heights on
the 3d, the situation was entirely in his hands after May 1. In a week's
fighting, and through the campaign made possible by the successes of
that week, he so changed the military situation that the Army of the
Potomac did not again undertake a march on Richmond for precisely
one year. It was undoubtedly the most remarkable victory he ever
achieved, and it increased greatly his well-established reputation both
in the eyes of the enemy and of the South.

Remarkable as was the victory, it was bought at an excessively great
cost. The toll of general officers was very heavy. Four brigades lost
eight successive commanding officers. Total Confederate casualties
numbered 13,156, of whom 1683 were killed, 9277 were wounded, and
2196 were prisoners of war. These losses, Lee told the President on May
7, reflected the difference in the strength of the opposing armies. The
killed and wounded, he explained, were "always in proportion to the
inequality of forces engaged." Hooker's losses, then of course unknown
to Lee, reached 16,845, a far smaller percentage of his total strength.

Precisely two years had elapsed since Lee had taken the decisive step
in mobilizing the Virginia volunteers. Two years of desperate contest,
lacking one month, lay ahead. He was midway his military career as a
Confederate commander when Jackson died. Much he had learned of
the organization and administration of an army, much of conciliating
rivals, much of arousing the best in men, much of creating the morale
of victory. In the hard school of combat he had mastered the art of the
offensive so fully, both in strategy and in tactics, that little seemed left
for him to acquire. But his military education was not yet completed.
On a hill near a little town in Pennsylvania, the bell of a quiet seminary
was calling him again to school to learn a new lesson, written red in
blood.

Who was to lead Jackson's corps and to act in his stead? Among the infantry officers of the Army of Northern Virginia were only four whom he seems to have considered for corps command—A. P. Hill, R. S. Ewell, R. H. Anderson, and John B. Hood. Lee regarded Hill as the best division commander he had. The man who had been closest to Jackson in his operations had been Ewell. There was strong sentiment for his appointment as the "logical successor" of Jackson. Anderson and Hood, Lee regarded as "capital officers" who were improving in the field. Lee believed they would make good chiefs of corps, if it was necessary to use them, but he did not prefer either of them to their seniors.

Outside the infantry then with the Army of Northern Virginia, only two other men could reasonably have been considered at the time. One was D. H. Hill and the other was "Jeb" Stuart. Hill was a tenacious fighter. Few division commanders could get more from a given number of men. Stuart was held by some to have exhibited qualities on May 3 that marked him as the best man in the army to be retained permanently in the command he had assumed on the night of May 2. But as Stuart recommended some one else for succession to Jackson's corps, it is hardly probable that he regarded himself as in line of promotion for that post. So far as the evidence shows, Lee did not consider him. This doubtless was because he regarded Stuart as indispensable where he was.

The choice narrowed to A. P. Hill and Ewell. In reality, it was hardly a choice, because Lee had long considered the corps too large to be handled by one man in the tangled country through which the army operated. He had desired to increase the number of corps and would have done so earlier had he been able to decide upon suitable commanders. He determined now to reorganize the army into three corps. Longstreet, of course, was to remain at the head of the First Corps; to Ewell, as Jackson's lieutenant, the Second Corps was to be entrusted; and for A. P. Hill a Third Corps was to be created. On May 20 Lee submitted the proposal to the President, and commended Hill and Ewell to his consideration.

In its consequences this was one of the most important resolves of Lee's military career. At the most critical hour of its history it placed two-thirds of the army under new corps leaders. A. P. Hill had never commanded more than one division in action, except for the confused hour after Jackson had been struck down. Hill, however, was devoted, prompt, and energetic, and deserved promotion. Ewell, Lee took at the valuation of others rather than on his own knowledge of the soldier. He had served directly under Lee something less than a month, and then always subject to Jackson's guidance. Lee had never had an opportunity of discovering the lack of self-confidence in Ewell, nor was he aware that Ewell's experience with Jackson had schooled him to obey the letter of orders and not to exercise discretion. Gettysburg was to show the results of Hill's inexperience and of Ewell's indecision in the face of discretionary orders.

The promotion of Hill and of Ewell being promptly authorized by Mr. Davis, Lee decided to apportion his troops equitably among the three corps he proposed to set up. Numerous promotions to succeed brigadier generals killed or disabled at Chancelorsville, or found incompetent, had likewise to be made.

The result was an almost complete reorganization of the army, as follows:

The First Corps was reduced to three divisions—McLaws's, Pickett's, and Hood's, in none of which was there any change.

The Second Corps, now Ewell's. included Early's, Johnson's, and Rodes's divisions. The four brigades of Early were unchanged. Johnson's division was under a commander who had served a very short time with Jackson and had never been with Lee except for some minor co-operation in the West Virginia campaign of 1861. Three of the four major units of this division were under new brigadier commanders —George H. Steuart, James A. Walker, and John M. Jones—and the fourth, Nicholls's, continued under its senior colonel because Lee was unable to find a man to succeed Nicholls. Here, then, was a revolutionized command for the famous old division that included the Stonewall brigade. It was hardly surprising that all the field officers of that brigade tendered their resignations. The third division of the Second Corps, under Rodes, contained one new brigade that had never fought with the Army of Northern Virginia. One of the other brigades was led by a colonel. Taken as a whole, the Second Corps, as reconstituted, was a difficult command for any man and especially for one like Ewell.

The Third Corps, that of A. P. Hill, comprised Anderson's, Heth's, and Pender's divisions. That of Anderson was in good hands, and its command had not materially changed. But Heth's division was led by a soldier who had joined the Army of Northern Virginia only in February. Two of the four brigades were strangers to the army. The third division, Pender's, had a new commander, and one of its brigades was under an officer who had just been promoted.

While this reorganization of the infantry was in progress, the battalion formation of the artillery was perfected, and the general reserve artillery was divided among the three corps. Weakened by the hard winter, the cavalry, too, had to be enlarged. With the patriotic co-operation of Major General Samuel Jones, commanding in southwest Virginia, Lee procured from that quarter a new and large brigade of horse under Brigadier General A. G. Jenkins, but neither this officer nor his men were accustomed to the type of cavalry fighting in which the rest of Stuart's command was experienced. Another cavalry brigade was also brought from western Virginia under Brigadier General John B. Imboden. This officer had been on irregular, detached duty, and many of his men had recently been recruited, some of them from the infantry service.

In short, the reorganization affected all three arms of the service. It involved the admixture of new units with old, it broke up many associations of long standing, and it placed the veteran regiments of a large part of the army under men who were unacquainted with the soldiers and with the methods of General Lee. The same magnificent infantry were ready to obey Lee's orders, but many of their superior officers were untried and were nervous under new responsibilities.

Lee had made what he considered to be the best selections from the officers available and he realized some if not all of the risks he took in subjecting the reorganized army to the early test of a great battle on alien soil. Even had he been wholly conscious of the danger he faced, the option of delay for the training of his new subordinates was denied him. He must strike quickly. Perhaps his state of mind was most fully disclosed in a few sentences of a letter he wrote Hood while the reorganization was under way. "I agree with you," he said, ". . . in believing that our army would be invincible if it could be properly organized and officered. There never were such men in an army before. They will go anywhere and do anything if properly led. But there is the difficulty—proper commanders—where can they be obtained? But they are improving—constantly improving. Rome was not built in a day, nor can we expect miracles in our favor." There it is: absolute confidence in the men who shivered and sweltered, endured hunger and tramped cheerfully over hard roads on bare feet, lay wounded and uncomplaining, or, like stoics, faced death on strange fields; absolute faith in the ranks, and consciousness of the limitations of the command, but, along with that, the patience and the hope of an intrepid soul.

CHAPTER X

Gettysburg

DURING the two weeks following the battle of Chancellorsville, Hooker made a few moves of no consequence, but he seemed to be receiving reinforcements as if the Washington government were determined to utilize his army for the major eastern offensive of the year. Around Vicksburg the front of the Federals was slowly advancing. In Tennessee Rosecrans was defying Bragg. In North Carolina a force appeared to be preparing for another drive against the railroads, and from Hampton Roads a small army was threatening the Peninsula of Virginia.

In what manner could the dwindling Confederate armies best be employed against the hosts that were concentrating as if to cut the South into bits that could be devoured at leisure? Longstreet maintained that Bragg should be strengthened to club Rosecrans; Secretary Seddon favored the dispatch of two of Longstreet's divisions to the Mississippi; Lee explained that, in his opinion, the Confederacy had to choose between maintaining the line of the Mississippi and that of Virginia. If he could procure sufficient troops and could draw General Hooker away from the Rappahannock, he proposed to assume the offensive and to enter Pennsylvania. He believed that the best defensive for Richmond was at a distance from it; he did not think it desirable to fight again on the Rappahannock, where he could not follow up his victory. Neither did he wish once more to carry his army into the ravaged counties near Washington. Even had Lee been willing to give battle in Virginia, he did not think he could subsist his troops there, whereas, if he marched into Pennsylvania he would find provisions in abundance. By crossing high up the Potomac he could draw the enemy after him, clear Virginia of Federals, and perhaps force the enemy to recall the forces that were troubling the south Atlantic coasts and threatening the railroads. Contact with the realities of war, moreover, might increase in the North the peace movement which seemed to be gathering strength. Of all the arguments that weighed with him, the most decisive single one was that he could no longer feed his army on the Rappahannock. He had to invade the North for provisions, regardless of all else.

While he was developing this plan, he was summoned to Richmond for conference. He spent May 14–17 there. Mr. Davis was much troubled at the time by calls for troops at Vicksburg, but when it came to a final choice between advancing into Pennsylvania or detaching troops from Lee to do battle on the Mississippi, the President favored a new invasion of the North.

Back on May 18 at his old headquarters near Hamilton's Crossing, Lee began to develop the details of his new adventure. He met with opposition from one man only—Longstreet. Longstreet insisted that if a campaign was to be undertaken in Pennsylvania it should be offensive in strategy but defensive in tactics. The event was to show that it would have been better if Lee had stood Longstreet before him and had bluntly reminded him that he and not the chief of the First Corps commanded the Army of Northern Virginia. Apparently, however, it never occurred to Lee that Longstreet was trying to dictate. Longstreet in his vanity mistook Lee's tact and politeness for acquiescence and went about his preparations for the move in the belief that the campaign was to be conducted in accordance with his idea.

Gathering sufficient strength for the offensive was a matter of provisions, of horses, and of additional men, not a question of morale, for the victory at Chancellorsville had raised the spirit of the army to the highest pitch. Any material increase in the infantry seemed almost a forlorn hope. Hood was returning with his full division and Pickett was at Hanover Junction with three of his four brigades, but all Lee's powers of persuasion had not sufficed to prevail upon President Davis to release the fourth brigade of Pickett or the three brigades that had been sent southward during the previous winter. Unless he could procure them, he would not have for the campaign as many as 75,000 officers and men of all arms—about 60,000 infantry, 4700 artillery and 10,200 cavalry. If the detached brigades were returned, Lee was willing to trust the army for its part in the great gamble of a second invasion of the North.

In the face of uncertainties—the safety of Richmond, the return of detached units, and the possibility of a sudden move by Hooker—Lee had to prepare for the defensive while hoping to be able to take the offensive. By the 23d he was satisfied that Hooker was making ready for another move. Four days later there were indications that the Federal general was about to advance by some of the fords on the upper Rappahannock. The apparent imminence of another battle on the south bank of the Rappahannock, where victory would be as barren as costly, made Lee more anxious than ever to launch his projected offensive in Pennsylvania. He was willing to take the other risks if he could be reasonably sure of the safety of Richmond and could recover his "lost brigades." The difference between a hazardous defensive and a practicable offensive resolved itself into the difference between the strength he then mustered and the strength he could command if those brigades were returned to him. Yet it was so easy for Hooker to engage Lee while the forces at Suffolk and West Point marched on Richmond! By May 30 Lee was almost persuaded that the time had passed when he could take the offensive, and as he was desirous of building up a force for the protection of the Richmond front, he urged on the Secretary of War that troops be called to Richmond from the Carolina coast, that the fortifications be strengthened, and that local-defense units be organized.

Three anxious days passed at the end of May, with the troops disposed either to start a march up the Rappahannock or to meet Hooker if he crossed the river. Then, unexpectedly, on June 2, there came a telegram from Richmond announcing that the troops previously at West Point, supported by a force from Gloucester and Yorktown, were marching northward. The destination of these Federals was not clear, but it was manifest that no immediate advance on Richmond was contemplated. Lee saw in this his opportunity. With Richmond no longer in serious danger, he could hope that the President would authorize him to call Pickett's division and Pettigrew's brigade from Hanover and start his manoeuvre around the Federal flank in the hope that he might enter Pennsylvania.

Orders were issued by Lee for an advance by part of the army the next day. Ewell was called to headquarters and given his instructions. Longstreet was present during the conference, on Lee's invitation, and insisted that if the army was to take the offensive it should do so south of the Potomac. Lee let Longstreet present his view fully, with few remarks on his own part, but with no intention whatever of sanctioning another battle on a field whence the Federals could easily withdraw to the Washington defenses.

On the morning of June 3 the enemy showed no sign of attacking, and McLaws's division was set in motion for Culpeper. On the morning of the 4th Rodes started toward Culpeper. Still there was no activity on the Stafford Heights. Emboldened by this, Lee withdrew Early and Johnson on the 5th and left only A. P. Hill on the Fredericksburg line. Scarcely had the last of Ewell's regiments wound their way over the hills than the Federals began to lay a bridge over the Rappahannock. It was done so ostentatiously as to raise suspicion. Lee reasoned that Hooker was either attempting to feel out Confederate strength or was to divert attention from some move on his own part, but he deemed it prudent to dispose Hill's forces to hold the line temporarily. On the 6th, the Federals not being strengthened, Lee became satisfied that Hill could cope with the troops in his front and ordered Ewell to advance. That afternoon Lee broke up headquarters at Hamilton's Crossing— for the last time, as it proved—and took the road his men marched.

Arriving on the morning of June 7 at Culpeper Courthouse, near which two of Longstreet's divisions and all three of Ewell's were encamped, Lee was more than ever convinced that his army must be reinforced if it was to execute successfully his plan of invasion. He telegraphed Davis a suggestion that a brigade from Richmond be moved to Hanover Junction to relieve Pickett, so that commander could bring Longstreet's third division forward. Lee urged, also, in a letter to the President, that Beauregard's troops from Charleston, S. C., either be sent to reinforce Johnston in Mississippi or to unite with the Army of Northern Virginia. He ordered Imboden's cavalry to organize a raid into northwest Virginia, and instructed Brigadier General A. G. Jenkins to prepare his brigade of horse from southwest Virginia for cooperation in the Shenandoah Valley.

Early June 9, Lee received a hurried report from Stuart that the enemy cavalry, with some infantry, was pouring across Beverley and Kelly's Fords, on both flanks of the Confederate outposts. Lee wrote Stuart where he could get infantry in case he needed it but urged him to conceal the presence of Confederate foot if possible. Soon it became apparent that the Federal horse coming from the direction of Kelly's Ford had outwitted Stuart's troopers on that road and were moving to get on the flank and in the rear of the Southern cavalry. Action centred around Fleetwood Hill, a long ridge running with the meridian just north of Brandy Station. Hour after hour, the opposing cavalry contended for this high ground. Lee left the management of the field to Stuart and had no fear of disaster, because he had sufficient infantry at hand to hurl the Federals back across the Rappahannock; but in the afternoon, as this battle of Brandy Station developed into the greatest cavalry engagement of the war, he ordered an infantry brigade to

report to General Hampton, and he rode forward in person to survey
the situation. Lee was shocked to meet his son Rooney being borne to
the rear with a severe wound in the leg. While he was doing what he
could to make his son comfortable, the battle ended in a retreat of the
Federals.

Lee had to contend with a more serious obstacle in the attitude of the
administration. In dispatches from the War Department a new concern
for the safety of Richmond was observable, together with a reluctance
to forward troops. This reluctance had led Lee on the 8th to offer to
return closer to Richmond if the government so desired. On the other
hand, he could not escape the general logic of an offensive-defensive
nor overlook the strategic advantage he had already gained through the
failure of the Federals to attack A. P. Hill at Fredericksburg. As he
read the Northern newspapers he was confirmed in his belief that the
projected campaign in Pennsylvania would strengthen the arguments of
the Northern peace party. His resolution held: he would send one
corps forward and await developments. If that did nothing more, it
would at least clear Milroy from the Valley and probably force the
Federals to abandon the line of the Rappahannock.

The plan of advance had been worked out before the vanguard had
left Fredericksburg. It called for the co-operation of Jenkins's cavalry
in preparing the way for a march to Winchester by Ewell. If Ewell was
unmolested, he was to mask Winchester and continue over the Potomac,
through Maryland, and into Pennsylvania. Longstreet was then to
advance northward on the eastern side of the Blue Ridge, so as to cover
the advance of A. P. Hill. When Hill was also in the Valley, Longstreet
was to follow him, and the cavalry were to hold the mountain gaps
until the advance into Pennsylvania had called all the Federals north
of the Potomac. It was a bold plan, but no more dangerous than others
Lee had successfully executed.

On the morning of the 10th the reconstituted Second Corps started
on its way. As Ewell's men turned westward Lee sat down to write the
President on the subject that had been so much in his mind since
Chancellorsville—the promotion of the peace movement in the North.
A most important letter it was for two reasons. It showed Lee alive to
the danger that the Southern cause would be lost because of the
superiority of Federal resources. Similarly, it disclosed Lee's simple
reasoning on politics, with which he had little acquaintance. He pointed
out that the intransigent attitude of the Southern newspapers was discouraging those Northerners who were arguing that the South would

return to the Union if the Washington government made peace. Then he said: "We should not conceal from ourselves that our resources in men are constantly diminishing, and the disproportion in this respect between us and our enemies, if they continue united in their efforts to subjugate us, is steadily augmenting." He went on to explain that the strength of the Army of Northern Virginia was declining, and he argued that an effort should be made to divide the North by encouraging the peace party. "Should the belief that peace will bring back the Union become general, the war would no longer be supported, and that, after all, is what we are interested in bringing about. When peace is proposed to us, it will be time enough to discuss its terms, and it is not the part of prudence to spurn the proposition in advance."

This letter was as ingenuous as it was sincere. So great was Lee's faith in the Southern people that he believed they would be willing to resume the war in case peace negotiations produced no better terms than a return to the Union. With less knowledge of the state of mind of the North, he thought that, in like conditions, a powerful element would be willing to concede the independence of the South. Unless this happened, he could see no other outcome than the ultimate defeat of the Confederacy. This was twenty-two months before Appomattox.

Following the dispatch of this letter there came a period of confusion as to the intentions of the Federals. The loss of time sustained by this uncertainty might be serious enough, Lee feared, to defeat the full execution of his plans. By the morning of June 15, however, the situation began to clear. A. P. Hill started Anderson's division for Culpeper confident that the Federals were really leaving the line of the Rappahannock. Ewell reported that he was preparing to attack Winchester, which he had found more strongly fortified than he had expected.

Ewell had been ordered not to delay his march for a siege. Consequently, Lee assumed that Ewell on the 15th was en route to Hagerstown. This would mean that the Army of Northern Virginia was spread out from north of Winchester to the lower Rappahannock. For a time there would be no force between Winchester and Culpeper except a few cavalry outposts. It was to meet just this situation that Lee had planned to advance Longstreet east of the Blue Ridge. On the 15th in a personal conference with that officer, followed by written orders later in the day, Lee outlined the details of this operation: Longstreet was to start with Hood's division and was to be followed by McLaws and then by Pickett, three brigades of whose division had now reached Culpeper.

Longstreet was to march to Markham and was to demonstrate, if he saw fit, against any Federal force he might encounter. Three brigades of cavalry were to operate on his front. His trains could move by Chester Gap into the Valley, where they would be safe from Federal raiders. Two brigades of cavalry were to be left behind to guard the fords of the Rappahannock and to cover the march of the Third Corps. By this Lee hoped to confuse the enemy as to his plan and also to facilitate the advance of Hill. Should an attempt be made to destroy Longstreet, he could easily retire to Ashby's or to Snicker's Gap and hold it against the enemy. In case of a Federal advance northward to head off Ewell in Pennsylvania, Longstreet could readily move into the Valley and hasten to Ewell's support. If all went well, the original plan of having Hill pass in rear of Longstreet could be executed without danger, and Longstreet's corps would then act as rearguard. There were thus to be four successive movements—Ewell's advance toward Hagerstown, Longstreet's march to the east of the mountain passes, Hill's tramp up the Rappahannock and thence along Ewell's route, and Longstreet's final withdrawal through the mountains and to the Potomac.

On the evening of the day that Longstreet left Culpeper, Lee received good news: Ewell had driven Milroy from Winchester the previous night and had captured some 4000 prisoners. Ewell's corps was now free to advance to the Potomac. Two of Hill's divisions were on the road to Culpeper, and the third was ready to leave Fredericksburg.

It was now time for Lee to move in person. By the 17th he broke up headquarters and rode to Markham. On his arrival, he found that Stuart had been engaged that day in hot actions at Aldie and Middleburg but had not established contact with the Federal infantry. From Hooker's failure to face him, Lee continued to assume that his adversary was moving toward the Potomac. Reports from some of the scouts on the 18th and 19th confirmed this, though it was not clear whether Hooker would make for Harpers Ferry, enter the Valley, or cross the river somewhere in the vicinity of Leesburg. In addition to this uncertainty, all operations were being slowed down by the scarcity of food, though Lee was keeping every wheel turning in the effort to gather provisions.

Lee must have reinforcements in position to move to Ewell's support the moment Hooker showed signs of crossing the Potomac. He had, therefore, to shape plans for quick execution in an emergency.

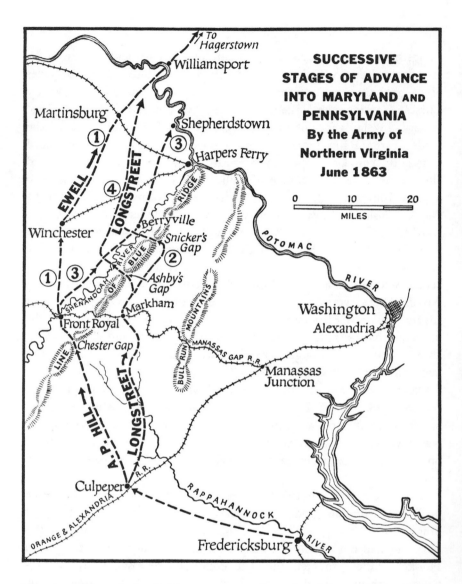

SUCCESSIVE STAGES OF ADVANCE INTO MARYLAND AND PENNSYLVANIA By the Army of Northern Virginia June 1863

The handling of the infantry presented no special problems, but as the cavalry was detached, Lee had a conference with Longstreet and Stuart to arrange for the movement of the mounted forces. There was not the least doubt in his mind as to the function of the main body of the cavalry: it should keep the enemy as far to the east as possible, protect the lines of communication, and supply information as to the movements of the enemy. To do these things the cavalry should operate on the right flank of the army.

But Stuart had a more ambitious plan. He proposed that he should move to Hooker's rear and annoy him if he attempted to cross the river. Should he find that Hooker was intent on going into Maryland, he could break off and rejoin the army. Longstreet approved this proposal, and Lee assented, in principle, but he told Stuart that when he discovered that Hooker was passing the river, he "must immediately cross himself and take his place on our right flank as we moved north." There the matter ended for the time.

On the 19th Lee passed through Ashby's Gap to Millwood, and the next day established headquarters at a point a short distance beyond Berryville where he determined to wait until Hill's corps came up. Longstreet was put on the alert to start for the Potomac and, through a misunderstanding of his orders, withdrew on the 20th from the mountain gaps and established himself west of the Shenandoah. By ill fortune the enemy selected the 21st for a general cavalry advance on Stuart and drove him back into Ashby's Gap. As the Federals had infantry support, there was danger that they might seize the pass and might pour into the Valley on Longstreet's rear when he began his march toward the Potomac. McLaws's division had to be sent back to prevent this. At daylight on the 22d, however, it was found that the Union infantry had withdrawn and that the cavalry was retiring eastward. Stuart followed vigorously.

Provided the army could be subsisted, it was the policy of wisdom to detain Hooker south of the Potomac, while Ewell, undisturbed, continued to collect supplies in Pennsylvania. So long as Hooker remained where he was, Lee could have many of the benefits of invasion with none of the risks and losses. If Hooker could steal even one march on Lee he might get across the river and perhaps interpose between Ewell and the remainder of the army. Lee already had had one unhappy experience with a division of force on the north side of the Potomac and he had no desire to repeat it. It was safest, on every count, to move to the Potomac without further delay. If this were done, Ewell could be permitted to continue his march toward the Susquehanna, because the remainder of the army would soon be within supporting distance. Anderson's division was ordered to the river; Ewell was instructed to move on if ready. He was to proceed in two columns. One was to advance by Greencastle and Chambersburg toward Harrisburg. The other was to march by Emmitsburg and Gettysburg toward York.

Before giving the order for the movement of Longstreet, Lee had to decide finally the question of the disposition of the cavalry with Stuart. As Lee reflected on Stuart's proposal to operate in rear of the

Federals during their advance northward he became apprehensive. Stuart might not be able to perform his principal mission of covering the right of the army. That Stuart might understand that this duty was all important, Lee instructed Major Charles Marshall, in answering a communication from Stuart, to cover the point. Probably because he knew Stuart's propensity for daring, spectacular raids, Lee decided to refer the question of Stuart's best route to Longstreet, along with the question on which Longstreet would properly have to pass—that of whether two brigades were sufficient to hold the passes. He sent the letter to Stuart under cover of a note to Longstreet, with instructions to forward the message to Stuart if he saw fit to do so.

The next day, June 23, Lee's scouts affirmed that the enemy was laying a brigade at Edwards' Ferry on the Potomac. If the information as to preparations for a crossing were correct, that would mean that if the Army of the Potomac was concentrating on Edwards' Ferry its long columns would be spread some distance southward on all the roads, making them impassable for Stuart. Therefore, Stuart would almost certainly be compelled to cross the Potomac east of Edwards' Ferry in order to perform his major duty of covering the right flank of the army after it entered Pennsylvania.

Hooker would require a long time to move his immense army across the Potomac. There was, consequently, no reason why Stuart could not ride around him, pass the river east of Edwards' Ferry, and reach the right flank of the Confederate column in Maryland before Hooker would be dangerously close. But the wisdom of a crossing east of Edwards' Ferry in passing over the Potomac was contingent on Stuart's being able to disorganize the Federal wagon trains and confuse the crossing without being materially delayed. If he lost his way, or became confused among the moving Federal columns, or stopped to indulge his fondness for fighting, he might be late. It was necessary, therefore, to make it plain to Stuart that while he could cross the Potomac east of Hooker's army, he must put his major mission first and must not attempt a ride around the Federal army if he were hindered in the attempt.

But suppose Hooker had no intention of making early use of the pontoon bridge at Edwards' Ferry? If the enemy were simply waiting, it was much more important that Stuart should be with the army on its advance into Pennsylvania than that he should remain east of the mountains in Virginia. Lee prudently decided to cover the operations of the cavalry in the contingencies that might develop and to explain once again that its main function was to cover the right of the army in Pennsylvania. Lee directed Marshall to do this in further instructions. In the situation that actually developed, Lee undoubtedly intended to give Stuart discretion, after midnight of June 24, to pass around the Federal rear, which meant crossing the Potomac east of Edwards' Ferry. The one proviso was that Stuart must not be so hindered in following the routes as to be delayed in performing his principal service in the campaign. Stuart was not to attempt to pass around the enemy's rear if he met with hindrance or delay. In case he did, he was to withdraw west of the mountains and follow the army into Pennsylvania.

Even when these orders had been issued to protect the flank of the army when it moved into Pennsylvania, Lee still looked about to see what further measures he could take to strengthen himself for the test that awaited him in the enemy's country. In the hope that Corse and Cooke might reinforce him, he urged the War Department to send them forward. One other possibility presented itself—the employment in his support of Beauregard's troops whom he had suggested, while still at Culpeper, that the President send either to Virginia or to join Johnston in the West. He now proposed formally that Beauregard come to Virginia in person, if with only a small force, and establish himself at Culpeper Courthouse.

After arriving opposite Williamsport, Lee received from the President a letter which endorsed Lee's views on the encouragement of the peace party in the North. In answering this on the morning of June 25, Lee reverted to his proposal that Beauregard be moved to Virginia. Already, he said, Federal apprehension for the safety of Washington was causing the Federals to recall troops for its defense. Lee said: "If the plan that I suggested the other day, of organizing an army, even in effigy, under General Beauregard at Culpeper Courthouse, can be carried into effect, much relief will be afforded." Then he quietly announced to the President what had doubtless been apparent to him from the time he had found that he would have to undertake his expedition with only the troops at his disposal: "I have not sufficient troops to maintain my communication, and, therefore, have to abandon them." The army would have to take the great risk of living off the country. He did not magnify his possible achievements as he closed his letter to the President. "I think," he said, "I can throw General Hooker's army across the Potomac and draw troops from the South, embarrassing their plan of campaign in a measure, if I can do nothing

more and have to return. I still hope that all things will end well for
us at Vicksburg. At any rate, every effort should be made to bring
about that result."

The supreme endeavor of the South to win its independence was
now to be made. In the midst of a heavy rain on the morning of
June 25, the bands struck up "Dixie," the cheering division began to
move, and the man who carried his nation's hope turned Traveller's
head into the Potomac.

A group of ladies under dripping umbrellas awaited Lee on the
Maryland side of the Potomac—to wish him victory on his second invasion of the North. The ladies desired to put a wreath around the
bowed gray neck of Traveller. Lee balked at this. Garlands were well
enough for Stuart . . . He was extremely indebted to the ladies for
their courtesy, but would they excuse him? Marylanders of the per-
suasive sex who had braved rain and radicals to do honor to a "rebel"
were not easily put off. A parley ensued, with the ladies insistent and
Lee resolute. It was compromised at length by giving the wreath to a
courier to carry for the General.

The friendly spirit of the invasion was somewhat the same the
next morning when Lee left his camp and rode through Hagerstown
en route to Chambersburg, whither Hill's and Longstreet's columns
were moving. From Hagerstown he rode northward and entered
Pennsylvania for the first time since the beginning of the war.

Lee established headquarters in a little grove on the road to Gettysburg. Here the atmosphere was not that of merrymaking, but of preparation for battle. Lee's first concern, on the 27th, was to assure the
safety of private property. He had issued orders on June 21 governing
the seizure of supplies for the army while in the enemy's country.
He had directed that all the necessities of the army should be met by
formal requisition on local authorities or by purchase and payment
in Confederate money. Where Confederate notes were refused, the
quartermasters were to issue receipts, setting forth the name of the
owner of the seized property, the quantity and the fair market value.
These instructions had been measurably respected by Ewell's troops,
but now that the whole of the army was in a district where Lee
expected it to remain for some time, the regulations were reiterated in
General Orders No. 73 for the guidance of the individual soldiers.
The orders were written, no doubt, with an eye to the encouragement
of the peace movement in the North; but they were drafted in sincerity
and they were enforced with vigor. There were no charges of rape and

UNION BATTERY ON THE EVE OF CHANCELLORSVILLE

Copyright by Review of Reviews

GENERAL J. E. B. STUART

few of plundering. The chief difficulty of the officers was in keeping hot, bareheaded soldiers from snatching civilian's hats as they marched through the crowd-lined streets of the little towns.

Regardless of hats, the army had to be ready for action. By the 27th Ewell was well advanced in two columns, one as far as Carlisle on the road to Harrisburg, and the other, which consisted of Early's division, within about six miles of York. Ewell's orders were to take Harrisburg if his force was adequate, and Early was under instructions to cut the railroad between Harrisburg and Baltimore and to destroy the bridges at Wrightsville and Columbia. Longstreet's and A. P. Hill's corps were encamped around Chambersburg and Fayetteville, in excellent health and full of confidence, far better shod and clad than when they had entered Maryland in 1862.

The general advance of the army was to be on Harrisburg, in order to draw the enemy out and to cut communications between East and West. The execution of the plan depended primarily on the arrival of Stuart's cavalry. Presumably, Hooker was still in Virginia. Otherwise Stuart would surely have notified Lee.

While waiting for Stuart, Lee checked his maps carefully by all the information he could get from Southern sympathizers and had a lengthy interview with Major General Trimble, who knew the country well. Trimble told him there was scarcely a square mile east of the mountains in Adams County that did not offer good positions for manoeuvre or for battle. Lee was pleased at the assurance: "Our army," he was quoted long afterwards by Trimble as saying, "is in good spirits, not overfatigued, and can be concentrated on any one point in twenty-four hours or less. I have not yet heard that the enemy have crossed the Potomac, and am waiting to hear from General Stuart. When they hear where we are, they will make forced marches to interpose their forces between us and Baltimore and Philadelphia. They will come up, probably through Frederick, broken down with hunger and hard marching, strung out on a long line and much demoralized, when they come into Pennsylvania. I shall throw an overwhelming force on their advance, crush it, follow up the success, drive one corps back on another, and by successive repulses and surprises, before they can concentrate, create a panic and virtually destroy the army."

Trimble expressed his belief that this could be done, because the morale of the troops had never been higher. "That is, I hear, the general impression," Lee answered. Then, as Trimble rose to go, Lee laid his hand on the map and pointed to a little town east of the mountains, Gettysburg by name, from which roads radiated like so many spokes. "Hereabout," he said, "we shall probably meet the army and fight a great battle, and if God gives us the victory, the war will be over and we shall achieve the recognition of our independence."

The 28th came, and still no word of the enemy, of Stuart, or of the cavalry that had been left behind to guard the passes of the Blue Ridge. As the day passed, Lee's wonder at the silence of Stuart increased, and when he retired for the night it must have been with amazement that an officer who was in the habit of reporting so promptly and so regularly should have sent no messenger since the army had crossed the Potomac on the 25th.

After 10 o'clock on the night of the 28th there came a rap on Lee's tent pole, and when Lee answered Major John W. Fairfax entered and announced that Harrison, one of Longstreet's scouts, had brought the startling news that Hooker was north of the Potomac. Lee was skeptical. "I do not know what to do," he said to Fairfax. "I cannot hear from General Stuart, the eye of the army. What do you think of Harrison? I have no confidence in any scout, but General Longstreet thinks a good deal of Harrison." Fairfax had no opinion and went his way. Later in the evening, Lee decided to talk with Harrison and sent for him. The spy said that he had left Longstreet at Culpeper and had gone to Washington, where he had picked up much gossip. Hearing that Hooker had crossed the Potomac, he had started for Frederick, walking at night and mingling with the soldiers during the day. At Frederick he had found two corps of infantry. Having learned that the Army of Northern Virginia was at Chambersburg, he had procured a horse and had hurried northward. On the way to Chambersburg he had ascertained that two more corps were close to South Mountain. Incidentally, he had heard that General Hooker had been replaced by Lee's old comrade and friend, Major General George Gordon Meade.

Lee heard Harrison through without a tremor, but he was profoundly concerned by the intelligence. There could hardly have been worse news. Lee had not fully carried out his design of abandoning his communications with Virginia. But if the Army of the Potomac was already at the foot of South Mountain, the new commander would almost certainly cross, move westward and destroy the Confederate communications. If the Federals got into Cumberland Valley, they might force Lee to conform and thereby rob him of the initiative. The situation instantly became one of gravity—and because of Stuart's unexplained absence, the army was blindfolded.

The whole army must be concentrated at once and must be moved east of the mountains so as to compel the Federals to follow and thereby abandon their threat to Lee's rear. By 7:30 A.M. Lee had so far developed his plan that he saw there was danger of delaying the movment by crowding too many troops on the road from Chambersburg eastward, so he modified Ewell's orders and directed him to march directly from Carlisle toward Cashtown or Gettysburg. Hill was to use the road that led over the mountains from Chambersburg to these towns, and he was to be followed the next day, June 30, by Longstreet, who was to leave one division to guard the rear until the arrival of Imboden's cavalry.

The day of the 29th had broken dark and stormy, and Lee's feelings were gloomy. A visitor found him restless and concerned during the day, but later he recovered his poise completely. When he went out to walk in the road for exercise, during the afternoon, his outward calm was as complete as ever and he announced quietly to some officers who attended him, "Tomorrow, gentlemen, we will not move to Harrisburg, as we expected, but will go over to Gettysburg and see what General Meade is after." When asked for his opinion of the latest change in the command of the Army of the Potomac, he answered that he thought the Federal cause benefited but that this was counterbalanced by the difficulties Meade would encounter in taking charge in the midst of a campaign. He said then, or soon thereafter, "General Meade will commit no blunder in my front, and if I make one he will make haste to take advantage of it."

Still with no news from Stuart, Lee speeded up the march on the morning of June 30. Thus far on the road no enemy had been encountered. Late in the evening of the 30th General Hill, who had ridden on to overtake his troops at Cashtown, sent back word that Pettigrew's brigade of Heth's division had gone on that day from Cashtown to Gettysburg to procure shoes. Near Gettysburg, Pettigrew had found Federal cavalry, and some of his officers reported that they had heard the roll of infantry drums beyond the town. Lee could hardly believe this report, and even if it were true he could do nothing until morning.

Dawn of July 1 broke with a gentle breeze and was sunshiny and clear, except for occasional showery clouds. Despite the uncertainty, Lee was cheerful and composed and called to Longstreet to ride with

him. The men of the First Corps were confident, and as they swung
into the road, doubtless every one of them shared the view Lee's
adjutant general had expressed in a letter two days before: "With
God's help we expect to take a step or two toward an honorable peace."

About six miles east of Chambersburg the head of the First Corps
found Johnson's division of Ewell's corps pouring into the road from
the northwest in obedience to Lee's order for a quick concentration.
Lee directed Longstreet to halt the First Corps and let Johnson have
the road. After a short wait, Lee proposed that they ride ahead, and,
with their staffs, he and Longstreet began to climb the mountain. As
they ascended there was audible an occasional distant rumble—artillery!
At first Lee imagined that it was simply a brush with cavalry, but his
lack of information irritated him. As they approached the crest of
the divide, the sound of firing came insistently from the east. Lee
could restrain himself no longer. Bidding Longstreet farewell, he
quickened Traveller's pace and hurried on to Cashtown, where he
met A. P. Hill, sick and very pale. Hill knew little, except that Heth's
division had gone ahead under instructions not to force an action if it
encountered the enemy until the rest of the army came up.

Hearing that Anderson's division was in the town, together with
the reserve artillery of the Third Corps, Lee thought that Anderson
might know something further and sent for him. Anderson had no
information that Lee had not already received. He left Anderson and
started again toward the sound of the guns, the opening guns of
Gettysburg.

Along a road he had never travelled before, Lee galloped toward
Gettysburg like a blinded giant. He did not know where the Federals
were, or how numerous they might be. Never had he been so dangerously in the dark. Louder and nearer was the sound of the artillery.
Soon infantry volleys added their treble to the bass of the guns. Smoke
was now visible on the horizon. At 2 o'clock, when he was still about
three miles from Gettysburg, he came into the open country and
found Pender's division deployed. In the distance action was visible.
Quickly putting binoculars to his eyes he studied the gray and green
panorama before him.

Lee's glasses must have fixed themselves quickly on the smoke that
was rising on either side of the Chambersburg road where it crossed
Willoughby Run. Evidently there had been an attack and a repulse.
The artillery was blazing away, and Heth's division was apparently
forming on a front about a mile in length. Two of Heth's brigades

were in bad order. Beyond them, across the run, where the smoke from the Union batteries was swelling, must be the Federal infantry— and how strong?

Soon Lee's presence became known, and officers began to bring him news. Heth had sent forward two of his brigades during the morning. They had pushed ahead vigorously and had driven the enemy back. Later the Federals had attacked in heavy force and had compelled them to retire. Heth was now resting his men preparatory to attacking again, and Hill had directed Pender to support him. Finding their opponents out of range, the Federal infantry had halted and had ceased firing. The artillery exchange was slowing down.

Lee was still so anxious not to bring on a general engagement that had there not been a sudden stir north of Gettysburg about 3 o'clock he would probably have forbidden an advance. The enemy began to move out troops in that direction; firing commenced briskly. Soon from the woods above Gettysburg a long gray line of battle emerged. Having heard the sound of Hill's engagement, Rodes had taken advantage of the cover on the ridge and was coming up almost on the right flank of the forces that had been engaged with Hill. It could not have happened more advantageously if this chance engagement had been a planned battle!

General Heth came up to Lee. "Rodes," said he, "is heavily engaged; had I not better attack?"

"No," said Lee, reasoning that little was to be gained and much was to be risked by committing himself to the offensive with only part of his forces. "No, I am not prepared to bring on a general engagement today—Longstreet is not up."

But the very gods of war seemed to wear gray that hot afternoon. Early's division of Ewell's corps had arrived on Rodes's left and was driving the Federals. At precisely the right place, and at exactly the right moment, a third blow was being delivered. Everything was working perfectly. As quickly as the situation changed with the arrival of Early, Lee's decision was reversed. So fair an opportunity was not to be lost. The men in the ranks were as willing as their commander. With a yell that echoed weirdly over the Pennsylvania hills, Heth's brigades swept eastward. Pender's troops moved across the ridge, joined with Heth, and charged irresistibly over Willoughby Run. Rodes pressed on; Early swept everything before him. In forty-five minutes the battle was over. The Federals were routed and hurled back toward the ridges south and east of Gettysburg. The town was

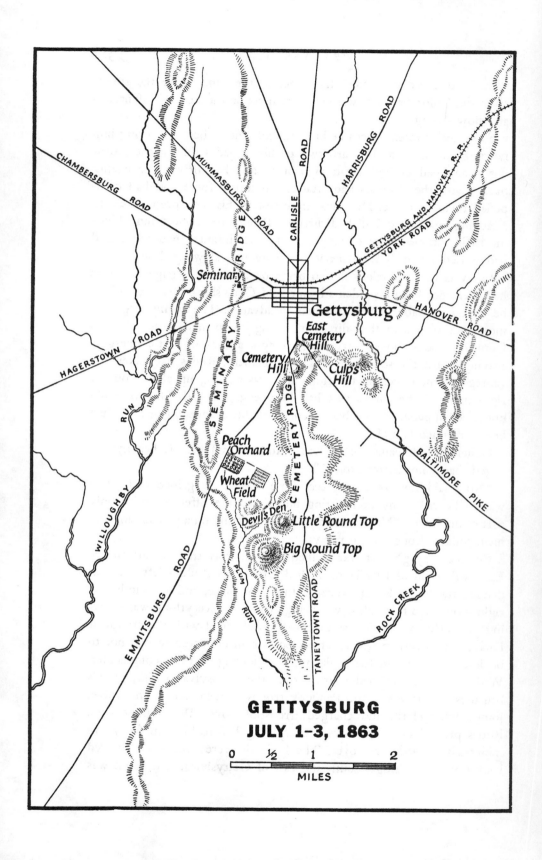

CHAMBERSBURG ROAD

MUMMASBURG ROAD

CARLISLE ROAD

HARRISBURG ROAD

GETTYSBURG AND HANOVER R. R.

YORK ROAD

Seminary

Gettysburg

HANOVER ROAD

East Cemetery Hill

HAGERSTOWN ROAD

Cemetery Hill

Culp's Hill

SEMINARY RIDGE

CEMETERY RIDGE

Peach Orchard

BALTIMORE PIKE

Wheat Field

Devil's Den

Little Round Top

Big Round Top

WILLOUGHBY RUN

EMMITSBURG ROAD

PLUM RUN

TANEYTOWN ROAD

ROCK CREEK

GETTYSBURG
JULY 1–3, 1863

0   ½   1   2

MILES

in Early's hands. A doubtful morning had ended in a smashing victory.

Riding hurriedly forward across Willoughby Run and up the next ridge, Lee halted near the point where the Chambersburg turnpike comes down from the ridge. Half a mile away lay the town of Gettysburg. South of it was a high cleared hill. Toward this hill, in confused and demoralized masses, the defeated Federals were retreating. On the hill were blue infantry reserves and artillery. If the ground could be seized at once and the Federals driven from it, the Confederates would control the whole position. Could this be accomplished without bringing on the general engagement that Lee was anxious to avoid until the entire army was up? Hill, who was unhappily sick, reported that his men were exhausted and disorganized. Ewell, then, must undertake the advance. Sending Ewell an account of what he saw, Lee told him it was only necessary to "push those people" to get possession of the hill, and he suggested that Ewell do so, if practicable, without committing the whole army to battle.

General Longstreet rode up. Lee pointed out to him the enemy's position, and Longstreet made a careful survey of the front with his field-glasses. Longstreet studied the terrain closely by the side of the chief with whom there had not been a ripple of disagreement since they had entered Pennsylvania; but when Longstreet turned to Lee, it was to assert his confidence in the plan he himself had formulated for offensive strategy and defensive tactics. Without waiting, apparently, for Lee to ask his opinion, Longstreet declared the field ideal for the course on which he had set his heart. "All we have to do," he later quoted himself as saying in substance, "is to throw our army around by their left, and we shall interpose between the Federal army and Washington."

Lee answered Longstreet at once: "If the enemy is there, we must attack him."

At some stage of the discussion Colonel A. L. Long returned from a reconnaissance in front of Cemetery Hill. Long reported that an attack would be hazardous and doubtful of success. About the same time, Lieutenant James Power Smith arrived with a message from Ewell. Ewell desired to inform the commander that General Rodes and General Early believed they could take Cemetery Hill if they were supported on the right and that "it would be well if Lee occupied at once the higher ground in front of our right, which seemed to command the Cemetery Hill."

"I suppose," Lee answered, "this is the higher ground to which these gentlemen refer," and, pointing to the front, he handed Smith his field-glasses. "You will find that some of those people are there now."

Then he turned to Longstreet: Where on the road were the troops of the First Corps? McLaws's division, Longstreet said, was about six miles away. Beyond that he was indefinite and noncommittal. Lee urged him to bring his corps up as rapidly as possible, and told Smith to tell Ewell that Lee did not then have troops to support him on the right but that Lee wished Ewell to take Cemetery Hill if it was possible. Longstreet did not like this either. He argued that if Lee intended to attack, he should do so immediately. Longstreet then had no more to say and presently rode off.

It was now about 5:30 P.M. Firing had ceased. There was no sign of any effort on the part of Ewell to storm Cemetery Hill. To ascertain the state of affairs on the front of the Second Corps, Lee rode to Gettysburg and found Ewell and Rodes together. He sat down with them to hear their reports. Their statements showed all too plainly that the new organization of the Second Corps was operating very clumsily. Two of Rodes's brigade commanders had failed badly in the attack that Lee had witnessed. Rodes had lost nearly 2500 men and found himself, at the end of the action, on ground from which he did not believe he could advance directly on Cemetery Hill. Early had a better position, but his progress had been held up by panicky reports from an inexperienced brigadier. Ewell had been irresolute. The fiery Trimble, who had joined Ewell and was acting as a volunteer aide, had at length lost all patience when Ewell, by his delay, had lost an opportunity of seizing easily the position on Cemetery Hill that was the key to victory.

"Can't you, with your corps, attack on this flank tomorrow?" Lee asked Ewell.

Ewell said nothing; Early took the floor. An attack, he contended, would be most costly and of doubtful issue. The ground was more favorable to an attack south of Gettysburg, Early maintained, and if an offensive there resulted in the capture of the Round Tops, the Confederates would dominate the entire field.

"Well," Lee said at length, "if I attack from my right, Longstreet will have to make the attack." Then he raised his head: "Longstreet is a very good fighter when he gets in position and gets everything ready, but he is so slow."

Lee was not wholly convinced that the chiefs of the corps were correct in their stand, but, tentatively, he accepted their view and left them, ere long, with the understanding that the attack was to be made on the right as early as practicable the next morning, and that the left wing was to press the enemy and pursue any advantage that might be gained. After Lee returned to Seminary Ridge he became dissatisfied with the decision he had reached and sought an opportunity of reviewing his whole problem. Word had been received—at last—from Stuart. He was at Carlisle. He would not, however, be available until late on the 2d. Lee would have about 50,000 infantry and some 2000 of Jenkins's cavalry available early on the morning of July 2. All the reinforcements he could hope to receive thereafter would be Stuart's weary horse and about 7000 infantry. If he was to take the offensive he must strike as soon as possible, and before the whole of the Federal army arrived in his front.

Strategically Lee saw no alternative to attacking the enemy before Meade concentrated, much as he disliked to force a general engagement so early in the campaign and at such a distance from Virginia. Tactically, what was the best plan? Late reconnaissance reports did not discourage an attack on the right. Lee's doubts increased on reflection. It seemed better to shorten the line, to concentrate heavily on the right, and to throw the three corps against that position than to operate on a long exterior line.

Having reached this conclusion, Lee sent a message to Ewell, telling him he should move during the night and reinforce that flank. In answer to this message, Ewell rode over late in the evening. He explained that if allowed to stay where he was, he believed that Johnson could capture Culp's Hill, which overlooked Cemetery Hill. This at once changed the outlook; for, obviously, if Ewell could take that eminence, the Second Corps could be profitably employed where it was. Lee therefore directed him to take it as soon as practicable.

Longstreet was with Lee during the evening while this change in plan was being matured. Lee gave him no positive order to attack at any particular point the next morning, yet Longstreet must have known that Lee wished the First Corps brought up as rapidly as possible. He must have understood, also, that Lee intended to attack as soon as it arrived. Lee simply followed his established practice when he refrained on the night of July 1 from giving Longstreet direct orders to have his men at the front by a given hour. The plan was discussed at Lee's headquarters and seemed to be fully understood. As Longstreet had to bring up his troops and deliver the major blow, whereas Ewell's men were already at hand for their lesser part in the enterprise, Lee decided to time Ewell's movements by Longstreet's. Toward midnight, a courier went off with orders to Ewell not to attack until he heard Longstreet's guns open.

"Gentlemen," said Lee to some of his weary officers, by way of final announcement, "we will attack the enemy as early in the morning as practicable."

Lee was at breakfast before daylight on July 2, and soon rode out to a post of observation on Seminary Ridge. Eagerly he put his glasses to his eyes and studied in the growing light the long hillside in front of him. He could not have asked for a better prospect than that which greeted him. The Federals were still on Cemetery Hill, but, so far as he could see, nearly all the ridge south of the hill was bare! The two corps that had been defeated the previous afternoon had not yet been strengthened. Ewell had intercepted a message during the night showing that Sykes's V Corps had been four miles east of Gettysburg at 12:30 A.M. and was to march at 4 o'clock. As this dispatch had been addressed to Major General H. W. Slocum it was to be assumed that Slocum's XII Corps was close at hand also. But neither corps was up yet—and if Longstreet was ready to attack, the ridge could be taken and the remnant of the I and XI Corps destroyed.

Lee turned and looked for Longstreet's veterans, who, by this time, should be shaping their gray lines along the slope from which they were to advance. But they were not there, not a man of them. Was the opportunity to be lost because of Longstreet's slowness? Would the V and XII Corps reach Cemetery Ridge before McLaws and Hood arrived opposite them? What could be done? Could Ewell attack meantime, and if not, would it be wise to revert to the plan formulated and rejected the previous day and to bring the Second Corps to the right in case Longstreet delayed so long that the full strength of the army would be required to drive from the heights the Federals who would soon occupy them? Feeling that golden minutes were slipping through his fingers, Lee hurried Major Venable off to Ewell to inquire what his prospects were and to tell him that the question was whether all the troops should be transferred to the right.

Soon after Venable had ridden off, General Longstreet arrived on the ridge. The head of his column was not far behind, but the start had been most leisurely and the two divisions were spread out for a long distance on the Chambersburg road. Longstreet renewed his argument for a turning movement to get between the enemy and Washington. Lee continued unshaken in his belief that a battle had become in a measure inevitable and that an instant offensive might yield so decisive a victory as to justify the risks.

Federal reinforcements began to file into position on Cemetery Ridge. Minute by minute their strength increased until it soon was apparent that, instead of occupying the ridge without resistance, Lee had to reshape his plans so as to take it in the face of the enemy's opposition and with the least interference from Cemetery Hill. As he studied the terrain, he observed that there were two excellent positions on the Emmitsburg road, which ran for part of its length on high ground between the two main ridges. One of these positions was directly west of Round Top and the other at a peach orchard on the farm of J. Want. Lee reasoned that if he extended his right until he was opposite Round Top, he would get beyond the Federal left. Then, by advancing up the Emmitsburg road, he could seize the peach orchard, plant his artillery there and cover an attack on that section of the ridge occupied by the foe.

To ponder this plan, Lee left Longstreet and walked alone among the trees. More Federals arrived on Cemetery Ridge and disappeared behind the fences that covered its sides. More glasses were fixed on them now, for numbers of Lee's officers were coming up to report. Soon General Hood arrived, ahead of his troops, and sought out Lee. "The enemy is here," Lee told him, "and if we do not whip him, he will whip us." Hood interpreted this to mean that Lee was anxious to attack forthwith, but Longstreet, who must have overheard the remark, hastened to say privately to Hood, "The General is a little nervous this morning; he wishes me to attack; I do no wish to do so without Pickett. I never like to go into battle with one boot off."

In the expectation that Longstreet would dispose his troops for an immediate attack, Lee now left him and rode over toward Gettysburg to see the situation on Ewell's front.

It must have been about 9 o'clock when Lee reached Ewell's headquarters in the outskirts of Gettysburg. Ewell was out reconnoitring. General Trimble was at hand and conducted him to the cupola of the almshouse. Thence Lee could see that the Federals on Cemetery Hill had improved their ground greatly during the night. "The enemy have the advantage of us in a short and inside line," he said, "and we are too much extended. We did not or could not pursue our advantage of yesterday and now the enemy are in a good position."

Probably this was Lee's diplomatic manner of suggesting that, though the Second Corps had failed to do all that it might have done on the 1st, it must not fail in decision and co-ordination now.

Lee was hoping that Longstreet would soon open the attack, and as the minutes passed in silence all along the front, he began to get restless. The enemy was rapidly strengthening his position, and the chances of a successful attack were fast slipping away. "What *can* detain Longstreet!" he exclaimed toward 10 o'clock. "He ought to be in position now."

As Lee rode back toward Seminary Ridge and at last located Longstreet, it was 11 o'clock or later. One glance was enough to show Lee he had been disappointed in his expectation that Longstreet would act to carry out his wishes. Longstreet had been content to wait in the face of the known wishes of the commanding general that he attack as early as practicable! It was incredible but it was the fact, and it left Lee no alternative to ordering the attack it was manifest Longstreet was endeavoring to delay. Lee therefore told Longstreet in plain terms what he wanted him to do and directed him to move against the enemy with the troops he then had on the field.

Still assuming, despite the delay, that his positive orders would be carried out, Lee did not wait to see them executed but rode off again to make a further reconnaissance. Soon, however, he met General Pendleton and learned that the enemy had been driven out by Wilcox's brigade, which had extended its front and was ready to co-operate in the attack Longstreet was to make. By this time, noon had passed. Still seeing nothing of Longstreet's deployment, Lee turned his horse's head once more and sought Longstreet out. He found that the columns had at last begun to move to the right. The reason for this further delay, it developed, was that although Lee had specifically ordered Longstreet to move with the troops then on the field, that officer had seen fit to wait about forty minutes for Law's brigade to come up.

Lee now rode with Longstreet, as he often did when he wished to hurry him along. As they tramped along, an officer came up from the right and reported the enemy moving troops toward Round Top, the great natural bastion on the left of the Federal line. "Ah, well," said Lee, "that was to be expected. But General Meade might as well have saved himself the trouble, for we'll have it in our possession before night."

It was 2 o'clock when McLaws's men filed past Wilcox's brigade. Soon Longstreet's men would be in position south of A. P. Hill, outflanking the extreme left of the Federal line, as Lee hoped. Then they were to attack astride the Emmitsburg road. If their advance reached a point opposite Anderson's division, without driving the Federals, Hill understood that he was to attack frontally. As the battle swept northward on Hill's front, Ewell was to await a favorable opportunity and, if he found it, was to storm the sides of Cemetery Hill. It was a difficult plan, and of such doubtful issue that there was small wonder that Lee's face took on "an expression of painful anxiety."

As Lee waited, Heth came up, to bear his commander company in the hour of contest; Long remained at hand; Hill did not leave; Colonel Arthur J. L. Fremantle of the venerable Coldstream Guards, who was watching vigilantly, lest he lose a single scene of the pageant he had crossed the ocean to observe later reported that the artillery opened, like the drums of a stirring overture to an opera that told of the struggle of demigods and heroes, and then, a band in Rodes's division, from a ravine on the left, began to play lively polkas and waltzes.

But the drama did not open immediately. Some of the performers had been delayed once more in reaching the stage. When the head of the First Corps was within a mile and a half of the ground where Hood's division finally deployed, Captain Samuel R. Johnston notified Longstreet that if the troops continued along the road, they would pass over the crest of a hill where their presence would be disclosed to the enemy. Johnston pointed out a shorter, concealed route across a nearby field. But Longstreet insisted that Johnston go on. When the head of the column reached the top of the hill, whence the signal station on Little Round Top could be seen, Longstreet halted it and, after a conference with General McLaws, decided to countermarch and seek a better route. No sooner was McLaws in sight of the ridge, about 3:30 o'clock, than he perceived that the Federal line extended far beyond his right. In all the time that had elapsed after Lee had signified his intention of attacking on the right, Longstreet had done nothing to verify the reconnaissance made early in the morning. The Confederate right had to be extended still farther.

Hood learned from scouts sent out by Law that he could work his way around the southern end of Round Top and take it in flank and rear. Law insisted that this would be a far less costly line of advance than up the Emmitsburg road, as Lee's orders contemplated. Hood agreed and sent back a messenger to acquaint Longstreet with the facts and to ask permission to turn Round Top. Willing as Long-

street had been during the morning to delay all action, in the hope
of forcing Lee to adopt his strategy, he was stubborn now in adher-
ing to the absolute letter of his instructions. Right or wrong, it was
Lee's battle, not his, and he did not propose to modify the commanding
general's plan, no matter how the situation had changed. Three times
Hood besought him to permit the easier move; three times Longstreet
refused.

Of all this, of course, Lee knew nothing. His first assurance that
the troops were in position came about 4 o'clock when Hood's right
brigade, that of Law, went forward under a floating cloud of smoke.
The advance was difficult, but progress was steady. But instead of
moving up the Emmitsburg road, with their right flank on the ridge,
as Lee had hoped, Hood's men were forced to fight their way directly toward the ridge and, where they could mount it, to turn to
the left. It was desperate going, and the volume and direction of
the fire showed they were encountering the stiffest resistance.

By this time, from the northeast, there swelled the roar of Ewell's
artillery. Evidently Ewell had heard Longstreet's guns and was making
the demonstration required by his orders; but of the effect of his
cannonade Lee could tell nothing. No infantry fire was audible from
that direction. On Lee's right, however, the battle was now drawing
closer to him and was partially visible through the smoke. About 5:30
McLaws's right brigade, under Kershaw, advanced skillfully against a
very difficult position in its front. Behind him Semme's brigade moved
quickly. Then, on McLaws's left, Barksdale's Mississippians followed
their leader across the field, his white hair streaming in the afternoon sun. Their charge was against the peach orchard, and their advance was made with a dash and precision that won the praise of
soldiers who had witnessed some of the most desperate assaults of the
war. A few minutes more and nearly everywhere Longstreet's men
were gaining ground.

If the advantage was to be pushed, Hill must now take up the
fight. As the general direction of the Emmitsburg road is from the
southwest to northeast, Hill's right division, that of R. H. Anderson,
would have to cover a much greater distance than had been traversed
by McLaws's division in reaching the road. The ground, moreover,
was cleared and exposed to a sweeping artillery fire. But Anderson's
four brigades were chafing at the delay. At the word of command,
the soldiers sprang to the charge. They brushed aside the skirmish
line; they reached the road; in a quick exchange of volleys they

drove the Federals back. Then down the slope they dashed to the ravine and, under a steadily increasing fire, began to mount the heights, only to be met by a new Federal line. Here, for nearly half an hour, Wilcox's men met charge after charge. Perry's men, on Wilcox's left, fought with equal valor.

While these two brigades of Hill's corps were fighting to hold their ground, Wright's Georgians moved forward on the left of Perry. Before he reached the road Wright observed that Posey's brigade, which was to cover his left, was not advancing. He halted his men and sent back word to Anderson, who assured him Posey would follow. Wright thereupon ordered the advance to continue. His troops hurled back the Federals in the road, crashed through their main line, and dashed up the ridge. They reached the crest and found themselves among the Federals' massed artillery. They forced the Federals from the high ground and drove them down into the gorge to the east. The grip of the Federals on the ridge was broken. If Wright could get support enough to extend the position he had so gallantly captured, the day would be won!

It was not to be. Perry's brigade had given ground on the right; on the left, Posey had not succeeded in reaching the road. Soon Wright found the Federals massing heavily for a counterattack, and he had to make his way back from the ridge as best he could, with heavy losses. Wilcox was forced to retire about the same time.

Had Ewell been able to achieve more? In the din of the action it had been impossible to tell whether the infantry of the Second Corps had been engaged. Just before darkness fell on the field, Rodes's men deployed west of Gettysburg and moved to the south-east, but they halted and ere long withdrew. This was the last phase of a tragedy in faulty co-ordination. At 6 o'clock, when the Confederate artillery had been almost silenced by the overpowering Union guns, Ewell had ordered Johnson's division forward against Culp's Hill. As Johnson fought his way upward, Early threw two brigades into action against East Cemetery Hill. Their attack was furious and they were soon within the Federal lines. But here, as with Wilcox and Wright, when they looked about for support, Early's men found none. Rodes's division, which was expected to join in the attack, moving on the right of Early, had been slow in deploying and had more ground to cover. When at length Rodes was in position to attack, Early was giving ground. The whole of the three days' battle produced no more tragic might-have-been than this twilight en-

gagement on the Confederate left. Had Rodes's 5000 been at hand to
support Early for even an hour, the Federal guns could have been
captured and turned on the enemy. Cemetery Hill would have been
cleared, and the ridge to the south could have been so enfiladed
that the Federals would have been compelled to evacuate it.

The day was a failure, yet not altogether a failure, and not a
failure that reflected on the valor of the men in the ranks. Troops
that had achieved this much, despite Longstreet's delay and Ewell's
failure to co-ordinate his attacks, could be counted on to do still more
if the whole strength of the army could be employed the next day.
Lee's confidence in his men, at the end of the second day, was as
great as it had ever been. Favorable ground had been gained. The
right seemed well anchored. George H. Steuart's gains on the left might
be enlarged. The ridge traversed by the Emmitsburg road had been
taken, the peach orchard was in Southern hands, and, as Lee saw it,
could be utilized to cover an assault on the position that Wright had
shown was not impregnable.

Enough troops were at hand for a supreme effort on the morning
of the 3d. Pickett's division had arrived within striking distance during
the afternoon and its commander had been told by Lee to rest his
men for the morrow. And Stuart, the wandering, much-missed Stuart,
had come up. For these reasons Lee determined to renew the battle
on the third day. He ordered the artillery made ready to open all
along the line as early as possible. He directed Ewell to renew his
attack at daylight. Lee sent orders for Longstreet to attack the next
morning. That assault would be decisive: Either Meade would be
beaten and the road to Baltimore and Philadelphia would be opened,
or . . .

In the early morning of July 3 a cannonade swept over the ridges
to tell that Ewell was preparing to attack. Lest delay again occur,
Lee rode to the headquarters of the First Corps. On the way he saw
nothing of Pickett's division, which he had ordered up from the
Chambersburg road. Neither did he observe any evidence of preparations for the offensive. When he reached Longstreet he discovered
the reason. "General," Longstreet began, "I have had my scouts out
all night, and I find that you still have an excellent opportunity to
move around to the right of Meade's army, and manoeuvre him into
attacking us." Weary as Lee must have been of Longstreet's contention, he listened patiently, and then, once again, told Longstreet
that he intended to attack. But Longstreet was not to be silenced. He

argued that no 15,000 men could be found who would be capable of storming the ridge. His argument was warm and lengthy.

Lee believed that a general assault along the right held out the highest promise of success. But he probably reasoned that if Longstreet did not have faith in the plan it would be worse than dangerous to entrust the assault to his troops alone. Lack of confidence is half of defeat. Lee put aside what he regarded as the best plan and improvised a second best. He would shift the front of the attack more to the centre. It seemed a reasonable thing to do, but, as the event proved, the shift subjected the assaulting column to a fire on both flanks. Ewell was notified that Longstreet's attack would be delayed until 10 A.M.

Lee rode with Longstreet toward the centre to study the ground and to see that the artillery was well posted. Longstreet had entrusted the placing of his corps of artillery to Colonel E. P. Alexander, perhaps the best artillerist in the Army of Northern Virginia. Altogether, about 125 guns would be available to protect the attack of the infantry. On the left Johnson had been assailed and had begun a counteroffensive before Ewell had received Lee's notice that Longstreet would not attack until 10 A.M. Johnson was wearing himself out and would be unable to co-operate when the great assault was launched. Co-ordination had failed again!

Lee was determined that nothing should be lacking in infantry preparation. Twice he rode the length of the line with Longstreet and then went over it again without him. Later Lee rode out in front of the right of Pettigrew's command with Longstreet and with Hill to arrange the last tactical details. The objective that Lee chose for the coming assault was a small grove of umbrella-shaped chestnut oaks.

Narrow the objective was, compared with the front of attack. The lines therefore would have to converge. Pickett's was to be the right division in the attack, with Kemper's brigade on the right in the first line and Garnett's on the left. Armistead was to be in support. Heth's division, under Pettigrew, was to form on Pickett's left, its four brigades from right to left being Archer's under Colonel B. D. Fry, Pettigrew's old brigade under Colonel J. K. Marshall, Davis's, and Mayo's (Brockenbrough's). Two brigades of Pender's division under Trimble were to be in support of Heth—Scales's on the right, led by Colonel W. L. J. Lowrance, and Lane's on the left. On the extreme right, in rear of Pickett's right flank, Wilcox was to be placed to meet any counterattack against the flank.

The artillery was to cover the charge by a concentrated bombardment. The infantry were not to start until the artillery fire had done its fullest execution. Meantime, the columns of assault were to be kept under cover. Longstreet was to be in general command, with authority to call on Hill for Anderson's division if he required it. When everything was ready, Longstreet was to have two cannon fired in quick succession as a signal for the bombardment to open. To him, also, was given the responsibility of deciding at what moment the infantry should start and when the batteries should limber up and follow.

The last preparations were complete. The time had come to give the order for the bombardment. Longstreet could not bring himself to do it. Instead, he wrote Colonel Alexander: "If the artillery fire does not have the effect to drive off the enemy or greatly demoralize him, so as to make our effort pretty certain, I would prefer that you should not advise Pickett to make the charge. I shall rely a great deal upon your judgment to determine the matter and shall expect you to let Gen. Pickett know when the moment offers."

Alexander was of the bravest of the brave, but he was unprepared to assume the responsibility he felt his chief was trying to unload on him. He demurred but, after an exchange of notes with Longstreet, finally wrote:

"General: when our fire is at its best, I will advise General Pickett to advance."

The silence on the field was almost complete. The Federal infantry were huddled behind the stone wall that ran along the ridge, or were blistering in the tall grass in front of the wall. The Southern infantry were idling under cover. They had ceased their usual banter, but in the memory of old triumphs, and in their unshakable faith in the leadership of Lee, they were as confident as ever they had been. Hungry, athirst, dirty, they waited under the noonday sun whose fiery course was to decide whether America was to be two nations.

At one o'clock, almost on the hour, the silence of the fields around Gettysburg was broken by a gun on the Emmitsburg road. It was the agreed signal for the opening of the bombardment. Instantly the gunners all along the line sprang to their loaded pieces, and in another moment the roar of the massed batteries shook the ridge. Orders were to fire in salvoes, and as the guns were discharged together the concussion told of a coming terror that would make men long for the lesser dangers of Gaines's Mill and of Sharpsburg. Soon the Federal batteries opened, eighteen guns from the very grove Pickett was to

charge, and up and down a line that lengthened until a front of fully
two miles was blazing in answer. The scene resembled the centre of
some furious thunderstorm.

Twenty minutes of this maddening bombardment, and the ammunition of some of the Confederate batteries was half gone, with no
diminution in the Federal fire. Alexander felt there was little hope of
silencing the enemy's fire and reasoned that unless the infantry moved
soon, the artillery would not be able to cover it. He scratched off
this note to Pickett:

> "General: If you are to advance at all, you must come at once
> or we will not be able to support you as we ought. But the enemy's
> fire has not slackened materially and there are still 18 guns firing
> from the cemetery."

Suddenly, through a rift in the smoke, Alexander saw Federal
batteries withdrawing from the vicinity of the little grove. At the same
instant the Federal fire began to fall off. Alexander scrawled to Pickett:

> "For God's sake come quick. The 18 guns have gone. Come
> quick or my ammunition will not let me support you properly."

A messenger dashed off through the smoke with the paper.

Pickett, at that moment, was in receipt of Alexander's previous dispatch. He read it and without a word passed it to Longstreet, who had
dismounted. Longstreet scrutinized it, but gave no order.

"General," said Pickett, anxiously, "shall I advance?"

Longstreet turned and looked away, and then, as if the effort cost
him his very heart's blood, slowly nodded his head.

Pickett shook back his long hair and saluted. "I am going to move
forward, sir," he said, and galloped off.

Fearing for the safety of all the ammunition the army had to
replenish the gaping caissons, General Pendleton ordered the wagons
to the rear and, a little later, recalled four of the nine eleven-pounder
howitzers that Alexander had not been able to employ in the bombardment but had intended to use in following up the advance. Alexander
must have been notified promptly of this, for when Longstreet rode to
him after Pickett had left Alexander told him that the howitzers were
gone and that ammunition was running low.

"Go and stop Pickett where he is," Longstreet said sharply, "and
replenish your ammunition."

"We can't do that, sir," Alexander said. "The train has but little. It would take an hour to distribute it, and meanwhile the enemy would improve the time."

"I do not want to make this charge," Longstreet said with deep emotion. "I do not see how it can succeed. I would not make it now but that General Lee has ordered it and is expecting it." With that he stopped, but he did not send word to Lee of the state of his ammunition.

The Confederate artillerists paused now, for the infantry had to pass through the batteries. The Federal guns continued for a few minutes and then they too reserved their fire. Three hundred yards behind Alexander's batteries, the infantrymen realized that their time had come.

Pickett galloped up, as debonair as if he had been riding through the streets of Richmond under the eye of his affianced. "Up, men," he called, "and to your posts! Don't forget today that you are from old Virginia!" Almost at the same moment, on the crest, Pettigrew called to Marshall, "Now, Colonel, for the honor of the good Old North State, forward." General Garnett, buttoned to the neck in an old blue overcoat and much too ill to take the field, mounted his great black horse and rode out in front of his column as it sprang into line. Kemper on his charger took position in advance of his willing regiments. Armistead shouted in a voice that had never failed to reach the farthest man in his brigade, "Attention, Second battalion, the battalion of direction! Forward, guide centre! March!"

Now the skirmish line was in the open. Now the front brigades were emerging from the woods. Once clear of the woods, at a word of command, the whole line was dressed until it was almost perfect in its formation. Nineteen battle flags were in sight, their red deepened by the sunlight, and the array seemed overpowering, but, as the smoke had lifted, those who looked on the right could see that the flank of Kemper was separated by almost half a mile from the left of Mc-Laws—as if inviting an enfilade fire in its advance, or a counterattack should it fail. Soon the supporting line was visible, too—and twenty-five more battle flags. Each unit moved as if the distance had been taped and marked for a grand review.

Two hundred yards forward and scarcely a shot. Then the Federal artillerists opened—not with the weakened fire that the supposed withdrawal of eighteen guns had led the Confederates to anticipate, but with the full fury of massed guns. Shells tore gaps in the line; flags began to go down; dead and writhing men littered the ground. But the charge continued at the same measured pace, with scarcely the fire of a single Southern musket.

Soon the skirmishers were brought to a stand at the post-and-plank fences along the Emmitsburg road. They disputed this barrier with the Federal skirmishers, who held their own until the main Confederate line was within one hundred yards. Then the enemy fell back. Beyond the second fence on the eastern side of the road Pickett's men were halted and the line was drawn again. Armistead was close behind now, the flanks of Garnett's and of Archer's brigades had met, and Pettigrew's two right brigades had kept their formation admirably. Davis had caught up, but Mayo's brigade was falling behind. Pettigrew's units were now under artillery fire and were suffering heavily.

Up the hill now and at double time! More colors go down; hundreds of men have fallen. Still the formation is excellent, and the front is heavy enough to cover the 250 yards that separate the Confederate right from the wall. Here is the Federal advanced line already, hidden in the tall grass. It fires and flees. A flash of flame, a roar, and the Federal infantry behind the stone wall has opened with their volley. The rebel yell rolls up the ridge in answer to the Federal challenge. Garnett is charging bayonets, pouring canister into Pettigrew. Only a hundred yards for Pickett now, hardly more for Pettigrew. "Fire!" cries Garnett, and his men for the first time pull trigger.

Twenty-five yards to the barrier in Garnett's front. The grimy faces of the Federal infantry can be seen where the smoke lifts for an instant. But the lines are all in confusion now. Armistead is now at the low barrier. His voice is ringing out above the din "Follow me!" Over the wall then, with the bayonet, and on to the crest of the hill! About 100 men of five brigades follow him into the *mêlée*, with butt and thrust, but they fall at every step. Marshall's men press on. The enemy is all around them. Where are the thousands who marched in that proud line from the woods? The right is in the air. And on the left—more Federals. The place is a death-trap; Armistead lies dead within the wall, his right hand still grasping his sword. Are there no reinforcements to drive the victory home? A few batteries have advanced, but their fire is weak and erratic. No support; no succor! Survivors are stumbling over the bodies of the dead; every minute sees the struggling remnants thinned.

From the right there is a rush and a volley; on the left the Federals loose an overwhelming blast of musketry; in front, they stand stubbornly behind the wall at the angle and on the crest. The column is surrounded; there is no escape except in abandoning the heights, won with so much blood and valor. Every man for himself! Uplifted hands for the soldier whose musket has been struck down, a white handkerchief here, a cry of "I surrender," and for the rest—back over the wall and out into the field again. The assault has failed. Men could do no more!

Down the ridge the Virginians made their way; straight across the field the men of Pettigrew's and of Trimble's divisions retired. Only a few kept the semblance of formation. A few Union soldiers came out in pursuit and aimed hungrily at the Confederates, but there was no immediate counterstroke. The repulse had been too costly. At last the survivors staggered to the cover of the low ground west of the batteries. There they found Lee astride Traveller. As soon as he had seen that the assault was failing, he had ridden out to rally the men and to share the ordeal of the counterattack, if one was to come. His one thought now was of those who had come back, dazed or wounded, from the ridge. With Longstreet and some staff officers he circulated among them.

All his self-mastery had been mustered for this supreme test, and he seemed to overlook nothing. He was still expecting a thrust by the enemy, and where he met a man whose wounds were light he told him, "Bind up your hurts and take a musket." A little way off Lee saw Pickett and hurried over to meet him. "General Pickett," he began, "place your division in rear of this hill, and be ready to repel the advance of the enemy should they follow up their advantage."

"General Lee, I have no division now, Armistead is down, Garnett is down, and Kemper is mortally wounded."

"Come, General Pickett," said Lee, "this has been my fight and upon my shoulders rests the blame. The men and officers of your command have written the name of Virginia as high today as it has ever been written before."

Presently General Wilcox came up. His losses had been heavy, and as he tried to explain the condition of his brigade, his emotion overwhelmed him. Lee shook his hand. "Never mind, General, all this has been my fault—it is I that have lost this fight, and you must help me out of it the best way you can."

The carnage had been frightful. From Pickett's division only one field officer had found his way back to the lines. All the others had

been killed or had been wounded and captured. Garnett had taken
in more than 1300 men and had lost 941. Pettigrew's brigade had but
a solitary staff officer to rally the remnant, and of his whole division
only 1500 or 1600 returned. The Thirty-eighth North Carolina could
muster a bare forty, under a first lieutenant, and Company A of the
Eleventh North Carolina, which had crossed the Potomac with one
hundred, had only eight men and a single officer.

Lee remained with Alexander more than half an hour, now in
the open and now behind the edge of the ridge, where the group of
horsemen could look over the crest without attracting the fire of the
enemy. Slowly, when it was all over, he rode toward headquarters.
The few batteries that had attempted to follow the charge were
gradually withdrawn, and after nightfall Alexander skillfully brought
all his guns back to Seminary Ridge. The infantry were recalled from
the right to a shorter line. They accomplished the manoeuvre with
no material interruption by the enemy.

Lee had no complicated strategic problem to solve now, no alternatives to ponder. Retreat was the only course. Orders were therefore
issued before the day was out to prepare for the withdrawal as soon
as the wounded and the wagon trains could be cleared.

After a long conference with A. P. Hill on the arrangements for
the retreat, Lee walked Traveller back through the sleeping camps
about 1 A.M. When he reached his own headquarters he was so weary
that he could hardly dismount.

Presently General Imboden addressed him in a sympathetic voice:
"General, this has been a hard day on you."

"Yes, it has been a sad, sad day for us," Lee answered mournfully.
Then he broke out with an excitement of manner that startled his
companion: "I never saw troops behave more magnificently than
Pickett's division of Virginians did today in that grand charge upon
the enemy. And if they had been supported as they were to have
been—but for some reason not yet fully explained to me, were not—
we would have held the position and the day would have been ours."

A pause, and then he exclaimed in a voice that echoed loudly and
grimly through the night, "Too bad! Too bad! Oh, too bad!"

Would Meade attack? If the Federals had the strength to take the
initiative, they would find the Confederates frightfully extended, bleeding, and almost without ammunition. Should the Union commander

withhold attack, another dawn would find Lee on his way back to Virginia.

Instead of following the long route back to Chambersburg and thence to Hagerstown, the army was to go southwestward to Fairfield and westward to Greencastle. Stuart was to send a brigade or two of cavalry to hold the passes west of Cashtown on the Chambersburg pike. The rest of the Confederate troopers were to use the Emmitsburg road and protect the rear and left flank of the army. The wounded were to leave as soon as practicable. Hill was to follow. Then Longstreet was to take up the march and was to guard the prisoners. Ewell would cover the rear. All the wagons not used in transporting the wounded were to form a single train, placed midway the column.

A hundred troublesome details absorbed the weary commander of the defeated army. In an effort to relieve himself of the burden of 4000 unwounded prisoners, he dispatched a flag of truce proposing an exchange, but Meade prudently declined. Engineers were sent back to select a line in rear of Hagerstown, in case the enemy pursued vigorously. The wounded were painfully assembled with great difficulty, and an artillery force was provided to supplement the escort, which consisted of Imboden's cavalry. A brief report was prepared for the President.

A torrential rain began to fall about 1 P.M. and delayed the start of the ambulance train. When at last the wounded were on their way, in rough wagons that were as torturing as the rack, fully 5000 sulkers and sick contrived to march with them. Lee could not readily prevent this, but he was most solicitous that no panic or sense of demoralization spread among the troops.

The next day, July 5, was sixteen daylight hours of purgatory. The rain was still falling heavily; the men were muddy, wet, and hungry. So slowly did the other corps drag themselves along the blocked road that it was 2 A.M. before Ewell left the field of Gettysburg, and 4 P.M. by the time he reached Fairfield, less than nine miles from his starting point. The rain continued during the night of July 5–6, but as the leading corps was then through the mountains it was able to move, unabashed, at greater speed than it had ever made before in putting distance between itself and its old adversary.

At 5 o'clock on the afternoon of the 6th, Longstreet's corps, which was then the van, succeeded in reaching Hagerstown. Lee rode with it and found that the ambulance train had arrived at Williamsport that day with the wounded. But the elements had again done battle against the South: the pontoon bridge below the town had been broken up by a raiding party, and the Potomac, swollen by the rains, was far past fording. The army, its wounded, and its prisoners, were cut off from Virginia soil. More than that, a mixed force of Federal cavalry and artillery had appeared in the rear and had threatened the capture of the wagons. But attack had been held off until Stuart had arrived with his cavalry. The Federals had then been repulsed. Despite this, the situation was worse than serious. Meade, in Lee's opinion, was certainly pursuing in the hope of attacking before he crossed the Potomac. Any long delay would involve another battle in Maryland, and a disaster with the river at flood would mean annihilation.

Lee's first thought was for his wounded. He gave orders that all the ferry-boats in the vicinity be collected so that he might use them in transporting the sufferers to the south bank. The wagons must wait, and if Meade attacked the army must prepare to give battle once more to the Federals. Fortunately, the engineers had found and had laid out an admirable defensive line.

The men in the ranks were not conscious of the danger they faced, or else they defied it. They were in sight of their own country once more and their morale seemed unimpaired. In the press of duties in front of Williamsport, Lee found the loss and suffering of his men brought home to him. On June 26, Rooney Lee had been taken from his bed at "Hickory Hill," Hanover County, by a Federal raiding party, and had been carried to Fort Monroe, where he was held as a hostage for the good treatment of some Federal officers who had been threatened with death as a measure of retaliation.

Not for a moment, however, did Lee let his concern for Rooney or his uneasiness for his troops shake his equanimity. No trace of resentment was there in his dealings with the men who had failed him. He greeted Longstreet cordially as "my old war horse." When FitzGerald Ross, another English observer and a captain in the army of Austria, came to call, Lee talked of Gettysburg as if all the fault had been his own. He told Ross that if he had been aware that Meade had been able to concentrate his whole army, he would not have attacked him, but that the success of the first day, the belief that Meade had only a part of his army on the field, and the enthusiasm of his own troops had led him to conclude that the possible results of a victory justified the risks. He added that his lack of accurate knowledge of the enemy's concentration was due to the absence of Stuart's cavalry. In writing to the President, he was full of fight and urged once more that Beauregard's army be brought to the upper Rappahannock for a demonstration on Washington.

This was written on the 8th of July. The next night an officer who had escaped from the Federals at Gettysburg arrived with news that the enemy was marching on Hagerstown. This confirmed Lee's belief that Meade intended to attack and he prepared accordingly. His cavalry were thrown out as a wide screen and the infantry were moved into the lines prepared for them.

The Federals had been approaching cautiously, but by the 12th they grew bolder. Lee's mind wavered between hope and anxiety.

His prayers seemed answered on the 13th. The resourceful Major J. A. Harman had torn down old warehouses and had constructed a number of crude boats that had been floated to Falling Waters, where some of the original pontoons had been recovered. With these a crossing had been laid. The river at Williamsport was still deep but fordable, at last, by infantry. Lee determined not to delay a day in reaching a wider field of manoeuvre on the south shore of the forbidding Potomac. To expedite his movement he decided to use both the ford and the pontoons—Ewell to cross by the former route, and the trains and the rest of the army by the bridge. Longstreet demurred at this withdrawal, because there was a chance of fighting a defensive battle on ground to his liking, but Lee overruled him and personally directed the preparations for the crossing.

That afternoon, as if to defeat the whole difficult enterprise, rain began to descend heavily, and by nightfall the river seemed to be pouring from the skies. At the ford there was much confusion. Nerves grew raw under the strain. A new road had been cut to the bridge at Falling Waters, and under the downpour this soon became so heavy that the wagons began to stall. Instead of the swift march for which Lee had hoped, there was a virtual blockade. Laboring teams struggled through the mire, and soldiers strained at the hub-deep wheels. Lee sat on his horse at the north end of the bridge, encouraging the men until even his strong frame grew weary. Toward morning the report was that Ewell's column soon would be in Virginia; but at Falling Waters dawn found the rear of the wagon train still swaying uneasily on the pontoon bridge. Longstreet and Hill were yet to cross. Leaving Longstreet to direct the movement on the north side of the river, Lee went to the southern shore to expedite the clearing of the bridge.

Finally only Hill and the cavalry remained behind. Lee's anxiety was not wholly relieved, for he believed it certain that Meade would attack

Hill. When Colonel Sorrel reported Longstreet's last file had passed, Lee bade him urge the Third Corps to make the utmost haste. Soon Sorrel came back and announced that the road was clear and that Hill was only three-quarters of a mile from the bridge.

"What was his leading division?" Lee inquired.

"General Anderson, sir," Sorrel answered.

"I am sorry, Colonel; my friend Dick is quick enough pursuing, but in retreat I fear he will not be as sharp as I should like."

At that moment the echo of a heavy gun rolled up the river gorge. "There!" the General exclaimed. "I was expecting it—the beginning of the attack!"

But instead of halting or stampeding at the sound, Hill's tired troops continued their steady tramp across the bridge. Ere long General Lee learned that only the rear division, Heth's, was in contact with the enemy, and that it was holding its own. Heth contrived to reach the river with no other loss than that of the stragglers and sick whom he had not been able to push on ahead of him.

The retreat was over! The Potomac stood between the battered Army of Northern Virginia and the disappointed Federals. As the army manifestly must have rest, Lee moved it on the 15th to the vicinity of Bunker Hill. He sent out men and horses, threshed wheat, carried it to the mills, ground it, and, with the beef captured in Pennsylvania, contrived to give a sufficient ration to the hungry army.

Before Lee could make more than a start in the never-ending work of reorganization, Meade crossed the Potomac east of the Blue Ridge and advanced his cavalry to the passes into Loudoun. Lee promptly made counter-dispositions and placed Longstreet in Manassas. A force left at Manassas Gap had an affair with the enemy, but drew off with no great difficulty. The Federals shifted to Warrenton, and from that base on the night of July 31–August 1 sent a cavalry column and some infantry across the Rappahannock. Confederate horse promptly opposed this advance, but Lee decided to transfer his whole army south of the Rapidan. This was accomplished by August 4, on which date the Gettysburg campaign may be said to have come to its conclusion, with the opposing troops holding almost the very ground whence Jackson had started the first stage of Lee's offensive a year previously.

Disappointment was general in Richmond, and there was much questioning throughout the South. Lee refused to accept this as justified; and remarked that little value was to be attached to popular judgment of victories or of defeats. "As far as I am concerned," Lee said of one series of hostile complaints, "the remarks fall harmless," but he felt that censure of the army did damage at home and abroad. As criticism spread, Lee was quick to absolve his men of all responsibility for failure to attain the full objective. The army, he wrote Mrs. Lee on July 15, "has accomplished all that could be reasonably expected. It ought not to have been expected to perform impossibilities, or to have fulfilled the anticipations of the thoughtless and unreasonable." He hoped that the final reports would "protect the reputation of every officer," and he was determined not to blame any of his subordinates. He felt that he had himself been at fault in expecting too much of the army. His confidence in it, he frankly confessed, had carried him too far. Overlooking all the tactical errors and all the mistakes due to the state of mind of his subordinates, he went straight to the underlying cause of failure when he said it was due primarily to lack of co-ordination.

After reflecting fully on the outcome in the comparative quiet of his camp at Orange Courthouse, he decided that he should ask to be relieved of the command of the army. In the course of a deliberately written letter to the President he said: "I therefore, in all sincerity, request Your Excellency to take measures to supply my place. I do this with the more earnestness because no one is more aware than myself of my inability for the duties of my position. I cannot even accomplish what I myself desire. How can I fulfill the expectations of others?"

He had not long to wait for the President's decision. August 12 or 13, Lee received from Mr. Davis a long answer in which the chief executive deplored the clamor of the times and then continued:

"But suppose, my dear friend, that I were to admit, with all their implications, the points which you present, where am I to find that new commander who is to possess the greater ability which you believe to be required? I do not doubt the readiness with which you would give way to one who could accomplish all that you have wished, and you will do me the justice to believe that if Providence should kindly offer such a person for our use, I would not hesitate to avail of his services . . .

"To ask me to substitute you by some one in my judgment more fit to command, or who would possess more of the confidence of the army, or of the reflecting men of the country, is to demand an impossibility . . ."

That ended it! Lee had to go on.

The discussion of Gettysburg, however, did not end with this private exchange of letters. It continued into the winter and to the close of General Lee's life. Lee made little comment on Gettysburg during the war. When it had ended, General Lee was still reticent in writing and speaking to strangers about Gettysburg or about any other of his battles, and never went further than to say to them that if the assault could have been co-ordinated success could have been attained. It is certain, however, that in the last years at Lexington, as Lee viewed the Gettysburg campaign he concluded that it was the absence of Jackson, not the presence of Ewell or Longstreet, that made the Army of Northern Virginia far less effective at Gettysburg than at Chancellorsville. And one afternoon, when he was out riding with Professor White, he said quietly, "If I had had Stonewall Jackson with me, so far as man can see, I should have won the battle of Gettysburg." That statement must stand. The darkest scene in the drama of Gettysburg was enacted at Chancellorsville when Jackson fell.

CHAPTER XI

The Spectre of Want and Disaster

"WE MUST now prepare for harder blows and harder work." In that spirit Lee faced the enemy after his return to Virginia. Weakened by 23,000 men, he was back in a devastated country and was forced to rely once again on Commissary General L. B. Northrop for the army's food. Because of this, he realized that he might be compelled to retreat nearer to Richmond, but he was not willing to relinquish the initiative to General Meade if he could take it himself.

As soon as the army settled down on the Rapidan, Lee undertook to bring it to offensive strength again. His first results were encouraging. The return of stragglers and of lightly wounded and the arrival of 3000 men, lent him temporarily from the army of Major General Samuel Jones, raised Lee's effective strength to 58,000 by August 10. But the limitations of man-power soon were apparent. The soldiers were almost barefooted; the supply of rations was menacingly short; the railroads were scarcely able to haul what the commissaries found; the equipment of the cavalry was in embarrassing disrepair and the horses received so little grain that they recovered slowly. Soon Jones's troops had to be ordered back, and the ranks were further reduced by furloughs Lee thought it prudent to grant. The end of August found the army stronger by only 2600 than it had been on the 10th.

On August 24, President Davis asked Lee to come to Richmond to discuss with him a new and menacing situation. Lee left Longstreet in charge and went immediately to the capital, where he remained, with one or two days' intermission, until September 7. He discussed with the President the means of preventing desertion and of procuring more corn for the animals attached to the army, and he had to advise on a large and critical problem of general strategy. In this crisis, the darkest the embattled South had yet known, what course held out the strongest promise of relief? That was the question President Davis discussed in

348

long, private conferences with the commander of the Army of Northern Virginia. The main choice, as Lee saw it, lay between attacking Meade and attacking Rosecrans in Tennessee. Which should be done? As Bragg could not take the offensive without additional troops, should he give ground or should he be reinforced from the Army of Northern Virginia? Lee's inclination was to assume the offensive against Meade. The President, it seems, at first leaned so strongly to this view that Lee ordered the army to be made ready for an advance. On September 2, however, the Federals entered Knoxville, the enemy's movement against Chattanooga developed, and the situation became so alarming that Davis concluded he must reinforce both Beauregard at Charleston, S. C., and Bragg from the Army of Northern Virginia. Lee acquiesced in the movement of two brigades to Charleston and in the dispatch of part of one corps to Tennessee. The President was anxious that Lee assume command on that front himself but left the question open while Lee hurried back to the Rapidan on September 7. Lee had decided to designate the First Corps, less Pickett's division, for the adventure in the West, and as he found Longstreet most anxious to go, he was confirmed in his opinion that it would be best to remain personally in Virginia, to detach Longstreet, and to leave the direction of affairs in Tennessee to officers familiar with the troops. Within twenty-four hours after he reached Orange, Lee had McLaws's and Hook's divisions of Longstreet's famous veterans on the road. Pickett was to follow.

There were reasons for concern on the line of the Rapidan. The activity of the Federal cavalry indicated that an attack might be brewing. Lee sent back all his surplus supplies to Gordonsville, in anticipation of an enforced withdrawal. He had already cautioned Davis to strengthen the Richmond fortifications and to expedite the erection of arsenals farther inland. He advocated haste in the completion of the railroad that was to link Danville, Va., with Greensboro, N. C. Otherwise, the Army of Northern Virginia might no longer be able to draw supplies from the south. And that would mean ruin.

Then, in a dark hour, the telegraph clicked off the announcement— as glorious as it was unexpected—that Bragg, with Longstreet's help, had struck Rosecrans at Chickamauga on September 19–20 and had thrown him in retreat on Chattanooga. A new crisis had passed. Hope rose in every Southern heart. If the victory could be followed up, the whole gloomy prospect might be transformed. Lee announced the success to his troops and wrote warm congratulations to Longstreet.

Jubilation over Chickamauga lasted only a few days. The Army of

Tennessee had exhausted itself in winning the battle and did not follow up its success. Rosecrans withdrew in safety to Chattanooga, and the Confederates were slow to follow. Longstreet's self-confidence began to evaporate, and he called loudly for the leadership of which he was later so critical in his review of Gettysburg. "Can't you send us General Lee?" he pleaded with the Secretary of War.

While Bragg's movements were still in doubt, Lee received reports on September 28 that the XI and XII Corps of the Army of the Potomac had been sent to reinforce Rosecrans. Now that the odds against him had been reduced, Lee began to consider the advisability of seizing the initiative once more. The ranks were thin, and the men were poorly clad and worse shod. Lee himself was far from well. But a movement against Meade would prevent the detachment of additional troops to the West. If, furthermore, Meade could be driven back to the Potomac and held there during the winter, northern Virginia would be spared the distresses of Federal occupation, the railroads would be more nearly safe from raiders, and the campaign of 1864 would open where Lee would have ample ground for manoeuvre without exposing Richmond.

Meade was north of Culpeper on a ridge that would serve as well for defense as for attack and had two corps extended to the Rapidan. In this position the enemy could not be assailed to advantage by a frontal attack. Lee determined to manoeuvre him from his position and to thrust at him when he found a favorable opening. This would necessitate a round-about march, if the movement was to be a surprise. Lee directed General Imboden to move up the Shenandoah Valley and to protect the flank of the army. Then Lee divided his cavalry, which had been reorganized into two divisions under Wade Hampton and Fitz Lee. Fitz Lee was to remain on the Rapidan to cover the army's rear until Meade retreated. Hampton's division, led by Stuart, was to move on the right. Supplies were to be sent up the Orange and Alexandria Railroad to Culpeper as soon as the road was opened by Meade's withdrawal.

When the time for the advance arrived, Lee's "rheumatism" in the back was so severe that he could not mount a horse, but he determined not to delay operations on that account. The corps of Ewell and A. P. Hill made their way through the hills toward Madison Courthouse, which was reached on the 10th. The appearance of Federal cavalry in front of Stuart that day showed the movement had been discovered and Lee could not hope to catch Meade off his guard. Stuart easily disposed of the cavalry outposts and cleared the road for the advance toward Culpeper on the 11th. When the army reached Stone House Mountain, Lee learned that Meade had evacuated his position and had put the Rappahannock between him and his pursuers. It was necessary to undertake a new turning movement to reach the Federals, but before this could be started the army had to be rationed. While the hungry columns rested by the roadside, Lee rode into Culpeper. His back was better and he could keep on his horse.

Meantime, on the 11th, the cavalrymen were having a most exciting day. Stuart had flushed the Federal horse early in the morning. Late in the day one of Stuart's officers reported that Fitz Lee had encountered Federal cavalry and was driving them in the direction of Brandy Station, while Stuart was pressing another column back toward the Rappahannock. Stuart and Fitz Lee joined near the scene of their action of June 9, and together fought a second battle of Brandy Station, almost as interesting as the first because of the soldierly co-ordination of horse artillery, cavalry, sharpshooters, and dismounted cavalry. By nightfall they had driven the enemy over the Rappahannock.

Lee's task on the morning of October 12 was to outflank Meade and to intercept him on his retreat up the Orange and Alexandria Railroad. The only roads available to Lee for this purpose led to Warrenton, so he chose that town as his immediate objective and set out from the vicinity of Culpeper on the morning of October 12, his front and right flank covered by Stuart's cavalry. Ewell's corps was to move by way of Jeffersonton and Sulphur Springs; Hill was to take the longer route via Woodville, Sperryville, Washington, Amissville, and Waterloo Bridge.

Early on the morning of October 13 Ewell's corps moved on Warrenton. Their march was not rapid because Lee knew that Hill had a longer route to pursue, and he did not desire to be in the presence of the enemy until the two corps were reunited. It was afternoon when he reached Warrenton, where Hill joined him about dark, too late to undertake a farther advance before nightfall. During the day Lee had received messages from Stuart through Fitz Lee, announcing that enemy troops were still at Warrenton Junction, but were burning stores. Stuart's notes indicated that he was close to the enemy. Then the flow of messages stopped. As the troops went into bivouac Lee waited long after his usual hour of retirement for further news. Had Stuart been cut off? Was the enemy approaching Warrenton?

About 1 o'clock a staff officer announced that a spy in Stuart's service, Goode by name, had arrived with a strange tale. Goode was much concerned: Stuart had found the enemy moving northward and had started back toward Auburn. As Stuart approached Auburn he discovered another Federal column moving northward. He took his men out of the road and hid them in a wood, but he was between two forces of the enemy and might be discovered at any time. He had sent Goode to inform General Lee of his plight and to ask that a force be sent to make an artillery demonstration west of the Auburn-Greenwich road.

Lee ordered Ewell to make the desired diversion at dawn. About daylight there came the sound of a brief cannonade from the direction of Ewell's approach, followed quickly by a more distant salvo, evidently Stuart's guns. It was apparent that part of the Army of the Potomac was close at hand, but there was little prospect that Meade would soon be overtaken.

The Confederates set out toward Bristoe, however, in high spirits. The march was long and the pace was fast. Shoes for bare feet, blankets for shivering shoulders, sutlers' delicacies for hungry stomachs—these were the spurs that hurried the regiments on. At Greenwich, Ewell gave Hill the direct road to Bristoe Station and, as he was familiar from boyhood with the ground, Lee rode with Ewell at the head of the Second Corps. About mid-afternoon, as he approached the railroad, Lee was greeted with a heavy outburst of firing on the left, infantry and artillery. Proceeding at once across country, he did not reach the area of action until fighting was over. Then he learned the grim details of as badly managed a battle as had ever been fought under the flag of the Army of Northern Virginia.

This is what happened: As his corps approached Bristoe Station, A. P. Hill observed a large force of the enemy on the near side and many more troops on the far side of Broad Run. The stretch of Broad Run above the railroad was almost directly in his front. He deployed Heth's division facing the stream, with the intention of crossing at once and pursuing the enemy. Only two brigades—Cooke's and Kirkland's—had been put in position when they received orders to attack immediately. The enemy across the run was moving hurriedly off at the time, and Poague's battalion was being advanced to shell the column. Just as Cooke started forward, a sharp fire broke out on his right. Throwing forward two companies to feel out the enemy, Cooke halted. Hill sent peremptory orders for Cooke to advance at once. Scarcely had he started than the whole of the railroad embankment on his right began to blaze with musketry. The embankment formed an ideal breastwork, and behind it Federal artillery was soon visible.

While the Confederates had been intent on pursuing the troops across the run, another Federal force had advanced up the railroad and had taken position where it could sweep Heth's flank. Cooke's brigade could do nothing but retreat or pivot on its right and attack the enemy behind the embankment. As Cooke was badly wounded, his senior colonel made a quick choice and ordered the charge. Kirkland made for the enemy in the cut. He, too, was wounded, but his men kept on. They reached the embankment and plunged over it, only to be driven back speedily or captured. Cooke's men gallantly approached the embankment but came under a heavy enfilade and failed to reach their objective. The two brigades fell back and in doing so uncovered a Confederate battery that had been placed, unknown to them, on the right of the road in rear of Cooke. The enemy promptly advanced and seized four of the guns.

Within forty minutes the battle was ended and night was falling. Two Confederate corps had been within striking distance and so disposed that if Hill's attack had been delayed even half an hour the Federals moving along the railroad could have been roughly handled and perhaps cut off. As it was, two brigades had been wrecked. Cooke's fine regiments had lost 700, and Kirkland's 602.

During that same morning of October 15, the cavalry reported that the enemy had retreated beyond Bull Run and was entrenching there. Should Lee follow? He was confident that if he did so he could turn Meade's position and either force him north of the Potomac or compel him to take refuge in the fortifications around Washington. Were the possible benefits worth the risks? Lee was disposed to answer in the negative.

Satisfied that he could accomplish little by staying in Meade's front, Lee started the army back toward the Rappahannock on October 18 and left the cavalry to watch the enemy. By noon of the 18th the army reached the Rappahannock, for its march was swift; but because of the slowness of the engineers, the pontoon bridge was not ready and the tired columns had to wait. At length the bridge was laid, and Lee crossed to the south bank with half the army. The other forces followed the next morning.

The whole movement was completed without interruption, except for an action that won the alluring name of the "Buckland Races." This affair was on October 19. Stuart made a stand in the vicinity of Buckland and was holding off the enemy when he received a dispatch from Fitz Lee. If Stuart fell back down the Warrenton road, Fitz Lee could assail the Federals' flank and perhaps rout them. Stuart retired until he reached Chestnut Hill. Hearing then the guns of Fitz Lee, he turned on Kilpatrick's cavalry, who retreated in great haste. Not until Buckland was reached did Stuart halt the chase. That Federals and Confederates were so close together on the stretch of seven miles gave the contest the nature of a race.

While the "Buckland Races" gave a saving touch of humor to the withdrawal, they did not relieve the expedition of failure. Lee had asked, in effect, whether the offensive could be resumed, and the answer, all too plain, was that it could not be with the limited forces he had and with his *matériel* as poor as it then was.

Back south of the Rappahannock, the Army of Northern Virginia was satisfied that the year's fighting had been ended. Meade was somewhat of the same mind. But Lee was not so sure that all was over for the winter. He presumed that Meade would advance again. On the possibility that supplies might be forthcoming for a limited offensive, he kept his pontoons on the Rappahannock. Simultaneously, he fortified a bridgehead on the north bank of the river.

Two weeks and more passed without important incident.

On November 5 outposts reported the enemy advancing to the Rappahannock, and by noon on November 7 Federal infantry was in front of the *tête-de-pont*, while a large column was moving to Kelly's Ford. As the ground on the south bank of the river at this ford was somewhat similar to that at Fredericksburg, Lee intended to permit Meade to cross and then to attack him in superior force by holding part of the Federals at Rappahannock Bridge.

When, therefore, Lee learned during the afternoon that the enemy had crossed at Kelly's Ford, in front of Rodes's division, he felt no particular concern. Johnson's division was ordered to reinforce Rodes, Anderson was brought up to support Early, who commanded the crossing, and the rest of Hill's corps was put on the alert. Early hurried across the pontoon bridge, and Lee busied himself with disposing two batteries of artillery that were at Rappahannock Bridge. On the arrival from the rear of Hoke's command, the leading brigade of Early's division, Lee ordered it over the bridge to support the troops already in position, but he declined to send more men to the north side. He believed that seven regiments would suffice to defend the bridgehead, inasmuch as the enemy could not advance on a longer front than the two brigades held.

In a short time dusk fell. Soon the Federal ordnance, which had achieved a cross-fire on the bridgehead, ceased. Shortly afterward flashes of musketry could be seen, but these were not long visible. This stoppage of fire convinced Lee that the Federals were merely making a demonstration, and he concluded that the action was over for the day. He rode back to headquarters, where he received the unwelcome news that the enemy had captured parts of two regiments at Kelly's Ford, had laid a pontoon bridge, and had sent a large force over to reinforce the first units. Then Early sent him almost incredible news from the *tête-de-pont:* After dark, the enemy had massed in strength, stormed the bridgehead and captured the whole force on the north side.

Lee saw that he must move back, and at once. Within a few hours after Early had reported the disaster at Rappahannock Bridge the army was retiring to a line that crossed the Orange and Alexandria Railroad two miles northeast of Culpeper and barred the road from Kelly's Ford by way of Stevensburg. On the morning of November 9 Lee again put the columns in motion and, on November 10, was back on the south side of the Rapidan.

The men went cheerfully to work building new huts, and contrived to make themselves comfortable after a fashion. Lee sought once more to get shoes for those who were barefooted and began a long correspondence with the commissary bureau concerning the rationing of the army. As he could not leave the army to go to the capital to discuss these matters with Mr. Davis, he requested the President to visit the army, and, during a period of rainy weather from November 21 to November 24, conferred with him on the situation.

For more than two weeks after the line of the Rapidan was manned, Meade showed no disposition to assume the initiative except for minor cavalry demonstrations. Then, on the night of November 24, Lee's spies reported suspicious movements. Lee's belief was that his able adversary, in making another thrust, would attempt, on crossing the Rapidan, to advance through the Wilderness of Spotsylvania in the direction of the Richmond and Fredericksburg Railroad. He now prepared to move quickly to the northeast in order to interpose between Meade and his objective.

November 26 disclosed the enemy moving toward Germanna Ford. As this was precisely what Lee had expected Meade to do, orders were issued for the Confederate movement to begin during the night. At 3 A.M. of the 27th, Lee left his headquarters and started for Verdiersville.

After establishing his headquarters at the Rhodes house, Lee walked down the plank road and found Stuart. In a brief conversation with his chief of cavalry, Lee directed him to cover the roads in the direction of Chancellorsville and Spotsylvania Courthouse, as the enemy was believed to be moving in that direction. General Early reported in person. Lee ordered him to continue his advance in the direction of Chancellorsville.

Early soon sent back word that General Hays had met Federal infantry at Locust Grove, about a mile and a half east of Mine Run. Early completed his dispositions, and put Rodes and Hays in line, opposite what appeared to be a strong force at Locust Grove. Instead, therefore, of having a race for Chancellorsville, with an enemy moving southeastward from the fords of the Rapidan, Lee found the Federals in his front and on his left flank.

About 1 P.M. Heth's division reached Verdiersville. Lee gave the men an hour's rest and then directed that they continue their march up the plank road toward Mine Run. Sometime after the last regiment of the division had filed past, Lee himself rode forward with his staff. When he had gone about two miles he found the division halted and heard firing ahead. In rear of Heth's line of battle, Lee waited. North of him a hot action was in progress.

General Stuart, in a note sent at 2 o'clock, expressed the belief that the enemy was advancing up the Rapidan. General Thomas L. Rosser reported that during the morning he had found the ordnance train of the I and V Army Corps on the plank road near Wilderness Tavern and that the wagons were headed for Orange Courthouse, not for Chancellorsville.

Was Meade, then, moving against the Army of Northern Virginia, rather than to the Richmond and Fredericksburg Railroad? It seemed probable, but until the purpose of the enemy was more fully disclosed Lee hardly dared hope that his numerically inferior army would have the opportunity of fighting a defensive battle. Added intelligence led him to conclude that the whole of the Army of the Potomac was in his front. It was not necessary to go in search of the enemy; the enemy was searching for him! For the first time since Fredericksburg the army was to have a chance of receiving the enemy's assaults. Lee determined not to advance against the strong position of the Federals that evening, but to withdraw to the west bank of Mine Run during the night and to await developments.

If Meade was of a mind to assume the offensive, Lee wished to meet it on the most favorable ground. On the 28th he ordered earthworks thrown up. But the enemy did not attack that day, nor the next, though he opened a heavy artillery fire on the 29th and threatened to assault. Lee could not believe that Meade had moved his whole army for a mere demonstration, so he continued to strengthen his earthworks, while the enemy set about to emulating him. That day witnessed the strange spectacle of two great armies exchanging occasional cannon shots and contenting themselves, for the rest, with seeing which of them could pile the higher parapets.

On the 30th, the weather still very cold, Stuart reported early that the enemy was forming line of battle on the south side of the Catharpin road. But once again expectations were deceived, and no general engagement occurred.

When the morning of December 1 came and went with no further sign of any intention on the part of the Federals to press the offensive, Lee determined to take the initiative himself. Before daybreak on December 2 the whole army was ready; Anderson and Wilcox were in position; the rest of the men were on the alert; the gunners were at their posts. As soon as it was light enough to see, the skirmishers looked eagerly through the woods for the Federal pickets. But they scanned the thickets in vain: The enemy was gone! Informed of the changed situation, the cavalry rode fast and hard, and the infantry followed through woods the retiring enemy had set afire. Meade, however, had a long lead, for he had started during the late afternoon of the 1st, and the chase was fruitless.

"I am too old to command this army," Lee said grimly, when he saw that his adversary had retreated, "we should never have permitted those people to get away."

Except for a troublesome raid by General W. W. Averell against the Virginia and Tennessee Railroad, beginning December 11, the Mine Run episode marked the end of active operations in 1863. It had been for Lee no such year of victory as '62. The bloody glory of Chancellorsville had been dimmed by defeat at Gettysburg; the limit of the manpower of the South had almost been reached; the spectre of want hung over the camps. From the time of the return to the line of the Rappahannock and Rapidan after the Pennsylvania campaign, the army had met with no major disaster, but it had scored no success. Taking Bristoe Station, the capture of the Rappahannock bridgehead and the movement to Mine Run as one campaign, Lee's losses had been 4255 and his gain had been nil.

Lee came back to his headquarters at Orange Courthouse to find other reason for distress than the escape of Meade unpunished from Mine Run. The public prints were full of alarming news from Tennessee. Bragg had waited in front of Chattanooga until he had been driven off by incredible Federal assaults on Lookout Mountain and Missionary Ridge, November 23–25. He then, the papers reported, had retreated to Dalton, where he had been relieved of command.

So fraught with disaster was this turn of events that Lee put aside his reserve and wrote the President on December 3 a letter of direct advice. He pointed out that the enemy might penetrate into Georgia "and get possession of our depots of provisions and important manufactories." He suggested that Beauregard be put at the head of the Army of Tennessee and that troops be drawn from Mobile, Mississippi, and Charleston. Then he laid down this general strategic policy: "I think that every effort should be made to concentrate as large a force as possible, under the best commander, to insure the discomfiture of Grant's army. To do this and gain the great advantage that would accrue from it, the safety of points practically less important than those endangered by his army must be hazarded. Upon the defence of the country threatened by General Grant depends the safety of the points now held by us on the Atlantic, and they are in as great danger from his successful advance as by the attacks to which they are at present directly subjected." Lee saw in December, 1863, the probability of what was to happen in December, 1864, and sought to prevent it by an immediate concentration.

The answer to this letter came in a telegram from the President: "Could you consistently go to Dalton . . ?" Davis asked. Lee did not want to make the exchange of commands. He did not feel that he had the strength to undertake an active campaign with a demoralized army in unfamiliar country. What was needed was an able, permanent commander who knew the officers and had the vigor to suppress their rivalries. Besides, if he left the Army of Northern Virginia, a new leader would have to be assigned to it, for Ewell was too feeble to direct it. It seemed, however, as if the President were determined to act, for on December 9 Lee received a summons to Richmond. Lee interpreted the message to mean that he was to be ordered to the far south. At that prospect, the affection Lee had formed for the Army of Northern Virginia asserted itself. In a hurried note to Stuart he wrote,

"My heart and thoughts will always be with this army," but there he stopped. His was not a nature to sentimentalize.

Lee departed that same day, December 9. Arriving in Richmond, he went to quarters his wife had rented on Leigh Street. They were in a two-story wooden house, a humble place compared with Arlington, but the first home of their own in which the members of the family had been able to gather since the outbreak of the war. As Lee sat down in this new abode, he must have heard many stories of the wanderings of the family during the exciting months when he could keep in touch with them only by hurried letters that often were delayed and sometimes went astray.

There were griefs enough. Mrs. Lee's condition was definitely worse, and though she still talked bravely of what she could do when she could walk again, she could not get about even with the aid of her crutches and had to use a rolling-chair. Rooney's capture was a constant grief to the family, and not least to his father. Charlotte's condition became daily more serious; all her vitality seemed to be gone. Custis Lee was unhappy, too. His brothers and kinsmen had been in nearly all the great battles of the Army of Northern Virginia; he had occupied a sheltered position as one of the President's aides, a post of honor, yet not to his liking. His great desire was to see field service, but his keen conscience made him feel that he should not undertake it without experience, nor did either he or his father consider that he should ask for a transfer.

Still another shadow hung over the household. Under a law passed by the U. S. Congress in June, 1862 (as amended February 6, 1863), direct taxes had been levied on real estate "in the insurrectionary districts within the United States." Commissioners were empowered, in case of default, to sell the property, and as the aim of the act was, in effect, to expropriate the holdings of Southern men in occupied territory, the officials held to the rule that they would only accept payment from the owners in person. On behalf of the Lees their cousin, Philip R. Fendall, tendered the taxes imposed on Arlington, $92.07 with a penalty of 50 per cent. The commissioners refused to receive the money and were preparing to issue a tax title to the United States. The old home, the centre of the life of the family, was about to be lost —for delinquent taxes in theory, by confiscation in fact.

Thus, when Lee came home that evening of December 9, he realized how heavily the war had smitten his family—their home had been lost, Mrs. Lee was almost helpless in her invalidism, one son was in prison, the General's brilliant first-born was unhappy because of his assignment, one daughter was dead in a far-off cemetery, and his only daughter-in-law was not far from death. Lee himself, who had entered the struggle in the full vigor of robust manhood, was aging hourly, his hair and beard white.

But there was little time to dwell on family woes. The question that had brought him to Richmond had to be discussed in long conferences with the President. Lee remained willing to assume the difficult task in Georgia if the President thought it proper to send him there. In talking with Senator B. H. Hill, he said simply: "I have no ambition but to serve the Confederacy and do all I can to win our independence. I am willing to serve in any capacity to which the authorities may assign me." But he held to his belief that others could accomplish more with the Army of Tennessee than he could hope to do, and when he found the President indisposed to name Beauregard to succeed Bragg, as he had originally advised, it seems probable that he urged the appointment of General Johnston to the command. There was some delay in a decision, while Mr. Davis waited for information from the Southwest, but by about the 15th it was settled that Lee would not be ordered to Dalton. On December 16 Johnston was assigned to the post with instructions to reorganize the army and to prepare for an offensive as soon as practicable.

General Averell was on another of his raids at the time. Though the officers at Lee's headquarters were loath to forward him all the stories that came in concerning the move, Lee learned enough to make him anxious to return to the army, but the Federals contrived to get quickly away after burning the station and the supplies at Salem, Va. There was, consequently, no special reason why Lee should hurry back to the Rapidan, and there were numerous personal reasons why he should spend Christmas with his family. Why should he not remain?

At Lee's camp, his aides were asking the same question and were not envious of his good fortune. But in accordance with his character to suppress personal desire when in conflict with the performance of his duty, on December 21, Lee appeared in camp. He had deliberately sacrificed his Christmas to set an example of obedience to duty.

It was a gloomy Christmas he had in his tent, oppressed by Mrs. Lee's condition and by Charlotte's illness, though the news from Charlotte had been somewhat encouraging. On the 26th Lee was hopeful that she might recover, but that evening he received from Custis a telegram announcing her death.

The first three months of 1864 were spent in a routine similar to that

which Lee had taken up after Burnside's "Mud March" in the winter of
1862–63. On February 22, Lee went to Richmond to confer with Mr.
Davis on the military outlook. He spent much time with the President
and with General Bragg, who had come to Richmond to act as Mr.
Davis's adviser. The visit was interrupted on February 29 by news
that General Kilpatrick and Colonel Ulric Dahlgren had launched a
raid on Richmond. Lee passed up the railroad only a few hours before
Dahlgren struck it, and once again narrowly escaped capture. Dahlgren
and Kilpatrick were repulsed at the Richmond defenses, and Dahlgren
was later killed in King and Queen County. On his body was found an
address to his soldiers, directing that the prisoners in Richmond be released, that the city be burned, and that President Davis and his Cabinet
be killed. This paper created an immense stir and prompted General
Lee to make formal inquiry of General Meade as to its authenticity.

These were the only operations of importance in northern and
central Virginia until Grant opened the Wilderness campaign in May,
1864.

There was abundant work, however, at headquarters. Lee the
strategist had to be Lee the diplomatist. It was his task to remove the
incompetent, to promote the deserving, to humble the arrogant, to
soothe the sensibilities of the disappointed, and to prepare the command once more for the cruel exactions of what might be the decisive
campaign.

The assignment of new officers to brigade and divisional command
had been under way since the close of the Gettysburg campaign. The
most important position to fill had been that of a successor to General
Pender. On August 1, Lee had recommended Brigadier General Cadmus
M. Wilcox. To succeed Pettigrew, he had chosen W. W. Kirkland, and
in the place of the fallen Semmes he had selected Goode Bryan. Perrin
had been given McGowan's old brigade, temporarily; John Pegram
had been assigned to that formerly led by William Smith. In the absence
of Rooney Lee, the able John R. Chambliss was named to head his
command, and in March, 1864, Brigadier General N. H. Harris was
designated to handle the brigade of Carnot Posey, who had died on
November 13, 1863, of wounds received at Bristoe Station. In making
these and all other promotions Lee was mindful not only of valor and
leadership displayed on the field but also of discipline maintained in
camp and on the march.

That the Army of Northern Virginia did not decline in morale during the winter of 1863–64 was due, first, to its previous record of victories. Soldiers who had triumphed at Second Manassas, at Fredericksburg, and at Chancellorsville refused to regard Gettysburg, Bristoe Station, and Rappahannock Bridge as anything more than a succession of unhappy accidents. The adaptability of the individual contributed, in the second place, to the army's morale during the same shivering months. The men's ingenuity increased in proportion to their hardships. Still a third factor was the invincible good cheer of the troops. The sternest experience was softened by their jokes, as in the case of the hungry infantryman who came upon a group of commissary officers seated under a clump of trees and enjoying an ample dinner. The soldier walked up to the fence that surrounded the grove, put his head through the palings, gazed longingly, and remarked with fine satire, "I say, misters, did any of you ever hearn tell of the battle of Chancellorsville?" An army that ate the meal of mirth could keep its morale even on the rancid bacon and cornbread that often formed its only ration. Religion was another factor in sustaining the spirit of the soldiers through the long, blusterous months on the Rapidan. That winter 15,000 men were converted, and many of them were fired with a faith that defied the battle.

Lee himself was a force no less potent in preserving the morale of the army. His methods were as simple as they were effective. They reflected his own character and his interest in the welfare of the men entrusted to him, and in no sense did they bespeak any ordered, calculating analysis of what would or would not inspire soldiers. He rode frequently among the camps. Sometimes the men would cheer him; more often they received him with a silence that was almost reverent. Yet they never hesitated to bring him their complaints, in the knowledge that he would always receive them as friends in a common cause. Lee's respect for the individuality of his men extended to their wants and their duties. He was quick to defend them against discrimination and against imposition. The spiritual needs of his men he supplied, also, as best he could. Some of his generals, less religious in nature than he, fell into the habit of making Sunday a time for reviews and festivities. He issued a general order for the better observance of the Sabbath. He went regularly to church, and not infrequently attended the chaplains' meetings. His regard for his men produced in them something akin to the idolatry of youth for greatness.

Typical of Lee was an incident late in the winter of 1863–64. A scout arrived at headquarters with reports of a heavy movement of troop trains along the Baltimore and Ohio. The scout, only a boy in years, had ridden one horse to death in order to reach Lee speedily and was close to collapse. Lee listened to him and left for a moment to issue an order. When he returned he found that the boy had toppled over from his camp-stool and had fallen half on the General's cot, in the deep sleep of exhaustion. Lee covered him and left him alone until his cramped position caused him to awaken, two hours later. Then the General supplied him with food and saw to it that he received proper care.

Perhaps the best tribute to him was paid when some of the infantry were discussing the *Origin of Species*, which had then been published less than four years. Darwinism had its warm advocates, but one soldier refused to accept the arguments. "Well, boys," he said, "the rest of us may have developed from monkeys; but I tell you none less than God could have made such a man as 'Marse Robert.' "

The material wants of the men who gave him this measure of admiration could not be supplied that winter. Some of the worst wear-and-tear in clothing and footgear had been offset by September, 1863, but as the fall advanced and the weather grew worse, the depletion of Confederate credits abroad and the capture of several ships loaded with quartermaster stores resulted in such a shortage that shoes were worn out faster than they could be replaced.

Worse even than the shortage of shoes and blankets was the lack of food for the men. By December the government had only twenty-five days' supply of beef and bacon east of the Mississippi and had no reserve whatsoever in Virginia. In January the shortage of cereals was almost as acute. The daily ration had to be cut to four ounces of bacon or salt pork, with only one pint of corn meal per man. There were weeks, of course, during which the rations of some of the units were ample, but the periods of want were so frequent and so prolonged that Lee had to inform the administration in the most sombre terms that ruin was threatened if the army was not rationed.

It was not Lee's nature to content himself with explaining to the administration inevitable consequences. Through the whole of the winter, he strove himself to correct these conditions. The subsistence of the troops became his first and greatest concern.

What could he do to get food for the men? First of all the improvement of the railroads and the better use of their rolling stock were essential. Lee had long foreseen the danger of a collapse of the railways.

One of his first orders after assuming command in March, 1862, had been designed to straighten out a railroad tangle, and now, with the crisis at hand, he conserved his rail transportation with the utmost care. Thanks to this co-operation, the energetic administration of a new quartermaster-general, A. R. Lawton, kept the wheels turning and prevented the collapse that would otherwise have occurred. In March, 1864, Lawton was able to report that the creaking lines were hauling more than at almost any other period of the war, though it was admittedly a "forced march."

Lee's second method of providing food for his men was through raids into western and southwestern Virginia. At his own head-quarters, he set an example of the utmost frugality. Luxuries sent by admirers he dispatched to the hospitals, and as protests were made, he replied simply, "I am content to share the rations of my men." Once when he had guests, he ordered middling bacon with the cabbage, but when the diners sat down, the meat was so scant that all of them politely declined it. The next day, recalling that the meat had not been eaten, he bade his steward bring it—only to be met with the confession that there had been no bacon at headquarters and that what he had seen the previous day had been borrowed and had been duly returned to its owner, untouched.

The shortage that Lee sought to ease by these measures extended equally to the feed for the horses. At the end of August, 1863, promises had been made that the army would be supplied with 3000 bushels of corn a day, but before the middle of November the amount had fallen off so heavily that Lee feared many animals would be lost during the winter. Ere long the supply declined to 1000 bushels a day and the hay and fodder were relatively even less. There was no misreading the ominous meaning of this slow starvation of the horses. The loss through hunger and disease was heavy. Longstreet had been unable to take all his batteries to Georgia for lack of horses to pull the guns. Half of the animals in Stuart's horse artillery were reported to have died during the winter, and a reduction in the number of his batteries seemed inevitable. Five days before the opening of Grant's offensive, May 4, 1864, Lee reported that he was unable to get the troops together for want of forage.

To the burden of maintaining the army's morale and of finding food for its personnel and horses was added the labor of recruiting the ranks for the coming campaign. The General saw his forces reduced by the departure of Longstreet's corps, then raised to around 48,000 men from October through December by the return of the wounded, and then diminished again by furloughs and detachments to around 35,000 at the middle of February.

Lee's chief hope of building up his army to effective fighting strength lay in procuring the return of the detached units. His next hope was in a sterner policy of conscription that would bring into the ranks those who were still evading military duty. It was manifest that a more drastic statute and more vigorous enforcement were necessary. Lee threw all his influence on the side of universal compulsory service. "The law," he wrote the President, "should not be open to the charge of partiality, and I do not know how this can be accomplished, without embracing the whole population capable of bearing arms, with the most limited exemptions, avoiding anything that would look like a distinction of classes. The exemptions of persons of particular and necessary avocations had better be made as far as possible by authority of the department rather than by special enactment."

Conditions were corrected to some extent by the act approved on February 17, 1864, which lowered the age-limit to seventeen and raised it to fifty years with the proviso that the oldest and youngest recruits should be organized for state defense. Much stronger regulations concerning exemptions and disability were put into effect the next month. Substitution was barred by another statute.

Having done his utmost through official channels to have the law made more effective, Lee had to rely, for the rest, on careful administration of the army to increase its combatant strength. His first measures, which took a wide diversity of form, were designed to prevent the wastage of the troops he had. He exercised great vigilance in refusing to issue furloughs except in accordance with the general policy he had laid down to send numbers of his men home in order to relieve the pressure on the commissary. The policy of keeping down wastage from the ranks Lee applied, in the same way, to all details for detached duty. He declined to detail men because their families had need of them, or because there were many brothers of the same family in the army. "It is impossible," he said, "to equalize the burdens of this war; some must suffer more than others."

Direct recruitment and re-enlistment were Lee's second method of internal administration for the maintenance of his armed strength. Taking care not to interfere with the regular work of conscription, he offered a thirty-day furlough to every private soldier who procured an able-bodied recruit. Everywhere that Lee could find a recruit, he sought to bring him into the ranks. Even the guards at Camp Lee in Richmond were called up.

His labor was ceaseless in keeping up the spirit of the men, in finding food for them, in saving the horses from starvation, and in trying to fill the ranks. No campaign wore on Lee with greater severity than did the cruel winter of 1863–64. Every resource of mind, all his physical energy, and all the character he had built up through his years of self-control he threw into the struggle to keep his army in condition to fight. He knew that success depended on calling out the full resources of the country. Determined to do his utmost to that end, he did not permit himself to think what might happen if the country was unwilling to make the necessary sacrifices. That he left to God. Submissive, though determined, he did not quail, even when he read that Lincoln had called for 700,000 new troops in March. Seven hundred thousand . . . and the Army of Northern Virginia could not hope to muster 65,000 when Meade crossed the Rapidan!

As the end of winter approached, Lee began to shape his plan for active operations. He no longer could be guided exclusively by what was desirable in Virginia. He had to consider what was practicable with his reduced supplies and weakened transport; and he had to adapt his scheme of operations to the increasing threat of a Federal invasion of Georgia.

How could this dangerous invasion be prevented? Johnston did not believe he should take the offensive until he was reinforced and sup-plied with more transportation. Longstreet concluded that the Con-federate armies must advance or be overwhelmed. The administration was for an aggressive policy but was unwilling to strip other parts of the Confederacy to swell Johnston's ranks. Lee was too busy with the problems of his own army to make a full study of the strategic involve-ments in Tennessee, and, as General Bragg was now chief military ad-viser to the President, Lee's inclination against volunteering advice to his superiors was stiffened by military etiquette. Longstreet wrote him often and at length. Longstreet's first proposal was that he be recalled to Lee, that one corps of the army be mounted, and that it be thrown in rear of Meade. Lee pointed out that this was impracticable and urged that Johnston and Longstreet attack the Federals. Longstreet next asked for sufficient horses to mount his corps and to operate in Ken-tucky. Lee thought an advance into Kentucky would be desirable, but horses could not be supplied without rendering immobile other armies of the Confederacy. Longstreet then advanced the remarkable proposal that Lee hold Richmond with part of his troops, take the rest to Kentucky, open an offensive there and leave Johnston free to move to Virginia. At this stage of the correspondence, Lee went to Richmond and learned the administration favored joint operations by Johnston and Longstreet in middle Tennessee. A few days later Longstreet arrived at Lee's headquarters and unfolded still another plan—that Beauregard be sent to join the First Corps and that these forces execute the proposed offensive into Kentucky.

This appealed to Lee as more feasible, and he urged that Longstreet present the proposal to the chief executive. Longstreet argued that it would be far better if Lee put forward the plan. Lee agreed to go to Richmond with Longstreet and to present the question to the President. He called on the President by himself Monday morning, March 14, but there is no record of what happened at this meeting. After dinner, he returned with Longstreet to Mr. Davis's office and the three of them discussed the situation in detail without arriving at any conclusion. Longstreet later wrote an account of this council in which he represented General Lee as much disgusted at the insistence of the President and General Bragg on a campaign into middle Tennessee. It is probable that Longstreet's zeal led him to exaggerate Lee's disappointment, for Lee as late as April 2 was in favor of the operation in middle Tennessee. His inclination, however, was to defer to the judgment of General Johnston who was on the ground.

After these conferences Lee spent a few days in Richmond with his family. The family had moved to "The Mess," a large house, now numbered 707 East Franklin, that had been used previously by Custis and some of his fellow staff officers. Rooney had at last been exchanged and had come home, almost broken-hearted over Charlotte's death. It took no small effort on the part of General Lee to get his son to pull himself together again and to resume his military duties. Custis's state of mind was much the same as before: anxious for field duty, he still had scruples about undertaking it without experience.

Back in the camps on the Rapidan, Lee thought for a few days that the shock of battle was to come in Tennessee, but by March 28 he concluded that the blow would fall in Virginia. Signs multiplied that the Federals were accumulating a large force in his front. As it became increasingly probable that the Unionists were detaching troops from

the western army for use in Virginia, Lee reasoned that this might give
Johnston a better opportunity for aggressive action, even though Longstreet was recalled to the Army of Northern Virginia. On April 7
Longstreet was ordered to return from Bristol, Va.-Tenn., to Charlottesville to await Lee's orders.

Lee's balancing of the ponderables on the military scales was accurate.
He could not realize that an imponderable was tipping the beam. That
imponderable was the influence of President Lincoln. The Richmond
government had discounted Lincoln's every moderate utterance and
had capitalized his emancipation proclamation in order to stiffen Southern resistance. The Confederate people had mocked him. Lee had made
the most of the President's military blunders and fears. But Lee had
been much more interested in the Federal field-commanders than in the
commander-in-chief. After the late winter of 1863–64, had Lee known
all the facts, he would have given as much care to the study of the
mind of the Federal President as to the analysis of the strategical methods of his immediate adversaries. For that remarkable man, who had
never wavered in his purpose to preserve the Union, had now mustered
all his resources of patience and of determination. Those who had
sought to lead him found he was leading them. His unconquerable
spirit was being infused into the North.

By April 3 Lee commenced preparations for meeting the army the
Federals were mustering. The Northern states were responding whole-
heartedly to the calls sent out in March for 700,000 men. Ulysses S.
Grant, a soldier equipped with abilities that complemented Lincoln's,
had been brought from the West and placed in command of all the
Union armies. The enemy could not move until the highways dried,
though there was every prospect that as soon as the ground was firm,
Grant would cross the river.

Lee studied reports from his spies and on April 16 was satisfied that
three attacks were in the making—a main assault across the Rapidan, a
diversion in the Valley, and an attack probably directed against
Drewry's Bluff on James River, so as to expose the water-line of
Richmond.

How could this offensive be met? Lee believed that much might be
accomplished by Confederate action in the West. The alternative to
this was an advance against Meade. His judgment now told him that
the prudent course was to bring Beauregard's army to defend Richmond and to hasten the movement of Longstreet's corps from Bristol.
This done, he desired to "move right against the enemy on the Rappa-

hannock." His confidence was not shaken by the strength of the Army of the Potomac or by the prestige of General Grant. If the flanking movement against Richmond could be successfully met, he said quietly, "I have no uneasiness as to the result of the campaign in Virginia."

The offensive if practicable, the defensive if inevitable—between these courses the government had to decide, and decide not only according to its judgment of the strategic situation but also according to its ability to supply the army. Johnston was still unprepared to take the offensive; the danger to Richmond from the east was increasing, while the threat against Charleston was formidable; the commissary could do little for the soldiers and the quartermaster general less for the horses. The administration had to compromise. Longstreet's movement was continued to Gordonsville so that he would be available in case of an attack on Richmond. Beauregard was hurried north and put in charge of forces between the James and the Cape Fear Rivers.

On the 18th Lee issued orders to prepare for movement. Hourly ears strained for the opening gun; but the enemy's advance was held up.

On the morning of May 2 Lee climbed to the observation post on Clark's Mountain and, after studying with his glasses the location of the corps spread out beneath him and the rolling fields of Culpeper, he told his companions that the enemy's crossing would be at Ely's or at Germanna—the fords that led into the Wilderness. He knew he could count on the valor of those who had fought the bloodiest battles that ever drenched America. The morale of the army was now at its finest fighting pitch. The spirit of the army was the spirit of its leader. "You must sometimes cast your thoughts on the Army of Northern Virginia," he told one of his young cousins, "and never forget it in your prayers. It is preparing for a great struggle, but I pray and trust that the great God, mighty to deliver, will spread over it His almighty arms, and drive its enemies before it."

CHAPTER XII

The Wilderness

AT 9 O'CLOCK May 4, 1864, the signal station atop Clark's Mountain spelled out the message that was the beginning of the end of the Confederacy: The enemy was streaming down the road to Germanna and to Ely's Ford. The campaign was opening at last.

Lee was expecting that the enemy would move against his right flank. He ordered A. P. Hill to leave R. H. Anderson's division to guard the approaches to the "Gordonsville loop" of the Virginia Central Railroad, with instructions to rejoin his corps as soon as it was certain that the enemy had disappeared from that front. Ewell was directed to have Ramseur's brigade cover the lower crossings of the Rapidan. The rest of Ewell's and Hill's corps Lee ordered eastward to meet the advance. Longstreet was told to move to Todd's Tavern, where he could form the Confederate right.

Lee started along the familiar Plank road with Hill's corps. Ewell took the parallel route of the turnpike nearer the Rapidan. The ranks of neither corps were full. They numbered around 28,000 men. In the two corps were perhaps 4000 artillery. In scattered units Lee could count about 8400 cavalry, though it was questionable whether the horses could stand the strain of open campaigning. When Longstreet came up and Anderson rejoined, Lee would muster of all arms between 61,000 and 65,000 with 213 guns. In discipline and experience, the combat-force was better than it ever had been. Sickness was negligible, despite the fact that the rations barely sufficed to sustain life. In leadership, it was very different from the army that had fought at Chancellorsville or at Gettysburg. But most of the general officers were capable men, and if some of them were lacking in experience, Lee had full assurance that their soldiers were not.

Lee's scouts reported that the enemy would move with 100,000, but Lee did not think Grant's force exceeded 75,000 and he was skeptical

370

concerning the reputed size of the army that was expected to make a flank attack on Richmond while Grant hammered on the line of the Rapidan and Rappahannock. Lee was not certain, either, whether Grant would follow Meade's example, and turn southwest toward the Central Railroad after crossing the Rapidan, or would emulate Hooker and march to the southeast, against the line of the Richmond, Fredericksburg and Potomac below Fredericksburg. If Grant moved toward the southwest, Lee could hold his old lines on Mine Run with a part of his force and manoeuvre with the rest. Should Grant advance to the southeast, he would have to pass through the Wilderness of Spotsylvania.

Lee hoped that this latter would be his opponent's line of advance. His plan was to catch Grant on the march, where numerical superiority would mean least. He was anxious to engage the new commander in the Wilderness, where Federal ordnance could not be employed. Lee determined to leave Grant alone until he was south of the river. Then he intended to attack, as soon as Longstreet came up. Lee bivouacked at Verdiersville, where his headquarters had been during the Mine Run campaign.

To Lee's camp fire couriers brought many messages, encouraging and disquieting. Davis telegraphed reinforcements were on the way. In another message, the President announced that a Federal force had landed at Bermuda Hundred on James River, close to the railroad that linked Richmond and Petersburg. General Imboden reported a Union force under General Sigel advancing up the Shenandoah Valley, probably moving against Lee's left flank. There was new evidence that General Averell was preparing a raid against the Virginia and Tennessee Railroad. The enemy was taking the offensive in four directions. Lee's view was not confused by minor operations. In a letter written before news of the landing at Bermuda Hundred, he told the President, "It seems to me that the great efforts of the enemy here and in Georgia have begun, and that the necessity of our concentration at both points is immediate and imperative."

While assuming that Grant would seek the initiative, Lee was not disposed to yield it. Longstreet reported that he hoped to be at Richards' Shop, six miles south of Verdiersville, by noon the next day, May 5. On this assurance, Lee determined to attack Grant.

Late in the night Stuart advised Lee that the enemy still was in the Wilderness. The next morning Lee became satisfied that the enemy intended to pass through its gloomy mazes in an effort to turn his

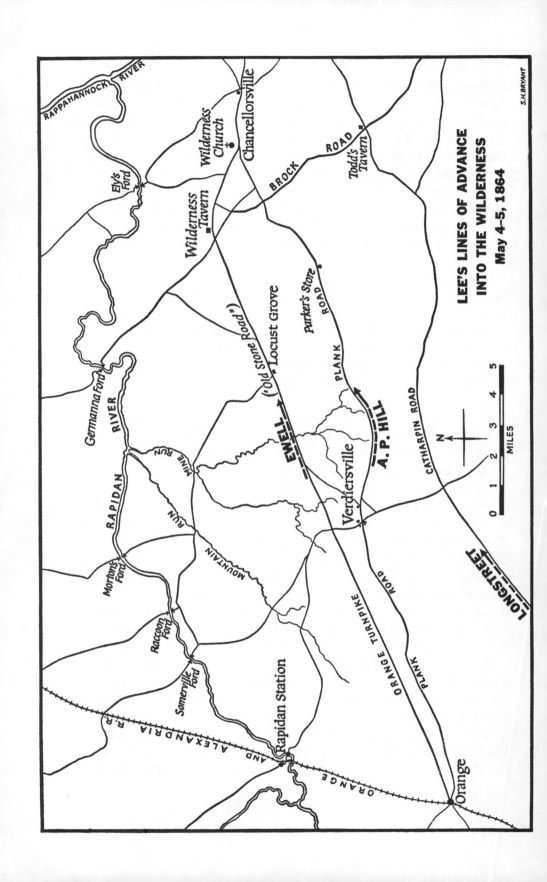

LEE'S LINES OF ADVANCE
INTO THE WILDERNESS
May 4-5, 1864

S.H.BRYANT

right. As this was precisely what he most desired, the prospect raised Lee's spirits.

Soon the Third Corps was ready to go forward. Lee rode at its head with A. P. Hill, preceded by Stuart and his cavalry. Not long after the column entered the Wilderness, Major Campbell Brown of Ewell's staff rode up and reported that the Second Corps was advancing along the old stone road and wished instructions. Lee sent word to Ewell, who was somewhat ahead of Hill, to regulate his advance by that of the Third Corps. While he did not absolutely forbid Ewell to meet the enemy, he expressed his preference that a major battle should not be precipitated until the arrival of Longstreet.

Shortly after 11 o'clock Ewell could see Federals crossing the turnpike by the route from Germanna Ford and moving in a southeasterly direction. About noon, however, there came from the direction of the old stone road the sound of heavy firing. Hill moved on and brushed aside a cavalry attack on his right flank. At this stage of the advance, the first tactical obstacle was encountered, an obstacle that played a large part in the fighting that followed: The course of the turnpike and that of the Plank road were diverging, and the space between them was now so wide that there was no contact between Hill's left on the Plank road and Ewell's right on the turnpike. Lee could not tell what the firing from Ewell's front indicated, or how the Second Corps was faring in an action that swelled steadily in violence.

For two miles Lee rode on ahead of Heth's division. Shortly before 3 o'clock, he reached a grove whence there was a view down the valley of Wilderness Run. Near the home of the widow Tapp he dismounted with Hill and Stuart to study the ground.

Lee was concerned at the separation of the two corps. There was danger that Grant would find the gap between Hill's left and Ewell's right. The Federals might pour into the unguarded area and turn the exposed flanks of both corps. As if to confirm this fear, a blue skirmish line deployed from the cover of some old-field pines. The Federals were as surprised at meeting graycoats as the Confederates were at seeing them and quickly withdrew.

Heth had scarcely been placed across the Plank road in line of battle, when the Federals attacked furiously. The woods were so thick that the enemy could scarcely be seen. The enemy's first onslaught was beaten off; but a second assault followed the first, and a third the second. Still the lines held.

Slowly the weight of attack began to shift to the Confederate right.

Lee reasoned that the Federals might be pulling away from Ewell. This might offer the Second Corps an opportunity of getting on the Federals' right and of reaching their line of supply from across the Rapidan. A message was sent to Ewell at 6 P.M. to make this move if possible. In case Ewell met resistance too heavy to be overcome, Lee planned to turn the Federal left, upon the arrival of Longstreet and of R. H. Anderson. Lee sent instructions to Longstreet to come up in support of Hill along the Plank road.

By the time these messages were on their way, a fourth and a fifth Federal attack had been made. Both had been repulsed, but they had been delivered with as much vigor as the Federals had ever displayed against the Army of Northern Virginia. Two divisions could not stand indefinitely against a repetition of these assaults. Lee sent Major H. B. McClellan of Stuart's staff to find General Field, whose division was heading Longstreet's advance, and to tell him to speed his march.

Night was drawing on when a new fury of fire came to Lee from the extreme right. This proved to be, in part, from Lane's brigade, which Wilcox had moved to meet a fresh threat there. Lane's was the last brigade Hill had at his disposal. Just as that grim fact became apparent word was received from Wilcox that the enemy was again pushing into the gap between his line and the right of Ewell. Reinforcements must be sent—but whence were they to come? The only troops not actually engaged were about 125 men of the Fifth Alabama battalion, who were guarding the prisoners. As quickly as possible, these Alabamians were hurried in, with a yell that must have created a false impression of their numbers. They hurled back the enemy. That was the last infantry attack. Firing died away after 8 P.M. Hill's estimate was that his 14,500 men had fought 40,000.

Ewell now sent a report that he, too, had been vigorously assailed. Jones's brigade of Johnson's division had been attacked about noon and had been thrown back on Battle, whose ranks had been disorganized. Daniel's brigade had been brought up and John B. Gordon, of Early's division, had delivered a brilliant counterattack. The corps had then been put in line of battle and had been instructed to throw up earthworks. The fighting had been so intense that the muskets of Pegram's brigade had become too hot to handle, but the enemy had suspended his attacks, and the Second Corps would be able, Ewell said, to hold its ground.

It had been a hard day's fighting. Significant was that the Federals

had not waited to be attacked but had advanced quickly to challenge
the Confederates. Grant obviously did not intend to allow the Army
of Northern Virginia to take the initiative and to assail him on the
march. Still, the enemy had been halted in the Wilderness, and Grant's
plan of moving around the right flank had been disclosed. That was
gain. During the afternoon Lee had considered attacking the next day
from his left, but Longstreet and Anderson could come up more
quickly on the right than on the left. Besides, there was more ground
for manoeuvring on the right. If the three divisions due to arrive during
the night could get on the Federal flank south of the Plank road, roll
up the Union line and throw Grant back against the fords of the
Rapidan, that would be the end of another "On to Richmond."

The lines of Heth and of Wilcox were badly disarranged. It was
desirable to straighten out the front and to establish entrenchments, but
this was impracticable. The simplest course seemed the safest—to leave
the men where they were and to relieve them with Longstreet's corps
upon its arrival. Field should be up by midnight. The line could be
taken over by comparatively fresh men, that dangerous gap between
Hill and Ewell could be filled, and the turning movement could be
begun at daylight.

Lee had just sat down to supper when Major H. B. McClellan made
his report. With suppressed indignation, he said that Field had refused
to accept the verbal orders and had stated he was under instructions
from General Longstreet to move at 1 A.M. Instead of arriving by
midnight, the head of Longstreet's corps would hardly reach the lines
until daylight, when the enemy would be astir.

When Lee learned this he did not communicate it to Wilcox or to
Heth. He probably reasoned that nothing was to be gained by arousing
the apprehension of the tired commanders. Nor did he order the front of
the Third Corps fortified, because he intended Longstreet's men to
take up and entrench a line drawn a short distance in rear of Wilcox
and Heth.

Sunrise found the Third Corps still scattered through the Wilderness,
with little semblance of a line. At 5 o'clock the Federal infantry opened
fire at close range and soon was attacking hotly. The Confederates made
such resistance as they could and contrived for perhaps half an hour
to retard the enemy. To their calls for assistance, Lee sent an urgent
appeal that they hold on until Longstreet was at hand. Soon stragglers
began to leave the front; presently Wilcox's line began to give ground;

then it went to pieces, except directly on the road, and men came pouring to the westward. It was a sudden crisis of a sort the army had never known except at Sharpsburg.

One glance showed Lee that the fate of the day and the control of the army were in the balance. Swiftly he ordered Taylor to prepare the wagon train for instant retreat in case the corps could not be halted. Then he hurried to help rally the retreating soldiers. Still men were rushing down the road and across the fields. A little more and the enemy would sweep on—what was there to stop him? Only the hope that Longstreet would come up at that moment!

Lee rode back into Mrs. Tapp's field. There were still Confederates east of the house—wounded men mostly. Should the artillery wait until these troops passed? Not one minute longer, Hill said, could the artillery delay! If it did, the guns would all be captured. But Poague's guns were already loaded; the command rang out; twelve belching pieces filled the woods with fire. Another round, and then another. The enemy only 200 yards away. Around Lee the choking smoke and excited cannoneers; behind him a wild scene of confusion. Then through the smoke, twenty or more ragged soldiers running with their muskets in their hands—not to the rear but into the space where Poague's guns were still vomiting grape. The Texans—Hood's Texans, of Longstreet's corps, just at the right place and at the right moment!

In rising excitement, Lee yelled to them to form line of battle at once. As the veterans sprang into position, a brigade of them now, he rode to the left of the line. He would lead them in the countercharge. The line started forward. He spurred Traveller through an opening in the gun pits, and was on the heels of the infantrymen. Then they realized what he intended to do. "Go back, General Lee, go back!" they cried. He paid no heed to them. "We won't go on unless you go back!" He did not hear them. Nothing stopped him until Colonel Venable arrived. Longstreet was at hand, Venable shouted; had he not better turn aside and give Longstreet his orders? Like a man coming out of a trance, Lee slowly pulled back his horse; he waved his hat to the onrushing Texans and went back to Longstreet—to be told bluntly that he should go farther behind the lines.

He left Longstreet to direct the counter-movement and busied himself with providing artillery support. Quickly, too, he began reforming Wilcox and Heth on the left of Longstreet. Most of the troops of the Third Corps had retreated only some 300 yards and now were ready to fight again. Lee sent them to fill the gap between their flank and Ewell's. Not long after Colonel William H. Palmer came galloping to report Hill had found a force between the Second and Third Corps and wished the loan of a brigade of Anderson's division in order that he might have enough men to capture the Federals who had ventured so far. Lee had given orders for Anderson to report to Longstreet and was loath to detach any part of the division without the knowledge of its temporary chief. He and Palmer rode together through the swelling accompaniment of a violent fire on a lengthening front and reached Longstreet just as Anderson's division was reporting, about 8 A.M. "General Hill," said Lee, "wants one of Anderson's brigades."

Old Pete was in his glory then. His troops were advancing faultlessly. "Certainly, Colonel," he said, addressing himself to Palmer, "which one will you take?" "The leading one," said Palmer, implying that all brigades of the Third Corps were equally good.

Palmer led the troops off, and Lee returned to follow the furious fighting up the Plank road. The counterattack of Longstreet's veterans had halted the Federals and now was forcing them back slowly toward temporary works. Before 10 o'clock the first stage of the battle was over. The Federal attack on Hill had been beaten off; the enemy on the whole of the Confederate right flank had been driven back beyond the positions he had occupied at the opening of the engagement; the front was momentarily stabilized.

What next? Lee had planned the previous evening to turn the Union left south of the Plank road. Now, General W. T. Wofford suggested to Longstreet that he use Anderson and part of his own corps to get on the left flank of the Federals. General M. L. Smith, the new chief engineer of the army, was sent to see if there was a route by which the turning movement could be executed. He found the cut of an unfinished railroad from Orange to Fredericksburg. Longstreet ordered his adjutant general, Lieutenant Colonel Moxley Sorrel, to conduct three brigades to the railroad cut, under Smith's direction, and to throw them against the enemy's flank which, Smith said, extended only a short distance south of the Plank road. Lee was willing for the manoeuvre to be made but left the execution entirely to the corps commander.

At length, about 11 o'clock, there swelled from the Confederate right the sudden roar of a new attack. Led by Colonel Sorrel, four brigades had moved to the railroad cut and now were advancing northward against the left of Meade's army. Soon the enemy's line was being rolled up. Some of the Union brigades were already routed. The victorious

Confederates were close to the Plank road; a general advance of the whole right wing was ordered. Longstreet had sufficient men. With their help and that of the troops already in line, Longstreet believed that Grant's army could be hurled back, a broken and confused mass, against the fords of the Rapidan. A tragic morning was trending to a glorious noon!

And now Longstreet's troops started forward again, some for a new flanking movement, some driving eastward to find the Federals who had retreated from the weakened front. Lee hastened toward the battle-line, in order to sustain Longstreet's attack with Hill's corps and with the artillery. When he reached the front, Longstreet, confident, almost exuberant, was just setting off with his entourage to follow the wild, cheering troops. And then a rattle of small arms up the road, a strong voice frantically crying "Friends," the sound of maddened horses galloping off, staff officers calling for surgeons . . . the Confederate troops parallel to the road evidently had fired on their own comrades advancing up it . . . some one had been hit. Longstreet had been wounded!

Colonel Sorrel came to give Lee the facts and say that Longstreet, coughing blood at every breath, urged Lee to continue the manoeuvre, which he had entrusted to General Field as ranking division commander of the corps. Lee rode to the temporary commander. He did not take the battle from Field's hands, but remained where the acting chief could consult him. The advantage had been pushed to the limit, and Longstreet had been wrong in assuming that he could hurl the enemy back to the Rapidan without disposing his troops anew. Recall of the flanking column and the drawing of a new line were exasperatingly slow tasks. Meantime the enemy was recovering from his near-panic and was bracing himself in strengthened works along the Brock road to meet a new assault. When the offensive could be renewed, it was 4:15, and the Federals could not be shaken.

Finding that nothing further could be achieved on the right, Lee rode over to the left, where, at 5:30 P.M., he found Ewell in consultation with Early and Gordon. Little had been accomplished all day by the Second Corps. Ewell and Early had nothing to propose, but Gordon said that he had found the extreme right of the Federal army exposed. He had asked permission to attack it but had not been allowed to do so. Early had been arguing against the proposal ever since Gordon had made it before 9 o'clock. Gordon had reconnoitred in person, he said, and had been several miles in the rear of the flank of the opposing force. His conviction was fixed that no troops were in support of the weak Federal right. On this statement of fact, Lee sided with Gordon and ordered him to attack. Gordon went forward with the ardor of youth. Having Robert D. Johnston's brigade in support, he swept a mile of the front of Sedgwick's corps, cut off the Army of the Potomac temporarily from its base across the Rapidan, and captured some 600 prisoners. But twilight caught the Confederates on the Union trenches and forced them back, with only their prisoners, their scant booty, and their tale of another lost opportunity. Night fell, such a night as even the Army of Northern Virginia had rarely known before. The woods were on fire in many places. Choking smoke was everywhere. It was war in Inferno.

The situation, in other respects, was not gloomy. Lee's casualties had been severe, but those of the Federals had been heavier. The enemy had been halted in his advance, repulsed on his centre, defeated on his left, and roughly handled on his right. In like circumstances Hooker had retreated: Would Grant?

The Confederates of the right wing built themselves stout entrenchments during the night and by the morning of the 7th had a strong front. But at dawn no attack came. Hours passed with only an exchange of picket fire. From the left of the Confederate line, General Early reported that the Union troops had abandoned their ground opposite his division and for part of the front of Johnson's command. This was significant. It meant that Grant had severed his line of communications via Germanna. That implied that he was not contemplating a retreat. History was failing to repeat itself. Grant was not willing to withdraw as Burnside and Hooker had done when they had been defeated. He had, however, to move before he exhausted the supplies in his wagons. In what direction was Grant going? If his purpose was to open a new line of supply, he would logically go to Fredericksburg; but if he intended an advance on Richmond, the direct road to Spotsylvania Courthouse was less than half as long as that by way of Fredericksburg.

The army must be ready to meet him. Lee directed General Pendleton to cut a way southward to the highway running from Orange Courthouse to Spotsylvania. This would give the Confederates an inner line, roughly parallel to that which the Federals would probably follow. Longstreet's corps would be the first to march over the new route to meet an advance on Spotsylvania.

But who was to lead that corps? The news from Longstreet was that his wound in the throat and shoulder would not necessarily be fatal, but months would elapse before he could resume his duties. It was no light matter to choose even a temporary successor to the senior corps commander. Three men in the army were entitled to be considered for the post—Early, Edward Johnson, and "Dick" Anderson. Much depended on the preference of the men of the First Corps: they must have the chief under whom they would fight best. To ascertain their sentiments Lee sent for Sorrel. Sorrel affirmed that Early probably was the ablest of the three under consideration but would be the most unpopular with Longstreet's men. Of Johnson he felt that some one personally known to the corps would be preferred. That brought the conversation around to Anderson. "We *know him*," Sorrel said, "and shall be satisfied with him." Lee probably preferred Early, but he could not ignore the considerations Sorrel urged and later in the day announced the temporary appointment of Anderson, with Mahone to command Anderson's division.

All day, of course, Lee studied closely every report on Grant's probable movements. Evidence had been cumulative that his adversary's objective was Spotsylvania. He sent Anderson orders to withdraw the First Corps from the line after dark and to put it in motion for the courthouse. Hill and Ewell were directed to follow Anderson.

Stealthily the Confederate skirmishers wormed their way through the shell-torn Wilderness on the morning of May 8. Cautiously the infantry peered over the rough entrenchments. Anxiously Lee waited word from the outposts. It came quickly. The Federals were gone from the Confederate left and centre. First reports indicated they had moved toward Fredericksburg. Lee so advised the War Department, but soon he received a dispatch from General Hampton stating the V Corps was on the road toward Todd's Tavern. That resort was on the road to Spotsylvania Courthouse. Lee at once set out for the courthouse and dispatched orders to Ewell to move the Second Corps to Shady Grove Church.

On his way Lee learned that A. P. Hill had become so sick overnight that it would not be possible for him to continue in command. Longstreet badly wounded on the 6th, Hill incapacitated on the 8th—two of the three corps passing into the hands of new men, and Ewell apt to collapse at any time! There could be no delay in filling Hill's place. Lee designated Early to act in his stead and arranged that Gordon should have command of Early's division.

By the time Lee reached Shady Grove Church his expectation of a Federal move to Spotsylvania had been realized: Anderson was al-

ready engaged hotly in defending it. Lee pressed on and reached the
vicinity of the courthouse before 2:30 P.M. There had been a race between his army and Grant's for Spotsylvania. Anderson had won,
though by the narrowest of margins. Both Fitz Lee and Rosser had
fought stubbornly during the morning. Federal assaults had been beaten
off with heavy loss to the enemy. It was a close escape. Anderson
deserved high credit, because he had started early and had pushed
on vigorously. Stuart had directed the defense around Spotsylvania
with the utmost skill. But behind these reasons for deliverance lay the
conclusion of Lee on the afternoon of the 7th that Grant would move
toward Spotsylvania. Had Lee not reasoned that his adversary would
march in that direction, Grant would have outgeneralled him.

There was a lull in the fighting after Lee arrived. As the afternoon
wore on, however, signs of a new effort to destroy Anderson began
to multiply. The VI Corps was reported to have come up to join the
V in a new assault. At 5 o'clock the storm broke. Over the fields
and through the woods, the long, heavy clouds of bluecoats swept.
But Confederate artillery was in position. Only on Lee's extreme right
did danger develop. But precisely at the moment it was needed, the
head of the Second Corps appeared on the road from Shady Grove.
It speedily broke up the enemy's flank attack, drove him back, and
put an end to the day's fighting.

General Lee would have his whole force again n front of the Army
of the Potomac on the morning of May 9. The movement from the
Wilderness was being completed without serious loss. The army still
stood between Grant and Richmond. That meant much. At the same
time, the enemy was in immense strength and seemed determined to
bear down all opposition. More than that, the other offensives in the
state were becoming serious. Nowhere was the pressure exerted by
the enemy lightening. A long campaign was in prospect. It was more
necessary than ever to conserve the Army of Northern Virginia. Lee
did not intend to abandon offensive strategy, if the enemy gave him an
opening, but as long as Grant continued to attack where he could be
repulsed without heavy Southern losses, it was to Lee's advantage to
maintain the defensive.

To prepare for this defensive, Lee was at his breakfast by 3 A.M.
on May 9. Longstreet's absence and Hill's illness put heavy demands
on his physique and on his intellect. Nevertheless, the line he drew when
Early brought up Hill's corps on the 9th showed his engineering skill
and military judgment unimpaired. Spotsylvania Courthouse lies on

a ridge between the Po and Ny Rivers and is a well-secured military position because the rivers, though they are not wide, are difficult to cross except where bridged.

To cover the courthouse and the three important roads that led southward from it, Lee drew a crude semicircle with the Po as its diameter. Several nights were spent in extending this front. When the line was completed the position was compact and thoroughly defensible, except for a long salient on the left centre. This was occupied by Johnson's division of the Second Corps and was to play a gloomy part in the conflict. Part of the front had open ground in the direction of the Federal advance. Elsewhere the chief weakness was that woods came close to the line. As far as practicable, abatis were set. The artillery was located with much care. Anderson held the left, Ewell the centre, and Early occupied the right.

Before Lee's field fortifications were carried as far as he desired, he had need of them. On the afternoon of the 9th, the enemy's skirmishers felt out Anderson's lines. Later in the day a strong force was reported on the south side of the Po. If this force advanced to the bend of the river it would be able to enfilade the extreme left of the Confederate line. And if the enemy continued to press eastward, south of the Po, he would reach the highway from Spotsylvania to Louisa Courthouse, along which Lee had placed his wagon train. The move, however, did put a relatively small part of the Federal army where it could be attacked. Lee made the most of this. He ordered Early to send one of his divisions to extend the left flank and to protect it from an enfilade and to dispatch another division south of the Po to assail the enemy advancing eastward. Heth's division, chosen for this purpose, moved early on May 10, found Federals that afternoon, and proceeded to attack. The Unionists at once began to withdraw, but some of the force held their ground and repulsed several assaults by Heth. In the end the Federals retired across the Po, leaving one gun and some prisoners in Confederate hands.

North of the Po, interest shifted to the point where the right of the First Corps joined the left of the Second. This part of the front had given Lee concern. On the 9th, General Lee had seen its weakness and, at the instance of General Ewell, had consented to its extension northward to include some high ground from which it was believed the Federal artillerists could dominate the Confederate position. This made that sector a great, irregular angle, with the apex to the

GENERAL AMBROSE POWELL HILL

GENERAL RICHARD STODDERT EWELL

north. The soldiers promptly dubbed it the "Mule Shoe." Lee had his
headquarters within the angle, some 150 yards in rear of Doles's brigade
of Rodes's division. This brigade occupied a position about midway
the northwest face of the salient and had a battery of the Richmond
Howitzers battalion supporting it. The condition that made the spot
vulnerable was that thick, low-hanging pine woods came within 200
yards of the works.

During the day several attacks against Anderson's lines were beaten
off. As the hot afternoon passed there were signs of Federal activity
nearer the centre. Toward 6 o'clock, heavy guns began to bombard
the western face of the salient. On the hour, the firing ceased. In about
ten minutes there was a wild cheer, followed by the opening of
infantry fire. Soon a courier hurried up to Lee with the news that
Doles's lines had been broken and the howitzers captured and that
the enemy was pouring into the salient.

Lee started forward to rally the men, but his staff protested. When
at length they dissuaded him from rushing directly into the action,
he said, "Then you must see to it that the ground is recovered." The
fire by this time was violent, but the Southern troops on either side of
the gap began to close in, and those who had been driven out reformed
on the second line. The Federals resisted with the utmost determination. They received no reinforcements, however, and were slowly
pushed out of the works. By nightfall the danger was past, and the
line had been restored. The Confederate loss was subsequently estimated at 650 but was probably higher.

To the end of the third day at Spotsylvania the attacks of the
enemy had been repelled. The margin of safety had been narrower
than usual, but there had been nothing to indicate any decline in the
prowess of the army. Its veterans suffered far less than did the Federals.
Still the enemy showed no disposition to suspend his assaults. More than
that, ugly news came from the rear. The Federal cavalry, now under
Major General Phil H. Sheridan, on the 9th had struck the Central
Railroad at Beaver Dam Creek, where two locomotives, three trains of
cars, most of the reserve stores and 504,000 rations of bread and 904,000
of meat had been destroyed. Then the Union horse had moved on
toward Richmond, while Stuart pushed the endurance of men and
mounts to the limit in an effort to get between Sheridan and Richmond.

May 11 dawned dark. Lee spent part of the morning examining the rear of Rodes's lines. He was convinced that the "Mule Shoe" could be held with the help of the artillery. He gave instructions, however, that if the enemy should attack in the vicinity of the salient, Gordon should advance Early's division in support without waiting for further orders.

During the early afternoon rain began to fall heavily. There were renewed demonstrations as if the Federals were planning to cross the Po again. Lee promptly ordered Early to send troops to the south of the river. Before Early began his move, surprising dispatches arrived from Rooney Lee, who was in rear of the enemy's left flank. He reported that the Federal wagons had been underway all night. It was impossible to tell, from the information forwarded, whether the move was southward in the direction of the Annas or in retreat to Fredericksburg. Lee felt he should prepare the army for instant movement. He directed that all guns in difficult, advanced positions should be brought off before nightfall, to prevent delay in case of sudden orders to march, and particularly ordered the artillery withdrawn from the "Mule Shoe" salient, as it had to come through thick woods by a single narrow and winding road.

The suspicions of the commanders within earshot seem to have been aroused during the evening by the unusual fact that the enemy's bands struck up about 11 o'clock and continued to play, in the rain and darkness, for hours on end. The music had scarcely died away, and the black of the night was just beginning to change to the gray of a cold, wet fog, when there came the rattle of heavy infantry fire from the salient. Riding to the front Lee soon encountered men running toward the rear. In a few moments, out of the salient, rode Major Robert W. Hunter, of the staff of General Johnson. Hunter shouted his message: "General, the line is broken at the angle in General Johnson's front!" Lee's expression changed instantly. Remembering that he had ordered Gordon to move his division forward to any point of the salient that might be threatened, he reined Traveller in. "Ride with me to General Gordon," he said, and turned to the left and rear. Perhaps on the way, Hunter had breath to tell him more—how the enemy had suddenly burst over the lines, how some of the infantry had found their charges useless because of the rain, how artillery that had been ordered back had arrived just in time for full twenty pieces to fall into the enemy's hands, how General Johnson had tried to keep the men together, and how the enemy had captured him and

General George H. Steuart and most of the division. There were thousands of bluecoats in the salient; the lines of the army were split in twain.

Two hundred yards brought Lee to the point where the left of Pegram's brigade was hurriedly forming. Still farther to the left was Gordon's brigade, under Colonel Clement A. Evans. These troops, and Johnston's four regiments, formed the whole of Early's division, which Gordon was temporarily commanding. Already Gordon had thrown out Johnston's entire brigade as skirmishers in the hope that they could hold off the enemy till the other units were ready to charge. Lee approved the dispositions the Georgian had made and directed him to proceed with the counterattack. As Gordon turned to complete his arrangements, Lee rode to the centre of the line. By this time a searching fire was penetrating the woods where the graycoats were taking position. Gordon himself had just escaped death from a bullet that grazed his coat. When he saw Lee's position, he realized that the General was preparing to join in the charge and he broke out dramatically, "General Lee, this is no place for you. Go back, General; we will drive them back." As Lee rode unwillingly back a few paces, he heard the clear voice of Gordon above the roar of the musketry: "Forward! Guide right!"

Gordon's line of battle disappeared in a dense growth. There was a wild burst of firing—next, a hoarse, quavering, rebel yell, and then comparative silence as the two lines came to grips, too close together to load and fire. As daylight came, Lee saw that Gordon was driving the Federals up the salient, but he discovered, almost simultaneously, that Gordon's lines were not long enough to cover the whole front. Others observed this before Lee could issue orders. Lane's North Carolinians rushed forward and halted the advance. Rodes threw Ramseur's brigade into action. Daniel supported Ramseur. Together they held back the flood for a time, but they were so inferior in number that Rodes began to call for reinforcements. Lee dispatched Colonel Venable to General Mahone with instructions that one brigade of Mahone be left to cover the crossing of the Po on Field's left flank and that the rest be dispatched to aid Rodes. The battle was now spreading, but the salient must be held, and, if possible, the lines must be restored.

Gordon's troops were fighting like men possessed and by this time were masters of the centre of the salient. Soon Scales and Thomas of Wilcox's division were with Lane on the right and were pushing the enemy back. By 6:30 it was apparent that the Federals were being held, and more than held, except on the left. There the battle was doubtful, for the Federals were still throwing in more and more troops. Rodes must have help—and quickly.

To provide it, Lee rode off in search of Mahone's division. He found Harris's brigade resting by the road. Lee ordered Harris forward to support Rodes and took his place by that officer's side to speed the march. The column soon came under artillery fire from long-range Federal batteries. Traveller became excited and began to rear wildly. Once as he did so a round shot passed under his girth only a few inches from Lee's stirrup. If the horse had not been in the air, the General would almost certainly have been killed. Harris's veterans were quick to see his danger. "Go back, General," they yelled, "Go back! For God's sake, go back!" His anxiety was apparent that day, but his battle-ire was aroused, and if he was not personally to have a hand in repelling the enemy from the salient, he must have guarantee that it would be done. So, simply but stubbornly, he answered their appeal. "If you will promise me to drive those people from our works, I will go back." The men shouted their agreement and started on more vigorously than ever. Harris's men did not arrive a moment too soon. Just as they reached Rodes at the doublequick, an aide galloped up from Ramseur to say that he could hold his ground only a few minutes longer unless help was forthcoming.

Before 9 o'clock McGowan's brigade was sent to support Harris. It gave Rodes enough rifles to halt the Federal advance. Then, gradually, the Federals were forced and driven over the parapet. In front of this they rallied once more and refused to be moved. The second phase of the battle was ended. The enemy had attacked successfully; the Confederate counterattack had cleared the salient.

What next? Should Lee permit the enemy to remain on the outer side of the parapet, separated from his men only by the length of a bayoneted gun? All his impulse prompted him to force the enemy back to the woods. Sound tactics dictated the same course. Word was passed to Gordon and to Rodes to keep their men at the parapet and to hurl the enemy back if they could. Gallantly they held to their task while Lee hastily examined the rest of the front. He decided he could not accomplish anything on his left. The Federals were already attacking there. Anderson beat them off, thanks to Alexander's readiness with his artillery, but he could not attempt an offensive. On the centre and right of Hill's corps, Lee found that no assaults had been delivered.

The enemy seemed absorbed in the operations against Ewell. Already Wilcox's work was over, and his part of the line was restored. His division and Heth's were available for a counterstroke.

On the front of the line of Hill's corps, south of the "Mule Shoe," was a projection styled Heth's salient. Troops moving from the right side of this salient would be unseen by the Federals in front of the "Mule Shoe," and if they reached an oak wood in front of their lines they would be on the flank of the Federals. Lane filed quietly into the woods opposite the right face of the salient and soon had his line at right angles to the enemy's front. Mahone's brigade under Colonel Daniel A. Weisiger was in support. The situation was promising. But before the two brigades could strike, the Federals advanced to attack the left face of Heth's salient. Lee watched them come forward. Hill's artillery opened; the infantry fired as soon as they could bring down their mark. Lane hit the Federals in flank.

The attack was quickly repulsed in what was the clearest advantage the Confederates had gained that day. By midafternoon the right was safe and the left could hold its own. Still the fight raged around the "Mule Shoe," which had now earned its more familiar name of the "Bloody Angle." The counterattack by Lane and Weisiger failed to shake the grip of the Federals on the outer side of the parapet. From every vantage-point, the Federal artillery poured its fire into the salient. The loss of life was staggering; some of the brigades, wet, bleeding, and decimated, were close to exhaustion.

Lee determined to make another effort to force the Federals from the parapet. Sending for General Lane, he complimented the conduct of that officer's sharpshooters earlier in the day. He was loath, he said, to send them into action again. Lane replied that he knew they would go wherever Lee ordered them. The sharpshooters were brought forward and greeted Lee with cheers as they passed him. They soon discovered, however, that the Federals had entrenched positions in front of Early. Two brigades were then thrown out—only to uncover a still stronger line that would bar any large-scale flanking operation from the Confederate right. The possibilities had been exhausted. The battle had to be fought out at the parapet of the salient until the defenders could be withdrawn to the gorge in the rear. Lee directed that the line at that point be completed forthwith.

Long after darkness had engulfed the rear of the salient, the flash of rifles, the roar of the Federal guns, and the appearance of weary, dazed, and bloody men from the front told of the fidelity with which the veterans of the Second Corps were obeying Lee's orders to hold the parapet. They had been fighting for sixteen hours and more, with no rest, no food. The dead filled the ditch and had to be piled behind it in a ghastly parados. The survivors waded in mud and gore, slipping now and then over the mangled bodies of their comrades. When it seemed that the remnant of the brigades could not endure even fifteen minutes longer, they would bite new cartridges, ram home the charges, fire over the paparet and drop back into the muck of the ditch to do the same thing over again, with trembling fingers and numbed arms. At last, about midnight, Lee sent them orders to fall back slowly to the new line.

It was nearly dawn on the 13th when the last of them passed through the gorge of the salient to new security—but security bought at a ghastly price. The Federals claimed to have taken over 3000. The casualties among the commanding officers had been terrific. In nine days' fighting, five general officers had been killed or mortally hurt, nine had been wounded, and two had been captured.

And this doleful list did not tell the whole story of that dreadful day. In the midst of the battle a messenger had arrived with news of Stuart's movements to head off Sheridan's raid before it reached Richmond. The anxious Southern troopers had intercepted the Federals at Yellow Tavern, seven miles north of Richmond, and had given battle there. Stuart had been in the fullest of the fight and had been shot through the body by a dismounted blue cavalryman. That had been on the afternoon of the 11th. The wounded Stuart had been borne into Richmond and was believed to be dying.

Stuart dying! The "eyes of the army" about to be destroyed. It was the worst calamity that had befallen the South since that May day, just a year previously, when "Stonewall" had breathed his last. Lee had to steel himself as he announced the news. He paused a moment and then he added in a shaken voice, "He never brought me a piece of false information." Later in the night another message brought the dreaded word: Stuart had died that evening. As quickly as he could, Lee retired to his tent to master his grief, and when one of Stuart's staff officers entered, a little later, to tell him of Stuart's last minutes, Lee could only say, "I can scarcely think of him without weeping!" To Mrs. Lee he wrote, "A more zealous, ardent, brave and devoted soldier than Stuart the Confederacy cannot have." Jackson dead, Stuart dead, Longstreet wounded, Hill sick, Ewell almost incapacitated—the men on whom he had most relied were going fast! He had to walk alone.

Still another woe that black night brought. In his raid on Richmond, Sheridan had cut the Richmond, Fredericksburg and Potomac Railroad. The army's communications with Richmond were thus interrupted. No supplies were arriving either for the men or for the animals. All this load of death, disaster, and threatened hunger Lee bore with so stout a heart that even those who knew him best did not realize that in its agonizing demands the day of the Bloody Angle was second only to the final day at Gettysburg. He did not admit the imminence of ruin or lament the things he could not control.

The rain that had drenched the struggling shoulders of the Army of Northern Virginia on the day of the grapple for the Bloody Angle seemed a mercy on the morning of May 13. It continued four full days after the end of the battle of the Bloody Angle. Large-scale operations were at a standstill. Consolidating the decimated bridges of Johnson's old division, Lee named John B. Gordon major general, with rank from the date of his great struggle to recover the Bloody Angle. Until Lee could decide on a new commander of the cavalry corps, for there could be no successor to the unique Stuart, he directed the separate divisions to report directly to army headquarters; and because he was well satisfied with the manner in which the divisions of the First Corps were being handled, he requested the cancellation of orders issued by the War Department for the return of Major General McLaws to his old command. The gaunt spectre of want was repulsed temporarily during these days of rest. By the 15th both the Central and the Richmond, Fredericksburg and Potomac railroads were running normally. Supplies were distributed in larger quantities, to the great satisfaction of the men.

Yet the situation remained grave. Casualties to date, though never fully reported, must have been well in excess of 15,000, and not a single regiment had arrived, except Johnston's brigade on May 6, to make good the losses. General Grant was believed to be receiving large reinforcements. There were fourteen brigades in the defenses of Richmond, Drewry's Bluff, and Petersburg, with one brigade of cavalry and an abundance of artillery; but Sheridan's cavalry was just below Malvern Hill, undefeated, Butler was pressing on toward Drewry's Bluff from the south side of the James, and Kautz's cavalry was now on a raid against the Richmond and Danville Railroad. Breckinridge had two brigades and one battalion of infantry in the Valley of Virginia and had called to him the cadet corps of the Virginia Military Institute. All that Lee thought he could get at the time was Hoke's old brigade, which had reached the Richmond line from North Carolina, and even this was denied him for the moment. President Davis did not believe it was safe to release any troops from around Richmond until Beauregard had launched against Butler an attack that Davis and Bragg were urging. The President suggested that Lee summon the troops in the Shenandoah Valley, but Lee considered this too risky.

There came the sunshine of good news almost at the time the clouds broke away in brighter weather. On the 15th, at New Market, Breckinridge met Sigel and with the assistance of the battalion from the Virginia Military Institute drove the invaders down the Valley. Lee was immensely pleased that the upper Valley was cleared and that one of the most serious threats against his flank had been relieved. Scarcely had the soldiers realized the importance of the success in the Valley than the telegraph reported an even finer victory: On the 16th, Beauregard attacked Butler below Drewry's Bluff and hurled him back to Bermuda Hundred Neck, where, in General Grant's expressive phrase, he was "as completely shut off from further operations directly against Richmond as if [he] had been in a bottle strongly corked." Lee, being confident of this, at once asked that some of Beauregard's troops be sent to him. He saw in Butler's distress the one opportunity in all the Southland of giving his army substantial reinforcements. Almost simultaneously came reports that Sheridan's raid against Richmond had ended, that Kautz had given up his attacks on the Richmond and Danville Railroad, and that Crook and Averell had started back into western Virginia from their operations against the Virginia and Tennessee railroad. Finally, on the 18th, as if to give climax to the changed situation, an attempted general assault through the Bloody Angle was broken up so quickly that the army scarcely realized General Grant had planned another 12th of May.

Relieved though he was, Lee was not for a moment misled as to the magnitude of the danger that still confronted him. In a dispatch to the President on the 18th, Lee summarized his view of the situation: "[Grant's] position is strongly entrenched, and we cannot attack it with any prospect of success without great loss of men which I wish to avoid if possible. The enemy's artillery is superior in weight of metal and range to our own, and my object has been to engage him when in motion and under circumstances that will not cause us to suffer from this disadvantage. I think by this means he has suffered considerably in the several past combats, and that his progress has thus far been arrested. I shall continue to strike him wherever opportunity presents itself, but nothing at present indicates any purpose on his part to advance. Neither the strength of our army nor the condition of our animals will admit of any extensive movement with a view to drawing the enemy from his position. I think he is now waiting for reenforcements . . . The importance of this campaign to the administration of Mr. Lincoln and to General Grant leaves no doubt that every effort and every sacrifice will be made to secure its success." Later in the day, Lee again gave the warning that more than once had induced the President to send him troops even when Richmond had seemed to be threatened: "The question," he said, "is whether we shall fight the battle here or around Richmond. If the troops are obliged to be retained at Richmond I may be forced back."

Abundant evidence was forthcoming on May 19 of the determination Lee credited his adversary. On the Confederate right the enemy seemed as strong as ever, but on the left there were indications that the enemy might be withdrawing. The turning movement that Lee had been suspecting since May 15 might be under way.

Lee ordered Ewell to demonstrate during the afternoon in front of his lines, but Ewell asked to be allowed to undertake a circuitous manoeuvre that would put him in rear of the Federal right flank. Lee gave permission. Not long after the Second Corps had started, Lee found that Ewell had sent back his artillery because of the badness of the roads. Realizing that this was inviting disaster, Lee sought to extend Early's left to cover Ewell's front. Very soon rapid firing announced that Ewell had encountered the foe. As his object was merely to discover whether Grant had abandoned that part of the front, Ewell prepared to withdraw, but before he could do so the Federals attacked him with much vigor. Happily, Hampton, who had screened Ewell's operation, had carried a battery of his horse artillery along with him, and he quickly disposed this to check the enemy. The onrush of the Federals was, however, so vigorous that Ramseur, without waiting for orders, delivered a counterattack with his brigade. In a short time Ramseur had to retire to the position from which he had started. There Pegram's brigade came up on his left and rectified the line, which Ramseur was able to hold until nightfall. The corps left about 900 killed, wounded, and missing in the enemy's lines—a heavy price to pay for the information that the enemy had not denuded his right.

On the morning of May 20, there was encouragement for Lee in a telegram received from Mr. Davis. The President announced that he had ordered Pickett's division and Hoke's brigade to march to Lee, though Beauregard was contending that Lee should fall back to the line of the Chickahominy for a better concentration of the defending forces. Wherever and whenever Grant moved, Lee would have five more brigades to employ against him.

Signs multiplied of impending southward movement by the Federals. Before 9 A.M. on May 21, General Lee knew that the enemy was moving toward Bowling Green and Milford. He had already concluded that Grant's new base would be at Port Royal, on the Rappahannock River, and he had Ewell's corps in position along the Po, prepared to move at the tap of a drum. The rest of the army was made ready to leave the Spotsylvania lines as soon as the Federals disappeared from in front of Early and of Anderson.

Where should the army seek to interpose itself between Grant and Richmond? That was the question Lee had to answer. The enemy had the lead—how much of a lead, it was impossible for Confederate headquarters to say with assurance. Grant would make for Richmond as fast as he could, and he must be met as far from the city as possible. Lee decided quickly to move back to the North Anna River. If the enemy struck from the north, he would have a river line from which to defend Hanover Junction and the Central Railroad. In case the enemy continued down the Mattapony, the Army of Northern Virginia could move from the North Anna to a new position behind the Pamunkey. There was but one objection to this stand on the North Anna: It was only twenty-three miles from Richmond—dangerously close. Lee would have preferred to bring north of the river the troops at Hanover Junction, and to give battle as far from Richmond as possible. But if he tried to operate between Spotsylvania and the North Anna, or followed the enemy eastward, some part of Grant's force might slip by and get between him and Richmond. The North Anna was the nearest position of strength that he could take up and be sure that his adversary would not easily slip around his flank.

Hanover Junction it was, then! He telegraphed instructions for the troops there to defend the place against raiders. The wagon trains started southward. Ewell was put in motion for Mud Tavern and the Telegraph road, on the way to the Junction. Orders were given

General Early to sweep his front and, if he found that the enemy had departed, to prepare to march. Similiar directions went to Field.

Lee himself moved his headquarters to the Southworth house, on the right bank of the Po, and there he remained, somewhat impatiently, to hear the outcome of the reconnaissance north of the river. General Hill rode up and reported that he was well enough to take up his duties again. Lee restored him to command and ordered Early to resume the leadership of his division under Ewell. Skirmishers resisted so vigorously a reconnaissance by General Wilcox that two brigades were sent after them and were soon engaged in a stiff fight. Field, too, encountered some opposition on his sector. Soon, however, Anderson was convinced that only a rearguard remained on the line, and he followed Ewell. As the evening drew on, several of Lee's general officers joined him at the Southworth house. To all of them Lee gave his final verbal orders. One by one the officers rode off. Lee remained alone with his staff and a few guides. Presently, with no more ceremony than if he were departing for an evening ride, he said to his companions, "Come, gentlemen.' Mounting silently, he touched the reins of Traveller and turned his head southward.

With Eustis Moncure by his side as a guide and with Colonel Taylor and W. G. Jesse, another guide, immediately behind, Lee rode through the night toward Traveler's Rest, midway between the Po and Ta Rivers. About 2 A.M. on the morning of the 22d, he came to the little house by the road where Doctor Joseph A. Flippo ministered to the ills of the countryside. Lee paused to rest his mount and to chat with Flippo, and then went on. When he reached the north side of Stevens' Mill pond he found his headquarters tents erected, with Ewell's troops resting nearby. Here he halted.

Lee rested for an hour or two and then, before dawn, summoned Moncure and sent him off with a dispatch to General Hampton, advising him of the army's progress and instructing him to hold the enemy in check and to fall back slowly toward Hanover Junction.

The troops of the Second Corps were now stirring. They had covered the seventeen miles to Dickinson's Mill almost without a halt, and they had relaxed only an hour or two, but they must press on. Proceeding with the troops, Lee was soon joined by Major Jed Hotchkiss, the capable topographical engineer of the Second Corps. Soon they reached the hills that look down on the crossings of the North Anna. The railroad bridge and Fox's Bridge on the Telegraph road were intact. A small Confederate garrison held the works that had been

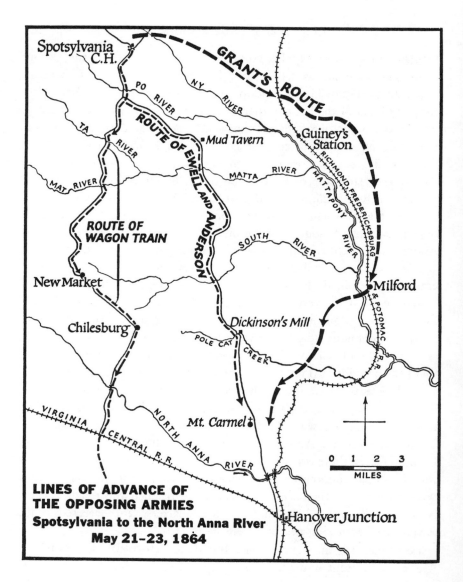

LINES OF ADVANCE OF
THE OPPOSING ARMIES
Spotsylvania to the North Anna River
May 21–23, 1864

erected to protect the wooden spans. The race to the new position had
been won. If Grant was headed in that direction, he would find the
stream between him and the Army of Northern Virginia.

Lee left orders for Ewell and Anderson to pass to the south bank
and to take position there, without destroying the spans or evacuating
the bridgeheads. With his staff he went on to Hanover Junction, three
miles southward, and there established headquarters in the southwest
angle of the crossing of the Richmond, Fredericksburg and Potomac
and the Central railroads.

The afternoon of the 22d passed without the appearance of any

Federal force, but Hampton reported that the Army of the Potomac was marching by Milford and that its objective seemed to be Hanover Junction. Lee hoped that it was. Now that he had occupied the Junction, he felt himself in position to move after Grant, whatever his adversary's line of march. He was anxious for Beauregard to join him, if possible, for an attack on the Army of the Potomac, because, as he wrote President Davis, "it seems to me our best policy to unite upon [Grant's army] and endeavor to crush it." He did not think it sound strategy to permit the enemy to reach the Chickahominy before the Army of Northern Virginia was reinforced by Beauregard. "His difficulties," he said of Grant, "will be increased as he advances, and ours diminished, and I think it would be a great disadvantage to us to uncover our railroads to the west, and injurious to open to him more country than we can avoid." If he could meet Grant where the larger numbers and the superior artillery of the enemy did not make the offensive hopeless, it was still his intention to attack—and as far from Richmond as practicable.

On the morning of May 23, Lee reconnoitred the ground on the south side of the river. He did not fortify extensively, probably because he knew he could not long retain a position close to the river. The Confederate cavalry outposts withdrew and bluecoats began to appear on the left bank of the North Anna about noon. Soon it was apparent that the enemy was in great force. Once again Lee had reasoned rightly concerning his opponent's objective; once again the Army of the Potomac had marched straight to a wall of waiting bayonets.

Ere long the enemy's artillery opened against the bridgeheads, and the Confederates answered. Opposite the railroad crossing and Fox's Bridge there were signs of Federal activity in ravines that could not be reached by the Southern guns. Nearly two miles upstream, at Ox Ford, Union troops gathered but made no attempt to cross. Here, Lee determined to make personal reconnaissance. He found some of the horse artillery in position with cavalry support, throwing up a light fortification. Across the North Anna the Federals were visible. Lee studied them carefully. Then he turned to the courier who had accompanied him. "Go back and tell General A. P. Hill to leave his men in camp," he said, "this is nothing but a feint; the enemy is preparing to cross below." He had scarcely returned to Hanover Junction before his prediction was fulfilled. There was a bend in the river opposite Jericho Mills, three miles above Ox Ford. About 3 o'clock

General Wilcox found that the enemy had crossed at the mill. He reported to General Hill, who ordered him to advance his division and to attack.

Wilcox formed his line opposite Noel's Station. The action opened briskly. By nightfall, however, the division was glad to withdraw— in the unhappy knowledge that the troops in its front were still on the south bank and were entrenching rapidly. It was a badly managed affair. Heth's division had been brought up during the afternoon but had not been successful in driving the enemy.

The action might mean that the enemy was preparing to cross the North Anna with his entire army. On the opposite flank, about 7:15 P.M., in the midst of a furious rainstorm, there was another move that might indicate a determination on Grant's part to force a crossing. From the ravines beyond the bridgeheads, the enemy swarmed forward and overwhelmed the small garrison. Between 100 and 200 men, who could not run the gauntlet over the bridges in the gathering darkness, were captured.

Was all this a ruse? On the theory that it might be, Lee directed Anderson to be ready if necessary to move the next morning. To prepare for an attack by the enemy on the front where the Army of Northern Virginia then stood, Lee decided to change his lines. He could not keep the enemy from moving to the south side opposite the bridges, for after he burned these the enemy could easily ford the river. Neither could Lee fight close to the river, on his right, because the Federal guns dominated the position. But there was one point where the ground favored Lee. That was in the centre, near Ox Ford. There the Confederates held the elevation and could prevent a Federal crossing. Lee determined on a novel system of defenses, a very wide inverted "V" with its apex to the north and both flanks well secured—the left by Little River and the right by swampy ground east of Hanover Junction. He was in position where he could reinforce one wing from the other, and as long as he held Ox Ford could compel Grant to fight with his wings separated. Lee was sanguine. His communications were shorter, and his strength was raised, at last, some 8500 by the arrival of all of Pickett's division, Hoke's old brigade, and Breckinridge's command. The opportunity for which he had been waiting might come the very next day. But before it developed, Lee was attacked by a violent intestinal complaint, brought on, no doubt, by bad food and long hours. He was loath, as always, to yield to sickness, and on the 24th he tried to transact army business as usual.

Union forces crossed to the south bank as soon as they discovered that the Confederates had drawn in their lines. This put the enemy precisely where Lee wanted him: If Grant tried to reinforce the right from the left, or *vice versa*, he would have to cross the river twice. The Confederate centre held stubbornly to Ox Ford. An attempt by Grant to force a crossing at that point was easily defeated. For a few hours opportunity beckoned. If Lee had been well enough to organize a strong attack he perhaps might have crushed the II Corps on his right or the V on his left; but hourly, as the Union entrenchments rose, his chances of success grew less.

Lee was worse on the 25th and confined to his tent, but he insisted on receiving reports and he carried on his official correspondence, in which there was not even a hint that he was sick. In his dispatches he was able to keep his measured tone. In his tent it was different. As he felt opportunity slipping away, his grip on himself weakened, and he had a violent scene with Colonel Venable, who argued some point with him. Lee could not, would not give up, but he broke out vehemently: "We must strike them a blow—we must never let them pass us again—we must strike them a blow." To Doctor Gwathmey he said of Grant, "If I can get one more pull at him, I will defeat him."

The opportunity was gone, however. The Unionists were too strong to be attacked and too cautious to assault the lines with their forces divided. The 25th passed with nothing more serious than a few demonstrations. To procure more rest than was possible at Hanover Junction, Lee moved his headquarters to Taylorsville.

The Federals did not wait long in the difficult position where Lee had placed them by drawing his inverted "V." On the morning of May 27 the enemy was found to have evacuated the south bank of the North Anna, and was marching down the north bank. Grant had declined the challenge to battle and was preparing to try again. Almost at the same time, cavalry outposts reported that the Federals were crossing at Hanovertown on the Pamunkey River. Grant had the cover of a river and was getting eight miles nearer Richmond, for Hanovertown is fifteen miles northeast the Confederate capital.

Lee did not waste an hour in hurrying to intercept this new effort. Ewell's corps was immediately set in motion toward Ashland, and Anderson, with Breckinridge, was ordered to follow him. Hill was to form the rearguard that evening.

The operation on the North Anna was not accounted a success because it did not compel Grant to give battle. Strategically, it accomplished far more than Lee could then foresee. It forced the Federal commander to abandon a direct move on Richmond from the north, and to leave Lee in command of communications with the Valley. No achievement of the entire campaign from the Rapidan to the James meant more in prolonging the struggle. But now Lee saw the battle brought back close to the fields where he had taken command not quite two years previously.

Lee rode with Ewell's corps toward Richmond on the morning of May 27. About mid-day he learned from the cavalry that the enemy seemed to be advancing from Hanovertown on the Pamunkey to Haw's Shop, an important crossroads ten miles northeast of Mechanicsville on the way to Richmond. Lee remembered that there was a fine defensive position on the ridge between Totopotomoy and Beaver Dam Creeks, the same ridge he had ordered Stuart to reconnoitre at the beginning of the famous "ride around McClellan." The columns were ordered in that direction, to intercept Grant and, if might be, to give him battle there.

He came in the afternoon to the vicinity of the Chickahominy River, just west of the upper waters of the Totopotomoy. There he received reports that only cavalry had been seen near Haw's Shop and that a column of infantry was moving along the south bank of the Pamunkey from Hanover Courthouse to Hanovertown. This information was much too indefinite to justify Lee in throwing the whole army to the northeast of Richmond, for this would leave open to the enemy the direct road from the north, via Ashland. Lee decided to halt the columns for the night so that they could be moved in whichever direction the advance of the enemy might develop.

Lee was now only nine miles by road from Richmond. He was determined to avoid a second siege of the capital. But proximity to the city was not without some advantages. It shortened his communications and lengthened those of his adversary. It gave him the promise of the assistance of the 5700 troops in the garrison of Richmond when he was close enough for the two forces to be consolidated. And he was now near the line of the Chickahominy, on which General Beauregard had said it would be possible to unite in an offensive. Lee was willing to move even closer to Richmond if Beauregard would designate the place where he would find it most convenient for the two forces to unite.

Still uncertain on May 28 whether Grant's advance would be down the Telegraph road or from the Pamunkey, Lee ordered the cavalry to make a forced reconnaissance across the Totopotomoy, in the direction of Haw's Shop, and to ascertain if the strong Federal horse in that quarter had infantry behind it. He had received the Fourth and part of the Fifth South Carolina Cavalry and had the assurance that the Sixth would soon arrive.

Later in the day he moved his headquarters to the Clarke house near Atlee's. He was so unwell by the hour he arrived there that he had to accept a room from the hospitable owner and transact army business indoors. It was the first time since the opening of the campaign that headquarters had not been under canvas. Sick as he was, Lee proceeded to dispose his troops with the greatest care.

The day passed without incident at headquarters, but in front of Haw's Shop the cavalry had a vigorous fight with Sheridan's command. The Confederates threw the enemy back against his supports, captured prisoners from the V and VI Corps, and thereby established the fact that Grant had much infantry south of the Pamunkey. But the gray troopers were greatly outnumbered and in the end were compelled to give ground.

Lee pondered the report the cavalry brought back. If Grant had two corps east of Haw's Shop, it was fairly certain that his main attack would not be down the Telegraph road. He had, however, three routes to Richmond from Haw's Shop. He could march northwestward and strike for the Central Railroad at Peake's Turnout; he could move directly westward against Atlee's; or he could turn south, across the Totopotomoy, enter the Old Church road, and make for Mechanicsville.

There was manifest advantage to the enemy in seizing the Central Railroad. At one stroke, Grant could again sever Lee's communications with western Virginia and re-establish for himself a rail line of supply from the Rappahannock. Lee applied his maxim that it was always well to expect the enemy to do what he should do, and he accordingly shifted the left of his line somewhat to the northeast, and closer to the Totopotomoy. Ewell was on the right along the Shady Grove road; Anderson was at an angle behind Ewell's left; then came Breckinridge; on the extreme left was Hill, covering the point where the road from Shady Grove to Hanover Courthouse crossed the Totopotomoy.

Lee had additional concern on the 29th. General Ewell's condition had become more serious and, in Lee's opinion, necessitated rest at a distance from the army. Early was left in charge and Ewell was given leave of absence. Beauregard had become alarmed over the activity of Butler on the Bermuda Hundred front and on the 27th had been uncertain whether the enemy was preparing to advance or withdraw. He was convinced that he was occupying twice as many troops as he had, and he so far convinced Mr. Davis of this that the President on the 28th hinted to General Lee that Beauregard might be doing as much good where he was as he could accomplish with the Army of Northern Virginia. Mr. Davis went out to Atlee's during the afternoon to discuss the situation, and, in the evening, Beauregard arrived. He maintained he could spare none of his 12,000 men. The conference ended amicably, but without result.

But the situation was changed over night. Early on the 30th the enemy began to disappear from the Confederate left and almost simultaneously there were signs of a new shift by Grant on the right of the Confederate line. Lee's most reliable scout reported that the Federals were moving along the road to Old Cold Harbor. Lee concluded that the Federals would fortify a line along the Totopotomoy and then, "will probably make another move by their left flank toward the Chickahominy," as he expressed it to Anderson.

The practical step seemed to be to strike at that part of Grant's army south of the Totopotomoy, in front of the Second Corps. That corps was in a good position and had already constructed two crossings over the fields to the Old Church road, on which the enemy was demonstrating with cavalry near Bethesda Church. When Early proposed to develop this situation by a vigorous attack, Lee at once approved.

Rodes was moved to the right and the action was opened. The burden of it fell on Early's old brigade. This command had been led by Brigadier General John Pegram until that officer had been wounded and then by Colonel Edward Willis of Georgia. As these veterans went forward, the Union cavalry quickly withdrew. Rodes's men passed into a broad field, swept back an opposing brigade, and immediately came under heavy fire. Their lines were torn by every round, for the Union gunners had the exact range. They charged desperately on, almost to the artillery position, and then were repulsed with slaughter. The failure of the attack was complete.

While Early was engaged at Bethesda Church, evidence began to accumulate that reinforcements from Butler were moving to Grant, via the White House on the Pamunkey River. The signal officer on the lower James reported that seventeen transports had passed down the river, carrying at least 7000 men. To save time that might be lost in transmitting the request through Richmond, Lee called directly on Beauregard for reinforcements. When that officer answered about nightfall that the War Department would have to decide what troops should be sent, Lee lost patience. "The result of this delay," he telegraphed the President, "will be disaster." The wheels of the War Department turned swiftly. Beauregard was ordered to dispatch Hoke by trains that would be sent him immediately; but before the call reached Beauregard, he, too, had concluded that the risk to Richmond was greater than that on his own line and he advised the department that Hoke's command was to start as soon as the movements of the enemy would permit.

CHAPTER XIII

The Twilight of the Confederacy

Now BEGAN the last great manoeuvres in the campaign from the Rapidan to the James, the manoeuvres that were to change the character of military operations in Virginia and substitute siege tactics for field strategy.

By dawn on May 31 the right, under Early, had been extended beyond the Old Church road, which led from the Federal position to Mechanicsville and thence to Richmond. The left rested on the Chickahominy swamp, west of Atlee's Station. The whole line had been well fortified and, if well supported by artillery, could be held by a comparatively small force of infantry. The works admirably covered the approaches to Richmond from the upper Pamunkey. But if Grant was moving by the left flank, it would be possible for him to swing around to the Chickahominy River and force the Army of Northern Virginia to stand siege in the Richmond defenses. That was the one thing above all others that Lee most desired to avoid, for he knew it could end only in defeat. He must extend his flank to save himself from being chained to Richmond. Fitz Lee's cavalry was already well beyond Early's exposed flank, holding the crossroads at Old Cold Harbor, the strategic importance of which Lee had learned in the campaign of the Seven Days. To support Fitz Lee, the commanding general directed Hoke's division toward Cold Harbor.

In mid-afternoon, Fitz Lee reported from Old Cold Harbor that the enemy was half a mile from that place and was advancing on it. General Lee thought he saw an opportunity for striking the blow he had so long wished to deliver. If he could attack the enemy at Cold Harbor, before the Federal left was in position, he might double it up. To this end, Anderson was taken from his position between Breckinridge and Early and was shifted during the later afternoon into Early's position and beyond it. Breckinridge extended his line somewhat to the

402

right and Early to the left to fill the gap made by Anderson's departure. Anderson was then quietly moved by the right flank until he was close to Beulah Church, which was about one mile northwest of Old Cold Harbor. Kershaw was in position early in the night; Pickett and Field were on the road behind Kershaw. Hoke's brigades were to file in on Anderson's right. Fifteen thousand Confederate infantry would be in the vicinity of Cold Harbor by daylight. The great day might be at hand.

About 7 o'clock on the evening of May 31 a significant message came from Fitz Lee. The enemy's cavalry had attacked his troopers and Clingman's brigade of infantry at Cold Harbor and had driven them from the crossroads. He thought Federal infantry were in his front. Infantry! Evidently, then, there was a race for Cold Harbor just as there had been for Spotsylvania Courthouse. Lee at once took the precaution of placing Hoke under Anderson and directed that Hoke's rear brigades be hurried to Cold Harbor. Lee doubtless wished to go himself, but he was still so weak that he had to ride in a carriage. The most he felt justified in doing was to advance his headquarters to Shady Grove, where he would be nearer the centre of operations in case Anderson's attack made a general offensive possible.

Hope might well have beaten high in the heart of Lee when he retired at Shady Grove on the evening of May 31. His plans had been well laid and the opportunity at Cold Harbor was great. When he arose on the morning of June 1, and strained his ears vainly for the sound of battle from his distant right, he had every reason to believe that the first courier from Anderson would bring great news.

It was far otherwise. The dispatch that finally reached him told a humiliating story of failure. Anderson attacked at dawn. The advance was led by Kershaw's veteran brigade under its ranking colonel, Lawrence M. Keitt of the Twentieth South Carolina, a green regiment that had recently joined the army. Keitt was a distinguished politician and had never been in close action. He dashed boldly forward, mounted on his charger, and was killed at the first onset. His raw regiment broke and forced the seasoned troops to give ground. Liaison between Anderson and Hoke was incredibly bad; Hoke did nothing; the attack failed and perhaps the greatest opportunity presented the army after May 6 was thrown away.

Bitterly as Lee must have been disappointed, he lost no time in repining. If he could not roll up the Army of the Potomac from his right, he must strengthen that flank to keep Grant from tying him down to the Richmond defenses. Breckinridge was ordered to Cold Harbor to reinforce and to extend the right. As it happened, Breckinridge was absent from his headquarters when the order reached him, and Heth's division of the Third Corps was changing position. An attack developed on Heth's front which held Breckinridge temporarily where he was and forced Lee to defer his own start for Cold Harbor. Cooke's brigade and Kirkland's, however, easily beat off the enemy. A little later, Breckinridge and Mahone cleared up the ground in their front and took about 150 prisoners. Almost at the same hour the cavalry that was covering the Confederate left met an advance by the Federal horse and drove it back in the dashing style of 1862.

These isolated attacks Lee took to be demonstrations to distract his attention, and some time after 4 o'clock he started for Cold Harbor. On his arrival he opened headquarters, probably in the field on the right of the Cold Harbor road, just west of the crossing of Powhite Creek at Gaines's Mill. Important events had happened during the afternoon. Fitz Lee had been forced back by superior numbers. This so threatened Anderson's right that he ordered Hoke to extend his flank southward beyond Old Cold Harbor. The key to this position was Turkey Hill. Knowing its strength, Lee had given instructions that it should be occupied fully, but Hoke did not extend his flank any great distance. He might have intended going farther in that direction, but immediately after he made the movement, the enemy attacked with vigor north of the road between New and Old Cold Harbor. The force of the Federal assault broke the lines between the left of Hoke and the right of Anderson. Clingman's brigade of Hoke's division gave way and Wofford's of Kershaw's division had to fall back, but Kershaw threw in two regiments and regained some of the ground. Hunton's brigade of Pickett's division was thereupon sent to Hoke. Working along the left flank of Hoke, the brigade almost closed the gap. The enemy withdrew after nightfall, but contact between Hoke and Anderson was practically lost, and confusion prevailed at Anderson's headquarters. Anderson's final dispatch of the day was that he had to be reinforced or his lines would be broken. Lee had already anticipated this need. Breckinridge should arrive in time to meet the attack expected at daylight.

But Lee had to look beyond his own army for the strength with which to resist the enemy on a longer line. He had been trying for days to effect joint action with Beauregard, and he had consistently failed, except for procuring Hoke's division. On June 1 he tried

diplomacy anew. He telegraphed Beauregard of Grant's shift toward
the James. Beauregard answered that he could not evacuate the south
side of the James unless the government was willing to abandon communications between Richmond and Petersburg. In Lee's opinion that
was not desirable, "but," he told Beauregard, "as two-thirds of Butler's
force has joined Grant, can you not leave sufficient guard to move
with the balance of your command to [the] north side of James River
and take command of right wing of army?"

At dawn on the 2d Lee awaited two developments—the arrival
of Breckinridge and the resumption of the attack; but he looked in
vain for Breckinridge and was relieved that the Federals withheld their
assaults. Anxious regarding Breckinridge, he set out for Mechanicsville. He covered the entire distance before he found the Kentuckian
at the village with his troops eating breakfast. It was explained that the
column had not started until after 10 P.M. from the Confederate left
and had then been so weary from its day's fighting that the men had
to rest every half hour. Major McClellan, who was acting as guide,
had no map, and in his ignorance of the country led the troops by
a long route.

Probably while he was at Mechanicsville, Lee learned that the
Federals had disappeared from opposite a part of the front of the Third
Corps. Reasoning that this meant a still heavier concentration around
Cold Harbor, he ordered Mahone and Wilcox to march at once for
the right and to take position beyond Breckinridge, who was to form
south of Hoke, between Old Cold Harbor and the Chickahominy.
Lee did not stop with this manoeuvre. If Grant was throwing division
after division to the Cold Harbor sector, he might readily be weakening his right; and there might be a chance to turn that flank. Lee
gave discretionary orders to Early to attack if he found a favorable
opening, and then he rode once more to Gaines's Mill. All was quiet
for the time, but a battle was brewing.

At last Breckinridge arrived and moved into position. Mahone and
Wilcox were now on the road, struggling with heat and dust and
thirst. After Mahone came up he probably went in support of Breckinridge. Wilcox arrived at 3 P.M. and took ground to the right and rear
of Hoke, where his men began immediately to entrench themselves.
Lee was not satisfied with the position of his right wing. The enemy
to the east dominated much of Turkey Hill, which Lee had especially
enjoined the commanders on the Confederate right to occupy. He had
only awaited the arrival of reinforcements to correct this. Soon, with

the support of two of Wilcox's brigades, Breckinridge was thrown forward and the enemy was cleared from the hill. This advance gave Lee artillery control of the bottom-land and secured his right against any turning movement, but to make that flank invulnerable he extended Wilcox on the right of Breckinridge until he was within half a mile of the river.

While making these dispositions, Lee was hopeful that Early had found opportunity of striking a blow on the Confederate left. There the Confederates had attacked, and had brushed aside a strong skirmish line but had been halted in front of heavy works thrown up northwest of Bethesda Church. Whatever was to be accomplished must be undertaken on the right.

There would assuredly be another bloody engagement on the morrow: could Beauregard spare as much as one brigade to help in winning a victory? It seemed doubtful, doubtful even whether Lee could retain all of the thin divisions he had. For here, on the evening of June 2, was a telegram from General Imboden at Mount Crawford, saying that Major General David Hunter, who had succeeded Sigel, had the previous day forced him from Harrisonburg in the Shenandoah Valley. If Hunter was moving up the Shenandoah, it might be necessary to send Breckinridge back with the two little brigades that were now occupying a critical sector south of the road between the two Cold Harbors.

A heavy rain had begun to fall before 4 o'clock on the afternoon of the 2d and continued during the night of the 2d–3d. All along the front, when the rain ceased and the shadows began to gray on the morning of June 3, the ragged veterans manned the trenches and stood on the alert. In exposed positions, the guns were charged and primed. Everywhere the feeling was the same: The enemy was surely coming! Why not? That thin, sprawling line was all that stood between him and Richmond. At headquarters, Lee was astir with the dawn, busily considering where he should locate his artillery south of the Chickahominy, in case the enemy moved in that direction. Circular orders were issued for the recall of the last man on extra duty. Every rifle would be needed behind the parapet that day.

Suddenly, at 4:30, there was a roar of cheers and a crash of musketry. An instant after, the thunder of guns swelled from the heights of the Chickahominy far over to the Confederate left. A general assault was on, a determined effort, backed by all the might of the Army of the Potomac, to break through, everywhere, anywhere—and to take the road into the city that woke from sleep startled at the loudest firing it had ever heard.

Lee could only listen to the din and speculate whether it would come closer, for he had not a single regiment in general reserve, and until he could ascertain where the Federal assaults were heaviest, he could not weaken one part of the line to strengthen another. The whole front was furiously engaged. Now the firing fell away, now it rose again. Shells were falling in the field where Lee's headquarters were located, and soon the wounded began to come back from the front, but they were not numerous. Stoutly, in that inferno, the lines must be holding.

Couriers and staff officers rode off to find the commanding generals on the line and to get reports. In half an hour the first of the messengers returned. On the front of Wilcox, no attack had been delivered. The enemy had reached Breckinridge's line and had broken through a bit of swampy ground, but Mahone had sent in Finegan and the old Maryland battalion and was restoring the front. A. P. Hill had shown Lee's courier the dead lying on one another where Grant had vainly assaulted. Hoke reported that the slain and wounded literally covered the ground and that, up to that time, he had not lost a single man in his division. On the sector held by the right of Kershaw successive assaults had been pushed with vigor but had been beaten off with ease. Favorable reports came from the centre and from the left.

On the front of the First Corps, attack followed attack with so much vigor that Anderson by 8 o'clock had counted fourteen. From the Confederate works the Federal officers could be heard commanding their men to advance, but as the bloody morning hours passed the only response would be a volley from the ground. The men realized it was futile to go on. By 11 o'clock the assaults on all parts of the line seemed to be suspended.

Lee turned to the grim task of seeing if he could replace the men who were still falling along the lines under Federal fire. Hoke had reported that he had captured prisoners from the XVIII Corps, which had joined Grant from Butler's army. This was what Lee had been expecting and it proved that the force in front of Beauregard had been greatly reduced. Lee put the facts before the President and added, "No time should be lost if reinforcements can be had." The administration was of the same mind and, in a terse exchange of messages, ordered Matt Ransom's brigade from Beauregard to Lee.

After 1 P.M. it was apparent that the enemy had abandoned all hope of successful general assaults. The Confederate wounded could be brought out and the lines put in order. On Breckinridge's front the works had been recaptured without heavy loss, so that the whole position was intact. Desultory firing continued until about nightfall. Then the enemy delivered a final attack, but was beaten off easily. The pickets kept up their nervous dispute and at intervals the artillery would open, but the battle was over. "Our loss today," Lee was able to write the President at 8:45, "has been small, and our success, under the blessing of God, all that we could expect."

Lee might have written much more, for while his own casualties had not exceeded 1200 to 1500 on the six miles of front, more than 7000 of Grant's men crowded the field hospitals or lay, in every attitude of agony, on the open ground, in the ditches and among the slashed trees. The repulse had been an incredible success. Although the Confederates did not know it at the time, the planned major assaults had been broken up within eight minutes after the advance had begun. It was, Colonel Venable recorded, "perhaps the easiest victory ever granted to the Confederate arms by the folly of the Federal commanders."

All day long June 4, the pitiful plea, "Water, water, for God's sake, water!" could be heard within the Confederate lines. No attack was made over the ground covered by these agonized men, but no request came from the Union side for a truce. Lee dispatched no flag, because virtually none of the casualties in front of his trenches had been among his own men. It was June 5 when Grant sent any message, and then he merely proposed that each army be privileged to put out relief parties when no action was on. Lee had to say, in answer to this unusual proposal, that it would lead to "misunderstanding and difficulty," and that when either army desired to remove the victims of battle it should ask for a suspension of hostilities. Grant could not bring himself to make this tacit admission of defeat until late on the 6th. The slow exchange of communications through the lines then delayed execution of the truce until the evening of June 7. By that time all except the ambulant wounded had died or had been removed at night by comrades.

The period of this correspondence and the five days that followed the burial of the Union dead were marked by no general action. The skirmishing, however, was constant, and several minor attacks were delivered by Lee, only to be halted before they reached the formidable Union positions. The Northerners, for their part, remained on the defensive. Some of the Confederates took this to mean that the Union high command had at last seen the futility of frontal assaults. Lee held a more cautious view, because of other operations undertaken by the enemy. On June 7 most of Sheridan's cavalry corps started for a raid up the Virginia Central Railroad. Lee at once detached Hampton and Fitz Lee with 4700 troopers in pursuit, leaving with the army only Rooney Lee's small division and Gary's mounted brigade of the Richmond garrison—a very serious division of force. It was an inevitable countermove, but it was to prove most costly. Lee observed that Sheridan started about the same time that Hunter began moving up the Shenandoah Valley. He assumed that these two advances were connected and reasoned that Grant might be waiting on the outcome, rather than halting because of exhaustion.

Lee did not, however, adopt the assault tactics his antagonist seemingly had abandoned temporarily. General Matt Ransom's brigade had been sent from the Bermuda Hundred front to strengthen the department of Richmond and indirectly had made good the losses at Cold Harbor. As long as Grant remained north of the Chickahominy the Confederate front was quite secure. But Lee did not think he could drive Grant out except by an assault on the Federal fortifications, and this he was anxious to avoid if possible.

As the armies watched each other, Lee had his first opportunity of fixing the status of the officers who had been named to succeed those fallen between the Wilderness and Cold Harbor. Under the new law permitting appointments with temporary rank, Anderson was promoted lieutenant general and Early was elevated to the same grade. Ewell was displeased at being supplanted but Lee did not think he could stand the hardships of active service and slated him to take charge of the department of Richmond. Major General Robert Ransom, whom Ewell was to succeed was sent to head the cavalry in western Virginia. Mahone was given temporary rank as major general to direct Anderson's division, and Ramseur was awarded the same honor with Early's division. Kershaw was designated as successor to McLaws in the First Corps.

Anything was a relief after the ghastly fighting of the preceding month, but nothing of the hilarity of winter quarters prevailed there in the sands and swamps of Hanover. Sharpshooting was worse than it had ever been. Vicious artillery fire broke out at intervals. Demonstrations were frequent. More serious, on every count, was a slow, daily shifting of the Federal line to the left in Grant's favorite manoeuvre. This kept

Lee's army constantly on the alert, lest the Federals slip by its right flank.

Bad news came from the Shenandoah Valley. At Piedmont on June 5, Hunter fell on the Confederate cavalry under Brigadier General W. E. Jones, killed him, routed his small force, and took 1000 prisoners. The next day Hunter occupied Staunton, where the Virginia Central crossed the Valley. Toward him, from Lewisburg, Brigadier General George Crook was moving along the railway, destroying it as he advanced. General Averell was following Crook with his cavalry. Rumor put the combined strength of these invaders at 20,000. Lee, anxiously consulted by the President, did not lose his strategical perspective. "It is apparent," he said, "that if Grant cannot be successfully resisted here we cannot hold the Valley— If he is defeated it can be recovered." He thought, however, that the Southern cause would best be served by returning Breckinridge and his command to Lynchburg. Breckinridge left about June 7 and reduced Lee's strength by approximately 2100.

Lee was satisfied that the force opposing Beauregard was very small. Beauregard, on the other hand, was becoming more and more alarmed. He interpreted Grant's shift to the left as designed to bring the Army of the Potomac to the James, and he was concerned over the appearance in the river of a large pontoon bridge.

A movement across the James had, indeed, become such a distinct possibility that Lee had now to reckon on four threats:

1. Grant was within nine miles of Richmond and might continue his hammering.

2. Grant might cross the James and crush Beauregard's 7900 men either at Bermuda Hundred, at Petersburg, or on both sectors.

3. Hunter might sweep the Valley and then move eastward with his force, now estimated at 15,000 instead of 20,000.

4. Sheridan might cut the Virginia Central Railroad and join Hunter or, having devastated midland Virginia, and having destroyed Lee's communications with the Valley, might return to Grant.

With 73,000 men in four areas of action, Lee was facing 125,000 to 130,000. These were odds of which Lee was not unmindful, but in his view, nothing that could happen in western Virginia or even, for the time being, at Petersburg, was as important as inflicting a defeat on the Army of the Potomac. No diversion clouded his vision. "We must destroy this army of Grant's before he gets to James River," he told Early. "If he gets there, it will become a siege, and then it will be a mere question of time."

On the afternoon of June 9 Lee received a message from General Bragg announcing that a surprise attack had been delivered that morning against Petersburg. He regarded the move against Petersburg as a reconnaissance and nothing more. Nevertheless, Lee set Matt Ransom's brigade in motion for the Confederate pontoons at Drewry's Bluff and Bragg ordered Gracie's brigade to the same crossing. As it developed, neither was required immediately at Petersburg. For, when the Federals had appeared in front of the defenses of the city, the district commander, Brigadier General Henry A. Wise, had mustered the few troops at his disposal and had manned the works facing the enemy. In Petersburg the tocsin had been sounded and the reserves in the city, men over forty-five and boys in their middle teens, had been called to defend the works that Wise could not cover. Even the prisoners in the jail had been released at their own request to share in the city's defense. On the left, the Federal infantry had done little more than make a demonstration, but on the right, Kautz's cavalry had attacked with vigor. The old men and the boys had beaten off one attack and had held up a second. Then the survivors had been compelled to retreat, but they had gained enough time for Beauregard to hurry up reinforcements. Kautz had quickly retreated, Dearing had followed him up, and the battle had been over.

What did this attack portend? Was it merely a bold raid against Beauregard's flank, or was it the preliminary of a movement to transfer the campaign to the south side of the James? The movement of the Army of the Potomac over the James was taken for granted by many. Lee, however, had to consider all other possibilities. He could not afford to weaken his front north of the Chickahominy on the assumption that his adversary had suddenly changed his strategy and his tactics. Nor could Lee overlook the chance that Grant might shift to the south of the Chickahominy and besiege Richmond between that stream and the James. Finally, Lee had to consider the likelihood that Grant would return the troops taken from Butler and undertake simultaneous operations up both banks of the James.

Either Lee had to attack or he had to concentrate on his right and prepare to move after Grant as soon as his adversary marched southward from the Cold Harbor line. Much as Lee desired to take the initiative, the first course was impracticable. He could only prepare for the next stage of the campaign by concentrating on his right. This he did by bringing Early from the left and putting him in rear of A. P. Hill.

Early took his new position on the 11th. The previous day Breckinridge had telegraphed that Hunter was moving up the Valley, either toward Lexington or toward the gaps that led to Lynchburg. Bragg was of opinion that the Valley should be cleared; Davis passed on the message to Lee. Lee answered that it was desirable to expel the enemy from the Valley, but that this would require him to detach a corps. "If it is deemed prudent," he said, "to hazard the defense of Richmond . . . I will do so." The next day the news was that Hunter had occupied Lexington on the 11th. Without further debate on the subject, Lee ordered Early to start on the morning of the 13th with his artillery and his 8000 infantry to meet Hunter. With good generalship, Early would have enough men to dispose of Hunter. Then Lee planned that Early should make a new demonstration against Washington and Baltimore. This, Lee hoped, would either compel Grant to attack the Army of Northern Virginia or force him to detach troops for the defense of the capital and give Lee prospect of a successful offensive.

By one of those coincidences that place the history of the Army of Northern Virginia among the most dramatic stories in the annals of war, Lee's skirmishers brought back the long-expected word at the very hour when the men of Early's corps were turning their faces westward: The long trenches in front of Cold Harbor were empty; Grant was gone. Immediately the order was given to take up the pursuit. Lee threw both corps across the Chickahominy, struck for the Charles City road and moved down it toward Riddell's Shop. Late in the afternoon contact with the enemy was established by Hill's corps and he was forced steadily eastward. Nightfall found the army extended southward from the White Oak Swamp. Lee was covering the approaches to Richmond between the lower Chickahominy and the James and at the same time had his right flank within ten miles of the pontoon bridge at Drewry's Bluff in case Grant moved across James River.

Darkness ended the pursuit on the evening of the 13th. Lee intended to attack with Hill's corps on the morning of June 14, but before the skirmishers advanced at dawn the enemy had departed.

It was impossible to ascertain with certainty the position or movements of the Federals. By maintaining strong guards at the crossroads,

Grant could screen his army as effectively as if he had taken ship and vanished down the James. For the first time since the opening of the campaign Lee was out of touch with his adversary. His cavalry was too scanty to make a reconnaissance in force and the infantry both too distant and too weak to attempt an advance.

Weighing all the probabilities suggested by such reports as he had, Lee wrote the President at 12:10 P.M. June 14:

> ". . . I think the enemy must be preparing to move South of James River . . . I apprehend that he may be sending troops up the James River with the view of getting possession of Petersburg before we can reinforce it. We ought therefore to be extremely watchful and guarded. Unless I hear something satisfactory by evening, I shall move Hoke's division back to the vicinity of the pontoon bridge across James River in order that he may cross if necessary. The rest of the army can follow should circumstances require it."

Information accumulated that Grant was on the James and that part of his forces were at Wilcox's Landing where the stream was narrow. Lee made his contemplated disposition of Hoke.

If Grant was going to cross the James the Army of Northern Virginia might be called upon to defend both sides of the river. It seemed desirable to retire closer to the Richmond entrenchments when messages from Beauregard raised a new doubt whether Grant was actually contemplating an early crossing of the James. Beauregard announced that transports were moving upstream. Lee decided not to draw back to the fortifications of Richmond on the night of the 14th. Instead, he kept his headquarters at Riddell's Shop and remained with his right flank in the direction of Malvern Hill.

The next morning, June 15, opened one of the most difficult periods in the history of the Army of Northern Virginia, a crisis that put Lee's military judgment to the supreme test. The enemy was active on his front but the ease with which the Federals were driven back renewed Lee's doubts whether Grant intended to attack on the north side of the James. As that, in turn, increased the probability of an attack on Petersburg, Lee felt that he should not hold Hoke any longer at the pontoon bridge but should send him forthwith to support Beauregard. He issued orders accordingly.

Very soon a courier arrived with dispatches from Bragg. These covered telegrams from Beauregard. The latest of them set forth that the return of Butler's forces and the arrival of Grant at Harrison's Landing rendered Beauregard's position "more critical than ever." Beauregard said: "If not reinforced immediately, enemy could force my lines at Bermuda Hundred Neck, capture Battery Dantzler, now nearly ready, or take Petersburg, before any troops from Lee's army or Drewry's Bluff could arrive in time." He concluded, "Can anything be done in the matter?" Lee had anticipated Beauregard's need by dispatching Hoke, and now he urged that Ransom be returned to Beauregard. Pending further developments, he decided to keep the remainder of the army, now reduced to six divisions, on the lines it then occupied.

So far as the records show, Lee received no further advices from Richmond that day. Beauregard reported new movements of the enemy in front of Petersburg in a series of dispatches to Bragg, but his files show no telegrams to Lee, though copies of two messages to Bragg were directed through Richmond to be forwarded to Lee. The second of these, 9:11 P.M., announced that the enemy had penetrated the lines at Petersburg. Johnson would be sent there to aid Hoke, Beauregard said, and Lee would have to look to the defense of Petersburg and of Bermuda Neck. The evidence is strong the message had not reached Lee when he was awakened at 2 A.M. on June 16 and handed this telegram from Beauregard: "I have abandoned my lines of Bermuda Neck to concentrate all my force here: skirmishers and pickets will leave there at daylight. Cannot these lines be occupied by your troops? The safety of our communications requires it. Five thousand or 6,000 men may do."

Manifestly, no soldier of Beauregard's distinction would be abandoning the Bermuda Hundred line and concentrating on Petersburg unless the enemy was likely to capture that city. But was it Grant or Butler, and in what strength? Being wholly in the dark, Lee could only act on the information Beauregard gave him. Lee did what he had done wherever Beauregard had made a call for troops in the face of an immediate threat: He sent them. Although the act would reduce his mobile force on the north side of the James to something between 21,000 and 24,000 infantry, plus the doubtful strength of the immobile Richmond garrison, he summoned Pickett's division from the vicinity of Frayser's Farm and directed it to cross the river at Drewry's Bluff and to occupy the lines. Anderson was instructed to proceed at once to Bermuda Hundred and to take charge on the exposed front. Beauregard was requested, if he could, to keep his skirmishers in position until these reinforcements arrived. It was only a request, for in dealing

GENERAL GEORGE E. PICKETT

FEDERAL DEAD AT GETTYSBURG, *July 1, 1863*

with Beauregard, Lee did not exercise the power, if indeed he knew it had been given him the previous day by the President, to direct the operations of all separate commands in Virginia and North Carolina—a definite if belated recognition of the need of a unified command.

One brigade of Pickett's division was speedily under way; the others were slow in taking the road. Lee broke up his headquarters at Riddell's Shop and followed the first troops. Shortly before 9:40 A.M., on the morning of June 16, he was south of the river, midway between his own army and Petersburg. Here he could supervise operations on the Bermuda Hundred front; but he had to rely on the telegraph for communication with Beauregard and on a line of couriers to Malvern Hill and beyond.

His first act on arriving was to advise Beauregard of his position and to inform him of the arrival of Pickett's division, with a request for what he needed most—intelligence as to what the enemy was doing. Before Beauregard could receive this message, one was handed Lee from Petersburg. Evidently Beauregard had sent earlier dispatches that had not been received, dispatches in which he had asked for reinforcements; but now he explained nothing except that he was being pressed and needed help. In the absence of specific information as to Beauregard's situation, Lee at 10:30 A.M. could only telegraph him in answer:

"Your dispatch of 9:45 received. It is the first that has come to hand. I do not know the position of Grant's army, and cannot strip north bank of the James. Have you not force sufficient?"

Shortly after 1 o'clock Lee heard from Anderson that he had encountered the enemy and was driving the Union skirmishers back. "It is to be presumed," wrote Anderson, "that he has possession of our breastworks opposite Bermuda Hundred." The commander of the First Corps went on: "I have not been able to communicate with our troops near Petersburg. If I find difficulty in clearing the road it will be impracticable for General Pickett to reach Petersburg."

A new complication, this! Regardless of how badly Beauregard might need reinforcements, if the road to Petersburg was blocked they could not be sent there speedily. More than that, as he would have to follow roundabout roads, Lee feared it would be a slow and costly business to "bottle" Butler again and to reopen the Petersburg turnpike. So, without delay, Lee ordered Field's division to cross at Drewry's Bluff and directed that Kershaw march his division to the north end of the pontoon bridge and await orders. Leaving the heavy artillery and the cavalry out of account, the comparative strength of the forces defending Richmond and those on the Drewry's Bluff–Petersburg front would now be: north side, 20,000 to 23,000; south side, 22,600.

Beauregard's next telegram explained only that Pickett had not reached his line at Bermuda Neck by 10:30 and that, at that hour, his pickets still held the second line, under orders to maintain it as long as practicable. Lee's information did not indicate that the pickets were still in position, and at 1:15 he telegraphed Beauregard that he feared their withdrawal had caused the loss of the line. He explained Anderson's movements and his plans to repossess the lines and concluded: "What line have you on your front? Have you heard of Grant's crossing James River?"

Soon it was 3 o'clock. Anderson was driving back the Federal skirmishers when Lee received a reassuring answer from Beauregard, written at 12:45 P.M.:

"Your dispatch of 10:20 received. We may have force sufficient to hold Petersburg. Pickett will probably need re-enforcements on the lines of Bermuda Hundred Neck. At Drewry's Bluff at 9 A.M. or later no news of Pickett's division."

Still not a word about the troops opposing Beauregard! Lee replied with a broad hint for more specific information and with a frank statement that he himself had no positive knowledge on Grant's crossing the river. In answer Beauregard only stated that the signal corps reported the movement of forty-two transports up the James in recent days. Lee now made specific inquiry on the all-important question: Had Grant been seen crossing the James? This time the answer was slow in coming. Down the Petersburg pike, Anderson's troops manoeuvred for the second line occupied that morning by the Federals and took the left of it about 6 P.M.

At last, there came a more specific telegram from Beauregard, written at 7 P.M.:

"There has been some fighting today without result. Have selected a new line of defences around city, which will be occupied tomorrow, and hope to make it stronger than the first. The only objection to it is its proximity to city. No satisfactory information yet received of Grant's crossing James River. Hancock's and Smith's corps are however in our front."

Lee must have held that sheet a long time in his hand and must have read it again and again—nothing in that to hint of disaster or even of acute danger. Was Lee to conclude that the main Federal army was still on the northside? It was a portentous question with which to close a day of doubt.

The first news that reached Lee on June 17 was altogether encouraging. At 11 o'clock the previous night Pickett's men had recaptured the first Confederate line on the left, from the Howlett House to Clay's Farm. From Petersburg Beauregard reported that he had repulsed two attacks during the night and had captured 400 prisoners, though he had not entirely regained his first position. For the time it seemed as if the situation was stabilized, with every prospect that Petersburg would be held, that the Bermuda Hundred front would be recovered in its entirety, and that the four divisions on the north side of the James would not be needed south of the river.

Ordering the immediate repair of the Richmond-Petersburg Railroad, a part of which had been broken by Butler's advance, Lee watched the operations to regain the southern end of the first line on Bermuda Hundred Neck, kept Beauregard advised of his progress, and made a personal examination of Trent's Reach on the James, where the Federals had sunk a number of vessels in the hope of preventing the descent of the Confederate ironclads from Richmond. All was going well when, shortly before noon, Lee received this message from Beauregard, written at 9 A.M.:

"Enemy has two corps in my front, with advantage of position. Impossible to recover with my means part of lines lost. Present lines entirely too long for my available forces. I will be compelled to adopt shorter lines. Could I not be sufficiently re-enforced to take the offensive [and] thus get rid of the enemy here? Nothing positive yet known of Grant's movements."

Lee could only answer: "Until I get more definite information of Grant's movements I do not think it prudent to draw more troops to this side of the river."

Presently Beauregard telegraphed for information as to the movements of the V Corps. He suggested that it had probably gone to meet Early and that the Petersburg line might be suddenly reinforced and the enemy in his front crushed. This did not look as if Beauregard were *in extremis.* Lee replied with such scanty facts as he had concerning the movements of the V Corps to June 14; and, as it seemed impossible to get any detailed facts from Beauregard concerning Grant's operations, he turned again to the north bank to see if the cavalry there could find out where the V, VI, and IX Corps were.

Anderson by this time held all the Confederate second line and most of the first, except for a stronghold on Clay's Farm. During the early afternoon, Pickett on the left and Field on the right were made ready to assault this central position so as to restore the front Beauregard had held prior to the 16th. Just as the assault was about to be made, the engineers reported that a line could be drawn in such a fashion as to make an assault unnecessary. Orders were sent to abandon plans for attack. These orders reached Field, but they did not arrive at Pickett's headquarters until his men were on the move. Not knowing that Field had been ordered to remain where he was, Pickett informed Gregg's brigade of Field's division that he would need its support on his right flank. Gregg conformed and, gave warning to the next brigade on his right that his flank would have to be guarded. Ere long the whole left of Field's division was sweeping forward with Pickett. The Federals made only a feeble resistance. Shortly after 4 o'clock the Confederate flag was again flying along the whole of the front opposite Bermuda Neck.

The road to Petersburg was now out of range of the enemy, and the railway would soon be repaired. This had not been done a moment too soon, for Beauregard was forwarding new and alarming dispatches. The enemy, he said, had carried another of the weak points on his old line and was concentrating on his right centre. He was collecting all available troops to resist until nightfall, when he hoped to take up new lines. "We greatly need re-enforcements to resist such large odds against us," he concluded. "The enemy must be dislodged or the city will fall."

There was nothing specific, even yet, as to what units had crossed to Petersburg, but Lee felt that Beauregard's situation was now serious. He ordered A. P. Hill to move to Chaffin's Bluff, and Kershaw was directed to move to the Bermuda Hundred line.

The next telegram from Beauregard, written at 5 P.M., read thus:

"Prisoners just taken report themselves as belonging to the Second, Ninth and Eighteenth Corps. They state that the Fifth and Sixth Corps are coming on. Those from Second and Eighteenth came here by transports and arrived first; others marched

night and day from Gaines' Mill and arrived yesterday evening.
The Ninth crossed at Turkey Bend where they have a pontoon
bridge. They say Grant commanded on the field yesterday. All
are positive they passed Grant on the road several miles from
here."

If all this were true, a clear course of action was marked out. But
was it true? Lee had a poor opinion of the information given by
prisoners and by untried scouts, and with the fate of Richmond at stake
he was not prepared to trust everything to this telegraphic summary of
the examination of miscellaneous prisoners by an unidentified officer.
At the same time, if the information was correct, then there was every
reason to expect an overwhelming assault on Petersburg as soon as the
Army of the Potomac could be disposed in Beauregard's front. Lee concluded that the weight of probability was much on the side of Beauregard's information and that the greater part of Grant's army was on
the south side of the river, but he did not feel himself justified in
abandoning the possibility of an attack on Richmond by an adversary
whose command of the river made it easy for him to move swiftly
large bodies of men.

Before 10 o'clock this message from Beauregard, written at 6:40 P.M.,
was handed him:

"The increasing number of the enemy in my front, and inadequacy of my force to defend the already much extended lines,
will compel me to fall within a shorter one, which I will attempt
to effect tonight. I may have to evacuate the city very shortly.
In that event I shall retire in the direction of Drury's [Drewry's]
Bluff, defending the crossing at Appomattox River and Swift
Creek."

If Beauregard were reduced to this plight and faced as long odds as
his previous telegram had indicated, then some further chance had to
be taken that Richmond might be captured by a surprise attack, or else
Petersburg would be lost. Lee ordered Kershaw to march early the
next morning to reinforce Beauregard and instructed A. P. Hill to move
to the Petersburg pike and there to await further orders.

About the time these orders were issued, Captain A. R. Chisolm of
Beauregard's staff arrived with the details of the Federal offensive:
Dearing's 1900 cavalry had been driven back on the morning of June
15 to the lines that had been erected in a crude half circle on the south

side of the Appomattox River, in front of Petersburg. The enemy advanced from the east and skirmished briskly until 7 o'clock that evening. Shortly after that hour the Federals broke through the line just south of the City Point Railroad and could undoubtedly have marched straight into Petersburg had he pressed on. By the morning of the 16th the Confederates were able to present a more formidable front. During the afternoon a general assault was delivered. This gained some advantage for the Federals though it brought them no decision. Beauregard put up an almost flawless defense. At intervals the Confederates counterattacked as if they had abundant strength, and on nearly the whole of the line they held the enemy at bay. On the 17th the Federals renewed their attacks with vigor and soon penetrated a gap in the front of Johnson's division. Then about sundown they smashed through the right centre of Johnson's division and doubtless would have doubled up the whole of Beauregard's line but for the arrival of Gracie's brigade. Gracie counterattacked, closed the gap, and halted the enemy. As Chisolm was describing this to Lee, Beauregard was drawing back to a new line, well-sighted but unpleasantly close to Petersburg.

Chisolm's report and Beauregard's hint of a possible evacuation of Petersburg, determined Lee to send Field's division as a further reinforcement to Beauregard. The outlook brightened momentarily, after this was ordered, for a later message from Beauregard told of a successful repulse of the last assaults of the enemy; but the next dispatch, dated 12:40 A.M. contained a new warning:

"All quiet at present. I expect renewal of attack in morning. My troops are becoming much exhausted. Without immediate and strong reinforcements results may be unfavorable. Prisoners report Grant on the field with his whole army."

Before morning Lee learned that the last of Grant's army had crossed over to the south of the James.

By 3:30 A.M., on June 18, the situation was clear for the first time since the enemy had disappeared on the morning of June 13. Lee proceeded to shift the remainder of his force to the new front, and rode swiftly toward Petersburg.

At 7:30 that morning, as the exhausted troops of Beauregard's command put aside their spades and took up their muskets on the new line they had constructed during the night they saw the glint of the bayonets of Kershaw's division coming through a ravine near Blandford cemetery. It was to their weary eyes the fairest sight of the entire war.

Field's division arrived at 9:30 A.M.; Hill's divisions were spread out on the Petersburg pike, fighting dust and thirst and marching at a furious pace. When they arrived, which would not be before night, they were to take position on the extreme right and were to extend the front well beyond the railroad that led from Petersburg to Weldon.

Lee reached Petersburg about 11 o'clock and rode out at once to join Beauregard. Together they went over the line that had been drawn the previous night. It was so close to Petersburg that when the enemy organized his front the city could be bombarded. Otherwise, Lee had no fault to find with it. Beauregard proposed an instant attack against the enemy's flank, but Lee rejected the idea, in the conviction that the troops were too much exhausted for combat.

The great and bloody campaign from the Rapidan to Petersburg had now ended in something closely akin to what Lee had most desired to avoid. He could not have forgotten that he had told Early: If Grant reached James River, "it will become a siege, and then it will be a mere question of time." With communications still open and the troops on the north side of the James well outside the Richmond defenses, it was not yet a siege, but that, too, was only a question of time.

The burdens Lee took up at Petersburg on June 18 occupied him daily. Each morning brought so much of anxiety that the evening found him weary. The crowded present gave him little time to think of the past. Yet there must have been rare hours when he could look back on the bloody wrestle from the Rapidan to Petersburg and would ask himself whether anything could have saved his army from the ordeal of the long and ghastly siege. Students of military history have been raising the same question ever since. Rarely has it been considered for what it fundamentally was—on one side an example of the costliness but ultimate success of the methods of attrition when unflinchingly applied by a superior force and, on the other, an impressive lesson in what resourcefulness, sound logistics, and careful fortification can accomplish in making prolonged resistance possible, even on a limited field of manoeuvre, by an army that faces oppressive odds.

Lee's object from the hour Grant started his columns down the Rapidan was clear: He would seek to catch his adversary on the march and to destroy him, or, if that was impossible, to keep him from reaching Richmond.

In seeking to attain his object, Lee was as heavily handicapped as a general well could be: His numbers were scarcely more than half those of his opponent; he had no prospect of large reinforcements; his artillery was inferior in weight of metal and in range to that of the enemy; the mounts of his cavalry could not endure hard service and could not be replaced when worn out; because of casualties and illness during the campaign, he had to change the commanders of two of his three corps and the senior officers of more than a third of his brigades; for eleven days he was himself almost incapacitated; he was once cut off from his base of supplies, lost his reserve food supplies, and, during the early stages of the campaign, had to subsist his men and feed his horses on rations that barely sustained life. At the very crisis of Grant's offensive, Lee was compelled to detach two brigades and then an entire corps. Save for a major disaster in the field, virtually everything happened to him that could operate to prevent the fulfillment of his mission.

From the Confederate point of view, the whole of the battle of the Wilderness presented a succession of dangers and difficulties. If they were met by Lee in such a manner as to leave no just ground for criticism except for his failure to fortify or to withdraw from the line of Heth and Wilcox on the night of the 5th, then the result manifestly is a credit to Lee's generalship. But that is not all. When an army that is numerically to its enemy as six to ten is able to inflict losses that are in the ratio of fourteen to seven, then a question is raised as to the skill with which the larger army is handled. Especially is this the case if most of the fighting occurs outside field fortifications. It is beyond the function of a biographer of Lee to criticise the skill of his opponents, but in reaching a fair appraisal of Lee's place as a soldier, the short-comings of his adversaries must sometimes be taken into account. How was it that Grant exposed his right as he did on the 6th of May? With so large an army at his disposal, why did he not more adequately cover his left flank south of the Plank road? One of three conclusions seems inevitable: General Grant was less skillful in this battle than his previous achievements would have led one to expect, or he was care-lessly contemptuous of Lee, or else he relied on the great superiority in numbers to the neglect of the finer qualities of leadership.

The transfer of the First Corps from the Wilderness to Spotsylvania on the night of May 7–8 to anticipate Grant's move to that point, has always been regarded as one of Lee's most brilliant achievements. In piecing information together, and in deciding that Grant was making for Spotsylvania, Lee did no more than he had done on a dozen oc-casions. The act was spectacular because the results were. A close study of his logistics on May 7–8 will show them to have been flawless.

The student of war who is interested in economy of force can hardly find a better field exercise than to go to Spotsylvania and try to locate, in the face of an imaginary enemy, a stronger line, except for the "Mule Shoe," than Lee drew. Thrown on the defensive with a smaller force, Lee sought to protect his men and to increase the effectiveness of their fire by giving them the full benefit of temporary earthworks. What had been done at Fredericksburg after the battle of December 13, 1862, on the left in the initial stage of the Chancellorsville campaign, in the forest along Mine Run, and in the Wilderness was done more elaborately across the fields and through the woods around Spotsylvania.

At Spotsylvania, as in the Wilderness, Lee was materially helped by the methods his antagonist applied. Grant did not hold literally to his boast, "I never manoeuvre." He did manoeuvre, but he did not manoeuvre well. The chief criticism that must be made of the Federal operations at Spotsylvania, however, is the manner in which Grant on May 12 continued to hurl troops into the Bloody Angle until the captured position was so crowded with men that they got in one another's way.

The transfer of the Army of Northern Virginia from Spotsylvania Courthouse to the North Anna was in some respects an even finer military performance than the move from the Wilderness that halted Grant at Spotsylvania. Lee's reasons for taking that position involved more than placing the Army of Northern Virginia once more between Grant and Richmond. By moving to the North Anna, and then fortifying so strongly that his opponent did not even attack him there, Lee deflected to the eastward the line of Grant's advance on Richmond. That was strategically of the greatest consequence because it meant that the Virginia Central Railroad remained in Confederate hands. Communications with Staunton could be reopened. Co-operation between Grant and Sigel's successor was rendered more difficult. A drive against the Federals in the Valley was facilitated, and the roads for a new invasion of Maryland were restored to the Confederacy. It is not too much to state that Lee's arrival at the North Anna ahead of Grant prolonged the war by saving a large part of Virginia to the Confederacy for another six months. Lee's position was defensively ideal, but it could only serve to force Grant to another movement by his left flank.

When that movement was made on May 27, Lee had suspected such a manoeuvre and had his cavalry disposed far down the Pamunkey to warn him of any advance in that direction. Being quickly advised of the appearance of the enemy at Hanovertown, Lee encountered no difficulty in making the move from the North Anna to the Totopotomoy. Nothing of great moment happened until Grant made his shift to Cold Harbor. Once Grant had started for Cold Harbor, Lee's task was to reach that point in sufficient strength to thwart Grant's turning movement and, if possible, to double up his left. The only question that arises here is whether Lee concentrated at Cold Harbor on June 1 as heavily as he should have. The actions at Cold Harbor on June 1 were poorly directed on the Confederate side, but from the time Lee himself arrived the battle was well-ordered. He anchored his right on the high ground above the Chickahominy and located his support lines opposite the weakest points in his front. Then he simply waited. When Grant attacked, the Union lines were mowed down with a slaughter worse than that inflicted on Pickett and Pettigrew at Gettysburg.

The success of Grant in crossing the James unhindered and the failure of Lee to reinforce Petersburg more quickly and more heavily, after the attack of June 15, have been very generally regarded as the most serious blemishes on Lee's military record, with the possible exception of his order for Pickett's charge at Gettysburg. Three facts, however, cancel most of what has been written about this aspect of the movement:

1. Lee expected Grant to cross the James.

2. He knew the approximate position of his adversary by the early afternoon of June 14.

3. He had ordered Hoke's division to the Confederate pontoon bridge at Drewry's Bluff eight hours before Grant's bridge at Wilcox's Landing was finished.

Lee was ready, in short, to begin the reinforcement of Beauregard before Grant had done more than utilize his available transports to strengthen Butler's army.

When new troops began to appear in front of Petersburg on June 15, Lee naturally was forced to rely on Beauregard as to their number and identification. Unfortunately, many of the reports that he received from Beauregard were belated, vague, and well-nigh equivocal. This was not altogether Beauregard's fault, but it proved a handicap to Lee. Beauregard was an experienced officer whose rank and judgment were to be respected. Not one request for men did he make with which Lee did not comply, from the time of the first threat until Beauregard, becoming optimistic, asked for reinforcements to undertake a counteroffensive that Lee did not approve. All this is a most material consideration in determining whether Lee did everything that could have been expected of him.

Beauregard's troops made a splendid fight in front of Petersburg and were handled by him with great skill and boldness. Nobody could have done better, favored though he was by some curious delays and by a most singular division of authority among the Federal commanders. He was aided, too, by good initial positions and by a strong force of well-employed artillery. It must be said, however—and in no derogation of his generalship—that the excellence of Beauregard's battle grew as the story was told. Lee and his veterans were so accustomed to fighting against long odds that they took them as a matter of course. Lee did Beauregard the compliment of assuming that his men could fight equally well and against like odds. A commander who had seen Sharpsburg, Second Manassas, Fredericksburg, Gettysburg, and the Bloody Angle could hardly become so excited over the attacks on Petersburg that he would risk the capture of Richmond, strip the north bank of the James, and increase a force of 27,000 in order to resist an attack by a force that Beauregard put down at two corps. Lee had heard the cry of "Wolf-wolf" so often from the southside during May that he may have been a little skeptical of Beauregard's reports.

This is the record. It speaks for itself. Lee unavoidably lost contact with Grant on June 13–14, but he was not outgeneralled nor taken by surprise. If he did not reinforce Beauregard heavily at Petersburg until the strength of the attacking force became known, he gave Beauregard in every instance the help that general asked for defense; he sent enough troops to Petersburg to hold it, without neglecting his major mission, that of insuring the safety of Richmond.

The balance of achievement is overwhelmingly to Lee's credit. So far as general strategy and headquarters tactics could influence the result, his generalship had never been finer, if, indeed, it had ever been quite so good. Wherever Grant advanced, there he found Lee's bayonets closing the road to Richmond. Yet even before the crossing of the James, time and numbers were having their effect. Lee did not lose the battles, but he did not win the campaign. He delayed the fulfillment of Grant's mission, but he could not discharge his own. Lee found few opportunities of attacking the enemy in detail or on the march, and in every instance where he assumed the offensive, except in the turning movement of May 6, he failed to achieve the results for which he had hoped. This was not because the Army of Northern Virginia fought

less well than before, but because the Army of the Potomac was relatively stronger and fought better. "Lee's Miserables" never behaved
with greater gallantry than in the Wilderness on May 5 and in recovering the Bloody Angle on May 12; but their numbers were smaller,
and in some subtle fashion General Grant infused into his well-seasoned
troops a confidence they had never previously possessed. There was,
likewise, an ominous decline in the standard of Confederate corps, divisional, and brigade command. Too many of the ablest officers had been
killed and were replaced by soldiers less skillful. After Longstreet was
wounded, every corps commander failed badly, at least once. Two
excellent new divisional commanders were developed in Kershaw and
Gordon. Ramseur and Mahone showed promise. But some of the
others did not fulfill expectations, and a few more were definitely
mediocre. The same was true of the brigade commanders. There was no
remedy for it and there could be no blame on Lee because of this, but
the sombre fact remained: troops were no longer led as they had been
in the period from Second Manassas through Chancellorsville. In the
largest sense, only Lee and the men in the ranks still made the army
terrible in battle.

When General Lee went to church in Petersburg on June 19, the
military problem in the solution of which he sought divine guidance
was as grave as any he had ever faced. The front of battle was now
twenty-six miles in length. The whole of this line had at all times to
be held. Lee was required, in the second place, to prevent the enemy
from seizing ground that would force the Confederates back into the
Richmond defenses; thirdly, he had to cover the capital against surprise
attack; and fourthly, he had to keep open the railroads.

Lee's force had been so reduced by casualties and detachments that
he had small chance of undertaking a sustained offensive unless Grant
should be guilty of some serious blunder and present an opening. Lee
believed, however, that he could defend Richmond from a direct assault delivered on the northside, provided he could keep the Richmond-
Petersburg Railroad in running order for the transfer of troops in an
emergency.

The one advantage of the Confederate commander was this: Grant
had approached Petersburg from the east. His lines ran north and south
and had not yet been extended to the southwest or to the west. Lee's
lines, on the Confederate left, paralleled Grant's, but as Lee had to
protect Petersburg fully, he drew his lines north and south and then
to the west. From the point where Lee's line curved to the westward

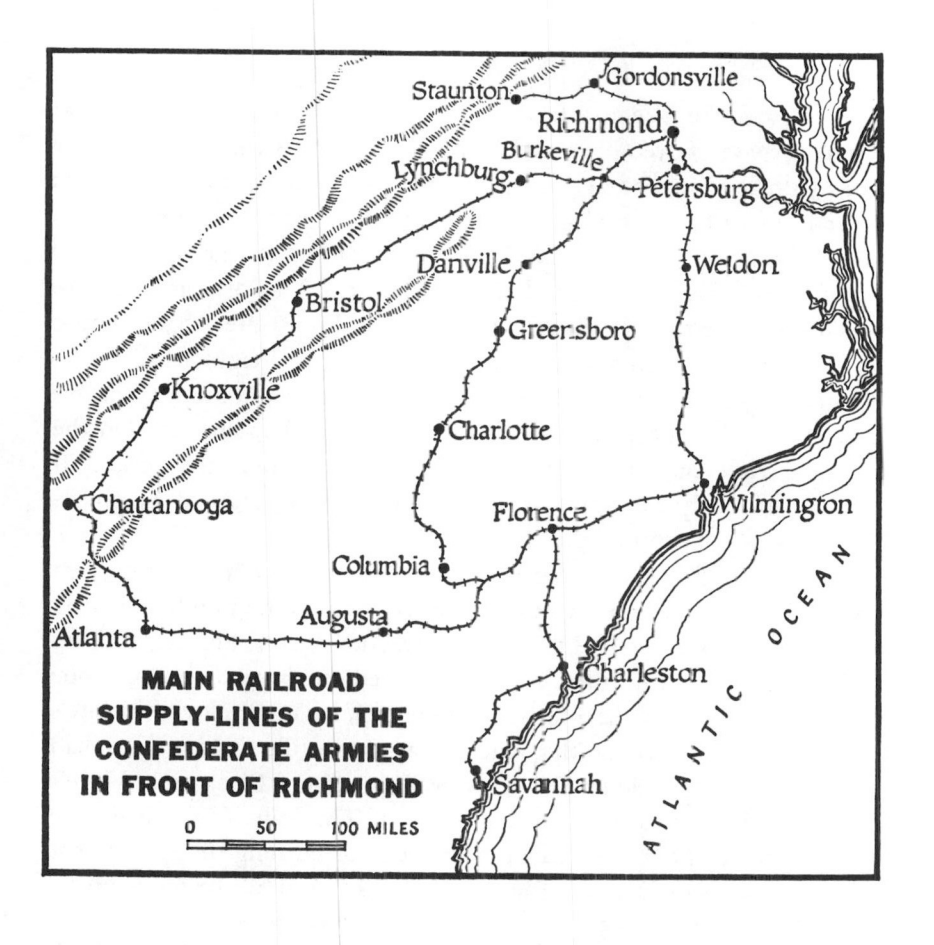

MAIN RAILROAD
SUPPLY-LINES OF THE
CONFEDERATE ARMIES
IN FRONT OF RICHMOND

0   50   100 MILES

the space between the two fronts widened until it became as much as
two miles. This gave Lee a freedom of manoeuvre on his right. He
employed his right division as a general reserve to strengthen the sector
to the east or to be moved across the James and aid Custis Lee, now
commanding the troops in Richmond.

Lee was almost entirely dependent on the railways to feed his army.
Surveying the lines of communication, he was satisfied that it would be
almost impossible to hold permanently the Petersburg and Weldon, the
northern end of which was less than three miles from the left of the
Federals. His aim was to keep the enemy from that railway until the
harvest in Virginia, or as long as he could do so without heavy loss.
Meantime, he urged that the Southside, the Richmond and Danville,
and the Piedmont railroads be supplied with ample rolling stock and
defended by the second-line reserves, so that these lines could supply
the army when the Petersburg and Weldon fell to the enemy.

On the 21st of June outposts reported an extension of the Federal lines toward the Weldon tracks. Simultaneously, Union cavalry was found to have started on a raid farther down the same road. Rooney Lee's troops were sent in pursuit of the raiders. Wilcox's division was moved out to take the place of the cavalry, but it found the enemy's infantry retiring. The next day Mahone thought he saw an opening for a flank attack. He found a gap between the II and VI Corps and quickly rolled up two strong Federal divisions. He skillfully drew back before night with more than 1600 prisoners, four guns and eight flags.

Encouraged by the evident low morale of the Federal infantry in this engagement, Lee projected an offensive near the Appomattox. On the 24th, he rode out and joined Beauregard to witness the action. It opened brilliantly but ended abruptly when the advance of Hagood's brigade was not supported.

This fiasco offset the success of the 22d. The net advantage of current operations depended on the outcome of the cavalry raid undertaken by the Federals on the 21st. Union horse reached Reams Station, tore up several miles of track there, and then started out in two columns, one to destroy the line of the Southside in the vicinity of Black-and-White's and the other to wreck the junction at Burkeville. Those who had moved to the Southside Railroad were driven from Black-and-White's and hurried off to join the other column. The joint force made for the bridge across Staunton River in the hope of burning the span, but it was repulsed valiently on June 25 by a handful of reserves under Captain L. B. Farinholt. On the 27th Lee's information was that the column was returning by a route chosen to bring the Federals back to the Weldon Railroad in the vicinity of Stony Creek.

General M. C. Butler reached Lee's headquarters that day, bringing cavalry reinforcements from Hampton. With Butler at hand, and the rest of Hampton's command coming up, Lee swiftly set a trap for the railroad wreckers. Butler was to place himself between the returning Federals and the Weldon Railroad. Hampton was to join him there. Mahone was advanced to Reams Station. Fitz Lee was to support him at that point with his division of cavalry. The plan worked perfectly. Butler and the rest of Hampton's division formed a junction with Rooney Lee. Together they drove the enemy on the 28th and headed him for Reams Station. Hampton pressed their rear, Mahone met them in front, and Fitz Lee struck their flank. The result was an utter rout, involving heavy Federal casualties, 1000 prisoners, thirteen guns, the wagon train and all the loot and Negroes that had been seized on the raid. This brilliant action gratified the army, and their heavy losses led the Federals to conclude that they no longer had a numerical superiority in cavalry. Federal commander Brigadier General James H. Wilson had, however, destroyed parts of two railways.

As continuous hot, dry weather forced a virtual suspension of large-scale operations toward the end of June, the only cheer in the army was over the good news of Early's advance down the Shenandoah Valley. When Early approached New Market and seemed to have a clear road to Harpers Ferry, Lee hoped for a time that a farther advance on Early's part might lead Grant to attack the Petersburg lines in the hope of compelling him to recall the expedition. And if Grant could be induced to attack, another Cold Harbor would be awaiting him.

Early's name was on every tongue late in June, and his prospects were discussed in every council and at every bivouac. He would be in position to threaten Washington. For a time he made a continent hold its breath. By July 4 he was at Harpers Ferry; on the 6th he crossed the old battlefield of Sharpsburg; the 9th saw him on the Monocacy, where he defeated Major General Lew Wallace; on the 11th he was within range of the forts defending Washington. His column was too feeble to venture an assault, and he had to withdraw on the 14th to Virginia soil, by way of White's Ford, above Leesburg. But he continued to demonstrate vigorously and on July 28 was able to anounce that he had again forced the enemy across the Potomac and was himself at Kernstown.

The outlook in the south became gloomy while Early's advance was raising hope in some hearts. General Johnston was manoeuvred from his strong position on Kennesaw Mountain and fell back close to Atlanta. There were hints that he intended to abandon Atlanta, also. President Davis had discovered in the winter of 1861–62 the proclivity of General Johnston for retreating, but he was slow to give ear to the clamor that now arose for the removal of that officer. Lee was not prepared for a crisis when he received on July 12 a cipher telegram from the President announcing that it was necessary to remove Johnston and asking what he thought of Hood as a successor. Lee knew little of the immediate reasons for the contemplated action of the President, but he knew the limitations of Hood. He accordingly wrote the chief executive:

"Telegram of today received. I regret the fact stated. It is a bad time to relieve the commander of an army situated as that of

Tenne. We may lose Atlanta and the army too. Hood is a bold
fighter. I am doubtful as to other qualities necessary."

This was as reserved as his counsel to the administration usually was
in everything that did not pertain to supplies or recruitment. Reading
between the lines, it was plain that he doubted the wisdom alike of
removing Johnston and of naming Hood. He must have had no little
misgiving when he learned on July 18 that Johnston had been ordered
to turn over the army to Hood. If Hood succeeded, there was hope for
the South. But if he failed, only the dwindling Army of Northern
Virginia stood before the Confederacy and ruin.

Wearily, along lines that were now becoming formidable earthworks,
the survivors of Lee's many battles awaited the next move of their adversary. An hour before each dawn every man stood at arms to repel
attack. Half an hour before dusk the whole of each regiment mounted
the fire step and remained there until dark. The sharpshooters became
so proficient on both sides that momentary exposure was almost certain
to result in a serious wound, if not in death. There was always, too, the
danger of an exchange of mortar shells. Heat, flies, and the stench of
the latrines made existence a torture.

Often the weary men thought they heard the sound of picks at work,
far underground. As early as July 1, General Alexander reported to
Lee his conviction that the enemy was mining. Countershafts were
sunk and listening galleries run out, but the engineers failed to encounter
Federal miners. Suspicion was strongest that the enemy was striking for
a position known as Elliott's salient, south of the Appomattox and
southeast of Blandford Cemetery.

On July 23 there were reports that Union troops had crossed to the
north side of the James. Lee thought it likely that they were intended
for no serious operations, but as a precaution the south side was almost
denuded by transfers. In front of Petersburg were left only about 18,000
infantry. To risk the very existence of this small force was to purchase
security for Richmond at a heavy price. Perhaps it was at this time
that Lee began to doubt whether it was wise to attempt indefinitely to
hold Richmond with his weakened army. Late in the night of July
29–30, after reading the dispatches from the north side, Lee became
satisfied that the enemy was merely making feints at other points and
was preparing to attack on the Petersburg sector. At 2 A.M. on the
30th, a general warning was sent down the trenches.

Then, at 4:44 on the morning of July 30, there came the sound of a mighty explosion, somewhere to the southeast of Petersburg. At 6:10 a galloping officer arrived from General Beauregard. On the front of Elliott's brigade, he said, the enemy had blown up the Confederate line, and under cover of a wild tornado of fire had thrown forward heavy columns into the crater formed by the upheaval of hundreds of tons of earth. The Federals were already in the works and at the moment might even be advancing straight on Cemetery Hill. Lee's orders were given almost as soon as the message was delivered. The line must be restored at once. General Mahone was to draw two brigades out of the line, unobserved by the enemy, and to hurry them to a position in rear of the gap in the fortifications. Lee hurried toward the front.

The explosion had occurred about the middle of Elliott's front. It had destroyed the front line for a distance of 135 feet and had left a crater some thirty feet deep, with a breadth, from front to rear, of ninety-seven feet. Nine companies, forming part of two South Carolina regiments, had been blown up, together with the men of Pegram's four-gun battery, which was stationed between the main earthworks and the cavalier trench. The enemy had crowded into the crater by the thousand, and had captured about thirty yards of the line to the right of it and some 200 yards to the left. Union flags floated also from the second line, though none of the Federals were yet over its parapet. Elliott's men had rallied quickly. On the left and behind the traverses that led from the first line to the second, they were keeping the Federals at bay. On the right, a fragment of Elliott's brigade had the support of Wise's men, who held a sector from which they could pour a fire into the crater and across the field leading to it. These two brigades, almost un-aided, had met the first onslaught and had prevented the enemy from extending his front. The artillery had gone into action quickly and was pouring a blasting fire into the crater.

Evidently the enemy was stopped, but for how long? Where were Mahone's two brigades? Moving up, their commander said. A third brigade had been ordered to join them. Were any other reinforcements available? None, except one regiment that Hoke was sending from the left and a few of Elliott's men, who had been placed in a sheltered ravine. Mahone must charge with what he had—and as quickly as he could file his men into the depression where the South Carolinians were waiting. The infantry fire had slackened somewhat by this time—it was now after 8—or else the ears of the combatants had been deadened to its rattle, but the artillery bombardment increased in violence every moment. Fourteen Union flags were visible now; Federal officers could be seen on the parapet of the second line, waving their swords and urging their men to come out of the ditch and charge up Cemetery Hill. How much more time would be required to get all the men into the countercharge? At last the word was given for the soldiers to move out of the ravine and to crouch in the open as they formed their line. Only one special instruction was given—that the troops should not fire till they were on the enemy.

Soon a Federal officer on the parapet seized a flag, called once more to his men to charge, and sprang down toward the open ground between him and the Confederates. Out from the works came his followers, their number swelling every second.

"Tell Weisiger to move forward," said Mahone on the instant.

But Weisiger had not waited for orders. He had shouted "Forward" and his 800 men, with some of the Georgia troops and a fragment of Elliott's brigade, raised the old rebel yell and started up the hill.

Up the hill the line swept, its ragged battle flags flying, with the fire of all the Confederate batteries redoubled as if in applause. "No quarter!" some foolish Federal cried, as they leaped into the rear work. They answered with one volley, jumped over the parapet, and fought it out with bayonet and clubbed musket. Only a few minutes of this and then, their lines irregular but unbroken, they rushed for the front trench. Thrust and counterthrust there, and soon, through the smoke, the red of their flags could be seen on the main parapet.

Most of the ground on the left was recovered in this charge; the gap was narrowed. Now for the right! Those of the Georgia brigade who had not assaulted with Weisiger were ordered forward to take the second line. They advanced, but met so heavy a fire that they drifted to the left and only reached the rear position already occupied by their comrades. Still the enemy held the crater.

One more effort must be made, this time by the third brigade of Mahone's division, Sanders's Alabamians, who had been summoned from the right. Arriving at 11 o'clock, they were disposed with care. Lee sent word to Sanders that he had no more troops available. If the Alabamians did not take the crater on the first assault, he said, he would re-form them and would lead them in person. The thing *had* to be done.

They were ready now. It was 1 o'clock. The order "Forward!" went down the line, and the men began to creep out from the ravine and up the hill. The artillery roared anew; shells screamed like frightened birds. Soon the men were in the open, where the enemy's fire began to tell. Directly up the incline they went, straight for the crater. Lee saw them reach the second line, from which the enemy had fled. They waited there only long enough to catch their breath and were about to dash into the crater when, at one point, a white flag was raised and the Federals surrendered. At another place on the crater rim the fighting kept up. Some of the Alabama troops lifted their caps on their ramrods just over the rim of the crater. A hundred bullets tore them to tatters, and the volley that was meant for the men was wasted. Immediately the Alabamians sprang into the crater, followed by soldiers from the other brigades of the division. The *mêlée* was like a battle of despairing demons. The sight of Negro troops, whom they now encountered in close action for the first time, seemed to throw Mahone's men into a frenzy. Bewildered by the onslaught, all the Federals who could do so fell back into a smaller pit, in front of which the explosion had raised an earthen barrier. The Confederates were preparing to follow them when there were wild cries, shouts, uplifted hands, frantic appeals, and a final surrender.

The "Battle of the Crater" was over. At 2:25, Lee was able to report to the War Department, "We have retaken the salient and driven the enemy back to his lines with loss." Mahone counted 1101 prisoners and Johnson's division had a lesser quota. Twenty flags were taken. The price paid by the Confederates was about 1500, of whom 278 lost their lives or were captured when the mine exploded. Lee was much gratified that so serious a threat had been repulsed with such unequal losses, and he said of the action, "Every man in it has today made himself a hero."

Bloody as had been the repulse of Grant at the Crater, Lee expected him to continue mining and pressed the work of driving countershafts. He learned on August 4 that Grant was moving troops down James River. The Federal commander had so entrenched himself that he could now send off troops and still hold his lines. Lee felt that if it were Grant's intention to overwhelm Early, it would be better to detach troops too than to risk the loss of Early's little army and of the Virginia Central Railroad.

Promptness was half of advantage; so, on August 6, Lee went to Richmond and held a conference with President Davis and General Anderson. The conclusion was to dispatch Kershaw's division of infantry and Fitz Lee's cavalry to northern Virginia under Anderson. Anderson should not join Early at once but should take position in Culpeper, where he could menace the flank and rear of the Federals in case they advanced up the Valley against Early. The troops moved the same day.

On August 14 the enemy attacked with vigor on the north side of

James River. The Federals seized the works near Fussell's Mill but were met by two regiments of dismounted cavalry, and when Field brought up a brigade of infantry the enemy was flanked and forced to retire. Lee had no troops to spare. His judgment told him that the Federal move might be a feint, but after assurance from Field that it was serious he ordered two brigades of infantry from the Petersburg front. Going to Chaffin's Bluff on August 15, Lee found that except for some cavalry fighting the Federals had not renewed the action, though they were manifestly very numerous and were fortifying. The enemy's delay gave Lee time to bring up troops that had been ordered from the south side, together with a scratch brigade from Pickett's division.

During the forenoon of the 16th, Lee heard from Field that the Federal cavalry had driven Rooney Lee's pickets from White Oak Swamp and had moved in force up the Charles City road. This was ominous news; the Federals were in rear of Field's left and on a direct road to Richmond. Lee at once sent a message to President Davis asking that the local defense troops be called out, and he prepared to take Field's left brigades and to throw them against the flank of the force on the Charles City road. For that purpose he rode along the advanced line, toward Field's position near Fussell's Mill. But before he could reach that point, and long before the tocsin was sounded in Richmond, the enemy had approached within fifty yards of the light Confederate works, to the left of the mill. Then, with a rush and a cheer, the Federals charged. Two Southern brigades broke, and a gap was torn in Field's front. In a quick counterattack, Field's division pushed the Union troops back and speedily recovered the works. A little later, on the Charles City road, more by chance than by fine logistics, the van of Hampton's division arrived to support Rooney Lee. The crisis ended as quickly as it had arisen.

Lee prepared a cavalry operation for the 18th to clear his left flank along the Charles City road. This was measurably successful, but before it was fully developed Beauregard telegraphed that a Federal column was moving toward the Weldon Railroad. By the morning of the 19th at least three divisions of Federal infantry were on the railroad, in the vicinity of Globe Tavern, three and a half miles south of the Confederate right at Petersburg. Later in the day indications pointed to a return to the south side of part of the troops that had been operating on Field's front. That same afternoon, A. P. Hill struck the enemy's column and captured 2700 prisoners. The Federals, however, kept their grip on the railroad and could not be dislodged.

The contingency Lee had anticipated from the time he took up the Petersburg line was at hand: The northern end of the Weldon Railroad from Rowanty Creek to Petersburg was definitely lost. The defense of the capital and the subsistence of the Army of Northern Virginia had now to depend on the full employment of the Southside and of the Richmond and Danville railroads. The loss of the Weldon road came, unfortunately, at a time when there was no corn either in Richmond or at the army depots around Petersburg. Lee at once set wagon trains to hauling supplies over the twenty miles of road that lay between Petersburg and Stony Creek, below the point where the railroad had been torn up by the Federals. He believed it would be possible to subsist the army until the Virginia corn crop was harvested.

Four days after Lee decided to abandon the effort to recover the Weldon Railroad, there came a dramatic epilogue. With Rooney Lee's division and his own, now under M. C. Butler, Hampton was operating west of the railway and in front of the Confederate right. A reconnaissance in force toward Reams Station, some four and a half miles south of Globe Tavern, showed Hampton that the Federals were tearing up the railroad near that point. He found that they were not well placed and asked the assistance of the infantry in making an attack. It was desirable, of course, that the enemy should not be left free to destroy the railroad indefinitely to the southward, for this would increase the distance between Petersburg and that part of the railroad still in Southern hands. Lee read Hampton's proposal sympathetically and decided to adopt it.

On August 24 infantry brigades were quietly moved beyond the right of the Confederate trenches. The next morning, with Hampton clearing the way, they advanced eastward. They found Hancock's II Corps in front of feeble works at Reams Station, entirely separated from the V Corps of Warren. An assault by Wilcox was repulsed. After a brief delay, part of his division and some of Heth's troops attacked farther to the left. They were brilliantly supported by Pegram's artillery and quickly stormed the right of the Federal lines. Simultaneously, Hampton worked his way around to the Federal left and, dismounting his men, threw them against the enemy. The victory was immediate and decisive, for the raw recruits in Hancock's corps behaved badly. Some 2000 were captured, along with nine guns, and the attempt of the Federals to destroy more of the railroad was abandoned. The Confederate infantry brought off their wounded, buried their dead, and returned the same night to Petersburg.

Like almost every other Confederate reverse during the investment of Petersburg, the loss of the Weldon road had its origin in the disparity of forces with which Lee had to defend so long a line. The fortunes of war, which in this case were but another name for numerical inferiority, were running strongly against him. He saw plainly that Grant's operations were designed to starve him out, and for this last, dreadful struggle he prepared himself as best he could with his ever-dwindling resources.

After the close of the battles for the Weldon Railroad, Lee returned to Chaffin's Bluff. He must have needed all his self-mastery to maintain his cheerfulness and his calm, for each day seemed to bring new anxieties and new perplexities, personal and official. Robert had been wounded on August 15, though not seriously; Custis's health was so uncertain that Mr. Davis was unwilling to assign him to duty in the Shenandoah Valley, where there was a vacancy in the cavalry; Mrs. Lee's condition was as bad as ever. The wear of war was showing on every arm of the service. For a hundred days, Lee told President Davis on August 29, there had not been one without casualties. In the midst of loss, alarms, and exhausting duty, Lee had to take up the old task of reorganization once again.

Hampton had shown so much energy and ability that he had been given command of all the cavalry on August 11. He made several excellent suggestions for its betterment. Hampton, moreover, took a hint from Lee that he might advantageously organize an expedition in rear of Grant's base at City Point, and from this he developed a plan for a raid that, on September 14, was brilliantly executed. It brought 2486 steers to the Confederate commissary at a time when there was only a fifteen-day supply of meat in Richmond for Lee's army.

Lee did not and could not misread the warnings of coming calamity, as written at Mobile, in front of Atlanta, and in the Shenandoah Valley. He did not urge on the government the evacuation of Richmond, for when its defense was his chief mission, his sense of discipline precluded any discussion of the subject. Yet it seems probable that he was beginning to consider the advisability of abandoning Richmond and Petersburg, of shortening his communications by retiring to the Staunton River, and of undertaking operations in an open country where he would have a wide field of manoeuvre.

Many of Lee's officers who had been wounded in the early stages of the campaign were now returning to duty. But attrition and exhaustion were daily becoming more serious. The local defense troops were being called out so often at Richmond that their absence interfered with the flow of munitions and the transaction of governmental business, yet in an emergency they could cover only a short sector of the defenses. Desertion, too, was disgracing and weakening the army. Morale was definitely declining. So great was the need for every private that Lee could not even furlough the Jewish soldiers for their religious observances.

For the dark emergency these conditions so tragically disclosed, Lee saw but one major policy the government could employ. That was the vigorous enforcement of the conscription act of February 17, 1864. Lee argued that this statute be applied to the letter. Urging that every man who was physically fit be brought into the field, he pleaded for the speedy organization of the reserves. In his letters he exhibited none of the deep feeling of the army at the injustice of exemptions, but nothing that he could say to speed up conscription before it would be too late, did he leave unsaid. Besides asking for 5000 Negro laborers to build roads and fortifications, he recommended that Negroes serve as teamsters and perform all possible labor that would release white men for combat service.

Lee began to speak very plainly concerning the inevitable results of unchecked attrition. His views were expressed only in confidential letters to the administration, but they more than hint that he believed the Southern cause was becoming hopeless. As early as August 23 he told the Secretary of War: "Without some increase of strength, I cannot see how we can escape the natural military consequences of the enemy's numerical superiority."

Scarcely had this warning been written than it was emphasized by a tragedy on the north side of the James, a tragedy that might have become a catastrophe. Lee had long been apprehensive of a heavy attack on that part of the defenses, where at the time he had barely 2000 men. He instructed Colonel W. Proctor Smith to build a new line of fortifications there, and on September 28 he ordered General Anderson to move north of the James and, under the direction of General Ewell, to assume command. The next morning, early, Lee received a telegram from Ewell announcing that the Federals had made a surprise attack on Fort Harrison and had captured it. This was one of the most important positions on the outer line of Richmond. Its loss was serious and might open the road to the capital. Lee forthwith notified Bragg and directed him to call out the local defense units and all other troops that could be assembled. Telegraphing Ewell to recover the fort, he sent at the same time for Field, whose troops were ordered to Hoke's division. Four regiments from Pickett were rushed to the northside. Rooney Lee was directed to move his division over, and six field batteries were given similar orders. As soon as these movements were under way, Lee went in person to the front. He considered a night attack to recover Fort Harrison, but he deferred operations until the morning of the 30th.

It was past noon when Hoke was in position to attack from a point slightly west of north, while Field was drawn up on a front northwest of the fort. Then the artillery opened for about half an hour. Field had about 500 yards to go, whereas Hoke could form in a ravine close to the towering earthworks the Federals held. Field threw out Anderson's brigade with instructions to advance as close as possible to the Federal position and then to lie down until he saw that he and Hoke's troops would reach the works at the same moment. Anderson did not tell his men they were to halt, and when they got orders to advance, they thought they were to drive their charge home. Seeing them rushing forward, Field had to send Bratton's and Perry's brigades in support. Concentrated fire forced Anderson back; Bratton and Perry were thrown into confusion, and the whole attack soon collapsed. Hoke must have realized that Field was attacking prematurely, but he waited until the agreed time and then delivered an assault, with the understanding that Bratton was to renew his attack at the same time. But co-ordination was not on the cards that day. Hoke was so quickly repulsed that Bratton did not make another attempt.

At this moment Lee arrived on the ground and rode along the ranks of Hoke's division as it formed again. Astride Traveller, he seemed oblivious to the fire, exposing himself recklessly. His hat was in his hand; his gray hair was shining in the afternoon light. A mighty cheer went up from the North Carolinians when they recognized him. He urged them to the charge. Fort Harrison was an important part of the defenses, he said, and he was sure the men could storm it if they would make one more earnest effort. They shouted their willingness to try, and, at the order, rushed out again—only to be repulsed a second time, in greater disorder and with heavier losses than before. But Lee persisted. The men did not refuse. As courageously as before, they went forward, but when they were again repulsed and hurled back, they were not far from panic and did not halt until they had reached cover. Fortunately the enemy did not attempt to follow the repulsed troops or to exploit his success. Gloomily Lee rode back to Chaffin's Bluff; re-

gretfully he had to report to the War Department the failure to recapture Fort Harrison.

While Lee was trying to recapture Fort Harrison, Hampton was
checking a Federal advance that might have carried to the Southside
Railroad. On the 29th, Butler's cavalry had been attacked and driven
back, but Rooney Lee's division arrived opportunely and reversed the
situation. It had been necessary to leave scarcely more than a picket
line on part of the Petersburg defenses. Lee saw plainly what this endless
extension of line involved. He wrote the Secretary of War a new appeal
for men in which, for the first time, he spoke of the fall of Richmond as
a possibility.

Early in October Lee undertook a movement to recover the exterior
line held by the Federals above Fort Harrison as an alternative to the
construction of a retrenchment between it and the line to the west. He
called out the local defense troops and put them in the works. Field
and Hoke were moved up the line, and Gary's cavalry and Perry's
brigade were marched beyond its northern end. The plan was that
Gary's men, dismounted, and the infantry of Perry's brigade were to
sweep down in rear of the line. Field was then to assault from the west
and, if successful in crossing the works, was to join the troops already
on the outer side of the exterior line; Hoke was thereupon to attack
from the inner side. The whole of the line was to be recovered as far
to the southward as the close artillery range of Fort Harrison.

On the 6th Lee had a conference with the President at Chaffin's Bluff
and on the morning of the 7th rode up to Field's front to see the action
open. Soon the advance began. Gary and the little remnant of the
Florida brigade pushed forward, turning the works; Field quickly
cleared the line and, pursuing the Federals, came upon them in a strong
position, well covered by abatis. At this stage of the advance Hoke
was to join in the attack from the western side of the exterior line, but
he either misunderstood his orders, was deterred by the obstacles in his
way, or was held back by the artillery fire of the enemy. Field attacked
again, but was repulsed while Hoke waited.

Lee was convinced that the Federals were planning a further extension of their lines on both flanks, and on the 10th of October he
issued a general warning. "We must drive them back at all costs," he
told his corps commanders, but to General Cooper he confided, in an
explanation of Grant's anticipated movement, "I fear it will be impossible to keep him out of Richmond." Abandoning all hope of recovering

Fort Harrison on the exterior works, he drew a retrenchment that cut
off the fort and secured the front. So it was, time after time, in the
battles of the late summer and autumn. On every field there were individual exploits as fine as those of '62. The veterans were as valiant as
ever. But, somehow, the old machine was not working as in earlier days!

It was an immense relief to Lee on October 19 to welcome Longstreet
back and to place in his experienced hands the defense of the north
side. Anderson was assigned command of Hoke's and of Johnson's divisions, which were informally organized as a separate Fourth Corps.
Longstreet was still unable to use his right arm, but he had learned to
write with his left hand and was fully capable of resuming command of
his old corps. He went vigorously to work strengthening his front.

General Early had retired up the Valley as far as Waynesboro, but
hearing that Sheridan had reduced his force, he had again advanced
northward. Lee had urged Breckinridge to reinforce Early, if possible,
so that Kershaw could be recalled, and on the 12th of October he
sent Early a lengthy letter of instructions, cautioning him not to employ his cavalry recklessly. In the exercise, however, of the discretion
given him, Early decided to assume the offensive, and on the 19th he
attacked Sheridan near Cedar Creek. The battle was his during the
forenoon, but in the afternoon some of his infantry broke, the enemy's
cavalry outflanked him, and he was forced into a disorderly retreat,
with the loss of twenty-three guns and about 3000 men. This meant all
prospect of a diversion in the Valley of Virginia was at an end. Grant
need have no further concern for Washington. Lee's old game of playing on Lincoln's fears for the safety of the capital could not be tried
again. More than that, it was doubtful whether Early, with the 12,000
men left him, could keep the enemy from completing the destruction
of the food supplies in the Valley, or even prevent his marching eastward over the mountains. Sheridan could reduce force to assist Grant;
Lee could not weaken Early except at great risk. A dark autumn was
growing blacker.

On his own front, Lee became apprehensive of a new attack, especially as the Federals were digging furiously on Dutch Gap Canal at
Bermuda Hundred Neck. On October 25–26, there were signs of an
increase in the Federal force on the north side of the James, and on the
morning of the 27th the enemy attacked vigorously. Simultaneously, Lee
received reports that Union troops had crossed Hatcher's Run on the
right of the Petersburg front and were moving toward the Boydton
plank road. The administration was profoundly alarmed and called the

last available reserves, the munition workers, and the cadets to the defenses.

Counter-operations on the south side had, of course, to be left to the judgment of A. P. Hill and Hampton. On the north side, Lee left the dispositions to Longstreet. And never did he have better reason to trust the military judgment of "Old Pete." The front opposite Fort Harrison had been carefully planted with subterra shells or "land mines," after the capture of that earthwork, so Longstreet had nothing to fear on that sector. Shrewdly reasoning that the Federals might be preparing to turn the upper end of the outer line, he boldly moved his infantry as far northward as the Williamsburg road and sent Gary's cavalry to occupy the fortifications on the Nine-Mile road. In the course of a few hours he competely repulsed the enemy and captured some 600 prisoners and 11 flags. No drive on the north side, during the whole of the investment of Richmond, had been broken up so readily.

On the south side the Federals crossed Hatcher's Run at Armstrong's Mill, and Rowanty Creek at Monk's Neck Bridge. Their numbers were large and their advance was rapid. Hampton met them by shifting his attack with skill and speed. Hill hurried Heth and Mahone from the line, where they had been on a quiet sector. The enemy reached Burgess's Mill, on Hatcher's Run, but as the two strong Federal corps failed to co-operate, the Confederates drove the Union troops back in confusion. The morning of October 28 found the Federals withdrawn to their lines and Hampton in possession of the field. Thus ended the most ambitious of the Federal attempts in 1864 to outflank the Richmond-Petersburg line. It closed with substantial Confederate victory.

Satisfied that the north side was temporarily safe, Lee started back on November 1 for Petersburg. On reaching Petersburg he allowed himself only a night's rest before starting out to examine the new line on the right. Johnson had been left to defend the front from the Appomattox to Battery 45 with only six brigades and one battalion. Three of Wilcox's brigades covered the right of the new line from Battery 45 to Hatcher's Run. Next he went down as far as Rowanty Creek, where he joined Rooney and Robert, then on outpost duty. It was as happy a meeting as times would allow.

Lee found that most of the soldiers in the trenches were in good health, though beginning to show physical weakness because of the poor ration. Sometimes their food was fairly abundant; more often the third of a pound of "Nassau bacon" that was issued with the daily pint of corn meal was so bad that the facetious affirmed the enemy let it pass the blockade in order to poison the army. Once, when transportation was interrupted, there was only a single issue of meat in four days. Firewood was scarce and green; soap was not to be had. Dirty and cold, the men dug themselves small caves in rear of the trenches, caves that were popularly known as "rat-holes" and officially styled "bomb-proofs," despite the oft-repeated experience that they were not "proof." The troops were beginning to lack even the means of defense. Percussion caps were running low. The Confederates in the advanced rifle-pits were limited to eighteen rounds per man, while the Federal pickets who fraternized with them between the lines complained that each of them was required to expend 100 rounds every twenty-four hours.

The distress of his soldiers wrung the heart of Lee, and the scantiness of their numbers gave him the deepest concern for the future. With all the troops on the works he could present, at best, only one man every four and a half feet. Desertion grew as ominously as a cancer. Reports told almost daily of men who had been unable to endure the ceaseless vigil of the freezing trenches and had crossed over the lines to safety, if to infamy. Lee had to be stern in the face of the steady loss of men, but if he were not sure that justice had been done a deserter, he would personally see to it that the man had the benefit of the doubt.

To meet the losses due to attrition and desertion, it was now apparent that the only hope lay in conscription and in the substitution of disabled soldiers and Negroes for the able-bodied white men who were on detail. Lee continued to urge the organization of Negroes in the service of supply. Detailed men were slow in arriving; conscripts were few. From Early Lee recalled Kershaw's division about November 14. There was some increase in the cavalry, but the shortage of horses was so great that of the 6200 troopers with Lee about 1300 were dismounted. For all the efforts of Lee, the President, and the War Department, the maximum strength of all arms reached in the return of November 30 was 60,753, exclusive of the Richmond garrison of something less than 6000. This was a gain, but not enough, in Lee's opinion, to give him any prospect of victory. "Unless we can obtain a reasonable approximation to [Grant's] force," he wrote the President early that morn, "I fear a great calamity will befall us."

In the far south were direful developments. After sending Forrest on a brilliant raid against Sherman's railroad communications, Hood decided to attempt to force Sherman out of Georgia by marching his army into Tennessee. This was, perhaps, the fatal military decision of the war. On November 16, while Hood tramped toward Nashville, Sherman boldly abandoned his communications with Tennessee and started on his march to the sea. For two weeks there was suspense; then, on November 30, Hood met Schofield at Franklin, Tenn., and in a wild, reckless, and wasteful battle threw him back on Nashville, where George H. Thomas was concentrating to destroy Hood and to leave Sherman free to move on Savannah. Bragg was forthwith sent southward from Wilmington with half the forces there, in the hope that he might organize a small army at Augusta, Ga., to check Sherman.

Grant speedily became most active again. There were signs of a new shift of troops to the north side of the James. All the signs pointed to another outflanking movement. Lee watched every move and studied carefully every spy's report. On December 5 the scouts brought in dark news: The well-led VI Corps, which had been fighting against Early, had rejoined Grant. Could Lee do anything to offset this turn of affairs? There was only one move he could make on the chessboard of war: As Grant had recalled part of his troops from Sheridan, Lee might bring back part of the Second Corps without subjecting Early to the threat of immediate destruction. Gordon's division was ordered to start for Petersburg. Early's division, now under John Pegram, followed it at once. Lee prepared to transfer Hoke to the southside again and to turn over his lines to Kershaw. When Gordon arrived he was marched through Petersburg and was placed on the extreme right. This hurried reconcentration made the odds less serious.

The Federals, on December 7, undertook a raid down the Weldon Railroad. Lee interpreted this to be an attempt to occupy Weldon. The enemy got as far as Belfield but could not cross the Meherrin River to Hicksford. When the Federals were forced to turn back, Hampton's cavalry skirmished hotly on their flanks and took some prisoners. A simultaneous demonstration on Hatcher's Run amounted to little.

Sherman's march to the sea was, meantime, progressing ominously, and the question of detaching troops from the Army of Northern Virginia became pressing. When he heard that the snow was six inches deep in the Shenandoah Valley, Lee, on December 14, ordered Rodes's division to Petersburg. This stripped Early of nearly his whole command, but it gave Lee some guarantee that if he had to dispatch a force to Georgia, he could replace a part of it. With its gallant commander left behind in his grave in the Valley, Rodes's division reached Petersburg on December 18. But the telegraph that told of his approach also brought dread tidings: On the 15th and 16th, Hood had met Thomas in front of Nashville and had been hopelessly routed. On the 19th a great armada from Hampton Roads arrived off Wilmington. The same day Beauregard announced from Savannah that Sherman was approaching and had demanded the surrender of the place. "The city," he said, "must be evacuated [as] soon as practicable."

Davis turned to Lee for counsel: What reinforcements could Lee send south? And should they go to Wilmington or to South Carolina? Lee concluded that the danger to Wilmington was more imminent and ordered Hoke's division to the North Carolina port. The movement of Hoke's division from Danville was incredibly slow, so slow that suspicion of treachery on the part of the Piedmont Railroad was widespread in the army. By Christmas Day only the leading brigade had reached Wilmington. For a time it looked as though the delay would be fatal, but, as it happened, the Federal attack was abortive, and on the 28th the fleet steamed away. But the good news that Wilmington was still open to the blockade runners meant little compared to the baleful tidings that on December 21 Sherman had marched into Savannah.

Hood's army a wreck; Georgia and the Gulf states cut off from Virginia; Sherman soon to be ready to march up the coast and to capture Charleston; the Army of the Potomac every day more powerful and better able to outflank Lee, no matter what his vigilance, or what his strategy; Sheridan free to return with his overwhelming cavalry—surely, when the last December sun of 1864 set over the Petersburg defenses it brought the twilight of the Confederacy.

CHAPTER XIV

Surrender? Not Yet

A NATION'S prayers, and not an individual's only, were needed as January, 1865, passed. Hourly along the line of thirty-five miles from the Williamsburg road to Hatcher's Run the pickets kept their rifles barking. Nightly each bomb could be traced like giants' fireworks. Never was there silence, never a day without casualties; yet there was no large action, largely because of the condition of the roads. Elsewhere, calamity followed on the heels of disaster. Before the middle of January it became apparent that Sherman would soon start from Savannah toward Charleston. Cavalry was much needed there. Lee dispatched Butler's division and authorized Hampton to go also, in the hope that his great reputation in South Carolina would bring new volunteers to the colors. In retrospect, Lee regarded this as the great mistake he made during the campaign, because it crippled him in dealing with subsequent Federal operations against his right flank. When the movement was ordered there seemed no alternative to it.

A great Federal fleet again appeared off Wilmington, convoying an infantry force on transports. Under General Alfred H. Terry, the troops were thrown ashore and on January 13 a bombardment of Fort Fisher was begun. Two days later, the Union flag was flying over the shattered works, and the last port of the Confederacy was closed.

With Wilmington lost and Sherman about to march northward, the alarm in Richmond grew into a frenzy. Davis was blamed, as the executive of a waning cause always is, both for what he had done and what he had failed to accomplish. Some now began to clamor for a dictator. Lee was to be the man. To his mind, the very suggestion was abhorrent and a reflection on his loyalty as a soldier and a citizen. At length, as a sort of desperate compromise with Congress, the President consented to the appointment of a general-in-chief and on February 6 named Lee to the office. The appointment came just when the negotiations for peace at the so-called Hampton Roads conference had failed and when the Federals were active on Lee's right flank.

Lee did not consider that his appointment conferred the right to assign generals to command armies. It was all he could do to watch Grant, to conserve the strength of his dwindling army, and to combat the dark forces of hunger and disintegration. In December the shortage of provisions had become more acute than ever. The commissary general confessed himself desperate, and a special secret report to Congress bore out his dark view of the South's resources.

In January heavy rains broke down the Piedmont Railroad, which linked Lee's army with the western Carolinas. Floods cut off supplies from the upper valley of the James. Lee then had only two days' rations for his men and already had scoured clean the country within reach of his foragers. On February 5 he had to march a heavy column to the extreme right to meet new Federal demonstrations on Hatcher's Run. For three nights and three days a large part of the Confederate forces had to remain in line of battle, with no meat and little food of any sort. The suffering of the men so deeply aroused Lee that he broke over the usual restraint he displayed in dealing with the civil authorities. "If some change is not made and the commissary department reorganized, I apprehend dire results," he wrote the Secretary of War. "The physical strength of the men, if their courage survives, must fail under this treatment." Within a few days, Northrop was succeeded by Brigadier General I. M. St. John, who had much distinguished himself by his diligent management of the mining and nitre bureau. St. John immediately organized a system by which supplies were to be collected from the farmers, hauled to the railroad and dispatched directly to the army, without being handled through central depots. Lee welcomed the change, and was encouraged by it to believe that if communications could be maintained, the army would be better fed.

When he was asked early in March for an appraisal of the military situation, he postulated everything, in his reply, on transportation and on the willingness of the people to make further sacrifices. "Unless the men and animals can be subsisted," he said, "the army cannot be kept together, and our present lines must be abandoned. . . . Everything, in my opinion, has depended and still depends upon the disposition and feelings of the people. Their representatives can best decide how they will bear the difficulties and sufferings of their condition and how they will respond to the demands which the public safety requires."

The representatives of Virginia in the Congress were brought together to answer Lee's question. He was present in Richmond and told them of lengthened lines and thinning forces, of privations, and of the scarcity of food. The Virginians replied that the people of the state, with loyalty and devotion, would meet any new demand, but they seemed to General Lee content with words. They proposed nothing; they did nothing. Lee said no more—the facts were warning enough—but he went from the building and made his way to his residence with distress and indignation battling in his heart. When dinner was over, his son Custis sat down by the fire to smoke a cigar and to read the news, but Lee paced the floor restlessly.

Suddenly he stopped in front of his son and faced him: "Well, Mr. Custis," he said, "I have been up to see the Congress and they do not seem to be able to do anything except to eat peanuts and chew tobacco, while my army is starving. I told them the condition the men were in, and that something must be done at once, but I can't get them to do anything, or they are unable to do anything." There was some bitterness in his tones.

The General resumed his promenade, but after a few more turns he again stopped in the same place and resumed: "Mr. Custis, when this war began I was opposed to it, bitterly opposed to it, and I told these people that unless every man should do his whole duty, they would repent it; and now they will repent."

Outraged as Lee was by the apparent incapacity of Congress, he warmly encouraged St. John to do his utmost in applying the methods of direct appeal the new commissary general had used with notable success in collecting nitre; but as Lee sought to find food for his men he saw new military difficulties added to those of transportation, weather, distress, and growing public despair. The danger of the destruction of all lines of communication with the South and the occupation of the only territory from which he was now drawing supplies were daily brought nearer and nearer.

Bound up, now as always, with subsistence for the men was the old, tragic question of provender for the horses during a winter when there was no pasturage. There was danger that the troops might remain where they were until they had no horses to move their trains. Yet Lee could not circumvent this by an early departure from Petersburg, because the mud was so heavy the teams could not pull the wagons.

He had to wait until the roads were better, even if he had to risk immobility then. What was true of the wagon trains applied also to the artillery. Many commands had to be consolidated and reorganized because there were not enough horses for all the batteries.

The cavalry suffered with the wagon train and with the artillery. Before the end of the winter Lee was uncertain whether he would be able to keep even a small cavalry force around Richmond. There was virtually nothing he could do to maintain the arm of service on which he had to depend not only for early information of the enemy's movements but also for the protection of his communications and for the safety of his right flank from a sudden turning movement. He was compelled to extemporize new tactics. Infantry were to be stationed as close as practicable to any point whence the enemy was expected to start a raid and were then to be moved rapidly to support the thin cavalry that might be thrown forward—a scheme that seems to have been proposed by Longstreet. This meant, of course, that the defensive line had to be weakened. It was a grim plight for an army that once had boasted a Stuart and stout squadrons of faultlessly mounted boys who had mocked the awkward cavalry of McClellan as they had ridden around his army.

Desertion continued to sap the man-power of the army. Desertions between February 15 and March 18 numbered 2934, nearly 8 per cent of the effective strength of the army. When men left they usually went home, but not a few of the weaker-spirited joined the enemy. The reasons for this wastage in an army that had been distinguished for nothing more than for its morale were all too apparent—hunger, delayed pay, the growing despair of the public mind, and, perhaps more than anything else, woeful letters from wives and families telling of danger or privation at home.

Despair had not entered every heart. If hundreds deserted, there were thousands who had resolved that neither hunger nor cold, neither danger nor the bad example of feebler spirits could induce them to leave "Marse Robert." Many of them "came to look upon the cause as General Lee's cause, and they fought for it because they loved him. To them he represented cause, country and all."

Although Lee had previously had a low opinion of the fighting quality of Negro troops, he saw now that the South must use them, if possible. After the beginning of 1865 he declared himself for their enlistment, coupled with a system of "gradual and general emancipation."

Congress debated long, but at last, on March 13, the President signed
a bill to bring Negroes into the ranks, though without any pledge of
emancipation. Bad as was the law, Lee undertook at once to set up
a proper organization for the Negro troops. While Congress had
argued, Virginia had acted in providing for the enrollment of Negroes,
slave and free, in the military service. On March 24 Lee applied for
the maximum number allowable under the statute of the commonwealth. "The services of these men," he said. "are now necessary to
enable us to oppose the enemy."

He urged on his lieutenants new economy of force and he strengthened his lines against sudden attack. Personal appeals were made to
returned prisoners of war to waive the usual furlough and to rejoin
their commands; all able-bodied men were taken from the bureaus;
all "leaves" for officers were suspended; new combat rules and revised
marching instructions were issued to meet changed conditions. All that
Lee had learned in nearly four years of war, all that his quiet energy
inspired, all that his associates could suggest or his official superiors devise—all was thrown into a last effort to organize and strengthen the
thin, shivering, hungry Army of Northern Virginia for the last grapple
with the well-fed, well-clad, ever-increasing host that crowded the
countryside opposite Lee's lines.

No food, no horses, no reinforcement! As that dread spectre of
ultimate defeat shaped itself, Lee did not content himself with reorganizing his army. Daily he wrestled with his strategic problem. Early
was still in the Shenandoah Valley with a few shivering *cadres* and
under orders to create the impression that his command was formidable.
Beauregard was seeking to muster a sufficient force to dispute Sherman's
advance. Bragg had some 6500 effectives in eastern North Carolina.
These were the only troops of any consequence left in the South
Atlantic states, except for the Army of Northern Virginia.

To dispose of Bragg and of Beauregard so that he could concentrate
all his strength against the ragged divisions that defied him in front of
Petersburg, Grant moved with swift assurance. Having halved the
Confederacy by seizing the line of the Mississippi and capturing
Vicksburg, Grant had then divided the eastern half by sending Sher-
man through Georgia. Now he brought from Tennessee some of the
troops that had wrecked Hood at Nashville. These he united with
Terry's below Wilmington and placed the whole under Major General
John M. Schofield to advance against Lee's lines of communication
along the seaboard from Weldon. If this operation were successful,

Virginia would be severed from the Carolinas; and if Sherman moved northward, joined Schofield, and marched with him to reinforce Grant, Lee would face three armies. By January 29 this danger had so far developed that Lee frankly warned the President. In case Grant were appreciably reinforced, he said, "I do not see how in our present position he can be prevented from enveloping Richmond."

There was at the time only one ray of light—the possibility of a negotiated peace. Three leading Southerners, Vice-President Stephens, Judge J. A. Campbell, and Senator R. M. T. Hunter, had gone to the Federal lines on the 29th and had proceeded to Hampton Roads. There they conferred unofficially with President Lincoln. The meeting, however, ended with no apparent possibility of an understanding.

On the day the disappointed Southern commissioners came back to Richmond, General Lee had to confess to President Davis that he could not send reinforcements to Beauregard, and that Beauregard, with such resources as he could muster, would have to make an effort to defeat Sherman "wherever he can be struck to most advantage." A little later he put the Secretary of War on notice: "You must not be surprised if calamity befalls us."

While the administration refused to face the dread reality, Schofield became a menace. Sherman was on the march. He entered Columbia, S. C., on February 17 and forced the evacuation of Charleston that night. Lee wrote on February 19: "It is necessary to bring out all our strength, and, I fear, to unite our armies, as separately they do not seem able to make head against the enemy. . . . I fear it may be necessary to abandon our cities, and preparations should be made for that contingency."

General Bragg, in North Carolina, was so discredited by previous failure in the field that he could not rally the people of that state. General Beauregard was in ill-health. He found that the militia of South Carolina would not cross the state line and that they consisted only of men who were soon exhausted on the march. There was direst need of a co-ordination of these forces under some man who had the military confidence of the Carolinas. Lee knew that Johnston held the good opinion of the people and was, perhaps, the only man who could bring out the last reserves. Mr. Davis did not have confidence in Johnston as an independent field commander. This would have kept Lee from acting in anything less than a final, overwhelming emergency, but now he asked the Secretary of War to order Johnston to report to him for assignment to duty. This was promptly done, as Mr. Davis explained, "in the hope that General Johnston's soldierly qualities may be made serviceable to his country when acting under General Lee's orders, and that in his new position those defects which I found manifested by him when serving as an independent commander will be remedied by the control of the general-in-chief."

On February 22 Lee placed Johnston in charge of operations in the Carolinas, with instructions to collect the scattered troops in those states and to attack Sherman on the march. If this proved an impossibility, then Johnston must join Lee or Lee must join Johnston, for Lee could not attempt to remain near Richmond once Sherman reached the Roanoke River.

Johnston speedily found that his army was suffering heavily from desertion. He could count only about 15,000 effectives. There was little likelihood that he could break away and get to Virginia. By the harsh logic of elimination, Lee must prepare to leave the Richmond front and to move toward Danville to unite his army with Johnston's. Their one hope would be to strike Sherman, to destroy him, and then together to face Grant. Before the end of the month the plan of a movement to Johnston was uppermost in Lee's mind.

The coming of March found about 50,000 men under Lee's immediate command. It was a pitiful army with which to face such crushing odds—so pitiful that when Longstreet reported that he believed Grant would confer with Lee on a peace plan, the consent of the President was procured and a letter proposing an interview was dispatched to Grant on March 2. Whatever hope Lee may have cherished of a favorable reception of his proposal was probably destroyed the day he wrote Grant. For on that same 2d of March, Sheridan overwhelmed the remnant of Early's force at Waynesboro. The Shenandoah Valley was irredeemably lost, and Sheridan was free to join Grant with his powerful mounted divisions.

This news shook Lee to the depths. What should he do? His obligations were both to his government and to those half-frozen soldiers in the trenches—which came first? Longstreet and A. P. Hill were distant. He could not discuss his problem with them, but must unburden himself. He sent for John B. Gordon, by this time one of his most trusted lieutenants. It was 2 o'clock when Gordon arrived. "In (Lee's) room," Gordon wrote, years later, "was a long table covered with recent reports from every part of the army. . . . He opened the conference by directing me to read the reports from the different commands as he should hand them to me, and to carefully note every important fact contained in them. The revelation was startling. Every report was bad enough, and all the distressing facts combined were sufficient, it seemed to me, to destroy all cohesive power and lead to the inevitable disintegration of any other army that was ever marshalled. . . . When I had finished the inspection of this array of serious facts, General Lee began his own analysis of the situation." Of his 50,000 men, only 35,000 were fit for duty; Grant must have 150,000; Thomas was sending 30,000 east. "From the Valley," said Lee, "General Grant can and will bring upon us nearly 20,000, against whom I can oppose scarcely a vedette." Schofield and Sherman between them probably had 80,000; Johnston could only count on 13,000 to 15,000. Adding all the Union forces together, there would soon be in the seaboard states 280,000 Federal troops, to whom the Confederacy could oppose only 65,000.

"This estimate ended," Gordon wrote, ". . . he again took his seat facing me at the table and asked me to state frankly what I thought under these conditions it was best to do—or what duty to the army and our people required of us. Looking at me intently, he awaited my answer."

"General," said Gordon, "it seems to me there are but three courses, and I name them in the order in which I think they should be tried:

"First, make terms with the enemy, the best we can get.

"Second, if that is not practicable, the best thing to do is to retreat—abandon Richmond and Petersburg, unite by rapid marches with General Johnston in North Carolina, and strike Sherman before Grant can join him; or,

"Lastly, we must fight and without delay."

"Is that your opinion?" Lee asked.

Gordon reiterated his views and deferentially asked if he might inquire how Lee appraised the outlook.

"Certainly, General," Lee answered. "You have the right to ask my opinion. I agree with you fully."

Lee explained that he did not feel that he, as a soldier, had the right to urge political action on the government. He did not tell Gordon that he had already written Grant, for that was a confidential matter between himself and the President, but at length Lee said he would go to see the President the next day, which, as a matter of fact, he had already planned to do.

Lee doubtless reviewed with the President the possibilities of nego-

tiating peace, but the discussion was probably cut short by the receipt
of Grant's reply to Lee's letter of March 2. "I would state," said he,
"that I have no authority to accede to your proposition for a conference on the subject proposed. Such authority is vested in the
President of the United States alone." Lee might have been willing
to negotiate on the basis of a restoration of the Union, but if he
canvassed this aspect of the subject with the President, he discovered
quickly that Mr. Davis was determined to have the Confederacy go
down in defeat rather than accept any terms that did not recognize
Southern independence.

The conversation turned to the dark necessity of evacuating Petersburg and Richmond. The chief executive faced this with unshaken
courage and, when Lee explained that he saw no alternative, Mr. Davis
asked why Lee delayed. Lee replied that his animals could not haul the
wagon-train until the muddy roads had dried somewhat. Then the
two debated the strategy of the inevitable retreat. Lee outlined the
plan he was formulating for a march to Johnston, a quick blow at
Sherman and then an attack on Grant. To accomplish this, it would
be necessary to build up a week's reserve of food in Richmond, to
accumulate depots of supplies along the railroads, and to issue more
corn to the horses even if this depleted the scant stock.

This gloomiest of interviews between Lee and the President occurred on Saturday. The next day Lee returned to Petersburg. To
Gordon, anxious to know the outcome of the conference, Lee explained what had happened.

"What, then, is to be done, General?" Gordon inquired.

Lee could only answer that they must fight.

In preparing to fight, Lee could not wait long, because Sheridan
would soon join Grant, and the overpowering Federal cavalry could
be employed to break Lee's communications with the South. On the
other hand, the horses had to be conditioned, and the depots must
be prepared so that the movement to join Johnston could be undertaken. The new commissary general went vigorously to work building up the reserve that Lee needed. St. John drew on the last food
stuffs that could be purchased, but he made the immediate outlook
for provisions better than it had been for weeks. The general plan of a
junction with the forces in North Carolina was examined and the alternatives were debated. By March 9 Lee concluded that no "marked
success" could be expected from Johnston's army. Two days later
Johnston wrote that if the Federal forces in North Carolina were

united, he could not prevent their march into Virginia. With this bad news Johnston coupled a suggestion: Would it be practicable for Lee "to hold one of the inner lines of Richmond with one part of your army, and meet Sherman with the other, returning to Richmond after fighting"? Lee began to canvass the possibility of detaching part of his forces to assist his old comrade in crushing Sherman.

In particular, Lee had General Gordon make a study of the Federal centre around Petersburg, in order to ascertain whether the lines could be broken. When Gordon reported that this was feasible, in the vicinity of the Federal Fort Stedman, Lee proceeded to work out a plan. He believed that if Gordon could penetrate the Federal lines after an assault by about half the army, one of two things would happen. Either General Grant would have to abandon the left of his line, or shorten his front. Then, when Sherman was near enough to be reached quickly, Lee could detach picked troops to Johnston, effect a junction and give battle to Sherman. If Sherman were beaten, Lee could then bring back his united forces to meet Grant. If Gordon did not succeed in breaking through the Federal lines, Lee would be in no worse plight for executing his previous general plan of joining Johnston with all his forces.

Lengthening March days brought no relief of any sort. Then, ominously, on March 23 Johnston reported that Schofield and Sherman had met at Goldsboro. "Sherman's course," Johnston telegraphed, "cannot be hindered by the small force I have. I can do no more than annoy him." The dreadful hour was drawing on. Sheridan, Lee believed, had already joined the Army of the Potomac. Grant was preparing to attack on the Confederate right. The Confederate commander could wait no longer. That night he gave his final approval to the plan for the attack on Fort Stedman.

Fort Stedman was on the high ground known as Hare's Hill, three-quarters of a mile southeast of the Appomattox. The place could boast of no particular strength. It had no bastion and immediately adjoined Battery 10, which was open in the rear. The terrain behind the fort was almost as high as the parapet.

The distance to Fort Stedman from the Confederate lines was 150 yards. Only 50 yards separated the pickets. The nearness of the fort, which made a surprise attack possible, was one of the reasons General Gordon selected Stedman as the object of his assault. As he studied the enemy's works from the Confederate front he saw what he took to be three Federal forts in the rear of Stedman. Behind these was an open space. He believed that he could reach this cleared ground, form there, and take the three works in reverse. If he could do this and could spread his troops to the right and to the left for a sufficient distance, he argued that he would divide the enemy's troops and could force the Federals to abandon that part of their fortifications to the south and southwest. In this way General Lee's immediate purpose would be served. The Federals would have to shorten their front, and the Army of Northern Virginia would have a lessened stretch of lines to defend. Troops could then be detached from Lee to help Johnston.

Before dawn of March 25, General Lee rode over from the Turnbull house to the hill where Gordon was standing ready to give the signal to the men who crowded the trenches beneath him. Almost on the second, at 4 o'clock, a single rifle, fired by a private at Gordon's word, sent the troops forward Lee could only wait on the hill and listen and hope. Very soon a message came from Gordon, who had followed the charging troops: the men were in Fort Stedman. The sound of the firing must soon have apprised Lee that the attacking columns had spread 400 or 500 yards on either side of the salient they had stormed.

The next news was of another sort: The officers of one party could not find the rear forts, on the seizure of which success of the enterprise depended. Another courier brought a similar report from the other advance parties. Then followed confused fighting. Soon it was apparent the Federals had rallied, were hurrying up reserves, and were pouring into Fort Stedman and the adjoining part of the line a fire that was holding up the advance. Lee saw that an attempt to storm the Federal redoubts would be risky and, even if not repulsed, would cost him heavily, so, about 8 o'clock, he ordered Gordon to withdraw to his own lines. As the disappointed troops made their way back, they came under a cruel fire that dropped hundreds in their tracks.

What Gordon had taken to be supporting forts were, in reality, old Confederate works. Confusion resulting from hunting non-existent forts had given the Federals time to rally in their well-constructed works. A smothering fire had been poured into those parts of the line that Gordon's men had occupied. Except at a very heavy loss of life it had not been possible to advance. And the failure of the attack was not all. Immediately following the repulse of Gordon's assaults, the Federals advanced along the whole right of Lee's position nearly to Hatcher's Run and took the entrenched picket lines. They captured about 800 prisoners and held their ground against all attempts to drive them back. The enemy was thus placed where he could launch a direct attack to break the Confederate front whenever he chose. The total haul of prisoners at the picket posts and at Fort Stedman was 2783. The Union estimate of gross Confederate casualties of 4800 to 5000 was not greatly exaggerated.

"I fear now," Lee wrote the President on the 26th, "it will be impossible to prevent a junction between Grant and Sherman, nor do I deem it prudent that this army should maintain its position until the latter shall approach too near."

Lee was thrown back on the plan of evacuating the Richmond line and of moving with his whole force to join the command in North Carolina. The retreat from Petersburg must begin. The sooner it was undertaken, the greater the prospect of eluding Grant. But there were obstacles to a speedy withdrawal. Gordon's men needed rest for the recovery of their morale. The administration was not ready to evacuate Richmond. The roads were still excessively bad. Lee had to wait. He was prepared for the retreat, but, for the moment, all he could do was to repeat what he had written Mrs. Lee before the outlook had become quite so dark: "I shall . . . endeavor to do my duty and fight to the last."

Reports on the 27th indicated that Federal movement was about to start and that it was directed against the upper stretches of Hatcher's Run. The railroad was the prime objective of any attempt Grant might make to drive Lee from Petersburg without a direct frontal assault. To reach the railroad, Grant's easiest course was to cross Hatcher's Run at a distance from Lee's lines, to march westward until he had reached a point beyond Lee's right flank, and then to strike northward.

Grant's easiest crossing was at Monk's Neck Bridge. Thence the way to the Southside Railroad led by Dinwiddie Courthouse and by Five Forks, where Lee already expected Grant's troops to appear. This route was only fifteen miles—say a march of a day and a half as the roads then were. To attempt to meet this advance by merely lengthening his front would be a prolongation of four miles, a distance Lee could not hope to cover adequately. Already he stretched his thin line almost as far as it would hold. On the twenty-seven and a half miles occupied by infantry, he could count an average of only 1140 men per mile.

What could Lee do with his scant force to meet the operation against his right? His first move, made on the 27th, was to transfer to that flank all the cavalry on the north side of the James, except

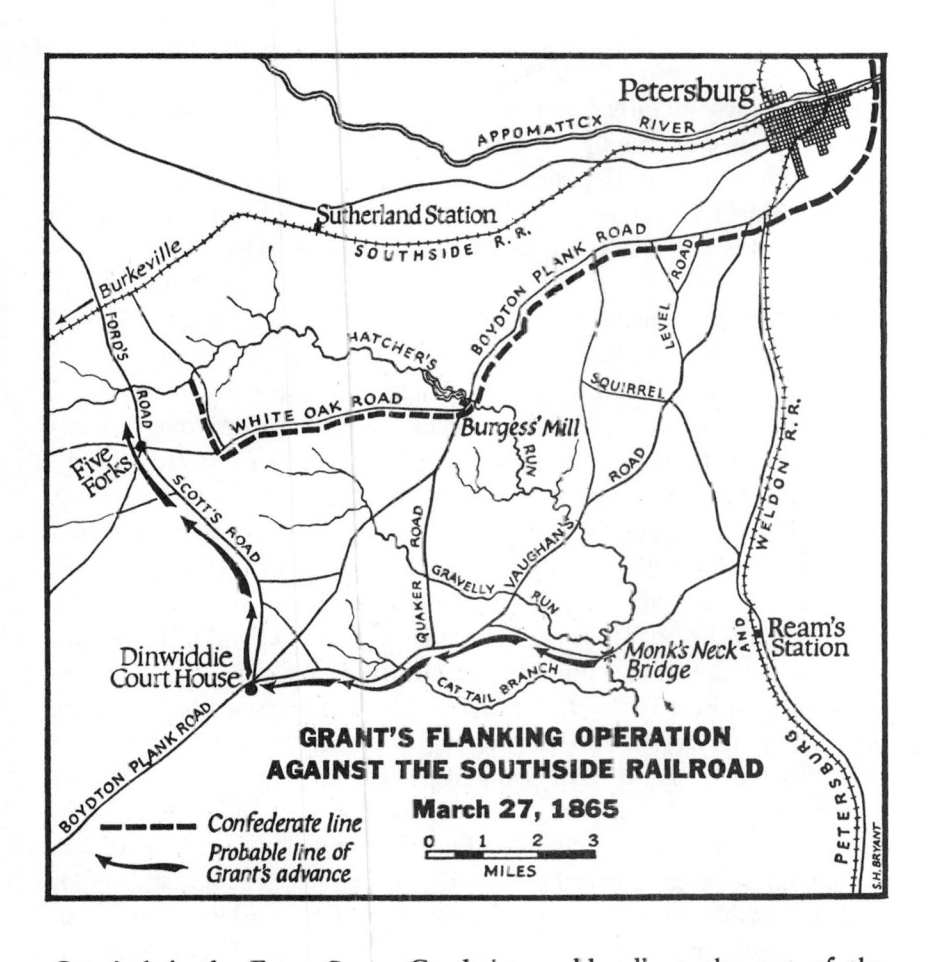

**GRANT'S FLANKING OPERATION
AGAINST THE SOUTHSIDE RAILROAD**

March 27, 1865

- - - - Confederate line
Probable line of
Grant's advance

0   1   2   3
MILES

Gary's brigade. From Stony Creek he could call up the rest of the
cavalry, when needed, and thus could concentrate all his mounted
troops on his extreme right. As a second step Lee executed a plan
he had adopted at Longstreet's suggestion—to support his cavalry attack with an advanced and quasi-independent force of infantry. He
knew he might have to increase this force, but he hoped if the enemy
attacked he could do this without being compelled to draw troops
from the line in such numbers as to make a break inevitable. The plan
was a compromise between a major detachment of force and a long
extension of front. Pickett's division was selected for this service with
the cavalry.

On the 28th Lee began to prepare for the movement of Pickett's
division to the right. He still had faith in his army and told the administration that it would have ten or twelve days in which to
evacuate Richmond. During the forenoon of the 29th Lee received
word that hostile cavalry and infantry had crossed Hatcher's Run.

From the early reports Lee was not certain of the immediate Federal objective. In the evening, as a heavy rain began to fall, word came from Anderson that the advancing Federals had extended their left to Dinwiddie Courthouse. Soon the outposts reported that Federal artillery had also gone with the infantry and cavalry. Darkness fell in a continued downpour, with no further indication of what was ahead, except that on a large part of the Petersburg front heavy Federal demonstrations were begun. These were continued all night.

Although no alarming news greeted Lee on the rainy morning of March 30, he became convinced that he would have to strengthen his extreme right still more. Any withdrawal from the line was exceedingly dangerous, but unless Lee was willing to have his right turned, what alternative was there? Grimly he ordered Gordon to take over two miles of trenches beyond the point where the flank of his troops rested; and then, having discharged the gloomy business of the army at headquarters, he rode out to the vicinity of Sutherland's. He found that Rooney Lee and Rosser had not arrived, but that Fitz Lee was advancing on Five Forks. Pickett had reached Anderson's headquarters and had reported to him on the night of the 29th. Lee promptly detached Pickett from Anderson and placed at Pickett's disposal Matt Ransom's and Wallace's brigades of Johnson's division, Anderson's corps, in addition to the three of Pickett's own division. Pickett was thereupon directed to march on Five Forks, to seize the initiative, and, with the cavalry, to march in the direction of Dinwiddie Courthouse for an attack on the flanking column of the enemy. Six of Pegram's twenty guns were to go with Pickett. The others were to remain at Burgess's Mill. By these orders Lee definitely set up the mobile force to protect the right flank, roughly 6400 infantry and 4200 cavalry. Having done this—all that he could do—Lee rode back to Petersburg. "Don't think he was in good humor," an observant young officer wrote in his diary.

Advancing to Five Forks, Fitz Lee saw nothing of the enemy. He then moved toward Dinwiddie Courthouse, quickly established contact with the Federal infantry and horse and, after beating off two attacks, drove them back on their reserves. This done, he returned to Five Forks, where he was to meet Pickett. Almost all the way to Five Forks that officer had had to drive the enemy from his front. When at length he arrived it was nearly sundown.

Fitz Lee and Pickett decided that as the remainder of the cavalry had not joined them, and as the men were very tired, having marched with little rest for eighteen hours, they would delay until the next morning, the 31st, the combined offensive General Lee had ordered. Two brigades were thrown out about three-quarters of a mile south of Five Forks to cover the front. To do this, the troops had, ominously enough, to drive back dismounted Federal cavalry who used repeating rifles and offered stiff resistance. Soon after, W. H. F. Lee and Rosser arrived at Five Forks with their cavalry.

On the morning of the 31st when Pickett and Fitz Lee were to advance against the enemy seeking to turn the Confederate right, General Lee rode down the line as far as the fortifications within the angle of Hatcher's Run. He found Union infantry in front of these works with their left "in the air" at a point about opposite the end of his own line. To take advantage of this carelessness, and to preclude the possibility of the Federals breaking through between Pickett's advancing column and Anderson's fortified position, Lee determined to attack and roll up the Union flank, though he had available for the task only four brigades.

It was raining when Lee made the arrangements for the attack. McGowan waited for the downfall to cease and then moved quietly out. He was getting himself into position, almost directly across the left flank of the infantry, under Lee's own eye, when firing broke out farther up the line. A lieutenant in Hunton's brigade, seeing the enemy, had sprung forward, had called on his men to follow him, and had opened the fight without waiting for orders. McGowan had perforce to launch his attack at once. The action had not progressed far when Lee saw that Hunton might lose contact with the troops on the line toward Petersburg, so he ordered Wise's brigade to take position on Hunton's left. These tactics were successful. The troops on the Federal flank were quickly doubled up and thrown back across a branch of a nearby stream, Gravelly Run. There the advance had to stop, however, as the Boydton plank road and strong Federal supports lay just beyond. Lee went with McGowan to the bank of the little watercourse, and after examining the terrain he determined to hold it if he could. He tried to get up some artillery and, if possible, some cavalry. Just then the left of the attacking forces began to waver in the face of a strong Federal counterattack. Lee had to consent to a withdrawal which, at the end of the day, brought the troops virtually back where they had been in the morning.

Lee reported to the War Department the developments of the day. He had heard nothing from Pickett and Fitz Lee, and apparently he had caught no sound of their fire, but later in the evening he received news of what had befallen them. The troops around Five Forks had advanced southward toward Dinwiddie Courthouse, taking the initiative from the enemy. After a hard fight they had driven back the Federals, who were so numerous that Fitzhugh Lee was satisfied they constituted the whole of the cavalry corps. Pushing on, the Confederates had come within about half a mile of the courthouse. There darkness had halted them, and thence Pickett reported to Lee. The showing of the men had been admirable. There was nothing to suggest either exhaustion or any wavering whatsoever.

The good showing made by his gallant old infantry did not deceive General Lee. He realized on the morning of April 1 that the situation was increasingly critical, even though his troops had, as yet, been defeated nowhere on the right. In one of his last letters from the field, he explained the situation to Mr. Davis. The enemy was on his flank and potentially in his rear and was in position, with superior cavalry, to cut both the Southside and the Richmond and Danville Railroads. "This," he said, "in my opinion obliged us to prepare for the necessity of evacuating our position on the James River at once, and also to consider the best means of accomplishing it, and our future course." There was no longer any hope, he left Mr. Davis to infer, that time would remain for a slow removal of supplies from Richmond.

Probably it was soon after he dispatched this letter—it certainly was not before—that Lee received a report from Pickett to the effect that he was being forced to withdraw from the vicinity of Dinwiddie Courthouse. This was bad news. As the Federals were certain to follow Pickett's withdrawal, every step of their advance would bring them toward Five Forks and thence dangerously close to the Southside Railroad. If the railroad was to be saved, Pickett could not afford to give much ground. Lee wrote Pickett: "Hold Five Forks at all hazards. Protect road to Ford's Depot and prevent Union forces from striking the Southside Railroad."

The routine of the morning completed, Lee rode out to the headquarters of Anderson's corps to watch developments there. He found that the troops which had been in Anderson's front the day before had moved to the right, in the direction of General Pickett's front, but, so far as the records show, he heard nothing more from Pickett himself.

While at the headquarters of Anderson's corps, Lee received from Longstreet a telegram concerning the withdrawal of troops from the north side of the James. Longstreet had no sure information, but he was inclined to think the Federals had diminished their force. As he apprehended the Federal gunboats could prevent any successful offensive on his part, he thought it better if any troops could be spared to reinforce the southside. Lee answered him with instructions to prepare for a troop movement to the Petersburg front if Longstreet found confirmation of the report that he faced reduced numbers.

At 4 o'clock that afternoon heavy firing was heard from the direction of Five Forks. Theoretically, a cavalry brigade was in liaison between the Confederate right and the mobile force under Pickett and Fitzhugh Lee; practically, the mobile force had been cut off from the Southern lines since it had begun operations. There was, consequently, no knowledge at Anderson's headquarters as to what the sounds of action really meant. It must have been 5 o'clock and after when a young cavalry captain brought Lee the first intimation of what had happened. He was followed by a messenger from Fitz Lee, who reported that the troops had been attacked in great force and that he had lost contact with Pickett.

Lee accepted the news as indicating a reverse, but he did not yet know that a dark and humiliating tragedy had been enacted around Five Forks in these grim stages: Pickett's withdrawal from in front of Dinwiddie Courthouse had been carried out in good order. Line of battle had been formed in the position at Five Forks from which the advance had begun. Fitz Lee thought the Confederate advance had broken up the Federal movement, at least temporarily. When he returned to Five Forks he was not looking for a Federal attack that afternoon. Pickett must have been of the same mind, for he went off with Fitz Lee to enjoy a shad-bake provided by General Rosser. In their absence, shortly before 3 P.M., Federals were seen making their way toward the Confederate left. Soon they swept overwhelmingly down on the 6000 infantry, who were badly placed and had very little artillery. Quickly the Union troops routed or captured a large part of them. The survivors retreated as best they could in the darkness to the Southside Railroad.

Thus, in two calamitous hours, the mobile force that Lee had established to protect his right flank was swept away and virtually ceased to be. The Federals reported the capture of 3244 men and four guns. The casualties were not large compared with those Lee had sustained in some of his great battles, but they were a very considerable fraction of his diminished army. His most strategic position had been lost.

The best Lee could do now was little enough, and it entailed new risks. Bushrod Johnson was ordered to proceed at once to Church Crossing and to support the cavalry. This meant the virtual abandonment of that part of the line within the bend of Hatcher's Run. It meant even more, for as the few remaining units were spread out, they were so thinned as almost to be helpless. From Battery Gregg to Hatcher's Run the men were from ten to twenty feet apart, and at some points still farther. A single regiment of Scales's brigade and the sharpshooters of McRae's, were all that could be put in the position that Wise's and Hunton's brigades had occupied. Lee's only chance of remanning the endangered works on the right was to bring Field's division of 4600 men from the north side of the James. He now ordered this, most urgently, and directed that Longstreet come with Field's men. In the last struggle he wanted near him that lieutenant, who, for all his stubborn self-opinion, was the best corps commander he had left. Lee must have put the extremity of his plight into that order, the text of which has been lost, for as it was transmitted through channels, it had an ominous ring. "It is important beyond measure," Longstreet's adjutant general wrote Field, "that no time be lost." The tocsin was sounded in the capital and all the local defense troops, together with the state cadets, were ordered out to man the works below Richmond. Ewell reassumed command on the northside.

Had Lee known early in the evening the magnitude of the disaster that had befallen Pickett he might have ordered the evacuation of the Petersburg line before daylight. Even as it was, with the enemy on his right flank and the river behind him, he must have had full knowledge that what little hope remained to him hung on the arrival of Longstreet before Grant assaulted.

South of the James River, on nearly 20 miles of line, Lee now had scarcely 16,000 infantry in position and none in reserve. From the Appomattox to Hatcher's Run, he had only 11,000. From Lieutenant's Run to the very end of his fortified position, where the Claiborne road crossed the western stretch of Hatcher's Run, he had no more than 12,500 infantry. These included the forces in the highly important position of Burgess's Mill. If Grant were held off one day longer, as he had been held off for nine months, there was still a chance of a safe withdrawal and a reconcentration. But if Grant turned the right, or discovered how thin was the line of infantry behind the works . . . then . . . but Lee could only tell General Grimes, who reported the weakness of his position, that he must do the best he could.

His orders given, Lee went to his quarters, but he slept little, if at all. Perhaps he caught the sound of the picket firing that broke out at 1:45 on the morning of the fateful 2d. Soon A. P. Hill came out from his quarters, which were a mile and a half nearer Petersburg than Lee's. About 4 o'clock Longstreet arrived. Lee was in bed, feeling unwell, but received Longstreet at once and reviewed for him the condition on the right. He directed Longstreet to take his troops, the instant they detrained, and to march for Hatcher's Run.

Suddenly Colonel Venable broke excitedly into the room. Wagons and teamsters, he said, were driving wildly down Cox's road toward Petersburg. An infantry officer had told him that Federal skirmishers had driven him from Harris's quarters, less than half a mile from Edge Hill.

From Harris's quarters? Why, the huts of the Mississippians were a mile and a half in the rear of the main line! If the enemy were there, then the Federals had broken the line—broken it at a point that would put them in rear of the whole of the Confederate right!

Instantly the General sprang from his bed and hurried to the door with Longstreet. It was an unusually dark morning. Distant objects were vague. But long lines of men, like those of skirmishers, were visible, moving slowly toward Edge Hill from the southwest. Were they retreating Confederates or advancing Union troops? Quick, Colonel Venable, mount and reconnoitre, and General Hill—but Hill was already running toward his horse. Away they galloped. Other officers leaped into their saddles and sped after them. Couriers lashed their lean and frantic horses as they dashed away with orders.

Then, for a few moments, the line that stretched across the gray fields halted as if in doubt. Soon, in the growing light, the color of the men's uniforms was visible—blue. They were Federals. Could Longstreet use Field's division to stop them? No, "Old Pete" had to answer: Word had not yet come that any of Field's regiments had arrived. The best that could be done for the moment was to rally the Confederate forces on Fort Gregg and Fort Baldwin.

Lee dressed quickly. When he reappeared, he was in full uniform and had on his sword. He rode down to the gate of Edge Hill and across the road, whence he had a good sweep of the country. He had not been there long when a number of staff officers came up. Some of them were of Hill's entourage, and with them was Hill's dapple-gray horse. But the commander of the Third Corps was not astride the animal. Instead, Sergeant G. W. Tucker rode him—Tucker, who was known throughout the army as Hill's daredevil courier. He told how Hill and himself had ridden on, after Colonel Venable had left them, and how they had encountered two Federals who answered their call for "Surrender" with rifle shots. Hill had been hit and had toppled out of his saddle. Tucker had seen him on the ground, motionless, had caught his horse and changed to it because the gray was fresher than his own mount. Lee listened intently. Tears came to his eyes: "He is at rest now," he murmured, "and we who are left are the ones to suffer." To Major General Heth, Hill's senior division commander, Lee dispatched the grim announcement, with orders to report at once in person. Heth was far down on the right and found the enemy between him and headquarters. As he failed to appear, Lee put the Third Corps under Longstreet.

After the first irruption of the Federals there was a period of comparative calm west and southwest of Edge Hill. The tide of blue seemed to be receding rather than advancing. It was probably at this time that Lee learned what had happened. The Federals had started bombardment during the night, and at 4:45 had assaulted along nearly the whole of the line from the Appomattox River to Hatcher's Run. Southwest of Fort Gregg, where the lines turned away toward Hatcher's Run, Thomas's and Lane's brigades of Wilcox's division had been overwhelmed. The van of the Federals had pushed to the Boydton plank road and beyond. These were the troops that had first been seen from Lee's headquarters.

Lee did not have all the details but he knew that the troops on Hatcher's Run were cut off from him, and he could see that beyond the right of Fort Gregg he practically had no line. The situation now presented two obvious problems. One was to hold Petersburg until night and then to get out with the troops still on the lines. The other was to effect a new concentration with the forces cut off on the right. He was not certain, shortly after 10 o'clock, that he would be able to maintain his position until night; but he determined, if he could hold out that long, to evacuate the whole front as soon as darkness fell, and to reconcentrate on the Richmond and Danville Railroad. He dictated a telegram for the Secretary of War, concluding significantly: "I advise that all preparation be made for leaving Richmond tonight. I will advise you later, according to circumstances." It was recieved in Richmond at 10:40. This was the dispatch that was carried to President Davis in Saint Paul's Church during the morning service. He read it, got up quietly, and left the building.

Lee maintained his equanimity. He was "self-contained and serene," wrote Colonel Taylor, and "he acted as one who was conscious of having accomplished all that was possible in the line of duty, and who was undisturbed by the adverse conditions in which he found himself."

New tests of his self-control lay ahead, for the Federals began to move forward again. Shell began to come over. One of them went through the house itself. Federal infantry were massing. Assaults were brewing. Soon Taylor and the telegraph operator were leaving the house. Musketry fire was mingling with the shell. Even the artillery was about to withdraw. Lee himself must turn his back on the enemy and go within the inner lines. Unwilling to start, he remained until the enemy was so close that Traveller had to be put to a gallop. A little way, and he reined in his gray, but evidently his cavalcade had been recognized, for the Federals pursued it with a hot fire. Soon a shell exploded only a few feet behind, killed a horse and scattered fragments.

Now came one of the most dramatic incidents of an overwhelming day. Some 400 to 600 troops of Wilcox's division and of Harris's brigade, were put into Fort Gregg and told to hold it to the last extremity. They made a Homeric defense. Using their few field guns as long as they could, they then employed their muskets, and in the final assault at 1 o'clock, their bayonets. Against them was directed a full division. When the Federals at last entered Fort Gregg, they found fifty-five dead and took about 300 prisoners, including the wounded.

Just before the attack on Fort Gregg began, Benning's brigade, the van of Field's division, reported to Longstreet and was put in to fill a gap on the Confederate right. Along with the men already on the line they fought desperately but against such heavy odds that their officers kept calling for reinforcements. Lee had each time to send the same answer—that he had none. The men must fight it out where they were. And they did.

As soon as he was reasonably sure that he could hold Petersburg until nightfall, Lee proceeded to arrange the details of the evacuation. The march was to be directed to Burkeville, and the point of reconcentration was to be Amelia Courthouse, forty miles from Petersburg on the railroad from Richmond to Danville.

The evacuation of Petersburg was to begin immediately after dark. All guns were to be out of the works in front of that city by 8 o'clock and were to be across the Appomattox by 3 A.M. The special orders were issued as rapidly as possible. The general order was drafted more slowly and was revised with care.

Its composition was interrupted by many calls for counsel and direction. Mr. Davis telegraphed that a move from Richmond that night would "involve the loss of many valuables, both for the want of time to pack and of transportation." Lee's nerves were beginning to feel the strain of a day in purgatory, and when he read the President's message he tore it into bits. "I am sure I gave him sufficient notice," he said, but he replied calmly that it was "absolutely necessary" to abandon the position that night.

Rumors of the proposed move were getting afoot. The naval commander at Drewry's Bluff had heard of the stir among the infantry, and as he had no orders from his department, he asked for suggestions, through Mahone, who held the adjacent lines. From the bureau of subsistence in Richmond came an inquiry to Colonel Cole as to the proper route for the reserve rations that had been accumulated. Reminders there were, in the midst of it all, that Petersburg was not the only city in anguish. From Lieutenant General Taylor in Alabama, Lee received telegrams predicting the fall of Mobile.

Another message now from the President: Would the Danville Railroad be safe that night? Lee thought so and notified him it could be used until the next day. The admission was gloomy, but so was the situation, yet Lee did not abate his efforts. He was still full of fight.

The afternoon was passing. Duties for the desperate night had to be apportioned. Lee called his staff together, explained the plans for the evacuation and assigned to each his work. When the dreadful day ended the lines were still holding. The enemy's attacks had died away, as if Grant knew that the morning would yield him the city, without the shedding of more blood. Soon after night fell, the troops began to move out of the city. Lee mounted Traveller and passed over the bridge to the north side of the Appomattox—for the last time as a soldier.

His heart was heavy but his manner was calm as he rode to the mouth of the Hickory road, where Gordon was to take the right fork and Longstreet the left if they slipped successfully away from their positions. Lee drew rein between the forks and superintended the movement. In darkness, the columns pressed on, with no drum for their step, no word from the sergeants. Their march was to the growl of the Federal guns on the lines and to the groan of heavily laden wagons. Lee waited till the rear was well closed up before he rode on.

Lee had with him probably not more than 12,500 infantry and on the whole of the front he had only from 28,000 to 30,000 infantry moving or preparing to move. After the heavy losses on the right on April 1 and the casualties of April 2 he could not have mustered even that number had not the local defense troops and many of the detailed men and convalescents quit Richmond and joined the retreat. Not all of these, of course, were efficient troops. Nor, for that matter, could all the units of the veteran army itself be accounted fit. The artillery counted about 200 guns, some on weak carriages, pulled by feeble horses in rotten harness. The wagons exceeded 1000, most with four animals. When the trains were fully spread out they occupied thirty miles of road, heavy impediments for an army whose escape required speed.

Despite this, the start was auspicious. After day broke on April 3 and the men had been rested by the roadside, a curious spirit, half elation, spread down the ranks. Lee himself appeared relieved that he was on open ground again and confident he would be able to reach Johnston. Everything, however, depended on a speedy and uninterrupted retreat.

There was nothing on the first day to indicate a rapid or vigorous pursuit, but if that lead of one day were lost all might be lost. When Grant found the direction of the army's retreat and set out after Lee, all the advantage would be with the Federals. Lee's immediate objective, Amelia Courthouse, could be reached before Grant could overtake him, but beyond Amelia Lee's road turned to the southwest, down the Richmond and Danville Railroad, and crossed the low trajectory of Grant's march. From Petersburg to Burkeville, Lee had to cover fifty-five miles. Grant's route from Sutherland Station to Burkeville was nineteen miles shorter. Lee's total distance to the Roanoke River, the nearest point where he could hope to meet Johnston, was 107 miles. Grant's was 88. In the knowledge that the time-factor would settle the campaign—and the war—Lee urged the troops to their best effort. The long line of ragged men streamed westward through the spring mud. Already some of the half-starved teams were collapsing as they tried to pull the heavy ordnance wagons. Men too weak to keep up with the column were beginning to straggle.

By nightfall on the 3d the troops from Petersburg had covered an average of not less than twenty-one miles. Longstreet had crossed Field's and Wilcox's men over the Appomattox at Goode's bridge and had taken up a line to the west of the bridge to cover the passage of the wagons and of the artillery. Gordon, who was behind Longstreet, acted as rearguard of the principal column the next day and the next. Mahone had left the Howlett Line a little before daylight on the 3d and was well on the road to Goode's bridge. Lee had heard nothing from Ewell, who was supposed to be marching to Genito bridge with Custis Lee's command and Kershaw's division.

After Pickett had been defeated at Five Forks, Anderson had started about dark on April 1 to go to Church Crossing, near Ford's Station on the Southside Railroad, to support the cavalry. Meantime, what was left of Pickett's command had proceeded to Exeter Mills in the hope of crossing the Appomattox and rejoining the army. At the mills, Pickett had found no bridge and had discovered the river too high to be forded. Anderson had reached Church Crossing at 2 A.M. on the morning of April 2 and had formed a junction with Fitz Lee's cavalry, but had received no word of Pickett. Pickett was located, very early in the morning of April 2, and he set out to march to Anderson, but he had not gone far before he met stragglers from Heth's and Wilcox's divisions. Pickett ascertained from these men what had happened and decided to continue up the river and join Anderson, who was moving toward Amelia Courthouse. That night, April 2, Hunton's brigade, which had been having hard fighting, rejoined Pickett. On the 3d, accompanied by the cavalry, Anderson, after a day of many disturbances, reached the vicinity of Bevill's bridge. There he caught up with Pickett.

During the time Pickett was marching up the Appomattox the broken parts of Wilcox's and Heth's divisions—McGowan's, Scales's, MacRae's, and perhaps some of McComb's stragglers—got together under General Heth at Sutherland's Tavern. They proceeded to construct a hasty line by piling up fence rails. Two attacks they beat off, but when the enemy turned their left flank and got in their rear they had to retreat hurriedly. Many were captured; a remnant got across the river. They kept moving, at intervals, until the night of the 3d, when they rejoined their divisions at Goode's bridge. Although there thus were three points of concentration—Church Crossing, Sutherland's Tavern, and Exeter Mills—Anderson, who had nearly all the cavalry of the army with him, could not get the troops together. Each command fought or marched alone, in an effort to escape. But now, at last, on the night of the 3d, Lee was in touch with all the units that had made their way from the Petersburg line, and he had no reason to suppose the forces from the Richmond and Howlett lines would not speedily overtake him. It looked as if the reconcentration would be effected at Amelia Courthouse with no further losses.

About 7 o'clock the next morning, Lee learned that the courier who had been sent to Ewell with orders the previous evening had reported that he had not been able to hear anything of the troops moving from Richmond. Lee sent the dispatch off again with a postscript in which he gave Ewell discretionary orders to cross the river where he could, and to move as soon as practicable to Amelia Courthouse.

Longstreet passed the rest of his command over Goode's bridge early in the morning of the 4th. He soon met enemy cavalry. Skirmishing began and continued intermittently on the left flank as the column moved toward Amelia Courthouse, eight and a half miles away. Lee himself crossed the stream shortly after 7:30. Lee rode on with the advance of Longstreet's corps. Gordon's veterans followed. The troops had now been out of the trenches thirty-six hours, with their wagon train strung out on the muddy roads behind them. The little bread and meat they chanced to have with them at the time of the Federal onslaught had been consumed. The men were hungry, and for such long marches as they were expected to make they needed ample food. The commissary general had carried out his instructions to collect a special reserve of rations in Richmond and had accumulated some 350,000 there. Lee's expectation was to supply the troops from this reserve as the men arrived at Amelia Courthouse. Then he expected to move directly down the railroad toward Danville. At other points on the railway, additional supplies were to be sent him. Having changed his base to Danville, his line of communications would be shortened hourly.

On reaching Amelia Courthouse, Lee's first thought was for the commissary stores. He found ordnance supplies in abundance—96 full caissons, 200 boxes of artillery ammunition, and 164 boxes of artillery harness—but no food. More than 30,000 hungry men were moving on a village where there was not an army ration!

This meant, at the least, a full day's delay, for the army must be fed, and the only way to do this was to halt the march, send wagons into the impoverished country round about, and impress what could be found. And a day's delay entailed the loss of the army's advantage in time. Even that might not be all. For if the enemy cut the railroad ahead of the army, where could rations be found for the next day, or the next? The possibilities alarmed Lee as had nothing that had occurred up to that time on the retreat. It was no easy task to disentangle wagons from the train and to send them out foraging over roads about which the teamsters knew nothing, but this was done at once. The only other thing Lee could do immediately to procure food was to order supplies sent up the railroad from Danville.

Proud as Lee must have been of the spirit his men displayed, he knew that it could not long be sustained in the face of continued hunger and attack. He must recover as many hours as he might of the day's lead he was losing. This could be done only by rapid marching. And rapid marching could be made possible only by a reduction of the wagon train and artillery. So, during the morning of the 4th, General Pendleton was set to work bringing down the artillery to the needs of the army, and Colonel Corley was directed to do the same thing with the wagons. The excess animals were to be used to help those that remained with the trains. The surplus guns were to be moved by rail to Danville, if practicable. The wagons that were not required with the troops were to be sent around the army in such a way that the army would be between them and the Federals. In case the artillery could not be sent by rail, it was to follow the route of the wagon trains.

The enemy was advancing. That was as ominous as the lack of provisions. South of the railroad and beyond Amelia, on the way to Burkeville, Federal cavalry were to be seen. Longstreet moved out Field, Wilcox, and Heth and attempted to bring on a fight, but he found the Unionists wary. Lee set out to reconnoitre behind the Fourteenth Virginia Cavalry, of Rooney Lee's division. He went some distance down the Avery Church road and soon found himself where the regiment was skirmishing with a Federal mounted outpost.

At nightfall, the Federals withdrew from in front of Amelia, and Longstreet's troops were able to leave their line of battle. But there was rest neither of mind nor of body for Lee. Now, at last, came word from Ewell. He had reached the Appomattox and had found no bridge on his designated route, but he had gone to Mattoax and reported from that point, telling General Lee that the engineers were planking the railroad bridge so that he could cross there. Lee answered with instructions and encouragement. He surmised that Ewell would have passed the stream by the time he wrote, 9 P.M., and in this he was not greatly mistaken. Kershaw of Longstreet's corps and the scratch division of Custis Lee, 6000 men altogether, were behind the Appomattox by night. Mahone, who had been holding the bridge at Goode's, passed over also and set out for Amelia.

The reconcentration was nearly complete. Should food be forthcoming on the morrow, the army could move down the railroad and might regain some of the time it had lost. If they had good fortune, the excess wagons and artillery on the right of the railroad might reach their destination unharmed. Although the odds were all against Lee, there was still a chance of escape: twenty-four hours would dim it or bring it nearer reality. The Staunton River, a strong line, was distant only four days' forced marching, and beyond it lay Danville, where a million and a half rations were stored.

On the morning of April 5, the wagons began to come in from foraging. One glance at them told the tale: they were almost empty. The farmers had scarcely anything to give or to sell. The country had already been stripped. It was a catastrophe. Now starvation seemed a stark reality. Wet and gloomy, the men were slow to take their places in the ranks and to test their last hope—that of marching down the road far enough to find the provisions ordered from Danville.

At length the surplus artillery and the wagons were started on their roundabout way to Danville. W. H. F. Lee's cavalry division was dispatched down the railroad. Gary's brigade was ordered to protect the wagon train. Gordon's infantry were to continue to cover the rear.

Then Longstreet began to move southwestward, behind a cavalry screen, toward Jetersville and Burkeville. He was followed by Mahone and Pickett. After them marched the rest of Anderson's troops. Ewell reported with Kershaw and Custis Lee from Richmond. He was put in rear of Anderson but did not move until later in the day. Fitz Lee was ordered to take his own division and Rosser's and to proceed in the direction of Paineville, near which the wagon train was supposed to be moving.

General Lee kept his headquarters at Amelia until the infantry were well on the road. About 1 P.M. he rode forward with Longstreet and about seven miles from Amelia came upon the enemy, entrenching on a well-chosen position. The Federals had overtaken Lee. The road of the army's escape was blocked.

This time Lee was the pursued and not the pursuer. Unless the Federal position could be quickly forced or turned, the hope of getting supplies from Danville was at an end. Hastening to the front, Lee found Rooney with some information as to Federal forces. They were Sheridan's men, the cavalryman reported and infantry were close by, moving in the general direction of Burkeville. Grim-faced and silent, Lee made a reconnaissance of the Federal position. Should he try once more the "antique valor" of his infantry? Should he stake everything on one last assault, and either win a crushing victory or die where the flags went down?

If he could not attack the Federal position, what should he do? He must speedily get provisions if he was to continue fighting. How could he victual the men and at the same time proceed with his retreat? The railroad supply-lines left to him before he had quit Petersburg had formed a rough Saint Andrew's cross. The lines met at Burkeville, the junction that had been in his mind since February. All that was left to him of the four arms of the cross was that from Burkeville toward Lynchburg. He determined to strike across to that "arm" of the cross, to order supplies down it from Lynchburg, and then, having fed his army, to turn southwestward in the direction of Danville again.

But how was he to get away from the enemy that stood across his path and was getting stronger every hour? He had lost his day's lead; he could regain it only by a night march. Orders were given accordingly.

Longstreet retraced his steps a short distance up the railroad and turned to the left. The other corps took the same general route—only to find the roads jammed and progress almost impossible. Federal cavalry had swept down upon the trains before they had reached Paineville and had driven off the guards. About 200 wagons had been burned, and 320 soldiers, in addition to 310 Negro teamsters, had been made prisoner. This attack on a narrow road in swampy ground stopped all movement of the trains. Six hours passed before the wheels of the wagons began to turn again. It was after night when the trains got to Paineville, only about ten miles from Amelia.

The forced night march of April 5–6, now Lee's chief hope of escape, almost immediately became a slow stumble over crowded roads where confusion ruled and panic easily was spread. The engineers had not considered the possibility of an advance on the road to Amelia Springs, and had not strengthened the bridge over a troublesome little stream known as Flat Creek. The bridge broke down and halted the artillery and the wagons, though the infantry could ford the watercourse and keep on.

Probably while he was waiting for the engineers to come up, a courier brought Lee a message from Gordon: two spies had been captured, and from one of them had been taken dispatches that Gordon considered sufficiently important to forward for inspection. The envelope was addressed to the Federal General Ord. Inside were two messages of no

great consequence, and a note to Ord dated "Jetersville, April 5, 1865
—10:10 P.M." It directed that officer to move at 8 A.M. the next
morning and to take a position from which he could watch the roads
between Burkeville and Farmville. "I am strongly of the opinion that
Lee will leave Amelia tonight to go south. He will be pursued at 6 A.M.
from here if he leaves. Otherwise an advance will be made upon him
where he is." This was signed. "U. S. Grant, lieut-genl."

There was no mistaking the meaning of this: Grant himself was at
Jetersville, Ord at Burkeville. The Army of the James as well as the
Army of the Potomac was nearby in sufficient strength to pursue or to
attack. The news showed the vigor of the pursuit and reinforced the
urgency of speed and still more speed. Lee remained at the crossing
until the engineers had given assurance that the material for repairing
the bridge was close at hand. Thence he rode on to Amelia Springs and
adjusted his dispositions, so far as practicable, to the new development.

The first danger was that the wagon train would slow the retreat of
the army so much that the rear troops might be cut off. There was no
way to be rid of the wagons because the roads were few. The wagons
had to be taken along, and the rear closed up as well as was possible.

The second danger was that Sheridan would destroy the wagon train
as it groaningly crept to the southwest the next day. The only defense
was caution in seeing that each command kept contact with the unit
ahead and, exercising the greatest vigilance, stood ready to beat off attacks. The condition presented by the captured dispatch could not be
removed strategically and had to be met tactically. With speed his one
remaining weapon, Lee was confirmed in his decision that the movement of the whole army must continue with only such brief rest as was
imperative. Desperate since he had reached Amelia Courthouse and had
found no provisions there, his situation might easily be rendered hopeless within twenty-four hours.

Commissary General St. John reported at headquarters while Lee was
at Amelia Springs. St. John had left Richmond not long before the
Federals had entered the city April 3, and he had been trying to hasten
forward the wagons he had loaded in Richmond with the provisions
he had not been able to send up the Danville Railroad on April 2. From
St. John, probably, Lee learned why the rations had not been awaiting
him at Amelia. He learned, also, that part of those that had been brought
from the evacuated capital had been captured by the Federals near
Clementown bridge. The only encouragement St. John could give was
that he had 80,000 rations at Farmville, nineteen miles away. Should

they be left at Farmville, asked St. John, or should they be moved farther down the railroad, closer to the army? Lee said frankly that the military situation made it impossible to answer. He apprehended that the Federal cavalry might reach the railroad before he did, and might destroy the train. St. John accordingly went on to Farmville to prepare for the coming of the army and for the issuance of rations there.

It was now the early morning of April 6. While Lee had been at Amelia Springs, the column had been moving painfully forward. Straggling was perceptibly worse. The number of broken-down teams was larger. As Lee rode to join Longstreet there was something akin to despair in the eyes that were turned on him, and there was delirium in the loyal cheers that greeted him.

Continuing to the vicinity of Rice, Lee awaited there the coming of the First Corps. Longstreet arrived during the forenoon with his men. "Old Pete" had information that some 600 or 700 mounted Federals had passed up the road toward Farmville. The object of these troops presumably was to burn the bridges over which part of Lee's army would pass. Longstreet immediately sent off cavalry in pursuit. Hearing, also, that the enemy was in force about four miles to the southeastward, he took up line of battle covering the roads to Rice and at right angles to the railway.

This intelligence of the nearness of the Federals was bad news for Lee. Still more ominous was a development about 10 A.M. The wagon train was assailed some two miles back on the road. The outlook was grim. With the column broken, the presence of Union cavalry on the flank of a far-spread wagon train meant danger and delay—at a time when speed was everything.

Lee examined the roads and the terrain around him. It was bad ground for a retreat. There could hardly have been a stretch of Virginia countryside better suited for an attack by cavalry on an encumbered column of infantry. Particularly dangerous was the ground northwest of Rice. There were located the two forks and the watershed of a little stream called Sayler's Creek that flows northward into the Appomattox.

In examining this ground General Lee rode during the early afternoon toward the mouth of Sayler's Creek. There he found himself with Roberts's cavalry brigade. This little command was watching something as ominous as it was unexpected—a fight in progress on the other side of the creek, between Gordon's corps and unidentified units of the enemy. Lee dismounted and took out his glasses to survey some white objects he saw in the distance.

A young captain came up at the moment. "Are those sheep or not?" Lee asked doubtfully.

"No, General," said the possessor of younger eyes, "they are Yankee wagons."

Lee looked again through his glasses and then said slowly: "You are right; but what are they doing there?" What did it mean that the Federal wagon trains were already up—and no word from Anderson or Ewell, who were marching ahead of Gordon?

Riding back in a few minutes, toward the line on which these corps should be moving, Lee soon met Colonel Venable. Venable told him that the enemy had captured the wagons that were between the branches of Sayler's Creek.

"Where is Anderson?" exclaimed General Lee. "Where is Ewell? It is strange I can't hear from them." Then he turned. "General Mahone," he said, "I have no other troops. Will you take your division to Sayler's Creek?"

Mahone gave the order; the men started, Lee and Mahone ahead of them. They came to the elevation overlooking the creek. Lee stopped and straightened himself in his saddle and stared at what he saw. It was such a sight as his eyes had never beheld: streaming out of the bottom and up the ridge were teamsters without their wagons, soldiers without their guns, and shattered regiments without their officers, a routed wreck!

"My God!" cried Lee, as if to himself; "has the army been dissolved?"

Mahone answered stoutly: "No, General, here are troops ready to do their duty."

Lee regained his poise on the instant. "Yes, General," he said, "there are some true men left. Will you please keep those people back?"

As Mahone hurried away to draw a line of battle, Lee spurred forward to rally the men who were running toward him. Either from the ground where the bearer had dropped it in his fight, or else from the hand of some color-bearer, Lee took a battle flag and held it aloft. There on Traveller he sat, the red folds of the bunting flapping about him, the soldiers in a mob in front of him, some wild with fear, some exhausted, some wounded. A few rushed on; others looked up and, recognizing him, began to flock around him as if to find shelter in his calm presence. Did it flash over him then that this was the last rally of the great Army of Northern Virginia?

Mahone soon returned and took the battle flag from the General's hand. Lee reached for his binoculars and began to study the valley and the hills beyond it, in the hope of discovering how he should dispose his thin line to halt the enemy's advance. The character of the *débâcle* was not yet known, but its magnitude was obivous. Ewell and Anderson had met disaster.

What should be done? Lee put the question to Mahone. Together they worked out a plan for Longstreet to march on to Farmville while Mahone held his position. Later in the night Mahone was to withdraw through the woods and cross the Appomattox on the Southside Railroad bridge. He was to hold the crossing until all had passed, and then the engineers were to burn both that high span and the lower wagon bridge. Colonel Talcott was assigned this duty.

Lee rode back to Longstreet's lines at Rice. The cavalry that had been sent off during the morning had overtaken the Federals who were aiming to burn the high bridge over the Appomattox, and had killed or captured nearly all of them. Longstreet's forces were intact, and Gordon's were still hotly and dangerous engaged. These and the cavalry were now nearly all that was left of the army.

In the fighting at Sayler's Creek Ewell had lost 2800, Anderson perhaps 1500. The two corps as fighting units virtually ceased to exist. Lee told only the sombre truth when he said to Pendleton, "General, that half of our army is destroyed."

As he had covered the rear, Gordon had been closely pursued. Once he was compelled to form line of battle along the hills at Deatonsville to retard the enemy until the road in front of him was clear for a mile. At an exceedingly bad crossing near the mouth of Sayler's Creek a direct assault was successfully repulsed. Soon afterward, however, the Federals who had overrun Ewell's front massed for a charge on Gordon. Once more he drove back his assailants, but finally his exhausted divisions broke, got across the creek as best they could, and formed again, after a fashion, on the west bank, in the darkness.

Gordon lost by capture some 1700. These brought the Federals' haul of prisoners to at least 6000. The day had cost Lee not less than 7000 and perhaps 8000 men. The Southern commander now had only six divisions that could be counted as fighting organizations and but two of these were of any size. The cavalry mounts were nearly dead, though the troopers were still capable of putting up a fight. The artillery was reduced by about 50 per cent in personnel and still further in guns. To oppose on the morrow four corps of infantry and four divisions of cavalry—a total of 80,000 men—Lee could not muster more than 12,000 reliable muskets and 3000 sabres.

Lee permitted himself no inferences that night. There was still a chance of escaping with what remained of the army, if he could rest and reorganize his men. He might still outmarch the enemy. He could cross to the north bank of the Appomattox, burn the bridges near Farmville, and give his men the repose that was now as much a necessity as food. So long as this chance was open to him, his sense of duty did not permit him to consider any alternative.

One relief, if only one, was in sight. General St. John had reached Farmville and had found the provisions sent from Burkeville, 80,000 rations of meal and about 40,000 of bread. St. John turned over all he had to Lee's commissary for issue to the troops, many of whom had received no regular rations since April 2. The starving time, it seemed, at last was over!

In the morning of April 7th Lee rode to the north side of the Appomattox to locate the troops that had escaped the disaster at Sayler's Creek and had been ordered to cross the Appomattox at High Bridge. He soon found Major General Bushrod R. Johnson, who reported that his division had been destroyed; but very shortly Lee saw marching toward him in good order the largest of its brigades, headed by General Wise. Behind Wise's brigade and the stragglers the survivors of Gordon's corps were moving up. They had crossed at High Bridge and would be ready to rejoin the rest of the army when Longstreet moved to the north side of the Appomattox.

Longstreet's troops were now coming into Farmville, and advanced units were marching to the northside, where they were to halt and cook their long-awaited rations. The cavalry was following them, with the understanding that when they had passed, the two bridges were to be burned. If this were done and if the two crossings at High Bridge had been destroyed, as previously ordered, then Lee would have at least some chance to rest his army and to resume his march ahead of the enemy.

All Lee's plans were suddenly set at nought. Federal infantry were already on the north bank of the river. A grievous blunder had been made. The wagon bridge had been lighted too late. Federals were moving easily over it. Mahone made an attempt to retake the bridgehead, but failed. General Lee exploded when he got word of the blunder. With vehemence unrestrained he voiced his opinion of the act and its authors. Lee's rage was soon subdued, however, and his mind was put to work to redeem once more the military mistakes of others.

Federal cavalry were pressing so closely behind the Confederates that Fitz Lee had to make a stand on the outskirts of Farmville and in the streets of the town to permit Longstreet's rearguard and the stragglers to clear the bridges. By 11 A.M. the advance of the fast-moving VI Corps was on the hills overlooking Farmville from the south. The bridges were fired and caught rapidly, before the Confederate cavalry could break off the skirmish and cross. The arrival of the Federals caused a near-stampede among the teamsters and scattered units on the north side of the river and prompted General Lee to order an immediate resumption of the retreat. The issue of rations had to be suspended. Envelopment was threatened; no time was to be lost.

Lee went up the road with Longstreet's column to the coal pits north of Farmville. There he found the cavalry and learned that the Confederates had located a ford and had crossed safely. He sat down under a tree and was resting when Federal cavalry advanced for another attack on the wagons. Under his eyes, the enemy's attack was broken up brilliantly. Lee's spirits were much improved by this success. "Keep your command together and in good spirits, General—don't let them think of surrender—I will get you out of this," he told Rooney.

Lee held the cavalry where it could meet another attack, and he sent Mahone's division to the position taken by the artillery which Alexander had sent forward to the point where the road of the Federal advance met the road of Lee's march. A little more than three miles north of Farmville, Mahone drew up line of battle, entrenched, and prepared to cover the passage of the wagons and of the army.

The army had virtually no start when Federal infantry began to appear in strength on Mahone's front. In the afternoon they tried to turn the division's left, which was almost "in the air." Gordon and Longstreet had to send Mahone help. He then beat off the attack and delivered a countercharge in which he took some prisoners. Lee could not presume on this momentary advantage. He dared not attempt an offensive against the troops that threatened his road. The start that had been so vigorously begun at the double-quick near Farmville came to a maddening halt within four miles and in plain sight of the enemy!

As darkness fell, Lee went to a cottage near Mahone's lines to spend the night. Longstreet soon joined him there. About half-past nine a courier came up with a dispatch. Lee opened it and read:

Headquarters Armies of the United States.
April 7, 1865—5 P.M.

General R. E. Lee,
Commanding C. S. Army:

General: The results of the last week must convince you of the hopelessness of further resistance on the part of the Army of

GENERAL GEORGE GORDON MEAD

GENERAL ULYSSES S. GRANT

Northern Virginia in this struggle. I feel that it is so, and regard it as my duty to shift from myself the responsibility of any further effusion of blood, by asking of you the surrender of that portion of the C. S. Army known as the Army of Northern Virginia.

Very respectfully, your obedient servant,

U. S. GRANT,
Lieutenant-General,
Commanding Armies of the United States.

General Lee silently passed it to Longstreet, who was sitting near him. Longstreet read it, also, and handed it back. "Not yet," he said.

Longstreet's answer bespoke his chief's mind. As long as there was a prospect of escape Lee felt it was his duty to fight on. He would not yield one hour before he must. With no reply to Longstreet, he wrote his answer:

7th Apl '65

Genl

I have recd your note of this date. Though not entertaining the opinion you express of the hopelessness of further resistance on the part of the Army of N. Va.—I reciprocate your desire to avoid useless effusion of blood, & therefore before considering your proposition, ask the terms you will offer on condition of its surrender

Very respy your obt. Servt
R. E. LEE
Genl

Lt. Genl. U. S. Grant
Commd Armies of the U. States

The wagons had passed on now and had halted in the neighborhood of New Store, nearly twenty miles from Farmville, but they were much scattered. The troops who still carried their muskets had hardly the appearance of soldiers as they wearily tramped along, their clothes tattered, their eyes sunken and lustreless, and their faces pale and pinched. Lee deemed it desirable to send ahead Gordon's tired men and the various scattered units and to bring from van to rear the corps of Longstreet which had suffered less and was in fair fighting condition. Nothing was left of the infantry now but the starved remnant of these two corps and a few small brigades. By 11 P.M. Gordon's men had passed up the road toward Lynchburg, and Longstreet resumed the march. The cavalry closed the rear. At 1 A.M., from New Store, the wagons started once again.

It was now Saturday, April 8. Lee's objective remained the same—Danville and union with Johnston—but his hope of attaining that objective had dwindled until now it hung on a double contingency. If Lee was to escape, he had to cross the watershed between the Appomattox and the James before the enemy closed the way. And if he was to keep his army from starvation, he had to meet at some point on the railroad over that watershed the trains of provisions. The most convenient place to reach the trains was where the road of his march crossed the railway at a station called after the county and the river, Appomattox.

Would Lee reach Appomattox Station before the Federals and would he procure food there or nearby? If he did, he might feed the men, turn south and even yet reach Danville and join General Johnston. But if he found the Federals across the watershed in sufficient strength to block his advance and to seize his provisions, that was the end.

Toward Appomattox Station the march continued slowly through the morning hours of the 8th. The Federals in the rear did not push the cavalry. The infantry were only a little disturbed on the left flank, and there only by horsemen. Lee's manner was as composed as ever. The situation was so quiet that General Lee halted during the forenoon to rest. General Pendleton approached and told him that a number of his officers had met the previous evening and had considered the situation. They had deputized Pendleton to acquaint Lee with their deliberations and to tell him that, in their opinion, he ought to stop the fighting and open negotiations for surrender. Pendleton did not say so, but the officers had acted in a desire to save Lee the humiliation of making the first move toward surrender. They were willing to assume the responsibility. Lee did not like the suggestion, and when General Pendleton talked of the interview shortly after it ended, he had the air of a man who had been decidedly snubbed and was embarrassed to have to tell of it.

During the early afternoon word came from Fitz Lee that his rearguard was about two miles behind the infantry and that the enemy was two miles behind him. Later a further dispatch from Fitz Lee brought news that the enemy's cavalry had reached Prospect Station, twenty miles east of Appomattox. They would arrive at Appomattox by 10 A.M. of the 9th at the earliest. The race to Appomattox would be close! The enemy's cavalry and the Confederate advance would get there within a few hours of each other.

Anderson was left without a command after the *débâcle* of Sayler's Creek. On the 8th he was formally relieved and notified that he could return to his home, or any other place he might select, and report thence to the Secretary of War. At the same time that Lee relieved Anderson of command, he took like action regarding Pickett and Bushrod Johnson, but the order concerning Pickett apparently never reached him.

About dark Lee received another note from Grant. Grant stated, in simple terms, that as peace was his great desire, the only condition on which he would insist would be that the officers and men who were surrendered should be disqualified to bear arms until properly exchanged. Grant added that he would meet Lee, or, he offered thoughtfully, would designate officers to meet others named by Lee to arrange the terms for the surrender of the Army of Northern Virginia.

Lee was not yet willing to consider surrender, but the hope of a general settlement that had shaped his action on receipt of Grant's first letter did not seem wholly destroyed by Grant's language. So, Lee wrote in his own hand this letter:

8h Ap^l '65

Genl

I recd at a late hour your note of today. In mine of yesterday I did not intend to propose the surrender of the Army of N. Va.— but to ask the terms of your proposition. To be frank, I do not think the emergency has arisen to call for the surrender of this Army, but as the restoration of peace should be the sole object of all, I desired to know whether your proposals would lead to that and I cannot therefore meet you with a view to surrender the Army of N. Va.—but as far as your proposal may affect the C. S. forces under my command & tend to the restoration of peace, I shall be pleased to meet you at 10 A.M tomorrow on the old stage road to Richmond between the picket lines of the two armies.

Very respy your Obt Sevt
R. E. LEE.
Genl.

Lt. Genl U. S. Grant
Comng Armies of the U. S.

This was delivered to General Humphreys' lines. Before it was dispatched, the leading brigades of Gordon's command, very weary, had halted at 3 P.M. about one mile from Appomattox Courthouse. Longstreet's corps stopped behind Gordon. Lee and his staff turned out from the road, with Longstreet and his officers, and made camp about two miles from the courthouse.

About 9 o'clock there came a sudden roar of artillery from the front. The enemy was across the line of the army's advance over the watershed! Lee sent orders to Fitz Lee to pass the cavalry to the front and directed him to report in person at headquarters. The rearguard proceeded to dig and to man field works across the road of the Federal pursuit.

Ere long Fitz Lee arrived, as did Gordon, on a like summons. With these and with Longstreet, began Lee's last council of war. Lee explained the condition of affairs as far as he knew it and read to his chiefs of corps the correspondence with Grant.

What, he then asked, did they advise him to do?

There could be only one answer from men who were determined to fight as long as any hope remained. That answer was to attempt to cut a way through. But if the Federal infantry stood in force across the road, too strong to be driven, the troops would then be virtually surrounded and only one thing remained—surrender. The word could not be avoided now.

Details were worked out quickly. The advance was to begin at 1 A.M. Fitz Lee was to drive the enemy from his front, wheel to the left, and cover the passage of the trains. Gordon was then to move ahead, and Longstreet was to close up and be ready to repel any attack by the forces moving on the Confederate rear. The orders were given. The conference was ended. Gordon and Fitz Lee rode off. Longstreet prepared to make his bed on the ground, when one of Gordon's staff officers returned to explain that his chief had neglected to ask where he was to halt and camp the next night. Did General Lee have any directions for him on this point?

"Yes," said Lee grimly. "Tell General Gordon I should be glad for him to halt just beyond the Tennessee line," some 175 miles away.

CHAPTER XV

Appomattox

SHORTLY after 1 o'clock, there came the weary staccato of the march. Soon the groups among the trees were awake. General Lee dressed himself faultlessly, and put on his handsomest sword and his sash of deep, red silk. "I have probably to be General Grant's prisoner and thought I must make my best appearance," he told General Pendleton, when that officer expressed his surprise at Lee's attire.

Then, about 3 o'clock, Lee started to the front, where the guns were announcing Gordon's preparation for an advance. Lee had not far to go, for what was left of the Army of Northern Virginia was now on and alongside a single road, the van not more than four miles from the rearguard. He had less than 8000 armed infantry left in the ranks.

It was 5 o'clock when the attack opened, about half a mile west of the courthouse. When Lee arrived in rear of Gordon's command the battle was on. The course of the action could not be seen. Lee waited until perhaps 8 o'clock, and then, as no word had come from Gordon, he sent Colonel Venable to ask what might be expected. Venable surveyed the situation hastily and soon was back with Gordon's report of it: "Tell General Lee," Gordon said, "I have fought my corps to a frazzle, and I fear I can do nothing unless I am heavily supported by Longstreet's corps."

Lee heard in silence this report, which was the more conclusive because Gordon was one of the most daring leaders in the Army of Northern Virginia. "Then," said Lee, oblivious to the presence of his staff officers about him, "there is nothing left me to do but to go and see General Grant, and I would rather die a thousand deaths."

His words meant the end! Men spoke in the grief of their hearts. "Oh, General," said one, "Oh, General, what will history say of the surrender of the army in the field?"

"Yes," answered Lee, simply, "I know they will say hard things of us: They will not understand how we were overwhelmed by numbers. But that is not the question, Colonel: The question is, is it right to surrender this army. If it is right, then I will take all the responsibility."

But he did not take it as calmly as his brave answer indicated. After a little, he sent a messenger for Longstreet. When Longstreet rode up, Lee told the chief of the First Corps how matters stood. What was Longstreet's view? Mahone was nearby, shivering. Lee asked for his opinion.

Soon Alexander appeared. Alexander proposed, as an alternative to surrender, that the men take to the woods with their arms, under orders to report to governors of their respective states. Lee saw much danger in this proposal to become guerillas. "General," he reasoned, "you and I as Christian men have no right to consider only how this would affect us. We must consider its effect on the country as a whole. Already it is demoralized by the four years of war. If I took your advice, the men would be without rations and under no control of officers. They would be compelled to rob and steal in order to live. They would become mere bands of marauders, and the enemy's cavalry would pursue them and overrun many sections they may never have occasion to visit. We would bring on a state of affairs it would take the country years to recover from. And, as for myself, you young fellows might go to bushwhacking, but the only dignified course for me would be to go to General Grant and surrender myself and take the consequences of my acts."

Lee paused, and then he added, "But I can tell you one thing for your comfort. Grant will not demand an unconditional surrender. He will give us as good terms as this army has the right to demand, and I am going to meet him in the rear at 10 A.M. and surrender the army on the condition of not fighting again until exchanged."

Alexander went away a humbler man. "I had not a single word to say in reply," he wrote afterwards. "He had answered my suggestion from a plane so far above it, that I was ashamed of having made it."

Lee seems to have unburdened himself somewhat by talking with his associates-in-arms, but he was still abstracted and sick at heart when he mounted Traveller at 8:30 or about that time. He was going to meet Grant, and if the Federal chief was not willing to discuss a general peace, then Lee would have to ask terms for the Army of Northern Virginia alone. Those terms were not to be negotiated: if his adversary so willed, they could be imposed.

The rendezvous that Lee had set with Grant, in his note of the

previous evening, was on the old state road, between the picket lines.
In that direction he now went, accompanied by Taylor, Marshall, and
Sergeant Tucker, chief courier of the Third Corps. Soon the four
riders came to a stout breastwork of logs that the Confederate rearguard had erected. The men recognized Lee and cheered him as he
passed through their line.

The courier then went ahead with his white flag. Marshall and Taylor
followed, and behind them, Lee. The group of horsemen had gone a
little more than half a mile when they saw Federal skirmishers approaching them. Marshall immediately went out in the expectation of meeting
General Grant and his staff. Instead, a single Union officer and his flag-
bearer came forward. The officer proved to be Lieutenant-Colonel
Charles A Whittier. Colonel Whittier had no verbal message from
General Grant and no instructions to conduct the party to a meeting
place. He merely brought a letter, which he delivered. He would wait,
he said, in case Lee wished to send an answer. Marshall jogged back
and gave the dispatch to Lee, who opened it and read as follows:

> *Headquarters Armies of the United States*
> *April 9 1865.*
>
> General R. E. Lee,
> Commanding C. S. Armies:
>
> General: Your note of yesterday is received. As I have no au-
> thority to treat on the subject of peace the meeting proposed for
> 10 A.M. today could lead to no good. I will state, however, Gen-
> eral, that I am equally anxious for peace with yourself, and the
> whole North entertain the same feeling. The terms upon which
> peace can be had are well understood. By the South laying down
> their arms they will hasten that most desirable event, save thou-
> sands of human lives, and hundreds of millions of property not yet
> destroyed. Sincerely hoping that all our difficulties may be settled
> without the loss of another life, I subscribe myself,
>
> > Very respectfully, your obedient servant,
> >
> > > U. S. GRANT,
> > > *Lieutenant-General U. S. Army.*

There was not to be even the poor comfort of an approach to the
surrender of the army of Northern Virginia through a discussion of
peace on all the fronts! The humiliation must be complete. Lee had to
make a formal and unqualified offer to yield up the arms of his men.

But he did not hesitate a moment. He faced that duty precisely as he met any other, in a determination to do his best for the soldiers, without any evasion or attempt to shield himself.

Disappointed that Grant had not come to meet him, he began to be apprehensive that his adversary had refused to appear because he now felt that he had the army virtually surrounded and could impose harsher conditions. Lee's misgivings may have been increased, when at that very moment, there came a roar of artillery from the front, as if the enemy were attacking.

He wrote his reply to Grant, which was hurriedly finished, as the sound of firing from the front grew ominously:

April 9th, 1865

General,

    I received your note of this morning on the picket line whither I had come to meet you and ascertain definitely what terms were embraced in your proposal of yesterday with reference to the surrender of this army. I now request an interview in accordance with the offer contained in your letter of yesterday for that purpose.

Very respectfully
Your obt. servt
R. E. LEE

Lt. Gen U. S. Grant
Comdg U. S. Armies

As Marshall carried the letter to Whittier he saw the Federal skirmishers again advancing. He knew that if they went forward a needless battle would occur, so he explained to Whittier the purport of the letter and told him he hoped hostilities might be suspended until the communication reached Grant. Whittier took the letter and went off, with a promise to bring an answer from his commanding general. Lee waited in the road.

Colonel Whittier soon returned and said he was directed to state that the attack had been ordered and his commanding officer had no discretion but must deliver it. Marshall asked Whittier to request his superior to read Lee's letter to General Grant, as the commanding officer might feel justified in suspending the order. Whittier disappeared again with this appeal.

Lee waited with his companions. The Federal skirmishers drew closer. A flag of truce came out from the Federal lines with a request that the Confederates withdraw, as the attack was about to be de-livered. It was probably through this messenger that Lee sent another note to Grant.

9th April 1865

General,

I ask a suspension of hostilities pending the adjustment of the terms of the surrender of this army, in the interview requested in my former communication today.

Very respectfully,
Your obt. servt.,

Lt. Gen. U. S. Grant   R. E. LEE
Comdg. U. S. Army.   *Genl.*

Lee waited under the flag of truce for an answer. He remained where he was until the head of the Federal column was not more than one hundred yards away. Then came a peremptory warning that he must withdraw immediately. Very reluctantly, Lee turned his horse's head and rode back through the Confederate rearguard, where he found Longstreet awaiting the Federals' attack. Just when it appeared certain that the action would open, Colonel Whittier appeared again under a white flag opposite Field's division. He brought a note from Meade, the text of which has been lost. As far as it can be reconstructed in-ferentially, the note expressed agreement to an informal truce on Meade's lines for an hour and suggested that Lee might be able to communicate more quickly with Grant if he sent a duplicate of his letter through some other part of the line.

Lee rode back toward the front. He stopped in a small apple orchard a short distance in advance of the line of battle. From this point Lee now sent Grant his third note of the day. This letter went even further than did Lee's earlier communication. It was because his experience of the morning had made him fearful of sterner terms and because his army could easily be destroyed, no matter how dearly the men sold their lives. Fitz Lee had gone off with nearly all the cavalry, determined that he would not share in the surrender. Gordon's troops had with-drawn from their advanced position. As the Federals had pressed closely in, what was left of the Army of Northern Virginia was almost en-veloped.

To Longstreet Lee confided his fear that Grant might demand stiffer terms, inasmuch as he had declined those offered the previous day.

Longstreet did not think so. He had known Grant intimately before the war and he told his chief that the Federal general would impose only such terms as Lee himself would in reversed circumstances.

And now, about 12:15 P.M., with another flag of truce, came a single staff officer, accompanied by a Confederate escort. "General Lee," said the escort, "allow me to introduce you to Colonel Babcock." Babcock delivered this letter:

> *Headquarters Armies of the U. S.*
> *April 9, 1865*

> *General R. E. Lee,*
> *Commanding C. S. Army:*

> Your note of this date is but this moment (11:50 A.M.) received. In consequence of my having passed from the Richmond and Lynchburg road to the Farmville and Lynchburg road I am at this writing about four miles west of Walker's church, and will push forward to the front for the purpose of meeting you. Notice sent on this road where you wish the interview to take place will meet me.

> Very respectfully, your obedient servant

> U. S. GRANT,
> *Lieutenant-General*

There was at least no suggestion of other terms than those that had been offered the day before! Babcock supplemented its considerate language with a courteous message: he had been sent by Grant to make any arrangement Lee might desire for a conference, whether within Union or Confederate lines.

In the company of Marshall, Babcock, and Tucker, the daring orderly, Lee started up the road, and beyond the thin and silent line of battle on the hillside. He was on his last ride as commander of the Army of Northern Virginia. Thirty-nine years of devotion to military duty had come to this . . . and this, too, was duty.

Grant had left it to him to select the place of meeting. Would Marshall go ahead and find a suitable house? After a while the orderly returned to say that Colonel Marshall had found a room for the conference. Lee went on and drew rein beyond the courthouse in the yard of a house on the road to Lynchburg. The residence belonged to Major Wilmer McLean, who had owned the farm on Bull Run where the first battle of that name had occurred. Major McLean had removed from that exposed position and had purchased a property at Appomattox—only to find that the march of the armies he had sought to avoid was now about to end, as it had begun, at his door.

Lee dismounted in the yard and walked toward the wide steps of the house. Entering the central hall, he turned into a typical parlor of a middle-class Virginia home. Colonel Marshall went with him. Colonel Babcock accompanied Lee, also, with the explanation that General Grant would soon arrive.

Half an hour passed, perhaps the longest half hour in Lee's life. About 1:30 o'clock there was a clatter in the road, the sound of the approach of a large body of mounted men. Babcock went to the door and opened it. A man of middle height, slightly stooped and heavily bearded, came in alone. He was dressed for the field, with boots and breeches mudbespattered. He took off his yellow thread gloves as he stepped forward. Lee had never seen him to remember him but he knew who he was and, rising with Marshall, he started across the room to meet General Grant. They shook hands quietly with brief greetings. Then Grant sat down at the table in the middle of the room, and Lee returned to his place. Marshall stood to the left and somewhat behind him. Babcock had a few whispered words with Grant, then went from the room. He soon was back, followed by a full dozen Federal officers. The newcomers arranged themselves behind Grant and in sight of Lee as quietly as boots and spurs and clanking swords permitted. Grant made no reference to their coming. Lee showed no sign of resentment at their presence.

The conversation began: "I met you once before, General Lee," Grant said in his normal tones, "while we were serving in Mexico, when you came over from General Scott's headquarters to visit Garland's brigade, to which I then belonged. I have always remembered your appearance, and I think I should have recognized you anywhere."

"Yes," answered Lee quietly, "I know I met you on that occasion, and I have often thought of it and tried to recollect how you looked, but I have never been able to recall a single feature."

Mention of Mexico aroused many memories. Grant pursued them with much interest. Lee felt the weight of every moment and brought Grant back with words that seemed to come naturally, yet must have cost him anguish that cannot be measured.

"I suppose, General Grant," he said, "that the object of our present meeting is fully understood. I asked to see you to ascertain upon what terms you would receive the surrender of my army."

Grant did not change countenance or exhibit the slightest note of exultation in his reply. "The terms I propose are those stated substantially in my letter of yesterday—that is, the officers and men surrendered to be paroled and disqualified from taking up arms again until properly exchanged, and all arms, ammunition and supplies to be delivered up as captured property."

Lee nodded an assent that meant more than his adversary realized. "Those," said he, "are about the conditions I expected would be proposed."

"Yes," Grant answered, "I think our correspondence indicated pretty clearly the action that would be taken at our meeting; and I hope it may lead to a general suspension of hostilities and be the means of preventing any further loss of life."

That was a theme that Lee's conception of his duty as a soldier would not permit him to discuss. The civil authorities had the sole power, he held, to make peace of the sort General Grant had in mind. So he merely inclined his head again.

Grant talked on of peace and its prospects. Lee waited and then, courteously, said: "I presume, General Grant, we have both carefully considered the proper steps to be taken, and I would suggest that you commit to writing the terms you have proposed, so that they may be formally acted upon."

"Very well, I will write them out."

Lee sat in silence as Grant called for his manifold orderbook, opened it, lit his pipe, puffed furiously, wrote steadily for awhile with his pencil, paused, reflected, wrote two sentences and then quickly completed the text. Lee sat as he was until Grant rose and put the book in his hands, with the request that he read over the letter. Lee took up the order book for a slow, careful reading:

> "*Appomattox C. H., Va.*
> *Apr. 9th, 1865.*

> "*Gen. R. E. Lee,*
> "*Comd. C. S. A.*

> "Gen.

> "In accordance with the substance of my letter to you of the 8th instant I propose to receive the surrender of the Army of N. Va. on the following terms, to-wit:

> "Rolls of all the officers and men to be made in duplicate, one

copy to be given to an officer designated by me, the other to be retained by such officer or officers as you may designate. The officers to give their individual paroles not to take up arms against the"

—At this point, Lee turned the page and read on—

"Government of the United States until properly and each company or regimental commander sign a like parole for the men of their command."

Lee stopped in his reading, looked up, and said to Grant: "After the words 'until properly,' the word 'exchanged' seems to be omitted. You doubtless intended to use that word."

"Why, yes," answered Grant, "I thought I had put in the word 'exchanged.'"

"I presumed it had been omitted inadvertently, and with your permission I will mark where it should be inserted."

"Certainly."

Lee felt for a pencil, but could not find one. Colonel Horace Porter stepped forward and offered his. Lee took it, thanked him, placed the book on the table, inserted the caret, and resumed his reading:

"The arms, artillery and public property to be parked and stacked and turned over to the officer appointed by me to receive them.

"This will not embrace the side arms of the officers, nor their private horses or baggage. This done each officer and man will be allowed to return to their homes not to be disturbed by United States authority so long as they observe their paroles and the laws in force where they may reside.

Very respectfully,

U. S. GRANT, *Lt Gl.*"

Lee looked up at Grant and said: "This will have a very happy effect on my army."

"Unless you have some suggestions to make in regard to the form in which I have stated the terms," Grant resumed, "I will have a copy of the letter made in ink and sign it."

Lee hesitated: "There is one thing I would like to mention. The cavalrymen and artillerists own their own horses in our army. Its organization in this respect differs from that of the United States. I would like to understand whether these men will be permitted to retain their horses."

"You will find," answered Grant, "that the terms as written do not allow this. Only the officers are allowed to take their private property."

Lee read over the second page of the letter again. His face showed his wish. His tongue would not go beyond a regretful "No, I see the terms do not allow it; that is clear."

Grant read his opponent's wish, and, with the fine consideration that prevailed throughout the conversation—one of the noblest of his qualities, and one of the surest evidences of his greatness—he did not humiliate Lee by forcing him to make a direct plea for a modification of terms that were generous. "Well, the subject is quite new to me. Of course, I did not know that any private soldiers owned their animals, but I think this will be the last battle of the war—I sincerely hope so— and that the surrender of this army will be followed soon by that of all the others, and I take it that most of the men in the ranks are small farmers, and as the country has been so raided by the two armies, it is doubtful whether they will be able to put in a crop to carry themselves and their families through the next winter without the aid of the horses they are now riding, and I will arrange it this way: I will not change the terms as now written, but I will instruct the officers I shall appoint to receive the paroles to let all the men who claim to own a horse or mule take the animals home with them to work their little farms."

It could not have been put more understandingly or more generously. Lee showed manifest relief and appreciation. "This will have the best possible effect upon the men," he said. "It will be very gratifying and will do much toward conciliating our people."

While Grant set about having his letter copied, Lee directed Marshall to draft a reply. In the wait that followed, Grant brought up and introduced the officers who had remained silent in the background. Lee shook hands with those who extended theirs and bowed to the others, but he spoke only to General Seth Williams, a warm friend during his superintendency at West Point.

When the introductions were over, Lee turned again to Grant. "I have a thousand or more of your men as prisoners, General Grant, a number of them officers whom we have required to march along with us for several days. I shall be glad to send them into your lines as soon as it can be arranged, for I have no provisions for them. I have, indeed, nothing for my own men. They have been living for the last few days principally upon parched corn, and are badly in need of both rations and forage. I telegraphed to Lynchburg, directing several train loads of rations to be sent on by rail from there, and when they arrive I should be glad to have the present wants of my men supplied from them."

There was a stir among the listeners at this remark, and they looked at Sheridan, for, unknown to Lee, he had the previous night captured at Appomattox Station the rations that had come down from Lynchburg. Those that had been sent up from Farmville had been found by the Federals farther down the road. Grant did not add to Lee's distress by a recountal of these seizures. He merely said, "I should like to have our men within our lines as soon as possible. I will take steps at once to have your army supplied with rations, but I am sorry we have no forage for the animals. We have had to depend upon the country for our supply of forage. Of about how many men does your present force consist?"

Lee reflected for a moment: "Indeed, I am not able to say. My losses in killed and wounded have been exceedingly heavy, and besides, there have been many stragglers and some deserters. All my reports and public papers, and, indeed, my own private letters, had to be destroyed on the march to prevent them from falling into the hands of your people. Many companies are entirely without officers, and I have not seen any returns for several days; so that I have no means of ascertaining our present strength."

Grant had estimated Lee's numbers at 25,000 and he asked, "Suppose I send over 25,000 rations, do you think that will be a sufficient supply?"

"I think it will be ample," Lee replied. "And it will be a great relief, I assure you," he added instantly.

By this time, Marshall had finished his draft of Lee's acceptance of Grant's terms. Lee made a few changes, and then had Marshall copy the document:

"*Lieut-Gen. U. S. Grant,*

"*Commanding Armies of the United States.*

"General: I have received your letter of this date containing the terms of surrender of the Army of Northern Virginia as proposed by you. As they are substantially the same as those expressed in your letter of the 8th instant, they are accepted. I will proceed to designate the proper officers to carry the stipulations into effect.

"Very respectfully, your obedient servant,"

Lee put his signature to this without a quiver. It was then about 3:45 P.M. The rest was casual and brief.

Lee rose, shook hands with General Grant, bowed to the spectators and passed from the room. He went through the hall to the porch, where several Federal officers at once sprang to their feet and saluted. Putting on his hat, Lee returned their salute and with measured tread crossed the porch. At the head of the steps, he drew on his gauntlets, and absently smote his hands together several times as he looked into space—across the valley to the hillside where his faithful little army lay. In a moment he aroused himself and, not seeing his mount, called in a voice that was hoarse and half-choked, "Orderly! Orderly!" Tucker answered from the corner of the house. Lee walked down the steps and stood in front of the animal while the man replaced the bridle. Lee mounted slowly and with an audible sigh. At that moment Grant stepped down from the porch on his way to the gate. Stopping suddenly, Grant took off his hat, but did not speak. The other Federals followed the courteous example. Lee raised his hat, without a word, and rode away to an ordeal worse than a meeting with Grant—the ordeal of breaking the news to his soldiers and of telling them farewell.

By no means all the men were prepared for the surrender. Such was the faith of the army in itself and in its commander that many were unwilling to believe the end had come. Lee came toward them as erect as ever, but with none of the composure that usually marked his countenance. The men started to cheer him, but somehow their cheers froze in their throats at the sight of him. They hesitated a moment, and then without a word they broke ranks and rushed toward him.

"General," they began to cry, "are we surrendered?"

The question was like a blow in the face. He tried to go on, but they crowded about him. The road was full of frenzied, famished faces. He had to halt and answer his soldiers. "Men," he said, "we have fought the war together, and I have done the best I could for you. You will all be paroled and go to your homes until exchanged." Tears came into his eyes as he spoke. He attempted to say more but his self-mastery failed him. Moving his lips in a choking "good-bye," he again essayed to ride on.

Each soldier reacted to it in his own fashion. Some wept. Others were dazed, as though they did not understand how the Army of Northern Virginia could surrender. To others, it was as the very end of the world. Some blasphemed and some babbled, but all who could crowded to say farewell to Lee. Catching hold of his hands, they looked

SPOTSYLVANIA, *May, 1864:* WAREHOUSE SERVING AS HOSPITAL

PETERSBURG, *April, 1865*

up at him and cried the more. In a confused roar, half-sob, half-ac-
clamation, they voiced their love for him, their faith in him, their good-
bye to him as their commander.

Then Lee retired a short distance away from the road, and there he
began to feel the reaction. He kept pacing up and down under a tree.
The staff officers did not disturb him. He walked and turned and
walked again and turned, battling with his own emotions.

Lee went about the duties of April 10 calmly but with an occasional
evidence of abstraction. He felt that he should prepare a report of the
campaign, and he sent a circular to the corps chiefs directing them to
prepare brief accounts of their operations from March 29 "to the
present time."

About 10 o'clock Lee called for the draft of a farewell address to
the army which he had instructed Marshall to write. Marshall had
been so occupied amid all the coming and going around the camp that
he had found no time for the task. Lee told him to go into his
ambulance, which had been drawn up near his headquarters tent, and
to stay there until he finished the document.

Soon came word that General Grant had ridden over to call on
him and that he had been stopped and told he must wait until General
Lee's instructions could be given the pickets. Chagrined at this display
of a lack of consideration for a distinguished visitor, Lee proceeded
at a gallop to meet Grant. He found him on a little knoll to the right
of the road to Lynchburg. Grant began by telling Lee that his interest was in peace and in the surrender of the other Confederate armies.
Lee replied that the South was a large country and that the Federals
might be compelled to march over it three or four times before the
war was entirely ended, but the Federals could do this because the
South no longer could resist. For his own part, he hoped there would
be no further sacrifice of life. Thereupon Grant said there was no
man in the South whose influence with the soldiers and with the people
was as great as Lee's, and that if Lee would advise the surrender of all
the armies he believed they would lay down their arms. Lee knew far
better than Grant possibly could the weakness of the Confederate
forces still in the field. But Grant's proposal had to do with a question that Lee felt he could not urge on his own initiative. He promptly
said that he could not advise the remaining Confederate armies without
first consulting the President. Grant understood Lee's viewpoint and
did not attempt to persuade him. The conversation lasted more than
half an hour and, according to Grant, was "very pleasant."

General Lee was returning to his camp when he met a cavalcade in blue and was greeted with a cheery "good morning, General" from a bearded man, who removed his cap as he spoke. The speaker recalled himself as none other than George Gordon Meade, commanding the Army of the Potomac, and an old friend of kindly days. Meade had ridden over on a visit of courtesy and, not finding Lee at headquarters, was starting back. Lee invited Meade to his tent and chatted with him for some time.

Later in the day Lee had another visitor in the person of the ablest of the Federal artillerists, General Henry J. Hunt. He found Lee "weary and care-worn, but in this supreme hour the same self-possessed, dignified gentleman that I had always known him." Lee conversed pleasantly with Hunt for half an hour, until General Wise and, after him, General Wilcox, came in.

After dining frugally with his staff, Lee had still other visitors and not a few routine duties. He received the formal terms of surrender, and from Grant's headquarters he got a copy of the Federal order under the terms of which paroled Confederates were to be allowed to pass through the Federal lines and to travel free on government transports and military railroads in order to reach their homes.

When Marshall had finished his pencilled draft of the farewell order, Lee went over it, struck out a paragraph that seemed to keep alive ill-feeling, and changed one or two words. Marshall then wrote a revised draft, which he had one of the clerks at headquarters copy in ink. General Lee signed this and additional copies made by various hands for the corps commanders and for the chiefs of the bureaus of the general staff. Other individuals made copies of their own which they brought to General Lee to sign as souvenirs. In hasty transcription and frequent reprinting the language of the order has assumed several versions. That which follows is from General Lee's letter book, into which it was copied, after Appomattox, by Custis Lee.

Hd. qrs. Army of N. Va.
April 10, 1865

General Orders

No. 9

After four years of arduous service marked by unsurpassed courage and fortitude, the Army of Northern Virginia has been compelled to yield to overwhelming numbers and resources.

I need not tell the brave survivors of so many hard fought battles, who have remained steadfast to the last, that I have consented to this result from no distrust of them; but feeling that valor and devotion could accomplish nothing that could compensate for the loss that must have attended the continuance of the contest, I determined to avoid the useless sacrifice of those whose past services have endeared them to their countrymen.

By the terms of the agreement, officers and men can return to their homes and remain until exchanged. You will take with you the satisfaction that proceeds from the consciousness of duty faithfully performed; and I earnestly pray that a Merciful God will extend to you His blessing and protection.

With an unceasing admiration of your constancy and devotion to your Country, and a grateful remembrance of your kind and generous consideration for myself, I bid you all an affectionate farewell.

(Sgd) R. E. LEE
Genl.

The next day, April 11, Lee began to receive the reports of his subordinates. Some of them were hurried and perfunctory, but others were well-considered. Those of the field officers concerned operations only. The general staff wrote in some instances of the problems of the retreat, and confirmed Lee's judgment as to the necessity of surrendering when he did. With this material and doubtless with Marshall's assistance, Lee set about preparing his own report. He sketched operations from the arrival at Amelia Courthouse to the surrender. The outcome was attributed primarily to failure to find at Amelia the provisions he expected would be there. The army, he explained, had been forced to halt a day in order to seek food in the surrounding country. "This delay," he said, "was fatal, and could not be retrieved." The nearest approach to blame for any individual was the statement, in reference to Sayler's Creek, that "General Anderson, commanding Pickett's and B. R. Johnson's divisions, became disconnected with Mahone's division, forming the rear of Longstreet."

Proceeding to the events that ended in the capitulation, he said of his action in accepting Grant's terms: "I deemed this course the best under all the circumstances by which we were surrounded. On the morning of the 9th, according to the reports of the ordnance officers, there were 7892 organized infantry with arms, with an average of 75 rounds of ammunition per man. The artillery, though reduced to sixty-three pieces, with ninety-three rounds of ammunition, was sufficient. These comprised all the supplies of ordnance that could be relied on in the State of Virginia. I have no accurate report of the cavalry, but believe it did not exceed 2100 effective men. The enemy was more than five times our numbers. If we could have forced our way one day longer, it would have been at a great sacrifice of life, and at its end I did not see how a surrender could have been avoided. We had no subsistence for man or horse, and it could not be gathered in the country. The supplies ordered to Pamplin's Station from Lynchburg could not reach us, and the men, deprived of food and sleep for many days, were worn out and exhausted." That was the closing sentence.

This report is dated April 12, "near Appomattox Courthouse," and it doubtless was finished and signed that morning. By the time it was completed Lee had said farewell to many of his officers, had given his autograph to some of them, had written his pledge not to take up arms against the United States "until properly exchanged," and had signed Taylor's individual parole, the only one that required his personal attention.

As the paroling had begun on April 10, Lee might have started home that day. He never explained why he remained until the 12th, but doubtless he stayed because he did not wish to leave his men to bear without him the humiliation of stacking their arms and giving over their cherished battleflags. He did not witness that sad ceremony on the morning of April 12, but he did not break camp till the surrender was over and his tearful soldiers had turned away from the field of their last parade.

Quietly he left his last headquarters and started home. With him rode Taylor, Marshall, and Major Giles B. Cooke, the last-named sick and in an ambulance lent by the Federals. Colonel Venable started with them but parted company very soon, as his route to reach his family was different from theirs.

As evening drew on, General Lee passed through Buckingham Courthouse, where he was identified and greeted. Two miles beyond the village he came to the bivouac of Longstreet. The two spent their last evening together and parted the next day to meet no more, though they continued to correspond irregularly. "My interest and affection for you will never cease," Lee wrote Longstreet the next January, "and my prayers are always offered for your prosperity."

The news of Lee's coming spread ahead of him. Women hastened to cook provisions and brought them out to the road, where they waited for him. On the 14th Major Cooke bade his chief farewell and turned off the road. Lee continued on his way. At evening Lee reached his brother's farm in Powhatan County. He was made welcome, of course, but as the house was crowded he insisted on using his tent. It was his final bivouac, the last night he ever slept under canvas.

The next morning the company was swelled by the arrival of Rooney Lee and the General's nephew, John Lee. Riders and vehicles soon got under way—there were twenty horses altogether—and went down the River road, through Powhatan and Chesterfield Counties. As they neared the capital of the dying Confederacy, in the midst of a spring downpour, General Lee and two of his officers went ahead of the wagons and of the ambulance. Ere long they reached Manchester, opposite Richmond.

The streets through which General Lee rode in Manchester cut off his view of Richmond until he was close to the James. Then he could see how deep and hideous were the scars on the city. Both bridges were gone: a line of Federal pontoons afforded the only crossing. Nearly the whole waterfront had been consumed in the fire of April 2–3 that had followed the evacuation. Arsenal, factories, flouring mills, tobacco warehouses, stores, dwellings—all were destroyed. On his left Belle Isle prison camp lay deserted. Beyond it the Tredegar Iron Works was intact, but east of it were blackened walls, sentinels over the once-busy plants that had supplied him with shell and with small arms. Thence eastward for nearly a mile fire had levelled the city. Scarcely a wall stood shoulder-high in the whole area, for safety had required the wrecking of those the flames and the fall of floors had left standing. The streets that had shown the proudest bustle in the days of the Confederacy now were mere tracks amid debris. Above them, was the capitol that Jefferson had designed, the capitol in which Houdon's statue of Washington stood, the capitol where Lee himself had received command of the Virigina troops, the capitol where Jackson's body had lain in state, the capitol through whose corridors had run the defiant voices of the Confederate Congress, swearing that the new nation should never know subjection. And now over its roof, in the easy pride of assured possession, the Union flag was flying. Against the gray sky of the dark April afternoon, above the waste and wretchedness of the city, that colorful flag must have seemed to dominate Richmond as the symbol of conquest.

General Lee probably was forced to wait at the pontoon bridge, for his wagons and companions overtook him and followed him across the river and up the streets of Richmond. He was anxious to avoid a demonstration of any sort. It had been the supposition of all loyal

Confederates that Lee would return directly to his family in Richmond. A certain informal lookout for him had been kept. Now word spread quickly that he was riding uptown. As many as could hurriedly turned out to see him.

He had put aside his best uniform and had on one that had seen long service, but he still wore a sword, though not the handsome weapon he had carried at Appomattox. His mount was Traveller. With him now rode five others. These officers also carried their side arms, but their horses were gaunt and jaded. Behind them rattled the General's old ambulance and the wagons the Federals had permitted the officers for the transportation of their effects. One of them, lacking a canvas, was covered with an old quilt. But those who looked at the sad little procession understood and choked and wept. Along a ride of less than a mile to the residence at 707 East Franklin Street the crowd grew thicker with each block. Cheers broke out, in which the Federals joined heartily. Hats went off, and uniform caps of blue along with them. General Lee acknowledged the greetings by uncovering repeatedly, but he was anxious to finish his journey as quickly as he could.

Arriving in front of the house, he turned his horse over to one of the men attending the wagons. In a moment, with his emotions strained almost to tears, he made his way to the iron gate, and up the granite steps. Bowing to the crowd, he entered the house and closed the door. His marching over and his battles done, Robert E. Lee unbelted his sword forever.

No scratch was on the sword that General Lee laid away that April day in Richmond. His weapon had never been raised except in salute. Rarely had it been drawn from its scabbard. Yet it was the symbol of a war, of an army and of a cause. Where it had been, the red banners of the South had flown. About it all the battles of the Army of Northern Virginia had surged. As he puts it down, to wear it no more, the time has come, not to fix his final place as a soldier, but to give an accounting of his service to the state in whose behalf alone he would ever have drawn his blade in fratricidal strife.

Had his sense of duty held him to the Union, as it held Winfield Scott and George H. Thomas, how much easier his course would have been! Never, then, after the first mobilization, would he have lacked for troops or been compelled to count the cost of any move. He would not have agonized over men who shivered in their nakedness or dyed the road with shoeless, bleeding feet. Well clad they would have been, and well fed, too. They would not have been brought down to the uncertain ration of a pint of meal and a quarter of a pound of Nassau bacon. The superior artillery would have been his, not his adversary's. On his order new locomotives and stout cars would have rolled to the front, swiftly to carry his army where the feeble engines and the groaning trains of the Confederacy could not deliver men. He would have enjoyed the command of the sea; so that he could have advanced his base a hundred miles, or two hundred, without the anguish of a single choking march. If one jaded horse succumbed on a raid, the teeming prairies would have supplied two. His simplicity, his tact, his ability, and his self-abnegation would have won the confidence of Lincoln that McClellan lost and neither Pope, Burnside, nor Hooker ever possessed. He would, in all human probability, have won the war, and now he would be preparing to ride up Pennsylvania Avenue at the head of a victorious army, on his way to the White House.

But he had held to the older allegiance, and had found it the way of difficulty. Always the odds had been against him. Not once, in a major engagement, had he met the Federals on even terms; not once, after a victory, had his army been strong enough to follow it up. To extemporize, to improvise, to reorganize—that had been his constant lot. There had been no single day when he had enjoyed an advantage he had not won with the blood of men he could not replace. His guns had been as much outranged as his men had been outnumbered. He had marched as often to find food as to confound his foe. His transportation had progressively declined as his dependence upon it had increased. The revolutionary government had been created as a protest against an alleged violation of the rights of the states, and it made those rights its fetish. When it required an executive dictatorship to live, it chose to die by constitutionalism. With poverty he had faced abundance; with individualism his people had opposed nationalism.

Desperate as his country's disadvantage had been, it had been darkened by mistakes, financial, political, and military. Of some of these he had not been cognizant; others he had protested to no purpose. From the first shot at Sumter he had realized that the South could only hope to win by exerting itself to the utmost; yet he had not been able to arouse the people from the overconfidence born at Bull Run. On the strategy of particular campaigns he had been heard and heeded often; on the larger strategy of full preparation, his influence had not been great.

Lee had himself made mistakes. Perhaps no one could have saved

Western Virginia in 1861, but he had failed to recover it. In his operations on that front and during the Seven Days, he had demanded professional efficiency of an amateur staff and had essayed strategy his subordinates had been incapable of executing. After Second Manassas he had overestimated the endurance of his men, and in Maryland he had miscalculated the time required for the reduction of Harpers Ferry. Longstreet had been permitted to idle away days that might have been spent in bringing his two divisions back to Chancellorsville to crush the baffled Hooker. Lee had erred in giving corps command to Ewell. Apart from the blunders of that officer and the sulking of Longstreet at Gettysburg, he had lost the Pennsylvania campaign because his confidence in his troops had led him to assume the offensive in the enemy's country before his remodelled machine had been adjusted to his direction. At Rappahannock Bridge he had misread the movements of the Federals, and in the Wilderness he had left Wilcox and Heth in a position too exposed for their weary divisions to hold. Wrongly he had acquiesced in the occupation of the Bloody Angle at Spotsylvania. Incautiously, that blusterous 11th of May he had withdrawn his artillery from Johnson's position. The detachment of Hampton and of Early had crippled him in coping with Grant when the Army of the Potomac crossed the James. He had strangely underestimated Sheridan's strength in the Shenandoah Valley, and he had failed to escape from Petersburg. These errors or failures exacted of the South some of its bravest blood.

Deeper still had been the defect of Lee's excessive amiability. He conceded too much in kind words or kinder silence to the excuses of commanders and to the arguments of politicians. Humble in spirit, he had sometimes submitted to mental bullying. Capable always of devising the best plan, he had, on occasion, been compelled by the blundering of others to accept the second best. He had not always been able to control men of contrary mind. His consideration for others, the virtue of the gentleman, had been his vice as a soldier.

Perhaps to this defect may be added a mistaken theory of the function of the high command. He believed that the general-in-chief should strive to bring his troops together at the right time and place and that he should leave combat to the generals of brigade and division. To this theory Lee steadfastly held from his opening campaign through the battle of the Wilderness. Who may say whether, when his campaigns are viewed as a whole, adherence to this theory of his function cost the army more than it won for the South? If this policy failed with Longstreet, it was gloriously successful with Jackson. If the failure at Gettysburg was partly chargeable to it, the victory at Chancellorsville was in large measure the result of its application.

When Lee's inordinate consideration for his subordinates is given its gloomiest appraisal, when his theory of command is disputed, when his mistakes are written red, when the remorseless audit of history discounts the odds he faced in men and resources, and when the court of time writes up the advantage he enjoyed in fighting on inner lines in his own country, the balance to the credit of his generalship is clear and absolute.

In three fast-moving months he mobilized Virginia. Finding the Federals, when he took command of the Army of Northern Virginia, almost under the shadow of Richmond's steeples, he saved the capital from almost certain capture and the Confederate cause from probable collapse. He repulsed four major offensives against Richmond and by his invasion of Pennsylvania he delayed the fifth for ten months. Ere the Federals were back on the Richmond line Lee had fought ten major battles. Six of these he had indisputably won. At Frayser's Farm he had gained the field but had not enveloped the enemy as he had planned. Success had not been his at Malvern Hill and at Sharpsburg, but only at Gettysburg had he met with definite defeat. During the twenty-four months when he had been free to employ open manoeuvre, he had sustained approximately 103,000 casualties and had inflicted 145,000. Chained at length to the Richmond defenses, he had saved the capital from capture for ten months. All this he had done in the face of repeated defeats for the Southern troops in nearly every other part of the Confederacy. These difficulties of the South would have been even worse had not the Army of Northern Virginia occupied so much of the thought and armed strength of the North. Lee is to be judged, in fact, not merely by what he accomplished with his own troops but by what he prevented the hosts of the Union from doing sooner elsewhere.

The accurate reasoning of a trained and precise mind is the prime explanation of all these achievements. Lee was pre-eminently a strategist, and a strategist because he was a sound military logician. It is well enough to speak of his splendid presence on the field of battle, his poise, his cheer, and his manner with his men, but essentially he was an intellect, with a developed aptitude for the difficult synthesis of war. The incidental never obscured the fundamental. The trivial never distracted. He had the ability to visualize his fundamental problem as though it had been worked out in a model and set before his eyes.

He projected himself mentally across the lines to the position of his adversary. What was the logical thing for his opponent to do? Assuming that the Federals had intelligent leadership, he said, "It is proper for us to expect [the enemy] to do what he ought to do." Every stir of his enemy along the line he canvassed both for its direct meaning and for its relation to other movements.

In assembling this information he was not more adept than many another capable general, and in studying it he was not more diligent, but in interpreting it he excelled. Always critical of the news that came from spies, he was cautious in accepting newspaper reports until he learned which correspondents were reckless or well-furnished with fact. A credulous outpost commander received scant attention when he forwarded countryside rumor; but Stuart's "sixth sense" Lee soon learned to appreciate.

Lee did not rely so much as has been supposed upon his knowledge of his adversaries. McClellan and Meade were the only Federal generals-in-chief with whom he had been closely associated before the war. The others, save Grant, were in command for periods so brief that he scarcely knew them before they were gone. Grant's bludgeoning tactics and flank shifts he quickly fathomed, but he was progressively less able to combat them as his own strength declined.

Having decided what the enemy most reasonably would attempt, Lee's strategy was postulated, in most instances, on a speedy offensive. His larger strategy, from the very nature of the war, was offensive-defensive, but his policy was to seize the initiative wherever practicable and to force his adversary to adapt his plans thereto.

Once he determined upon an offensive, Lee took unbounded pains to execute it from the most favorable position he could occupy. Of his great aptitude for reconnaissance and of the wise strategic employment, in combat, of ground that had been previously selected, or occupied from necessity, enough has already been said in comment on particular campaigns. Lee's career does not prove that a soldier must be a great military engineer to be a great strategist, but it does demonstrate that if a strategist is an engineer as well he is doubly advantaged.

If Lee on occasion seemed "slow" to his restless and nervous subordinates, it was because some unvoiced doubt as to the enemy's plan or his own best position still vexed his mind. For when his military judgment was convinced, he begrudged every lost hour. Herein was displayed the fourth quality that distinguished his strategy, namely, the precision of his troop movements, the precision, let it be emphasized, and not the speed nor always the promptness of the march. The army as a whole, under Lee's direction, could never cover as much ground in a given time as the Second Corps under Jackson or under Ewell. Lee, however, could calculate with surprising accuracy the hours that would be required to bring his troops to a given position. After the Seven Days' campaign had acquainted him with his men and their leaders, Lee made only three serious mistakes in logistics. One of these was in the time required to occupy Harpers Ferry and to reconcentrate the army at Sharpsburg. The next was in calculating when the First Corps would arrive at Gettysburg, and the third was in estimating the hour at which that same corps would overtake A. P. Hill in the Wilderness. In two of these three instances, Lee based his advance on Longstreet's assurances, which were not fulfilled. Against these three cases of the failure of Lee's logistics are to be set his transfer of the Army of Northern Virginia to meet Pope; the movement down the Rappahannock to confront Burnside at Fredericksburg; the quick and sure detachment of Anderson and then of Jackson at Chancellorsville; the convergence of Hill's and of Ewell's corps at Gettysburg; the march from the Wilderness to Spotsylvania; the shift to the North Anna, and thence to the Totopotomoy and Cold Harbor, and the careful balancing of force north and south of the James during the operations against Petersburg —the list is almost that of his battles. Had his mastery of this difficult branch of the art of war been his only claim to distinction as a soldier, it would of itself justify the closest scrutiny of his campaigns by those who would excel in strategy.

His patient synthesis of military intelligence, his understanding employment of the offensive, his sense of position and his logistics were supplemented in the making of his strategy by his audacity. Superficial critics, puzzled by his success and unwilling to examine the reasons for it, have sometimes assumed that he frequently defied the rules of war, yet rarely sustained disaster in doing so because he was confronted by mediocrity. Respect for the strength of his adversaries, rather than contempt for their abilities, made him daring. Necessity, not choice, explains this quality. A desperate cause demanded desperate risks; nothing more surely explains Lee, the commander. Yet if "daring" is an adjective that has to be applied to him again and again, "reckless" is not. His daring was measured in terms of probable success. If the reward did not seem worth the risk, nothing could move him—except the knowledge that he had no alternative. From the Seven Days to Gettysburg, his daring increased, to be sure, as well it might, with his army performing every task he set before it; but the period after Gettysburg affords proof, almost incontrovertible, that he never permitted his daring to become recklessness.

These five qualities, then, gave eminence to his strategy—his interpretation of military intelligence, his wise devotion to the offensive, his careful choice of position, the exactness of his logistics, and his well-considered daring. Midway between strategy and tactics stood four other qualities of generalship that no student of war can disdain. The first was his sharpened sense of the power of resistance and of attack of a given body of men; the second was his ability to effect adequate concentration at the point of attack, even when his force was inferior; the third was his careful choice of commanders and of troops for specific duties; the fourth was his employment of field fortification.

Once he learned the fighting power of his army, he always disposed it economically for defense, choosing his position and fortifying it with the utmost care, so as to maintain adequate reserves—witness Fredericksburg. Only when his line was extended by the superior force of the enemy, as at Sharpsburg and after the Wilderness, did he employ his whole army as a front-line defense. In receiving attack, he seemed to be testing the resistance of every part of his line, and if he found it weakening, he was instant with his reserves. Over and again, in the account of some critical turn of action, it is stated that the reserves came up and restored the front. Behind this, almost always, was the most careful planning by Lee. On the offensive it was different. "It is only by the concentration of our troops," he said in November, 1863, "that we can hope to win any decisive advantage." He applied the principle to every offensive. It was his custom to hurl forward in his assaults every man he could muster, on the principle that if enough weight were thrown against the enemy, there would be no need of reserves. Only when he was doubtful of the success of an assault did he deliberately maintain a reserve. In partial attacks he somehow learned precisely what number of men would be required, with such artillery preparation as he could make, and he rarely failed until the odds against him became overwhelming.

For swift marches and for desperate flank movements, Lee relied on the Second Corps as long as Jackson lived; to receive the attack of the enemy he felt he could count equally on the First. Within the corps he came to know the distinctive qualities of the different divisions, and even among the divisions he graded the brigades. He was guided less in this, perhaps, by the prowess of the men than by the skill and resourcefulness of the different general officers, and he shaped his course according to his knowledge of the type of leadership he could anticipate.

Whether that leadership was good or bad, Lee gradually developed fortifications to support it. The earthworks he threw up in South Carolina were to protect the railroad he had to employ in bringing up his army. Those built around Richmond, in June, 1862, were designed to protect the approaches from siege tactics and to permit heavy concentration north of the Chickahominy. The works were too light to withstand the continued hammering of siege guns, but they served admirably to cover his men and to discourage assault. They were midway between permanent fortifications of the old type and the field fortifications he subsequently employed. His digging of trenches in the open field, while actively manoeuvring, began with the first stage of the Chancellorsville campaign. After May, 1864, when increasing odds forced him unwillingly to the defensive, he made the construction of field fortifications a routine of operations. The trenches served both a strategical and tactical object. They were strategical in that they made it possible for him to detach troops for manoeuvre; they were tactical in that they enabled him successfully to resist a superior force with a steadily diminishing army.

As a tactician, Lee exhibited at the beginning of hostilities the weaknesses that might be expected of one who had been a staff officer for the greater part of his military career. Until he lost many of his most capable officers he held strictly to his theory of the function of the high command—that of bringing the troops together in necessary numbers at the proper time and place. Yet he continued to learn the military art as the war progressed, and of nothing did he learn more than of tactics. He overcame his lack of skill in the employment of his cavalry. In the end he was deterred from elaborate tactical methods only because he did not believe the brigade commanders could execute them.

Predominant as was strategy in the generalship of Lee from the outset, and noteworthy as was his later tactical handling of his troops on the field of battle, it was not to these qualities alone that he owed the record he closed that day when he unbelted his sword after Appomattox. It had been as difficult to administer the army as to use it successfully in combat. Never equipped adequately, or consistently well-fed after the early autumn of 1862, the Army of Northern Virginia had few easy marches or ready victories. Lee had to demand of his inferior forces the absolute best they could give him. The army's hard-won battles left its ranks depleted, its command shattered by death or wounds, its personnel exhausted, its horses scarcely able to walk, its transportation broken down, its ammunition and its commissary low. Its victories could not be pressed.

On him fell the burden of an endless reorganization that is a part of his title to fame. Out of the wreckage of battle, time after time, he contrived to build a better machine. He did not work by any set formula in administering the army, but by the most painstaking attention to the most minute details. Hungry men had to be restored by better rations: if the commissary could not provide them, he would seek them in the surrounding country. Rest was imperative: he would choose a strategically sound position, where the troops could have repose without uncovering the approaches to Richmond. To select men to succeed the general officers who fell in action, he would confer with those who knew the colonels of the regiments and he would examine each officer's record for diligence, for capacity, and for sobriety. Had the men worn out more shoes than they had been able to capture from the enemy? Then he would present their plight to the administration and would continue writing till the footgear was forthcoming, or else he would organize his own cobblers. If state pride demanded that troops from the same area be brigaded together and commanded by a "native son," he might disapprove the policy, but he would shift regiments and weigh capabilities until the most grumbling congressman and the most jealous governor were satisfied. The very soap his dirty men required in the muck of the Petersburg trenches was the subject of a patient letter to the President. His mobilization of Virginia, though it was among his most remarkable achievements and afforded sure evidence of his rating as an administrator, was equalled by the speed and success of his reorganization of the army after the Seven Days, after Sharpsburg, and after Gettysburg.

One aspect of his skill in administration deserves separate treatment as a major reason for his long-continued resistance. That was his almost uniform success in dealing with the civil government, a sometimes difficult business that every military commander must learn. Although the front of his army may be where the general-in-chief can direct every move, its rear stretches back far beyond the most remote bureau of the War Department. Few generals are ever much stronger than their communications with the authorities that sustain them, and few are greater than the confidence they beget. It was by the good fortune of former association that Lee had the esteem of President Davis; it was by merit that he preserved that good opinion, by merit plus tact and candor and care. During the war, General Lee received a few sharp messages from Mr. Davis; yet it cannot be said that Lee found Davis a difficult man with whom to deal. This was because Lee dominated the mind of his superior, yet applied literally and loyally his conviction that the President was the commander-in-chief and that the military arm was subordinate to the civil. He reported as regularly to the President as Stuart or Jackson reported to him. He rarely made a move without explaining his full purpose to the President in advance. In judgment he always deferred to Mr. Davis. Although he was entrusted with the defense of the capital of the Confederacy, and had constantly to seek replacements, Lee never put the needs of his army above those of the Confederacy.

Dealing with four Secretaries of War in order—Walker, Benjamin, Seddon, and Breckinridge—Lee encountered little or no friction. To each of the secretaries Lee reported and before each of them he laid his difficulties. Usually he was candid with them as to his plans. Only when secrecy was imperative was Lee ever restrained in addressing the war office.

With Congress, Lee had little directly to do. Perhaps it was fortunately so. He often captivated politicians, and at one time, it will be remembered, he virtually acted for the administration in dealing with that difficult and positive individual, Governor Zebulon Vance of North Carolina; but Lee had seen too much of Congress in Washington to cherish any illusions regarding it in Richmond. He had an ineradicable distrust of politicians. Although he rarely broke the bounds of his self-imposed restraint, he was convinced that Congress was more interested in exemptions than in inclusions in the conscript laws. In the winter of 1864–65, he thought the lawmakers were playing politics when the existence of the Confederacy depended upon the enlistment of every able-bodied man.

Next among the reasons for Lee's success as a soldier is probably to be ranked his ability to make the best of his subordinate officers. Lee had some of the best graduates of West Point among his officers. He saw to it that such men held the posts of largest responsibility. Yet these officers were not all of outstanding ability, nor were they sufficient in number to command the divisions, much less the brigades. He had to entrust the lives of many thousands of his men to those who had received no advanced training in arms prior to 1861. Perhaps Lee's most difficult labor was that of taking a miscellaneous group of Southern individualists, ranging in capacity from dullness to genius, and of welding them into an efficient instrument of command.

No commander ever put a higher valuation on the innate qualities of leadership. He was not quick to praise, but he was sparing in criticism. Unless a man was grossly incapable, he was slow to relieve him of command. He preferred to suffer the mediocrity he knew than to fly to that of which he was not cognizant. Indecision, notorious ill-temper, intemperance, and a pessimistic, demoralizing outlook were the qualities he most abhorred in a soldier. "I cannot trust a man to control others who cannot control himself," he said. For personal cowardice he had a soldierly scorn, but he rarely encountered it.

The more a soldier was capable of doing, the more Lee demanded of him. Never brusque unless with extreme provocation, Lee was least suave and most exacting with those whose conception of duty he knew to be as high as his own. Once he got the true measure of Jackson, he would have considered it a reflection upon that officer's patriotism to bestow soft words or to make ingratiating gestures. He had a personal affection for the praise-loving Stuart, but he rarely put flattery or flourishes into his letters to that remarkable officer. Yet when a dull brigadier or a stupid colonel came to his quarters, Lee did his utmost to hearten him. For young officers he always had kind words and friendly, considerate attention, except when it was manifest that they needed a rebuke.

All that can be said of Lee's dealings with his officers can be said in even warmer tones of his relations with the men in the ranks. They were his chief pride, his first obligation. Their distress was his deepest concern, their well-being his constant aim. His manner with them was said by his lieutenants to be perfect. Never ostentatious or consciously dramatic, his bearing, his record of victories, his manifest interest in the individual, and his conversation with the humblest private he met in the road combined to create in the minds of his troops a reverence, a confidence, and an affection that built up the morale of the army. And that morale was one of the elements that contributed most to his achievements. The men came to believe that whatever he did was right —that whatever he assigned them they could accomplish. Once that belief became fixed, the Army of Northern Virginia was well-nigh invincible. There is, perhaps, no more impressive example in modern war of the power of personality in creating morale.

The final major reason for Lee's successes in the face of bewildering

odds was his ability to maintain the hope and the fighting spirit of the
South. The confidence aroused by the first victory at Manassas sustained
the South until the disasters at Fort Henry and Fort Donelson. Thereafter, for a season, the belief was strong that Europe's need of cotton
would bring recognition and intervention. As months passed with no
hopeful news from France or from England, the Southern people
looked to their own armies, and to them alone, to win independence.
Vicksburg fell; the Confederacy was cut in twain. The expectations
raised by the victory at Chickamauga were not realized. The Army of
Tennessee failed to halt the slow partition of the seceded states. Gradually the South came to fix its faith on the Army of Northern Virginia
and on its commander. Elsewhere there was bickering and division; in
Virginia there was harmony and united resistance. The unconquered
territory was daily reduced in area, but on the Rapidan and the Rappahannock there was still defiance in the flapping of each battle flag. The
Southern people remembered that Washington had lost New York
and New England, Georgia and South Carolina, and still had triumphed.
Lee, they believed, would do no less than the great American he most
resembled. As long as he could keep the field, the South could keep its
heart. Morale behind the line, not less than on the front of action, was
sustained by Lee.

The qualities that created this confidence were essentially those that
assured Lee the unflagging aid of the President, the loyalty of his lieutenants, and the enthusiastic devotion of his men. But the order in
which these qualities were esteemed by the civil population was somewhat different. Mr. Davis and the corps commanders knew that Lee
was better able than any other Southern soldier to overthrow the
plans of the enemy; the men in the ranks were satisfied he would shape
his strategy to defeat the enemy with the least loss to them. The people
in the Southern towns and on the farms of the Confederate states saw,
in contrast, a series of military successes they were not capable of interpreting in terms of strategy or of tactics. But for them the war had
taken on a deeper spiritual significance than it had for some of those
who faced the bloody realities of slaughter. They saw in Lee the
embodiment of the faith and piety they believed a just Heaven would
favor. The army, seeing him in battle, put his ability first and his character second. The civilian population, observing him from afar, rated
his character even above his ability.

These, then, would seem to be the signal reasons why Lee so long
was able to maintain the unequal struggle of a Confederacy that may

have been foredoomed to defeat and extinction. The tactics he employed in the 1860's belong to the yesterday of war, but the reasons for his success remain valid for any soldier who must bear a like burden of responsibility, whether in a cause as desperate or where the limitless resources of a puissant government are his to command.

When the story of a soldier is completed, and the biographer is about to leave the last camp-fire of a man he has learned to respect and to love, he is tempted to a last word of admiring estimate. May he not, by some fine phrase, fan into enduring flame the spark of greatness he thinks he has discovered in the leader whose councils he has in spirit shared? May he not claim for him a place in the company of the mighty captains of the past? Yet who that reverences historical verities can presume to say of any soldier who rises above the low shoulders of mediocrity, "In this he outshone or in that he rivalled another who fought under dissimilar conditions for a different cause in another age?" Circumstance is incommensurable: let none essay to measure men who are its creatures. Lee's record is written in positive terms; why invoke comparatives? The reader who can appraise the conditions under which he fought can appraise the man. Others need not linger at the door or watch him take off his sword, or strain to hear the words he spoke to Mrs. Lee in the first moment of their meeting.

CHAPTER XVI

The Call to Lexington

GENERAL LEE did not break down when he sat down behind the closed door of the house in Franklin Street, a paroled prisoner of war. He was exhausted in body, heavy of heart, and troubled for the future of the defeated Southern people. Outwardly he seemed merely a very tired man who had passed through a bitter experience about which he did not wish to talk, though he would converse freely on other subjects. He spent long hours in bed and for some days did not leave the house.

Meantime the agonized city was close to chaos. The old government and the familiar landmarks were gone. Nobody had any money and few had any provisions. The public supplies of the Confederacy and the stock of the principal stores had been destroyed or looted. Many of the people were dependent for food on the relief agencies set up after the Federals had entered Richmond. No trains were running. The mail system had been wiped out; the telegraph was in the hands of the Federals. Only one newspaper was being printed, and that one, *The Whig*, had turned coat. The people did not know how Johnston's army was faring, nor what had become of the Confederate troops in Virginia who were not at Appomattox, nor when and how the thousands of prisoners who were eating out their hearts in Northern camps would get home again. The days were torture and the nights were dread. Everywhere was suspense or despair, a tension heightened on the one side by suspicion that the South inspired the assassination of Lincoln, April 14, 1865, and on the other by resentment that so foul a charge could be credited.

Then, slowly, the city began again to live. The survivors of Appomattox limped back and continued to arrive until there were in the city between 10,000 and 15,000 former Confederates. Negroes flocked in. The railroads were repaired and tourists descended in swarms. There was, so far, no work for any one. Returned soldiers walked the streets but might not stop and talk one to another, for after the murder of

President Lincoln orders had been given that no more than two men should be allowed to foregather in a public place. They needed leadership, did those Confederates. No country was theirs and no cause, and they looked often and wistfully at the tall brick residence on Franklin Street, because, in defeat as in victory, they regarded Lee as their leader. In front of the house a Federal sentinel usually stood, while a changing knot of curious strangers peered at the windows. The staid building was as much the centre of that stricken city as ever his tent had been headquarters.

The people did not let him sit long in the back parlor to rest from the strain those last months had put upon his arteries and heart. His own people came to him, to comfort and to be comforted. Old officers called to bid their chieftain farewell, some of them bound for distant states, and convinced they would never see him again. Ministers and public men asked his counsel. Friends of his daughters came to beg souvenirs. Others wished to see the face of Lee, or if they might not behold him in the flesh, they wanted pictures. Photographers importuned him— among them Brady, for whom he sat in the rear of his home. It was a stern picture. The jaw was strongly set and a shadow both of anguish and of defiance lingered on his face. Journalists dogged him. Federal officers climbed his steps, some from ill-concealed curiosity and some to pay an honest tribute to him as soldier and as man.

Not one of all these visitors observed in General Lee any evidence of collapse, or even the slightest wavering in his self-control. Men saw new lines in his face and sadness in his eyes, but if they were discerning, they were quick to observe that this did not come from any rage at his defeat or from any personal humiliation over the surrender. He grieved then and to the end of his days, sometimes so deeply that he had to get up from his bed and pace the floor until he was weary, but it was never in self-pity. The sorrows of the South were the burden of his life. Not a day in the last five years of his life can be understood unless it be remembered that the weight on his heart was that of others' woes.

He had no intention of further, futile resistance. Throughout his life he had submitted himself to existing authority, and he would do so now. But what of the future of the South, and what of those thousands of hotblooded young men who had fought so passionately against the Union they were now commanded to respect? He must shape his course to serve them.

On April 26 Johnston surrendered. A week thereafter the Army of the Potomac approached Richmond in all its might. Ahead of the endless divisions rode General Meade. In Meade's entourage was Markoe Bache, who happened to know Custis Lee and called on him. In some way, the suggestion of a visit by Meade to Lee was made, whereupon Custis, of course, said that his father would be glad to see the General. On May 5, the forthright commander called and had a long conversation with Lee. In the frankness of old friendship, he urged Lee to take the oath of allegiance, not only to establish his own status, but for the influence his action would have on the South. Lee replied, in the same spirit, by telling Meade that he had no objections to renewing allegiance to the United States, and that he intended to submit to their authority, but that he did not propose to change his footing as a paroled prisoner of war until he knew what policy the Federal Government intended to pursue toward the South.

What Lee had said, he had determined from the very day of surrender to make the first rule of his conduct. No matter what happened, he would not abandon Virginia, as many heavy-hearted Confederates were planning to do. He would remain with his state and share her fate. "Now, more than at any other time," he told a friend, "Virginia and every other state in the South needs us. We must try and, with as little delay as possible, go to work to build up their prosperity." He similarly counselled others. If men asked his counsel, he would advise silence, hard work, quiet behavior and avoidance of everything that might arouse the spirit of resistance or react against the defenseless. When visitors denounced the Federals, his was the first voice of moderation and his the first acknowledgment of generosity "General Grant has acted with magnanimity," he said.

Where and how could he best lead the life he had shaped for himself? He was not penniless, for he had saved some of his modest investments; but their yield was uncertain and not enough to maintain the family in Richmond, even had he desired to stay there. His inclination and his financial circumstances alike disposed him to leave the old capital. "I am looking for some little quiet house in the woods," he wrote General Long, "where I can procure shelter and my daily bread if permitted by the victor. I wish to get Mrs. Lee out of the city as soon as practicable."

Late in May, he rode out of Richmond for a visit of a few days at Pampatike, home of his cousin Colonel Thomas H. Carter. Lee chatted about the farm he wished to purchase. Colonel Carter recommended Clarke County if the General desired a grass country and Gloucester if he preferred salt-water. Lee declared for the grass.

It was at Pampatike that Lee saw for the first time President Johnson's proclamation of May 29. In this document, to all except fourteen designated classes of Confederates, amnesty and pardon were offered those who would take a specified oath to support the constitution and laws of the United States. Full property rights, other than in slaves, were to be restored every man who took the oath. Those like Lee, in the excepted classes of the prominent, were privileged to make special application for individual pardon, with the assurance that "clemency will be liberally extended as may be consistent with the facts of the case and the peace and dignity of the United States."

This was a declaration of the sort for which Lee had been waiting before deciding whether he would take the oath. The statement of the President's intentions greatly relieved General Lee's mind. It opened a way, he thought, for the South's recovery. Her people realized the Confederacy was dissolved, and most of them were willing to accept the outcome. President Johnson's offer indicated that the administration was not to impose the harsh law of the conqueror and would not visit retribution upon the disarmed South. An early return to a union of all the states accordingly became in General Lee's eyes as desirable for the South as it was logical for people of a common stock who had settled the issues that divided them. Lee knew that the men who had looked to him in battle were looking to him now. As he had sought to set them an example during the life of the Confederacy, he must do no less in the hour of its death.

When Lee arrived back in Richmond he heard that District Judge John C. Underwood had called on a Federal grand jury sitting in Norfolk to indict him and other Confederates for treason against the United States. The threat of criminal proceedings raised a question that puzzled him: Would his decision to ask for a pardon be regarded as an effort to escape trial? He adopted a direct expedient: he would enter his application for pardon, under the amnesty, but he would make it contingent on the non-prosecution of the charges against him. If he was to be brought to the bar he would not ask for pardon but would face the charge and accept the outcome. For the sake of the tens of thousands of Southern men who held paroles similar to his own, he would endeavor to have the terms of their surrender respected. He would address his communication to General Grant, the officer who had taken his parole, and he would enclose in it his application to the President for pardon. But how would General Grant view the matter? On reflection, Lee decided to make verbal inquiry through his friend Reverdy Johnson, United States senator from Maryland, who had supported the Union cause yet was a firm advocate of reconciliation. In a few days Lee learned that Grant would insist that the paroles be respected, and would endorse Lee's application for pardon, which he urged him to make.

This was the letter he then wrote Grant:

Richmond, Virginia, June 13, 1865.

Lieutenant-General U. S. Grant,
Commanding the Armies of the United States.

General: Upon reading the President's proclamation of the 29th ult., I came to Richmond to ascertain what was proper or required of me to do, when I learned that, with others, I was to be indicted for treason by the grand jury at Norfolk. I had supposed that the officers and men of the Army of Northern Virginia were, by the terms of their surrender, protected by the United States Government from molestation so long as they conformed to its conditions. I am ready to meet any charges that may be preferred against me, and do not wish to avoid trial; but, if I am correct as to the protection granted by my parole, and am not to be prosecuted, I desire to comply with the provisions of the President's proclamation, and, therefore, inclose the required application, which I request, in that event, may be acted on. I am, with great respect,

Your obedient servant,

R. E. LEE.

The enclosed application to the President was in this language:

Richmond, Virginia, June 13, 1865.

His Excellency Andrew Johnson,
President of the United States.

Sir: Being excluded from the provisions of the amnesty and pardon contained in the proclamation of the 29th ult., I hereby apply for the benefits and full restoration of all rights and privileges extended to those included in its terms. I graduated at the Military Academy at West Point in June, 1829; resigned from the United States Army, April, 1861; was a general in the Confederate Army, and included in the surrender of the Army of Northern Virginia, April 9, 1865. I have the honor to be, very respectfully,

Your obedient servant,

R. E. LEE.

News that General Lee had asked for a pardon soon became known. Many of those who had fought with General Lee reasoned that they could safely follow his leadership in this particular and could accept the President's amnesty. But there were die-hards who did not understand and swore they would never follow his example. No single act of his career aroused so much antagonism. Twenty years after his death some of the "unreconstructed" Southerners were still insistent that Lee had erred, and, by asking a pardon, had admitted a fault.

The possibility of Lee's trial for treason created as much talk as his application to Johnson. Offers of legal help came quickly, and were gratefully acknowledged. Holding to the view expressed in his letter to Grant—that paroled prisoners of war could not be brought to trial— he exerted himself chiefly to allay the resentment of his friends over the course the Federal authorities threatened to take in dealing with him. General Grant upheld Lee's view that paroled prisoners of war could not be tried for treason so long as they observed their paroles. Grant also transcribed in a letter to Lee his "earnest recommendation" to the President that Lee's application for amnesty and pardon be allowed.

No early action to quash the indictment was taken, but Lee was not arrested and prosecution was not begun. By the end of July, Lee was about convinced that the treason indictment would not be pressed and that he would not soon be granted a pardon. He was right. The individual pardon was never granted.

Pardon or no pardon, treason or no treason, Lee felt he must now set an example by going to work. He did not even own the house in which his family was then sheltered. It belonged to John Stewart, a Scotch philanthropist of Richmond. With characteristic generosity and thoughtfulness, Mr. Stewart offered the place to Mrs. Lee for as long as she was willing to stay there, and stipulated that he would take only Confederate money, in accordance with the terms of the original lease. Appreciative as General Lee was of his landlord's kindness, he did not desire to remain in the city and did not feel that he could live on the bounty of Mr. Stewart. Nor did he feel that he could accept any of the numerous other offers of hospitality that came to him. He wrote a Britisher: "I cannot desert my native state in the hour of her adversity. I must abide her fortunes, and share her fate." He would not consider entering politics. There is no evidence to show that he canvassed the outlook for his old specialty, engineering. He believed that agriculture offered the best opportunity of the Southern soldier who had no profession and no money, and he often commended that vocation to his old soldiers. He withheld a final decision about buying a place, however, probably in view of his uncertainty as to the treason proceedings.

While he waited, there came a letter from Mrs. Elizabeth Randolph Cocke, a widow of wealth and station, who resided at Oakland, a fine estate in Cumberland and Powhatan Counties, on the south side of the James River, some fifty-five miles above Richmond. She had a vacant cottage on a quiet part of her Powhatan property; would the General and his family use it, and the land that went with it, at their pleasure? Her letter was so cordial that the family accepted.

The General's spirits were visibly raised at the near prospect of getting away from crowds and callers, bustle, and bluecoats. Finally, the preparations for departure were complete. The family, one afternoon between June 26 and June 30, went down to "the Basin," a few squares below their home, and took the packet-boat up the James River.

A week at Oakland and then to Derwent, two miles away, the property Mrs. Cocke had placed at his disposal. It was a plain tenant's house, with two rooms above and two below, and had an "office" in the yard. Mrs. Cocke had equipped it with furniture from Oakland and had given it a simple air of comfort, which was heightened by a fine grove of trees. The neighborhood was secluded, the land was poor, and the summer was hot, but the large, hard-working family of Palmores, who surrounded Derwent, supplied butter and vegetables to supplement frequent baskets from Oakland. Lee was more than content.

His social nature he commanded as usual at Derwent. He read nothing about the war and felt no desire to do so. But he was acutely conscious of the sufferings of the Southern people, he agonized over the mistreatment of President Davis, and, willingly or not, he dwelt in memory on the achievements of his soldiers, who had been proud to style themselves "Lee's Miserables." He urged his principal lieutenants to write their memoirs and planned himself a history of his campaigns as "the only tribute that can now be paid to the worth of [the army's] noble officers and soldiers."

His materials for the history were meagre. He had copies of his reports through the Gettysburg campaign, but most of the later reports had been burned on the retreat from Petersburg. The archives of the Confederate War Department had been seized. His one hope was that he could recover from other sources something of what had been lost. On July 31, in a circular letter to a number of his general officers, he set forth his purpose to record the story of his men's valor, and asked for any reports, orders, or returns his comrades might have or might be able to procure for him. The subject continued to be a theme of considerable correspondence during the months that followed.

This work apart, the contention that was rising again as ominously as in 1861 he desired to avoid. But just as there had been brought to Arlington Judge Robertson's message from Governor Letcher that had thrown him into the struggle for Southern independence, so now one day in August there came up the road to Derwent a tall and bulky gentleman with another summons to service for Virginia and the South.

The visitor was John W. Brockenbrough, rector of Washington College, Lexington, Va., and teacher of a private school of law in that town. To the complete surprise of General Lee he stated that on August 4 the trustees of Washington College had unanimously elected the General president of the institution, and wished to know if he would accept. The salary was to be $1500 per annum, plus a house and garden and one-fifth of the tuition fees of the students, which were raised to $75 each.

The conversation between General Lee and Judge Brockenbrough unfortnately was not reported by either of them. All that is known is that when the judge started back to Lexington he had the General's promise to consider the call. As Lee canvassed the idea it seemed that the summons was providential, in that it offered him both a livelihood and an opportunity of service to his people. The spiritual aspect of the work appealed to him strongly.

Soon he wrote his conditional acceptance in this letter:

Powhatan County, August 24, 1865.

Gentlemen: I have delayed for some days replying to your letter of the 5th inst. informing me of my election by the Board of Trustees to the Presidency of Washington College, from a desire to give the subject due consideration. Fully impressed with the responsibilities of the office, I have feared that I should be unable to discharge its duties to the satisfaction of the trustees or to the benefit of the Country. The proper education of youth requires not only great ability, but I fear more strength than I now possess, for I do not feel able to undergo the labour of conducting classes in regular courses of instruction. I could not, therefore, undertake more than the general administration and supervision of the institution. There is another subject which has caused me serious reflection, and is, I think, worthy of the consideration of the Board. Being excluded from the terms of amnesty in the proclamation of the President of the U. S., of the 29th May last, and an object of censure to a portion of the Country, I have thought it probable that my occupation as the position of President might draw upon the College a feeling of hostility; and I should, therefore, cause injury to an Institution which it would be my highest desire to advance. I think it the duty of every citizen, in the present condition of the Country, to do all in his power to aid in the restoration of peace and harmony, and in no way to oppose the policy of the State or General Government directed to that object. It is particularly incumbent on those charged with the instruction of the young to set them an example of submission to authority, and I could not consent to be the cause of animadversion upon the College.

Should you, however, take a different view, and think that my services in the position tendered to me by the Board will be advantageous to the College and Country, I will yield to your judgment and accept it; otherwise, I must most respectfully decline the office.

Begging you to express to the trustees of the College my heartfelt gratitude for the honour conferred upon me, and requesting you to accept my cordial thanks for the kind manner in which you have communicated their decision,

I am, gentlemen, with great respect,
Your most obt servt.,

R. E. LEE.

Messrs. John W. Brockenbourgh [sic], *Rector, S. McD. Reid, Alfred Leyburn, Horatio Thompson, D.D., Bolivar Christian, T. J. Kirkpatrick, Committee.*

The trustees promptly relieved General Lee of all instructional duty and expressed their agreement with his views. The question of his future work was settled. The effect on Lee was immediate. Idleness and uncertainty were at an end. He had a task and he would discharge it. He began to set even more vigorously than before the example he thought the South required.

The South was inspired by his choice, and so were the men who had elected him. They had acted in the first instance on a remark attributed to one of General Lee's daughters. Mary—that the people of the South were willing to give her father everything he might need but that no offer had been made of any position in which he could earn a living for himself and his family. After they had voted to offer the presidency to General Lee, they had sat for a few minutes as if stunned by their own temerity. Now that they had his acceptance, they prepared to work with him and to raise funds for the restoration of the college.

They may well have felt that their new president was out of scale with their institution. Washington College at that time was a name, a site, a small body of faithful men, and little besides. Established in 1749, at Greenville, Augusta County, as the Augusta Academy, it had been the pioneer classical school in the Valley of Virginia. At the first meeting of the trustees after the Battle of Lexington, the name of the institution was changed to Liberty Hall. In 1796 George Washington gave the school the hundred shares of stock in the James River Company which the general assembly of Virginia had voted him. In gratitude, the trustees thereupon resolved to call the institution Washington Academy. Following a fire in 1802, it was moved to Lexington, and on January 2, 1813, it was chartered as Washington College. On April 18, 1861, the Unionist president of the college, Doctor George Junkin, tendered his resignation. Before his successor could be chosen, the war broke out. The students of 1861 volunteered as a unit, joined Jackson at Winchester, and fought through the war, many of them in the Stonewall brigade. The plant of the school suffered in the struggles. Hunter's raiders looted Washington College. Its library was scattered past recovery. The laboratory equipment was broken up or carried away. The end of the war found the buildings in such disrepair that some were scarcely habitable. In the summer of 1865 so dire was the plight of the college that the institution was as nearly dead as it could be without causing its supporters to abandon it altogether. But with Lee as their leader, the trustees were willing to carry on.

On September 15, 1865, General Lee started for Lexington on Traveller. The trustees met on September 20, the second day after his arrival. A committee was at once appointed to wait on the General and to escort him to the meeting place. On his arrival he was welcomed by the rector and was introduced to the members. After he retired, the trustees discussed a number of measures for his comfort. They felt that they owed him the best they could give him because he had been willing to take the presidency, but they felt, at the same time, that they were acting for the whole South in doing him honor. They never relaxed in their consideration for him. The minutes of the board are a continuing record of unremitting kindness.

For his inauguration, arranged for October 2, the trustees had planned a great occasion, by which the college and General Lee's connection with it would be advertised to the country. But the General did not desire the ceremonies to be elaborate, and out of deference to his wishes, unpretentious exercises were held.

He quickly established a routine of duty. Rising early at the Lexington Hotel, where he resided until the arrival of his family, he proceeded afoot to the college. Before 7:45 he was at chapel for the fifteen-minute services, which he invited the ministers of the principal Lexington churches to hold in rotation. From 8 until 1 or 2 P.M. he attended to labors on the campus. The afternoons were generally given over to social duties or to exercise, chiefly rides out of town on Traveller. Unless there were religious or academic exercises that he felt called upon to attend, he remained in his room at the hotel after supper. He usually retired at 10.

Having no clerk in his office and very little help on the campus, he was forced to transact in person even the least important matters of college business. To endless, close economies, he was compelled to give direct, continuing attention. On him fell, likewise, the supervision of all improvements to the grounds and of all repairs to the buildings. After the faculty came to know him better, some of the members would protest against the amount of work the General performed.

General Lee had no plans for enlarging the curriculum when he assumed charge of the college, but his own training, his long experience in construction, his four years of hourly grappling with the harsh realities of war, and his knowledge of the needs of the South, combined, very soon, to give him definite opinions concerning the instruction the college should offer. Lee was a believer both in the classics and in the pure sciences. But he did not think that these of themselves sufficed to meet the needs of the impoverished South, whose first problems were those of economic recovery and enlarged trade. Accordingly, Lee acquiesced without reservation in a plan that had been under consideration to provide wider training for the students by the immediate creation of additional departments.

Taxing as was his new life, General Lee found time to answer the multitude of letters that reached him on subjects unrelated to the affairs of the college. Punctilious in his correspondence, he never left a letter unanswered when he thought the writer would expect a reply. Some solicited help, some sought positions, and some asked for letters of recommendation.

Many of his former comrades wrote him in answer to his request for material to be used in his projected book on the Army of Northern

Virginia. "I hope both you and Johnston," he told Beauregard, "will write the history of your campaigns. Everyone should do all in his power to collect and disseminate the truth in the hope that it may find a place in history, and descend to posterity." The assembling of material was not to be an easy task, soon finished, because, as he wrote a Northern publishing house, "It will be some time before the truth can be known, and I do not think that period has yet arrived." Despite difficulties, he held to his undertaking during 1866, because he believed he owed it to his men to chronicle their deeds. He is reported to have said to some of his friends, "I shall write this history, not to vindicate myself, or to promote my own reputation. I want that the world shall know what my poor boys, with their small numbers and scant resources, succeeded in doing."

The hardest letter Lee had to write that winter was one in answer to Mrs. "Stonewall" Jackson. On a visit to Lexington she brought for his perusal the manuscript of a *Life* of her dead husband, written by his former chief of staff, Major R. L. Dabney. Lee read it over, as he said, for the delight of the narrative, but had neither the heart nor the time to review critically the long text; yet when Mrs. Jackson asked for its return, Lee could not wholly overlook the facts that in his zeal for the fame of his chief, Major Dabney had made some claims that were at variance with Lee's recollection of the facts. With great care he wrote a tactful correction, but the circumstances of its composition made the letter seem vague to those unfamiliar with the operations.

In correspondence, college duties, and a very simple social life, the autumn of 1865 wore away and the winter came. Custis was with the General at the hotel now, having been elected professor of civil engineering at the Virginia Military Institute, but Mrs. Lee and her daughters had not yet come, as their house was still unready. Lee pushed the repairs as rapidly as he could. On the morning of December 2, General Lee had the pleasure of welcoming his wife and daughters at the packet landing. They arrived aboard the private boat of the president of the canal, and were accompanied by Robert E. Lee, Jr. Riding on Traveller, with the family in a carriage, General Lee escorted them to the house, where the thoughtful wife of a member of the faculty had arranged breakfast.

With great interest the young people went over the old residence. Although the best had been made of scant materials, the effect of the extemporized furnishings was, on the whole, somewhat odd. Mrs. Lee asserted her authority with promptness. The General submitted as cheerfully to domestic authority as ever he had to Congress and President. With his family about, his spirits rose visibly. "My father appeared bright and even gay," wrote Robert E. Lee, Jr., who had not seen him since the day at Pampatike. The General went to work vigorously to make the house attractive for his family. As soon as the weather permitted, he planted shrubs and roses, set out trees, repaired the stable, built walks, and prepared a vegetable garden. "In a short time," chronicled the son, "we were quite comfortable and very happy." There were no regrets in the family because he had declined an offer of $10,000 a year to act as titular head of an insurance company, while remaining at the college.

Christmas came and passed, a very different Christmas from that dreadful season in the Petersburg trenches twelve months before. With the New Year, Lee had to make a hard trip to Richmond. On December 4, 1865, the general assembly of Virginia had met, undisturbed as yet by a hostile Congress. Friends of education decided to make an appeal to it on behalf of the colleges. Several of these institutions had bonds guaranteed by the state and were dependent on the interest for a part of their support. This interest had stopped with the collapse of the Confederacy: the schools were anxious that the legislature make good the arrears and resume payment. A demonstration before the committee of the house of delegates on schools and colleges was arranged, and General Lee was asked to appear with Colonel Bolivar Christian, of the board of trustees, in behalf of Washington College, which owned $88,000 of the bonds.

It was a mission of a sort from which every sensibility of Lee's nature shrank, but it had to be performed. The General travelled to Richmond, where he arrived on January 11, 1866. The next day Lee went with Christian before the committee. After his associate had explained the plight of the institution, Lee arose. He had little to add, he said, to what Mr. Christian had told the committee. Perhaps it did not matter at all what he said: the members of the committee heard him with their hearts rather than with their ears. He was still their chieftain, not to be denied, and they took a short recess in order that they might greet him.

As Agnes Lee was then in Richmond, the General had a pleasant time with her and with Richmond friends. He remained in Richmond for about a week, helping to make friends for the bill to aid the colleges, and left for home, at last, on a day when snow was sifting ominously down. It was a rough, perhaps a dangerous, journey, but it was not in vain. The general assembly passed an act for the relief of the institutions, by which some $28,000 of interest was distributed among them.

Other financial assistance was at hand, also. Before General Lee had gone to Richmond, Reverend S. D. Stuart, one of the agents of the school, had returned from Baltimore, where he had raised $9000 toward the endowment of the presidency. Reverend Doctor W. S. White simultaneously collected $8000 from friends of the institution in the Valley of Virginia. Still another representative, Reverend E. P. Walton, had established headquarters at Memphis, Tenn., and was meeting with liberal responses to his appeal for the school. About the same time, as a result of one of the few letters of direct solicitation that Lee had written, Cyrus H. McCormick became interested in the college. He was a native of Rockbridge County, in which the institution was located, and he had made the first grain reaper in a shop not many miles from Lexington. On January 6, 1866, the board was told that Mr. McCormick had given $10,000 to the endowment fund. This was a great donation for the times, and was received with the thanks of the college. These funds relieved somewhat a dark financial situation. Increasing fees paid by the students, who were coming in ever-larger number, also eased somewhat the school's distress.

During the winter of 1865–66 distresses came with satisfactions. Mistreatment of President Davis was a load on Lee's heart. The politicians had taken the saddle in Washington. Stern "reconstruction" legislation was in the making. A "test oath" was being devised to keep out of office all those who had fought or had enacted laws for the South.

Contrary to his wishes, and in a manner most obnoxious to him, the General was now unexpectedly brought into contact with the men who were shaping laws against the South. On December 13, 1865, Congress had agreed on the appointment of a joint committee to "inquire into the condition of the states which formed the so-called Confederate States of America, and report whether they, or any of them, are entitled to be represented in either house of congress." Sub-committees had been named for the various geographical divisions of the South. That on Virginia, North Carolina, and South Carolina had Senator Jacob M. Howard of Michigan as its chief inquisitor. He and his associate began taking testimony on January 23, 1866, and continued at intervals until April 19.

General Lee's name had frequently come into the testimony of the

THE RUINS OF RICHMOND

committee. The committee could not resist the temptation to summon to Washington the man who was "at the head of the rebellion." On February 17, he was called before the committee, was sworn, and then was examined by Howard. The interrogation occupied two hours. General Lee did not want to testify, and though he was resolved to lose neither his dignity nor his temper, he was determined to say no more than was demanded of him. Explaining at the first opening that he lived "very retired" and had little communication with politicians, he gave only the most general, cautious answers to Howard's inquiries about the sentiment of the people on reunion, the payment of taxes, and the treatment of the Negro. His testimony was not of a sort to charge editorial bombs, and it received no more than casual mention in the news columns. If the committee had any other motive than curiosity in summoning him as a witness, it failed to accomplish its purpose.

If the journey had any effect on Lee, it was to deepen his taciturnity on public questions. "I have thought from the time of the cessation of hostilities," he wrote Mrs. Davis, shortly after his return to Lexington, "that silence and patience on the part of the South was the true course; and I think so still. Controversies of all kinds will, in my opinion, only serve to continue excitement and passion, and will prevent the public mind from acknowledgment and acceptance of the truth."

College duties and correspondence alike grew heavier with the spring. Lee's interest in his work was increasing and his zeal for education was becoming more pronounced. He wrote after his return from Washington:

"I consider the proper education of (the South's) youth one of the most important objects now to be attained, and one from which the greatest benefits may be expected. Nothing will compensate us for the depression of the standard of our moral and intellectual culture, and each state should take the most energetic measures to revive its schools and colleges, and, if possible, to increase the facilities of instruction, and to elevate the standard of living."

It was during this period that Lee first began to doubt whether he could write the history he had projected the previous summer. He continued to collect material and to urge his old comrades to gather it, but from most sources Lee found the haul very scanty. "It will be difficult to get the world to understand the odds against which we fought," he wrote Early, "and the destruction, or loss, of all the returns from the army embarrasses me very much."

Circumstances combined to round out a session that marked a definite advance. A struggling college that opened with four professors and a thin platoon of students was able to print a catalogue that listed 146 matriculates and a faculty for the next year of 14 members, exclusive of the president. In scope, its curriculum had been virtually doubled. Schools of Engineering and of Law had been established. For the inquiring student, the library had been partially restored. The election of courses had been made the privilege of every one, and the honor system in its fullness had been established.

The financial campaign had been vigorously prosecuted. The trustees proceeded to expand and improve the college plant as the endowment increased. Provision for the enclosure of the college grounds was made. A superintendent of grounds and buildings was chosen, as was a clerk to the faculty. Without the president's knowledge, his salary was doubled and was put at $3000. Fifteen hundred dollars were appropriated for new scientific equipment. Ambitious plans were made for the erection of a new dormitory for 100 men. A new chapel was authorized, at a cost not to exceed $10,000. Appropriation was made for gymnastic apparatus, repairs to the professors' houses were ordered, and a resolution was adopted for the construction of "a mansion" for the president, as soon as the funds were available. A college that had been very near death was to live again with a vigor it never had known.

The summer passed very quietly. Building and repairs at the college occupied much of the General's time. Although remaining in Lexington himself, he sent Mrs. Lee to the Rockbridge Baths, eleven miles from the town, and as often as he could, he rode over to see her.

One day that September (1866), while General Lee was riding on the road to the Rockbridge Baths, he stopped at a roadside spring. He found some young men there who recognized him instantly, handed him a drink of water, and then told him about themselves. They were from Tennessee, they explained, and were prospective students at Washington College. Might they give him their introductions from General Ewell and others of his former officers? Lee read the letters and inquired of the boys whither they were bound. To Rockbridge Baths, they said, to spend part of the time before the opening of college. Lee forthwith wrote and delivered them a line to the proprietor of the springs, John A. Harmon. "My dear Major," it read, "These are some of my new boys. Please take care of them."

That note did more than win for the Tennesseans the most cordial of welcomes at the baths; it displayed as well the spirit in which General Lee regarded the students of Washington College. He held them as his "boys" in his labor with them and in his hopes for them.

His "boys" were not all boys. In fact he never called them "boys" to their faces. In private conversation as in official dealings, each was "Mister." Many of them were veterans of his own campaigns and wore beards. A few of them were reckless and violent, hardened by their experience in war and loose in their habits. College to them was a minor adventure, endurable only because it offered opportunities for wassailing in the bars of the town and for hunting the defiant fox in the hills around Lexington. Other ex-soldiers, serious-minded, were typified by a young man who tramped all the way to the campus from Alabama, bringing with him his father's gold watch and three hundred dollars, all the family could raise for his schooling. These students worked with a zeal that set a standard for the college, and as they had obeyed General Lee's orders during the war, they cheerfully submitted themselves to his discipline now. They were indifferent to dress, had no money to waste, and were anxious to equip themselves as rapidly as possible for their careers. The third group consisted of boys who were just coming of the age to enter college and had not seen service in the army— "yearlings" they were styled by the veterans. Sons of rich men and of poor, they differed little, except in preparation, from those who crowd the registrars' offices today.

For the well-being of a student-body so diversified and so difficult to handle, General Lee felt an obligation that sometimes weighted him down. By diligent correspondence, he solicited work in summer for boys who needed money with which to complete their college course. Some students who could not get summer work or raise money among their friends were accepted on credit, evidenced solely by their notes of hand.

General Lee initiated the honor system very soon after he came to Lexington, and made it the basis on which all students were received. Faculty visitation of dormitories and all forms of espionage were abolished. If any breach of discipline occurred or any injury was done to college property, he expected the students who were involved in it to report to him. "We have no printed rules," Lee told a new matriculate who asked for a copy. "We have but one rule here, and it is that every student must be a gentleman." The first and the final appeal was to the student's sense of honor. He drew a clear and constant distinction between military rule and self-controlled obedience to constituted authority. One of his oft-repeated maxims was, "Obedience to lawful authority is the foundation of manly character."

The first application of the great fundamental—"be a gentleman"—was to the students' habits of study. The General countenanced no idleness. Even under the elective system, all students had to take at least fifteen hours of classroom work each week, and every man was required to belong to one or the other of the two literary societies. General holidays were few. He knew that the presence of most of the students represented some one's sacrifice in those difficult times, and he was determined that students should not waste what others had sweated to provide.

Lee's second application of the code of a gentleman was to the general deportment of the students. Unostentatiously and with few preachments, but hourly and earnestly, Lee sought the elevation of the boys' morals rather than the mere repression of vice. At the same time he waged active war on liquor. He had seen too much of the ill-effects of alcohol in the army not to make him regard it as a dangerous enemy.

Good habits of worship Lee ranked with those of study and of general deportment. Compulsory chapel attendance he abolished at the close of his first year at the college, but he was always anixous that the students should be present and he sought various ways of assuring this. He always was at chapel himself, sitting in the same place, next the wall on the north side of the new building, in the second pew from the front. The college Y.M.C.A., which he did much to organize, always had his encouragement, his contribution, and his praise in his annual report. He invited the ministers of the town to act in turn as chaplain, and jointly to meet the students at the opening of the session. Painstakingly he prepared and sent each Lexington pastor a list of the matriculates of his faith, and he encouraged the clergymen to keep in touch with them.

To keep the peace was the last of the four simple requirements General Lee made of "his boys" in obedience to the first law of being a gentleman. Respect for good order meant something in the late sixties. For Lexington presented a field of more serious contention than the customary clashes between town and gown, or between the college boys and the "tooth picks," as the students for some obscure reason styled the local youths. The town had a Federal garrison part of the time, and was not always fortunate in the commander of the troops. Several times it seemed that issues were made by the military authorities simply to embarrass Lee. The students flashed with wrath whenever they thought that the General was being assailed. To protect him, they would balk at nothing. Lee, therefore, had constantly to keep the students in hand.

These, then, were the things he required of "his boys"—that they be gentlemen in all things, that they study faithfully, that they hold to high moral standards, that they "remember their Creator," and that they keep the peace.

What he required of himself in his dealings with them was not so simple. He put his emphasis, first of all, on the individual. When a boy came to college for the first time, and entered his office to report, the General always rose to welcome him and greeted him with a graciousness that made the strange lad comfortable. The boy might not see General Lee again, except at chapel or on the walks. But he was not forgotten, and when he met the president, he was always addressed by name.

The faculty met every week and reported those who were derelict. In his office he received these delinquents, who usually were loath to discuss afterwards what happened between them and the General. The treatment probably was fitted to the patient, and usually it was administered in a few sentences, with a gentleness that impressed the student more than sternness would have done. Some of the things told them there might be maxims for the guidance of youth in every age. For a youngster who was in rebellion against authority, he put a life-rule in a single sentence: "You cannot be a true man until you learn to obey." The General did not mingle with the students, as a rule, but he made them feel that he had a personal interest in them. They felt his influence, did those boys of his, from the first time they went into his office to register. Although not actually afraid of him, they were most anxious not to offend him. Standing in awe of him, they yet had an exalted affection for him. Some of them thought they saw in his face the whole tragedy of the war, but the discerning knew he had kindness and humor of a kind.

Lee's influence over his students did not end when he handed them their degrees and declared them graduates of Washington College. It followed them and helped to shape their lives through the difficult years of poverty that preceded the South's recovery. He said of them: "My only object is to endeavor to make them see their true interest, to teach them to labor diligently for their improvement, and to prepare themselves for the great work of life."

It was not easy to watch the welfare of nearly 400 boys, and it was not always pleasant to keep in hand all the small details and close economies of a poor, overcrowded college. The weight of his people's sorrow lay on his heart, all the while, and in his mind he sometimes had to do battle with many memories. He was sustained in it all by the self-mastery that was, in large sense, one expression of his religion. Belief in God's mercy and submission to His will, in a faith that never seemed to be troubled by doubt, were stronger after Appomattox, if that were possible, than before. The General had family prayers every morning before breakfast, but his own spiritual life was bound up with the daily Bible reading and with special seasons of private devotions. The Bible was to him the book of books. Thus far it is easy to proceed in analyzing Lee's religion in after-war days. Beyond this it is not possible to go. Simple as was his soul, he had "meat to eat that ye know not of."

The session of 1866–67 opened on September 13 with a greatly increased registration. Before the end of March the enrollment had risen to 345, and by commencement it was 399. The students were more serious than had come to Lexington the previous autumn. The behavior of the boys gave General Lee little concern until early spring. The faculty was worked hard but was recruited during the winter. The trustees, at General Lee's instance, had put first among the construction projects of the college the erection of the new chapel. General Lee devoted himself to building the structure economically and within the allowed appropriation. With Custis's assistance, he gave to it daily supervision and the experience gained in dealing with labor when he had been an army engineer.

Autumn slipped away and with winter came a gloomier outlook for Virginia and the rest of the South. Congress and the President had disagreed bitterly over reconstruction. The committee that had heard General Lee and a host of witnesses had reported in April. On the basis of its findings, an elaborate plan was being built up to force the Southern states to acquiesce in the enfranchisement of the Negroes as a condition of readmission to the Union. The government that had been functioning reasonably well in Virginia was now threatened with overthrow.

Lee displayed deep concern over the prospect. He said: "The Radical party are likely to do a great deal of harm, for we wish now for good feeling to grow up between North and South . . . They are working as though they wished to keep alive by their proposals in Congress the bad blood in the South against the North."

The scope and content of Federal legislation were still undetermined in the early winter of 1866–67, but it was manifest that the vindictive spirit of Thaddeus Stevens and his radical followers was triumphing over the wise policy of reconciliation that Lincoln had devised and Johnson had sought to apply. Twenty months after Appomattox, the political prospect of the South was far gloomier than it had been at the time of the amnesty proclamation, issued before the paroled Southern soldiers had all found their way home.

These were the conditions in which General Lee received, during December, 1866, a letter from Sir John Dalberg Acton, later Lord Acton. The British historian asked for an expression of Lee's views on the constitutional issues involved in secession and on the longer political outlook, in order that he might counsel wisely the editors of a new British review. General Lee took pains with his answer.

General Lee believed that the rights of the states must be preserved, though the right of secession admittedly was no longer among them. He did not think the Federal Government had the authority under the Constitution to dictate suffrage requirements to the states, though he was entirely willing that the prohibition of slavery should be written into the Constitution. He held that the Southern states could not be denied their civil rights and their places in Congress under the theory of an indestructible Union, a theory which the North itself supported.

Like most Southerners, Lee supported President Johnson, and of course opposed the program of the Radicals. In July, 1866, he had written: "Everyone approves of the policy of President Johnson, gives him his cordial support, and would, I believe, confer on him the presidency for another term, if it was in his power." In October, 1867, he told Longstreet, who seemingly desired his endorsement of some move in support of the Republicans, "While I think we should act under the law and according to the law imposed upon us, I cannot think the course pursued by the dominant political party the one best for the interests of the country, and therefore cannot say so, or give them my approval." When Longstreet took a contrary course, and joined the Republicans, Lee said "General Longstreet has made a great mistake."

Despite the gloom of the political outlook, Christmas, 1866, was a pleasant season for the Lees. Rooney did not come up for the holidays, and Mildred was with friends in Maryland, but the other girls and Custis were at home, and Robert arrived on December 20.

Young Lee brought a familiar friend with him—none other than the sorrel mare, Lucy Long, that Jeb Stuart in the fall of 1862 had given his chief. From that time until the spring of 1864, the General had used her alternately with Traveller. Broken down then by hard riding and scanty feed, the mare had been sent out to Henry County, Virginia, to recuperate. Lee recalled her before the opening of the Appomattox campaign, but never received her. In some way she reached Essex County, Virginia, where she was sold to an honest man. Her resemblance to the General's war-time mare having been noted, Lee learned of her whereabouts, proved her identity, and paid for her out of consideration for Stuart's memory. The horse was brought to young Robert Lee's during the autumn and was kept there until nearly Christmas.

Lee gave Lucy Long good care, of course, employing her chiefly as a riding horse for his daughters, but personally he almost always used Traveller. That silent veteran of his campaigns had a place in the General's heart next after his God, his country, his family, his veterans, and his boys. The charger spent much of his time in the front yard of Lee's house, and he always received his master with the same toss of the head that had acknowledged the soldiers' cheers during the war. Such was his loyalty to Traveller that it was an ominous sign of his approaching end when Lee had to admit that the trot of his steed was getting harder. Rightly enough, on the day that Lee was buried, the horse followed directly behind the hearse.

The new year, 1867, brought a call. There still was hope that Congress would leave President Johnson free to permit Virginia to elect a governor without military interference. Several possible conservative nominees were suggested. General Lee was the most conspicuous of them. It was not a new proposal. By the end of January, 1867, sentiment for Lee was so strong that Judge Robert Ould wrote to know if he would accept the nomination. The General replied at once. He was appreciative, he wrote the judge, but he preferred private life, which he thought was better suited to his condition and age.

Evidently he gave thought to the proposal. Although he had told Ben. Hill during the war that his talents were military, not civil, he might, in other circumstances have looked favorably on Judge Ould's suggestion. He may have been influenced unconsciously by the fact that his father had been governor of Virginia after the Revolution. One of Mrs. Lee's ambitions for him was that he should end his career with the same honor.

Very shortly after General Lee answered Judge Ould, the political outlook changed grimly for the worse. The Radicals in Congress triumphed decisively over President Johnson, and in the face of his veto, passed the First Reconstruction Act on March 2, 1867. In a supplementary law of March 23 this was elaborated.

These two statutes subordinated to army officers the government of ten Southern states, Virginia among them. The states themselves ceased to exist for the time, in the eyes of the Federal Government, and became military districts. On March 13 the Act was proclaimed in Virginia. On that day, the proud Old Dominion became Military District No. 1. Dictatorial power was vested in the soldier who had for some time been in charge of the Union forces garrisoning Virginia, Major General John M. Schofield.

What should Virginians do about this harsh legislation?

Thousands looked to Lee for guidance. He had followed the newspapers the previous year, but he would not permit himself to be brought into the controversy through the public prints. However, in at least one instance, an accurate though unauthorized statement of his views was printed in a newspaper soon after the passage of the Reconstruction Act.

It was this public statement that prompted him, in answer to an inquiry from Judge Ould, to express his opinion of Virginia's duty. Under date of March 29, 1867, he wrote: "When the Sherman bill became a law & its execution imperative, I considered it right & just to the people of the State, that it should be submitted as required for their action, & that the call for a convention should be legitimately & properly made. I have never read the bill passed by the Senate of Virginia for that purpose, & do not know its provisions; but if there was then a difference of opinion as to the proper mode, there can be none since the passage of the supplemental bill; & I think all persons entitled to vote should attend the polls & endeavour to elect the best available men to represent them in the convention, to whose decision every one should submit. The preservation of harmony & kind feelings is of the utmost importance, & all good citizens should exert themselves to secure it & to prevent the division of the people into parties. The interests of all are inseparably connected & can only be preserved by our united wisdom & strength. I think it useless to offer arguments to show the propriety of this course. Its advantages are too manifest . . ."

As the wrath of the South rose in resentment of the Federal legislation, Lee had to urge his view with tact. He refused to despair of the future, though "greater calamity," in his opinion, might yet result from the misunderstanding between the sections. And in June he wrote Rooney, in language curiously rhetorical for him, "Although the future is still dark, and the prospects gloomy, I am confident that, if we all unite in doing our duty, and earnestly work to extract what good we can out of the evil that now hangs over our dear land, the time is not distant when the angry cloud will be lifted from our horizon and the sun in his pristine brightness again shine forth."

Within the college, the session of 1866–67 passed quickly, amid the exactions of a thousand duties. Visitors came in the usual numbers. Among them was William Swinton, author of *The Campaigns of the Army of the Potomac*, who was then collecting from Confederate leaders material he used in his *Twelve Decisive Battles of the War*. "He seems to be gentlemanly," Lee confided to Rooney, in manifest relief, after Swinton's departure, "but I derive no pleasure from my interviews with book-makers. I have either to appear uncivil or run the risk of being dragged before the public." Lee himself found time, too, to think once again of the history of his campaigns he still hoped to write, though he had told Acton he was progressing slowly "in the collection of the necessary documents."

In March occurred the session's gravest breach of discipline. Some of the students heard there was to be a speech making to the Negroes and, boy-like, five of them determined to attend. One of the group foolishly took a pistol with him. They went to the Freedmen's Church and, finding it dark, decided that the meeting must be at the schoolhouse, so they tramped thither. On their arrival, the student who carried the pistol approached a window to see if there was a gathering within. Immediately a Negro accosted him, cursed him, and made a motion as if to draw a weapon. The student took out his own firearm and started to beat the Negro, but presently desisted and went away with his companions. In some manner he eluded arrest, but the four others were brought before the mayor and were tried. As soon as General Lee heard of the affair, he summoned the quartet who had been in court. When they came, the student who had been engaged in the altercation also appeared. In accordance with the honor system of the college, he explained the circumstances, and assumed the entire blame. He was promptly expelled and the others were reprimanded. Three weeks later the assistant superintendent of the Freedmen's Bureau wrote General Lee on the subject, apparently determined to make an issue of it, but he dropped the matter, it seems, after Lee wrote him the facts in the case.

A month before commencement, President Davis was released on bail from his long confinement at Fort Monroe. The news that Davis was at last free from prison, General Lee received with relief and thankfulness. He wrote the former executive: "You can conceive better than I can express the misery which your friends have suffered from your long imprisonment, and the other afflictions incident thereto. To none has this been more painful than to me, and the impossibility of affording relief has added to my distress. Your release has lifted a load from my heart which I have not words to tell, and my daily prayer to the great Ruler of the world is, that He may shield you from all future harm, guard you from all evil, and give you the peace which the world cannot take away. That the rest of your days may be triumphantly happy is the sincere and earnest wish of your most obedient, faithful friend and servant."

It was General Lee's custom, during the meetings of the trustees, to report and then to retire in order that the board might be under no restraint in debating his recommendations. While he was absent from the room at the June meeting, the building committee was instructed to contract at once for the erection of a new house for the president at a cost of $12,000, later raised to $15,000. General Lee did not think this should be done, and argued that other improvements should have precedence, but there was no gainsaying the trustees.

If the second year offered no such dazzling comparisons as could have been made at the end of the session of 1865–66, it was because the transformation had already occurred. The school, Lee had written in March, was progressing as well as could be expected. He believed at the time that in another year he would have done all he could at the college and that he could retire to "some quiet spot" east of the mountains where he could prepare a home for Mrs. Lee and his daughters. Confinement, he had told an old friend, "agrees less with me even than labour in the field."

CHAPTER XVII

The Beginning of the End

As COLLEGE work at the end of the session of 1866–67 was better organized than it had been the previous summer, the General could take a vacation, a needed one, for he had been almost continuously at work since he had moved to Lexington, nearly two years before.

First there came a trip to a lovely mountain, the Peaks of Otter, about thirty miles away, in Bedford County. It was undertaken on horseback with his daughter Mildred, who had returned home after a lengthy visit in Maryland.

Mrs. Lee's condition had not been favorable during the spring. Her invalidism was so confirmed that she wrote, "The greatest feat I can expect to accomplish will be to walk across my room without crutches & even that I have no hope of accomplishing." The General felt, as he had in peaceful years before the war, that a change of scene would do her good and that the mineral waters of some popular "springs" might relieve her rheumatism. He left the choice of a resort to her, and she selected the Greenbrier White Sulphur, "merely on the ground, I believe," the General wrote Rooney, "that she has never tried those waters, and, therefore, they might be of service to her." As soon as he got back from the Peaks of Otter, he began to make his preparation to take her to the spa—a long, bone-breaking journey by railroad and conveyance over the mountains.

Some time in July the party set out, Mrs. Lee, Agnes, Miss Mary Pendleton, and Custis. At the time the family reached White Sulphur, this resort consisted of a rambling central hotel, a huge wooden structure with long, wide porches, beyond which were rows of small cottages, each of them usually occupied by a single family. General Lee had the Harrison Cottage in Baltimore Row, and around him he found many whom he had known in the old days before the Potomac had become a chasm. He ate in the main dining room, at a table with

W. W. Corcoran of Washington, Mildred Lee, Miss Pendleton, and Custis. Mrs. Lee's meals were served in her cottage.

The social impulse of the General was always strong, and now, in renewed contact with long-separated friends, it asserted itself vigorously. Young gallants at the springs admired him, of course, but kept at a distance, for he over-awed them. The older men, in some instances, he purposely avoided, because they were forever talking of the war and of politics, two subjects he considered it his duty to leave alone. With the women guests, particularly the girls, he seemed less reserved.

The centre of the social life of "The White" was the parlor of the main hotel. It was a vast place, nearly always thronged. On the evening of his arrival, it was expected that the General would come into the parlor, and there was some hurried consultation as to how he should be received. Some honor, of course, must be shown him, but would applause embarrass him? Before the question could be answered, Lee entered. There was a moment's hush, and then, as if by common impulse, every one rose and remained silent and standing until he took a seat. After that, assured that no demonstration would be made, he went regularly into the parlor, and as often as he did so, he was surrounded by groups of young women, with whom he talked, half-seriously, half-jestingly. If new girls came to the hotel, he saw that they were made to feel at home. The homeliest and least known were as sure to receive his courteous attention as the fairest or the most aristocratic.

Lee's quiet participation in the promenades and his talk with guests occupied only a small part of the long summer days. "There are some 500 people here," he wrote Robert in August, "very pleasant and kind, but most of my time is passed alone with Traveller in the mountains." Sometimes he had companions or found them. Often his entire ramble was in solitude, but not in loneliness, for it was a rule with him always to occupy his hours of exercise with pleasant meditations and with a study of whatever beauty he might find.

Those weeks at the White were not entirely made up of restful rides and light talk. Northern people were beginning to visit the springs again: they did not always show the spirit of reconciliation, nor were they received with it. The women were more resentful than the men, and as they were much more numerous, any vindictiveness on the part of the Northerners was met with something akin to social ostracism. Against every manifestation of this spirit General Lee felt he should exert himself publicly. If former Federal officers avoided him, through consideration for his sensibilities, he quite subordinated the past to the present in a desire to see Southern hospitality vindicated and the strangers put at ease. He was thoughtful, too, in dealing with the Northern ladies, also, and sought, as far as he could, to break up the ice of animosity.

Before the time came to leave "The White," at the end of three weeks, General Lee was taken sick. In a short while, he recovered sufficiently to ride over to the Old Sweet, whither the family then moved, for it was the fashion of the day to go to two or three springs in a season. After his arrival, his physical distress grew into a real illness, superinduced, as Lee thought, by a cold. His recovery was slow, and the seizure, whatever its nature, left him feeble. Fortunately, the quarters were quite comfortable.

While the General was slowly getting better, some of the mountaineers came to the hotel with fruit for sale. When they saw their old commander—for they were survivors of his army—they forgot their trade and raised the rebel yell. And after the General acknowledged their tribute by shaking hands with each of them, they insisted that he accept the contents of their baskets. Such incidents were of frequent occurrence: wherever he went he met men who had served under him. Whether they had saved something from their country's wreck or were fighting with black poverty, they wanted to do what they could and to give him what they had, to show their affection for him.

Early in September it was arranged that Custis should escort home his mother, his sister, and Miss Pendleton, and that the General should return by a more leisurely journey, halting for his health at three resorts on the way. He reached Healing Springs on September 10, and was still so much indisposed that he had to remain there until the 13th or 14th. He then went on by easy stages and reached Lexington on the 17th.

He had been away from the college almost continuously since its close the previous June. As he had rested he should have been reestablished in health; but there had begun to creep more frequently into his letters an occasional sentence indicating his belief that he was getting old and that the end was not far distant. In contrast to his oldtime gaiety, he wrote the "Beautiful Talcott," who was still beautiful despite war and time, "Trouble and distress seem to pervade every part of the world, and peace and happiness are secure in none."

Rooney Lee, it will be remembered, had lost his young wife, Charlotte Wickham, during December, 1863, while he was a prisoner of war. In 1867, when he was thirty, Rooney began to pay attention to Miss Mary Tabb Bolling, a daughter of G. M. Bolling of Petersburg, Va. By August of that year it was known in the Lee family that Rooney hoped to marry her. His father heard the news with interest, for he had met her during the siege of Petersburg and liked her. After the General had returned from the springs in September, word came that the charming lady had capitulated to the cavalryman.

As soon as the approximate date for the wedding was set, the General was most warmly urged to attend the ceremonies. His mind was reluctant. He had not yet entirely recovered from the illness of the summer. But his chief reason for declining, though he may not have realized it, lay very much deeper, in his most personal and most profound reactions to the outcome of the war. He had never been disturbed about his own fate and he had never pitied himself. He had agonized, however, over the plight of the Southern people, so many of whom, in person or by letter, had poured out their sorrows to him. The grief that many saw in his face after the war was theirs. For none was that grief keener than for the people of Petersburg, that stout-souled city of grim memory. In them he saw the suffering of the whole South. Never did he think of them otherwise than with the deepest sorrow, and he dreaded to visit again the scenes of his travial of soul during the last winter of the war.

But what would be the wedding of a Lee if the General were not present?

While the arrangements for the wedding were being matured, General Lee was served with a *subpoena* to appear as a witness on November 26 at the Federal circuit court in Richmond. Custis was summoned, also. Either by chance or else to save a second trip, the ceremonies were set for November 28, during the week the General was to appear in Richmond.

Accompanied by Custis, he reached Richmond on the afternoon of November 25, and went to the Exchange Hotel, where Rooney was awaiting him. Lee had been to the city only once since 1865, and on that visit he had kept much in retirement. Now he felt he could allow himself social pleasure without making himself conspicuous. After supper, on his first evening at the hotel, when he attempted to go through the lobby, he was at once surrounded by men who knew him and had served under him. Strangers and Northerners joined the crowd that sought to shake his hand. It was the first time since the war that a promiscuous crowd in any Southern city had the opportunity of showing its affection for him, and its admiration of the course he had pursued after Appomattox. He may have been surprised and moved by this spontaneous warmth of welcome, but he was destined to discover that every other city of the South had the same feeling for him.

During the course of the evening, Lee went to Judge Ould's, and there, for the first time since March of 1865, he saw Jefferson Davis. The former President had come to Richmond to appear before the Federal court on the treason charge. "[He] looks astonishingly well," General Lee wrote Mrs. Lee, "and is quite cheerful. He inquired particularly after you all."

The next day General Lee presented himself at the Federal building. He found Mr. Davis there, ready to be tried if the government chose, and he had a long and pleasant chat with his former chief as they waited. The expectation had been that the chief justice would come down from Washington and sit with Judge Underwood, but as Chase did not appear, all that could be done was to impanel a grand jury.

The jury was "mixed," white men and Negroes, and it was harangued at length by the judge. Upon its retirement, the clerk read the list of witnesses. Lee's name came first. Spectators grew silent, awaiting his answer. They were disappointed, for the General was in another room at the moment and did not hear the crier. The district attorney rose immediately and explained obligingly that Lee was in the city and would be ready at any time to go before the grand jury. Other witnesses were thereupon called. For the remainder of November 26, Lee was overwhelmed with visitors. Every one knew he was in Richmond; every one, it seemed, was anxious to call on him. He spent an exceedingly busy ten hours and must have been as weary as he was gratified.

The grand jury did not summon the General again until the next day. Ushered in at 2 P.M., he was subjected to the jury's inquisition. He was, of course, an unwilling witness. Judging from the indictment returned on March 26, 1868, the evidence he was required to give the jurors had to do solely with known military movements, which the grand jury presented as proof of armed insurrection against the authority of the United States. Apparently there was no effort to probe into the personal relations of President Davis and General Lee, and no attempt to bring out any of the inner history of the Confederacy. The whole of the treason proceedings, in fact, dealt with facts familiar to every American of the time. After his two hours in the jury room, General Lee was excused from further attendance.

The following afternoon, November 28, he joined the large wedding party that was to go to Petersburg. Perhaps the restraint of the jury room was still upon him. Doubtless memories, as bitter as brave, had been aroused by the questioning of the grand jury. All these were revived as the train made its way southward. The wedding guests were chattering and laughing, as youth has a right to do; the General sat silent and sad-faced.

The brakes were grinding, the train was stopping: it was Pocahontas, a scattered settlement on the north bank of the river. The moment the wheels ceased turning there came a crash of sound—music, a band, the notes of the Marseillaise. The performers had come over to do him honor and had been waiting in the station. They played through the French anthem the Southern soldiers had loved, and then they climbed aboard the train. Slowly over the river and through the town the train was pulled to the Washington Street Station, which was crowded. The windows of Jarratt's Hotel nearby and the streets and roadway around it were jammed. People started cheering the moment General Lee appeared, and they opened their applauding, smiling ranks as he walked to the curb, where his host, General William Mahone, had a carriage with four white horses awaiting him. Around the vehicle surged the throng, acclaiming him, rejoicing to see once more the man whose thin line had so long kept their city safe. The final defeat was forgotten in the memory of the victories won against odds so commanding.

Three hours before the ceremony, the people of Petersburg began to gather at the church, more perhaps to see General Lee than to witness the ceremony. The crowd thronged the street. At last the guests began to arrive—first of all, General Lee. Behind General Lee were General and Mrs. Mahone. Presently came Miss Bolling and her ten bridesmaids. A like number of the friends of Rooney were at hand to support him in his happy ordeal. It was a gathering of the Lee clan, for besides the General, the groom, and Mildred, there were in attendance Custis, Robert, and Fitz Lee, the nephew.

After the wedding came the supper, in the most lavish style of the old Dominion. Dutifully the next morning, before any of the Mahones had descended to breakfast, the General penned a lengthy letter to his wife. He lunched with the Bollings. They had passed word that their friends might call on the General that afternoon, and those who revered him came by scores. In the evening an affair was given in honor of the bride. The General attended—he did not absent himself from any of the entertainments—and he seemed to enjoy himself greatly.

Every one knew, apparently, that the General was to journey back to Richmond on Saturday, November 30. As he went to the station they crowded the highways of Petersburg once again to bid him farewell. The train conveying him to Richmond pulled out amid a roar of cheers.

He spent Sunday quietly in Richmond and on the morning of December 2, with Custis and Robert he went down James River to Brandon, home of his cousins, the Harrisons. An all-too-brief night and part of a day were pleasantly passed at Brandon. Then he came back to Richmond by steamer, spent Thursday, December 5, at Hickory Hill, the Wickham home in Hanover County, and on December 6 started for home, which he reached on December 7.

It was the longest absence from college Lee thus far had allowed himself during the session, and it marked a definite transition in his state of mind. He was far happier after this visit and more willing to travel and to mingle with his people again. Prior to the journey to Petersburg he had been oppressed by the poverty, losses, and misery of the Southern people. He had travelled little after he had come to Lexington and he did not know how the South was reviving, or in what spirit it was adjusting itself to the reconstruction. Then, almost overnight, he found himself in a new atmosphere. Instead of distress, idleness, and vain regret, he found good cheer, industry, and a courageous acceptance of the outcome of the war, along with pride in the old cause and affection for those who had led it. A letter to Rooney gave expression to a sense of relief that was reflected in all Lee's correspondence and counsel thereafter:

> "When I saw the cheerfulness with which the people were working to restore their condition, and witnessed the comforts with which they were surrounded, a load of sorrow which had been pressing upon me for years was lifted from my heart."

The college, meantime, had opened auspiciously and uneventfully for the session of 1867–68, with an enrollment that exceeded 400 by October 4 and climbed before June to a total of 410.

Lee was kept busy with his administrative duties, which continued so heavy that he protested every absence from his office involved an accumulation of work. Agnes and Mary were both away in Maryland for the greater part of the winter. Mildred, the one-time absentee, not only kept house, but had in addition the care of another Mildred, daughter of General Lee's brother, Charles Carter Lee. Two of her brothers, the General's nephews, took their meals with the family that winter while rooming elsewhere and attending college. Custis continued to live with his parents and taught in the Virginia Military Institute. Mildred was so busy that she had little time to go out with the General, who consequently had to take his exercise alone. Christmas passed quietly, with Robert up from the Tidewater.

The gloom of a dark, wet winter was deepened early in February by the most unpleasant happening of General Lee's entire administration of the college. On North River there was a long stretch that afforded excellent skating in cold weather. Students and townspeople thronged it. On the afternoon of February 4, one E. C. Johnston, a former Federal soldier, went down to the river to enjoy the ice. He had come to Lexington in the autumn of 1865 as an agent of the American Missionary Association and had established some schools for the instruction of freedmen. From this work, he had turned to storekeeping, but his affiliations with the Negroes made him somewhat notorious and distinctly unpopular. He was accustomed to carry a pistol and had it with him that day.

Soon after Johnston got on the ice he noticed that other skaters shunned him. He went on for something more than a mile and then, turning a bend, came in view of a crowd that included town boys of various ages and a number of students from the college. Some of them knew the reputation of Johnston as one who consorted with the blacks, and they commenced to hoot and to yell at him—"just as the rebels used to yell when making a charge in the army," Johnston subsequently narrated. The object of this contempt skated past the crowd, without a word on his part or any act of violence on theirs. He went on to the dam, and then he started back up the river. His tormentors resumed their jibes at once. Johnston kept on toward them, and a lad of about twelve hurled the most insulting of epithets at him.

Johnston lost his head. He caught hold of the youngster, drew his pistol and threatened to shoot him if he repeated the words. The boy's older brother and probably some others came up immediately. Johnston thereupon released his grip and started off, pursued by the crowd, which began to abuse him hotly. The Northerner foolishly tried to dispute with them and thereby sharpened their language. In the excitement, some of the youths cried "Hang him" and "Drown him." He finally got off the river. Pelted with ice and clods as he went away, he reached shelter in safety, with sundry bruises and bumps, but with no serious injuries to show for his misadventure. That night a group of unidentified men came to his place of business, beat upon the door, rattled the shutters, and shouted insults. After a while, arousing no one, they went away. Johnston, as it happened, was not in the building at the time.

If General Lee heard anything of the episode, it probably was no more than that a Northern radical had drawn a pistol on a little boy and had been driven from the ice. Johnston, however, was out for revenge. He went forthwith to the mayor of the town, J. M. Ruff, and gave his version of the affair. His assumption apparently was that all those he had encountered on the river were students. He demanded protection and called upon the mayor to punish the guilty. In the absence of specific charges against any named student, the mayor told Johnston that he could not control the college boys. Johnston then reported the matter to the military authorities. Word of it reached Brigadier General Douglas Frazer, the assistant military commissioner for the district. General Frazer communicated with his superior, Brevet Major General O. B. Willcox, commanding the sub-district of Lynchburg. General Willcox came at once to Lexington and investigated. He talked with Johnston and with various witnesses to the affray, and also with the mayor, whom he thought "lacking in energy and determination but . . . well disposed." Then he went to see General Lee and, for the first time, acquainted him with the fact that Johnston considered he had been insulted by members of the student-body because he was a Northerner. General Willcox supplied the names of three students who were alleged to have been involved. General Lee immediately began an inquiry into the facts. Finding that two of the accused boys had been engaged in the affair, he directed one of them to withdraw immediately, and wrote the parents of the other to remove him from college. The third young man, who had been present but had not participated in the row, applied for permission to leave the institution and was allowed to do so. This action was taken by General Lee without calling the faculty together and while General Willcox was still in town. It was coupled with assurance to the Federal commander that he would expel any student guilty of disorderly conduct. General Willcox went back to Lynchburg well satisfied.

Here the matter might have ended, but for the feeling of Johnston and some of his friends that he had been badly treated. They endeavored to strike back—at General Lee, at the school and at General Willcox, whose refusal to take extreme measures had incensed them.

Washington College that winter had boldly launched in the North a promising campaign for financial support. Reverend E. P. Walton had charge of the solicitation and tactfully prevailed upon more than thirty New Yorkers of prominence to unite in a call for a meeting on the evening of March 3 in Cooper Institute. It was one of the first gatherings that came together in the North after the war to assist a Southern college directed by former Confederates.

Henry Ward Beecher closed the meeting with a characteristic speech in which he urged the cause of education. He pleaded for Washington College, because it was in Virginia and because Lee was its president. He would not withhold his support from any Southern school, but for this one his sympathies were strong. No one regretted the course which General Lee had chosen in former days more than he, the speaker, did. But if he had been born in Virginia, brought up amid her institutions, educated in a Southern college, he might have been prompted to take a course just as bad or erratic as did Lee or Johnston. Lee was now pleading for mental bread for his students. Mr. Beecher spoke with great earnestness and was much applauded.

Apparently, no collection was taken before adjournment, but the meeting was altogether as good an introduction to the people of New York as could have been asked. If it had been followed by similar endorsements from a few other leading men of the North it might have meant much to Washington College. The gathering, however, aroused the wrath of some of the old abolitionists who at that time knew nothing of the Johnston incident. *The New York Independent* of March 12 made the rally the text for an editorial article on "Education at the South."

It was the duty of the North, said the paper to help the South in education, but when it came to "supporting a college of which the late commander of the Confederate army is the president, we must respectfully decline." *The Independent* commented: "Is there any evidence that Washington College, under the presidency of Gen. Lee, is anything else than a rebel school, in which a loyal student would be subjected to insult and persecution? The friends of freedom at the North will be likely, we think, to demand an answer to this question before contributing to its support." If believers in education wanted to promote that cause in the South, let them help Berea College, Kentucky, where instruction was given "last year [to] more than three hundred students—of whom something over half were colored, the most advanced class in the South."

When the issue containing this article reached Lexington, one of Johnston's friends, who signed himself "A Resident of Lexington," wrote a very bitter letter to the periodical, instancing the treatment of that young man as further proof of what *The Independent* had charged. *The Independent* printed this letter, and its editor commented: "In view of facts like these, which come to us from a responsible source, we should think that every man who has given a cent to Gen. Lee's college would see and feel that he has been imposed upon, and that his money has been worse than thrown away."

Fortunately for the college, however, its anonymous critic, the "Resident of Lexington," had trod on the toes of General Willcox, and had hinted that the Federal commander had been much too lenient in the Johnston case. This aroused one of Willcox's admirers, "L," probably Captain Lacey of his staff. This officer wrote *The New York Tribune* a correct account of the affair, which *The Independent* had the grace to reproduce. "This correction," wrote "L," "will, I trust, be sufficient to exonerate General Lee, but for whom and the cause of education, so essential to the welfare of the South, I should not notice the letter and article referred to . . ."

Johnston saw this letter and he returned to the charge in a long argumentative communication to *The Independent*. While Johnston's final defense apparently did not circulate beyond the columns of *The Independent*, the first letter from Lexington and the accompanying editorial comment of the periodical were copied widely. Other publications joined in denunciation of the college. Among others, the Yale College weekly, *The Courant*, reproduced the initial article from *The Independent*. Until that time General Lee had taken no notice of the attacks, but he did write the New Haven paper. "I regret," said he, "that such an accusation against any literary institution in the country should have been copied in *The Yale Courant*. The statements of the 'Resident of Lexington' have been repeatedly denied, and I had hoped that a letter from an officer of the army, published in *The New York Tribune* of 20th April, would have satisfied all fair-minded persons of their injustice. As it gives all the facts in the case, and will have more weight than anything I could say, I enclose a slip from *The Lexington Gazette*, which republished it. Very respectfully, your obedient servant." *The Courant* promptly and generously made the *amende honorable*.

Mr. Walton got pledges and cash amounting to $4300 in New York, including $1000 from Henry Ward Beecher, Gerrit Smith's $200, and $100 each from John A. Griscom, Samuel J. Tilden, and Jas. W. Mc-Culloh. But it is quite likely that the vehemence of the attacks prompted the college to withdraw its agent and to abandon the canvass. The agitation exhibits, moreover, one reason why General Lee avoided all public appearances and every act that might lead to controversy. The temper of the time was not suited to co-operation between North and South. Every effort to that end, no matter how honestly planned or how sincerely undertaken, was certain to spur extremists, North and South.

The hard, wet winter was accompanied by much sickness in Lexington. Mrs. Lee suffered more than usual. The General took such exercise as he could get and he found much satisfaction, one March day, in following the ploughs of a neighboring farmer around the circuit of his fields. He caught cold, however, and had to admit, when the rough weather was past, that he had "not been as well . . . as usual," but he still delighted in his occasional rides on Traveller.

A prospect that depressed him was the approaching trial of President Davis. Going to Richmond as an unwilling witness in the proceedings was a "painful errand" for General Lee, even though it held out the prospect of meeting with his sons. As the time for the expected trial drew on, his tone was serious. "God grant," said he, "that, like the impeachment of Mr. Johnson, it may be dismissed." On May 1, 1868, Lee went to Richmond, under summons, only to find the proceedings deferred until June. He took advantage of his proximity to his sons, and paid them a brief visit.

Lee was in Richmond again on June 3 when Mr. Davis's case was due to be called and Chief Justice Chase was expected to be present. By agreement, when the Davis case was reached on the docket it was postponed to November 30. As Rooney was one of his fellow-witnesses, the General had opportunity of seeing him while he was in the old capital, but once again he hastened back to Lexington, this time in order to be present during the examinations.

In gratifying contrast to the two calls to Richmond, and coming between them, was a mission to Lynchburg, on May 20, 1868, to attend the annual council of the Protestant Episcopal Church of Virginia, as a lay delegate from Grace Church, Lexington. The next two days must have been busy, for Lee was named a member of three committees, that on the state of the Church, that on Church salaries, and that on a memorial to his old friend, Bishop William Meade. On the last day of the council meeting, the General was nominated a delegate to the general convention of the Protestant Episcopal Church, the highest honor the council could pay one of its members, but he was not elected, doubtless because he did not feel he could attend.

Examinations crowded the days that followed Lee's June trip to Richmond. Then came commencement. The college had a graduating class of fourteen—two in civil engineering, seven bachelors of law, five bachelors of arts—and it staged for them the most elaborate ceremonies that had been held since the war. The chapel was formally dedicated on June 14, much to General Lee's satisfaction, and the baccalaureate sermon was preached by the president's former Richmond rector, Doctor Charles Minnigerode.

General Wade Hampton was commencement guest, as orator before the literary societies. Lee arranged his engagements so that he could entertain the South Carolinian at dinner, and with him he talked frankly of the war. It was one of the few occasions after 1865 on which he did so. Their exchange ranged far—back to the beginning of the struggle and to their decision to share the fortunes of the South. Then it was that Lee made the simple observation that is the surest answer to all those who have contended that he hesitated before resigning from the United States army in 1861: "I did only what my duty demanded," he said. "I could have taken no other course without dishonor. And if all were to be done over again, I should act in precisely the same manner."

So ended the third session at Lexington under Lee's presidency. It had brought its vexations and its disappointments, and it had witnessed the only serious attack made on General Lee and the college during his administration. Although the endowment had not been increased largely, the year, financially, had not been very difficult, and scholastically it had been the best since the war. To Lee, along with some sorrows and sickness, it had brought new satisfactions. He made no move to resign as he had intimated the previous year he might do when the session of 1867–68 closed. Instead, as his devoted associates saw, his love for the college increased with each year. He showed that feeling very positively when he received a call to accept the vice-chancellorship and active administration of the University of the South, but with a few polite words he declined the offer.

The summer of 1868 began with the suggestion of a high honor—nothing less than that General Lee be made the Democratic nominee for the presidency of the United States. It was a qualified proposal, to be sure, for it was postulated on the assumption that the Democrats had to name a soldier to defeat General Grant. *The New York Herald* put Lee's name forward in an editorial that read in part as follows:

"But if the Democratic Committee must nominate a soldier—if it must have a name identified with the glories of the war—we will recommend a candidate for its favors. Let it nominate General R. E. Lee. Let it boldly take over the best of all its soldiers, making no palaver or apology. He is a better soldier than any of those they have thought upon and a greater man. He is one in whom the military genius of this nation finds its fullest development. Here the inequality will be in favor of the Democrats for this soldier, with a handful of men whom he had moulded into an army, baffled our greater Northern armies for four years; and when opposed by Grant was only worn down by that solid strategy of stupidity that accomplishes its object by mere weight."

Lee must have smiled at this article, if he saw it, but he had little time and perhaps little heart for smiling that summer. Sickness dogged the family. Mrs. Lee had become nervous and had been brooding so much over the plight of the South under military rule that her husband had feared she would aggravate her physical condition. Agnes had been sick while in Maryland, and was said to be looking very unwell. The General planned to take all of them away, and after he had comfortably established them at the springs Mrs. Lee preferred, he intended to go on with Mildred to the White Sulphur and to drink its waters for his rheumatism.

It was July 14 before the first stage of this journey could be undertaken and the family moved to the Warm Springs. All might have gone well had not Mildred contracted a low, debilitating fever which the doctor diagnosed as typhoid. Her mother, of course, could not nurse her. The burden fell on the General and on Agnes. It was August 14 before Mildred was pronounced convalescent, and even then she was so weak she could not speak. When she recovered sufficiently to travel, the General took her and the rest of the family from the Warm to the Hot Springs, and, after a few days, went on with Mildred to the White Sulphur.

He found a large gathering of former Confederates there, including many of his old generals and not a few of the civil officials of the dead government. Nearly all of them were talking politics. Grant and Schuyler Colfax had been nominated by the Republicans. Against them the Democrats had entered Governor Horatio Seymour and Francis P. Blair. Recent as was the war, some of the Democrats believed that they had a chance of electing their candidates. Lee had little part in these discussions. In fact, he avoided politics so sedulously that more than one of his comrades complained privately that he was distinctly cool to them.

Whether it was that the air was too heavily surcharged with politics or that Lee was exhausted by his long nursing of Mildred, he did not enjoy the social life of "The White" so much as he had the previous summer. He tried to be enthusiastic about the place and the company, but he left early in September for the Hot Springs, and by September 14 was back home. He was soon deep in the heavy work incident to the registration of the students and the reopening of the college on September 17.

Except for a trip of two days to the fair at Staunton in October, Lee did not leave Lexington during the fall and winter. From the beginning of the session to the second week in April, 1869, he missed only one faculty meeting. In contrast to the hard, unhappy summer, it was a pleasant time, broken by the coming and going of kinspeople. The General's nephew, Edward Lee Childe, journeyed over from Paris and was a welcome guest in October. Rooney and his wife, coming in November, were much entertained. At Christmas, Robert arrived for a stay of two weeks, and all the girls were at home. Only Rooney, of the six children, was absent. It was the last time as many as five of them were together during Lee's lifetime. The General had much delight in their company. Robert and his father were much together during this visit. They frequently inspected the new "president's house" that was now nearing completion on the same ridge with the old residence. They rode out together, too, Lee on Traveller and Robert on Lucy Long. The General's health seemed excellent and his spirits were high.

Shortly after the Christmas parties broke up, the last word was written in the treason proceedings that had been initiated almost four years before. President Davis had never been brought to trial because of legal difficulties that Chief Justice Chase saw in the way of the prosecution. The proceedings were halted in a motion to quash the indictment, and on which the court divided. On December 5, 1868, the division was certified to the Supreme Court of the United States. The general amnesty proclamation of December 25 followed in less than three weeks and of course operated to stop the prosecution of any former Confederate for treason. On February 15, 1869, the indictments against General Lee, Rooney, Custis, and Fitz Lee, fourteen other general officers of the Confederacy, and nineteen other persons, were nolle prossed.

This formal dismissal of the indictments passed almost unnoticed. Nor did the amnesty proclamation in a material way change Lee's status, though he could no longer be accounted a paroled prisoner of war. In one respect the adoption of the Fourteenth Amendment offset the amnesty in that it barred him from state or Federal office of any sort. When the new constitution of the state was ratified and the test-oath was eliminated he could have qualified to vote, but he did not do so. He did not die disfranchised, in the strict sense of the word, nor as a paroled prisoner of war, often as this has been asserted, but he did end his days disbarred from office.

The only effect of the amnesty proclamation on Lee was to make it possible for him to undertake the recovery of property seized at Arlington. The silver already had been sent to Lexington and was in daily use. Through the efforts of Mrs. Britannia Kennon, virtually all the portraits at the Custis mansion had been removed to Tudor Place, Georgetown, and after the war had been forwarded. But the Washington relics had been left at Arlington in 1861. Some of them were stolen and carried away by individuals, as were the small personal belongings of the Lees, found in the house by marauding Federal soldiers. When General McDowell took over Arlington as a Federal post, the servant in charge told him of the depredations that had occurred. To save the remaining effects of Washington, General McDowell removed them to the Department of the Interior. Placed on exhibit at the Patent Office, with the legend "Captured at Arlington," they constituted a rather pitiful display—a pair of candelabra, part of a set of china that Lafayette had given Mrs. Washington, a punch bowl, a looking-glass, a washstand, a "dressing bureau," a few of Washington's tent poles and pins, a little of his bed clothing and a pair of his breeches, with a waistcoat—nothing that had any value apart from its association with the first President.

In the winter of 1868–69, Captain James May, of Illinois, saw the relics, thought they should be returned, and consulted some of his friends in the administration. All of them agreed that it was proper to restore the articles to Mrs. Lee. The President had power to take this action, under existing law, and was sounded out. Captain May was satisfied Johnson would not withhold his consent. Captain May accordingly wrote Mrs. Lee on February 9, 1869, suggesting that she apply for the relics. Mrs. Lee of course sought the counsel of the General, and he approved of her proceeding as Captain May suggested. She addressed a brief application to the President on February 10, under cover to Captain May. He delivered it to Secretary O. H. Browning of the Department of the Interior, who brought it to the President's attention at a cabinet meeting. The chief executive and all his advisers were unanimously for complying with Mrs. Lee's request, and the Secretary of the Interior was authorized to deliver the goods to Mrs. Lee upon proper identification.

News of the prospective restoration of the relics was printed on February 26, 1869, in *The Washington Evening Express*. Unfortunately, it was erroneously stated that General Lee had made the application, that the relics had been taken from "the Arlington House, General Lee's estate," and that they were to be placed in the hands of some person deputized by the General to receive them. On the basis of this publication, General John A. Logan, of Illinois, introduced into the United States House of Representatives on March 1, 1869, a resolution calling on the committee on public buildings and grounds to ascertain "by what right the Secretary of the Interior surrenders these articles so cherished as once the property of the Father of his Country to the rebel general-in-chief."

The committee held a hurried hearing, with Captain May and Secretary Browning as the principal witnesses. On March 3, a few hours before the Congress adjourned *sine die*, the committee reported a resolution that the Washington relics were the property of the United States and that any attempt on the part of the administration "to deliver the same to the rebel General Robert E. Lee is an insult to the loyal people of the United States." The articles should remain in the Patent Office, the resolution concluded, and should not be delivered to any one without the consent of Congress.

General Lee must have felt keenly this action by Congress, but his observations upon it were brief. "[The relics] were valuable to [Mrs. Lee]," he wrote, "as having belonged to her great-grandmother, and having been bequeathed to her by her father. But as the country desires them, she must give them up. I hope their presence at the capital will keep in the remembrance of all Americans the principles and virtues of Washington." He was even more philosophical about the property that had been carried away from Arlington by private persons. "From what I have learned," said he, "a great many things formerly belonging to General Washington . . . in the shape of books, furniture, camp equipage, etc., were carried away by individuals and are now scattered over the land. I hope the possessors appreciate them and may imitate the example of their original owner, whose conduct must at times be brought to their recollection by these silent monitors. In this way, they will accomplish good to the country."

A more serious matter occupying General Lee's attention that winter was the settlement of the Custis estate, of which he was still active executor. Lee had liberated the slaves of his father-in-law during the winter of 1862–63. The other requirements of the will General Lee had not been able to carry out. Arlington, which had been sold for delinquent taxes on January 11, 1864, was now the property of the United States and had been set aside as a soldiers' cemetery. The price paid was $26,860, but the money was merely transferred from one government account to another. The "Four-Mile" tract had similarly passed out of the hands of the family. At the end of the war, General Lee had been of the opinion that Smith's Island had shared the fate of Arlington and the "Four-Mile" property. He therefore considered that the only realty left to the estate was Romancoke, which Mr. Custis had left to Robert, and the White House, which had been bequeathed to Rooney. Each of these farms contained 4000 acres and had been given subject to the condition that if the sale of certain other real estate and the labor of the slaves did not yield enough to pay the legacies to the grand-daughters, these two farms were to be worked and part of the proceeds set aside until the full amount of $40,000 had been realized.

General Lee's first impulse after the war had been to wait, trusting that his civil rights would be restored and that he could proceed to clear the estate, though, meantime, he asked a friendly attorney to investigate the case. As the prospect of a pardon faded out, he still hoped that he might redeem Arlington, which he assumed the government had sold in the belief that the estate was his. Lee could do nothing to prevent the award to the government of a tax-sale title, which was allowed on September 26, 1866.

Lee had strong attachment to the soil, and though he did not complain because the misfortunes of war had fallen heavily on his wife and children, he had lasting interest in the old family properties and a deep love for them. Cherishing these feelings, he was only deterred from an active effort to recover Arlington by his failure to find any practical means of attaining his result, though there was a general feeling in the spring of 1868 that the property would be returned. In January, 1869, J. S. Black of Washington, a lawyer and publicist of high position, volunteered his services in proceedings for the restoration of the former Custis property. The case demanded abilities as distinguished as those of Black, because in addition to the involvements of the tax sale, there were prospective complications owing to the fact that Custis Lee had not taken, and did not propose to take, his grandfather's "name and arms," as required under the Custis will.

Lee accepted Mr. Black's offer with a hearty "I thank you." He explained that he had no personal property interest in Arlington and that his desire simply was to turn it over to the rightful heir. He was willing to go to law for Mrs. Lee's and Custis's sake, but he did not wish to enter into litigation that would arouse dark passions, to no good purpose.

Meantime, it was discovered that though Smith's Island had been sold for delinquent taxes on June 15, 1864, it could be recovered under Virginia law. Action was accordingly instituted, and on April 23, 1868, the court returned the property to the Custis estate. Lee now suggested that Rooney and Robert visit the island and devise some plan for its use or disposition. Whatever they recommended, he would approve. Good business dictated that unless a better offer could be had, the two sons should take the island in hand and should make what they could from it. A friendly agent, Hamilton S. Neale, accordingly advertised the property, and on December 22, 1868, receiving no higher bid, sold it for $9000 to W. H. F. and R. E. Lee, Jr. The General took the note of his sons for the principal, payable without interest in thirteen years. From his own funds he took an equivalent amount and transferred it to his daughters, as part of the legacy due from their grandfather's estate. The net result of the sale of the island to his sons was that the daughters received a third of their legacy, the boys got the island and the General lost the interest on $9000.

The family, of course, had never been able to live after the beginning of the war as it had lived in the sumptuous, earlier years. Simplicity had been a virtue during the days of the Confederacy; thereafter it was a necessity. When the Confederacy fell, $20,000 of Lee's securities, about one-fourth of his estate, became worthless. For the first year of his presidency, living had been most spartan, with no luxuries and little travel. After the first session at Lexington the increase in General Lee's salary from $1500 to $3000, plus his share of tuition fees, of course relieved his finances somewhat. For 1866–67 the college paid him a total of $4756, but he did not change his style of living. The only difference was in his provision of more extensive summer vacations for his family.

The General had a horror of debt and he prudently avoided it by living within his income, however small it was. Nothing is more impressive, in the intimate annals of the family, than the absence of complaints about hard living or lack of money. It was a theme they tacitly avoided. The repeated business offers that came to him seem to have awakened no yearnings. The household was content to live modestly and to share the hardships of the time, and Lee himself was even more determined than before 1861 to save all he could. For the protection of his wife and daughters he spent no more than necessity and duty claimed of him. He was successful in his thrift and invested wisely in good securties. Never so poor a man as he was supposed to be after the war, he died worth some $88,000.

To only one business enterprise did General Lee give his active support. That was Valley Railroad Company. And then he was induced to participate because he thought the undertaking would help the college and the town.

Lexington was without railroad connection. The nearest station was Goshen, twenty-three miles distant, over a nightmare of a road. As an alternative, the traveller had nothing except the James River and Kanawha Canal, along which the canal boat crept for twelve hours to Lynchburg, fifty miles away. Once, when asked by a visitor to recommend the best way from Lexington to the outer world, Lee replied: "It makes but little difference, for whichever route you select, you will wish you had taken the other." Lexington had long dreamed of a railroad up the Shenandoah Valley, and after the close of the war actively agitated it. The Baltimore and Ohio was interested in the possibilities of the territory.

The counties along the proposed line were willing to market $1,200,000 of securities and to subscribe the proceeds to stock of the corporation. For the purchase of a bond issue, sufficient to cover the rest of the construction cost, the promoters looked to Baltimore, Md.

The leaders of the enterprise arranged to appear before the business men and council of that city. They appealed insistently to General Lee to accompany them. He did not feel he was suited for this sort of undertaking, but he was so importuned that he thought it would appear "ill-mannered and unkind to refuse." So, on April 20, 1869, he set out for Baltimore with a delegation that included most of the notables of that part of Virginia.

They reached Baltimore on the evening of April 21, and were received with much cordiality. Inevitably, the visit took on something of a public nature. Aside from those who were curious to see a celebrity, numerous Lee and Custis kinsfolk resided in Baltimore, as did many friends who had been cherished since the days of his residence there in 1849–52. All of them wanted to greet the General.

On the morning of April 22 the delegation organized by electing General Lee chairman. Shortly after noon on the 23d, the General went to the Corn and Flour Exchange. When Lee entered he was welcomed with cheers and was given a seat facing the president's chair. That afternoon at 4 o'clock the delegation appeared before the city council. Admission was by card, but the building was jammed with an interested audience, of whom a fourth were women. Before this assemblage General Lee had to read a memorial which he had prepared with care before he left Lexington. The formal presentation of this paper being the only business before the meeting, the councilman who had introduced the General announced that opportunity would be given for the ladies to meet him. Then began a gruelling half-hour, the worst, no doubt, that Lee had passed since Appomattox itself. The end of the line was reached at last, however, and Mayor Banks escorted Lee to the street, where another throng greeted him with high huzzahs.

Cheers did not build railroads. "The delegates have had a pleasant time in Baltimore," said the *American*, "and will probably go away with plenty of fair promises, of which those made upon the part of the Council are not likely to be fulfilled; certainly not until the banks cease to protest the notes of the city, and it has some money in its treasury." The paper went on to argue that Baltimore was not financially in condition to subscribe, and that if she were, Virginia as yet gave no assurance that the investment would be secure.

General Lee remained in Baltimore a few days after the hearing. There were friends he wished to see and a particular mission he had to perform: he wanted to purchase Mrs. Lee a small carriage, in which

ROBERT E. LEE: *May, 1869*

THE DEATH MASK

she could be placed easily and driven comfortably. He found what he desired and wrote her of it with manifest pleasure. On Sunday, April 25, he went to Saint Paul's Episcopal Church. Word of his presence spread and brought a great crowd to the door. When he left the building, at the close of the service, all hats were off and he had to walk for a long distance between lines of sympathizing people.

Lee's pleasant stay in Baltimore came to a close on May 1, when he travelled to Washington in order to pay his respects to President Grant. This was done on suggestion from the White House. Lee went without any questionings, and without any loss of equanimity. He had no apologies to make and he felt no embarrassment in meeting again the man to whom he had surrendered. Appomattox had put no stigma on his soul. "We failed," he wrote an old friend, not long before he called on Grant, "we failed, but in the good providence of God apparent failure often proves a blessing." The exact range of the conversation can only be surmised. It probably consisted only of a brief social exchange. In fifteen minutes the two shook hands again and Lee left, to meet Grant no more.

The General went by steamer from Washington to Alexandria. He had never set foot on her streets from the time he left for Richmond in 1861 until he came ashore that day at the boat landing, on his homeward journey from Baltimore, and started to walk to the town house of Mrs. A. M. Fitzhugh of Ravensworth, widow of Mrs. Lee's maternal uncle. Recognized and warmly greeted as he went along, he found at Mrs. Fitzhugh's his sister-in-law, Mrs. Sydney Smith Lee, and his nephew Fitz, of the cavalry. His brother Sydney soon came up from his farm on the Potomac to meet him. It was the first time they had been together since they had left Richmond after the close of the war.

Then followed three happy days. General Lee loved Alexandria. The townspeople began to call on him in such numbers that they almost swamped Mrs. Fitzhugh's house. It became necessary to arrange a reception at a local hotel, Green's Mansion House. No announcement of the reception had been published, and no invitations had been sent out, but half the town came to greet him. For more than two hours the line was unbroken. The callers must have numbered two or three thousand. Here, as everywhere else during the Alexandria visit, the cordiality of the General's greeting was remarked. He was "at home," and free of the reserve that sometimes was hard to distinguish from diffidence.

On the morning of May 7, the General left for home and arrived on the 8th, after an absence of eighteen days. Scarcely was the General at home before he felt compelled to leave once more. The Lexington church had again named him as delegate to the council, which met that year in Fredericksburg, and he did not think he should decline. Word of his coming spread. The brave little city turned out to do him honor. Although it was nearly midnight when his train arrived, the station was jammed, and the people instantly raised the rebel yell as it had not been heard there since 1863.

A committee of the town's leading men called on the General the next day and asked if he would consent to a reception in order that the people of the town might greet him. He declined. Having come to Fredericksburg to attend a religious meeting, he said, he did not think he should make any personal appearance. As usual, the General took no part in the debate of the council, though he was a member of the committee on the state of the church, and of the committee on clerical support.

From Fredericksburg, after the council ended on May 29, the General went to Richland and paid a two-day visit to his brother and intimate, Sydney Smith Lee, whom he had recently seen in Alexandria. Hurrying back, he reached Lexington late in the night of June 1 in time to attend the final examinations. He was rushing about faster than his heart would stand, but he made no complaint and, for the time, felt no ill-effects.

He returned in time for an event to which the family had long been looking forward: the new home—"the president's house," as General Lee always styled it to avoid the impression that it was his own, was finished and ready for occupancy. A two-story building, with a wide centre hall, it was very comfortable though not architecturally impressive.

The house was occupied by General Lee for only sixteen months and a half, and, except for the sombre fact that he died there, it has fewer associations with him than is possessed by the "old president's house," the next residence on the hill. It was a place of pleasantness to the Lees. They had more space, larger convenience, and room for every member of the family. The General soon found the spot he liked best—the space in front of the large windows in the dining room, whence he could look across the campus and, in the other direction, over the fields to the mountains that always delighted his eyes.

As the session of 1868–69 closed, a wordy, angry campaign was being conducted over the new state constitution that had been drawn by a motley convention as one of the conditions of Virginia's readmission to the Union. Radicals and Negroes had controlled the convention and had drafted a document that provided universal suffrage and in almost the same clause disfranchised thousands of Confederates by paraphrasing the language of the Fourteenth Amendment to the United States Constitution. These provisions were far milder than those the extreme radicals had originally adopted, but they would have kept from office in Virginia nearly all those best qualified to fill it. There was danger that conservative white men would vote against the constitution and thereby prolong military rule in Virginia, rather than submit to the enfranchisement of the Negroes and the disfranchisement of themselves. Fortunately, after the convention adjourned, this possibility was suggested: If Virginia would satisfy the first demand of the Radicals by granting the franchise to Negroes, might not Congress be prevailed upon to sanction a separate vote of the people on the offensive sections disfranchising Confederates and prescribing a test oath? If that were done, native white men might cast their ballots for the rest of the new constitution and assure its adoption. This would fulfill the last harsh requirement of the short-sighted Reconstruction Act. Then Virginia might be readmitted to the Union without being delivered for a generation into the hands of the Radicals and the enfranchised blacks. This proposal was duly formulated and was presented to General Grant, who regarded it favorably. Through the patient efforts of an able committee, a separate vote on the disfranchising sections of the new organic law was sanctioned by Congress and was authorized in an executive proclamation which set July 6, 1869, as the date for the election of a governor and a legislature and for the rejection or ratification of the constitution.

Was it the policy of wisdom for conservative white men to vote for the constitution, less the objectionable clauses, and thereby accept the Negro as a voter, in order to get rid of military rule? The question was put to General Lee in the midst of the campaign and was answered directly: "I have great reluctance to speak on political subjects," he said, "because I am entirely withdrawn from their consideration, and therefore mistrust my own judgment. I have, however, said in conversation with friends, that, if I was entitled to vote, I should vote for the excision of the obnoxious clauses of the proposed constitution, and for the election of the most conservative eligible candidates for Congress and the legislature. I believe this course offers the best prospect for the solution of the difficulties in which the state is involved, accessible to us. I think all who can should register and vote." This letter was not printed, but General Lee's opinion apparently became known and contributed to the desired result. The body of the constitution was ratified, and the two objectionable sections were rejected by approximately 40,000 votes. A governor of moderate views and a conservative legislature were elected. On January 26, 1870, the President signed the bill readmitting Virginia to the Union. The next day Military District No. 1 passed into the limbo of unhappy memories.

About the time General Lee returned from Fredericksburg he completed a labor on which he had long been engaged—the editing of his father's *Memoirs of the War in the Southern Department*. Lee seems to have contemplated a general revision of the work, but he soon gave up all ambitious editorial designs. He had to put his task aside and take it up again repeatedly. In the spring of 1869 he finished the new material for the book. Even then the concluding paragraphs show some signs of haste. Late in 1869 the book was published, and in 1870 it was reissued. Lee's receipts from it were given his brother Carter, who had supplied most of the letters.

The sketch of "Light-Horse Harry" Lee that preceded the text is the longest single composition from the pen of his most distinguished son, but from no point of view can it be accounted an effective piece of writing. The picture one gets at the end does less than justice to the man and to his record. Reading the sketch, one can understand why Gamaliel Bradford, in citing another paper by Lee, admitted that it went a long way toward reconciling him to the General's failure to write a history of his campaigns. The shortcomings of this solitary venture into biography are the more remarkable in view of General Lee's conversation about his father, conversation that was most entertaining and rich in diverting anecdote. Lee's letters were nearly always smooth, and sometimes were written in a style that makes the reader's heart beat a trifle faster. But when he came to formal composition, most of the grace and all the spontaneity of his style disappeared. What he wrote became ponderous and dull.

Slow as was the preparation of this new edition of his father's *Memoirs*, General Lee's accumulation of material for a history of his own campaigns lagged still more. He found much difficulty in locating documents, especially those relating to the matter he most desired to establish accurately, the comparative strength of the Union and Confederate armies. "If the truth were told just now," he said in the spring of 1868, "it would not be credited." He did not believe an impartial history could be written at so early a date, and he was discouraging to biographers. Although he never wholly abandoned his project, he accumulated few reports and returns after 1866 and made no start at composition.

At the commencement of 1869, thirty-eight students were awarded degrees, and some financial progress was recorded. Vigor in furthering the campaign for funds was now urged once again by the trustees; without it, golden plans for making the college more useful to the country could not be started.

These plans were set out for the approval of the trustees by the president and faculty in several papers that embody the fullest expression of General Lee's theory of education. The starting point was the deep conviction of General Lee that for all its poverty and distress, the South must promote general education. To General John B. Gordon, he stated his premise: "The thorough education of all classes of the people is the most efficacious means, in my opinion, of promoting the prosperity of the South." Education, he believed, was the best endowment of youth: "We must look to the rising generation for the restoration of the country." He did not except the Negroes from the list of those whom education would help.

Cultural studies he considered a most desirable element of education, but from the beginning of his work at Lexington he saw the South's need of better training in the sciences. With that in mind, he divided the School of Natural Philosophy, enlarged the instruction in chemistry, as already indicated, and built up a department of engineering. As time passed and he saw that the struggling South required men trained for the vocations as well as for the professions, his thought was given increasingly to what was styled "practical education," in the phrase of the day.

At their meeting in June, 1868, the trustees had authorized the faculty to work out an extension of the scientific departments. The faculty, in turn, had named a committee to prepare a report, under the direction of Lee. This was presented and considered at a special meeting of the board in March, 1869, and was then made public. At the annual meeting in June, 1869, the project was approved in most of its details and was given its final form. Three new departments were projected—agriculture, commerce, and applied chemistry. In addition, the report recommended the development of the engineering schools to include training in mechanical engineering. With the proposed department of applied chemistry, this would so broaden the instruction that three branches would be taught—civil engineering, mechanical engineering, and mining engineering and applied chemistry. English and French were to be taught with all the engineering courses.

Along with the extension of the scientific departments, the faculty report recommended the establishment of "press scholarships," not exceeding fifty, to "young men intending to make practical printing and journalism their business in life; such scholarships to be free from tuition and College fees, on condition that when required by the Faculty, they shall perform such disciplinary duties as may be assigned them in a printing office or in the line of their professions to a time equal to one hour in each working day."

These plans, like those General Lee had received when he came to Lexington, were pervaded with the ideals of Christianity. Taught in no course, religion was to be inculcated through all of them. Lee had come to Lexington as much a missionary as an educator. When he had told Pendleton in 1865 that he would not hesitate to give his services to the college, if he thought he could be of any "benefit" to the youth of the South, he had used the word as much in its moral as in its educational sense. He meant precisely what he said in an oft-quoted remark: "If I could only know that all the young men in the college were good Christians, I should have nothing more to desire. I dread the thought of any student going away from college without becoming a sincere Christian."

If General Lee had lived longer and the funds had been found, still other educational ideals doubtless would have been developed at Washington College. As it was, the program of 1869 represents the scene at its widest before the curtain dropped.

Poverty prevented its full attainment in the General's time, but Lee's plan was definite and advanced. It attracted much attention, particularly in the emphasis placed on "practical education." *The New York Herald* predicted that the movement was "likely to make as great an impression upon our old fogy schools and colleges as [General Lee] did in military tactics upon our old fogy commanders in the palmy days of the rebellion." The faculty did not labor in vain or follow to no purpose the leadership of the president. Washington College became a mighty force in Southern education. Defeated in war, Lee triumphed in his labor to upbuild the South.

The decline in Lee's health had become serious by June, 1869. He had to consider his physical condition in making his plans for the summer. He hoped that he might visit Rooney and Robert after the college closed and return to Lexington for the annual meeting on July 13 of the Educational Association of Virginia. But new college officers were to begin their duties July 1 and would require some coaching. He stayed in Lexington, which he found so quiet and pleasant, with the students away, that he wished he could remain there all summer. The Educational Association duly convened at the college. General Lee made no address and served on none of the committees.

Very soon after the convention closed, the General took Mrs. Lee to the Rockbridge Baths. Scarcely had Lee reached the springs when he received news that his brother Sydney Smith Lee had died at Richland. The General set out immediately but had to contend, as usual, with very poor transportation. When he arrived at Alexandria, on the evening of July 24, it was to find that the funeral had occurred late the previous afternoon. Lee was much shaken by the sudden taking of a brother he had loved to the end of his life as warmly as in the days of their boyhood in that some old city.

Robert was with him and he prevailed on the General to return home by way of the White House. Lee reached there on July 30. The General did not think his daughter-in-law was looking well and he believed that her baby, his namesake, would be the better for a trip to the mountains. So he prevailed on young Mrs. Lee to go to the springs with him. He was pleased at the prospect of having the young mother and her child in his care. On August 2 the mother went to Petersburg, to see her family for a day, while the General and Rooney awaited her in Richmond. As always happened now, whenever he was away from Lexington, visitors began to pour in on Lee in such numbers that he was compelled to hold an impromptu reception in the parlors of the Exchange Hotel. The next day, August 3, he set out for the springs, and safely delivered the mother and the youngster to Mrs. Lee. Obedient to his doctor's order, the General departed in a few days for the White Sulphur. He took with him Mildred and Agnes, who found a gay season in progress. Late in arriving, he had but a short stay at the springs, and before the end of August he was back in Lexington. His business was heavy after September 16, when the college opened. The session got smoothly underway and passed with few incidents. Its chief feature was the vigorous continuance of the campaign for endowment.

The life of the family was very pleasant that fall. Mrs. Rooney Lee and the General's little grandson, Robert, remained in Lexington for some time after they left the springs. Edward Childe paid another visit at the end of September. Mrs. Lee's health was no better but she was able to ride out with the General, on sunny autumn afternoons, in the carriage he had purchased for her the previous spring in Baltimore. These were their last rides together.

The symptoms that marked the beginning of the end commenced about October 22, 1869, and at first were simply those of another severe cold, which kept Lee indoors. He was better within a week and on November 2 was able to take a ride on Traveller and to confer with the faculty, but he was again confined to the house for a few days, and when he was allowed to go out once more, his weakness was pronounced and he felt a certain depression of spirits. Truth was, his doctors by this time had diagnosed his malady as the same "inflammation of the heart-sac" from which in 1863 he had suffered much. This was attended now by rheumatism of the back, right side, and arms. Apparently the physicians did not explain to him the nature of his trouble, but he knew his heart was affected. He confided this to Custis, and told his eldest son that he considered himself doomed, but he said nothing of it to any other member of the family.

As Christmas approached he wrote cheerfully to Rooney, who could not come to Lexington for the holidays, and he sent a message to Robert in the same spirit. On New Year's Day he kept open house to his friends. He still had strength for his correspondence and he was able, too, to see visitors, bidden and unbidden.

As the winter wore along, the General's free movement was greatly hampered by his physical condition. He rode out when the weather was favorable, but he could not walk much farther than to his office. Constantly in pain, he was unable to attend to anything beyond his college duties and his necessary correspondence. He insisted he was better, as February passed, but by the middle of March he was less optimistic and had reached the conclusion that if the spring brought no improvement, he would resign.

The professors of the college realized how serious his condition had become. Individually, from time to time, they urged him to take a long rest. Feeling that it was his sense of duty and his unwillingness to burden them that kept him from going away, they arranged among themselves a division of his college work and wrote him a letter in which they asked him to take a vacation and to spend it in travel for his health. It is quite likely that the suggestion of travel was made after conference with his physicians, who were very anxious for him to seek a climate where he would be less liable to contract colds.

Upon the delivery of this communication from the faculty, Lee's doctor and his family united with the professors in new importunities. On March 22, 1870, he notified the faculty that he had decided to take their suggestion and that he would name Professor Kirkpatrick to act as president in his absence.

Lee promptly decided where he would go. He had long desired to visit the grave of his daughter, Annie, near the White Sulphur Springs, Warren County, North Carolina. ". . . I have always promised myself to go [there]," he told Rooney, "and I think, if I am to accomplish it, I have no time to lose." From Warrenton he purposed to go to Savannah, and on his return journey he intended to stop and see his sons. His daughter Agnes was to accompany him.

CHAPTER XVIII

Strike the Tent

ON THE afternoon of Thursday, March 24, General Lee left Lexington. If it had been a quiet journey on which he set out, it might have benefited him greatly and might perhaps have prolonged his life. As it was, his two months of travel probably hastened his death. Much of his time had to be spent on the railroads, and many of his days were crowded with all the incidents of a triumphant progress, full of excitement and most injurious to an impaired heart. Still, if his sands were running out so swiftly that a few months were of no great moment, there could not have been a more fitting close. Was he preparing to face his Maker? Did he ask himself if he had walked humbly in the ways of God's appointing? Had he chosen rightly and counselled with prudence after the war? If, on his knees in prayer, he put these heart-searching questions, the South was ready to answer them for him. The last and most beautiful chapter of his life was opening.

In its initial stage his travel was retired. He reached Richmond on the afternoon of March 25. Too weak to go visiting, he remained quietly at the hotel and saw only the personal friends who called. Saturday he had a two-hour examination by three physicians.

In Richmond the General encountered Colonel John S. Mosby of the renowned partisan rangers. "The general was pale and haggard," Mosby subsequently wrote, "and did not look like the Apollo I had known in the army." They exchanged greetings, and a little later Colonel Mosby called at the General's room for a chat.

Mosby was soon back for a second visit, bringing with him a man whose presence recalled the tragedy of Gettysburg and the dread day of Five Forks—General George E. Pickett. Mosby had met Pickett, by chance, and when he had remarked that he had called on their old commander, Pickett had said that he would pay his respects if Mosby would return with him, but that he did not want to be alone with Lee.

The General had not seen Pickett since Appomatox, and he had conducted no correspondence with him. From Mosby's account it would seem that General Lee received Pickett with his full reserve, a reserve that could be icy and killing though coupled always with perfect courtesy. Sensing the unpleasantness of the meeting, Mosby got up in a few moments and Pickett followed him. Once outside the room, Pickett broke out bitterly against "that old man" who, he said, "had my division massacred at Gettysburg."

A more welcome visitor was Colonel J. L. Corley, who had been Lee's chief quartermaster, an able and devoted man. Without hinting that he thought General Lee needed an escort, Colonel Corley decided he should accompany his old chieftain on his journey, and diplomatically prevailed upon the General to let him make the arrangements to attend him southward from Charlotte, where he offered to meet him on an agreed date. It was a service of the most considerate sort, and it contributed immeasurably to lessen the discomfort of the trip.

On the afternoon of March 28 the General and his daughter left Richmond for Warrenton, N. C. They reached their objective the same night and received warm welcome at Ingleside, the home of Mr. and Mrs. John White. The next morning the Whites supplied the General and his daughter with masses of white hyacinths, and Captain William J. White placed a team and vehicle at their disposal that they might go unaccompanied to the cemetery.

Now began the public part of the tour—public not because Lee desired it so, but because the people heard of his coming and insisted on honoring him. The General left Warrenton March 29. The journey continued by way of Raleigh, Salisbury, Charlotte, and Columbia. At Charlotte, the faithful Colonel Corley reported himself. "Namesakes appeared on the way, of all sizes. Old ladies stretched their heads into the windows at way-stations and then drew back and said, 'He is mighty like his pictures' "—so Agnes wrote her mother. Columbia, S. C. presented a great crowd. All the Confederate veterans had been mustered and, with a large number of other citizens, had been marched in procession to the station. In the crowd was General E. Porter Alexander. But there were no war reminiscences now, only smiles and handshakes and cheers. General Lee was forced to go to the platform, where he was met with a roar. He bowed his acknowledgments but made no speech.

On the evening of March 30 he reached Augusta, Ga., where he expected to spend the night, before going on to Savannah. Lee was

weary and yielded to the appeal that he remain in Augusta a day and
not attempt to go on to Savannah the next morning. But if it was rest
he sought, he did not find it. He had to hold a reception nearly the
whole of the forenoon. "Crowds came," Agnes wrote her mother
"Wounded soldiers, servants, and workingmen even. The sweetest little
children—namesakes—dressed to their eyes, with bouquets of japon-
ica—or tiny cards in their little fat hands—with their names." Among
the callers were friends of other days, and several of Lee's old generals, among them Lafayette McLaws, A. R. Wright and W. M.
Gardner. The people must have thronged Lee, for it is recorded that
a boy of thirteen, who wished to see him, had to worm his way
through the crowd until, at length, he stood by the side of the General and looked up at him in wondering reverence. This lad's name
was Woodrow Wilson. The next day, April 1, the General and his
daughter left the hotel with Colonel Corley for Savannah.

At some point on the journey of 160 miles to the familiar city of
Lee's first engineering labors, a reception committee came aboard.
It included former Quartermaster General Lawton, General J. F.
Gilmer, who had been chief engineer of the War Department,
Andrew Lowe, and others. The General left the train at Savannah
to face one of the largest crowds that ever assembled to welcome
him. The people overflowed the train shed. His escort had difficulty
in making a way for him to the open barouche that was in waiting
for him. Cheer followed cheer, until the General had to rise and bow
his acknowledgments. The Negroes of the city and some of the Federal garrison joined cheerfully in the demonstration.

A drive about the town the next morning, April 2, was followed
by calls on the families he knew. After that came a dinner with a
number of his comrades, among them General Joseph E. Johnston,
General Lawton, and General Gilmer. It was the first time Lee had
seen Johnston since the war. The two were photographed together
in the familiar picture that shows them grizzled, old and feeble.

Lee was happy to greet old friends and to make new. Particularly
was he pleased when the Mackays got back to town and reopened
their familiar house in Broughton Street. But he found the pace
too hard, and in his letters home expressed regret that he had undertaken the long journey. "I wish I were back," he said, though he much
appreciated the hospitality shown him.

He had decided to go down into Florida on April 8, and on the
way to visit Cumberland Island, where his father was buried, but

Agnes fell sick and that prevented his departure until Tuesday, April 12. He set out then aboard the steamer *Nick King,* which ran leisurely between Savannah and Palatka on the Saint John's River. With him and his daughter went his Savannah host, Andrew Lowe. At Brunswick, where the people turned out to see him, the party was joined by William Nightingale, grandson of General Nathanael Greene and successor to the ownership of Dungeness, the estate on which "Light-Horse Harry" Lee had died. When the boat tied up at Cumberland Island they went ashore to the burial ground. ". . . Agnes decorated my father's grave with beautiful fresh flowers," Lee wrote, and added simply: "I presume it is the last time I shall be able to pay to it my tribute of respect. The cemetery is unharmed and the grave is in good order, though the house of Dungeness has been burned and the island devastated."

Entering historic Saint John's River, Lee and his daughter about 4 o'clock on the afternoon of Wednesday, April 13, touched at Jacksonville, Fla. People streamed aboard until the *Nick King* was almost swamped. As many more remained disappointed on shore, unable to get on the ship. To satisfy them, the General was asked to go on deck. When he walked out and stood where he could be seen, a strange thing happened: a complete silence fell on the throng, a silence of admiring reverence, as if the people thought it would be worse than discourtesy to applaud the old chieftain who embodied in their eyes the cause for which they had fought. ". . . The very silence of the multitude," reported *The Jacksonville Union,* "spoke a deeper feeling than the loudest huzzas could have expressed." At Palatka, Lee met another old friend not seen since Appomattox—Colonel R. G. Cole, chief commissary of the Army of Northern Virginia.

Lee then determined not to return home by the most direct route, but to visit Charleston, S. C., and friends in Tidewater Virginia. On the morning of April 25 he left Savannah for Charleston, accompanied now only by Agnes, whose health was giving her father some concern. The political situation in South Carolina was tense at this time, and General Lee was anxious to escape all demonstrations that might heat blood and provoke a clash. Accordingly, he hoped that word of his coming might not precede him, but a telegram was sent by some admirer a short time before the train was due to reach the Carolina city, and a company of his friends met him at the station. Within a few hours the whole city began to clamor for a glimpse of him. That evening the Post Band serenaded. The next morning his old friends began to call. A delegation came to ask if he would agree to hold a reception at one of the hotels, in order to give the public an opportunity of greeting him. He excused himself, but he could not escape the admiring homage of the people.

On April 28 the General left Charleston for Wilmington. Arriving at the brave old town that must have revived dark memories of Fort Fisher, he was escorted by the cadets to the home of George Davis, who had been attorney general in the Confederate cabinet. A night of quiet, and then another day of crowds and receptions. Friends by the score called on him at the Davis house.

On April 30 Lee left Wilmington and went by way of Weldon to Portsmouth, Va., where he was to take the ferry across the Elizabeth River to Norfolk. As usual, word of his coming had preceded him and had brought a vast throng to the station. When he left the train a new surprise awaited him: Wilmington had welcomed him with a line of cadets; Portsmouth received him with a roaring salute. And, as a fitting companion when artillery was barking, there in the van of the crowd, waiting to greet his old chief, was Colonel Walter H. Taylor. At Norfolk, amid the din of welcoming shouts, with the rebel yell as a sharp, continuing accompaniment, the General was escorted to a carriage and was driven off quickly with Colonel Taylor. His Norfolk stopping-place was the fine, quiet home of Doctor William Selden.

The Seldens tendered Lee a reception on the night of May 4, when many of his old soldiers came to shake his hand and to gaze once more—and for the last time—on his calm countenance. They represented every station in life and many units of the Army of Northern Virginia. This dinner, the reception, and a professional conference with Doctor Selden, who was a physician of high standing, consumed nearly all the General's strength. On May 5 he quietly left the city on the steamer that ran up the James to the river plantations he intended to visit.

First he stopped again at the lower of the three Harrison estates called Brandon. The mistress of Lower Brandon, Mrs. Isabella Ritchie Harrison, and her kin were people he had known long and affectionately. The atmosphere was that he loved best. There were no crowds to cheer him, no receptions to tire him. He could relax—almost for the first time since March 24, when he had left Lexington. He drove to the other Brandons, saw all his friends and connections in the neighborhood, went to church on Sunday, May 8, wrote a few family letters and enjoyed the delights of the place.

From Brandon, Lee went to Shirley, by pre-arrangement with Hill Carter. He spent there the better part of two days in much happiness of soul. No record of his stay at Shirley remains except the epigram of one of the daughters of the house: "We regarded him with the greatest veneration . . . We had heard of God, but here was General Lee!"

While the General had been in Savannah, Mrs. Lee had carried out a long-cherished plan of visiting Rooney at the White House. Lee planned to join her there and to visit his sons on their farms. He left the old Carter plantation on Thursday, May 12, and arrived at Rooney's home that evening.

Aside from a few familiars, there were no other guests at the White House. The General was free to rest and to play with his small grandson and namesake, to whom he was much attached. During his stay he rode over alone to spend a brief time with his bachelor son Robert at his plantation. Lee's only other visit was to White Marsh, the home of Doctor Prosser Tabb, in Gloucester County. Lee took the train for Richmond on the morning of May 22, ten days after his arrival at the White House. Agnes accompanied him, and Robert went up for the day as a filial guard of honor.

From May 22 to May 26 the General remained in Richmond. Much of his time was given over to medical examination by the Richmond doctors who had gone over him before he began his Southern tour. He had to endure, also, what must have seemed, in prospect, equally distasteful—measurement for a bust that was to be made of him. But the young artist who did the work was gentle, deft, and considerate, a cultured man and a good conversationalist. The General and he soon understood each other. When the sculptor, E. V. Valentine, remarked that the war had greatly altered his fortunes, General Lee answered quietly—his humor was never boisterous—that "an artist ought not to have too much money." Later, as the conversation turned again to adversity, Lee observed, "Misfortune nobly borne is good fortune." Valentine at the time thought this was original with General Lee, but subsequently, in reading the *Meditations of Marcus Aurelius*, he found the sentence there. ". . . No more appropriate epitaph," wrote Mr. Valentine, "could be carved on the tomb of the great Virginian."

The artist at length completed his measurements, and explained that he would have to go to Lexington to do the modelling, and could do so either immediately or in the autumn. Lee replied that he would have more leisure later on but that Valentine had better make the visit at once. He gave no reasons, but the young statuary understood that Lee thought his end was near at hand. On May 26, Lee left Richmond for the last time. He reached home on the morning of May 28, two months and four days from the time he had left. Physically, he was little the better for the tour. He had enjoyed his trip up the Saint John's River more than any other part of his tour, and when he had returned to Savannah he had felt improvement, but he found some of his symptoms aggravated.

The visits to Charleston and Wilmington had been particularly wearing, because so many social events had been crowded into so brief a time. Reports that he had heart disease had now become public property, and at Wilmington he had told friends that he was sure his ailment was of the heart and that it was incurable. He had begun to gain some ground from the time he had gone to Brandon. In fact, if he had not sought quiet when he did, it is altogether probable that he would have died on the road. Now that he was home, though he seemed buoyed up for the time, there was no real improvement: his malady was progressive.

Precisely what that malady was, his physicians were neither agreed nor positive. The diagnosis of simple pericarditis tentatively made in 1870 did not adequately explain his symptoms. The illness of 1863, from which his trouble dated, may have been an acute pericarditis. Later, he probably had a combination of maladies. His serious heart condition was almost certainly angina pectoris rather than "rheumatism," as he thought. This angina may have been accompanied by a chronic adhesive pericarditis. In addition he had some arthritis and a hardening of the arteries, which was rapid after 1866.

The psychological effect of the southern tour on Lee himself is not easily determined, because he said very little about it. In general, the effects were cumulative of those that followed his visit to Petersburg in 1867, when he had seen how the Southern people were shaking off the war. The only difference was that he now felt his end was at hand. He had paid his final visit of respect to the grave of his daughter and to the burial-place of his father and the early home of his mother. For the last time he had greeted many of those who had executed his orders and had fought his battles. He had consciously said farewell.

Scarcely had the General settled himself at home than Valentine made his promised visit to model the bust. Lee offered him one of the first-floor rooms of his residence as a temporary studio, but the sculptor preferred not to disturb the family, and found a vacant store under the hotel that he could utilize. There, on a low platform, Lee sat for Valentine, with the understanding that nobody but Custis or Professor White was to be admitted. Lee was not comfortable during this ordeal. Often, unconsciously, he would put his hand to his heart, as if in pain, but he made no complaint.

There was little time for rest. The date for the college commencement was approaching. Final examinations kept the president for long hours. Then followed the formal exercises and the meeting of the trustees, a rather important meeting, at that. Lee reported at length on the work of the year. The commencement itself was brilliant.

Lee must have been heartily tired of doctors' examinations by this time, but he yielded now to a new request that he go to Baltimore and consult Doctor Thomas Hepburn Buckler.

On June 30, 1870, just a week after the trustees adjourned, General Lee set out for Baltimore alone. He received a two-hour examination at the hands of Doctor Buckler, who was more encouraging than some of the other physicians had been. "He says he finds my lungs working well, the action of the heart a little too much diffused, but nothing to injure. He is inclined to think my whole difficulty arises from rheumatic excitement, both the first attack in front of Fredericksburg and the second last winter. Says I appear to have a rheumatic constitution, must guard against cold, keep out in the air, exercise, etc., as the other physicians prescribe. . . . In the meantime, he has told me to try lemon-juice and watch the effect."

On July 14, he crossed the Potomac for the last time, southward bound. At the Mansion House in Alexandria, he put up for the night. On the 15th he had a conference with his old attorney, Francis L. Smith, about the possible recovery of Arlington, but he got little encouragement. At the instance of Mr. Smith, Lee removed from the hotel to the lawyer's residence, where many of his friends came to "pay their respects," in the good old phrase of the times.

That afternoon he went to Cassius Lee's home, which was his headquarters for a round of visits—parting calls in the most sombre sense—to old friends in the neighborhood of Arlington. In the company of Cassius Lee, whom he had known all his life in closest intimacy, the General felt none of the restraint he usually displayed in talking about the past. Together, with no audience except Cassius Lee's silently attentive sons, they ranged the years. When they came to the dark era of blood, Cassius Lee questioned and the General explained. They talked of Jackson, and Lee told how the failure of "Stonewall" to get on McClellan's flank had forced him to fight the battle of Mechanicsville, lest the Federals on the other side of the Chickahominy sweep into Richmond. But he must have had ample praise for Jackson, for he expressed the belief that if his great lieutenant had been with him at Gettysburg that battle would have been a Confederate victory. "Jackson," said he, "would have held the heights which Ewell took on the first day." Ewell he accounted a good officer, but one who would not occupy a position beyond the town.

Cassius Lee asked him why he had not moved on Washington after the second battle of Manassas. The General answered: "Because my men had nothing to eat. I could not tell my men to take that fort"—pointing to the nearby ramparts of Fort Wade—"when they had nothing to eat for three days. I went to Maryland to feed my army."

Who was the ablest Federal general he had opposed? He did not hesitate a moment for the answer. "McClellan, by all odds," he said emphatically.

This was the fullest conversation on military matters that General Lee ever had after the war, and is the only one of which a measurably adequate record exists. Lee's reticence in discussing the war was always noticeable and extended to his correspondence.

So far as is known, he wrote only two general letters on his campaigns. The more lengthy was in answer to some inquiries from W. M. McDonald, who was writing a school history. In this letter, dated April 15, 1868, Lee explained why he went into Maryland in 1862, and why he chose to stand on the hills behind Fredericksburg rather than to dispute Burnside's crossing. "As to the battle of Gettysburg," he went on, "I must again refer you to my official accounts. Its loss was occasioned by a combination of circumstances. It was commenced in the absence of correct intelligence. It was continued in the effort to overcome the difficulties by which we were surrounded, and it would have been gained could one determined and united blow have been delivered by our whole line. As it was, victory trembled in the balance for three days, and the battle resulted in the infliction of as great amount of injury as was received, and in frustrating Federal plans for the season."

Perhaps in those two days with Cassius Lee, in the summer of 1870, he talked more of his battles than in all the rest of his post-bellum career. And it was with less heaviness of heart. Five days were spent in the pleasant company of Alexandria friends; then on the morning of July 19 the General went to Ravensworth until July 25 and then returned home.

General Lee's doctors were determined that his duties should not exhaust him; so, on August 9 they packed him off to the Hot Springs. Lee forthwith, as in duty bound, consulted the resident physician, who prescribed thermal treatment and predicted that, if the patient stayed long enough, the results would be good. The General held faithfully to the "spouts" and "broilers" that were supposed to benefit rheumatism, but he did not enjoy them. Nor did he find much solace in the company at the springs.

The General felt somewhat improved as his stay was prolonged, but on August 29 he left the springs for Staunton, to attend a meeting of the stockholders of the Valley Railroad. The project for the construction of this line was now slowly taking shape. Colonel M. G. Harmon, the president of the company, had done much, but on the morning of August 30 he announced that he could not stand for re-election and that he desired General Lee be named his successor.

Lee, of course, had no wish to take on new burdens and had no great faith in the enterprise. "It seems to me," he wrote Cyrus H. McCormick, "that I have already led enough forlorn hopes." When, however, old friends and associates insisted that he and he alone could make a success of a carrier that would serve the Valley, help the town of Lexington, and benefit the college, he accepted the post. His salary, which had not been fixed, and may not even have been mentioned until after he consented to take the place, was put at $5000 a year.

Upon the conclusion of the stockholders' meeting, General Lee returned to Lexington. The college session was scheduled to be opened shortly, and many preliminaries had to be arranged. Meetings required his direct attendance, or his accessibility in case the trustees wished to consult him. Despite the strain, he began to feel stronger and soon accounted himself definitely better. On Thursday, September 15, came the formal opening of the session.

Three days after the opening of the session of 1870-71 the fifth anniversary of General Lee's arrival in Lexington occurred. His hair was entirely white now and his gait was slow. Once the most erect of men, he was beginning to stoop in the shoulders. The nervous strain of the war and the difficult exercise of a stern self-control during reconstruction had proved too much for even his stout system. Although he was only sixty-three, he was an old man.

Yet none of the work he had done since the summer of 1865 had the shadow of senescence upon it. On the contrary, nothing more surely exhibits the strength of his intellect than the sustained quality of his labors and the continued sureness of his judgment during years when a similar physical condition would have been accompanied, in the case of most men, by a progressive mental decline. He had taken a feeble, old-fashioned college and had made it a vigorous pioneer in education, the admiration of the South. Although that had demanded hourly thought and many months of grinding labor, it had not been his chief contribution to his country since the close of the war. His example had been more important than his administration. He had meant less to education than to reconciliation. Denounced and lied about, in a time more difficult than any America had ever known except in the most baffling period of the Revolution, he had preached his gospel of silence and goodwill, of patience and hard work.

Had he left Virginia in 1865 many of the best men of the South might have emigrated with him, and those who remained might have been under the domination of Negroes and carpet baggers for a generation. Instead, the Confederates came to consider it as much the course of patriotism to emulate General Lee in peace as it had been to follow him in war. More than any other American, General Lee kept the tragedy of the war from being a continuing national calamity.

Like a soldier in action, General Lee regarded his taking off as probable at any time, but he had no special premonitions and he made no deliberate preparations for the great adventure. He worked on from September 18 to September 27 in accordance with a precise and busy schedule. On September 27 he attended faculty meeting as usual. The next morning, September 28, he completed his morning's work, and was just stepping out from his office when he met Percy Davidson, a sophomore from Lexington, who had with him a small picture of Lee, which a girl had asked him to get the General to autograph. Davidson explained this and added that as Lee was leaving, he would come some other time. "No," said Lee, "I will go right back and do it now." He returned and signed his name for the last time.

Then he went out again and shut the door behind him, to open it no more in life. From the office he walked slowly home, ate his dinner, and slept for a short time in his armchair. It was chilly after dinner and rain began to fall steadily. Lee should have stayed at home to protect himself against a cold, but he did not feel he should miss vestry meeting. Lee insisted on going, and took no precaution against the weather other than to put on his old military cape. He walked through the rain and went directly into the church auditorium. There was no heat in the building and no smaller room into which the vestrymen could retire. They had to sit in the pews, cold and damp.

Chatting a few minutes with his associates, the General at 4 o'clock called the meeting to order. The discussion was close and tedious. Sitting with his cape about him, Lee presided, but, as usual, did not attempt to influence the deliberations. After they had discussed possibilities for a new church building, the vestrymen began to subscribe a fund to raise Doctor Pendleton's salary. Lee was tired by this time, and despite the chill of the place, his face was flushed, but he waited in patience. All the vestrymen contributed; the clerk cast the total and announced how much was still needed to reach the desired sum. It was $55, considerably more than the part of one who already had contributed generously, but Lee said quietly, "I will give that sum."

Seven o'clock had struck, the hour at which, in so many of his battles, darkness had put an end to the fighting. The end had come now—not on a field of blood, but in the half-gloom of a bare little church, where the talk was of a larger house of prayer, and the only reminders of the days of strife were the cape and the weary, lined face of the old leader, and the military titles by which some of the vestrymen addressed one another. High command, great fame, heart-anguish, galling burdens had ended in this last service—to plan a little church in a mountain town, and to give of his substance to raise the pay of a parson who had been his loyal lieutenant in arms.

Bidding his associates good night, Lee walked home alone. He went to the dining room, where Mrs. Lee was waiting for him. She saw something unusual in his face and told him he looked chilly. "Thank you," he said in his normal voice, "I am warmly clothed."

It was rare that he, the promptest of men, should delay a meal half an hour, and as he often teased wife and daughters about their tardiness, Mrs. Lee from her rolling-chair smilingly challenged him: "You have kept us waiting a long time, where have you been?"

He made no reply. Taking his usual position in front of his chair, he opened his lips to say grace. But the familiar words would not come. Another instant and he sank back to his seat.

"Let me pour you out a cup of tea," said Mrs. Lee, "you look so tired."

He tried to answer but could make no intelligible sound. On the instant he must have realized that his summons had come, for a look of resignation lighted his eyes. Then he carefully and deliberately straightened up in his chair. If it was the "last enemy" he had to meet now, he would face him mindfully and erect.

The family sent immediately for his physicians, Doctor H. T. Barton and Doctor R. L. Madison. In a short time they hurried into the room. The General was placed on the couch. His outer garments were removed. "You hurt my arm," he said, and pointed to the shoulder that had long been paining him.

The physicians' examination showed no paralysis. He was very weak, had a tendency to doze, and was slightly impaired in consciousness. The doctors decided that he had what they termed "venous congestion," an impairment of the circulation that now would probably be termed a thrombosis. A bed was at once brought from the second floor and set up for him. Placed upon it, he turned over and went into a long and tranquil sleep, from which his physicians hoped he would awake much improved.

He was better the next day, though still very drowsy, but manifestly required careful nursing and close watching. The dining table was removed and the room was turned into a sick-chamber. Friends and members of the faculty began a regular round of waiting at his side. He lay quietly, now awake, now asleep, always on the borderline of the unconscious. Ere long, he responded to the treatment the doctors prescribed, and physically he seemed to improve. Taking his medicine regularly and eating with some appetite, he soon was able to turn over in bed and could sit up to swallow. The attendants' questions he understood and would answer. His replies were monosyllables, but his family explained that he always was silent in sickness.

Word spread that he was ill. The trustees' meeting had been called for September 29, the day after the General was stricken, and with their usual consideration for him they named a committee to express the board's regret at his absence and to consider the advisability of urging him to take a six-months' rest. Newspapers were quick to make inquiries and were able on September 30 to report him much improved.

Apprehension battled with hope. The doctors remained confident, and Mrs. Lee talked of the time "when Robert gets well," but in her heart she was haunted by the look that had come into his eyes when he had tried vainly to answer her at the supper table and then had sat upright. "I saw he had taken leave of earth," she afterwards wrote.

A week passed, and General Lee's improvement, though slight, was apparent and seemed to be progressive. On October 8 a Richmond paper quoted his physicians as saying he would soon be out again. He still talked very little, and once, when Agnes started to give him his medicine, he said: "It is no use." But she prevailed upon him to take it. Conscious of nearly all that went on around him, he was manifestly glad to have the members of the family come in to see him. He did not smile during his whole illness, but he always met greetings of his wife and children with the pressure of his hand.

On the morning of October 10, Doctor Madison thought his patient was mending. "How do you feel today, General?" he inquired.

"I . . . feel . . . better," said Lee, slowly but distinctly.

"You must make haste and get well; Traveller has been standing so long in the stable that he needs exercise."

The General shook his head deliberately and closed his eyes again.

That afternoon, without warning, his pulse began to flutter. His breathing became hurried. Exhaustion was apparent. The evening brought no improvement. At midnight he had a chill, and his condition was so serious that Doctor Barton had to warn the family.

Lee refused medicine and nourishment the next day, even from his daughters, but despite the confusion of his mind, self-discipline still ruled, and when either of his doctors put physic to his mouth he would swallow it. During the morning he lapsed into a half-delirium of dreams and memories. ". . . His mind wandered to those dreadful battlefields." He muttered unintelligible words—prayers, perhaps, or orders to his men. Sometimes his voice was distinct. "Tell Hill he *must* come up," he said, so plainly and emphatically that all who sat in the death-chamber understood him.

His symptoms now were aggravated. Mrs. Lee, in her rolling-chair, took her place by his bed for the last vigil and held his moist hand. His pulse continued weak and feeble; his breathing was worse. By the end of the day the physicians admitted that the fight was lost: the General was dying. They could only wait, not daring to hope, as he lay there motionless, save for the rapid rise and fall of his chest.

At last, on October 12, daylight came. The watchers stirred and made ready to give place to those who had obtained a little sleep. Out of the windows, across the campus, the students began to move about, and after a while they straggled down to the chapel to pray for him. Now it was 9 o'clock, and a quarter past. His old opponent, Grant, was sitting down comfortably to breakfast in the White House. With axe or saw or plough or pen, the veterans of Lee's army were in the swing of another day's work. For him it was ended, the life of discipline, of sorrow, and of service. The clock was striking his last half-hour. In some corner of his mind, not wrecked by his malady, he must have heard his marching order. Was the enemy ahead? Had that bayoneted host of his been called up once again to march through Thoroughfare Gap or around Hooker's flank or over the Potomac into Maryland . . . moving . . . moving forward? Or was it that the war was over and that peace had come?

"Strike the tent," he said, and spoke no more.

There he lies, now that they have shrouded him, with his massive features so white against the lining of the casket that he seems already a marble statue for the veneration of the South. His cause died at Appomattox; now, in him, it is to have its apotheosis. Others survive who shared his battles and his vigils, but none who so completely embodies the glamour, the genius, and the graces with which the South has idealized a hideous war. His passing sets a period to the bloodiest chapter in the history of his country.

Tomorrow a slow-footed procession will form to carry his body to the chapel of the college. Ere the silent undertaker screws down the lid of the coffin, let us look at him for the last time and read from his countenance the pattern of his life.

Because he was calm when others were frenzied, loving when they hated, and silent when they spoke with bitter tongue, they shook their heads and said he was a superman or a mysterious man. Beneath that untroubled exterior, they said, deep storms must rage; his dignity, his reserve, and his few words concealed sombre thoughts, repressed ambitions, livid resentments. They were mistaken. Robert Lee was one of the small company of great men in whom there is no inconsistency to be explained, no enigma to be solved. What he seemed, he was—a wholly human gentleman, the essential elements of whose positive character were two and only two, simplicity and spirituality.

Fortunate in his ancestors, Lee was fortunate most of all in that he inherited nearly all their nobler qualities and none of their worse. His line was not crossed in a century and a half with one that was degenerating. If blood means anything, he was entitled to be what he fundamentally was, a gentleman.

The first reference to Robert E. Lee in an extant letter is the significant statement of his father that "Robert was always good and will be confirmed in his happy turn of mind by his ever-watchful and affectionate mother. Does he strengthen his native tendency?" Penned when the boy was ten, this language registered the impression the absent father had formed when Robert was not more than seven years of age. The stamp of character must, then, have been upon him from childhood. When he emerges dimly as a personality, in the later days of his cadetship at West Point, many of his essential qualities are apparent. Thereafter he exhibits every characteristic that later distinguished him. Subsequent change in his character was negligible and is simply the development of the man by challenging circumstance. Of this there can be no question.

He had a strong and normal nervous system that was invigorated by a simple outdoor life. Although there is no evidence that Mrs. Ann Lee had any secret dread that her son would develop the recklessness of his father, there is abundant proof that, with tactful wisdom, she inculcated in him from childhood the principles of self-control. From earliest adolescence he had upon him the care of his mother. George Washington, the embodiment of character, was his hero, made real and personal in the environment of Alexandria. At West Point his ambition to excel in his class led Lee to subject himself willingly and with a whole heart to a discipline that confirmed every excellence he had acquired at home. Physically more developed than most of the cadets, he had from the outset a better appreciation of what the training of the academy was intended to accomplish. All his early assignments to engineering duty were of a sort to impose responsibility. These circumstances did not destroy his sunny exuberance of spirit, but they set his character so early and so definitely that it did not change with years or woes.

Whether it was at the Des Moines Rapids, or during his superintendency of West Point, or in the president's house at Washington College—wherever he was in full four decades when the burden of battle was not on him—an old acquaintance would have observed little difference in his daily outlook, his nature, or his manners. Only in few particulars was the man who went to that last vestry meeting at the Episcopal church in Lexington unlike the lieutenant who bantered the "Beautiful Talcott" at Old Point in the moments he was not watching the contractors who might circumvent the government. His buoyant bearing had given place to a calmer cheerfulness, which might have been the case with any man who has bridged the chasm that divides the twenties of life from the sixties, even though no river of blood has flowed through the chasm. He was changed, also, in that, after 1865, he put out of his heart the military career that long had fascinated him. All the misgivings he had felt before the war regarding the pursuit of arms were confirmed by five years at Lexington.

In his labor he was swift and diligent, prompt and accurate, always systematic and instinctively thrifty. His ambition was in his labor, whatever its nature. He did not covet praise. Blushing to receive it, he assumed that others would blush when he bestowed it, and he spared what he thought were their feelings, though no man was quicker to appreciate and, at the proper time, to acknowledge the achievement of others. Place and advancement never lured him, except as promotion held out the hope of larger opportunity and better provision for his family. Even then he was meticulous regarding the methods he would employ to further himself financially, and he would never capitalize his name or draw drafts on the good opinion of friends or public. Yet he had all his life the desire to excel at the task assigned him. That was the urge alike of conscience, of obligation, of his regard for detail, and of his devotion to thoroughness as the prime constituent of all labor. He never said so in plain words, but he desired everything that he did, whether it was to plan a battle or to greet a visitor, to be as nearly perfect as he could make it. No man was more critical of his own performance because none demanded more of himself. The engineer's impulse in him was most gratified if something was to be created or organized, but if it concerned another's happiness or had a place in the large design of worth-while things, he considered the smallest task proper to perform. Only the useless was irksome.

He endured interruption of his work without vexation. Rarely was

he embarrassed in his dealings with men. He met every visitor, every
fellow-worker, with a smile and a bow, no matter what the other's
station in life. Always he seemed to keep others at a judicious distance
and did not invite their confidences, but he sought as a gentleman
to make every right-minded person comfortable in his presence. With
a tact so delicate that others scarcely noticed it, when he was busy
he kept conversation to the question at issue, and he sought to make
his interviews brief; but even so, his consideration for the sensibilities
of others cost him many a precious hour. Wrangles he avoided, and
disagreeable persons he usually treated with a cold and freezing
courtesy. Should his self-control be overborne by stupidity or ill-
temper, his eyes would flash and his neck would redden. His rebuke
would be swift and terse, and it might be two hours or more before
he was completely master of himself. Whoever visited him meantime
would perhaps find him irascible, though sure to make amends. Exacting of his subordinates, he still reconciled himself often to working with clumsy human tools. Resentments he never cherished. When
he found men unworthy of his confidence, he made it his practice
to see them as little as possible and to talk to them not at all. Silence
was one of his strongest weapons. During the war he summarized his
code when he wrote these words on a scrap of paper that nobody
saw until after his death:

> "The forbearing use of power does not only form a touch-
> stone, but the manner in which an individual enjoys certain ad-
> vantages over others is a test of a true gentleman.
> "The power which the strong have over the weak, the employer
> over the employed, the educated over the unlettered, the experi-
> enced over the confiding, even the clever over the silly—the for-
> bearing or inoffensive use of all this power or authority, or a
> total abstinence from it when the case admits it, will show the
> gentleman in a plain light. The gentleman does not needlessly and
> unnecessarily remind an offender of a wrong he may have com-
> mitted against him. He can not only forgive, he can forget; and
> he strives for that nobleness of self and mildness of character
> which impart sufficient strength to let the past be but the past.
> A true man of honor feels humbled himself when he cannot help
> humbling others."

Those who look at him through the glamour of his victories or
seek deep meaning in his silence will labor in vain to make him appear complicated. His language, his acts, and his personal life were

simple for the unescapable reason that he was a simple gentleman.

Simple and spiritual—the two qualities which constitute the man cannot be separated. The strongest religious impulse in his life was that given him by his mother.

The theology of his youth had a vehemence and an emotionalism alien to his nature. He was content until he was past forty-five to hold to the code of a gentleman rather than to the formal creed of a church. After that time, first his sense of dependence on God for the uprearing of his boys during his long absences from home, and then the developing tragedy of the war, deepened every religious impulse of his soul.

And what did religion imply for him as he sent Pickett's men up Cemetery Ridge, as he rode to the McLean house, as he read of Military District No. 1, and as he looked down from the chapel platform at the scarred faces and patched garments of his students?

To answer that question is to employ the terms of a theology that now seems to some outworn and perhaps archaic. It was, however, the *credo* of a man who met the supreme tests of life in that he accepted fame without vanity and defeat without repining. To understand the faith of Robert E. Lee is to fill out the picture of him as a gentleman of simple soul. For him religion blended with the code of *noblesse oblige* to which he had been reared. Together, these two forces resolved every problem of his life into right and wrong. There cannot be said to have been a "secret" of his life, but this assuredly was the great, transparent truth, and this it was, primarily, that gave to his career its consistency and decision. Over his movements as a soldier he hesitated often, but over his acts as a man, never. There was but one question ever: What was his duty as a Christian and a gentleman? That he answered by the sure criterion of right and wrong, and, having answered, acted. Everywhere the two obligations went together; he never sought to expiate as a Christian for what he had failed to do as a gentleman, or to atone as a gentleman for what he had neglected as a Christian. He could not have conceived of a Christian who was not a gentleman.

Kindness was the first implication of religion in his mind—the instinctive kindness of a heart that had been schooled to regard others. His was not a nature to waste time in the perplexities of self-analysis; but if those about him at headquarters had understood him better they might often have asked themselves whether, when he brought a refreshing drink to a dusty lieutenant who called with dispatches, he was discharging the social duty of a host or was giving a "cup of cold water" in his Master's name. His manner in either case would have been precisely the same.

Equally was his religion expressed in his unquestioning response to duty. In his clear creed, right was duty and must be discharged. "There is," he wrote down privately for his own guidance, "a true glory and a true honor: the glory of duty done—the honor of the integrity of principle." He probably never summed up this aspect of his religion more completely than in that self-revealing hour before he started to meet General Grant, when he answered all the appeals of his lieutenants with the simple statement: "The question is, is it right to surrender this army? If it is right, then I will take all the responsibility." It was a high creed—right at all times and at all costs—but daily self-discipline and a clear sense of justice made him able to adhere to it.

Humility was another major implication of his religion. So lofty was his conception of man's duty to his Maker and to his neighbors, so completely did his ambition extend, all unconsciously, into the realm of the spirit, that he was never satisfied with what he was. Those who stood with him on the red field of Appomattox thought that his composure was due to his belief that he had discharged his full duty, and in this they were partially correct; but he always felt, with a sincerity no man can challenge, that he had fallen immeasurably short of his ideal of a servant of God.

Born of this humility, this sense of unworthiness in the sight of God, was submission to Divine will. There was nothing of blind fatalism in his faith. Resignation is scarely the name for it. Believing that God was Infinite Wisdom and Eternal Love, he subjected himself to seeming ill-fortune in the confidence that God's will would work out for man's good. Nothing of his serenity during the war or of his silent labor in defeat can be understood unless one realizes that he submitted himself in all things faithfully to the will of a Divinity which, in his simple faith, was directing wisely the fate of nations and the daily life of His children. This, and not the mere physical courage that defies danger, sustained him in battle; and this, at least equally with his sense of duty done, made him accept the results of the war without a single gesture of complaint.

Of humility and submission was born a spirit of self-denial that prepared him for the hardships of the war and, still more, for the dark destitution that followed it. This self-denial was, in some sense, the spiritual counterpart of the social self-control his mother had inculcated in his boyhood days, and it grew in power throughout his life. His own misfortunes typified the fate of the Confederacy and of its adherents. Through it all, his spirit of self-denial met every demand upon it, and even after he went to Washington College and had an income on which he could live easily, he continued to deny himself as an example to his people. Had his life been epitomized in one sentence of the Book he read so often, it would have been in the words, "If any man will come after me, let him deny himself, and take up his cross daily, and follow me." And if one, only one, of all the myriad incidents of his stirring life had to be selected to typify his message, as a man, to the young Americans who stood in hushed awe that rainy October morning as their parents wept at the passing of the Southern Arthur, who would hesitate in selecting that incident? It occurred in Northern Virginia, probably on his last visit there. A young mother brought her baby to him to be blessed. He took the infant in his arms and looked at it and then at her and slowly said, "Teach him he must deny himself."

That is all. There is no mystery in the coffin there in front of the windows that look to the sunrise.

INDEX

INDEX

1. Simberg/Jonathan Silver: Julianna's wedding
2. Blank Rome – s/o in Philly

3. Wolfe –
※ Seungjin Joo – New York State bar

results –   1.) love leaves move away
              2.) me to move away/$2
              3.) gaslighting me
              4.)